The Ten Grounds Sutra

The Daśabhūmika Sūtra

To refrain from doing any manner of evil,
to respectfully perform all varieties of good,
and to purify one's own mind—
This is the teaching of all buddhas.

The Ekottara Āgama Sūtra
(T02 n.125 p.551a 13–14)

A Note on the Proper Care of Dharma Materials

Traditional Buddhist cultures treat books on Dharma as sacred. Hence it is considered disrespectful to place them in a low position, to read them when lying down, or to place them where they might be damaged by food or drink.

The Ten Grounds Sutra

The Daśabhūmika Sūtra

The Ten Highest Levels of Practice
On the Bodhisattva's Path to Buddhahood

As Translated from Sanskrit by Tripiṭaka Master Kumārajīva (*c* 410 CE)

An Annotated English Translation by Bhikshu Dharmamitra

A Trilingual Edition (Chinese / English / Sanskrit)

Kalavinka Press
Seattle, Washington
www.kalavinkapress.org

Kalavinka Press
8603 39th Ave SW
Seattle, WA 98136 USA
(www.kalavinkapress.org)

Kalavinka Press is associated with the Kalavinka Dharma Association, a non-profit organized exclusively for religious educational purposes as allowed within the meaning of section 501(c)3 of the Internal RevenueCode. Kalavinka Dharma Association was founded in 1990 and gained formal approval in 2004 by the United States Internal Revenue Service as a 501(c)3 non-profit organization to which all donations are tax deductible.

Donations to KDA are accepted by mail and on the Kalavinka website where numerous free Dharma translations and excerpts from Kalavinka publications are available in digital format.

Edition: 10GKJ-SA-0919-1.0-Chinese/English/Sanskrit
Kalavinka Buddhist Classics Book 11a

ISBN: 978-1-935413-11-0 / Library of Congress Control #: 20199029480

Library of Congress Cataloging-in-Publication Data

Names: Kumārajīva, -412? translator. | Dharmamitra, Bhikshu, translator.
Title: The Ten grounds sutra : the Daśabhūmika sūtra : the ten highest levels of practice on the Bodhisattva's path to Buddhahood / as translated from Sanskrit by Tripiṭaka Master Kumārajīva (ca 410 ce) ; an annotated English translation by Bhikshu Dharmamitra..
Description: A trilingual edition (Chinese/English/Sanskrit) | Seattle, Washington : Kalavinka Press, 2019. | Series: Kalavinka Buddhist classics; book 11a | Includes bibliographical references. | Summary: ""The Ten Grounds Sutra" (Trilingual) is an annotated English Translation by Bhikshu Dharmamitra of Tripitaka Master Kumārajīva's circa 410 ce Sanskrit-to-Chinese translation of the Daśabhūmika Sūtra. This sutra describes in great detail the ten highest levels of bodhisattva practice on the path to buddhahood. This trilingual edition (English / Chinese / Sanskrit) includes the facing-page simplified and traditional Chinese texts along with the entire appended P. L. Vaidya Sanskrit text. The Sanskrit section headings are inset in all three languages for easy mutual correlation"-- Provided by publisher.
Identifiers: LCCN 2019029480 | ISBN 9781935413110 (paperback)
Subjects: LCSH: Tripiṭaka. Sūtrapiṭaka. Avataṃsakasūtra. Daśabhūmikasūtra--Criticism, interpretation, etc. | Bodhisattva stages (Mahayana Buddhism)
Classification: LCC BQ1632.A1 D43 2019 | DDC 294.3/85--dc23
LC record available at https://lccn.loc.gov/2019029480

Kalavinka Press books are printed on acid-free paper.
Cover and interior designed by Bhikshu Dharmamitra.
Printed in the United States of America

Dedication

Dedicated to the memory of the selfless and marvelous life of the Venerable Dhyāna Master Hsuan Hua, the Guiyang Ch'an Patriarch and the very personification of the bodhisattva's six perfections.

Dhyāna Master Hsuan Hua

宣化禪師

1918–1995

About the Chinese Text

This translation is supplemented by inclusion of the Chinese source text on verso pages in both traditional (above) and simplified (below) scripts. For the traditional character version, variant readings from other canonical editions are found as an appendix in the back of the book, and where I have incorporated those variants into the translation, they are usually signaled with an endnote along with my rationale for making the emendation. The traditional-character Chinese text and its variant readings are from the April, 2004 version of the Chinese Buddhist Electronic Text Association's digital edition of the Taisho Buddhist canon. The simplified-character Chinese text is as downloaded from the online Qianlong Chinese Buddhist Canon on July 23, 2018 (http://www.qldzj.com/).

Those following the translation in the traditional Chinese version should be aware that the original Taisho scripture punctuation contained in this 2004 edition is not traceable to original editions, is not reliable, and is probably best ignored altogether. (In any case, accurate reading of Classical Chinese should never depend on a previous editor's punctuation.)

About the Sanskrit Text

The Sanskrit text is included as an appendix in the back of the book. Use of the digital Sanskrit text is by the kind permission of Dr. Miroj Shakya, Project Director of the Digital Sanskrit Buddhist Canon. The Sanskrit text itself is the edition edited by P. L. Vaidya and published by The Mithila Institute of Post-Graduate Studies and Research in Sanskrit learning.

To ease the reader's correlation of the Sanskrit texts with both the English translation and the facing-page Chinese, J. Rahder's alphabetical section headings are embedded in curly braces within all versions of the text (Chinese, English, and Sanskrit).

Outlining in This Work

The ten chapter titles in this work are from the Taisho Chinese text. All other outline headings originate with the translator. Buddhist canonical texts are often so structurally dense that they are best navigated with the aid of at least a simple outline structure such as I have supplied here.

Acknowledgments

The accuracy and readability of this translation have been greatly improved by many corrections, preview comments, and editorial suggestions generously contributed by Bhikkhu Bodhi, Feng Ling, and Nicholas Weeks.

Expenses incurred in bringing forth this publication were underwritten by generous donations from Craig and Karen Neyman, Madalena Lew, Shuyu Yang, Jiajing Li, Kam Chung Wong, Loritta Chan, David Fox, Upasaka Guo Ke, Yuen-Lin Tan, the BDK English Tripiṭaka Project, and others. Sponsorship of Adobe Indesign book layout was provided by Anagarika Mahendra.

Use of the digital Sanskrit texts is by the kind permission of Dr. Miroj Shakya, Project Coordinator of the Digital Sanskrit Buddhist Canon Project.

Were it not for the ongoing material support provided by my late guru's Dharma Realm Buddhist Association and the serene translation studio provided by Seattle's Bodhi Dhamma Center, creation of this translation would have been impossible.

Additionally, it would have been impossible for me to produce this translation without the Dharma teachings and personal inspiration provided to me by my late guru, the awesomely wise and compassionate Dhyāna Master Hsuan Hua, the Guiyang Ch'an patriarch, Dharma teacher, and exegete.

Finally, I owe an immense debt of gratitude to the members of the liver care and transplant teams at Seattle's University of Washington Medical Center who cured me of liver cancer in 2010 and gave me a liver transplant several months later. In particular, if it weren't for over a decade of wonderfully attentive and compassionate care by Dr. Renuka Bhattacharya, medical director of UW's liver transplant program, the kindness and skill in three major surgeries by my transplant surgeon, Dr. Jorge Reyes, and the marvelous generosity of an anonymous liver donor, I would have died a half dozen years ago and thus never could have completed the scriptural translations I have produced in the last eight years.

List of Abbreviations

AN	Aṅguttara Nikāya
BB	Buddhabhadra (T278)
BCSD	Hirakawa's *Buddhist Chinese-Sanskrit Dictionary*
BDK	Bukkyo Dendo Kyokai English Tripiṭaka
BHSD	Edgerton's *Buddhist Hybrid Sanskrit Dictionary*
BR	Bodhiruci (T1522)
CBETA	Chinese Buddhist Electronic Text Association's digital edition of the Taisho Chinese Buddhist canon.
DN	*Dīgha Nikāya*
DR	Dharmarakṣa (T278)
DSBC	Digital Sanskrit Buddhist Canon's digitized edition of *Daśabhūmikasūtram*, edited by P. L. Vaidya.
HH	Venerable Hsuan Hua
KB	Kumārajīva assisted by Buddhayaśas (T286)
KJ	Kumārajīva
LTX	Li Tongxuan (李通玄)
MDPL	*Materials for a Dictionary of the Prajñāpāramitā Literature*
MLDB	*The Middle Length Discourses of the Buddha*
MN	*Majjhima nikāya*
Mppu	*Mahāprajñāpāramitā upadeśa*
MW	Monier Williams' *A Sanskrit-English Dictionary*
N	Nāgārjuna
PDB	Princeton Dictionary of Buddhism
QL	Qing Liang (唐清涼山大華嚴寺沙門澄觀)
QLSC	Qing Liang's *Huayan Shuchao* (大方廣佛華嚴經疏鈔會本. L130 no. 1557)
SYMG	The Song, Yuan, Ming, Gong editions of the Chinese Buddhist canon.
SA	Śikṣānanda (T279)
SD	Śīladharma (T287)
T	Taisho Chinese Buddhist Canon via CBETA (Version 2004. ed.) Taibei)
VB	Venerable Bhikkhu Bodhi
XHYJL	*Xin huayanjing lun* (新華嚴經論 – T36, no. 1739) by Li Tongxuan.

General Table of Contents

Directory to Chapter Subsections

Translator's Introduction

As a continuation of my efforts to bring forth translations of important bodhisattva path texts from the golden age of Classic Indian and Chinese Mahāyana Buddhism, I present here my English translation of *The Ten Grounds Sutra* (*Daśabhūmika-sūtra*) as translated into Chinese from Sanskrit in the early 5th century by Tripiṭaka Master Kumārajīva with the assistance of Tripiṭaka Master Buddhayaśas. The subject of this scripture is the bodhisattva's progress through ten "grounds," "planes," or "levels" of spiritual path cultivation as he ascends from his initial state as a common person ensconced in cyclic existence up to that of a fully enlightened buddha who has reached the utmost, right, and perfect enlightenment.

There is no agreement on the actual origin of this *Ten Grounds Sutra* text. According to the tradition, it was originally the "Ten Grounds" chapter of the immense *Avataṃsaka Sutra,* but later circulated independently as *The Ten Grounds Sutra.* A number of academics prefer to think that it was first an independently circulating scripture which was only later included in the *Avataṃsaka Sutra.* In any case, in addition to the later Sanskrit, Tibetan, and Mongolian editions of this text, there are six relatively early surviving Chinese editions as follows:

Dharmarakṣa (*c.* 297), T 283;
Kumārajīva assisted by Buddhayaśas (c. 408–412 CE),[1] T 286;
Buddhabhadra (*c.* 418–20 CE), as *Avataṃsaka Sutra* Ch. 22, T 278;
Bodhiruci (*c.* 508–511 CE), embedded in Vasubhandu's commentary, T 1522;
Śikṣānanda (*c.* 695–699 CE), as *Avataṃsaka Sutra* Ch. 26, T 279;
Śīladharma (*c.* 790 CE), T 287.

There have been several translations of this text into English in one or another of its classical contexts, as follows:

Megumu Honda from the Sanskrit of the *Daśabhūmika-sūtra;*[2]
Buddhist Text Translation Society (partial) of Śikṣānanda's rendering of the *Avataṃsaka Sutra*'s Chapter 26;
Thomas Cleary, supposedly (but not really) from Śikṣānanda's edition of the *Avataṃsaka Sutra,* this as Chapter 26 of his *Flower Ornament Scripture.*[3]

The Megumu Honda translation was done in 1961–62 when he was still a student at Yale, and, although perhaps useful for beginning students of Sanskrit, its utility is diminished by the author's early difficulties with both Sanskrit and English.

The BTTS effort is so far only a partial, consisting as it does of a translation of the first four of the ten grounds. I have been advised by a member of that translation team that, as of July, 2018, the tentative publication date for the rest of the Ten Grounds chapter is still two or more years away.

Regarding this *Ten Grounds Sutra* itself, Thomas Cleary's translation, although represented as a translation of Chapter 26 of the Śikṣānanda edition of the *Avataṃsaka Sutra,* is instead apparently a loose translation of the P. L. Vaidya Sanskrit edition of the *Daśabhūmika-sūtra.*

Although there are other schemas describing the levels of cultivation through which one passes in cultivating the bodhisattva path, the "ten grounds" arrangement described in this text is really quite standard for the Classic Indian Mahāyana tradition. As listed in the introductory section of this chapter, these ten levels of progress along the bodhisattva path are as follows:

1) The Ground of Joyfulness (*pramuditā*);
2) The Ground of Stainlessness (*vimalā*);
3) The Ground of Shining Light (*prabhākarī*);
4) The Ground of Blazing Brilliance (*arciṣmati*);[4]
5) The Difficult-to-Conquer Ground (*sudurjayā*);
6) The Ground of Direct Presence (*abhimukhī*);
7) The Far-Reaching Ground (*dūraṃgamā*);
8) The Ground of Immovability (*acalā*);
9) The Ground of Excellent Intelligence (*sādhumatī*);[5]
10) The Ground of the Dharma Cloud (*dharma-megha*).

Each of these grounds is correlated with the practice of one of these ten perfections:

The perfection of giving (*dāna-pāramitā*);
The perfection of moral virtue (*śīla-pāramitā*);
The perfection of patience (*kṣānti-pāramitā*);
The perfection of vigor (*vīrya-pāramitā*);
The perfection of *dhyāna* meditation (*dhyāna-pāramitā*);
The perfection of wisdom (*prajñā-pāramitā*);
The perfection of skillful means (*upāya-pāramitā*);

The perfection of vows (*praṇidhāna-pāramitā*);
The perfection of powers (*bala-pāramitā*);
The perfection of knowledge (*jñāna-pāramitā*).

There are also other correlations between particular grounds and important bodhisattva skills and capacities. Examples include:

The four means of attraction on the first four grounds;
The thirty-seven enlightenment factors on the fourth ground;
The four truths on the fifth ground;
The twelve links of conditioned arising on the sixth ground;
The unproduced-dharmas patience on the eighth ground;
The four unimpeded knowledges on the ninth ground.

According to this text, as the bodhisattva moves from one level to another in his cultivation of the ten grounds, he sees more and more buddhas, manifests more and more bodhisattva transformation bodies attended by bodhisattva retinues, and appears as a bodhisattva king in higher and higher stations of existence. This bodhisattva kingship phenomenon begins with his appearance as a king over the continent of Jambudvīpa on the first ground after which he appears as a king over all four continents on the second ground, appears as a king of the Trāyastriṃśa Heaven on the third ground, and so forth, finally culminating with his appearance as a king of the Akaniṣṭha Heaven on the tenth ground.

There were a number of difficulties that I encountered in translating this sutra from Chinese, most of which involve ambiguities in meaning introduced by the limitations of Chinese language in accurately reflecting Sanskrit technical term nuances. This problem is well evidenced by the particular Chinese-language technical term translations chosen by Kumārajīva. (The challenges I encountered in translating Śikṣānanda's "Ten Grounds" chapter of the *Avataṃsaka Sutra* were nearly identical.) Fortunately, because I could consult the surviving Sanskrit edition, it was for the most part possible to trace the antecedent Sanskrit terms and then choose somewhat more accurate English technical term translations than would have resulted from simply trying to translate Kumārajīva's terms directly from Chinese. Relative clarity in this matter was aided somewhat by J. Rahder's *Glossary*.[6] Even though the P. L. Vaidya Sanskrit edition dates from roughly a millennium after the Śikṣānanda and Kumārajīva editions, I think it is still mostly valid to rely on it for this purpose because, even as aspects of meaning at the sentence and paragraph level of the Sanskrit manuscript morph over time with each recopying or transcription from memory, technical terms still tend to remain unchanged. The same cannot be said for the actual text of the scripture because we can readily observe very obvious differences between the Sanskrit edition and the very early Śikṣānanda and Kumārajīva editions.

The first and most obvious problem is the difficulty which the Chinese translations have in reliably reflecting the difference between technical terms such as *jñāna* (knowledge, cognition, etc.) and *prajñā* (wisdom). In an ideal translation world, Kumārajīva and Śikṣānanda would have very rigorously stuck with simply *zhi* (智) for "*jñāna* / knowledge" and *zhihui* (智慧) for "*prajñā* / wisdom," but this is not the case, especially in the translation of verse lines where the need for extreme economy in composing Chinese 5- or 7-character verse lines where it often became necessary to shorten *zhihui* (智慧) to simply *zhi* (智), thereby accidentally obscuring for the Chinese reader the difference between "wisdom" and "knowledge." I found that this problem was fairly easily overcome through consulting the Sanskrit.

Other technical terms which initially produced difficulties due to the widely varying and sometimes deceptive Chinese translations were *adhyāsaya* (usually "higher aspirations," etc.), *āśaya* (usually "intentions," "resolute intentions," "dispositions," "inclinations," etc.), and *adhimukti* (usually "resolute beliefs," "resolute faith," "convictions," etc.). Had I not closely tracked the Sanskrit text, it would have been nearly impossible to accurately translate these terms and preserve their distinctions.

Due to the particular need of specialists and advanced students to closely track and distinguish technical terms and other issues such as these, at least in the multilingual editions of my translation, I am including under the same cover not only the facing-page Chinese simplified and traditional texts, but also (in the back of the book) the Sanskrit text. Use of the digital Sanskrit text is by the kind permission of Dr. Miroj Shakya, Project Coordinator of the Digital Sanskrit Buddhist Canon Project. The Sanskrit text itself is the edition edited by P. L. Vaidya and published by The Mithila Institute of Post-Graduate Studies and Research in Sanskrit learning. To ease the reader's correlation of the Sanskrit text with both the English translation and the facing-page Chinese, I have embedded the alphabetical Sanskrit section headings within all versions of the text (Chinese, English, and Sanskrit). These very helpful alphabetical section markers originate with Johannes Rahder who embedded them in his 1923 and 1926 editions of the *Daśabhūmika-Sūtra*.[7] In all cases I have placed these alphabetical section headings within the texts in bolded reduced-font "curly brackets" or "braces" as follows: **{A}**, **{B}**, **{AA}**, etc.

In bringing forth this translation, I making no claims to absolute accuracy. Though I have been assisted by critical comments from about a half dozen colleagues, it is still possible that there is room for improvement even after going through the manuscript so many times. I hope that readers who notice errors or infelicities will favor me with constructive email criticism via the Kalavinka website. I hope that this edition will at least encourage a deeper study of this text by students of the Dharma.

Bhikshu Dharmamitra
Seattle
July 4, 2019

Introduction Endnotes

1. Citing Kusugai, Richard Robinson (*Early Mādhyamika in India and China*, p. 76) says that Kumārajīva is said to have "procrastinated about starting work on the *Daśabhūmika* until Buddhayaśas joined him in the undertaking." Buddhayaśas arrived in Chang'an in 408, so the translation must date from around that time.
2. Sinor, D., Raghu Vira, Honda, Megumu, & Permanent International Altaistic Conference. (1968). *Studies in South, East, and Central Asia : Presented as a memorial volume to the late Professor Raghu Vira* (Śata-piṭaka series ; v. 74). New Delhi: International Academy of Indian Culture.
3. Cleary, T. (1984). The Flower Ornament Scripture : A Translation of the Avatamsaka Sutra. Boulder : [New York]: Shambhala Publications ; Distributed in the U.S. by Random House.
4. SA,SD, and Prajñā all translate the name of this *bhūmi* as "the Ground of Blazing Intelligence" (焰慧地). This appears to be the result of an error arising from misinterpreting the Sanskrit name (*arciṣmatī*) by mistaking a suffix indicating possession (*-mat* modified to agree with the feminine noun *bhūmi* to become *-matī*) for a completely unrelated word that means "intelligence," "intellect," "mind" (*mati*). (BB, BR, KB, and the Tibetan all recognize *–matī* as a possessive suffix and hence accord with the Sanskrit meaning.) I have chosen to "bridge" the problem by translating the name of this ground as "the Ground of Blazing Brilliance" in order to allow both meanings the be reflected in the word "blazing" and thus more or less accurately translate both the (seemingly erroneous) SA translation and the correct meaning of the Sanskrit.
5. There seem to be two distinctly different understandings of the meaning of this ground:

   DR, SA, BB, BR, SD, and Prajñā all translate the name of this *bhūmi* as "the Ground of Excellent Intelligence" (善慧地). DR translates that same meaning slightly differently: (善哉意). The Tibetan translation also corresponds to this with "the Ground of Excellent Insight" (*legs pa'i blo gros*). Strictly speaking, one could infer that most of these renderings appear be the result of an error arising from misinterpreting the Sanskrit name (*sādhumatī*) by mistaking a suffix indicating possession (*-mat* modified to agree with the feminine noun *bhūmi* to become *-matī*) for a completely unrelated word that means "intelligence," "intellect," or "mind" (*mati*).

Of all of the Chinese and Tibetan translators, it appears that the Kumārajīva-Buddhayaśas translation team may have been the only one to render the name of this *bhūmi* more or less in accordance with the above-referenced "strictly correct" interpretation of the Sanskrit term as "the Ground of Sublime Goodness" (妙善地). The KB edition only employs the possibly erroneous Chinese and Tibetan default rendering once (in its initial listing of the ten bodhisattva grounds), but otherwise accords with the strictly grammatically correct interpretation of the term throughout its detailed discussion of the ninth *bhūmi* itself.

6. Glossary of the Sanskrit, Tibetan, Mongolian, and Chinese Versions of the Daśabhūmika-Sūtra. Compiled by J. Rahder. (Buddhica, Documents et Travaux pour l'Étude du Bouddhisme publiés sous la direction de J. Przyluski; Deuxième Série; Documents—Tome I). Paris: Librarie Orientaliste Paul Geuthner, 1928.

7. On page vii in his Introduction to his *Glossary of the Sanskrit, Tibetan, Mongolian and Chinese Versions of the Daśabhūmika-Sūtra,* Rahder says, "capital letters between brackets refer to the sections of the chapters as indicated in my edition (1926)." (They are also present in his 1923 edition of the *Daśabhūmikasutra* that was published together with the *Bodhisattvabhūmi* with only the minor oversight of having left out "A" and "B" at the very beginning of the first *bhūmi.*)

T10n0286_p0497c01║
497c02║ No. 286 [Nos. 278(22), 279(26), 285, 287]
497c03║ 十住經卷第一
497c04║
497c05║ [16]後秦[17]龜茲國[18]三藏鳩摩羅[19]什譯

正體字

大乘华严部・第0101部十住经六卷姚秦三藏法师鸠摩罗什共佛陀耶舍译
・ 经名 ・ 卷数 ・ 跋序
・ 品名 ・ 品数 ・ 译作者字体：大号 中号 小号
十住经卷第一
欢喜地第一
十住经卷第二
离垢地第二明地第三
十住经卷第三
焰地第四难胜地第五现前地第六
十住经卷第四
远行地第七不动地第八
十住经卷第五
妙善地第九法云地第十上
十住经卷第六
法云地第十下
十住经卷第一

简体字

The Ten Grounds Sutra

The Daśabhūmika Sūtra

(Taisho T10, no. 286, pp. 497c01–535a20)

Translated from Sanskrit to Chinese in the Later Qin Era[1]
by Tripiṭaka Master Kumārajīva[2] from the State of Kucha.[3]

Chinese to English Translation by Bhikshu Dharmamitra

正體字

497c06‖ 歡喜地第一
497c07‖ {A}如是我聞。一時佛在他化自在天王宮摩尼
497c08‖ 寶殿上。與大菩薩眾俱。皆於阿耨多羅三藐
497c09‖ 三菩提。不退轉。從他方界。俱來集會。此諸菩
497c10‖ 薩。一切菩薩。智慧行處。悉得自在。諸如來智
497c11‖ 慧入處。悉皆得入。善能教化一切世間。隨時
497c12‖ 普示神通等事。於念念中。皆能成辦具足一
497c13‖ 切菩薩所願。於一切世[20]界一切劫一切國土。
497c14‖ 常修諸菩薩行。具足一切菩薩所有福德智
497c15‖ 慧。而無窮盡。能為一切。而作饒益。能到一
497c16‖ 切菩薩智慧方便彼岸。能示眾生生死及涅
497c17‖ 槃門。不斷一切菩薩所行。善遊一切菩薩禪
497c18‖ 定解脫三昧。神通明慧。諸所施為。善能示現
497c19‖ 一切菩薩無作神足。皆悉已得。於一念頃。能
497c20‖ 至十方諸佛大會。

简体字

欢喜地第一

如是我闻：一时，佛在他化自在天王宫摩尼宝殿上，与大菩萨众俱，皆于阿耨多罗三藐三菩提不退转，从他方界俱来集会。此诸菩萨，一切菩萨智慧行处悉得自在，诸如来智慧入处悉皆得入，善能教化一切世间，随时普示神通等事，于念念中皆能成办具足一切菩萨所愿，于一切世界、一切劫、一切国土常修诸菩萨行，具足一切菩萨所有福德智慧而无穷尽，能为一切而作饶益，能到一切菩萨智慧方便彼岸，能示众生生死及涅槃门，不断一切菩萨所行，善游一切菩萨禅定解脱三昧神通明慧，诸所施为善能示现，一切菩萨无作神足皆悉已得，于一念顷能至十方诸佛大会，

Chapter One
The Joyfulness Ground[4]

I. The Introductory Section

A. The Setting and Audience

{A} Thus I have heard. At one time, the Buddha was residing in Maṇi Jewel Hall within the palace of the Paranirmita Vaśavartin Heaven King together with an assembly of great bodhisattvas, all of whom were irreversible in their progression toward *anuttarasamyaksaṃbodhi*. They had all assembled there from the realms of other regions.

B. The Great Bodhisattvas and Their Qualities

These bodhisattvas had all achieved sovereign mastery in those places where all bodhisattvas' wisdom is practiced and had all entered into all those places that all *tathāgatas'* wisdom enters.[5] They were well able to teach the inhabitants of all worlds and were freely able at any time to everywhere manifest the spiritual superknowledges and other such phenomena.

In each and every mind-moment, they were entirely able to perfectly accomplish what all bodhisattvas have vowed to accomplish. In all worlds, in all kalpas, and in all lands, they always cultivated all of the bodhisattva practices and endlessly carried on the perfection of all bodhisattvas' merit and knowledge.

They were able to act for the benefit of all and were able to reach the perfection of all bodhisattvas' wisdom and skillful means. They were able to reveal for beings the gateway leading from *saṃsāra* to nirvāṇa and never desisted from coursing in the practices of all bodhisattvas.

They skillfully roamed in all of the bodhisattva's *dhyāna* concentrations, liberations, samādhis, spiritual superknowledges, and clear knowledges.[6] In all the endeavors to which they devoted themselves, they were well able to manifest all of the bodhisattva's effortlessly-implemented bases of psychic powers,[7] all of which they had already acquired.

In but a single mind-moment, they were able to go forth to the great assemblies of all buddhas throughout the ten directions

正體字

勸發諮請。受持法輪。常以
497c21‖ 大心。供養諸佛。常能修習諸大菩薩所行事
497c22‖ 業。其身普現無量世界。其音遍聞。無所不至。
497c23‖ 其心通達。明見三世一切菩薩。所有功德。具
497c24‖ 足修習。如是諸菩薩摩訶薩功德無量無邊。
497c25‖ 於無數劫。說不可盡
497c26‖ 其名曰金剛藏菩薩摩訶薩。寶藏菩薩。蓮華
497c27‖ 藏菩薩。德藏菩薩。蓮華德藏菩薩。日藏菩薩。
497c28‖ 月藏菩薩。淨月藏菩薩。照一切世間莊嚴藏
497c29‖ 菩薩。智慧照明藏菩薩。妙德藏菩薩。栴檀德
498a01‖ 藏菩薩。華德藏菩薩。優鉢羅華德藏菩薩。天
498a02‖ 德藏菩薩。福德藏菩薩。無[1]閡清淨[2]智德藏
498a03‖ 菩薩。功德藏菩薩。那羅延德藏菩薩。無垢藏
498a04‖ 菩薩。離垢藏菩薩。種種樂說莊嚴藏菩薩。大
498a05‖ 光明網藏菩薩。淨明威德王藏菩薩。

简体字

劝发咨请受持法轮，常以大心供养诸佛，常能修习诸大菩萨所行事业，其身普现无量世界，其音遍闻无所不至，其心通达明见三世一切菩萨，所有功德具足修习。

如是诸菩萨摩诃萨功德无量无边，于无数劫说不可尽。其名曰：金刚藏菩萨摩诃萨、宝藏菩萨、莲华藏菩萨、德藏菩萨、莲华德藏菩萨、日藏菩萨、月藏菩萨、净月藏菩萨、照一切世间庄严藏菩萨、智慧照明藏菩萨、妙德藏菩萨、栴檀德藏菩萨、华德藏菩萨、优钵罗华德藏菩萨、天德藏菩萨、福德藏菩萨、无碍清净智德藏菩萨、功德藏菩萨、那罗延德藏菩萨、无垢藏菩萨、离垢藏菩萨、种种乐说庄严藏菩萨、大光明网藏菩萨、净明威德王藏菩萨、

wherein they entreated them to initiate teachings, freely posed queries to them, and received and retained the teachings brought forth through the turning of the Dharma wheel.[8]

They always devoted their great minds to presenting offerings to all buddhas and they remained ever able to cultivate the works practiced by all great bodhisattvas. Their bodies manifested in countless worlds. Their voices were universally heard, reaching everywhere without exception. Their minds had achieved a penetrating level of comprehension whereby they were able to clearly see all bodhisattvas of the three periods of time. They perfectly cultivated and practiced all the meritorious qualities. The meritorious qualities of these bodhisattva *mahāsattvas*[9] were so measureless and boundless that they could never be completely described even in countless kalpas.

C. The Names of the Bodhisattvas in Attendance

Their names were:[10]

Vajragarbha Bodhisattva Mahāsattva;
Jeweled Treasury Bodhisattva;
Lotus Treasury Bodhisattva;
Treasury of Qualities Bodhisattva;
Treasury of Lotus Qualities Bodhisattva;
Solar Treasury Bodhisattva;
Lunar Treasury Bodhisattva;
Pure Moon Treasury Bodhisattva;
Treasury of Adornments Illuminating All Worlds Bodhisattva;
Treasury of Wisdom[11] Illumination Bodhisattva;
Treasury of Sublime Qualities Bodhisattva;
Treasury of Candana's Qualities Bodhisattva;
Treasury of Floral Qualities Bodhisattva;
Utpala Blossom Treasury Bodhisattva;
Treasury of Celestial Qualities Bodhisattva;
Treasury of Merit Bodhisattva;
Treasury of Unimpeded Pure Knowledge Qualities Bodhisattva;
Treasury of Meritorious Qualities Bodhisattva;
Treasury of Nārāyaṇa's Qualities Bodhisattva;
Treasury of Stainlessness Bodhisattva;
Treasury of Defilement Transcendence Bodhisattva;
Treasury of Adornment with All Forms of Eloquence Bodhisattva;
Great Brilliance Net Treasury Bodhisattva;
Treasury of the King of Pure Light's Awesome Qualities Bodhisattva;

正體字

大金山
498a06‖ 光明威德王藏菩薩。一切相莊嚴淨德藏菩
498a07‖ 薩。金剛焰德相莊嚴藏菩薩。焰熾藏菩薩。宿
498a08‖ 王光照藏菩薩。虛空無[＊]閡妙音藏菩薩。陀羅
498a09‖ 尼功德持一切世間願藏菩薩。海莊嚴藏菩
498a10‖ 薩。須彌德藏菩薩。淨一切功德藏菩薩。如來
498a11‖ 藏菩薩。佛德藏菩薩。解脫月菩薩。如是等菩
498a12‖ 薩摩訶薩。無量無邊。不可思議。不可稱說。金
498a13‖ 剛藏菩薩摩訶薩。而為上首
498a14‖ {B} 爾時金剛藏菩薩摩訶薩。承佛威神。入菩薩
498a15‖ 大智慧光明三昧。{C} 即時十方世界。於一方。過
498a16‖ [3]十億佛土微塵數世界乃有如來。名金剛藏。
498a17‖ 如是次第。十億佛土微塵數諸佛。皆現其身。
498a18‖ 名金剛藏。十方世界。皆亦如是。同聲讚言。
498a19‖ 善哉善哉。金剛藏。乃能入是菩薩大智慧光
498a20‖ 明三昧。如是十方世界微塵數等諸佛。皆同
498a21‖ 一號。加汝威神。又盧舍那佛。本願力故。又汝
498a22‖ 有大智慧故。

简体字

大金山光明威德王藏菩萨、一切相庄严净德藏菩萨、金刚焰德相庄严藏菩萨、焰炽藏菩萨、宿王光照藏菩萨、虚空无碍妙音藏菩萨、陀罗尼功德持一切世间愿藏菩萨、海庄严藏菩萨、须弥德藏菩萨、净一切功德藏菩萨、如来藏菩萨、佛德藏菩萨、解脱月菩萨。如是等菩萨摩诃萨，无量无边，不可思议，不可称说，金刚藏菩萨摩诃萨而为上首。

尔时，金刚藏菩萨摩诃萨，承佛威神，入菩萨大智慧光明三昧。即时十方世界，于一方过十亿佛土微尘数世界乃有如来，名金刚藏；如是次第，十亿佛土微尘数诸佛皆现其身，名金刚藏。十方世界，皆亦如是，同声赞言："善哉！善哉！金刚藏，乃能入是菩萨大智慧光明三昧。如是十方世界微尘数等诸佛，皆同一号，加汝威神。又卢舍那佛，本愿力故。又汝有大智慧故，

Treasury of the King of the Great Golden Mountain of Light's Awesome Qualities Bodhisattva;
Treasury of Adornment With the Pure Qualities of All Marks Bodhisattva;
Treasury of Adornment With Vajra Flames' Marks Bodhisattva;
Treasury of Blazing Flames Bodhisattva;
Treasury of the Constellation Kings' Radiance Bodhisattva;
Treasury of the Unimpeded Sublime Sound of Emptiness Bodhisattva;
Treasury of Dhāraṇī Qualities and Vows Sustaining All Worlds Bodhisattva;
Treasury of Oceanic Adornment Bodhisattva;
Treasury of a Sumeru of Qualities Bodhisattva;
Treasury of the Purification of All Meritorious Qualities Bodhisattva;
Tathāgata Treasury Bodhisattva;
Treasury of Buddha Qualities Bodhisattva;
And Liberation Moon Bodhisattva.

Bodhisattva *mahāsattvas* such as these were present there in measureless, boundless, inconceivable, and indescribable numbers.[12] Vajragarbha Bodhisattva Mahāsattva served as their head.

D. Vajragarbha Enters Samādhi and Countless Buddhas Manifest

{B} At that time, Vajragarbha Bodhisattva Mahāsattva aided by the Buddha's awesome spiritual power, entered "the bodhisattva's great wisdom light samādhi."[13] {C} Then, off in one of the directions among the worlds of the ten directions, beyond worlds as numerous as the atoms in ten *koṭis*[14] of buddha lands, there immediately appeared a Tathāgata named Vajragarbha. And in this same manner, there were in sequence buddhas as numerous as the atoms in ten *koṭis* of buddha lands, all named Vajragarbha, who manifested their bodies. And so it was as well in all worlds of the ten directions.

E. The Buddhas Praise Him and Encourage Him To Teach the Ten Grounds

All of them together, as if with a single voice, uttered their praises, saying:

It is good indeed, good indeed, Vajragarbha, that you are now able to enter the great wisdom light samādhi. In this way, buddhas as numerous as the atoms in the worlds of the ten directions, all of them of the same name, augment your awesome spiritual power.

This is also due to the power of the original vows of Rocana Buddha,[15] also because you possess great wisdom,[16] and also so

正體字

又與一切菩薩不可思議。諸佛
498a23‖ 法明。所謂。{D}令入智慧地故。攝一切善根故。善
498a24‖ 分別選擇一切佛法故。廣知諸法故。決定說
498a25‖ 諸法故。無分別智善分別故。一切世間法不
498a26‖ 能污故。出世間善根清淨故。得不可思議智
498a27‖ 力故。得一切智人智處故。又得菩薩十地故。
498a28‖ 如實說菩薩十地差別故。分別說無漏法不
498a29‖ 著故。大智慧光明。善擇以自莊嚴故。令入具
498b01‖ 足智門故。隨所應住次第說故。得無[*]閡樂
498b02‖ 說光明故。具足大無[*]閡智[4]地不忘失菩[5]薩
498b03‖ 心故。教化成就一切眾生性故。得一切遍至
498b04‖ 決定智故。{E}又金剛藏。汝當說此法門差別。所
498b05‖ 謂。

简体字

又与一切菩萨不可思议诸佛法明，所谓：令入智慧地故，摄一切善根故，善分别选择一切佛法故，广知诸法故，决定说诸法故，无分别智善分别故，一切世间法不能污故，出世间善根清净故，得不可思议智力故，得一切智人智处故，又得菩萨十地故，如实说菩萨十地差别故，分别说无漏法不著故，大智慧光明善择以自庄严故，令入具足智门故，随所应住次第说故，得无碍乐说光明故，具足大无碍智地不忘失菩萨心故，教化成就一切众生性故，得一切遍至决定智故。又金刚藏，汝当说此法门差别，所谓：

that you will bestow upon all bodhisattvas the inconceivable Dharma light of all buddhas, in particular doing so:

{D} To cause their entry into the grounds of wisdom;[17]

To facilitate their gathering of all roots of goodness;

To enable their skillful differentiation and selection of all dharmas of the Buddha;

To enable their vast knowing of all dharmas;

To enable their decisively resolute explication of all dharmas;

To cause their skillful differentiation with non-discriminating knowledge;

To ensure that they cannot be defiled by any worldly dharma;

To facilitate their purification of roots of world-transcending goodness;

To enable their acquisition of the inconceivable powers of knowledge;

To enable their acquisition of the sphere of knowledge of those possessed of all-knowledge;

To also cause their acquisition of the bodhisattva's ten grounds;

To present a reality-accordant explanation of the differentiating aspects of the bodhisattva's ten grounds;

To present a differentiating explanation of the non-attachment associated with the dharmas that are free of the contaminants;[18]

To enable their own adornment through skillful analysis using the light of great wisdom;

To cause their entry into the gateway of fully accomplished knowledge;

To enable them to provide sequential explanations appropriate to the circumstances in which they abide;

To facilitate their acquisition of the light of unimpeded eloquence;

To cause their complete fulfillment of the grounds of great unimpeded knowledge without ever losing the bodhisattva's resolve;

To enable their teaching and complete development of all realms[19] of beings;

And also in order to cause their acquisition of definitive knowledge that reaches everywhere.

{E} Additionally, Vajragarbha Bodhisattva, you should explain the differentiating aspects associated with these Dharma gateways, doing so:

正體字

諸佛神力故。汝能堪受如來神力故。自善
498b06‖ 根清淨故。清淨法性性故。饒益眾生性故。令
498b07‖ 眾生得清淨法身智身故。於一切佛得受記
498b08‖ 故。得一切世間最高大身故。過一切世間道
498b09‖ 故。出世間善根清淨故。{F} 即時十方諸佛。示金
498b10‖ 剛藏真實無上佛身。與無障礙樂說之辯。與
498b11‖ 善分別清淨智慧。與善憶念不忘。與善決定
498b12‖ 意。與遍至一切智處。與諸佛無壞力。與諸佛
498b13‖ 無所畏不怯弱。與諸佛無礙智分別諸法善
498b14‖ 開法門。與一切諸佛上妙身口意所作。{G} 何以
498b15‖ 故。以得菩薩大智慧光明三昧法故。亦是菩
498b16‖ 薩本願力故。志心清淨故。智慧明白故。善集
498b17‖ 助道法故。善修本事故。能持無量念故。信解
498b18‖ 清淨光明法故。

简体字

诸佛神力故，汝能堪受如来神力故，自善根清净故，清净法性性故，饶益众生性故，令众生得清净法身智身故，于一切佛得受记故，得一切世间最高大身故，过一切世间道故，出世间善根清净故。”

即时十方诸佛，示金刚藏真实无上佛身，与无障碍乐说之辩，与善分别清净智慧，与善忆念不忘，与善决定意，与遍至一切智处，与诸佛无坏力，与诸佛无所畏不怯弱，与诸佛无碍智分别诸法善开法门，与一切诸佛上妙身口意所作。何以故？以得菩萨大智慧光明三昧法故，亦是菩萨本愿力故，志心清净故，智慧明白故，善集助道法故，善修本事故，能持无量念故，信解清净光明法故，

On account of the Buddhas' spiritual powers;
To be able to take on the Tathāgata's spiritual powers;
To facilitate purification of one's own roots of goodness;
To purify the realms of the Dharma realm;[20]
To benefit the realms of beings;
To cause beings to acquire the pure Dharma body and knowledge body;
To enable the receiving of the prediction from all buddhas;
To enable acquisition of the most lofty and grand body in the entire world;
To enable stepping beyond all worldly paths;
And also to facilitate purification of world-transcending roots of goodness.

F. The Buddhas Bestow Qualities and Abilities on Vajragarbha

{F} The Buddhas of the Ten Directions then immediately bestowed the following things on Vajragarbha Bodhisattva:

They bestowed the genuine and unsurpassable body of a buddha;[21]
They bestowed the skill of unimpededly eloquent discourse;
They bestowed skillfully differentiating pure wisdom;[22]
They bestowed the ability to skillfully remember and never forget;
They bestowed a skillfully decisive intelligence;[23]
They bestowed the bases for universally extensive omniscience;
They bestowed all buddhas' powers of invincibility;
They bestowed the fearlessnesses and absence of timidity;[24]
They bestowed all buddhas' unimpeded knowledges[25] that distinguish all dharmas and skillfully open the Dharma gateways;
And they also bestowed all buddhas' supremely sublime functions of body, speech, and mind.

{G} Why did this occur?:

This was due to his acquisition of the bodhisattva's great wisdom light samādhi;
Due to the power of the bodhisattva's original vows;
Due to the purification of his higher aspirations;[26]
Due to the brilliantly pristine purity of his wisdom;[27]
Due to his having well accumulated the dharmas constituting the provisions assisting realization of the path;[28]
Due to his having skillfully cultivated karmic works in the past;
Due to his ability to sustain a measurelessly capacious memory;
Due to his resolute faith[29] in the pure and radiant Dharma;

正體字

善得陀羅尼門無分別故。以
498b19‖ 智印善印法性故。{H}爾時十方諸佛。皆伸右手。
498b20‖ 摩金剛藏菩薩頂。{I}金剛藏菩薩。即從三昧起。
498b21‖ {J}起已。告諸菩薩言。諸佛子。是諸菩薩事。先皆
498b22‖ 善自決定。無有過無分別。清淨明了。廣大如
498b23‖ 法性。究竟如虛空。遍覆一切十方諸佛世界
498b24‖ 眾生。為救度一切世間。為一切諸佛神力所
498b25‖ 護。何以故。諸菩薩摩訶薩。入過去諸佛智地。
498b26‖ 亦入未來現在諸佛智地。諸佛子。何等是諸
498b27‖ 菩薩摩訶薩智地。諸佛子。菩薩摩訶薩智地。
498b28‖ 有十。過去未來現在諸佛。已說。今說。當說。
498b29‖ 為是地故。我如是說。何等為十。一名喜地。二
498c01‖ 名淨地。三名明地。四名焰地。五名難勝地。六
498c02‖ 名現前地。七名深[6]遠地。八名不動地。九名
498c03‖ 善慧地。

简体字

善得陀罗尼门无分别故，以智印善印法性故。

尔时，十方诸佛皆伸右手，摩金刚藏菩萨顶。金刚藏菩萨即从三昧起，起已告诸菩萨言：“诸佛子，是诸菩萨事，先皆善自决定，无有过无分别，清净明了，广大如法性，究竟如虚空，遍覆一切十方诸佛世界众生，为救度一切世间，为一切诸佛神力所护。何以故？诸菩萨摩诃萨，入过去诸佛智地，亦入未来、现在诸佛智地。

“诸佛子，何等是诸菩萨摩诃萨智地？诸佛子，菩萨摩诃萨智地有十，过去、未来、现在诸佛已说、今说、当说，为是地故，我如是说。何等为十？一名喜地，二名净地，三名明地，四名焰地，五名难胜地，六名现前地，七名深远地，八名不动地，九名善慧地，

Due to his skillful acquisition of the *dhāraṇī*[30] gateways that are free of discriminations;
And it was also due to his being well-sealed by the seal of knowledge of the Dharma realm.[31]

G. Vajragarbha Emerges from Samādhi and Speaks of the Ten Grounds

{H} At that time, the Buddhas of the Ten Directions all extended their right hands and rubbed the crown of Vajragarbha Bodhisattva's head. {I} Vajragarbha Bodhisattva then immediately arose from samādhi. {J} Having emerged, he then informed the bodhisattvas:

Sons of the Buddha, as for these endeavors of all bodhisattvas, from the very beginning, they have all involved definite resolve and have remained entirely free of faults and free of discriminations. They have been pure, utterly brilliant, as vast as the Dharma realm itself, and as ultimately far-reaching as empty space. They have universally extended to cover all beings in all buddha worlds of the ten directions. They have been undertaken for the sake of rescuing and liberating the inhabitants of all worlds and have been carried forth under the protection of the spiritual powers of all buddhas.

And how has this come to be? All bodhisattva *mahāsattvas* enter the grounds of knowledge of all buddhas of the past and also enter the grounds of knowledge of all buddhas of the future and the present.

1. Vajragarbha Sets Forth the Names of the Ten Grounds

Sons of the Buddha, what are the grounds of knowledge of the bodhisattva *mahāsattvas*? Sons of the Buddha, the grounds of knowledge of the bodhisattvas are ten in number. All buddhas of the past, future, and present have proclaimed them, do now proclaim them, and shall proclaim in the future. It is for the sake of these very grounds that I set forth such a proclamation as this. What then are the ten? They are:[32]

First, the Ground of Joyfulness;
Second, the Ground of Stainlessness;
Third, the Ground of Shining Light;
Fourth, the ground of Blazing Brilliance;
Fifth, the Difficult-to-Conquer ground;
Sixth, the Ground of Direct Presence;
Seventh, the Far-Reaching Ground;
Eighth, the Ground of Immovability;
Ninth, the Ground of Excellent Intelligence;[33]

正體字

十名法雲地。諸佛子。是十地者。三世
498c04‖ 諸佛。已說。今說。當說。我不見有諸佛國土不
498c05‖ 說是菩薩十地者。何以故。此十地。是菩薩最
498c06‖ 上妙道。最上明淨法門。所謂。分別十住事。
498c07‖ 諸佛子。是事不可思議。所謂。菩薩摩訶薩。隨
498c08‖ 順諸地智慧。[7] {K} 是時金剛藏菩薩摩訶薩。說諸
498c09‖ 菩薩十地名已。默然而住。不復分別義趣。爾
498c10‖ 時一切菩薩眾。聞說[8]菩薩十地名已咸皆渴
498c11‖ 仰。欲聞解釋。各作是念。何因何緣。金剛藏菩
498c12‖ 薩。說菩薩十地名已。默然而住。不更解釋。時
498c13‖ 大菩薩眾中。有菩薩摩訶薩。名解脫月。知諸
498c14‖ 菩薩。心之所念。以偈問金剛藏菩薩言
498c15‖ 淨智念慧人　何故說菩薩
498c16‖ 諸地名號已　默然不解釋 {1}
498c17‖ 今諸大菩薩　心皆懷猶豫
498c18‖ 何故說是名　而不演其義 {2}

简体字

十名法云地。诸佛子，是十地者，三世诸佛已说、今说、当说。我不见有诸佛国土不说是菩萨十地者。何以故？此十地，是菩萨最上妙道、最上明净法门，所谓分别十住事。诸佛子，是事不可思议，所谓菩萨摩诃萨随顺诸地智慧。”

是时，金刚藏菩萨摩诃萨，说诸菩萨十地名已，默然而住，不复分别义趣。

尔时，一切菩萨众闻说菩萨十地名已，咸皆渴仰，欲闻解释，各作是念：“何因何缘，金刚藏菩萨说菩萨十地名已，默然而住，不更解释？”

时，大菩萨众中，有菩萨摩诃萨，名解脱月，知诸菩萨心之所念，以偈问金刚藏菩萨言：

“净智念慧人，　何故说菩萨，
诸地名号已，　默然不解释？
今诸大菩萨，　心皆怀犹豫，
何故说是名，　而不演其义？

Tenth, the Dharma Cloud Ground.

Sons of the Buddha, all buddhas of the three periods of time have proclaimed these ten grounds in the past, do proclaim them in the present, and shall also proclaim them in the future. I have not seen that there exists any buddha land anywhere wherein these ten bodhisattva grounds have not been proclaimed. And why is this? These ten grounds constitute the bodhisattvas' most supreme and sublime path and the most supreme gateway into Dharma's light and purity. We refer here to the differentiation of the matters pertaining to these ten stations.

Sons of the Buddha, these matters are inconceivable. We refer here to the wisdom[34] of the bodhisattva *mahāsattvas* as they progress through the grounds.

2. Vajragarbha Bodhisattva Falls Silent

{K} Then, having set forth the names of the bodhisattvas' ten grounds, Vajragarbha Bodhisattva Mahāsattva fell silent, remained in place, and did not proceed to present a differentiating explanation of their meanings and import.

H. The Congregation Is Caused to Wonder Why There Is No Explanation

At that time, having heard the names of the bodhisattvas' ten grounds, the entire congregation of bodhisattvas all gazed up at him with thirst-like anticipation, wishing to hear him set forth an explanation. They all had this thought, "Due to what causes and what conditions does Vajragarbha Bodhisattva, having set forth the names of the bodhisattvas' ten grounds, then fall silent and remain in place without presenting any further explanation?"

I. Liberation Moon Bodhisattva's First Request for Dharma Teaching

At that time, within that congregation of bodhisattvas, there was a bodhisattva *mahāsattva* named Liberation Moon. Knowing the thoughts in the minds of those bodhisattvas, he then employed verses to inquire of Vajragarbha Bodhisattva, asking:[35]

"O mindful and sagacious man possessed of pure knowledge,
why do you, having uttered the names
of the bodhisattvas' grounds,
then fall silent without proceeding to explain them? {1}

Now, the great bodhisattvas
are all beset by thoughts of hesitation,
Why is it that you utter these names
and yet refrain from proclaiming their meanings? {2}

正體字

498c19║ 大智諸菩薩　咸皆欲聽聞
498c20║ 如是諸地義　願為分別說 {3}
498c21║ 是諸菩薩眾　清淨無瑕穢
498c22║ 安住堅[9]實法　具足智功德 {4}
498c23║ 皆以恭敬心　瞻仰於仁者
498c24║ 願欲聞所說　如渴思甘露 {5}
498c25║ 金剛藏菩薩　聞說是事已
498c26║ 欲令大眾悅　即時說頌言 {6}
498c27║ 諸菩薩所行　第一難思議
498c28║ 分別是諸地　諸佛之根本 {7}
498c29║ 微妙甚難見　非心所能及
499a01║ 從佛智慧出　若聞[1]則迷沒 {8}
499a02║ 持心如金剛　深信佛智慧
499a03║ 以為第一妙　心無有疑難
499a04║ 遠離計我心　及心所行地
499a05║ 如是諸菩薩　爾乃能聽聞 {9}
499a06║ 寂滅無漏智　分別說甚難
499a07║ 如畫於虛空　如執空中風 {10}
499a08║ 我念佛智慧　第一難思議

简体字

大智诸菩萨，咸皆欲听闻，
如是诸地义，愿为分别说。
是诸菩萨众，清净无瑕秽，
安住坚实法，具足智功德，
皆以恭敬心，瞻仰于仁者，
愿欲闻所说，如渴思甘露。
金刚藏菩萨，闻说是事已，
欲令大众悦，即时说颂言：
诸菩萨所行，第一难思议，
分别是诸地，诸佛之根本。
微妙甚难见，非心所能及，
从佛智慧出，若闻则迷没。
持心如金刚，深信佛智慧，
以为第一妙，心无有疑难。
远离计我心，及心所行地，
如是诸菩萨，尔乃能听闻。
寂灭无漏智，分别说甚难，
如画于虚空，如执空中风。
我念佛智慧，第一难思议，

These greatly wise bodhisattvas
all wish to hear
the meanings of such grounds as these.
Please distinguish and explain them for their sakes. {3}

This entire congregation of bodhisattvas
is pure and free of flaws or defilements.
They abide securely in the solid and genuine Dharma
and are entirely complete in knowledge and meritorious qualities. {4}

With reverential minds,
they all gaze longingly up to you, O Humane One,
wishing to be able to hear what you will proclaim,
just as those beset by thirst long for the elixir of sweet-dew." {5}

J. Vajragarbha Explains His Silence

Then, Vajragarbha Bodhisattva,
having heard him speak on this matter
and wishing to please those in that great assembly,
immediately uttered verses, saying: {6}

The matter of the practices of all bodhisattvas
is the most difficult of subjects to fathom.
A differentiating explanation of these grounds,
the very origin of all buddhas, {7}

is a matter subtle, sublime, and extremely difficult to perceive.
This is not something that is accessible to thought.
It comes forth from the wisdom of the Buddha and is such that,
if one hears it, one may become submerged in confusion. {8}

Those whose minds have a capacity for retention as solid as vajra,
who possess a profound faith in the wisdom[36] of the Buddha,
and who take it to be the most supremely sublime—
It is these whose minds would remain free of doubts and difficulties.

Those who have transcended thoughts conceiving of a self
and the grounds wherein thought is active—
it is only bodhisattvas of this sort
who are then capable of hearing this. {9}

As for the quiescent knowledge that is free of contaminants,
a differentiating explanation of it would be extremely difficult.
It would be like painting a mural in space
or like seizing the wind as it moves through empty space. {10}

As I bring to mind the wisdom of the Buddha,
the foremost among all inconceivable subjects,

正體字

499a09‖ 眾生少能信　　是故我默然 {11}
499a10‖ {L} 解脫月菩薩。聞說此已。語金剛藏菩薩言。佛
499a11‖ 子。是大菩薩眾。深心清淨。善行菩薩道。善集
499a12‖ 助道法。善能供養恭敬諸佛。於無量佛。多種
499a13‖ 善根。成就無量[2]深厚功德。離癡疑悔。無有
499a14‖ 貪著及諸結[＊]閡。深心信解。安住不動。於是
499a15‖ 法中。不隨他教。是故佛子。當承佛力。敷演此
499a16‖ 義。是諸菩薩。於是深法。皆能證知。時解脫
499a17‖ [3]月。欲重宣此義。而說偈言
499a18‖ 　願說安隱法　　菩薩無上行
499a19‖ 　分別於諸地　　令智慧清淨
499a20‖ 　眾智淨無垢　　安住深信解
499a21‖ 　於諸無量佛　　證知十地義
499a22‖ {M} 爾時金剛藏菩薩言。

简体字

众生少能信，　　是故我默然。”

解脱月菩萨闻说此已，语金刚藏菩萨言：“佛子，是大菩萨众，深心清净，善行菩萨道，善集助道法，善能供养恭敬诸佛，于无量佛多种善根，成就无量深厚功德，离痴疑悔，无有贪著及诸结碍，深心信解安住不动，于是法中不随他教。是故，佛子，当承佛力，敷演此义。是诸菩萨，于是深法，皆能证知。”

时，解脱月欲重宣此义，而说偈言：

“愿说安隐法，　　菩萨无上行，
分别于诸地，　　令智慧清净。
众智净无垢，　　安住深信解，
于诸无量佛，　　证知十地义。”

尔时，金刚藏菩萨言：

I see that there are but few beings able to believe in this.
It is for these reasons that I remain silent. {11}

K. Liberation Moon Bodhisattva's Second Request for Dharma Teaching

{L} Having heard him declare this, Liberation Moon Bodhisattva then addressed Vajragarbha Bodhisattva, saying:

O Son of the Buddha, as for those within this congregation of great bodhisattvas, they:

Are possessed of pure resolute intentions;[37]
Have well practiced the bodhisattva path;
Have well assembled the provisions for realization of the path.[38]
Have been well able to make offerings to and revere all buddhas;
Have extensively planted roots of goodness under countless buddhas;
Have perfected measurelessly many extremely well-developed meritorious qualities;
Have abandoned delusions, doubts, and regrets;
Are free of covetous attachments and the hindrances associated with the fetters;
Have developed securely established and unshakable resolute intentions and resolute faith;
And, as they abide in this Dharma, do not follow other sorts of teachings.

Therefore, O Son of the Buddha, aided by the Buddha's powers, you should extensively expound on the meaning of these things. These bodhisattvas are all able to realize and understand these profound dharmas.

At that time, Liberation Moon Bodhisattva, wishing to restate this idea, then spoke verses, saying:

Please explain these dharmas ensuring peace and security,
the bodhisattva's supreme practices,
by presenting differentiating explanations of the grounds,
thereby causing their wisdom to become purified.

The knowledge of this congregation is pure and free of defilement.
They are securely established in deep resolute faith,
have dwelt in the company of incalculably many buddhas, and
will realize and understand the ten grounds' meanings.

L. Vajragarbha Further Explains His Reticence to Teach This Dharma

{M} At that time, Vajragarbha Bodhisattva then responded, saying:

正體字

[4]佛子。是諸大眾。雖皆
499a23‖ 清淨。離癡疑悔。於此事中。不隨他教。其餘樂
499a24‖ 小法者。聞是甚深難思議事。或生疑悔。是人
499a25‖ 長夜。受諸衰惱。我愍此等。是故默然。爾時金
499a26‖ 剛藏菩薩。欲明了此義。而說偈言
499a27‖ 是眾雖清淨　深[5]智離疑悔
499a28‖ 其心已決定　不復隨他教
499a29‖ 無動如須彌　不亂如大海
499b01‖ 其[6]餘不久行　智慧未明了
499b02‖ 隨識不隨智　聞已生疑悔
499b03‖ 彼將墜惡趣　愍念故不說
499b04‖ {N}解脫月菩薩言。佛子願承佛力。善分別此不
499b05‖ 可思議法佛所護念事。令人易信解。所以者
499b06‖ 何。善說十地義。十方諸佛。法應護念。一切
499b07‖ 菩薩。護是事故。勤行精進。何以故。是菩薩。
499b08‖ 最上所行。得至一切諸佛法故。譬如所有經
499b09‖ 書。皆初章所攝。

简体字

“佛子，是诸大众，虽皆清净离痴疑悔，于此事中不随他教。其余乐小法者，闻是甚深难思议事，或生疑悔，是人长夜受诸衰恼。我愍此等，是故默然。”

尔时，金刚藏菩萨欲明了此义，而说偈言：

“是众虽清净，　深智离疑悔，
其心已决定，　不复随他教，
无动如须弥，　不乱如大海。
其余不久行，　智慧未明了，
随识不随智，　闻已生疑悔，
彼将坠恶趣，　愍念故不说。”

解脱月菩萨言：“佛子，愿承佛力，善分别此不可思议法佛所护念事，令人易信解。所以者何？善说十地义，十方诸佛，法应护念。一切菩萨护是事故，勤行精进。何以故？是菩萨最上所行，得至一切诸佛法故。譬如所有经书，皆初章所摄，

O Son of the Buddha, although those in this congregation are all pure, have abandoned delusion, doubts, and regrets, and do not follow others' teachings with regard to these matters, still, when others who delight in lesser dharmas hear of extremely profound and inconceivable matters such as these, they may well bring forth doubts and regrets about them. People such as these will then be bound to undergo all manner of ruin and torment for a long time. It is because I feel pity for people such as these that I have therefore become silent.

At that time, Vajragarbha Bodhisattva, wishing to fully clarify this meaning, thereupon uttered verses, saying:

Although those in this assembly are pure,
are deeply knowledgeable, have abandoned doubts and regrets,
are already possessed of decisive resolve,
are not inclined to again follow others' teachings,
are as unshakable as Mount Sumeru,
and are as imperturbable as the great ocean,

still, there are yet others not of long duration in their practice
whose wisdom has not yet become utterly brilliant,
who follow consciousness rather than knowledge,
and who, on hearing this, will generate doubts and regrets.
They will then be bound to fall into the wretched destinies.
It is out of pity for them that I therefore become silent.

M. Liberation Moon Bodhisattva's Third Request for Dharma Teaching

{N} Liberation Moon Bodhisattva then said:

O Son of the Buddha, aided by the powers of the Buddha, please skillfully differentiate these inconceivable dharmas, these matters borne in the protective mindfulness of the Buddhas, and thus allow others to easily develop resolute faith in them.

And why? When it comes to the skillful explanation of the meaning of the ten grounds, the Dharma of the buddhas of the ten directions requires that they should extend their protective mindfulness to all bodhisattvas in this circumstance. It is due to their receiving such protection in these matters that those bodhisattvas are then able to pursue diligent and vigorous practice.

And why is this? This is because these matters constitute the most supreme practices undertaken by these bodhisattvas, for these are the means that allow them to finally succeed in reaching the dharmas of all buddhas. This is analogous to the circumstance holding for all literature wherein, in every case, the bases of its creation are entirely subsumed in one's initial alphabet[39] and

正體字

初章為本。無有一字不入初
499b10‖ 章者。如是佛子。十地者。是一切佛法之根
499b11‖ 本。菩薩具足。行是十地。能得一切智慧。是
499b12‖ 故佛子。願說此義。諸佛護念。加以神力。令人
499b13‖ 信受。不可破壞。爾時解脫月菩薩。欲顯此義。
499b14‖ 而說偈言
499b15‖ 善哉智慧子　清淨行具足
499b16‖ 願說十地行　所入十地法
499b17‖ 具足於智慧　得以成菩提
499b18‖ 所有十方佛　最勝人中尊
499b19‖ 皆共護念汝　說是十地義
499b20‖ 十地為根本　是名智行處
499b21‖ 亦為究竟道　佛無量法聚
499b22‖ 譬如諸文字　皆攝在初章
499b23‖ 諸佛功德智　十地為根本
499b24‖ {O} 爾時諸菩薩。一時同聲。以偈請金剛藏菩薩言
499b26‖ 上妙智慧人　樂說無有量
499b27‖ 德重如山王　哀愍說十地 {12}

简体字

初章为本，无有一字不入初章者；如是，佛子，十地者，是一切佛法之根本，菩萨具足行是十地，能得一切智慧。是故，佛子，愿说此义，诸佛护念，加以神力，令人信受不可破坏。”

尔时，解脱月菩萨欲显此义，而说偈言：

善哉智慧子，　清净行具足
愿说十地行，　所入十地法，
具足于智慧，　得以成菩提。
所有十方佛，　最胜人中尊，
皆共护念汝，　说是十地义。
十地为根本，　是名智行处，
亦为究竟道，　佛无量法聚。
譬如诸文字，　皆摄在初章，
诸佛功德智，　十地为根本。”

尔时，诸菩萨一时同声，以偈请金刚藏菩萨言：

“上妙智慧人，　乐说无有量，
德重如山王，　哀愍说十地。

that initial alphabet serves as their very origin, for there is not even a single alphabetical character not already subsumed within that initial alphabet.

In this same manner, O Son of the Buddha, these ten grounds constitute the very origin of all dharmas of the Buddha. It is through the bodhisattva's complete practice of these ten grounds that he is able to gain all-knowledge.

Therefore, O Son of the Buddha, please do explain the meaning of these. The Buddhas shall provide their protective mindfulness and shall bestow the aid of their spiritual powers whereby others will be caused to develop indestructible faith and acceptance.

At that time, Liberation Moon Bodhisattva, wishing to completely set forth his meaning, thereupon uttered verses, saying:

It would be good indeed, O Son of Wisdom
perfectly fulfilled in the pure practices
if you would please present an exposition of the ten grounds' practices
together with the dharmas of the ten grounds that one enters
whereby one reaches perfection in wisdom
and through which one gains the realization of bodhi.

All buddhas of the ten directions,
those most supreme of those honored among men—
They all join in affording you protective mindfulness
as you explain the ten grounds' meanings.

The ten grounds constitute their very origin.
These are the very bases of the implementation of knowledge.
and also constitute the ultimate path
and the repository of the Buddha's measurelessly many dharmas.

They are analogous to the alphabetic characters of all literature
that are all subsumed even in one's initial alphabet.
Just so, the ten grounds constitute the very origin
of all of the Buddha's meritorious qualities and knowledge.

N. The Bodhisattva Congregation Joins in Requesting This Teaching

{O} At that time, all of the bodhisattvas present there, at the same time and with a single voice, uttered verses requesting Vajragarbha Bodhisattva to speak, saying:

O man of supreme and sublime wisdom
whose eloquence is measureless
and whose virtue is as weighty as the king of mountains—
Feeling sympathetic kindness, please explain the ten grounds. {12}

正體字

499b28‖ 戒念慧清淨　說是十地義
499b29‖ 十力之根本　無[*]閡智本行 {13}
499c01‖ 戒定慧功德　集在仁者心
499c02‖ 憍慢諸邪見　皆悉[7]已滅盡
499c03‖ 是眾無疑心　[8]唯願聞善說 {14}
499c04‖ 譬如渴思水　如飢思美食
499c05‖ 如病思良醫　如蜂欲食蜜
499c06‖ 我等亦如是　聞甘露法味 {15}
499c07‖ 是故曠大意　願開初地門
499c08‖ 乃至第十地　次第為我說 {16}
499c09‖ {P}爾時釋迦牟尼佛。從眉間白毫相。放菩薩力
499c10‖ 明光焰。百千阿僧祇光。以為眷屬。放斯光已。
499c11‖ 普照十方諸佛世界。靡不周遍。三惡道苦。皆
499c12‖ 得休息。悉照十方諸佛大會。說法之眾。顯現
499c13‖ 如來不思議力。是光明。遍照十方諸佛大會。
499c14‖ 諸菩薩身已。於上虛空中。成大光明雲臺。十
499c15‖ 方諸佛。亦復如是。從眉間白毫相。俱放菩薩
499c16‖ 力明光焰。百千阿僧祇光。以為眷屬。

简体字

戒念慧清净，　说是十地义，
十力之根本，　无碍智本行。
戒定慧功德，　集在仁者心，
憍慢诸邪见，　皆悉已灭尽，
是众无疑心，　唯愿闻善说。
譬如渴思水，　如饥思美食，
如病思良医，　如蜂欲食蜜，
我等亦如是，　闻甘露法味。
是故旷大意，　愿开初地门，
乃至第十地，　次第为我说。”

尔时，释迦牟尼佛从眉间白毫相，放菩萨力明光焰，百千阿僧祇光以为眷属。放斯光已，普照十方诸佛世界靡不周遍，三恶道苦皆得休息；悉照十方诸佛大会说法之众，显现如来不思议力。是光明遍照十方诸佛大会诸菩萨身已，于上虚空中，成大光明云台。十方诸佛亦复如是，从眉间白毫相，俱放菩萨力明光焰，百千阿僧祇光以为眷属，

You of moral virtue, mindfulness, and purified wisdom—
please explain the meaning of these ten grounds
which constitute the very origin of the ten powers
and the foundational practices for gaining unimpeded knowledge. {13}

The qualities of moral virtue, concentration, and wisdom
are all gathered in the mind of the Humane One.
Arrogance and all erroneous views
have already been utterly extinguished.
This congregation is entirely free of doubting thoughts
and wishes only to hear you skillfully explain this. {14}

In this, they are like the thirsty in their yearning for water,
like the hungry imagining delicious food,
like the sick thinking of an especially good physician,
and like bees desiring to feast on honey.
We are all just like this
in our wishing to hear the flavor of the sweet dew Dharma. {15}

Therefore, you of such a vast mind—
Please open the gates to the first ground
as well to the rest of them including the tenth ground,
expounding on them in sequence for our sakes. {16}

O. The Buddha Emits Brilliant Light From Between His Eyebrows

{P} At that time, Śākyamuni Buddha emitted from the white hair mark between his eyebrows "the brilliant flaming light of bodhisattva powers," a light attended by a retinue of a hundred thousand *asaṃkhyeyas*[40] of light rays. After he had emitted this light, it then everywhere illuminated all buddha worlds of the ten directions, having none that it did not entirely pervade. The sufferings of the three wretched destinies all subsided. It entirely illuminated the great assemblies of all buddhas of the ten directions as well as the multitudes attending upon their proclamation of the Dharma while also revealing the inconceivable powers of the Tathāgatas.

After this light had everywhere illuminated the bodies of all bodhisattvas in the great assemblies of all buddhas of the ten directions, it then ascended into space wherein it formed an immense terrace of light clouds.

P. All Buddhas Emit Light That Utters Verses Requesting Dharma

The Buddhas of the ten directions proceeded in this very same way with every one of them emitting "the brilliant flaming light of bodhisattva powers," a light attended by a retinue of a hundred thousand *asaṃkhyeyas* of light rays. It everywhere revealed

正體字

499c17‖ 普現如來不思議力。悉照一切諸佛大會。及照娑婆
499c18‖ 世界。釋迦牟尼佛大眾。并照金剛藏菩薩摩
499c19‖ 訶薩。及師子座。照已。於上虛空中。成大光明
499c20‖ 雲臺。時諸大光明雲臺中諸佛神力故。而說
499c21‖ 偈言
499c22‖ 無等等諸佛　功德如虛空
499c23‖ 十力無畏等　最尊世間[9]主
499c24‖ 於釋迦佛前　而現此神力 {17}
499c25‖ 以佛力開現　法王師子藏
499c26‖ 說諸地所行　諸地義差別
499c27‖ 承諸佛力說　無有能壞者 {18}
499c28‖ 若人聞法寶　則為諸佛護 {19}
499c29‖ 漸次具諸地　得[10]以成佛道 {20}
500a01‖ 若人堪任聞　雖在於大海
500a02‖ 及劫盡火中　必得聞此經 {21}
500a03‖ 若人癡疑悔　終不能得聞 {22}
500a04‖ 是故今佛子　說諸地智道
500a05‖ 入勢力觀法　次第而修行
500a06‖ 得至於[*]餘地　各得所利益
500a07‖ 利一切世間　願說勿令斷 {23}

简体字

普现如来不思议力，悉照一切诸佛大会，及照娑婆世界释迦牟尼佛大众，并照金刚藏菩萨摩诃萨及师子座；照已，于上虚空中，成大光明云台。时，诸大光明云台中诸佛神力故，而说偈言：

无等等诸佛，　功德如虚空，
十力无畏等，　最尊世间主，
于释迦佛前，　而现此神力。
以佛力开现，　法王师子藏，
说诸地所行，　诸地义差别，
承诸佛力说，　无有能坏者。
若人闻法宝，　则为诸佛护，
渐次具诸地，　得以成佛道。
若人堪任闻，　虽在于大海，
及劫尽火中，　必得闻此经，
若人痴疑悔，　终不能得闻。
是故今佛子，　说诸地智道，
入势力观法，　次第而修行，
得至于余地，　各得所利益，
利一切世间，　愿说勿令断。

the inconceivable powers of the Tathāgatas, entirely illuminated the great assemblies of all buddhas, and also illuminated the great assembly of the Sahā World's Śākyamuni Buddha while also shining on both Vajragarbha Bodhisattva Mahāsattva and his lion throne. Having provided this illumination, it then ascended into empty space wherein it formed an immense terrace of light clouds. Then, due to the spiritual power of the Buddhas, from the midst of this light cloud terrace there came forth a voice uttering verses, saying:

The Buddhas, the equals of the unequaled,
who are like empty space[41] in their possession of qualities
that include the ten powers, the fearlessnesses, and the rest—
These most revered of all the lords of the world
appear here before Śākyamuni Buddha
and manifest these spiritual powers. {17}

Employ here the powers of the Buddhas to open and show
the treasury of the Dharma King, the Lion among Men.
Proclaim the practices taken up on the grounds
and the distinctions in meaning associated with the grounds.
Taking on the powers of the Buddhas, proclaim here
what is invulnerable to refutation by anyone. {18}

If a person is able to hear the jewel of Dharma,
he will be protected by all buddhas. {19}

When one gradually and sequentially perfects the grounds,
he shall then succeed in gaining buddhahood. {20}

If there is anyone capable of hearing this,
even though he is out in the midst of the great ocean
or in the middle of the kalpa-ending fire,
he will still definitely be able to hear this scripture. {21}

If there is anyone who, deluded, has doubts or misgivings,
he will never be able to succeed in hearing it. {22}

Therefore, O Son of the Buddha, now is the time
for you to expound on the grounds' path of knowledge,
its entry, its strengths, its contemplation dharmas,
its sequences, how to cultivate and practice them,

and how then to succeed in reaching the other grounds,
showing too the benefits arising by successfully reaching each one.
That you might thus bestow benefit on everyone in the entire world,
please explain these matters. Do not allow them to be cut off. {23}

正體字

500a08‖ {Q} 爾時金剛藏菩薩。觀察十方。欲令大眾。增益
500a09‖ 信敬。而說偈言
500a10‖ 諸佛聖主道　微妙甚難解
500a11‖ 非思量所得　[*]唯智者行處
500a12‖ 其性從本來　寂然無生滅 {24}
500a13‖ 從本以來空　滅除諸苦惱
500a14‖ 遠離於諸趣　等同涅槃相
500a15‖ 無中亦無後　非言辭所說
500a16‖ 出過於三世　其相如虛空 {25}
500a17‖ 諸佛所行處　清淨深寂滅
500a18‖ 言說所難及　地行亦如是
500a19‖ 說之猶尚難　何況以示人 {26}
500a20‖ 諸佛之智慧　離諸心數道
500a21‖ 不可得思議　非有陰界入
500a22‖ 但以智可知　非識之所及 {27}
500a23‖ 如空迹難說　何可示其相
500a24‖ 十地義如是　非無邊心知 {28}
500a25‖ 是事雖為難　發願行慈悲
500a26‖ 漸次具諸地　非心所能及 {29}

简体字

尔时，金刚藏菩萨观察十方，欲令大众增益信敬，而说偈言：

“诸佛圣主道，　微妙甚难解，
非思量所得，　唯智者行处。
其性从本来，　寂然无生灭，
从本以来空，　灭除诸苦恼，
远离于诸趣，　等同涅槃相，
无中亦无后，　非言辞所说，
出过于三世，　其相如虚空。
诸佛所行处，　清净深寂灭，
言说所难及，　地行亦如是，
说之犹尚难，　何况以示人？
诸佛之智慧，　离诸心数道，
不可得思议，　非有阴界入，
但以智可知，　非识之所及，
如空迹难说，　何可示其相？
十地义如是，　非无边心知。
是事虽为难，　发愿行慈悲，
渐次具诸地，　非心所能及。

Q. Vajragarbha's Preliminary Verses on the Difficulty of This Explanation

{Q} At that time, Vajragarbha Bodhisattva regarded the ten directions and, wishing to cause those in that immense assembly to develop increased faith and reverence, thereupon set forth verses, saying:

The path of the Buddhas, the lords among the Āryas,
is subtle, sublime, extremely difficult to comprehend,
and inaccessible to realization through thought's deliberations,
It is a region coursed in only by those possessed of knowledge.
Its essential nature, from its origins on forth to the present,
is quiescently still and without either production or extinction. {24}

From its origins on forth to the present, it is that emptiness
wherein all sufferings and torments are utterly extinguished.
It departs far beyond all of the destinies of rebirth
and is characterized by its identity with nirvāṇa itself.

In it, there is no middle and no end.
It is not amenable to description through words and phrases.
It transcends the three periods of time
and, in character, is comparable to empty space. {25}

This region wherein the Buddhas course
is that of purity and deep quiescent cessation.
It is difficult for verbal descriptions to approach it.
So too it is with the practices coursed in on the grounds.
If even describing them remains such a difficulty,
how much the more so would it be to reveal them to others. {26}

The wisdom of the Buddhas[42]
transcends the path of the mental factors,
cannot be conceived of by thought or described in words, and
is not a place wherein aggregates, sense realms, or sense bases exist.
One can only come to know it through knowledge
as it is not such as can be reached through the consciousnesses. {27}

It is as difficult to describe as the track [of a bird[43]] through the air.
How then could one succeed in revealing its aspects?
The meanings associated with the ten grounds are just like this.
They are not such as a mind not boundlessly vast can ever know. {28}

Although these matters are difficult,
one brings forth vows, coursing thence in kindness and compassion.
One's gradual fulfillment of practice on the ten grounds
is not such that the mind can reach it. {29}

正體字

500a27‖ 如是諸地行　微妙甚難見
500a28‖ 不可以心知　當承佛力說
500a29‖ 汝等當恭敬　咸共一心聽 {30}
500b01‖ 諸地相入行　修習出法門
500b02‖ 於無量億劫　說之不可盡
500b03‖ 今如實略說　其義無有餘 {31}
500b04‖ 一心恭敬待　今承佛力說
500b05‖ 大音唱因喻　義名不相違 {32}
500b06‖ 佛神力無量　今皆在我身
500b07‖ 我之所說者　如大海一[1]渧 {33}

简体字

如是诸地行，　微妙甚难见，
不可以心知，　当承佛力说。
汝等当恭敬，　咸共一心听：
诸地相入行，　修习出法门，
于无量亿劫，　说之不可尽，
今如实略说，　其义无有余。
一心恭敬待，　今承佛力说，
大音唱因喻，　义名不相违。
佛神力无量，　今皆在我身，
我之所说者，　如大海一渧。”

This sort of practice on the grounds
is subtle, sublime, and especially difficult to perceive.
One cannot know them through the mind.
One must take on the powers of the Buddhas to describe them.
You should all now attend to this with reverence
wherein everyone joins together in single-minded listening. {30}

The practices one utilizes in entering the grounds and their aspects
as well as the Dharma gates one cultivates in going forth therein—
Though one might discuss them for countless *koṭis* of kalpas,
one could still never be able to reach the end of their explanation.
Now I will present a reality-accordant summary discussion
of their meanings, leaving nothing therein unaddressed. {31}

Attend upon it with single-minded reverence
as, receiving the power of the Buddhas, I proceed here to speak
with the great voice, proclaiming in a manner reliant on analogies
the concepts and designations in a mutually non-contradictory way. {32}

In doing so, the immeasurably vast spiritual powers of the Buddhas
shall now all reside here within my person.
Even so, that upon which I proceed to expound here
will be comparable only to a single drop in what is a vast sea. {33}

正體字

500b08‖ {R} 金剛藏菩薩。說此偈已。告於大眾。諸佛子。若
500b09‖ 眾生。厚集善根。修諸善行。善集助道法。供養
500b10‖ 諸佛。集諸清白法。為善知識所護。入深廣心。
500b11‖ 信樂大法心。多向慈悲。好求佛智慧。{S} 如是眾
500b12‖ 生。乃能發阿耨多羅三藐三菩提心。為得一切
500b13‖ 種智故。為得十力故。為得大無畏故。為得具
500b14‖ 足佛法故。為救一切世間故。為淨大慈悲心故。
500b15‖ 為向十方無餘無[*]閡智故。為淨一切佛國令
500b16‖ 無餘故。為於一念中知三世事故。為自在轉
500b17‖ 大法輪廣示現佛神力故。{T} 諸菩薩摩訶薩。生
500b18‖ 如是心。

简体字

金刚藏菩萨说此偈已，告于大众：“诸佛子，若众生厚集善根，修诸善行，善集助道法，供养诸佛，集诸清白法，为善知识所护，入深广心、信乐大法心，多向慈悲，好求佛智慧。如是众生，乃能发阿耨多罗三藐三菩提心，为得一切种智故，为得十力故，为得大无畏故，为得具足佛法故，为救一切世间故，为净大慈悲心故，为向十方无余无碍智故，为净一切佛国令无余故，为于一念中知三世事故，为自在转大法轮广示现佛神力故，诸菩萨摩诃萨生如是心。

II. The Main Doctrinal Teaching Section

A. The First Ground: The Joyfulness Ground

1. Vajragarbha Lists the First Ground's Qualifications & Motivations

{R} Having uttered these verses, Vajragarbha Bodhisattva then informed the great assembly:

Sons of the Buddha, if there is a being:

Who has assembled thick roots of goodness;
Who has cultivated the good practices;
Who has well accumulated the dharmas facilitating realization of the path;[44]
Who has made offerings to the Buddhas;
Who has assembled the white dharmas of pristine purity;
Who has been under the protection of the good spiritual guide;
Who has entered the resolute and vast intentions;
Who has become resolutely disposed toward the great Dharma mind;[45]
Who has for the most part tended toward implementation of kindness and compassion;
And who delights in seeking the Buddha's wisdom—

{S} A being such as this then becomes capable of bringing forth the resolve to gain *anuttarasamyaksaṃbodhi,* doing so:

For the sake of acquiring the knowledge of all modes;
For the sake of gaining the ten powers;
For the sake of gaining the great fearlessnesses;
For the sake of achieving the complete fulfillment of the dharmas of buddhahood;
For the sake of rescuing all worlds;
For the sake of purifying the mind of great kindness and great compassion;
For the sake of proceeding toward the unimpeded knowledge of everything without exception throughout the ten directions;
For the sake of bringing about the purification of all buddha worlds without exception;
For the sake of knowing in the space of a single mind-moment all phenomena throughout the three periods of time;
And for the sake of turning the wheel of the great Dharma with sovereign mastery, thus broadly manifesting the spiritual powers of the Buddha.

{T} All bodhisattva *mahāsattvas* bring forth this very sort of resolve.

正體字

諸佛子。是心以大悲為首。智慧增上。
500b19‖ 方便所護。直心深心淳至。量同佛力。善籌量
500b20‖ 眾生力佛力。趣向無[＊]閡智。隨順自然智。能受
500b21‖ 一切佛法。以智慧教化。{U} 廣大如法性。究竟如
500b22‖ 虛空。盡於後際。諸佛子。菩薩生如是心。即
500b23‖ 時過凡夫地。入菩薩位。生在佛家。種姓無可
500b24‖ 譏嫌。過一切世間道。入出世間道。住菩薩法
500b25‖ 中。在諸菩薩數。等入三世如來種中。畢定究
500b26‖ 竟阿耨多羅三藐三菩提。{V} 菩薩住如是法。名
500b27‖ 住歡喜地。以不動法故。諸佛子。菩薩摩訶薩。
500b28‖ 住是歡喜地。多喜多信。多清淨

简体字

诸佛子，是心以大悲为首，智慧增上，方便所护，直心深心淳至，量同佛力，善筹量众生力、佛力，趣向无碍智，随顺自然智，能受一切佛法，以智慧教化，广大如法性，究竟如虚空，尽于后际。诸佛子，菩萨生如是心，即时过凡夫地，入菩萨位，生在佛家，种姓无可讥嫌，过一切世间道，入出世间道，住菩萨法中，在诸菩萨数，等入三世如来种中，毕定究竟阿耨多罗三藐三菩提。菩萨住如是法，名住欢喜地，以不动法故。

“诸佛子，菩萨摩诃萨住是欢喜地，多喜多信，多清净

2. The Qualities of the Bodhisattva's Resolve

Sons of the Buddha, this resolve:

Takes the great compassion as foremost;

Takes wisdom as its predominant condition;

Is guarded by skillful means;

[Is sustained by] by consummately realized higher aspirations and resolute intentions;[46]

Is invested with a capacity commensurate with the powers of the Buddha;

Is accompanied by skillful assessment of beings' powers and the Buddha's powers;

Is directed toward unimpeded knowledge;

Is accordant with spontaneous knowledge;[47]

Is able to incorporate all dharmas of the Buddha in using wisdom in transformative teaching;

And is as vast as the Dharma realm, as ultimately extensive as empty space, and so enduring as to reach the very end of future time.

3. The Consequences of Generating the Bodhisattva Vow

{U} Sons of the Buddha, when the bodhisattva brings forth just such a resolve as this, he immediately:

Passes beyond the grounds of the common person;

Enters the station of the bodhisattva;

Becomes born into the clan of the Buddhas;

Acquires a lineage that none can disparage;

Passes beyond all worldly paths;

Enters the world-transcending path;

Dwells in the bodhisattva dharmas;

Abides in the ranks of the bodhisattvas;

Equally enters the three periods of time;

And becomes definitely bound for the ultimate realization of *anuttarasamyaksaṃbodhi* in the lineage of the Tathāgatas.

{V} The bodhisattva who dwells in dharmas such as these is known as one who dwells on the Ground of Joyfulness, this on account of the dharma of imperturbability.

Sons of the Buddha, the bodhisattva *mahāsattva* who abides in this Ground of Joyfulness is endowed with:

Abundant joy;

Abundant faith;

Abundant purity;

正體字

多踊悅。多調
500b29‖ 柔多堪受。不好鬪諍。不好惱亂眾生。不好瞋
500c01‖ 恨。{W}諸佛子。諸菩薩。住是歡喜地。念諸佛故
500c02‖ 生歡喜心。念諸佛法故生歡喜心。念諸菩薩
500c03‖ 摩訶薩故生歡喜心。念諸菩薩所行故生歡
500c04‖ 喜心。念諸波羅蜜清淨相故生歡喜心。念諸
500c05‖ 菩薩與眾殊勝故生歡喜心。念諸菩薩力不
500c06‖ 可壞故生歡喜心。念諸如來教化法故生歡
500c07‖ 喜心。念能為利益眾生故生歡喜心。念一切
500c08‖ 佛一切菩薩所入智慧門方便故生歡喜心。
500c09‖ {X}諸佛子。菩薩復作是念。我轉離一切世間[2]界
500c10‖ 生歡喜心。入一切佛平等中生歡喜心。遠[3]離
500c11‖ 凡夫地生歡喜心。近到智慧地生歡喜心。

简体字

多踊悦，多调柔多堪受，不好斗诤，不好恼乱众生，不好瞋恨。诸佛子，诸菩萨住是欢喜地，念诸佛故生欢喜心，念诸佛法故生欢喜心，念诸菩萨摩诃萨故生欢喜心，念诸菩萨所行故生欢喜心，念诸波罗蜜清净相故生欢喜心，念诸菩萨与众殊胜故生欢喜心，念诸菩萨力不可坏故生欢喜心，念诸如来教化法故生欢喜心，念能为利益众生故生欢喜心，念一切佛、一切菩萨所入智慧门方便故生欢喜心。

“诸佛子，菩萨复作是念：‘我转离一切世间界生欢喜心，入一切佛平等中生欢喜心，远离凡夫地生欢喜心，近到智慧地生欢喜心，

Abundant ebullience;
Abundant pliancy;
Abundant tolerance;
[Abundant] disinclination to disputatiousness;
[Abundant] disinclination to harming or interfering with other beings;
And [abundant] disinclination to anger.[48]

4. The Bases For the First Ground Bodhisattva's Joyfulness

{W} Sons of the Buddha, those bodhisattvas who dwell on this Ground of Joyfulness:

Have joyful thoughts due to calling to mind the Buddhas;
Have joyful thoughts due to calling to mind the Dharma of the Buddhas;
Have joyful thoughts due to calling to mind the bodhisattva *mahāsattvas*;
Have joyful thoughts due to calling to mind the conduct practiced by the bodhisattvas;
Have joyful thoughts due to calling to mind the characteristic purity of the *pāramitās*;
Have joyful thoughts due to calling to mind the bodhisattvas' especially supreme qualities in comparison to those of everyone else;
Have joyful thoughts due to calling to mind the indestructibility of the bodhisattvas' powers;
Have joyful thoughts due to calling to mind the teaching methods of the Tathāgatas;
Have joyful thoughts due to calling to mind the ability to be of benefit to beings;
And have joyful thoughts due to calling to mind the gateways to wisdom[49] and skillful means entered by all buddhas and all bodhisattvas.

{X} Sons of the Buddha, the bodhisattva also brings forth this thought:

I have joyful thoughts due to having turned away from and abandoned all worldly states;
I have joyful thoughts due to entering the uniform equality of all buddhas;
I have joyful thoughts due to departing far from the grounds of the common person;
I have joyful thoughts due to drawing close to the grounds of knowledge;[50]

正體字

斷
500c12‖ 一切惡道生歡喜心。與一切眾生作依[4]止生
500c13‖ 歡喜心。近見一切諸佛生歡喜心。生諸佛
500c14‖ 境界生歡喜心。入一切諸菩薩數生歡喜心。
500c15‖ 我離一切驚怖毛竪等生歡喜心。{Y}所以者何。
500c16‖ 是菩薩摩訶薩。得歡喜地。所有諸怖畏。即皆
500c17‖ 遠離。所謂。不活畏。惡名畏。死畏。墮惡道畏。
500c18‖ 大眾威德畏。離如是等一切諸畏。何以故。是
500c19‖ 菩薩。離我相故。尚不貪身。何況所用之事。是
500c20‖ 故。無有不活畏也。心不悕望供養恭敬。我應
500c21‖ 供養眾生供給所須。是故無有惡名畏也。離
500c22‖ 我見。無我相故。無有死畏。又作是念。我若死
500c23‖ 已生。必不離諸佛菩薩。是故無有墮惡道畏。
500c24‖ 我所志樂。無與等者。何況有勝。是故無有大
500c25‖ 眾威德畏也。

简体字

断一切恶道生欢喜心，与一切众生作依止生欢喜心，近见一切诸佛生欢喜心，生诸佛境界生欢喜心，入一切诸菩萨数生欢喜心。我离一切惊怖毛竖等生欢喜心！’所以者何？是菩萨摩诃萨得欢喜地，所有诸怖畏即皆远离，所谓：不活畏、恶名畏、死畏、堕恶道畏、大众威德畏，离如是等一切诸畏。何以故？是菩萨离我相故，尚不贪身，何况所用之事？是故无有不活畏也。心不希望供养恭敬，我应供养众生供给所须，是故无有恶名畏也。离我见，无我相故，无有死畏。又作是念：‘我若死已生，必不离诸佛菩萨。’是故无有堕恶道畏。我所志乐，无与等者，何况有胜？是故无有大众威德畏也。

I have joyful thoughts due to severing all vulnerability to entering any of the wretched destinies;
I have joyful thoughts due to becoming a refuge for all beings;
I have joyful thoughts due to drawing near to and seeing all buddhas;
I have joyful thoughts due to being born into the domain of the Buddhas;
I have joyful thoughts due to entering the ranks of all bodhisattvas;
And I have joyful thoughts due to leaving behind the fear of all circumstances that would cause hair-raising terror.

5. The First Ground Bodhisattva's Five Kinds of Fearlessness

{Y} Why is it that when this bodhisattva *mahāsattva* gains the Ground of Joyfulness, all types of fearfulness are immediately left far behind? In particular, they are:

The fear of failing to survive;
The fear of a bad reputation;
The fear of death;
The fear of falling into the wretched destinies;
And the fear of the awesomeness of great assemblies.[51]

He leaves behind all such forms of fearfulness. And why is this? It is because this bodhisattva has abandoned any perception of a self.[52] He does not even covet his own body. How much the less might he covet whatever things it happens to use. As a consequence, he has no fear of failing to survive.

His mind does not cherish any hope of receiving offerings or reverence from anyone, but instead thinks, 'I should make offerings to beings of whatever they require. Therefore he has no fear of a bad reputation.

He has abandoned any view conceiving of the existence of a self. Because he has no perception of the existence of a self,[53] he has no fear of death.

He also has this thought: 'When, after I have died, I am reborn, I most certainly will not take rebirth somewhere apart from the Buddhas and the bodhisattvas.' As a consequence of this, he has no fear of falling into the wretched destinies.

He thinks: "The object of my resolve and that in which I delight have no equal anywhere, how much the less might there be anything that could be superior to it?" Consequently, he has no fear of the awesomeness of great assemblies.

正體字

諸佛子。如是菩薩。離諸驚怖毛
500c26‖ 竪等事。{Z}諸佛子。是菩薩。以大悲為首。深大心
500c27‖ 堅固。轉復勤修一切善根。{AA}所謂。以信心增
500c28‖ 上。多行淨心。解心清淨。多以信心。分別起
500c29‖ 悲愍心。成就大慈。心不疲懈。以慚愧。莊嚴。
501a01‖ 成就忍辱柔和。敬順諸佛教法。信重尊貴。{BB}日
501a02‖ 夜常修善根無厭。親近善知識。常愛樂法。求
501a03‖ 多聞無厭。如所[1]觀法正觀。心不貪著。不求
501a04‖ 利養名聞恭敬。一切資生之物。心無慳悋。常
501a05‖ 生[2]實心。無有厭足。{CC}貪樂一切智地。常欲得
501a06‖ 諸佛。力無畏不共法。

简体字

诸佛子，如是菩萨离诸惊怖毛竖等事。

“诸佛子，是菩萨以大悲为首，深大心坚固，转复勤修一切善根，所谓：以信心增上，多行净心，解心清净；多以信心，分别起悲愍心，成就大慈心不疲懈；以惭愧庄严，成就忍辱柔和；敬顺诸佛教法，信重尊贵，日夜常修善根无厌；亲近善知识，常爱乐法，求多闻无厌，如所观法正观；心不贪著，不求利养名闻恭敬，一切资生之物，心无悭吝；常生实心，无有厌足，贪乐一切智地，常欲得诸佛力、无畏、不共法，

Sons of the Buddha, bodhisattvas of this sort have left behind the fear of circumstances that would cause hair-raising terror as well as all such fearsome circumstances.

6. The Bodhisattva's Grounds Purifying Practices

{Z} Sons of the Buddha, this bodhisattva takes the great compassion as what is foremost and is possessed of a profound and vast resolve that is solid. Thus he redoubles his diligent cultivation of all roots of goodness, specifically doing so:

{AA} Through making faith predominant;

Through extensive practice of pure thought;[54]

Through possessing pure convictions;[55]

Through extensive reliance on the faith-imbued mind in making differentiating judgments;

Through bringing forth the mind imbued with compassion and kindly pity;

Through perfection of the great kindness;

Through remaining free of any tendency to become weary or to withdraw from his efforts;

Through being adorned with a sense of shame and dread of blame;

Through achieving consummate proficiency in patience and mental pliancy;

Through respectfully according with the Buddhas' teaching dharmas with strong faith and veneration;

{BB} Through always and insatiably cultivating roots of goodness day and night;

Through drawing near to good spiritual guides;

Through always cherishing and delighting in the Dharma;

Through insatiably pursuing extensive learning;

Through carrying forth right contemplation accordant with the Dharma one has learned;[56]

Through refraining from mental attachments;

Through not seeking offerings, renown, or reverence from others;

Through remaining free of miserliness regarding life-supporting material possessions;

Through always and tirelessly bringing forth jewel-like resolve;[57]

{CC} Through happily striving to reach the ground of all-knowledge;

Through always questing to gain realization of the Buddha's powers, fearlessnesses, and exclusive dharmas;

正體字

求助諸波羅蜜法。離諸
501a07‖ 諂曲。如說能行。常行實語。不污諸佛家。不捨
501a08‖ 菩薩學戒。生薩婆若。心不動如大山王。不樂
501a09‖ 一切世間諸事。成就出世間善根。集助菩提
501a10‖ 分法。無有厭足。常求勝中勝道。諸佛子。菩薩
501a11‖ 摩訶薩。成就如是淨治地法。名為安住菩薩
501a12‖ 歡喜地。{DD}菩薩如是。安住歡喜地。發諸大願。生
501a13‖ 如是[3]決定心。所謂。我當供養一切諸佛。皆
501a14‖ 無有餘。一切供養之具隨意供養。心解清淨。
501a15‖ 發如是大願。廣大如法性。究竟如虛空。盡未
501a16‖ 來際。盡供養一切劫中所有諸佛。以大供養
501a17‖ 具。無有休息。{EE}又一切諸佛。所說經法。皆悉受
501a18‖ 持。攝一切諸佛阿耨多羅三藐三菩提故。一
501a19‖ 切諸佛。所教化法悉皆隨順。一切諸佛法皆
501a20‖ 能守護。發如是大願。廣大如法性。究竟如虛
501a21‖ 空。盡未來際。盡皆守護一切劫中一切佛法。
501a22‖ 無有休息。

简体字

求助诸波罗蜜法；离诸谄曲，如说能行，常行实语；不污诸佛家，不舍菩萨学戒，生萨婆若心不动如大山王；不乐一切世间诸事，成就出世间善根，集助菩提分法无有厌足，常求胜中胜道。

“诸佛子，菩萨摩诃萨成就如是净治地法，名为安住菩萨欢喜地。菩萨如是安住欢喜地，发诸大愿，生如是决定心，所谓：‘我当供养一切诸佛，皆无有余。’一切供养之具随意供养，心解清净。发如是大愿，广大如法性，究竟如虚空，尽未来际，尽供养一切劫中，所有诸佛以大供养具无有休息。又一切诸佛所说经法皆悉受持，摄一切诸佛阿耨多罗三藐三菩提故，一切诸佛所教化法悉皆随顺，一切诸佛法皆能守护。发如是大愿，广大如法性，究竟如虚空，尽未来际，尽皆守护一切劫中一切佛法无有休息。

Through seeking to acquire the dharmas assisting proficiency in the *pāramitās;*

Through abandoning all flattery and deceptiveness;

Through being able to practice in accordance with what has been taught;

Through always practicing truthful speech;

Through never defiling the house of the Buddhas;

Through never relinquishing the moral precepts in which the bodhisattvas train;

Through bringing forth a resolve set on realization of all-knowledge that is as unshakeable as the king of mountains;

Through finding no pleasure in any worldly matters as he perfects the world-transcending roots of goodness;

Through insatiably gathering together the dharmas comprising the factors assisting realization of bodhi;

And through always striving to achieve realization of the most supreme of all superior paths.

Sons of the Buddha, the bodhisattva *mahāsattva* who completely develops such dharmas for purifying the grounds as these thereby becomes established on the bodhisattva's Ground of Joyfulness.

7. The Bodhisattva's Ten Great Vows

{DD} The bodhisattva who becomes established in this manner on the Ground of Joyfulness makes all of the great vows entailing the generation of just such decisive resolve. Specifically, they are:[58]

"I vow that I shall make gifts of every sort of offering to all buddhas without exception, freely making such offerings with pure resolute faith." In making such a great vow as this, his implementation of it is as vast as the Dharma realm and as extensive as empty space as he continues on until the end of future time, exhaustively making offerings of every sort of great gift to all buddhas.

{EE} He also vows that he will uphold and preserve the scriptural Dharma proclaimed by all buddhas, that he will take on the realization of the *anuttarasamyaksaṃbodhi* of all buddhas, that he will always accord with the Dharma taught by all buddhas, and that he will always be able to protect and preserve the Dharma of all buddhas. In making such a great vow as this, his implementation of it is as vast as the Dharma realm and as extensive as empty space as he continues on incessantly until the end of future time, exhaustively protecting and preserving the Dharma of all buddhas in every kalpa.

正體字

{FF}又一切世界。一切諸佛。從兜率天。
501a23‖ 來下入胎。及在胎中。初生時。出家時。成佛道
501a24‖ 時。悉當勸請轉大法輪。示入大涅槃。我於爾
501a25‖ 時。盡往供養。攝法為首。三時轉故。發如是
501a26‖ 大願。廣大如法性。究竟如虛空。盡未來際。盡
501a27‖ 一切劫。奉迎供養一切諸佛。無有休息。{GG}又一
501a28‖ 切諸菩薩所行。廣大高遠。無量不可壞。無有
501a29‖ 分別。諸波羅蜜所攝。諸地所淨。生諸助道法。
501b01‖ 有相無相道。有成有壞一切菩薩。所行諸
501b02‖ 地道。及諸波羅蜜本行。教化令其受行。心得
501b03‖ 增長。發如是大願。廣大如法性。究竟如虛空。
501b04‖ 盡未來際。盡一切劫中。諸菩薩所行。以法教
501b05‖ 化[4]成熟眾生。無有休息。{HH}又一切眾生。若有
501b06‖ 色若無色。若有想若無想。若非有想非無想。
501b07‖ 若卵生若胎生。若濕生若化生。三界繫入於
501b08‖ 六道。在一切生處。名色所攝。為教化[*]成[熱>熟]
501b09‖ 一切眾生。

简体字

又一切世界一切诸佛，从兜率天来下入胎，及在胎中，初生时，出家时，成佛道时，悉当劝请转大法轮；示入大涅槃，我于尔时尽往供养，摄法为首三时转故。发如是大愿，广大如法性，究竟如虚空，尽未来际，尽一切劫奉迎供养一切诸佛无有休息。又一切诸菩萨所行，广大高远，无量不可坏，无有分别，诸波罗蜜所摄，诸地所净，生诸助道法，有相无相道，有成有坏，一切菩萨所行诸地道，及诸波罗蜜本行，教化令其受行，心得增长。发如是大愿，广大如法性，究竟如虚空，尽未来际，尽一切劫中，诸菩萨所行，以法教化成熟众生无有休息。又一切众生，若有色、若无色、若有想、若无想、若非有想非无想、若卵生、若胎生、若湿生、若化生，三界系入于六道，在一切生处，名色所摄，为教化成熟一切众生，

{FF} He also vows that, in all worlds, with the arrival of all buddhas, when they come down from the Tuṣita Heaven, enter the womb, abide in the womb, are first born, leave behind the home life, and then gain buddhahood, in every case he will entreat them to turn the great wheel of the Dharma, vowing too that, when they manifest entry into the great nirvāṇa, "I will in every case go there, make offerings, and serve as a leader in the compilation of their Dharma," vowing to do these things in order to facilitate [the Dharma wheel's] turning throughout the three periods of time. In making such a great vow as this, his implementation of it is as vast as the Dharma realm and as extensive as empty space as he continues on until the end of future time and throughout all kalpas, incessantly raising up offerings to all buddhas.

{GG} He also vows that he will teach all of the practices coursed in by the bodhisattvas, so vast, lofty, and far-reaching, so immeasurable, indestructible, and free of discriminations, those practices that are subsumed within the *pāramitās*, that are purified on the grounds, that generate the dharmas assisting realization of the path, that constitute the path of signs and the path of signlessness, teaching how they may conduce to success and how they may lead to ruination, teaching the path of the grounds coursed in by all bodhisattvas, teaching too the *pāramitās'* foundational practices, teaching these things to others in a manner whereby they are caused to take up their practice and bring forth increased resolve. In making such a great vow as this, his implementation of it is as vast as the Dharma realm and as extensive as empty space as he continues on until the end of future time and throughout all kalpas, incessantly employing the practices coursed in by all bodhisattvas to provide teaching in accord with Dharma for the ripening of beings.

{HH} He also vows that he will teach all beings, whether possessed of form or formless, whether possessed of perception, free of perception, or abiding in a state of neither perception nor non-perception, whether egg-born, womb-born, moisture-born, or transformationally born, teaching them all, no matter to which of the stations in the triple world they have become connected, no matter in which of the six destinies of rebirth they have taken birth, no matter in which place they have taken rebirth, thus teaching all who are subsumed in the sphere of name-and-form, proceeding thus for the sake of teaching and ripening all beings, for the sake of influencing

正體字

斷一切世間道。令住佛法。集一切
501b10‖ 智慧。使無有餘。發如是大願。廣大如法性。究
501b11‖ 竟如虛空。盡未來際。盡一切劫。教化一切眾
501b12‖ 生。無有休息。{II}又一切世間。廣狹極高。無量不
501b13‖ 可分別。不可移動。不可說麁細。正住倒住。首
501b14‖ 足相對。平坦圓方。隨入如是世間。智如帝網。
501b15‖ 經幻事差別。如是十方。世界差別。皆現前知。
501b16‖ 發如是大願。廣大如法性。究竟如虛空。盡未
501b17‖ 來世。盡一切劫。如是世界。皆現前[5]淨知。無
501b18‖ 有休息。{JJ}又[6]以一切佛土。入一佛土。一佛土。
501b19‖ 入一切佛土。一一佛土。無量光明莊嚴。離諸
501b20‖ 垢穢。具足清淨道。有無量智慧。眾生悉滿其
501b21‖ 中。常有諸佛大神[7]通力。隨眾生心。而為示
501b22‖ 現。發如是大願。廣大如法性。究竟如虛空。盡
501b23‖ 未來際。盡一切劫。清淨如是國土。無有休息。
501b24‖ {KK}又一切菩薩。同心同學。共集諸善無有怨嫉。
501b25‖ 俱緣一事。

简体字

断一切世间道令住佛法，集一切智慧使无有余。发如是大愿，广大如法性，究竟如虚空，尽未来际，尽一切劫，教化一切众生无有休息。又一切世间广狭极高，无量不可分别，不可移动，不可说粗细，正住倒住，首足相对，平坦圆方，随入如是世间，智如帝网经幻事差别，如是十方世界差别皆现前知。发如是大愿，广大如法性，究竟如虚空，尽未来世，尽一切劫，如是世界皆现前净知无有休息。又以一切佛土入一佛土，一佛土入一切佛土，一一佛土无量光明庄严，离诸垢秽具足清净道，有无量智慧众生悉满其中，常有诸佛大神通力，随众生心而为示现。发如是大愿，广大如法性，究竟如虚空，尽未来际，尽一切劫，清净如是国土无有休息。又一切菩萨同心同学，共集诸善无有怨嫉，俱缘一事

them to cut off their coursing through all the destinies of worldly existence, for the sake of influencing them to abide in the Dharma of the Buddha, for the sake of influencing them to accumulate all-knowledge,[59] teaching all of them without exception. In making such a great vow as this, his implementation of it is as vast as the Dharma realm and as extensive as empty space as he continues on until the end of future time and throughout all kalpas, incessantly teaching all beings.

{II} He also vows to directly know all of the differentiating aspects of all worlds throughout the ten directions, including all aspects of those worlds that are wide, narrow, extremely towering, of so countlessly many varieties one could never distinguish them all, including those that are immovable, and those that are indescribably coarse, subtle, upright, inverted, formed with their crowns and bases opposing each other, flat, spherical, or cubical, thus being able in this knowing to freely enter the knowledge of all such worlds, knowing them as existing in a manner comparable to appearances in the net-like canopy of Indra wherein things manifest like the phenomena in a conjuration. In making such a great vow as this, his implementation of it is as vast as the Dharma realm and as extensive as empty space as he continues on until the end of future time and throughout all kalpas, incessantly carrying on the direct and complete knowing[60] of all such worlds.

{JJ} He also vows to bring about the purification of all buddha lands wherein all buddha lands enter a single buddha land, a single buddha land enters all buddha lands, and each and every buddha land is adorned with measurelessly many radiant phenomena, wherein they all become filled with measurelessly many wise beings[61] who have abandoned all defilements and perfected the path of purification, and wherein he always possesses the power of all buddhas' great superknowledges, accords with the mental dispositions of beings, and thus appears for their sakes. In making such a great vow as this, his implementation of it is as vast as the Dharma realm and as extensive as empty space as he continues on until the end of future time and throughout all kalpas, incessantly purifying lands such as these.

{KK} He also vows that he will be of like mind with and pursue the same studies as all other bodhisattvas, joining together with them in the accumulation of every sort of goodness, remaining free of enmity or jealousy toward them, that when all are engaged in a single endeavor, he will maintain thoughts of

正體字

等心和合。常不相離。隨意能現佛
501b26‖ 身。[8]自於心中。悉能解知諸佛。神力智力。常
501b27‖ 得隨意神通。悉能遊行一切國土。一切佛會。
501b28‖ 皆現身相。一切生處。普生其中。有如是不可
501b29‖ 思議大智慧。具足菩薩行。發如是大願。廣大
501c01‖ 如法性。究竟如虛空。盡未來[9]世。盡一切劫。行
501c02‖ 如是大智慧道。無有休息。{LL}又乘不退輪。行一
501c03‖ 切菩薩道。身口意業[10]所作不空。眾生見者。
501c04‖ 即必定佛法。聞我音聲。即得真實智慧道。有
501c05‖ 見我者。心即歡喜。離諸煩惱。如大藥樹王。為
501c06‖ 得如是心。行諸菩薩道。發如是大願。廣大如
501c07‖ 法性。究竟如虛空。盡未來[*]世。盡一切劫。行
501c08‖ 不退道。所作不空。無有休息。{MM}又於一切世界。
501c09‖ 皆得阿耨多羅三藐三菩提。於一毛頭。示身
501c10‖ 入胎。出家坐道場。成佛道。轉法輪。度眾生。
501c11‖ 示大涅槃。現諸如來大神智力。

简体字

等心和合常不相离，随意能现佛身，自于心中悉能解知诸佛神力、智力，常得随意神通，悉能游行一切国土，一切佛会皆现身相，一切生处普生其中，有如是不可思议大智慧具足菩萨行。发如是大愿，广大如法性，究竟如虚空，尽未来世，尽一切劫，行如是大智慧道无有休息。又乘不退轮行一切菩萨道，身口意业所作不空，众生见者即必定佛法，闻我音声即得真实智慧道，有见我者心即欢喜离诸烦恼，如大药树王。为得如是心，行诸菩萨道，发如是大愿，广大如法性，究竟如虚空，尽未来世，尽一切劫，行不退道，所作不空无有休息。又于一切世界皆得阿耨多罗三藐三菩提，于一毛头示身入胎、出家、坐道场、成佛道、转法轮、度众生、示大涅槃、现诸如来大神智力，

equal regard toward them, maintaining harmonious relations with them, never becoming mutually estranged from them, being able as well to manifest buddha bodies according to what suits the needs of others, being able in one's own mind to completely understand and know the domains, spiritual powers, and powers of cognition of all buddhas, always being able to freely employ spiritual superknowledges to roam at will to all lands, manifesting the appearance of one's body in the assemblies of all buddhas, being able as well to everywhere take up births into all stations of rebirth, being possessed of all such inconceivably great wisdom, and perfecting the practices of the bodhisattvas. In making such a great vow as this, his implementation of it is as vast as the Dharma realm and as extensive as empty space as he continues on until the end of future time and throughout all kalpas, incessantly carrying forth the practice of just such a great path of wisdom.

{LL} He also vows that he will take up the irreversible turning of the wheel of Dharma, that he will course in the bodhisattva path, that, of all of his physical, verbal, and mental actions, none will be such as are done in vain, that any being who merely sees him will thereby immediately become bound for definite success in the Buddha's Dharma, that, "Any being who so much as hears my voice will thereby immediately become bound for success in the path of genuine wisdom,"[62] that, "Any being who merely lays eyes on me will immediately be filled with joyous delight and abandon afflictions," that, in this, he will become like the great king of medicine trees, and that, in order to develop such resolve as this, he will course in the bodhisattva path. In making such a great vow as this, his implementation of it is as vast as the Dharma realm and as extensive as empty space as he continues on until the end of future time and throughout all kalpas, incessantly coursing along in the path of irreversibility, ensuring that none of his actions will have been done in vain.

{MM} He also vows that he will gain the realization of *anuttarasamyaksaṃbodhi* in all worlds, that even in those places manifesting within the tip of a single hair, he will manifest entry into the womb, leaving behind the home life, sitting in the *bodhimaṇḍa*, gaining buddhahood, turning the wheel of Dharma, bringing about the liberation of beings, and manifesting the appearance of entering the great nirvāṇa, that he will manifest the great spiritual and cognitive powers of

正體字

隨一切眾生。
501c12‖ 所應度者。念念中。得佛道度眾生。滅苦惱。知
501c13‖ 一切法。如涅槃相。以一音聲。令一切眾生。皆
501c14‖ 使歡喜。示大涅槃。而不斷菩薩所行。示眾生
501c15‖ 大智地。使知一切法皆是假偽。大智慧大神
501c16‖ 通。自在變化故。發如是大願。廣大如法性。究
501c17‖ 竟如虛空。盡未來際。盡一切劫。得佛道事。求
501c18‖ 大智慧。大神通等。無有休息。諸佛子。菩薩住
501c19‖ 歡喜地。以十願為首。生如是等百萬阿僧祇
501c20‖ 大願。{NN}以十不可盡法。而生是願。為滿此願。勤
501c21‖ 行精進。何等為十。一眾生不可盡。二世間不
501c22‖ 可盡。三虛空不可盡。四法性不可盡。五涅槃
501c23‖ 不可盡。六佛出世不可盡。七諸佛智慧不可
501c24‖ 盡。八心緣不可盡。九起智不可盡。十世間道
501c25‖ 種法道種智慧道種不可盡。

简体字

随一切众生所应度者，念念中得佛道度众生灭苦恼，知一切法如涅槃相，以一音声令一切众生皆使欢喜，示大涅槃而不断菩萨所行，示众生大智地使知一切法皆是假伪，大智慧、大神通自在变化故。发如是大愿，广大如法性，究竟如虚空，尽未来际，尽一切劫，得佛道事，求大智慧、大神通等无有休息。

“诸佛子，菩萨住欢喜地，以十愿为首，生如是等百万阿僧祇大愿，以十不可尽法而生是愿，为满此愿勤行精进。何等为十？一、众生不可尽，二、世间不可尽，三、虚空不可尽，四、法性不可尽，五、涅槃不可尽，六、佛出世不可尽，七、诸佛智慧不可尽，八、心缘不可尽，九、起智不可尽，十、世间道种、法道种、智慧道种不可尽。

the *tathāgatas*, that he will adapt to the circumstances of all individual beings and that, according to what is appropriate for their liberation, he will, even in every successive mind-moment, manifest realization of the buddha path, facilitate the liberation of beings, and bring about the extinguishing of their suffering and afflictions, that he will gain the cognition that realizes all dharmas are characterized by identity with nirvāṇa, that, employing a single voice, he will be able to cause all beings to become established in joyfulness, that, even though he manifests entry into the great nirvāṇa, he will nonetheless never cut off his coursing in the bodhisattva practices, that he will reveal to beings the grounds of great knowledge, that he will cause them to realize all dharmas are in every case false and deceptive, accomplishing these endeavors by resort to great wisdom,[63] great superknowledges, and freely manifested spiritual transformations. In making such a great vow as this, his implementation of it is as vast as the Dharma realm and as extensive as empty space as he continues on until the end of future time and throughout all kalpas, incessantly persisting in accomplishing the works associated with the path to buddhahood, in seeking great wisdom,[64] and in acquiring the great spiritual powers and other such realizations.

Sons of the Buddha, the bodhisattva dwelling on the Ground of Joyfulness takes these ten vows as foremost while also generating additional hundreds of myriads of *asaṃkhyeyas* of other great vows. {NN} He employs ten infinity dharmas to facilitate the generation of these vows, doing so to instigate the diligent practice of vigor for the sake of bringing these vows to fulfillment. What then are those ten? They are:

First, beings cannot end;
Second, worlds cannot end;
Third, empty space cannot end;
Fourth, the Dharma realm cannot end;
Fifth, nirvāṇa cannot end;
Sixth, the buddhas' coming forth into the world cannot end;
Seventh, the Buddhas' wisdom[65] cannot end;
Eighth, conditions taken as objects of mind cannot end;
Ninth, the arising of knowledge cannot end;
Tenth, the varieties of worldly paths, the varieties of Dharma paths, and the varieties of paths of wisdom[66] cannot end.

正體字

如眾生盡。我願
501c26‖ 乃盡。如世間盡。如虛空盡。如法性盡。如涅
501c27‖ 槃盡。如佛出世盡。如諸佛智慧盡。如心緣
501c28‖ 盡。如起智慧盡。如道種盡。我願乃盡。而眾
501c29‖ 生實不可盡。世間虛空。法性涅槃。佛出世。
502a01‖ 諸佛智慧。心緣起智道種。實不可盡。我是
502a02‖ 諸願福德亦不可盡。{OO}諸佛子。菩薩決定。發是
502a03‖ 大願。則得利安心。柔軟心。調順心。善心。寂
502a04‖ 滅心。和潤心。直心。不亂心。不嬈心。不濁心如
502a05‖ 是則成信者。樂[1]心信相。分別功德。信諸佛
502a06‖ 本所行道。信行諸波羅蜜而得增長。信善入
502a07‖ 諸地得殊勝功德。信得成佛十力。

简体字

如众生尽，我愿乃尽；如世间尽，如虚空尽，如法性尽，如涅槃尽，如佛出世尽，如诸佛智慧尽，如心缘尽，如起智慧尽，如道种尽，我愿乃尽。而众生实不可尽，世间、虚空、法性、涅槃、佛出世、诸佛智慧、心缘、起智、道种实不可尽，我是诸愿福德亦不可尽。

"诸佛子，菩萨决定发是大愿，则得利安心、柔软心、调顺心、善心、寂灭心、和润心、直心、不乱心、不娆心、不浊心，如是则成信者，乐心信相分别功德，信诸佛本所行道，信行诸波罗蜜而得增长，信善入诸地得殊胜功德，信得成佛十力，

[Accordingly, he vows that]:

If beings were to come to an end, then my vows might come to an end. If the worlds were to come to an end, if empty space were to come to an end, if the Dharma realm were to come to an end, if nirvāṇa were to come to an end, if the Buddhas' coming forth into the world were to come to an end, if the Buddhas' wisdom[67] were to come to an end, if the conditions taken as objects of mind were to come to an end, if the arising of wisdom were to come to an end, and if the varieties of paths were to come to an end, then my vows might come to an end.

However, in truth, beings cannot possibly ever come to an end. So, too, the worlds, empty space, the Dharma realm, nirvāṇa, the Buddhas' coming forth into the world, the Buddhas' wisdom,[68] conditions taken as objects of mind, the arising of knowledge, and the varieties of paths—none of them could ever possibly come to an end. Consequently, the meritorious qualities associated with these vows cannot possibly ever come to an end, either.

8. The Mental Qualities & Faith Acquired by the 1st Ground Bodhisattva

{00} Sons of the Buddha, once the bodhisattva has brought forth that resolve through which he makes these great vows, he then acquires:[69]

The beneficent mind;
The supple mind;
The subdued and adaptive mind;
The mind inclined toward goodness;
The quiescent mind;
The harmoniously smooth mind;
The straight mind;
The unscattered mind;
The undisturbed mind;
And the unsullied mind.

If one is of this sort, he becomes one possessed of faith who delights in the aspects of the mind of faith and distinguishes their respective meritorious qualities. [In particular]:[70]

He has faith in the path originally coursed in by the Buddhas;
Has faith in being able to develop the practice of the *pāramitās*;
Has faith in being able to thoroughly enter into the grounds especially superior qualities;
Has faith in being able to perfect the ten powers of the Buddha;

正體字

信具足四
502a08‖ 無所畏。信不共法不可壞。信諸佛法不可思
502a09‖ 議。信諸佛力無中無邊。信諸如來無量行門。
502a10‖ 信從因緣以成果報。舉要言之。信諸菩薩普
502a11‖ 行諸佛功德智慧威神力等。{PP} 諸佛子。菩薩作
502a12‖ 是念。諸佛正法。如是甚深。如是離相。如是
502a13‖ 寂滅。如是空。如是無相。如是無作。如是無
502a14‖ 染。如是無量。如是廣大。如是難壞。{QQ} 而諸凡
502a15‖ 夫。心墮邪見。為無明癡冥。蔽其慧眼。常立
502a16‖ 憍慢幢。墮在渴愛網。隨順諂曲。常懷慳嫉。而
502a17‖ 作後身生處因緣。多集貪欲。瞋恚愚癡。起諸
502a18‖ 重業。嫌恨猛風。吹罪心火。

简体字

信具足四无所畏，信不共法不可坏，信诸佛法不可思议，信诸佛力无中无边，信诸如来无量行门，信从因缘以成果报。举要言之，信诸菩萨普行诸佛功德智慧威神力等。

“诸佛子，菩萨作是念：‘诸佛正法，如是甚深，如是离相，如是寂灭，如是空，如是无相，如是无作，如是无染，如是无量，如是广大，如是难坏。而诸凡夫，心堕邪见，为无明痴冥蔽其慧眼，常立憍慢幢，堕在渴爱网，随顺谄曲，常怀悭嫉，而作后身生处因缘；多集贪欲、瞋恚、愚痴，起诸重业；嫌恨猛风，吹罪心火

Has faith in being able to achieve perfect fulfillment of the four fearlessnesses;
Has faith in the indomitable dharmas exclusive to the Buddhas;
Has faith in the inconceivable Dharma of the Buddhas;
Has faith in the Buddhas' powers as transcendent of either any middle or polar extremes;
Has faith in the Tathāgata's countless gateways of practice;
And has faith in realizing the fruits [of the path] as a consequence that results from their respective causes and conditions.

To speak of it in terms of the essentials, he has faith in the universally applied bodhisattva practices as well as the meritorious qualities, wisdom,[71] powers, and other attributes of the Buddhas.

9. The Bodhisattva's Reflective Contemplation on Dharma and Beings

{PP} Sons of the Buddha, the bodhisattva has the following thought:

The right Dharma of the Buddhas is characterized by:

Such extreme profundity;
Such transcendence of signs;
Such quiescence;
Such emptiness;
Such signlessness;
Such wishlessness;
Such non-defilement;
Such measurelessness;
Such vastness;
And such insurmountability.

{QQ} And yet common people:

Allow their minds to fall into wrong views;
Allow their wisdom eyes to be covered over by the darkness of ignorance;
Always raise up the banner of arrogance;
Fall into the net of craving;
Follow the course of flattery and deceptiveness;
Always embrace miserliness and jealousy through which they create the causes and conditions for their subsequent stations of rebirth;
Extensively accumulate those desires, hatreds, delusions whereby they create all manner of heavy karma;
So set the fierce wind of their hatefulness and animosity blowing upon the flames of the mind inclined toward

正體字

常令熾盛。有所
502a19‖ 施作。皆與顛倒相應。欲流有流。[2]無明流。見
502a20‖ 流相續起。心意識種於三界地生苦惱牙。{RR}所
502a21‖ 謂。名色和合。增長六入。諸[3]入外塵。相對生
502a22‖ 觸。觸因緣故。生諸受。[4]深樂受故生渴愛。渴
502a23‖ 愛增益故。生取。取增長故。復起後有。有因緣
502a24‖ 故。有生老死憂悲苦惱。如是因緣。集諸苦聚。
502a25‖ 眾生受諸苦惱。是中無我無我所。無作者無
502a26‖ 受者。無知者。如草木瓦石。又亦如影。凡夫
502a27‖ 可愍。不知不覺。而受苦惱。{SS}菩薩於此。見諸眾
502a28‖ 生不免諸苦。即生大悲智慧。是諸眾生。我等
502a29‖ 應救。

简体字

常令炽盛；有所施作，皆与颠倒相应，欲流、有流、无明流、见流相续起，心意识种于三界地生苦恼芽，所谓：名色和合增长六入，诸入外尘相对生触，触因缘故生诸受，深乐受故生渴爱，渴爱增益故生取，取增长故复起后有，有因缘故有生老死忧悲苦恼。如是因缘集诸苦聚，众生受诸苦恼；是中无我、无我所、无作者、无受者、无知者，如草木瓦石，又亦如影。凡夫可愍，不知不觉而受苦恼。’菩萨于此，见诸众生不免诸苦，即生大悲智慧：‘是诸众生，我等应救。’

karmic offenses that they are always caused to blaze intensely;

Become such that, whatever actions they pursue are reflections of the inverted views;[72]

And become such that the flood of desire, the flood of becoming, the flood of ignorance, and the flood of views[73] continuously generate seeds associated with the mind and mental consciousness in the field of the three realms of existence that in turn grow forth the sprouts of suffering and affliction.

{RR} Specifically, this occurs as follows:

The conjunction of [the aggregates of] name-and-form[74] then leads to the development of the six sense bases.[75]

The paired conjunctions of the sense bases with their corresponding objective sense dusts generate contact.

Because of the cause and condition of contact, there then occurs the arising of feelings.

Because of a deep delight in feelings, there then occurs the generation of desire.

Because of increased desire, there then follows the generation of grasping.

Due to an increase in grasping, there then follows the production of subsequent existence.

Because of the causes and conditions inhering in existence, there then occur birth, aging, worry, sorrow, suffering, and the afflictions.

It is through causes and conditions such as these that they accumulate such a mass of suffering. In this circumstance wherein beings undergo all manner of suffering and affliction, there is no self, nothing belonging to a self, no agent of actions, no one who undergoes anything at all, and no one who is possessed of any knowing awareness. This circumstance is just as if consisting solely of shrubs, trees, tiles, and stones. It is also comparable to mere reflections.

These common people are so pitiable. In all of this, they are unknowing and unaware and thus become bound to undergo such suffering and affliction.

10. The Bodhisattva's Resolve, Renunciation, and Grounds Purification

{SS} At this point, observing that these beings are unable to avoid all these sufferings, the bodhisattva immediately brings forth wisdom in association with the great compassion, thinking, "We should all strive to rescue these beings." He also wishes to cause

正體字

又欲令住畢竟佛道之樂。即生大慈智
502b01‖ 慧。{TT}菩薩摩訶薩。隨順如是大慈悲法。以深妙
502b02‖ 心。住在初地。於一切物。無所貪惜。尊重諸佛
502b03‖ 大妙智故。學行大捨。即時所有可施之物。盡
502b04‖ 能施與。所謂。穀麥庫藏。金銀摩尼珠。車𤦲。
502b05‖ 馬瑙琉璃珊瑚琥珀。珂貝瓔珞。嚴身之具。諸
502b06‖ 珍寶等。及象馬車乘。輦輿人民。奴婢眷屬。國
502b07‖ 土城邑。聚落廬舍。園林遊觀。妻子男女。一切
502b08‖ 所愛。皆悉捨與頭目耳鼻。支節手足舉身皆
502b09‖ 與。深重佛智故。而不貪惜。菩薩摩訶薩。住
502b10‖ 於初地。能行大捨。{UU}是菩薩。以大悲心大捨心。
502b11‖ 救一切眾生故。轉勤推求世間出世間利益
502b12‖ 勝事。心無疲懈。是故菩薩。生無疲倦功德。於
502b13‖ 諸經書。能自開解。是故。生知經書功德。得如
502b14‖ 是知經書智慧。善能籌量。應作不應作。於上
502b15‖ 中下眾生。隨宜而行。隨有依止來親近者。隨
502b16‖ 力利益。

简体字

又欲令住毕竟佛道之乐，即生大慈智慧。菩萨摩诃萨随顺如是大慈悲法，以深妙心住在初地，于一切物无所贪惜，尊重诸佛大妙智故学行大舍，即时所有可施之物尽能施与，所谓：谷麦库藏、金、银、摩尼珠、砗磲、玛瑙、琉璃、珊瑚、琥珀、珂贝、璎珞、严身之具、诸珍宝等，及象马车乘、辇舆、人民、奴婢眷属、国土城邑、聚落庐舍、园林游观、妻子男女，一切所爱皆悉舍与，头目耳鼻、支节手足举身皆与，深重佛智故而不贪惜。菩萨摩诃萨住于初地能行大舍，是菩萨以大悲心、大舍心，救一切众生故，转勤推求世间、出世间利益胜事心无疲懈。是故菩萨生无疲倦功德，于诸经书能自开解，是故生知经书功德，得如是知经书智慧，善能筹量应作不应作，于上中下众生随宜而行，随有依止来亲近者，随力利益。

them to be able to abide in the happiness of the Buddha's ultimate path and so immediately brings forth wisdom in association with the great kindness.

{TT} When, in accordance with the dharmas of the great kindness and the great compassion, the bodhisattva *mahāsattva* avails himself of deep and marvelous resolve and abides on the first ground, he becomes free of any covetous cherishing for anything at all and, out of profound veneration for the great and marvelous knowledge of the Buddhas, cultivates the great relinquishing through which he is immediately able to entirely give away everything that can be given. This includes his food and seed grains, the contents of his storehouses and treasuries, gold, silver, *maṇi* jewels, agate, carnelian, lapis lazuli, coral, amber, precious shells, jewel necklaces, adornments for the body, all manner of precious jewels and such, as well as elephants, horses, carriages, rickshaws, workers, servants, members of his own retinue, states, cities, villages, shelters, parks, forests, viewing terraces, wives, children, both male and female, and whatsoever else one might hold dear, relinquishing all of these things. He is also able to give away even his own head, eyes, ears, nose, limbs, hands, feet, and entire body, giving all of these things because of his profound esteem for the knowledge of the Buddha, doing so without retaining any possessive cherishing for them. The bodhisattva *mahāsattva* who dwells on the first ground is thereby able to carry forth the practice of the great relinquishing.

{UU} Utilizing the mind of great compassion and the mind of great relinquishing in his striving to rescue all beings, this bodhisattva redoubles his efforts aimed at implementing all forms of worldly and world-transcending beneficial endeavor and perseveres in this tirelessly.

As a consequence of this, this bodhisattva develops the quality of tirelessness through which he is able to open forth and comprehend all of the scriptural texts. He thereby develops the qualities associated with knowing the contents of the scriptures and acquires the wisdom[76] arising from such knowledge of the scriptural texts. He becomes able then to well assess how he should and should not proceed in relation to beings of superior, middling, and inferior capacities and thus accords with what is appropriate in subsequent related endeavors. He then accords with whoever comes to rely on and draw close to him, adapting to their capacities in his efforts to benefit them.

正體字

是故菩薩。生世智功德。得世智功德。
502b17‖ 則知時知量。慚愧莊嚴。修習自利利彼之道。
502b18‖ 是故則生慚愧功德。如是功德行中。精勤修
502b19‖ 行。心不懈退。是精進不退功[5]德。即時得堪
502b20‖ 受力。得堪受力已。勤行供養諸佛。隨佛所說。
502b21‖ 如說而行。諸佛子。是菩薩。悉知生起如是清
502b22‖ 淨地法。所謂。信慈悲捨不疲惓。知諸經書。善
502b23‖ 解世法。慚愧堪受力。供養諸佛。如所說行。
502b24‖ {VV}又是菩薩。住歡喜地。[6]以發願故。廣見於諸
502b25‖ 佛。數百數千數萬億那由他佛。菩薩見諸佛
502b26‖ 時。心大歡喜。深心愛敬。以菩薩樂具。供養諸
502b27‖ 佛。及供養僧。

简体字

是故菩萨生世智功德，得世智功德则知时知量；惭愧庄严，修习自利利彼之道，是故则生惭愧功德；如是功德行中，精勤修行心不懈退；是精进不退功德，即时得堪受力；得堪受力已，勤行供养诸佛，随佛所说，如说而行。

“诸佛子，是菩萨悉知生起如是清净地法，所谓：信慈悲，舍不疲惓，知诸经书，善解世法，惭愧堪受力，供养诸佛，如所说行。又是菩萨住欢喜地，以发愿故，广见于诸佛，数百、数千、数万亿那由他佛。菩萨见诸佛时，心大欢喜，深心爱敬，以菩萨乐具供养诸佛，及供养僧，

Thus it is that the bodhisattva develops the qualities associated with worldly knowledge. Having acquired these qualities associated with worldly knowledge, he then becomes aware of what constitutes correct timeliness and correct measure in these endeavors. Then, graced with a sense of shame and dread of blame, he cultivates the path of benefiting self and benefiting others. Because of this, he develops the qualities associated with possessing a sense of shame and dread of blame.

In his implementation of these qualities, he engages in the intensely diligent cultivation of irreversible resolve.[77] Through this quality of vigor in irreversible resolve, he immediately acquires the power of enduring fortitude. Having acquired this power of enduring fortitude, he then diligently engages in making offerings to all buddhas, according with whatever the Buddha has taught, and practicing in accord with whatever the Buddha has taught.

Sons of the Buddha, thus it is that this bodhisattva comes to comprehensively know all of the dharmas through which one brings forth such purification of the grounds, namely:[78]

Faith;
Kindness;
Compassion;
Renunciation;
Indefatigability;
Knowledge of the scriptures and texts;
Thorough comprehension of worldly dharmas;
A sense of shame and dread of blame;
The power of fortitude;
The making of offerings to the Buddhas while practicing in accordance with the teachings.[79]

11. The Bodhisattva's Seeing and Serving of Countless Buddhas

{VV} Furthermore, due to having made vows, this bodhisattva dwelling on the Ground of Joyfulness obtains a vast vision of the Buddhas, thereby becoming able to see the Buddhas, seeing many hundreds, seeing many thousands, or seeing even many myriads of *koṭis* of *nayutas* of buddhas. When the bodhisattva sees the Buddhas, his mind is filled with great joyfulness and deep-minded cherishing reverence. He then makes offerings to the Buddhas of whatsoever things would be pleasing to bodhisattvas, also making offerings to their Sangha assemblies as well. He then

正體字

以是福德。皆[回>迴]向阿耨多羅三
502b28‖ 藐三菩提。是菩薩。因供養諸佛故。生教化眾
502b29‖ 生法。多以二攝。攝取眾生。所謂。布施愛語。
502c01‖ 後二攝法。但以信解力。行未善通達。是菩薩。
502c02‖ 隨所供養諸佛。教化眾生。皆能受行清淨地
502c03‖ 法。如是諸功德。皆自然迴向薩婆若。轉益明
502c04‖ 顯。堪任有用。譬如佛子。金師鍊金。隨以火
502c05‖ 力。調柔可用。增益光色。如是菩薩。隨供養
502c06‖ 諸佛。教化眾生。受行清淨諸地之法。此諸功
502c07‖ 德。皆自然迴向薩婆若。轉益明顯。隨意所用。
502c08‖ {WW}又諸佛子。菩薩摩訶薩。於初地中。相貌得果。
502c09‖ 應從諸佛菩薩善知識所。諮受請問。[7]成地之
502c10‖ 法。不應[8]厭。廢是菩薩。住初地中。應於諸佛
502c11‖ 菩薩善知識所。諮受請問第二地中相貌

简体字

以是福德皆回向阿耨多罗三藐三菩提。是菩萨因供养诸佛故，生教化众生法，多以二摄摄取众生，所谓：布施、爱语。后二摄法，但以信解力行，未善通达。是菩萨随所供养诸佛，教化众生皆能受行清净地法，如是诸功德皆自然回向萨婆若，转益明显，堪任有用。譬如，佛子，金师炼金，随以火力，调柔可用，增益光色；如是菩萨随供养诸佛，教化众生，受行清净诸地之法，此诸功德皆自然回向萨婆若，转益明显，随意所用。

“又诸佛子，菩萨摩诃萨于初地中相貌得果，应从诸佛菩萨善知识所，咨受请问成地之法，不应厌废。是菩萨住初地中，应于诸佛菩萨善知识所，咨受请问第二地中相貌

dedicates the merit of these offerings to his eventual realization of *anuttarasamyaksaṃbodhi.*

12. The Bodhisattva's Practice of the Means of Attraction

Due to having made offerings to the Buddhas, this bodhisattva develops the dharmas through which one carries out the teaching of beings, for the most part using two of the means of attraction in his drawing beings forth. Specifically, these are giving and pleasing words. He only employs the remaining two means of attraction[80] in a manner commensurate with his own powers of faithful comprehension, for his practice of them has not yet reached a state of state of consummate skillfulness.

In a manner corresponding to the offerings he has made to the Buddhas and his efforts in the teaching of beings, this bodhisattva in all cases becomes able to take on the practice of the dharmas involved in purifying cultivation of the grounds. He naturally dedicates all the merit from these actions to all-knowledge. As he proceeds in this fashion, they increase in their shining brightness to the point where they can be put to use.

13. The Bodhisattva's Grounds Purification Compared to Refining Gold

Sons of the Buddha, this circumstance is analogous to that of a goldsmith who, in his refining of gold, employs the power of fire in the smelting and softening of gold through which it becomes increasingly radiant and lustrous. So too it is with the bodhisattva who, commensurate with his making of offerings to the Buddhas and his teaching of beings, takes on the practice of those dharmas used in the purifying cultivation of the grounds and then naturally dedicates all the merit therefrom to the acquisition of all-knowledge. As they become ever more brightly radiant, he thus becomes able to freely put them to use however he wishes.

14. The Bodhisattva's Acquisition of Further Knowledge of the Grounds

{WW} Furthermore, Sons of the Buddha, with regard to the first ground, the bodhisattva *mahāsattva* should consult, present requests for clarification, and receive instruction regarding its characteristic aspects and acquired fruits, seeking teachings on the dharmas involved in success on this ground, insatiably requesting these teachings from buddhas, bodhisattvas, and good spiritual guides.

As he dwells on the first ground, this bodhisattva should consult, present requests for clarification, and receive instruction regarding the second ground's characteristic aspects and

正體字

得
502c12‖ 果無有厭足。如是第三。第四第五。第六第七。
502c13‖ 第八第九。第十地中。相貌得果。應從諸佛菩
502c14‖ 薩善知識所諮受請問成十地法。無有[9]廢厭。
502c15‖ 是菩薩。悉應善知諸地逆順法。善知諸地成
502c16‖ 壞。善知諸地相貌因[10]果。善知諸地得捨。善
502c17‖ 知諸地清淨行分。善知諸地從一地至一地
502c18‖ 行。善知諸地是處非是處。善知諸地轉所住
502c19‖ 處。善知諸地初事後事差別。善知諸地得不
502c20‖ 退轉相。乃至善知一切菩薩清淨地法。善知
502c21‖ 入如來智地。諸佛子。如是諸菩薩。善知諸地
502c22‖ [11]相未發初[12]地乃至十地。知無障[*]閡。得諸地

简体字

得果，无有厌足。如是第三、第四、第五、第六、第七、第八、第九、第十地中相貌得果，应从诸佛菩萨善知识所咨受请问成十地法，无有废厌。是菩萨悉应善知诸地逆顺法，善知诸地成坏，善知诸地相貌因果，善知诸地得舍，善知诸地清净行分，善知诸地从一地至一地行，善知诸地是处非是处，善知诸地转所住处，善知诸地初事后事差别，善知诸地得不退转相，乃至善知一切菩萨清净地法，善知入如来智地。诸佛子，如是诸菩萨善知诸地相，未发初地乃至十地，知无障碍，得诸地

acquired fruits, insatiably requesting these teachings from buddhas, bodhisattvas, and good spiritual guides. So too should he proceed in these requests for teachings regarding the characteristic aspects and acquired fruits associated with the third, fourth, fifth, sixth, seventh, eighth, ninth, and tenth grounds. Thus it is that he should request teachings on successful development of the dharmas associated with the ten grounds, insatiably requesting these teachings from buddhas, bodhisattvas, and good spiritual guides.

This bodhisattva should then:

Thoroughly know with respect to all of the grounds those dharmas that are either contradictory or conducive to their successful cultivation;

Thoroughly know the circumstances conducing to success or to ruination of progress on the grounds;

Thoroughly know the characteristic aspects of the causes and effects associated with the grounds;

Thoroughly know what is involved in the successive acquisition and relinquishing of each of the grounds;

Thoroughly know the practice aspects associated with purification of the grounds;

Thoroughly know with respect to all the grounds the practices involved in progressing from any single ground to the next ground;

Thoroughly know with respect to all of the grounds what is and is not the correct station;

Thoroughly know with respect to the grounds what is involved in changing the station in which one is abiding;

Thoroughly know with respect to the grounds the distinctions in initially-occurring and subsequently-occurring phenomena;

And thoroughly know with respect to the grounds the characteristic signs of achieving irreversibility, and so forth until we come to his thoroughly knowing of all of the dharmas involved in purification of the grounds and his thoroughly knowing what is involved in entering the ground of the Tathāgata's knowledge.

Sons of the Buddha, so it is that the bodhisattvas thoroughly know the characteristic signs associated with all of the grounds from that point wherein one has not yet gained the first ground on through to the tenth ground, possessing unimpeded knowledge of these things. It is through their acquisition of the light

正體字

502c23‖ 智慧光明故。能得諸佛智慧光明。諸佛子。如
502c24‖ 大商主。多將賈人。欲至大城。應先問道路。
502c25‖ 退還過咎。在道利害。未發初處。知道宿時。
502c26‖ 乃至善知到彼城事。能以智慧。思惟籌量。具
502c27‖ 諸資用。令無所乏。正導人眾。得至大城。於險
502c28‖ 道中。免諸患難。身及諸人。皆無憂惱。諸佛
502c29‖ 子。菩薩摩訶薩。亦復如是。[13]住初地。而善知。
503a01‖ 諸地逆順法。乃至善知淨一切菩薩清淨地
503a02‖ 法。善知入如來智地
503a03‖ 爾時菩薩。集大福德智慧資糧。為眾生商主。
503a04‖ 隨宜教化。令出生死險難惡處。示安隱道。乃
503a05‖ 至令住薩婆若智慧大城。無諸[1]衰惱。是故諸
503a06‖ 佛子。菩薩摩訶薩。常應心不疲惓勤修諸地
503a07‖ 本行。乃至善知

简体字

智慧光明故，能得诸佛智慧光明。

“诸佛子，如大商主，多将贾人欲至大城，应先问道路、退还过咎、在道利害、未发初处、知道宿时，乃至善知到彼城事，能以智慧思惟筹量，具诸资用令无所乏，正导人众得至大城，于险道中免诸患难，身及诸人皆无忧恼。诸佛子，菩萨摩诃萨亦复如是，住初地而善知诸地逆顺法，乃至善知净一切菩萨清净地法，善知入如来智地。尔时菩萨集大福德智慧资粮，为众生商主，随宜教化，令出生死险难恶处，示安隐道，乃至令住萨婆若智慧大城无诸衰恼。是故，诸佛子，菩萨摩诃萨常应心不疲惓，勤修诸地本行，乃至善知

of wisdom in relation to the grounds that they become able to acquire the light of all buddhas' wisdom.[81]

15. The Bodhisattva's Path Knowledge Compared to a Caravan Guide

Sons of the Buddha, this circumstance is analogous to that of a great leader of merchants who is preparing to lead forth many merchants wishing to reach some great city. In such a circumstance, he needs to first inquire about the roads, about any possibly ruinous conditions that might require turning back, and about any circumstances on the road by which anyone might be harmed.

Even before first setting out, he finds out in advance where one will be able to rest each night and comes to thoroughly know all of the matters related to successfully reaching that city. He develops the ability to employ his wisdom[82] and reasoned assessments in the preparation of all of the provisions they will use, thus ensuring that they will not fall short of anything they need as he correctly leads that group of people on through to successful arrival at that great city. He thereby ensures that, while on that dangerous road, they will be able to avoid calamitous difficulties that might befall either himself or any of the others, thus making sure that everyone may remain free of worry or affliction.

Sons of the Buddha, the bodhisattva *mahāsattva* is just like this. Even while dwelling on the first ground, he comes to thoroughly know all of the grounds' contradictory and conducive dharmas and so forth on through to his thoroughly knowing all bodhisattva's grounds-purification dharmas and his thoroughly knowing entry into the ground of the Tathāgata's knowledge.

At this time, the bodhisattva sees to the accumulation of the provisions consisting of great merit and wisdom.[83] He then proceeds to serve beings like that leader of merchants. Thus he then accords with what is appropriate in teaching them and influencing them to escape the dangers, difficulties, and wretched destinies of *saṃsāra*'s cyclic births and deaths and shows them the safe and secure path, continuing to do so until he causes them to dwell in the great city of the wisdom[84] of all-knowledge wherein they become free of any vulnerability to ruin or affliction.

Therefore, O Sons of the Buddha, the bodhisattva *mahāsattva* should always bring forth tireless resolve in his diligent cultivation of all of the foundational practices associated with the grounds, doing so on through to the point where he thoroughly

正體字

入如來智地。諸佛子。是名略
503a08‖ 說菩薩摩訶薩。入歡喜地門。廣說則有無量
503a09‖ 百千萬億阿僧祇事。{XX}菩薩摩訶薩。住在此地。
503a10‖ 多作閻浮提王。豪貴自在。常護正法。能以
503a11‖ [2]布施。攝取眾生。善除眾生慳貪之垢。常行
503a12‖ 大施。而不窮匱所作善業。若布施若愛語。若
503a13‖ 利益若同事。是諸福德。皆不離念佛。不離念
503a14‖ 法。不離念諸菩薩摩訶薩伴。不離念諸菩薩
503a15‖ 所行道。不離念諸波羅蜜。不離念十地。不離
503a16‖ 念諸力無畏不共法。乃至不離念具足一切
503a17‖ 種智。常生是心。我當於一切眾生之中。為首
503a18‖ 為勝。為大為妙。為上為無上。為導為將。為師
503a19‖ 為尊。

简体字

入如来智地。

“诸佛子，是名略说菩萨摩诃萨，入欢喜地门，广说则有无量百千万亿阿僧祇事。菩萨摩诃萨住在此地，多作阎浮提王，豪贵自在，常护正法，能以布施摄取众生，善除众生悭贪之垢，常行大施而不穷匮。所作善业，若布施、若爱语、若利益、若同事，是诸福德皆不离念佛，不离念法，不离念诸菩萨摩诃萨伴，不离念诸菩萨所行道，不离念诸波罗蜜，不离念十地，不离念诸力、无畏、不共法，乃至不离念具足一切种智。常生是心：‘我当于一切众生之中，为首、为胜、为大、为妙、为上、为无上、为导、为将、为师、为尊，

knows the means used in entering the ground of the Tathāgata's knowledge.

16. Vajragarbha's Final Statements About the 1st Ground Bodhisattva

Sons of the Buddha, this constitutes a summary discussion of the bodhisattva *mahāsattva*'s entry into the gateway of the Ground of Joyfulness. Were one to take up an extensive discussion of this, this would involve the treatment of countless hundreds of thousands of myriads of *koṭis* of *asaṃkhyeyas* of specific topics.

17. The Bodhisattva's Social Station and Dharma Practice

{XX} The bodhisattva *mahāsattva* dwelling on this ground often becomes a monarch reigning over the continent of Jambudvīpa who is a member of the aristocratic nobility that, acting with sovereign freedom, is able to draw forth beings through great giving.[85] He is skilled in doing away with beings' filth of miserliness as he always practices great giving and never lessens the good karmic works in which he engages.

a. The Bodhisattva's Mindfulness

No matter whether he is engaged in the meritorious practices of giving, pleasing words, beneficial actions, or joint endeavors, still:

He never departs from his mindfulness of the Buddha;
He never departs from his mindfulness of the Dharma;
He never departs from his mindfulness of all of his companions among the bodhisattva *mahāsattvas*;
He never departs from his mindfulness of the path practiced by the bodhisattvas;
He never departs from his mindfulness of the *pāramitās*;
He never departs from his mindfulness of the ten grounds;
He never departs from his mindfulness of the powers, the fearlessnesses, and the dharmas exclusive to buddhas;
And so forth until we come to his never departing from his mindfulness of the quest to completely perfect his realization of the knowledge of all modes.

b. The Bodhisattva's Aspiration to Serve Beings

He always has this thought: "For all of these beings, I should serve them as a leader, as one who is supreme in this, as one who is grand, as one who is sublime, as one who is superior, as one who is unsurpassably superior, as one who serves them as a guide, as one who serves them like a general, as one who serves them as a teaching master, as one who is worthy of their reverence, and

正體字

乃至於一切眾生中。為依止者。諸佛子。
503a20‖ [3]是菩薩摩訶薩。若欲捨家。勤行精進。須臾
503a21‖ 之間。於佛法中。便能捨家妻子五欲。得出家
503a22‖ 已。勤行精進。須臾之間。得百三昧。得見百
503a23‖ 佛。知百佛神力。能動百佛世界。能飛過百佛
503a24‖ 世界。能照百佛世界。能教化百佛世界眾生。
503a25‖ 能住壽百劫。能知過去未來世各百劫事。能
503a26‖ 善入百法門。能變身為百。於一一身。能示百
503a27‖ 菩薩。以為眷屬。{YY}若以願力。自在示現。過於此
503a28‖ 數。若干百千萬億那由他不可計知。爾時金
503a29‖ 剛藏菩薩摩訶薩。欲重明此義。而說偈言
503b01‖ 若有諸眾生　厚修[4]集善根
503b02‖ 成就於白法　親近於諸佛

简体字

乃至于一切众生中为依止者。’

“诸佛子，是菩萨摩诃萨，若欲舍家勤行精进，须臾之间于佛法中，便能舍家妻子五欲；得出家已勤行精进，须臾之间得百三昧，得见百佛，知百佛神力，能动百佛世界，能飞过百佛世界，能照百佛世界，能教化百佛世界众生，能住寿百劫，能知过去、未来世各百劫事，能善入百法门，能变身为百，于一一身能示百菩萨以为眷属；若以愿力，自在示现过于此数，若干百千万亿那由他不可计知。”

尔时，金刚藏菩萨摩诃萨欲重明此义，而说偈言：

“若有诸众生，　厚修集善根，
成就于白法，　亲近于诸佛，

as one who serves them in other such ways up to and including serving them as one upon whom they can rely."

c. The Result of the Bodhisattva's Leaving the Household Life

Sons of the Buddha, if this bodhisattva *mahāsattva* wishes to relinquish the home life, once he applies himself to this, with but a moment's application of effort, he will become able to relinquish the home life along with his wife and children and the five desires. Having succeeded in leaving the home life under the auspices of the Buddha's Dharma, then, through but a moment's application of diligent effort:

He will be able to acquire a hundred samādhis, see a hundred buddhas, and know a hundred buddhas' spiritual powers;
He will be able to cause tremors throughout a hundred buddha worlds;
He will become able to fly across the span of a hundred buddha worlds;
He will become able to illuminate a hundred buddha worlds;
He will become able to teach the beings within a hundred buddha worlds;
He will become able to abide for a lifespan of a hundred kalpas;
He will become able to know the events of a hundred kalpas of both the past and the future;
He will become able to skillfully enter a hundred gateways into the Dharma;
He will become able to create a hundred transformation bodies;
And he will be able to manifest a hundred bodhisattvas to serve in the retinue of each of them.

{YY} Were he to avail himself of the power of vows, he could freely manifest these phenomena in even greater numbers so large that one could never count them even in however many hundreds of thousands of myriads of *koṭis* of *nayutas* of kalpas one might attempt to do so.[86]

18. Vajragarbha Bodhisattva's Summarizing Verses

At that time, wishing to reiterate and clarify these meanings, Vajragarbha Bodhisattva Mahāsattva then uttered verses, saying:

If there be any being
who liberally cultivates the accumulation of roots of goodness,
who perfects a hundred dharmas,
who draws close to the Buddhas,

正體字

503b03‖ 清淨信力大　隨順慈悲心
503b04‖ 如是人能發　無量之佛智 {1}
503b05‖ 諸佛一切智　無量力清淨
503b06‖ 堪受力堅牢　成就諸佛法
503b07‖ 悲心救世間　淨修諸佛國
503b08‖ 敷演轉法輪　發此無上願 {2}
503b09‖ 一念知三世　而無有別異
503b10‖ 種種時差別　以示於世間
503b11‖ 略說則盡求　諸佛之功德
503b12‖ 發於廣大心　猶若如虛空 {3}
503b13‖ 悲心智慧首　方便[5]合修行
503b14‖ 淨信深心故　其力無有量
503b15‖ 心向無障礙　而不隨他教
503b16‖ 同諸佛平等　而生於大心 {4}
503b17‖ 諸佛子當生　如是之[6]實心
503b18‖ 即離凡夫行　入於佛所行
503b19‖ 即生如來家　無有可譏嫌
503b20‖ 則同於諸佛　必成無上道 {5}
503b21‖ 生如是心時　即便得初地
503b22‖ 其心不可動　猶若如山王

简体字

清净信力大，　随顺慈悲心，
如是人能发，　无量之佛智。
诸佛一切智，　无量力清净，
堪受力坚牢，　成就诸佛法。
悲心救世间，　净修诸佛国，
敷演转法轮，　发此无上愿。
一念知三世，　而无有别异，
种种时差别，　以示于世间。
略说则尽求，　诸佛之功德，
发于广大心，　犹若如虚空。
悲心智慧首，　方便合修行，
净信深心故，　其力无有量。
心向无障碍，　而不随他教，
同诸佛平等，　而生于大心。
诸佛子当生，　如是之实心，
即离凡夫行，　入于佛所行；
即生如来家，　无有可讥嫌；
则同于诸佛，　必成无上道。
生如是心时，　即便得初地，
其心不可动，　犹若如山王。

whose power of pure faith is immense,
and who accords with the minds of kindness and compassion—
A person such as this is capable of bringing forth
the immeasurably vast knowledge of the Buddha. {1}

Questing to acquire the all-knowledge of the Buddhas,
their incalculably vast powers and purity,
with solid and enduring power of endurance,
he perfects all dharmas of the Buddhas,

with the mind of compassion, he rescues those in the world,
purifies all of the buddha lands,
turns the wheel of Dharma through its extensive proclamation,
and brings forth this most unexcelled of vows. {2}

In order, in a single mind-moment, to know the three periods of time,
and yet still have no discriminations in this regard,
in order to manifest within the world
in all of the various sorts of eras, each distinct from the other,

and, to state it briefly, in order to strive
to acquire all of the Buddhas' meritorious qualities,
he brings forth the vast resolve
that is comparable in its scope to empty space. {3}

Taking the compassionate mind and wisdom as foremost,
cultivating in conjunction with skillful means,
due to having pure faith and resolute intentions,
his powers in this become immeasurably vast.

In whatever he turns his mind to, he is unimpeded
so that he need not rely on the instruction from others.
In these matters, he achieves parity with the Buddhas
and thereby brings forth the great resolve. {4}

All sons of the Buddha should give birth to
just such a jewel-like[87] resolve as this.
By this, one immediately abandons the actions of a common person
and enters into the conduct engaged in by the Buddha.

One thus immediately achieves birth into the family of the Buddhas
that is beyond any bases for criticism or censure,
and then will become the same as the Buddhas
by being definitely bound to gain the unsurpassed enlightenment. {5}

When one gives birth to just such a resolve as this,
he thereupon immediately gains the first ground.
His resolve therein is as unshakeable
as the king of mountains.

正體字

503b23‖ 是菩薩便有　大喜相顯現
503b24‖ 其心常清淨　堪受於大事 {6}
503b25‖ 心不樂鬪訟　不好惱眾生
503b26‖ 無有瞋恨心　樂慚愧恭敬
503b27‖ 又習行直心　守護於諸根
503b28‖ 常念救世間　念求諸佛智
503b29‖ 心生於歡喜　我當得此事 {7}
503c01‖ 得於歡喜地　即過五恐怖
503c02‖ 不活畏死畏　及與惡名畏
503c03‖ 三惡道怖畏　大眾威德畏
503c04‖ 以不貪著我　及與我所故
503c05‖ 是諸佛子等　遠離諸怖畏 {8}
503c06‖ 常行慈悲心　恒有信恭敬
503c07‖ 慚愧功德備　晝夜增善法
503c08‖ 樂功德實利　不樂於諸欲 {9}
503c09‖ 如有所聞法　能常善思惟
503c10‖ 無有貪著行　斷諸利養心
503c11‖ 常樂於菩提　一心求佛智
503c12‖ 行諸波羅蜜　離於諂曲心 {10}

简体字

是菩萨便有，　大喜相显现，
其心常清净，　堪受于大事。
心不乐斗讼，　不好恼众生，
无有瞋恨心，　乐惭愧恭敬。
又习行直心，　守护于诸根，
常念救世间，　念求诸佛智。
心生于欢喜，　我当得此事，
得于欢喜地，　即过五恐怖，
不活畏死畏，　及与恶名畏，
三恶道怖畏，　大众威德畏。
以不贪著我，　及与我所故，
是诸佛子等，　远离诸怖畏。
常行慈悲心，　恒有信恭敬，
惭愧功德备，　昼夜增善法。
乐功德实利，　不乐于诸欲，
如有所闻法，　能常善思惟。
无有贪著行，　断诸利养心，
常乐于菩提，　一心求佛智。
行诸波罗蜜，　离于谄曲心，

This bodhisattva then has
the signs of great joyfulness manifest in him.
His resolve is thenceforth always pure
and is such that it can take on great endeavors. {6}

His mind finds no pleasure in disputatiousness,
is not fond of tormenting beings,
is entirely free of hateful thought,
and delights in a sense of shame, dread of blame, and respectfulness.

He also practices straight-mindedness,
guarding his sense faculties,
always bearing in mind rescuing those in the world,
and bearing in mind his quest for the Buddhas' knowledge.
Thus his mind becomes joyful
and he thinks: "I am bound to achieve success in these matters." {7}

When he gains the Ground of Joyfulness,
he immediately passes beyond five types of fearfulness:
Fear of failing to survive, the fear of death,
the fear of ill-repute,
the fear of the three wretched destinies,
and the fear of the awesome virtue of great assemblies.

It is due to having no covetous attachment to a self
or anything belonging to a self
that the sons of the Buddha
become able to abandon all forms of fearfulness. {8}

He always puts into practice the kind and compassionate mind,
is constantly possessed of faith and reverence,
is replete in a sense of shame, a dread of blame, and the qualities,
and, both day and night, increases the good dharmas.
He delights in genuine benefit provided by meritorious qualities
and does not delight in any of the desires. {9}

Whatever dharma he has happened to hear,
he is able to always subject to skillful contemplation.
He has no behavior motivated by covetous attachment
and has cut off all ideation pertaining to offerings or support.

He always delights in bodhi
and strives single-mindedly to acquire the Buddha's knowledge.
He practices all of the *pāramitās*
and abandons all thought tending toward flattery or deviousness. {10}

正體字

503c13‖ 隨說而能行　安住實語中
503c14‖ 不污諸佛家　不捨菩薩學
503c15‖ 遠世間事業　樂利於世間
503c16‖ 求善法無厭　精進轉增益 {11}
503c17‖ 諸菩薩如是　好樂諸功德
503c18‖ 而發於大願　求欲見諸佛
503c19‖ 護法至佛所　行菩薩妙行 {12}
503c20‖ 化一切眾生　淨一切佛土
503c21‖ 我佛國土中　滿諸大菩薩
503c22‖ 諸菩薩同心　見聞皆不空
503c23‖ 一切微塵中　諸佛成佛道 {13}
503c24‖ 發於如是等　無量無邊願
503c25‖ 是願無窮盡　如虛空眾生
503c26‖ 法性世涅槃　諸佛出智慧 {14}
503c27‖ 心緣起智種　我願如是住 {15}
503c28‖ 如是發大願　心柔軟調順
503c29‖ 能信佛功德　而觀於眾生
504a01‖ 知從因緣起　則生慈悲心
504a02‖ 即於苦眾生　我當救度之 {16}

简体字

随说而能行，　安住实语中。
不污诸佛家，　不舍菩萨学，
远世间事业，　乐利于世间。
求善法无厌，　精进转增益，
诸菩萨如是，　好乐诸功德。
而发于大愿，　求欲见诸佛，
护法至佛所，　行菩萨妙行。
化一切众生，　净一切佛土，
我佛国土中，　满诸大菩萨。
诸菩萨同心，　见闻皆不空，
一切微尘中，　诸佛成佛道。
发于如是等，　无量无边愿，
是愿无穷尽，　如虚空众生，
法性世涅槃，　诸佛出智慧，
心缘起智种，　我愿如是住。
如是发大愿，　心柔软调顺，
能信佛功德，　而观于众生，
知从因缘起，　则生慈悲心，
即于苦众生，　我当救度之。

He is able to practice in accordance with what has been proclaimed,
and establishes himself securely in truthful speech.
He never defiles the house of the Buddhas,
never relinquishes the bodhisattva training,

distances himself from worldly endeavors and karmic actions,
and delights in bestowing happiness and benefit in the world.
He seeks out good dharmas insatiably
and vigorously quests for ever-increasing progression. {11}

In this way, the bodhisattvas
are fond of and delight in all meritorious qualities
and bring forth their great vows
by which they aspire to see the Buddhas,
vow to protect the Dharma, to go wherever the Buddhas dwell,
and vow to practice the bodhisattva's marvelous practices. {12}

They vow to engage in teaching that matures all beings,
vow to take up the purification of all buddha lands,
vow that "My buddha land shall be
one that is filled with great bodhisattvas,"

vow, "I shall maintain a mind the same as that of all bodhisattvas,
shall become one who, if but heard or seen, it shall not be in vain,
and I shall bring it about that, even within every single atom,
buddhas shall appear, showing their realization of buddhahood." {13}

He brings forth vows such as these,
vows that are incalculable and boundless in their reach.
These vows are as endless
as empty space, as beings,
as the Dharma realm, as the worlds, as nirvāṇa,
as the coming forth of buddhas, as their wisdom,[88] {14}

as objects of mind, as arisings of knowledge, and path's variations.[89]
He vows: "My vows shall endure in a manner equal to these." {15}

Thus it is that they bring forth great vows,
carrying them forth with pliant, subdued, and concordant minds.
They are able to maintain faith in Buddha's meritorious qualities and,
in their contemplations with regard to beings,

realize that their circumstances arise from causes and conditions,
whereupon they bring forth the minds of kindness and compassion,
and thus immediately reflect with regard to suffering beings:
"I should rescue them and bring them to liberation." {16}

正體字

504a03‖ 為是眾生故　而行種種施
504a04‖ 所謂妙國土　上妙諸珍寶
504a05‖ 象馬及車乘　眷屬與人民
504a06‖ 頭目及手足　肌肉施無悔 {17}
504a07‖ 求種種經書　心無有疲惓
504a08‖ 得解其義趣　能隨世而行
504a09‖ 慚愧堪受心　漸令得增長
504a10‖ 能以恭敬心　供養無量佛 {18}
504a11‖ 智者於日夜　如是常修行
504a12‖ 善根得明了　猶如成鍊金
504a13‖ 菩薩住是地　能了知十住
504a14‖ 展轉修行時　無有諸障礙 {19}
504a15‖ 譬如賈客主　欲利諸商人
504a16‖ 先問道路中　諸險艱難事
504a17‖ 菩薩住初地　應知諸地行
504a18‖ 而無有障礙　能至於佛地 {20}
504a19‖ 住是初地中　多作閻浮王
504a20‖ 善知於諸法　常行慈悲心
504a21‖ 如法而化導　一切皆信敬
504a22‖ 勸令行布施　以求佛智慧 {21}

简体字

为是众生故，　而行种种施，
所谓妙国土，　上妙诸珍宝，
象马及车乘，　眷属与人民，
头目及手足，　肌肉施无悔。
求种种经书，　心无有疲惓，
得解其义趣，　能随世而行，
惭愧堪受心，　渐令得增长，
能以恭敬心，　供养无量佛。
智者于日夜，　如是常修行，
善根得明了，　犹如成炼金。
菩萨住是地，　能了知十住，
展转修行时，　无有诸障碍。
譬如贾客主，　欲利诸商人，
先问道路中，　诸险艰难事。
菩萨住初地，　应知诸地行，
而无有障碍，　能至于佛地。
住是初地中，　多作阎浮王，
善知于诸法，　常行慈悲心，
如法而化导，　一切皆信敬，
劝令行布施，　以求佛智慧。

For the sake of these beings,
he then engages in all the different sorts of giving,
specifically relinquishing to them marvelous lands,
all sorts of supremely wondrous and precious jewels,

elephants, horses, carriages,
his retinue, the services of his countrymen,
and even his head, eyes, hands, feet,
and flesh, relinquishing them all with no regrets. {17}

He seeks to acquire knowledge of the many different scriptures,
doing so with tireless mind,
gains an understanding of their meanings and purport,
and is able to practice them in a manner adapted to the world.

The sense of shame, the dread of blame, the mind of forbearance—
He gradually brings about growth in these,
and is able to bring forth a reverential mind
in making offerings to countless buddhas, {18}

The wise, both day and night,
always carry forth their cultivation in this manner,
thus causing their roots of goodness to shine brightly,
just as when one engages in the refinement of gold.

The bodhisattva who dwells on this ground
becomes able to understand all ten of the grounds
so that, as his cultivation progresses,
he has nothing that obstructs his advancement. {19}

He is comparable to a leader of traveling traders
who, wishing be of benefit to all those merchants,
first inquires about the conditions encountered on the road and
what sorts of hazardous and difficult circumstances they may meet.

The bodhisattva dwelling on the first ground
should learn all of the practices associated with the grounds
so that he will remain free of all obstacles
and be well able to arrive at the ground of buddhahood. {20}

One who dwells on this first ground
often becomes a monarch on the continent of Jambudvīpa
who is skillful in his knowing of all dharmas
and always employs the minds of kindness and compassion.

He thereby teaches and leads in accordance with the Dharma,
causing everyone to bring forth faith and reverence,
encouraging them to engage in the practice of giving,
and thereby strive to acquire the Buddha's wisdom.[90] {21}

正體字

504a23‖ 菩薩若捨國　佛法中出家
504a24‖ 勤行於精進　即得百三昧
504a25‖ 及見百諸佛　震動百國土
504a26‖ 光明照百國　飛行亦如是 {22}
504a27‖ 化百土眾生　入於百法門
504a28‖ 念知百劫事　示現百種身
504a29‖ 能以百菩薩　眷屬而示現
504b01‖ 若以其願力　過是數無量 {23}
504b02‖ 今明初地義　但以略解說
504b03‖ 若欲廣說者　億劫不能盡
504b04‖ 是初菩薩地　名之為歡喜
504b05‖ 利益眾生者　今已分別說 {24} [1]◎

简体字

菩萨若舍国，　佛法中出家，
勤行于精进，　即得百三昧，
及见百诸佛，　震动百国土，
光明照百国，　飞行亦如是，
化百土众生，　入于百法门，
念知百劫事，　示现百种身。
能以百菩萨，　眷属而示现，
若以其愿力，　过是数无量。
今明初地义，　但以略解说，
若欲广说者，　亿劫不能尽。
是初菩萨地，　名之为欢喜，
利益众生者，　今已分别说。”

If the bodhisattva chooses to relinquish his country,
leave the home life, and enter the Buddha's Dharma,
through diligent practice pursued with vigor,
he immediately succeeds in acquiring a hundred samādhis,

in being able to see a hundred buddhas,
in being able to cause tremors in a hundred lands,
in being able to illuminate a hundred lands,
and in being able to fly across just such an expanse. {22}

He becomes able, too, to teach the beings in a hundred lands,
to enter a hundred gateways into the Dharma,
to call to mind the events of a hundred kalpas,
and manifest a hundred bodies

while also being able to bring forth a hundred bodhisattvas
to manifest in the retinue of each of them.
If he avails himself of his power of vows,
he is able to exceed these numbers by an incalculably great amount. {23}

In this clarification of the ideas related to the first ground, I now
merely offer a summary explanatory description.
If one wished to present an expansively comprehensive description,
one could not complete it even in a *koṭi* of kalpas.

This first of bodhisattva grounds,
is known as the station of joyfulness.
I hereby now conclude this differentiating discussion
of this one who bestows such benefit on beings. {24}

The End of Chapter One

正體字

504b06║ ◎[2]離垢地第二
504b07║ 一切菩薩眾　聞說上地義
504b08║ 其心皆清淨　歡喜無有量{1}
504b09║ 各於所坐處　踊住虛空中
504b10║ 脫身上妙衣　以散金剛藏{2}
504b11║ 咸皆稱讚言　善哉金剛藏
504b12║ 大智無所畏　善說菩薩地{3}
504b13║ 解脫月大士　知眾心清淨
504b14║ 欲聞第二地　相貌之所說{4}
504b15║ 即請金剛藏　大智願解說
504b16║ 第二地相貌　一切皆欲聞{5}
504b17║ {A}爾時金剛藏菩薩摩訶薩。語解脫月菩薩言。
504b18║ 佛子。[3]諸菩薩摩訶薩。已具足初地。欲得第
504b19║ 二地者。當生十心。何等為十。一柔軟心。二調
504b20║ 和心。

简体字

十住经卷第二

离垢地第二

一切菩萨众，　闻说上地义，
其心皆清净，　欢喜无有量，
各于所坐处，　踊住虚空中，
脱身上妙衣，　以散金刚藏，
咸皆称赞言：“善哉金刚藏，
大智无所畏，　善说菩萨地！”

解脱月大士，　知众心清净，
欲闻第二地，　相貌之所说，
即请金刚藏：“大智愿解说，
第二地相貌，　一切皆欲闻！”

尔时，金刚藏菩萨摩诃萨，语解脱月菩萨言：“佛子，诸菩萨摩诃萨已具足初地，欲得第二地者，当生十心。何等为十？一、柔软心，二、调和心，

Chapter Two
The Stainlessness Ground

B. The Second Ground: The Stainlessness Ground

1. The Second Ground's Introductory Verses and Dharma Request

Once that entire assembly of bodhisattvas
had heard the explanation of the previous ground's meaning,
their minds all became purified
and they experienced boundless joyfulness. {1}

From the places in which they sat,
they ascended upwards and stood in empty space,
removed their marvelous upper cloaks
and scattered them down before Vajragarbha. {2}

They all then praised him in unison, saying:
"It is good indeed, Vajragarbha,
that the greatly wise and fearless one
so well explains the grounds of the bodhisattva." {3}

The greatly eminent master, Liberation Moon,
knowing that the minds of those in the assembly were pure
and desirous of hearing, with respect to the second ground,
an explanation of its characteristic aspects, {4}

then immediately requested this of Vajragarbha, saying:
"O Greatly Wise One. We pray that you will please explain
the characteristic aspects of the second ground,
for everyone here wishes to hear this explained." {5}

2. Vajragarbha Commences the Second Ground's Explanation

{A} At that time, Vajragarbha Bodhisattva Mahāsattva replied to Liberation Moon Bodhisattva, explaining thus:

3. The Ten Resolute Intentions as Bases for Entering the 2nd Ground

O Son of the Buddha, those bodhisattva *mahāsattvas* who have already completely fulfilled their practice on the first ground and who then wish to succeed in reaching the second ground should bring forth ten types of resolute intentions[91] to facilitate this. What then are those ten? They are as follows:[92]

First, the resolute intention to be gentle;
Second, the resolute intention to be harmonious;

正體字

三堪受心。四善心。五寂滅心。六真心。
504b21‖ 七不雜心。八無貪恪心。九快心。十大心。{B}若諸
504b22‖ 菩薩摩訶薩。已具足初地。欲得二地者。先當
504b23‖ 生是十心。{B}諸佛子。菩薩欲住是離垢地。從本
504b24‖ 已來。離一切殺生。捨棄刀[4]杖。無瞋恨心。有
504b25‖ 慚有愧。於一切眾生。起慈悲心。常求樂事。尚
504b26‖ 不惡心惱於眾生。何況麁惡。{C}離諸劫盜。資生
504b27‖ 之物。常自滿足。不壞他財。若物屬他。他所受
504b28‖ 用。他所攝者。於是物中。一草一葉。不與不
504b29‖ 取。何況過者。{D}離於邪婬。自足妻色。不求外
504c01‖ 欲。屬他女人。尚不生心。何況從事。

简体字

三、堪受心，四、善心，五、寂灭心，六、真心，七、不杂心，八、无贪吝心，九、快心，十、大心。若诸菩萨摩诃萨已具足初地，欲得二地者，先当生是十心。

“诸佛子，菩萨欲住是离垢地，从本已来，离一切杀生，舍弃刀杖，无瞋恨心，有惭有愧，于一切众生起慈悲心，常求乐事，尚不恶心恼于众生，何况粗恶？离诸劫盗，资生之物常自满足，不坏他财，若物属他、他所受用、他所摄者，于是物中一草一叶不与不取，何况过者？离于邪淫，自足妻色，不求外欲，属他女人尚不生心，何况从事？

Third, the resolute intention to be capable;
Fourth, the resolute intention to be good;
Fifth, the resolute intention to be serene;
Sixth, the resolute intention to be genuine;
Seventh, the resolute intention to be unmixed [in moral purity];
Eighth, the resolute intention to be unattached;
Ninth, the resolute intention to be happy;[93]
And tenth, the resolute intention to be magnanimous.

If bodhisattva *mahāsattvas* already perfectly fulfilled in the first ground's practices wish to succeed in reaching the second ground, they must first develop these ten types of resolute intentions.

4. The Bodhisattva's Observance of Ten Courses of Good Karmic Action[94]

a. Avoidance of Killing

{B} Sons of the Buddha, the bodhisattva wishing to abide on the Ground of Stainlessness, from the very beginning on up to the present, has already abandoned the killing of beings, has already cast aside swords and staves, has already developed a mind free of hatefulness, has already imbued himself with a sense of shame and dread of blame, has already brought forth the minds of kindness and compassion for all beings, has already always sought to bring about circumstances conducing to their happiness, and has never even produced evil thoughts envisioning his inflicting distress upon other beings, how much the less might he have engaged in any of the coarse forms of such evildoing.

b. Avoidance of Taking What Is Not Given

{C} He has abandoned all forms of theft, is always easily satisfied regarding life-sustaining possessions, and does deprive others of their valuables. As for whatever is owned by someone else, used by someone else, or appropriated by someone else, he will not take any such thing that has not been given to him, not even a blade of grass or a leaf. How much the less might he take anything of greater significance than that.

c. Avoidance of Sexual Misconduct

{D} He has abandoned sexual misconduct, has naturally found satisfaction in relationship with his own wife, and does not seek to indulge desires elsewhere. Regarding women are under the protection of others, he does not even have those sorts of thoughts, how much the less might he pursue such affairs.

正體字

{E}離於妄
504c02‖ 語。常真語實語。諦語[5]隨語。不作憎惡妄語。
504c03‖ 乃至夢中。尚不妄語。何況故作妄語。{F}離於兩
504c04‖ 舌。無破壞心。此聞不向彼說。彼聞不向此說。
504c05‖ 於鬪諍離散人中。常好和合。{G}離於惡口。所有
504c06‖ 言語。[6]麁[7][麩-夫+黃]苦惡。令他瞋惱。[8]又以瞋慢。令
504c07‖ 他怖畏惱熱。不[9]愛不喜。自壞其身。亦壞於
504c08‖ 他。如是等語。皆悉捨離。所有言[10]語。甚可喜
504c09‖ 樂。美妙悅耳。能化人心。和柔具足。多人愛
504c10‖ 念。能令他人歡喜悅樂。常出如是之語。{H}離於
504c11‖ 綺語。常自守護所可言說。應作不作。常知時
504c12‖ 語實語。利益語順法語。籌量語不為戲樂語。
504c13‖ 乃至戲笑。尚不綺語。何況故[11]作。

简体字

离于妄语，常真语、实语、谛语、随语，不作憎恶妄语，乃至梦中尚不妄语，何况故作妄语？离于两舌，无破坏心，此闻不向彼说，彼闻不向此说，于斗诤离散人中常好和合。离于恶口，所有言语不粗犷苦恶令他瞋恼，不以瞋慢令他怖畏恼热，不爱不喜自坏其身亦坏于他，如是等语皆悉舍离；所有言语甚可喜乐，美妙悦耳能化人心，和柔具足多人爱念，能令他人欢喜悦乐，常出如是之语。离于绮语，常自守护所可言说应作不作，常知时语、实语、利益语、顺法语、筹量语、不为戏乐语，乃至戏笑尚不绮语，何况故作？

d. Avoidance of False Speech

{E} He has abandoned false speech and always practices genuine speech, reality-based speech, speech reflecting truth, and direct speech.[95] He does not tell hate-filled lies and does not even commit false speech in his dreams, how much the less might he deliberately tell a lie.

e. Avoidance of Divisive Speech

{F} He has abandoned divisive speech and remains free of any intent to disparage others. Thus he does not tell that person what he heard from this person and does not relate to this person what he has heard from that person. In circumstances involving people engaged in disputes who have become estranged, he is always favors harmoniousness.

f. Avoidance of Harsh Speech

{G} He has abandoned harsh speech, including all speech that is coarse, fierce, bitter, and vile, which incites others to hatred, or which, attended by glowering or arrogance, incites fearfulness, affliction, or heated anger in others. This includes speech that would not please others, that no one would enjoy, that could bring harm to himself, or that could bring harm to others. He has entirely cast aside and abandoned all such forms of speech as these.

Whatever he says is of a sort that others might find extremely delightful, that is fine, sublime, and pleasing to the ear, that is able to transform the minds of others, that is perfectly infused with harmoniousness and softness, that the multitude would cherish and remember, and that has the capacity to cause others to be delighted, pleased, and happy. He always practices these very sorts of speech.

g. Avoidance of Frivolous Speech

{H} He has abandoned frivolous speech[96] and always guards against errors in what he might say, assessing it as to whether it should or should not be pursued. He is always aware of the importance of speech that is timely, speech that is truthful, speech that is beneficial, speech that accords with the Dharma, and speech that involves careful reflection. He does not engage in merely comedic speech and even when indulging in humor, he still refrains from merely frivolous speech, how much the less might he actually deliberately practice it.

正體字

{I}不貪他物。
504c14‖ 若有屬他。他所貪著。他所攝用。不作是念。我
504c15‖ 當取之。{J}離瞋害心。嫌恨心。迫熱心等。常於眾
504c16‖ 生。求好事心。愛潤心。利益心。慈悲心。{K}離
504c17‖ 於占相。習行正見。決定深信罪福因緣。離於
504c18‖ 諂曲。誠信三寶。生決定心。菩薩如是。常護善
504c19‖ 道。{L}作是思惟。眾生墮諸惡道者。皆由十不善
504c20‖ 道因緣。我今當自住十善法。亦當為人說諸
504c21‖ 善法。示正行處。何以故。若人自不行善。為他
504c22‖ 說法。令住善者。無有是處。{M}又是菩薩。復深思
504c23‖ 惟。行十不善道因緣故。則墮地獄畜生餓鬼。
504c24‖ 行十善道因緣故。

简体字

不贪他物，若有属他、他所贪著、他所摄用，不作是念：‘我当取之。’离瞋害心、嫌恨心、迫热心等，常于众生求好事心、爱润心、利益心、慈悲心。离于占相，习行正见，决定深信罪福因缘。离于谄曲，诚信三宝生决定心。

“菩萨如是常护善道，作是思惟：‘众生堕诸恶道者，皆由十不善道因缘。我今当自住十善法，亦当为人说诸善法，示正行处。何以故？若人自不行善，为他说法令住善者，无有是处。’又是菩萨复深思惟：‘行十不善道因缘故，则堕地狱、畜生、饿鬼。行十善道因缘故，

h. Avoidance of Covetousness

{I} He does not covet the possessions of others. Regarding whatever belongs to someone else, whatever is the object of another's own covetous attachment, or whatever has been appropriated by someone else for their own use, he does not think: "I should take that thing."

i. Avoidance of Ill Will

{J} He abandons thoughts inclined toward hatred or injury, thoughts of begrudging enmity, and thoughts intended to persecute and anger others. With respect to other beings, he always entertains thoughts seeking fine circumstances for them, fond thoughts, thoughts motivated to benefit them, and thoughts motivated by kindness and compassion.

j. Avoidance of Wrong Views

{K} He abandons practices such as divination, consistently maintains right views, and possesses definite and profoundly deep belief in causes and conditions as the determinants of karmic offenses and merit. He abandons all flattery and deviousness, possesses sincere faith in the Three Jewels, and brings forth decisive resolve.

It is in this manner that the bodhisattva always guards his adherence to the courses of good karmic action.

5. The Bodhisattva's Reflections on Ten Good and Bad Karmic Actions

{L} He reflects in this manner:

> Those beings who fall into the wretched destinies in every case do so due to causes and conditions associated with the unwholesome courses of karmic action. I should now dwell within the dharmas of the ten good karmic deeds and should also explain all good dharmas for their sakes, revealing for them the bases of right practice. And why should I proceed in this manner? It is because, if one were to fail to personally practice goodness himself and yet nonetheless expected that he could cause others to dwell in goodness simply by explaining such dharmas for their sakes, it would be impossible to succeed in this.

a. Reflections on their Generation of the Six Rebirth Destinies

{M} Contemplating yet more deeply, this bodhisattva also thinks:

> It is due to the causes and conditions associated with practicing the ten courses of unwholesome karmic action that beings fall into the hell realms, into the animal realms, and into the realms of the hungry ghosts. It is due to the causes and conditions

正體字

則生人處。乃至有頂處生。
504c25‖ 又是十善道。與智慧和合修行。心劣弱者。樂
504c26‖ 少功德。厭畏三界。大悲心薄。從他聞法。至聲
504c27‖ 聞乘。{N}復有人。行是十善道。不從他聞。自然得
504c28‖ 知。不能具足大悲方便。而能深入眾因緣法。
504c29‖ 至辟支佛乘。{O}復有人行是十善道。清淨具足。
505a01‖ 其心[1]廣大無量無邊。於眾生中。起大慈悲。
505a02‖ 有方便力。志願堅固。不捨一切眾生故。求佛
505a03‖ 大智慧故。清淨菩薩諸地故。能淨諸波羅蜜
505a04‖ 故。能入深廣大行。{P}又能清淨行是十善道。乃
505a05‖ 至能得佛十力。四無所畏。四無礙智。大慈大
505a06‖ 悲。乃至具足一切種智。集諸佛法。是故我等。
505a07‖ 應行十善道。常求一切智慧。{Q}是菩薩。復作是
505a08‖ 思惟。

简体字

则生人处，乃至有顶处生。又是十善道，与智慧和合修行。心劣弱者，乐少功德，厌畏三界，大悲心薄，从他闻法至声闻乘。复有人行是十善道，不从他闻自然得知，不能具足大悲方便，而能深入众因缘法，至辟支佛乘。复有人行是十善道，清净具足，其心广大无量无边，于众生中起大慈悲，有方便力，志愿坚固，不舍一切众生故，求佛大智慧故，清净菩萨诸地故，能净诸波罗蜜故，能入深广大行，又能清净行是十善道，乃至能得佛十力、四无所畏、四无碍智、大慈大悲，乃至具足一切种智，集诸佛法。是故我等应行十善道，常求一切智慧。’是菩萨复作是思惟：

associated with practicing the ten courses of good karmic action that beings are then born into the station of human rebirth and are born into the other stations of rebirth on up to the station at the peak of existence.

b. Reflections on Generation of the Fruits of the 3 Vehicles' Paths

Also, if these ten courses of good karmic action are cultivated in conjunction with the wisdom, then, in the case of those whose resolve is inferior and weak, who take pleasure in lesser levels of merit, who abhor and fear existence in the three realms, whose mind of great compassion is but slight, and who have heard the Dharma from others, their cultivation ultimately culminates in the Śrāvaka-disciple Vehicle.

{N} There are yet others who practice the ten courses of good karmic action who do not derive their understanding through hearing teachings from others, who spontaneously develop knowing awareness on their own, who are unable to completely perfect the skillful means associated with the great compassion, and who become able to deeply penetrate the many dharmas of causes and conditions. For these, their course of cultivation ultimately leads them to the Pratyekabuddha Vehicle.

{O} There are yet others who are consummately pure in their practice of the ten courses of good karmic action, whose minds are measurelessly and boundlessly vast, who have brought forth great kindness and great compassion for beings, who possess the power of skillful means, and whose resolve in their vows is solid. Because they do not forsake any being, because they strive to acquire the Buddha's great wisdom, because they engage in purifying cultivation of the bodhisattva grounds, and because they are able to purify their practice of the *pāramitās*, they are then able to enter the deep and vast practices.

{P} There are yet others who are able to engage in the purifying practice of these ten courses of good karmic action even up to the point that they are able to acquire the Buddha's ten powers, four fearlessnesses, four unimpeded knowledges, the great kindness, and the great compassion, and then finally reach the point where they achieve complete fulfillment of the knowledge of all modes and accumulate all dharmas of the Buddha. Therefore, we should all course in the practice of the ten good karmic deeds and should always strive to acquire all-knowledge.

c. Reflections on the 10 Transgressions' 10 Karmic Retributions

{Q} This bodhisattva additionally contemplates thus:

正體字

此十不善道。上者地獄因緣。中者畜生
505a09|| 因緣。下者餓鬼因緣。於中殺生之罪。能令眾
505a10|| 生墮於地獄畜生餓[2]鬼。若生人中。得二種果
505a11|| 報。一者短命。二者多病。劫盜之罪。亦令眾
505a12|| 生。墮於地獄畜生餓鬼道。若生人中。得二種
505a13|| 果報。一者貧窮。二者共財不得自在。邪婬之
505a14|| 罪。亦令眾生墮於地獄畜生餓鬼道。若生人
505a15|| 中。得二種果報。一者婦不貞良。二者得不隨
505a16|| 意眷屬。妄語之罪。亦令眾生。墮三惡道。若

简体字

‘此十不善道，上者地狱因缘，中者畜生因缘，下者饿鬼因缘。于中杀生之罪，能令众生堕于地狱、畜生、饿鬼，若生人中得二种果报：一者、短命，二者、多病。劫盗之罪，亦令众生堕于地狱、畜生、饿鬼道，若生人中得二种果报：一者、贫穷，二者、共财不得自在。邪淫之罪，亦令众生堕于地狱、畜生、饿鬼道，若生人中得二种果报：一者、妇不贞良，二者、得不随意眷属。妄语之罪，亦令众生堕三恶道，若生人中得二种果报：一者、多被诽谤，二者、恒为多人所诳。两舌之罪，亦令众生堕三恶道，若生人中得二种果报：一者、得弊恶眷属，二者、得不和眷属。恶口之罪，亦令众生堕三恶道，

The highest level of transgression in these ten courses of unwholesome karmic action produces the causes and conditions for descent into the hell realms. The middling level of transgression in them produces the causes and conditions for descent into the animal realms. The lowest level of transgression in them produces the causes and conditions for descent into the realms of the hungry ghosts.

Of these, the karmic offense of killing is able to cause beings to descend into the realms of the hell realms, animal realms, and hungry ghost realms. If they are then able to gain rebirth into the human realm, they encounter two kinds of retribution: First, a short lifespan. Second, extensive illness.

The karmic offense of stealing also causes beings to descend into the destinies of the hell-dwellers, animals, and hungry ghosts. If they are then able to gain rebirth into the human realm, they encounter two kinds of retribution: First, they are poverty-stricken. Second, they have any wealth they possess held in common with others so that they remain unable to freely use it.

The karmic offense of sexual misconduct also causes beings to descend into the destinies of the hell-dwellers, animals, and hungry ghosts. If they are then able to gain rebirth into the human realm, they encounter two kinds of retribution: First, their spouse is not virtuous. Second, they acquire a retinue that fails to be responsive to their wishes.

The karmic offense of false speech also causes beings to descend into the three wretched destinies. If they are able to gain rebirth into the human realm, they encounter two kinds of retribution: First, they are often slandered. Second, they are constantly deceived by many people.

The karmic offense of divisive speech also causes beings to descend into the three wretched destinies. If they are able to gain rebirth into the human realm, they encounter two kinds of retribution: First, they acquire a corrupt and evil retinue. Second, they acquire a discordant retinue.

The karmic offense of harsh speech also causes beings to descend into the three wretched destinies. If they are able to gain rebirth into the human realm, they encounter two kinds of retribution: First, they always hear unpleasant sounds. Second, whatever conversations they are able to engage in constantly involve disputation.

The karmic offense of frivolous speech also causes beings to descend into the three wretched destinies. If they are able to

正體字

505a17‖ 生人中。得二種果報。一者多被誹謗。二者恒
505a18‖ 為多人所誑兩舌之罪。亦令眾生墮三惡道。
505a19‖ 若生人中。得二種果報。一者得弊惡眷屬。二
505a20‖ 者得不和眷屬。惡口之罪。亦令眾生墮三惡
505a21‖ 道。若生人中。得二種果報。一者[3]常聞惡音。
505a22‖ 二者所可言說恒有諍訟。綺語之罪。亦令眾
505a23‖ 生墮三惡道。若生人中。得二種果報。一者所
505a24‖ 有言語。人不信受。二者有所言說。不能分了。
505a25‖ 貪欲之罪。亦令眾生。墮三惡道。若生人中。得
505a26‖ 二種果報。一者多欲。二者無有厭足。瞋惱之
505a27‖ 罪。亦令眾生。墮三惡道。若生人中。得二種果
505a28‖ 報。一者常為他人。求其長短。二者常為他所
505a29‖ 惱害。邪見之罪。亦令眾生。墮三惡道。若生人
505b01‖ 中。得二種果報。一者常生邪見之家。二者其
505b02‖ 心諂曲。諸佛子。如是十不善道。皆是眾苦大
505b03‖ 聚因緣。{R}菩薩復作是念。我等何故。不遠離是
505b04‖ 十不善道行十善道。亦令他人行此善道。{S}如
505b05‖ 是念已。即離十不善道。安住十善道。亦令他
505b06‖ 人。發心住[4]於善道。{T}是菩薩。爾時於一切眾生
505b07‖ 中。生安隱心。樂心慈心。悲心憐愍心。利益
505b08‖ 心

简体字

若生人中得二种果报：一者、常闻恶音，二者、所可言说恒有诤讼。绮语之罪，亦令众生堕三恶道，若生人中得二种果报：一者、所有言语人不信受，二者、有所言说不能分了。贪欲之罪，亦令众生堕三恶道，若生人中得二种果报：一者、多欲，二者、无有厌足。瞋恼之罪，亦令众生堕三恶道，若生人中得二种果报：一者、常为他人求其长短，二者、常为他所恼害。邪见之罪，亦令众生堕三恶道，若生人中得二种果报：一者、常生邪见之家，二者、其心谄曲。’

“诸佛子，如是十不善道，皆是众苦大聚因缘。菩萨复作是念：‘我等何故不远离是十不善道，行十善道，亦令他人行此善道？’如是念已，即离十不善道，安住十善道，亦令他人发心住于善道。是菩萨尔时，于一切众生中，生安隐心、乐心、慈心、悲心、怜愍心、利益心、

gain rebirth into the human realm, they encounter two kinds of retribution: First, their utterances are neither believed nor accepted by others. Second, whatever they utter is perceived by others to be deficient in clarity.

The karmic offense of covetousness also causes beings to descend into the three wretched destinies. If they are able to gain rebirth into the human realm, they encounter two kinds of retribution: First, they are beset by many desires. Second, they are insatiable.

The karmic offense of ill will also causes beings to descend into the three wretched destinies. If they are able to gain rebirth into the human realm, they encounter two kinds of retribution: First, they are always subjected to fault-finding by others. Second, they are always subjected to torment and injury by others.

The karmic offense of wrong views also causes beings to descend into the three wretched destinies. If they are able to gain rebirth into the human realm, they encounter two kinds of retribution: First, they are always reborn into a household ruled by wrong views. Second, their minds tend toward flattery and deviousness.

Sons of the Buddha, so it is that the ten courses of unwholesome karmic action constitute the causes and conditions for an immense aggregation of the many sorts of suffering.

d. Renunciation of 10 Bad Actions & Rousing of 10 Altruistic Minds

{R} The bodhisattva also thinks: "Why do we not leave these ten courses of unwholesome karmic action behind and instead practice the ten courses of good karmic action while also influencing others to practice these ten courses of good karmic action?"

{S} Having thought in this manner, he then immediately leaves behind the ten courses of unwholesome karmic action, abides securely in the ten courses of good karmic action, and also causes others to bring forth the resolve to abide in the courses of good karmic action. {T} With respect to all beings, this bodhisattva then brings forth:[97]

A mind intent on ensuring their peace and security;
A mind intent on establishing them in happiness;
A mind of kindness;
A mind of compassion;
A mind of kindly pity;
A beneficial mind;

正體字

守護心。師心大師心。我所有心。{U}作是念。是
505b09‖ 諸眾生。墮於邪見。隨逐邪心。行邪險道。甚可
505b10‖ 憐愍。我等應令是眾生。[5]住正見道。如實法
505b11‖ 中。{V}是諸眾生。常共瞋恨鬪諍。分別彼我。我等
505b12‖ 應令是眾生。[6]住無上大慈中。{W}是諸眾生。無
505b13‖ 有厭足。常貪他人財物。恒以邪命自活。我等
505b14‖ 應令是眾生。住於清淨身口意業。{X}是諸眾生。
505b15‖ 隨逐貪欲瞋恚愚癡因緣。常為種種煩惱大
505b16‖ 火之所燒然。不求得出方便。我等應令是眾
505b17‖ 生。滅諸煩惱大火。安置清涼之處。{Y}是諸眾生。
505b18‖ 常為無明黑闇所覆。入大黑闇。遠離智慧光
505b19‖ 明。入於生死大險道中。隨逐種種邪見。我等
505b20‖ 應令是眾生。使得無礙清淨慧眼。以是眼故。
505b21‖ 知一切法如實相。得不隨他教。[7]一切如實無
505b22‖ 障礙智。{Z}是諸眾生。墮在生死險道中。將[8]墮
505b23‖ 地獄畜生餓鬼深坑。入惡邪見網中。為種種
505b24‖ 愚癡叢林所覆。隨逐虛妄邪道逕路。常為愚
505b25‖ 癡之所盲冥。遠離有智導師。非是出道。謂為

简体字

守护心、师心、大师心、我所有心，作是念：‘是诸众生堕于邪见，随逐邪心行邪险道，甚可怜愍！我等应令是众生，住正见道如实法中。是诸众生常共瞋恨斗诤，分别彼我；我等应令是众生，住无上大慈中。是诸众生无有厌足，常贪他人财物，恒以邪命自活；我等应令是众生，住于清净身口意业。是诸众生随逐贪欲、瞋恚、愚痴因缘，常为种种烦恼大火之所烧燃，不求得出方便；我等应令是众生，灭诸烦恼大火，安置清凉之处。是诸众生，常为无明黑闇所覆，入大黑闇，远离智慧光明，入于生死大险道中，随逐种种邪见；我等应令是众生，使得无碍清净慧眼，以是眼故，知一切法如实相，得不随他教一切如实无障碍智。是诸众生堕在生死险道中，将堕地狱、畜生、饿鬼深坑，入恶邪见网中，为种种愚痴丛林所覆，随逐虚妄邪道迳路，常为愚痴之所盲冥，远离有智导师，非是出道谓为

A protective mind;
A mind that sees them as teachers;
A mind that sees them as great teaching masters;
And a mind that sees them as like himself.

6. His Reflections on the Plight of Beings & Resolve To Rescue Them

{U} He then thinks in this manner:

These beings have fallen into wrong views, pursue the course of wrong thinking, and travel wrong and dangerous paths. In this, they are extremely pitiable. We should cause these beings to instead abide in the path of right views and in dharmas that accord with reality.

{V} They are always embroiled in mutual hatred and disputation. They distinguish between others and themselves. We should cause these beings to abide in the unsurpassable great kindness.

{W} These beings are insatiable, always covet the wealth and possessions of others, and constantly sustain themselves through wrong livelihoods. We should cause these beings to abide in pure actions of body, speech, and mind.

{X} These beings pursue the causes and conditions of desire, hatred, and delusion. They are always burned by the great blazing fire of the many different sorts of afflictions and never seek to acquire the means to escape. We should cause these beings to extinguish the great flames of the afflictions and become securely established in the station of clarity and coolness.

{Y} These beings are always covered over by the darkness of ignorance. They have entered the great darkness and have left behind the light of wisdom. Having entered the greatly hazardous path of *saṃsāra,* they follow all different sorts of wrong views. We should cause these beings to acquire the unimpeded purified wisdom eye. Using this eye, they can know all dharmas in accordance with their true character so that, without needing to rely on others' instruction, they can acquire the unimpeded knowledge of all things in accordance with reality.

{Z} These beings have fallen into the hazardous paths of cyclic births and deaths and are on the verge of plummeting into the deep chasm of the hells, hungry ghosts, and animals. They have entered the net of evil and wrong views wherein they are covered over by the dense forest of the many different sorts of delusions. They follow the roads of false and erroneous paths. They are always blinded by stupidity and depart far from wise spiritual guides. What is not a path of escape, they take to be the

正體字

505b26‖ 出要。墮惡魔道。隨順魔意。遠離佛意。我等應
505b27‖ 令是眾生。度於生死險道艱難。安處令住一
505b28‖ 切智人無畏大城。無諸衰惱。{AA}是諸眾生為諸
505b29‖ 煩惱暴水所沒。常為欲流有流。見流無明流
505c01‖ 所漂。常隨生死。相續不絕。入大愛河。為諸煩
505c02‖ 惱勢力所食。不能得求出要之道。常為欲覺
505c03‖ 瞋覺惱覺惡虫所害。又為身見水[9]虫羅刹所
505c04‖ 執。入於五欲深流洄澓諸難之中。為喜愛淤
505c05‖ 泥之所染污。我慢陸地之所焦枯。無所歸趣。
505c06‖ 於十二入怨賊聚落。不能得出。不遇導師能
505c07‖ 正度者。我等應於是眾生。生大慈悲。以大善
505c08‖ 根力。而拔濟之。得安隱處。離諸驚怖隱沒。住
505c09‖ 一切智慧寶洲。{BB}是諸眾生。深心貪著。多有憂
505c10‖ 悲苦惱患難。憎愛所縛。欲械所繫。入於三界
505c11‖ 無明稠林。我等應令是眾生。遠離一切三界
505c12‖ 所著。令住離相無礙涅槃。

简体字

出要，堕恶魔道，随顺魔意，远离佛意；我等应令是众生，度于生死险道艰难，安处令住一切智人无畏大城，无诸衰恼。是诸众生为诸烦恼暴水所没，常为欲流、有流、见流、无明流所漂，常随生死相续不绝入大爱河，为诸烦恼势力所食，不能得求出要之道，常为欲觉、瞋觉、恼觉恶虫所害，又为身见水虫罗刹所执，入于五欲深流洄澓诸难之中，为喜爱淤泥之所染污，我慢陆地之所焦枯，无所归趣，于十二入怨贼聚落不能得出，不遇导师能正度者；我等应于是众生生大慈悲，以大善根力而拔济之，得安隐处，离诸惊怖隐没，住一切智慧宝洲。是诸众生深心贪著，多有忧悲苦恼患难，憎爱所缚，欲械所系，入于三界无明稠林；我等应令是众生，远离一切三界所著，令住离相无碍涅槃。

actual means of escape. They fall into the paths of evil *māras*,[98] obey the will of Māra, and depart far from the intentions of the Buddha. We should cause these beings to cross beyond the difficulties of *saṃsāra*'s hazardous destinies to a secure place by influencing them to dwell in the omniscient ones' great city of fearlessness that is free of the adversity or afflictions.

{AA} These beings have all become submerged in the great flood of the afflictions. They are always tossed along in the flood of desire, the flood of existence, the flood of views, and the flood of ignorance and so always follow the course of cyclic births and deaths, doing so continuously and without respite. They have entered the great river of love wherein they are devoured by the power of the afflictions, remaining entirely unable to find a route to serve as a means of escape.

They are always injured by the evil serpents of desire-ridden thought, hate-filled thought, and thoughts intent upon harming others. They are also seized by the river-serpent *rākṣasa* of the view imputing the existence of a true self in association with one's body.[99] They have entered into the disastrous circumstance of being caught in the deep and swiftly roiling whirlpools of the five desires. They have become dirtied and defiled by the mud of ardent love. They are roasted and withered on the plain of pride in self. They have no place in which to seek refuge, have entered into the village of the hostile insurgents of the twelve sense fields and remain unable to succeed in escaping.

They have been unable to encounter a spiritual guide who can enable their rightly-guided liberation. We should bring forth great kindness and great compassion for these beings and employ the power of great roots of goodness to extricate and rescue them so that they might then be able to dwell in a peaceful and secure location on the jeweled isle of all-knowledge, well apart from their present submersion in the midst of terrifying circumstances.

{BB} The minds of these beings have deep-seated inclinations toward covetous attachment, are extensively beset with the calamitous difficulties inflicted upon them by worry, lamentation, and bitter affliction. They have become tied up by the bonds of hatred and love, are tethered by the shackles of desires, and have entered the dense forest of the ignorance characteristic of existence in the three realms. We should cause these beings to abandon their attachments within the three realms of existence and should cause them to abide in the nirvāṇa that transcends signs and is free of obstacles.

正體字

{CC}是諸眾生。深著我
505c13‖ 我所。於五陰欅窟。不能自出。常隨四倒。依
505c14‖ 六入空聚。為四大毒蛇之所侵害。為諸煩惱
505c15‖ 眾賊所殺。受此無量諸苦惱者。我等應令是
505c16‖ 眾生。離一切貪著。令住空無我智道。所謂。涅
505c17‖ 槃斷一切障礙。{DD}是諸眾生。其心狹劣。樂於小
505c18‖ 法。遠離無上一切智慧。以是貪著小乘心故。
505c19‖ 不求無底大乘出法。我等應令是眾生。住廣
505c20‖ 大心。無量無邊諸佛法中。所謂無上大乘。諸
505c21‖ 佛子。是菩薩。如是隨順持戒力。善能廣生大
505c22‖ 慈悲心。{EE}是菩薩。住離垢地。得見數百佛。數千
505c23‖ 萬億那由他諸佛。見諸佛已。以衣被飲食。臥
505c24‖ 具醫藥。資生之物。供養諸佛。於諸佛所。生恭
505c25‖ 敬心。復受十善道。受已乃至得阿耨多羅三
505c26‖ 藐三菩提。終不中失。是菩薩。若干多百多千。
505c27‖ 乃至多百千萬億劫。遠離慳貪破戒垢故。淨
505c28‖ 修布施持戒。

简体字

是诸众生深著我、我所，于五阴欅窟不能自出，常随四倒依六入空聚，为四大毒蛇之所侵害，为诸烦恼众贼所杀，受此无量诸苦恼者；我等应令是众生，离一切贪著，令住空无我智道，所谓涅槃断一切障碍。是诸众生其心狭劣，乐于小法，远离无上一切智慧，以是贪著小乘心故，不求无底大乘出法；我等应令是众生，住广大心无量无边诸佛法中，所谓无上大乘。’

“诸佛子，是菩萨如是随顺持戒力，善能广生大慈悲心。是菩萨住离垢地，得见数百佛，数千万亿那由他诸佛。见诸佛已，以衣被、饮食、卧具、医药、资生之物供养诸佛，于诸佛所生恭敬心，复受十善道，受已乃至得阿耨多罗三藐三菩提，终不中失。是菩萨若干多百、多千，乃至多百千万亿劫，远离悭贪破戒垢故，净修布施持戒。

{CC} These beings are deeply attached to self and the possessions of a self and remain unable to escape on their own from the cave of the five aggregates. They always follow the four inverted views and abide in the empty village of the six sense bases in which they are assailed and injured by the poisonous serpents of the four great elements, and are slain by the many thieves of the afflictions. As for those who are afflicted by these countless sufferings, we should cause these beings to abandon their covetous attachment and then abide in the path to the cognition of the emptiness and absence of a self, namely in nirvāṇa's severance of all obstacles.

{DD} The minds of these beings are narrow and inferior. They delight in small dharmas and depart far from the unexcelled state of all-knowledge. Because they are covetously attached to the Small Vehicle, they fail to avail themselves of the dharmas of transcendence offered by the unfathomably deep Great Vehicle. We should cause these beings to abide in the vast resolve and within the realm of the measureless and boundless Dharma of the Buddhas, that is to say, within the unexcelled Great Vehicle.

Sons of the Buddha, this bodhisattva, in accordance with his power to uphold the moral precepts, is well able to bring forth vast resolve in his exercise of the mind of great kindness and the mind of great compassion.

7. The Bodhisattva's Seeing and Serving of Countless Buddhas

{EE} This bodhisattva who dwells on the Ground of Stainlessness succeeds in being able to see many hundreds of buddhas on up to many thousands of myriads of *koṭis* of *nayutas* of buddhas. Having succeeded in seeing the Buddhas, he makes offerings to the Buddhas wherever they dwell and brings forth the reverential mind as he presents offerings consisting of robes, food and drink, bedding, medicines and whatever other things are useful in sustaining their lives.

Additionally, he takes on the ten courses of good karmic action and, having taken them on, never lets his practice lapse at any point along the way, continuing on in this manner all the way to his realization of *anuttarasamyaksaṃbodhi*. Because this bodhisattva has already abandoned the filth of miserliness and transgressions against moral precepts for many hundreds, many thousands, and so forth until we come to many hundreds of thousands of myriads of *koṭis* of kalpas, he maintains purity in his cultivation of giving and the upholding of the moral precepts.

正體字

諸佛子。譬如成鍊真金。在礬石
505c29‖ 中。諸一切[10]垢盡。轉復明淨。菩薩亦如是。住
506a01‖ 是離垢菩薩地中。多百多千。乃至無量百千
506a02‖ 萬劫[1]離慳貪破戒垢故。淨修布施持戒。菩薩
506a03‖ 爾時。於四攝法中。愛語偏多。十波羅蜜中。
506a04‖ 戒波羅蜜偏勝。餘波羅蜜。非不修集。但隨地
506a05‖ 增長。諸佛子。是名菩薩摩訶薩第二離垢地。
506a06‖ 菩薩住是地中。多作轉輪聖王。為大法王。廣
506a07‖ 得法力。七寶成就。有力自在。能除一切眾生
506a08‖ 慳貪破戒之垢。以善方便。令眾生住於十善
506a09‖ 道中。為大布施。而不窮盡所作善業。若布施
506a10‖ 若愛語。若利益若同事。皆不離念佛。不離念
506a11‖ 法。

简体字

诸佛子，譬如成炼真金在矾石中，诸一切垢尽转复明净；菩萨亦如是，住是离垢菩萨地中，多百、多千乃至无量百千万劫，离慳贪破戒垢故，净修布施持戒。菩萨尔时，于四摄法中，爱语偏多；十波罗蜜中，戒波罗蜜偏胜，余波罗蜜非不修集，但随地增长。

“诸佛子，是名菩萨摩诃萨第二离垢地。菩萨住是地中，多作转轮圣王，为大法王，广得法力，七宝成就，有力自在，能除一切众生慳贪破戒之垢，以善方便令众生住于十善道中，为大布施而不穷尽。所作善业，若布施、若爱语、若利益、若同事，皆不离念佛，不离念法，

8. The Bodhisattva's Grounds Purification Compared to Refining Gold

Sons of the Buddha, this process is analogous to the smelting of real gold wherein, when one places it together with *kāsīsa*,[100] all of its impurities are entirely driven off and it manifests a more radiant degree of purity. So too it is with the bodhisattva residing on the Ground of Stainlessness who, for many hundreds, many thousands, and so forth until we come to incalculably many hundreds of thousands of myriads of kalpas, has separated himself from the filth of miserliness and transgressions against the moral precepts and has engaged in the purifying cultivation of giving and in the observance of the moral precepts.

9. The Bodhisattva's Practice of Means of Attraction and Pāramitās

During his time as a bodhisattva, among the four means of attraction, he has most extensively cultivated "pleasing words" and, among the ten *pāramitās*, he has become especially supreme in the practice of the moral-virtue *pāramitā*. In this, it has not been the case that he fails to cultivate and accumulate proficiency in the other *pāramitās*. Rather, he simply accords with the growth in them that corresponds to his level of practice on this ground.

10. Vajragarbha's Final Statements About the 2nd Ground Bodhisattva

Sons of the Buddha, this is what constitutes the character of the bodhisattva *mahāsattva*'s abiding on the second ground, the Ground of Stainlessness.

a. The Bodhisattva's Station and Dharma Practice

The bodhisattva dwelling on this ground often becomes a wheel-turning sage king serving as a great Dharma sovereign who has developed vast powers in the Dharma, who is abundantly endowed with the seven precious things, who is possessed of masterfully exercised powers, who is able to rid all beings of their defilements associated with miserliness and transgressions against the moral precepts, who employs skillful means to cause beings to abide in the ten courses of good karmic action, who carries on the practice of great giving and, in this, endlessly pursues the good karmic deeds in which he is perpetually engaged.

b. The Bodhisattva's Mindfulness

No matter whether it be in his practice of giving, pleasing words, beneficial actions, or joint endeavors, he never departs from his mindfulness of the Buddha, never departs from his mindfulness of the Dharma, never departs from his mindfulness of his companions among the bodhisattva *mahāsattvas* never departs from

正體字

不離念諸菩薩摩訶薩伴。不離念諸菩薩
506a12‖ 所行道。不離念諸波羅蜜。不離念十地。不離
506a13‖ 念諸力無畏不共法。乃至不離念具足一切
506a14‖ 種智。常生是心。我當於一切眾生之中。為首
506a15‖ 為勝。為大為妙。為上為無上。為導為將。為
506a16‖ [2]師為尊。乃至於一切眾生中。為依止者。諸佛
506a17‖ 子。是菩薩摩訶薩。若欲捨家勤行精進。須臾
506a18‖ 之間。於佛法中。便能捨家妻子五欲。得出家
506a19‖ 已。勤行精進。須臾之間。得千三昧。得見千
506a20‖ 佛。知千佛神力。能動千佛世界。能飛過千佛
506a21‖ 世界。能照千佛世界。能教化[3]千世界眾生。
506a22‖ 能住壽千劫。能知過去未來世各千劫事。能
506a23‖ 善入千法門。能變身為千。於一一身。能示千
506a24‖ 菩薩。以為眷屬。若以願力自在示現。過於此
506a25‖ 數。若干百千萬億那由他不可計知。

简体字

不离念诸菩萨摩诃萨伴，不离念诸菩萨所行道，不离念诸波罗蜜，不离念十地，不离念诸力、无畏、不共法，乃至不离念具足一切种智。常生是心：‘我当于一切众生之中，为首、为胜、为大、为妙、为上、为无上、为导、为将、为师、为尊，乃至于一切众生中为依止者。’

“诸佛子，是菩萨摩诃萨，若欲舍家勤行精进，须臾之间，于佛法中，便能舍家妻子五欲；得出家已，勤行精进，须臾之间，得千三昧，得见千佛，知千佛神力，能动千佛世界，能飞过千佛世界，能照千佛世界，能教化千世界众生，能住寿千劫，能知过去、未来世各千劫事，能善入千法门，能变身为千，于一一身能示千菩萨以为眷属；若以愿力，自在示现过于此数，若干百千万亿那由他不可计知。”

his mindfulness of the path coursed in by the bodhisattvas, never departs from his mindfulness of the *pāramitās*, never departs from his mindfulness of the ten grounds, never departs from his mindfulness of the powers, the fearlessnesses, and the dharmas exclusive to the Buddhas, and so forth on up to the point where he never departs from his mindfulness of progression toward complete fulfillment of the knowledge of all modes.

c. The Bodhisattva's Aspiration to Serve Beings

He always thinks, "I should become a leader among beings, one who is supreme, one who is great, one who is marvelous, one who is superior, one who is unsurpassable, one who serves them as a guide, as a general, as a teacher, as one worthy of their veneration, and as one who serves them in other such ways up to and including serving them as one upon whom all beings can rely."

d. The Result of the Bodhisattva's Leaving the Household Life

Sons of the Buddha, if this bodhisattva *mahāsattva* wishes to leave behind the home life and take up the diligent practice of vigor, he will be able in but a moment of abiding in the Dharma of the Buddha to relinquish his household, his wife and children, and the five desires. Having succeeded in leaving the home life, taking up the diligent practice of vigor, in but a moment:

> He will be able to acquire a thousand samādhis, see a thousand buddhas, and know a thousand buddhas' spiritual powers;
> He will be able to cause tremors in a thousand buddha worlds;
> He will be able to fly across the span of a thousand buddha worlds;
> He will be able to illuminate a thousand buddha worlds;
> He will be able to teach the beings in a thousand worlds;
> He will be able to abide for a lifespan of a thousand kalpas;
> He will be able to know the events of a thousand kalpas of the past and the future;
> He will be able to skillfully enter a thousand gateways into the Dharma;
> He will be able to create a thousand transformation bodies;
> And he will be able to manifest a thousand bodhisattvas to appear in the retinue of each and every one of them.

Were he to avail himself of the power of vows, he could freely manifest these phenomena in even greater numbers so large that one could never count them even in however many hundreds

正體字

爾時金
506a26‖ 剛藏菩薩摩訶薩。欲重明此義。而說偈言
506a27‖ 菩薩柔軟心　調和堪受心
506a28‖ 善心寂滅心　真心不雜心
506a29‖ 無有貪恪心　快心與大心
506b01‖ 得是十心已　入於第二地 {6}
506b02‖ 菩薩住是地　成就諸功德
506b03‖ 常離於殺生　不惱於一切
506b04‖ 常離於劫盜　不生邪婬心
506b05‖ 實語不兩舌　不惡口綺語 {7}
506b06‖ 他人所有物　不生於貪心
506b07‖ 不惱於眾生　直心行正見
506b08‖ 無有憍慢心　亦無諂曲心
506b09‖ 柔軟不放逸　護持諸佛教 {8}
506b10‖ 所有劇苦惱　地獄與畜生
506b11‖ 餓鬼熾然身　皆從惡心有
506b12‖ 我今已永離　如是諸惡事 {9}
506b13‖ 行於真實理　寂滅之善法
506b14‖ 從人至有頂　所有受樂處

简体字

尔时，金刚藏菩萨摩诃萨，欲重明此义，而说偈言：

“菩萨柔软心，　调和堪受心，
善心寂灭心，　真心不杂心，
无有贪吝心，　快心与大心，
得是十心已，　入于第二地。
菩萨住是地，　成就诸功德，
常离于杀生，　不恼于一切，
常离于劫盗，　不生邪淫心，
实语不两舌，　不恶口绮语，
他人所有物，　不生于贪心，
不恼于众生，　直心行正见，
无有憍慢心，　亦无谄曲心，
柔软不放逸，　护持诸佛教。
所有剧苦恼，　地狱与畜生，
饿鬼炽然身，　皆从恶心有；
我今已永离，　如是诸恶事，
行于真实理，　寂灭之善法。
从人至有顶，　所有受乐处，

of thousands of myriads of *koṭis* of *nayutas* of kalpas one might attempt to do so.[101]

11. Vajragarbha Bodhisattva's Summarizing Verses

At that time, Vajragarbha Bodhisattva Mahāsattva wishing to again clarify the meaning of this, thereupon uttered verses, saying:

The bodhisattva develops the gentle mind,
the harmonious mind, the capable mind,
the mind imbued with goodness, the serene mind,
the genuine mind, the unmixed mind,

the unattached mind,
the happy mind, and the magnanimous mind.
Once he has acquired these ten kinds of minds,
he succeeds in entering the second ground. {6}

The bodhisattva dwelling on this ground
perfects all of the meritorious qualities,
always abandons the killing of beings,
and does not inflict distress on any of them.

He always abandons stealing,
does not produce thoughts inclined toward sexual misconduct,
practices truthful speech, refrains from divisive speech,
and does not engage in harsh speech or frivolous speech. {7}

With regard to the possessions of others,
he has no covetous thoughts,
does not visit anguish on any being,
and, employing the straight mind, courses in right views.

He has no arrogant thoughts
nor does he indulge flattering or devious thought.
He is pliant-minded and refrains from neglectfulness,
while protecting and upholding the Dharma of the Buddhas. {8}

Realizing that all those severe sufferings and torments
endured in the hell realms, in the animal realms,
and by the hungry ghosts in their flaming bodies
all come into existence due to evil thought,
He thinks, "I have now already eternally abandoned
all such circumstances associated with practicing what is evil. {9}

Practice in accordance with genuine principles,
the good dharmas associated with quiescence,
and all circumstances in which one may experience happiness,
from the human realm on up to the peak of existence,

正體字

506b15|| 禪樂三乘樂　皆從十善生 {10}
506b16|| 如是思惟已　心常不放逸
506b17|| 身自持淨戒　亦教人令持
506b18|| 遍觀諸眾生　種種受苦惱
506b19|| 如是愍念已　轉生深悲心 {11}
506b20|| 凡夫甚可愍　墮在諸邪見
506b21|| 心多懷瞋恨　常好起諍訟
506b22|| 常樂於五欲　貪求無有厭
506b23|| 起三毒因緣　我應度此等 {12}
506b24|| 深覆愚癡闇　墜生死險道
506b25|| 入大邪見網　[4]墜於[5]世籠檻
506b26|| 常為諸魔賊　煩惱之所壞
506b27|| 此等甚可愍　我應度脫之 {13}
506b28|| 沒深煩惱水　四流所漂漫
506b29|| 具受於三界　百種諸苦毒
506c01|| 住五陰深樔　生我我所心
506c02|| 我為度此苦　當勤修行道 {14}
506c03|| 捨無上佛慧　生於下劣心
506c04|| 令住佛大智　發無量精進 {15}
506c05|| 菩薩住此地　集無量功德

简体字

禅乐三乘乐，　皆从十善生。
如是思惟已，　心常不放逸，
身自持净戒，　亦教人令持。
遍观诸众生，　种种受苦恼，
如是愍念已，　转生深悲心：
‘凡夫甚可愍，　堕在诸邪见，
心多怀瞋恨，　常好起诤讼，
常乐于五欲，　贪求无有厌，
起三毒因缘，　我应度此等！
深覆愚痴闇，　坠生死险道，
入大邪见网，　坠于世笼槛，
常为诸魔贼，　烦恼之所坏，
此等甚可愍，　我应度脱之！
没深烦恼水，　四流所漂漫，
具受于三界，　百种诸苦毒，
住五阴深樔，　生我我所心，
我为度此苦，　当勤修行道！
舍无上佛慧，　生于下劣心，
令住佛大智，　发无量精进。’
菩萨住此地，　集无量功德，

including the bliss found in *dhyāna* and in the Three Vehicles—
This all arises through practicing the ten good karmic deeds." 10}

Having concluded such deliberations,
his mind always refrains from neglectfulness
as he personally maintains purity in the moral precepts
and also teaches others, thus inspiring them to uphold them as well.

He contemplates how all beings everywhere
undergo all the different sorts of suffering and anguish, and,
having thus been moved to pitying mindfulness of their plight,
develops an ever stronger mind of profound compassion for them. {11}

Thinking, "Common people are so very pitiable.
Having descended into all manner of wrong views,
their minds so often cherish hatefulness
and are ever fond of disputation.

They always delight in the five objects of desire
and lust after them insatiably,
thereby generating causes and conditions linked to the three poisons.
I should strive to liberate these very sorts of beings." {12}

"Deeply submerged in the darkness of stupidity,
they have fallen into the perilous destinies of cyclic births and deaths.
They have entered into the great net of erroneous views
and have tumbled down into the cage of worldly existences.

They are always assailed and brought to ruin
by the afflictions instigated by Māra's marauders.
Such beings as these are so extremely pitiable.
I should strive to bring about their liberation. {13}

"They have become submerged in the deep waters of the afflictions
and are engulfed and swept along in the four floods.
Within the three realms of existence, they undergo in their entirety
all of the hundred varieties of sufferings' poisons.

They abide in the deep cave of the five aggregates,
wherein they form conceptions of a self and the possessions of a self.
In order to bring about their liberation from this suffering,
I must diligently cultivate the path. {14}

"For these who forsake the unexcelled knowledge of the Buddha
and bring forth inferior and mean thoughts,
I must bring forth measureless vigor
to cause them to abide in the Buddha's great knowledge." {15}

The bodhisattva who dwells on this ground
accumulates an immeasurably great stock of meritorious qualities,

正體字

506c06‖ 得值遇諸佛　承事而供養
506c07‖ 以是因緣故　善根轉明淨
506c08‖ 猶如好真金　鍊之以礬石 {16}
506c09‖ 佛子住此地　常作轉輪王
506c10‖ 令諸眾生等　住於十善道
506c11‖ 從初發心來　所修[*]集諸福
506c12‖ 願以救世間　令得佛十力 {17}
506c13‖ 若欲捨王位　出家行學道
506c14‖ 勤心行精進　得入千三昧
506c15‖ 得見數千佛　供養聽受法 {18}
506c16‖ 菩薩住此地　能示如是事
506c17‖ 若以其願力　示諸神通事
506c18‖ 度脫於眾生　過此數無量 {19}
506c19‖ 常為諸世間　勤求好事者
506c20‖ 具足解說此　第二地已竟 {20} [6]◎
506c21‖ 十住經卷第一

简体字

得值遇诸佛，　承事而供养。
以是因缘故，　善根转明净，
犹如好真金，　炼之以矾石。
佛子住此地，　常作转轮王，
令诸众生等，　住于十善道。
从初发心来，　所修集诸福，
愿以救世间，　令得佛十力。
若欲舍王位，　出家行学道，
勤心行精进，　得入千三昧，
得见数千佛，　供养听受法，
菩萨住此地，　能示如是事。
若以其愿力，　示诸神通事，
度脱于众生，　过此数无量。
常为诸世间，　勤求好事者，
具足解说此，　第二地已竟。”

succeeds in encountering the Buddhas,
in serving them, and in thereby making offerings to them.

It is on the basis of these causes and conditions
that their roots of goodness shine ever more brightly in their purity
just as happens with the finest real gold
when it is refined with the aid of *kāsīsa*. {16}

The son of the Buddha who dwells on this ground
tends to always become a wheel turning monarch
who causes the various classes of beings
to abide within the ten courses of good karmic action.

All of that merit that he cultivates and accumulates
from when he brings forth the initial resolve on forward—
He vows to employ it in rescuing those who abide in the world
and in influencing them to acquire the ten powers of the Buddha. {17}

If he wishes to relinquish the royal throne
to leave behind the home life and course in the study of the path,
and if, with diligent resolve, he courses in the practice of vigor,
he then succeeds in acquiring entry into a thousand samādhis,
in seeing many thousands of buddhas,
in making offerings to them, and in hearing and receiving Dharma. {18}

The bodhisattva dwelling on this ground
becomes able to manifest in just such circumstances as these.
If he avails himself of his power of vows,
the phenomena linked to his manifesting spiritual superknowledges
and to his bringing about the liberation of beings
then exceed these numbers to an immeasurably great degree. {19}

As for those herein who always act for the sake of those in the world,
diligently striving to create the finest of circumstances for them—
This concludes the explanation of these matters
as they relate to this second ground. {20}

End of Chapter Two

正體字

506c24‖ 十住經卷第二 506c25‖506c26‖ [7]後秦[8]三藏鳩摩羅什[9]譯
506c27‖ ◎[10]明地第三
506c28‖ 諸菩薩聞是　不可思議行
506c29‖ 心皆大歡喜　恭敬無有量
507a01‖ 即時虛空中　雨眾名華香
507a02‖ 如雲而垂下　供養金剛藏{1}
507a03‖ 咸讚言善哉　善哉[念>金]剛藏
507a04‖ 善說諸大人　護持淨戒行
507a05‖ 於諸眾生中　深有憐愍心
507a06‖ 敷演解說是　第二地行處{2}
507a07‖ 菩薩微妙行　真實無有異
507a08‖ 是諸菩薩等　清淨之行[1]處
507a09‖ 為一切眾生　常求諸好事
507a10‖ 第二淨明地　今已解說竟{3}
507a11‖ 天人恭敬者　願說第三地
507a12‖ 善示智所作　菩薩之所行{4}
507a13‖ 願說諸大人　云何行布施
507a14‖ 持戒及忍辱　精進行禪定

简体字

明地第三

诸菩萨闻是，　不可思议行，
心皆大欢喜，　恭敬无有量。
即时虚空中，　雨众名华香，
如云而垂下，　供养金刚藏，
咸赞言善哉：“善哉金刚藏，
善说诸大人，　护持净戒行！
于诸众生中，　深有怜愍心，
敷演解说是，　第二地行处，
菩萨微妙行，　真实无有异。
是诸菩萨等，　清净之行处，
为一切众生，　常求诸好事。
第二净明地，　今已解说竟，
天人恭敬者，　愿说第三地，
善示智所作，　菩萨之所行。
愿说诸大人，　云何行布施，
持戒及忍辱，　精进行禅定，

Chapter Three
The Shining Light Ground

C. The Third Ground: The Shining Light Ground

1. The Third Ground's Introductory Verses and Dharma Request

When all those bodhisattvas had heard this discourse on these
inconceivable practices of the bodhisattva,
their minds all became greatly joyful
and became filled with immeasurably great reverence.

Then, from the midst of space, they immediately
rained down the many sorts of fine flowers and incense
that then draped down like clouds,
presenting their offerings to Vajragarbha. {1}

All in unison, they praised him, exclaiming, "It is good indeed,
good indeed, Vajragarbha,
that you have so well proclaimed how the great personages
guard and maintain their practice of purity in the moral precepts.

With a mind deeply imbued with kindly pity
toward all beings,
you have set forth this expansive proclamation explaining
the second ground's realm of practice. {2}

"You have explained these bodhisattvas' sublime practices
that are true, real, and free of anything that deviates,
have explained as well the realm of the practice of purity
coursed in by all such bodhisattvas as these,

and have always sought the finest circumstances
for all beings.
Thus this explanation of all such matters
related to the second ground of radiant purity has come to an end. {3}

"The devas and humans abiding here in reverence
pray that you will proceed to discuss the third ground,
skillfully revealing the endeavors of the wise
and that which the bodhisattvas practice therein. {4}

"We pray you will explain with regard to these great personages
just how it is that they practice giving,
the upholding of moral precepts, patience,
vigor, and how they practice *dhyāna* concentration,

正體字

507a15‖ 智慧與方便　並及慈悲心
507a16‖ 云何行是法　清淨於佛行{5}
507a17‖ 解脫月菩薩　語金剛藏言
507a18‖ 菩薩至三地　當以何等心{6}
507a19‖ {A}金剛藏菩薩摩訶薩。語解脫月菩薩言。佛子。
507a20‖ 諸菩薩摩訶薩。深淨心行第二地已。欲得第
507a21‖ 三地。當以十心得入第三地。何等為十。一淨
507a22‖ 心。二猛利心。三厭心。四離心。五不退心。六
507a23‖ 堅心。七明盛心。八無足心。九快心。十大心。
507a24‖ {B}諸佛子。是菩薩摩訶薩。以是十心。得入第三
507a25‖ 地。能觀一切有為法如實相。所謂。無常苦空。
507a26‖ 無我不淨。

简体字

智慧与方便，　并及慈悲心？
云何行是法，　清净于佛行？”

解脱月菩萨，　语金刚藏言：
“菩萨至三地，　当以何等心？”

金刚藏菩萨摩诃萨，语解脱月菩萨言：“佛子，诸菩萨摩诃萨，深净心行第二地已，欲得第三地，当以十心得入第三地。何等为十？一、净心，二、猛利心，三、厌心，四、离心，五、不退心，六、坚心，七、明盛心，八、无足心，九、快心，十、大心。诸佛子，是菩萨摩诃萨，以是十心得入第三地，能观一切有为法如实相，所谓无常、苦、空、无我、不净，

wisdom, and skillful means
as well as the minds of kindness and compassion,
and how it is, in practicing these dharmas,
they carry on purifying cultivation of the practices of the Buddha." {5}

Liberation Moon Bodhisattva
then addressed Vajragarbha, saying,
"In the case of a bodhisattva who has arrived at the third ground,
of which types of mind should he avail himself?" {6}

2. Vajragarbha Commences the Third Ground's Explanation

{A} Vajragarbha Bodhisattva Mahāsattva then informed Liberation Moon Bodhisattva, saying:

3. The Ten Resolute intentions as Bases for Entering the Third Ground

O Son of the Buddha, in the case of the bodhisattva *mahāsattvas* who have already completed their profoundly pure-minded practices on the second ground and who then aspire to reach the third ground, they should then avail themselves of ten types of resolute intentions[102] through which they may achieve entry into the third ground. What then are these ten? They are:[103]

First, the resolute intention set on purity;
Second, the resolute intention set on intense acuity;
Third, the resolute intention set on renunciation;
Fourth, the resolute intention set on abandonment;
Fifth, the resolute intention set on irreversibility;
Sixth, the resolute intention set on solidity;
Seventh, the resolute intention set on flourishing brilliance;
Eighth, the resolute intention set on unquenchable zeal;
Ninth, the resolute intention set on happiness;
And tenth, the resolute intention set on magnanimity.

{B} Sons of the Buddha, this bodhisattva *mahāsattva* employs these ten minds to gain entry into the third ground.

4. The Bodhisattva's Contemplation of All Conditioned Dharmas

Through his contemplations, he becomes able to see the true character of all conditioned dharmas. Specifically, he observes that they are characterized by:

Impermanence;
Suffering;
Emptiness of intrinsic existence;
Absence of anything constituting a self;
Impurity;

正體字

不久敗壞。不可信相。念念生滅。又
507a27‖ 不生不滅。不從前際來。不去至後際。現在不
507a28‖ 住。{C}菩薩如是。觀一切有為法真實相。知此諸
507a29‖ 法。無作無起。無來無去。而諸眾生憂悲苦惱。
507b01‖ 憎愛所繫。無有停積。無定生處。但為貪恚癡
507b02‖ 火所然。增長後世苦惱火聚。無有實性。猶
507b03‖ 如幻化。{D}見如是已。於一切有為法。轉復厭離。
507b04‖ 趣佛智慧。是菩薩。知如來智慧不可思議。不
507b05‖ 可稱量。有大勢力。無能勝者。無有雜相。無有
507b06‖ 衰惱憂悲之苦。能至無畏安隱大城。不復轉
507b07‖ 還。能救無量苦惱眾生。

简体字

不久败坏，不可信相，念念生灭；又不生不灭，不从前际来，不去至后际，现在不住。菩萨如是观一切有为法真实相，知此诸法无作无起，无来无去，而诸众生忧悲苦恼憎爱所系，无有停积，无定生处，但为贪恚痴火所燃，增长后世苦恼火聚，无有实性犹如幻化；见如是已，于一切有为法转复厌离，趣佛智慧。

“是菩萨知如来智慧不可思议、不可称量，有大势力无能胜者，无有杂相，无有衰恼忧悲之苦，能至无畏安隐大城不复转还，能救无量苦恼众生。

Inability to long endure;
Certainty of ruination;
Unreliability;
Production and destruction in each successive mind-moment;
And also by being neither produced nor destroyed, by not having coming forth from any point in the past, by not going forth to any point in the future, and by not abiding in the present moment.

{C} It is in this manner that the bodhisattva contemplates the true character of all conditioned dharmas. He thus knows these dharmas:

As uncreated;
As non-arising;
As neither coming nor going;
As being such that, even so, beings experience worry, sorrow, suffering, and anguish on their account;
As bound up with hatred and love;
As involving ceaseless accumulation;
As being such that beings have no fixed station of rebirth;
As being such that beings may only be burned up in the fires of covetousness, hatred, and stupidity;
As increasing the bonfire of suffering and torments undergone in future lifetimes;
And as like magical conjurations in their absence of any true nature.

5. The Bodhisattva's Renunciation & Quest For Buddha's Knowledge

{D} Having observed all this, he redoubles the strength of his renunciation of all conditioned dharmas and his striving to progress toward the Buddha's wisdom. This bodhisattva realizes that the wisdom of the Tathāgata:[104]

Is inconceivable;
Is immeasurable;
Is possessed of immense power;
Is insuperable;
Is characterized by absence of admixture with anything else;
Is free of the sufferings of ruination, anguish, worry, or sorrow;
Is capable of reaching all the way to the great city of fearlessness and security;
Is irreversible;
And is able to rescue countless suffering beings.

正體字

{E}如是見知佛智無量。
507b08‖ 見有為法無量苦惱。於一切眾生。轉生殊勝
507b09‖ 十心。何等為十。眾生可愍。孤獨無救。貧窮
507b10‖ 無所依止。三毒之火。熾然不[2]息。閉在三有
507b11‖ 牢固之獄。常住煩惱諸惡刺林。無正觀力。於
507b12‖ 善法中。欲樂心薄。失諸佛妙法。而常隨順生
507b13‖ 死水行。驚畏涅槃。{F}是菩薩。見眾生如是多諸
507b14‖ 衰惱。發大精進。是諸眾生。我應救。我應解。
507b15‖ 應令清淨。應令得脫。應著善處。應令安住。應
507b16‖ 令歡喜。應知所宜。應令得度。應使滅苦。{G}菩薩
507b17‖ 如是。善遠離一切有為法。深念一切眾生。見
507b18‖ 諸佛一切智有無量利益。即時欲具佛智慧

简体字

如是见知佛智无量，见有为法无量苦恼，于一切众生转生殊胜十心。何等为十？众生可愍，孤独无救，贫穷无所依止，三毒之火炽然不息，闭在三有牢固之狱，常住烦恼诸恶刺林无正观力，于善法中欲乐心薄，失诸佛妙法，而常随顺生死水行，惊畏涅槃。是菩萨见众生如是多诸衰恼，发大精进：‘是诸众生，我应救，我应解，应令清净，应令得脱，应著善处，应令安住，应令欢喜，应知所宜，应令得度，应使灭苦。’

“菩萨如是善远离一切有为法，深念一切众生，见诸佛一切智有无量利益，即时欲具佛智慧

6. The Bodhisattva's Ten Sympathetic Mental Intentions Toward Beings

{E} Having thus observed that the knowledge of the Buddha is immeasurably vast and having observed that conditioned dharmas involve immeasurably vast suffering and anguish, he then brings forth ten especially supreme types of mental intentions toward all beings.[105] What then are these ten? They are worthy of pity because:[106]

They are alone, with no one who might come to their rescue;
They are poverty-stricken and have no one to rely on;
They are ceaselessly burned by the fires of the three poisons;
They are confined in the solidly-constructed prison of the three realms of existences;
They always abide in the forest of the afflictions' wickedly injurious thorns;
They are bereft of the power of correct contemplation;
They possess only feeble aspirations to cultivate the dharmas of goodness;
They have lost the marvelous Dharma of the Buddha;
They always follow the course of the flowing stream of cyclic births and deaths;
And they are frightened at the prospect of entering nirvāṇa.

7. The Bodhisattva's Generation and Practice of Great Vigor

{F} Observing that beings are beset by just so very many sorts of ruinous torments, this bodhisattva brings forth great vigor, thinking with regard to these beings:[107]

I should rescue them;
I should liberate them;
I should cause them to develop purity;
I should cause them to gain liberation;
I should see to their becoming situated in a place of goodness;
I should cause them to abide securely;
I should cause them to become joyful;
I should cause them to know what is most fitting;
I should cause them to succeed in reaching liberation;
I should influence them to achieve the cessation of suffering.

{G} So it is that the bodhisattva skillfully abandons all conditioned dharmas and becomes deeply mindful of all beings. He sees that the omniscience of the Buddhas has countless benefits. Hence, because he immediately wishes to equip himself with the wisdom

正體字

507b19‖ 救度眾生故。勤行菩薩道。作是思惟。以何因
507b20‖ 緣。以何方便。是諸眾生。墮在大苦諸煩惱中。
507b21‖ 當拔出之。使得永住畢竟常樂。{H}即時知住無
507b22‖ 礙解脫智慧中者。乃可得此是無礙智慧解
507b23‖ 脫不離通達諸法如實智。無行行慧。如是智
507b24‖ 慧之明。從何而得。當知不離多聞決定智慧。
507b25‖ 復作是念。無礙解脫等諸佛法。以何為本。不
507b26‖ 離聞法為本。{I}菩薩如是念已。一切求法時。轉
507b27‖ 加[3]精進。日夜常樂聽法。無有厭足。心無休
507b28‖ 息。喜法愛法。依法隨法。重法究竟法。歸法
507b29‖ 救法。隨順行法。{J}菩薩如是。方便求法。所有。
507c01‖ 珍寶。財物金銀等庫藏無所[4]匱惜。

简体字

救度众生故，勤行菩萨道，作是思惟：‘以何因缘？以何方便？是诸众生，堕在大苦诸烦恼中，当拔出之，使得永住毕竟常乐，即时知住无碍解脱智慧中者，乃可得此是无碍智慧解脱，不离通达诸法如实智，无行行慧？如是智慧之明，从何而得？当知不离多闻决定智慧。’复作是念：‘无碍解脱等诸佛法，以何为本？不离闻法为本。’菩萨如是念已，一切求法时转加精进，日夜常乐听法无有厌足，心无休息，喜法、爱法、依法、随法、重法、究竟法、归法、救法、随顺行法。

“菩萨如是方便求法，所有珍宝财物、金银等库藏无所匮惜，

of the Buddha in order to rescue and liberate beings, he diligently practices the bodhisattva path.

He then has this thought: "Using which causes and conditions and which skillful means should I extricate these beings who have fallen down into the afflictions associated with immense suffering so that I may cause them to abide forever in ultimate and eternal bliss?"

{H} He then immediately realizes that it is only through coming to abide in the unimpeded wisdom of liberation that one can accomplish this. He realizes, too, that this unimpeded wisdom of liberation is inseparable from the knowledge that penetratingly comprehends dharmas in accordance with reality which is the practice wisdom that cognizes the non-existence of any [inherently existent] action at all.[108]

[He also thinks]: "From what does one acquire the light of such wisdom as this? One should realize that it is inseparable from the definitive wisdom associated with extensive learning."

He again reflects, "What constitutes the very origin of unimpeded liberation and the other dharmas of the Buddha? They are inseparable from hearing the teaching of Dharma. That is their origin."

{I} Having thought in this manner, whenever there is an opportunity to advance his quest for Dharma, the bodhisattva brings forth ever increasing vigor to the point that, day and night, he always insatiably and tirelessly:[109]

Delights in hearing the Dharma,
Finds joy in the Dharma;
Cherishes the Dharma;
Relies upon the Dharma;
Accords with the Dharma;
Deeply esteems the Dharma;
Strives to achieve the ultimate realization of the Dharma;
Takes refuge in the Dharma;
Rescues the Dharma;
And complies with the practice of the Dharma.

{J} It is in this manner that the bodhisattva employs such skillful means in pursuit of the Dharma. As for of any of the precious jewels, wealth, material possessions, gold, silver, or contents of storehouses and treasuries, he has none of them that he sees as difficult to obtain or worthy of cherishing esteem. He does not

正體字

於此物
507c02‖ 中。不生難想。但於說法者。生難遭想。為求
507c03‖ 法故。於內外物。無不能捨世間所有可布施
507c04‖ 者。所謂。國土人民眷屬。田業財物。摩尼寶珠。
507c05‖ 金銀庫藏。象馬輦輿。眾寶瓔珞。諸嚴身之具。
507c06‖ 妻子男女。及支節手足。耳目鼻舌。舉身施與。
507c07‖ 無所愛惜。又為求法故。於說法者。盡心恭敬。
507c08‖ 供養給侍。破除憍慢。我慢大慢。諸惡苦惱。
507c09‖ 無理等事。悉能忍受。深求法故。若得一句。
507c10‖ 未曾聞法。勝得滿三千大千世界珍寶。得聞
507c11‖ 正法一偈。勝得轉輪聖王。釋提桓因。梵天王
507c12‖ 處。無量劫住。是菩薩。若有人。來作是言。我
507c13‖ 與汝佛所說法一句。能淨菩薩所行道。令汝
507c14‖ 得聞。若能入大火坑受大苦者。當以相與。是
507c15‖ 菩薩作是念。我受一句法故。尚於三千大千
507c16‖ 世界火坑。從梵天投下。何況墮小火坑。我等
507c17‖ [5]求法應盡受一切諸地獄苦。

简体字

于此物中不生难想，但于说法者生难遭想。为求法故，于内外物无不能舍，世间所有可布施者，所谓国土、人民眷属、田业财物、摩尼宝珠、金银库藏、象马辇舆、众宝璎珞、诸严身之具、妻子男女，及支节手足、耳目鼻舌，举身施与无所爱惜。又为求法故，于说法者尽心恭敬，供养给侍。破除憍慢、我慢、大慢，诸恶苦恼无理等事，悉能忍受。深求法故，若得一句未曾闻法，胜得满三千大千世界珍宝；得闻正法一偈，胜得转轮圣王、释提桓因、梵天王处无量劫住。是菩萨，若有人来作是言：‘我与汝佛所说法一句，能净菩萨所行道，令汝得闻。若能入大火坑受大苦者，当以相与。’是菩萨作是念：‘我受一句法故，尚于三千大千世界火坑，从梵天投下，何况堕小火坑？我等求法，应尽受一切诸地狱苦，

conceive of such things as rare, for he only conceives of those who explain the Dharma as rarely encountered.

Were it to be for the sake of seeking the Dharma, there is nothing then in the sphere of inward or outward possessions that he would not be able to relinquish. No matter what there is in the world that one might be able to give as a gift, be it countries, peoples, retinues, agricultural labor, wealth, material possessions, precious *maṇi* pearls, gold, silver, storehouses, treasuries, elephants, horses, carriages, necklaces made of the many sorts of jewels, every sort of physical adornment, one's wife, sons, daughters, or one's limbs, feet, hands, ears, eyes, nose, tongue, or entire body, he would be able to give away all of these without retaining any cherishing for them.

Additionally, for the sake of seeking the Dharma, he does everything he can think of to pursue the respectful making of offerings, supplying and serving whoever speaks the Dharma. He eliminates all arrogance, pride in self, and great pride. He is able to endure being subjected to every sort of evil, suffering, torment, and unprincipled circumstance for the sake of fulfilling his deeply sincere quest to acquire the Dharma.

Were he to merely be able to acquire a single sentence of Dharma he had never heard before, he would consider that to be superior to acquiring precious jewels sufficient to completely fill a great trichiliocosm.

Were he to simply be able to hear but a single stanza of right Dharma, he would consider that to be superior to becoming a wheel-turning sage king or to ascending to the station of a Śakra Devānām Indra or of a king of the Brahma Heaven wherein he might reign for countless kalpas.

If someone came before this bodhisattva and spoke these words: "I will bestow on you a single sentence of Dharma spoken by the Buddha by which you will be able to purify your cultivation of the path practiced by bodhisattvas. However, I will only allow you to hear it if you are able to enter a huge fire pit and endure immense suffering. If you can do that, I will give it to you."

This bodhisattva would then have this thought:

> If I were to be able to receive but a single sentence of such Dharma, I would even leap from the height of the Brahma Heaven down into a fire pit the size of a great trichiliocosm. How much the less might I shrink from descending into such a relatively small fire pit as this. In our seeking of the Dharma, we should be able to entirely endure even all the sufferings of the

正體字

猶應求法。何況
507c18‖ 人中。諸小苦惱。為求法故。發如是心。又如所
507c19‖ 聞法。心常喜樂。悉能正觀。{K}是菩薩。聞諸法
507c20‖ 已。降伏其心。於空閑處。心作是念。如說行
507c21‖ 者。乃得佛法。不可但以口之所言。菩薩如是。
507c22‖ 能住明地。即離諸欲惡不善法。有覺有觀。離
507c23‖ 生喜樂。入初禪。滅覺觀。內清淨心一處無覺
507c24‖ 無觀。定生喜樂。入二禪。離喜故。行捨心念
507c25‖ 安慧身受樂。諸賢聖。能說能捨。常念受樂。入
507c26‖ 三禪。斷苦斷樂故。先滅憂喜故。不苦不樂。行
507c27‖ 捨念淨。入四禪。是菩薩。過一切色[6]相。滅一
507c28‖ 切有對[*]相。不念一切別異[*]相故知無邊虛
507c29‖ 空。

简体字

犹应求法，何况人中诸小苦恼！’为求法故发如是心。又如所闻法，心常喜乐，悉能正观。

“是菩萨闻诸法已，降伏其心，于空闲处心作是念：‘如说行者乃得佛法，不可但以口之所言！’菩萨如是能住明地，即离诸欲恶不善法，有觉有观，离生喜乐，入初禅；灭觉观，内清净心一处，无觉无观，定生喜乐，入二禅；离喜故行舍心，念安慧身受乐，诸贤圣能说能舍，常念受乐，入三禅；断苦断乐故，先灭忧喜故，不苦不乐，行舍念净，入四禅。是菩萨过一切色相，灭一切有对相，不念一切别异相故知无边虚空，

> hell realms. Even then, we should still pursue the acquiring of Dharma. How much the less might one shrink from these lesser sufferings and torments encountered in the human realm.

For the sake of seeking the Dharma, he is able to bring forth just such resolve as this. Also, whatever Dharma he hears causes his mind to feel ever joyful and he is able to make it all the focus of right contemplation.

{K} Having heard the Dharma, this bodhisattva proceeds to subdue his mind. In a secluded location, he guides his mind in thoughts such as this: "It is only through cultivating in a manner concordant with what one has been taught that one may acquire the Buddha's Dharma. One cannot accomplish this solely through the spoken word."

8. The Bodhisattva's Conquest of the Meditative Absorptions

So it is that the bodhisattva is able to abide on the Ground of Shining Light. He immediately separates himself from all desires and from all evil and unwholesome dharmas, whereupon, still possessed of ideation and possessed of mental discursion, experiencing joy and bliss arising through separation, he enters the first *dhyāna*.

Then, extinguishing ideation and mental discursion, establishing himself in inward purity, focusing his mind in a single place, becoming free of ideation and free of discursion, and experiencing joy and bliss arising through concentration, he enters the second *dhyāna*.

Due to separating himself from joyfulness, coursing in equanimity in the sphere of the formative factors aggregate, being possessed of mindfulness, establishing himself in discerning knowing, experiencing physically-based bliss the likes of which the Worthies and the Āryas are able to say of it that one is able to maintain equanimity toward it, and always abiding in mindfulness as he experiences such bliss, he enters the third *dhyāna*.

Due to cutting off suffering and cutting off bliss and on account of having earlier extinguished both sorrow and joy, experiencing neither suffering nor bliss, and coursing in equanimity and mindfulness that are pure, he enters the fourth *dhyāna*.

Due to going beyond all perceptions[110] of form, extinguishing all perceptions of [sensory] impingement, and not bearing in mind any perceptions of differentiation, this bodhisattva acquires a knowing awareness of boundless space and then immediately

正體字

即入虛空無色定處。過一切虛空[＊]相。知
508a01‖ 無邊識。即入識無色定處。過一切識[＊]相。知
508a02‖ 無所有。即入無所有。無色定處。過一切無所
508a03‖ 有處。知非有想非無想安隱。即入無色非有
508a04‖ 想非無想處。但隨順諸法行故。而不樂著。{L}是
508a05‖ 菩薩。以慈心高廣無量。無瞋[1]無恨無惱害。
508a06‖ 以信解力。遍滿一方。二方。三方四方。四維上
508a07‖ 下。亦復如是。悲心喜心捨心。高廣無量。無瞋
508a08‖ 恨無惱害。以信解力。遍滿一方。第二[2]三。四
508a09‖ 方四維上下。亦復如是。{M}是菩薩。有種種神通
508a10‖ 力。能動大地。一身為多身。多身為一身。現滅
508a11‖ 還出。

简体字

即入虚空无色定处；过一切虚空相，知无边识，即入识无色定处；过一切识相，知无所有，即入无所有无色定处；过一切无所有处，知非有想非无想安隐，即入无色非有想非无想处；但随顺诸法行故而不乐著。是菩萨以慈心高广无量，无瞋无恨无恼害，以信解力遍满一方、二方、三方、四方，四维、上、下亦复如是；悲心、喜心、舍心高广无量，无瞋恨无恼害，以信解力遍满一方、第二三四方、四维、上、下亦复如是。

“是菩萨有种种神通力，能动大地，一身为多身，多身为一身，现灭还出，

enters the formless realm absorption corresponding to the station of [boundless] space.

Going beyond the perception of everything as empty space, he develops a knowing awareness of boundless consciousness and then immediately enters the formless realm absorption corresponding to the station of boundless consciousness.

Going beyond the perception of everything as consciousness, he develops a knowing awareness of the existence of nothing whatsoever and thus immediately enters the formless realm absorption corresponding to the station of nothing whatsoever.

Going beyond the station of nothing whatsoever, he develops a knowing awareness of the stability constituted by a state of neither perception nor non-perception and thus then immediately enters the formless realm absorption corresponding to the station of neither perception nor non-perception.

Because he only accords with the practice of dharmas, he does not indulge any pleasure-based attachments.

9. The Bodhisattva's Development of the Four Immeasurables

{L} Employing the mind of kindness developed to the point of loftiness, vastness, and immeasurability, this bodhisattva becomes entirely free of hatred, free of enmity, free of any tendency to annoy or harm others, and, employing the power of resolute belief, he expands that contemplation until it pervades one direction, two directions, three directions, four directions, the four midpoints, the zenith, and the nadir in just the same manner.

He also cultivates the mind of compassion, the mind of sympathetic joy, and the mind of equanimity until they are lofty, vast, immeasurable, free of hatred, free of enmity, and free of any tendency to annoy or harm others. Through the power of resolute belief, he expands those contemplations until, in just the same way, they pervade one direction, two directions, three directions, four directions, the four midpoints, the zenith, and the nadir.

10. The Bodhisattva's Development of the Spiritual superknowledges

{M} This bodhisattva possesses the power of all different sorts of spiritual superknowledges by which:

He is able to cause the entire great earth to tremor;
He is able to create many bodies from his own single body;
He is able to make those many bodies become a single body, either making them become manifest or making them disappear and return to invisibility;

正體字

石壁山障。皆能徹過。如行虛空。於虛空
508a12‖ 中。加趺而去。猶如飛鳥入出於地。如水無異。
508a13‖ 履水如地。身出烟焰。如大火聚。日月有大神
508a14‖ 德威力。而能以手。捫摸摩之。身力自在。乃至
508a15‖ 梵世。是菩薩。以清淨天耳。過於人耳。悉聞人
508a16‖ 天音聲遠近。是菩薩。以他心智。如實知他心。
508a17‖ 染心如實知染心。離染心如實知離染心。瞋
508a18‖ 心離瞋心。癡心離癡心。垢心離垢心。小心大
508a19‖ 心。散亂心如實知散亂心。定心不定心。縛心
508a20‖ 解心。有上心無上心。如實知有上心無上心。

简体字

石壁山障皆能彻过如行虚空，于虚空中跏趺而去犹如飞鸟，入出于地如水无异，履水如地，身出烟焰如大火聚，日月有大神德威力，而能以手扪摸摩之，身力自在乃至梵世。是菩萨以清净天耳过于人耳，悉闻人天音声远近。是菩萨以他心智，如实知他心，染心如实知染心，离染心如实知离染心，瞋心离瞋心、痴心离痴心、垢心离垢心、小心大心、散乱心如实知散乱心，定心不定心、缚心解心、有上心无上心如实知有上心无上心，

He is able also to go directly through the obstructions of rock, cliffs, and mountains just as easily as if they were empty space;
He is able to travel in full lotus through the air just as bird does;
He is able to enter into and emerge from solid ground no differently than if it were merely water;
He is able to walk across the surface of the water as if it were solid ground;
He is able to emit smoke and flames from his body just as if he had become a great bonfire;
He is able to employ the awesome power of his great spiritual virtue to reach up and stroke the sun and moon;
And he is able to freely exercise his personal powers all the way up to the Brahma Worlds.

11. The Bodhisattva's Heavenly Ear

This bodhisattva employs the purified heavenly ear in a manner exceeding the powers of the human ear so that he is able to entirely hear all of the sounds of both humans and devas, whether they be far or near.

12. The Bodhisattva's Knowledge of Others' Thoughts

Using the knowledge of others' thoughts, this bodhisattva knows in accordance with reality the thoughts in the minds of others. When they have thoughts defiled [by desire], he knows in accordance with reality that they are thoughts defiled [by desire]. When they have thoughts that have abandoned defilement [by desire], he knows in accordance with reality that they are thoughts that have abandoned defilement [by desire].[111] He knows when they have thoughts affected by hatred or thoughts that have abandoned hatred, when they have thoughts affected by delusion or thoughts that have abandoned delusion, when they have defiled thoughts or thoughts that have abandoned defilement, and when they have petty thoughts or great thoughts.

When they have thoughts that are scattered and disordered, he knows in accordance with reality that they are thoughts that are scattered and disordered. So too, he knows when they have concentrated thoughts or unconcentrated thoughts and when they have thoughts that are in bondage or have thoughts that are liberated.

When others have surpassable thoughts or unsurpassable thoughts, he knows in accordance with reality that they have

正體字

508a21‖ 如是以自心知他心。是菩薩。念知宿命。諸所
508a22‖ 生處。所謂。一世二世。三四五世。乃至十二十
508a23‖ 三十。四十五十。乃至百世千世。萬世百千萬
508a24‖ 億那由他世。一劫二劫。乃至百千萬億那由
508a25‖ 他無量劫數。其中諸劫。無量成壞。於諸劫中。
508a26‖ 所經因緣。悉能念知。我生彼處。如是種族。如
508a27‖ 是姓名。如是飲食。如是苦樂。如是久住。我於
508a28‖ 彼死。生於此間。於此間死。生於彼間。如是種
508a29‖ 種。相貌因緣。悉能念知。是菩薩。天眼清淨
508b01‖ 過於人眼。見眾生生死。形色好醜善惡。貧賤
508b02‖ 富貴。趣善惡道。隨業受報。皆如實知。所謂
508b03‖ 是諸眾生。成就身惡業。成就口惡業。成就意
508b04‖ 惡業。[3]距逆賢聖。

简体字

如是以自心知他心。是菩萨念知宿命诸所生处，所谓一世、二世、三四五世，乃至十、二十、三十、四十、五十，乃至百世、千世、万世、百千万亿那由他世，一劫、二劫乃至百千万亿那由他无量劫数，其中诸劫无量成坏，于诸劫中所经因缘，悉能念知。我生彼处，如是种族，如是姓名，如是饮食，如是苦乐，如是久住；我于彼死，生于此间，于此间死，生于彼间，如是种种相貌因缘，悉能念知。是菩萨天眼清净过于人眼，见众生生死、形色好丑、善恶、贫贱富贵、趣善恶道，随业受报皆如实知，所谓：是诸众生成就身恶业，成就口恶业，成就意恶业，距逆贤圣，

surpassable thoughts or unsurpassable thoughts. In this way, he uses his own mind to know the minds of others.

13. The Bodhisattva's Recall of Past Lives

This bodhisattva remembers with respect to past lifetimes all of the places in which he has taken rebirth, remembering this with respect to a single lifetime, two lifetimes, three lifetimes, four lifetimes, five lifetimes, up to ten, twenty, thirty, forty, and fifty lifetimes, and so forth on up to a hundred lifetimes, a thousand lifetimes, and a myriad lifetimes, remembering even a hundred thousand myriads of *koṭis* of *nayutas* of lifetimes. He knows them as they have transpired across the course of one kalpa, two kalpas, and so forth on up to a hundred thousand myriads of *koṭis* of *nayutas* of measureless kalpas, knowing too with respect to all of those kalpas all of the causal circumstances he passed through during those kalpas' innumerably many creation phases and destruction phases.

He is able to remember them all, recalling: "I was born in that place, belonged to this type of clan, was a member of a family bearing this surname, consumed just such food and drink as this, endured just such sorts of suffering and happiness as these, and dwelt there for just this long, after which I died in that location, was then reborn again in this circumstance, then died in this circumstance and was reborn again in yet another circumstance." Thus it is that he is able to entirely remember with regard to all of those causal circumstances all of the many different sorts of physical appearances that he bore.

14. The Bodhisattva's Heavenly Eye

This bodhisattva employs the purified heavenly eye in a manner exceeding the powers of the human eye so that he is able to entirely observe the births and deaths of other beings, observing whether they were of fine or hideous physical appearance, whether they were inclined toward goodness or evil, whether they were poverty-stricken and of only low social station or were wealthy and of aristocratic social station, whether they then proceeded toward the good destinies or toward the wretched destinies, undergoing retributions in accordance with their karmic deeds. He knows all of these things just as they really are, specifically knowing with regard to these beings how, because they have created bad physical karmic deeds, have created bad verbal karmic deeds, have created bad mental karmic deeds, have obstructed and gone against the Worthies and the Āryas, have

正體字

受邪見教。起罪業因緣故。
508b05‖ 身死墮惡道。生在地獄。是諸眾生。成就善身
508b06‖ 業。善口業。善意業。不逆賢聖。信受正見。行
508b07‖ 善業因緣故死後生善處天上。是菩薩。於諸
508b08‖ 禪定。解脫三昧。能入能出。而不隨生。但見何
508b09‖ 處。有助菩提法處。以願力故。能生其中。{N}是
508b10‖ 菩薩。住明地中。見數百千萬億那由他諸佛。
508b11‖ 恭敬供養尊重讚歎。衣服飲食。臥具醫藥。親
508b12‖ 近諸佛。聽受經法。聽受法已。隨力而行。是菩
508b13‖ 薩。爾時觀諸法不生不滅眾緣而有。{O}於百千
508b14‖ 萬億劫所集欲縛。漸得微薄。一切有縛。一切
508b15‖ 無明縛。皆悉微薄。不復積集。不積集故。斷
508b16‖ 於邪貪邪瞋邪癡。

简体字

受邪见教，起罪业因缘故，身死堕恶道生在地狱。是诸众生成就善身业、善口业、善意业，不逆贤圣，信受正见，行善业因缘故，死后生善处天上。是菩萨于诸禅定解脱三昧，能入能出而不随生；但见何处有助菩提法处，以愿力故能生其中。

“是菩萨住明地中，见数百千万亿那由他诸佛，恭敬供养，尊重赞叹，衣服、饮食、卧具、医药，亲近诸佛听受经法，听受法已随力而行。是菩萨尔时观诸法不生不灭，众缘而有，于百千万亿劫所集欲缚渐得微薄，一切有缚、一切无明缚皆悉微薄，不复积集；不积集故，断于邪贪、邪瞋、邪痴。

accepted teachings characterized by wrong views, and have generated causes and conditions associated with karmic offenses, they have then fallen at death into the wretched destinies and have thus been reborn in the hells.

So too is he able to observe how beings, because they have created good physical karmic deeds, have created good verbal karmic deeds, have created good mental karmic deeds, have refrained from any action obstructive of the Worthies and the Āryas, have believed in and taken on right views, and have cultivated the causes and conditions of good karmic actions, after they die, they are then born into good stations of existence, including up in the heavens.

15. The Bodhisattva's Vow-Determined Rebirth Apart From the Dhyānas

This bodhisattva is able to enter and emerge from the *dhyāna* absorptions, samādhis, and liberations while still not acquiescing in taking on their corresponding stations of rebirth. Rather, he simply observes which places present him with the bases for carrying out his cultivation of the dharmas assisting the realization of bodhi and then, availing himself of the power of his vows, he is able to take rebirth in just such circumstances.

16. The Bodhisattva's Seeing and Serving of Countless Buddhas

{N} This bodhisattva who dwells on the Ground of Shining Light sees many hundreds of thousands of myriads of *koṭis* of *nayutas* of buddhas and pays reverence to them, makes offerings to them, venerates them, and praises them. He presents them with robes, food and drink, bedding, and medicines. He draws close to the Buddhas, listens to and takes in the Dharma of the sutras, and then, having listened to and taken in the Dharma, he puts it into practice in a manner befitting his powers to do so.

17. The Bodhisattva's Purification & Its Comparison to Refining Gold

This bodhisattva then contemplates all dharmas as neither produced nor destroyed and as existing through the conjunction of a multitude of conditions.

{O} The bonds of desire that he has created across the course of hundreds of thousands of myriads of *koṭis* of kalpas gradually become attenuated and all of the bonds of becoming and all of the bonds of ignorance also become attenuated. They are no longer accumulated. Because they are no longer accumulated, he entirely severs wrong desire, wrong hatred, and wrong delusion.

正體字

諸佛子。譬如真金。巧師鍊
508b17‖ 治。轉更精好。光明倍勝。菩薩亦如是。住在明
508b18‖ 地。不集三縛故。斷於邪貪邪瞋邪癡。諸善根。
508b19‖ 轉增明淨。是菩薩。忍辱心柔軟心。美妙心不
508b20‖ 壞心。不動心不濁心。不高心不下心。一切所
508b21‖ 作不望報心。他少有作當生報心。不諂曲心。
508b22‖ 不染亂心。轉勝明淨。爾時菩薩。於四攝法中。
508b23‖ 愛語利益偏多。十波羅蜜中。忍辱波羅蜜。精
508b24‖ 進波羅蜜轉多。餘助菩提法。皆轉明淨。諸佛
508b25‖ 子。是名諸菩薩第三明地。{P}菩薩摩訶薩。住是
508b26‖ 地中。多作釋提桓因。智慧猛利。能以方便因
508b27‖ 緣。轉諸眾生。令離[4]淫欲。所作善業。若布施
508b28‖ 若愛語。若利益若同事。皆不離念佛念法。乃

简体字

诸佛子，譬如真金，巧师炼治，转更精好，光明倍胜；菩萨亦如是，住在明地，不集三缚故，断于邪贪、邪瞋、邪痴，诸善根转增明净。是菩萨忍辱心、柔软心、美妙心、不坏心、不动心、不浊心、不高心、不下心、一切所作不望报心、他少有作当生报心、不谄曲心、不染乱心，转胜明净。尔时菩萨于四摄法中，爱语利益偏多；十波罗蜜中，忍辱波罗蜜、精进波罗蜜转多，余助菩提法皆转明净。

“诸佛子，是名诸菩萨第三明地。菩萨摩诃萨住是地中，多作释提桓因，智慧猛利，能以方便因缘，转诸众生令离淫欲。所作善业，若布施、若爱语、若利益、若同事，皆不离念佛、念法，

Sons of the Buddha, it is just as with real gold which, when it is refined by a skilled artisan, it becomes ever more pure and fine and shines with doubly increased radiance. So too it is with the bodhisattva dwelling on the Ground of Shining Light who, because he no longer accumulates three types of bonds, cuts off all wrong desire, wrong hatred, and wrong delusion. His roots of goodness then become ever more radiantly purified.

This bodhisattva's inclination to be patient, his inclination to be gentle, his inclination to be beautifully sublime, his inclination to remain indestructible, his inclination to remain imperturbable, his inclination to remain unmuddled, his inclination to refrain from elevating himself, his inclination to refrain from judgments of "superiority," his inclination to refrain from judgments of "inferiority," his inclination to not seek gratitude for anything he does, his inclination to reward even the smallest deeds done by others, his inclination to refrain from flattery or deviousness, his inclination to remain undefiled and unconfused—all of these become ever more purified.[112]

18. The Bodhisattva's Practice of Means of Attraction and Pāramitās

At this time, among the dharmas constituting the four means of attraction, the bodhisattva focuses more strongly on the practice of "pleasing words" and "beneficial actions," whereas, among the ten *pāramitās*, he focuses more strongly on the patience *pāramitā* and the vigor *pāramitā*.[113] As for the remaining dharmas assisting the realization of bodhi, they all become ever more radiantly purified.

19. Vajragarbha's Final Statements About the 3rd Ground Bodhisattva

Sons of the Buddha, this is what constitutes the third bodhisattva ground, the Ground of Shining Light.

a. The Bodhisattva's Station and Dharma Practice

{P} The bodhisattva dwelling on this ground often becomes Śakra Devānām Indra. Using wisdom that is fiercely sharp, he is able to use the causes and conditions of skillful means to turn beings in such a way that they are influenced to abandon sensual desire.

b. The Bodhisattva's Mindfulness

In all of the good karmic deeds he does, whether in the sphere of "giving," "pleasing words," "beneficial actions," or "joint endeavors," he never departs from his mindfulness of the Buddha, mindfulness of the Dharma, and so forth until we come to his never

正體字

508b29‖ 至不離念具足一切種智。常生是心。我當何
508c01‖ 時於眾生中。為首為尊。乃至於一切眾[5]生。
508c02‖ 為依止者。是人若欲勤加精進。於須臾間。能
508c03‖ 得十萬三昧。乃至能示十萬菩薩。以為眷屬。
508c04‖ 隨其願力。神通自在。不可算數。若干百千萬
508c05‖ 億那由他劫。[6]不可計知。爾時金剛藏菩薩。
508c06‖ 欲令此義轉明故。而說偈言
508c07‖ 菩薩以是心　能得第三地
508c08‖ 淨心猛厭心　離心不退心
508c09‖ 堅心堪受心　快心及大心
508c10‖ 以如是等心　得入於三地 {7}
508c11‖ 智者住明地　觀有為作法
508c12‖ 不淨無常苦　無我壞敗相
508c13‖ 無有牢固性　不久念念滅
508c14‖ 如是思惟知　無有來去相 {8}

简体字

乃至不离念具足一切种智。常生是心：‘我当何时，于众生中为首为尊，乃至于一切众生为依止者？’是人若欲勤加精进，于须臾间，能得十万三昧，乃至能示十万菩萨以为眷属；随其愿力，神通自在不可算数，若干百千万亿那由他劫不可计知。”

尔时，金刚藏菩萨欲令此义转明故，而说偈言：

“菩萨以是心，　能得第三地，
净心猛厌心，　离心不退心，
坚心堪受心，　快心及大心，
以如是等心，　得入于三地。
智者住明地，　观有为作法，
不净无常苦，　无我坏败相，
无有牢固性，　不久念念灭，
如是思惟知，　无有来去相。

departing from mindfulness of his quest to achieve complete fulfillment of the knowledge of all modes.

c. The Bodhisattva's Aspiration to Serve Beings

He always brings to mind the thought, "Oh, when will I be able to become among beings, one who serves them as a leader, and one who is worthy of veneration?" and so forth until we come to his thinking, "Oh, when will I be able to become for all beings one upon whom they can rely?"

d. The Consequences of the Bodhisattva's Vigor and Vows

If this person wishes to apply himself to the diligent practice of vigor, then, in but a moment's time, he will be able to acquire a hundred thousand samādhis and so forth until we come to his being able to manifest a hundred thousand bodhisattvas to serve in his retinue. In accordance with the power of vows, through sovereign mastery in the spiritual superknowledges, he could manifest these phenomena in incalculable numbers so large that one could never count them even in however many hundreds of thousands of myriads of *koṭis* of *nayutas* of kalpas one might attempt to do so.

20. Vajragarbha Bodhisattva's Summarizing Verses

At that time, wishing to make his meaning even more clear, Vajragarbha Bodhisattva then uttered verses, saying:

By using the types of resolute intentions, the bodhisattva
becomes able to succeed in reaching the third ground:
the pure mind, the intensely acute mind, the mind of renunciation,
the mind of abandonment, the non-retreating mind,

the solid mind, the mind capable of withstanding whatever comes,[114]
the happy mind, and the magnanimous mind.
Employing such types of mind as these,
he succeeds in entering the third ground. {7}

One who is wise, dwelling on the Ground of Shining Light,
contemplates conditioned and created dharmas
as impure, impermanent, suffering,
devoid of self, as characterized by being bound to perish,

as having no enduring or solid nature,
as not lasting long, and as destroyed in each succeeding moment.
He meditates upon them in this way and realizes that
they are characterized as well by having no coming or going. {8}

正體字

508c15‖ 見諸有為法　如病如癰瘡
508c16‖ 愛心所纏縛　生諸憂悲苦
508c17‖ 但為貪恚癡　猛火所焚燒
508c18‖ 從無始世來　熾然常不息 {9}
508c19‖ 即時於一切　三界生厭離
508c20‖ 惡賤有為法　心無所貪著
508c21‖ 但求諸佛智　無量無邊限
508c22‖ 甚深難思議　清淨無諸苦 {10}
508c23‖ 如是見佛智　無諸苦惱已
508c24‖ 哀愍諸眾生　貧窮無福慧
508c25‖ 三毒火常然　無有救護者
508c26‖ 墮在地獄中　百種苦所切 {11}
508c27‖ 放逸凡夫人　沒諸煩惱聚
508c28‖ 盲冥無所見　失諸佛法寶
508c29‖ 常隨生死水　無怖空怖畏
509a01‖ 我於是眾生　當勤度脫之 {12}
509a02‖ 精進求智慧　為作饒益者
509a03‖ 思惟何方便　可以得救護
509a04‖ [1]唯有諸如來　深妙無礙智
509a05‖ 此智何為因　[*]唯從智慧生 {13}

简体字

见诸有为法，　如病如痈疮，
爱心所缠缚，　生诸忧悲苦，
但为贪恚痴，　猛火所焚烧，
从无始世来，　炽然常不息。
即时于一切，　三界生厌离，
恶贱有为法，　心无所贪著，
但求诸佛智，　无量无边限，
甚深难思议，　清净无诸苦。
如是见佛智，　无诸苦恼已，
哀愍诸众生，　贫穷无福慧，
三毒火常然，　无有救护者，
堕在地狱中，　百种苦所切！
放逸凡夫人，　没诸烦恼聚，
盲冥无所见，　失诸佛法宝，
常随生死水，　无怖空怖畏，
我于是众生，　当勤度脱之。
精进求智慧，　为作饶益者，
思惟何方便，　可以得救护？
唯有诸如来，　深妙无碍智，
此智何为因？　唯从智慧生。

He observes that all conditioned dharmas
are comparable to a sickness, like an abscess, and like a sore,
that beings are bound up in the bonds of their love-obsessed minds,
that they generate all manner of worry, sorrow, and suffering,

that their existence is only one of being burned up
by the fierce flames of covetousness, hatred, and stupidity,
and that, from the onset of their beginningless lifetimes onward,
this blaze has always burned on incessantly. {9}

He immediately renounces
everything in the three realms of existence
and feels revulsion for all conditioned dharmas.
His mind then remains free of covetous attachments.

He devotes himself solely to acquiring the knowledge of the Buddhas
that, immeasurable and boundless,
is extremely profound, difficult to conceive of, difficult to describe,
pure, and free of all forms of suffering. {10}

Having seen in this way that the Buddha's knowledge
is free of all suffering and anguish,
he feels sympathetic pity for all beings
in their poverty-stricken state bereft of merit and wisdom,

for they are always burned by the fires of the three poisons,
have no one to rescue and protect them,
and have become bound to fall down into the hell realms
wherein they are sliced by the hundred kinds of sufferings. {11}

These neglectful common people
have become immersed in a mass of afflictions,
are blind, totally unable to see,
and have lost the jewel of the Buddha's Dharma.

They forever follow the flowing currents of cyclic births and deaths
and have no fear of that, yet remain fearful of emptiness.
He then thinks, "I should be diligent
in bringing about the liberation of these beings {12}

and hence should vigorously pursue wisdom
in order to become one who benefits them."
He contemplates which skillful means, if employed,
could be successful in rescuing and protecting them,

realizes that it can only be that quality of the Tathāgatas,
their profound, sublime, and unimpeded knowledge,
and thus ponders, "What does such knowledge take as its cause?"
and then realizes, "It can only arise from wisdom." {13}

正體字

509a06‖ 思惟是智慧　但從多聞生
509a07‖ 如是籌量已　勤求多聞法
509a08‖ 日夜常精進　聽受無厭惓
509a09‖ 讀誦愛樂法　[*]唯法以為貴 {14}
509a10‖ 為欲求法故　以諸珍寶等
509a11‖ 所親愛妻子　隨意諸眷屬
509a12‖ 國土及城邑　資生諸好物
509a13‖ 歡喜而施與　心無所戀惜 {15}
509a14‖ 頭目耳鼻舌　牙齒及手足
509a15‖ 支節[2]身血肉　心肝及髓腦
509a16‖ 以此等施人　猶不以為難
509a17‖ 若得聞正法　是為最甚難 {16}
509a18‖ 假令有一人　語此菩薩言
509a19‖ 汝今若能入　是大猛火聚
509a20‖ 然後當與汝　諸佛所說法
509a21‖ 聞已即歡喜　自投於火聚 {17}
509a22‖ 設使大千界　火聚滿其中
509a23‖ 須彌梵世下　不足以為難
509a24‖ 若為求一句　諸佛所說法
509a25‖ 救諸苦惱者　得之甚為難 {18}

简体字

思惟是智慧，　但从多闻生，
如是筹量已，　勤求多闻法，
日夜常精进，　听受无厌惓，
读诵爱乐法，　唯法以为贵。
为欲求法故，　以诸珍宝等，
所亲爱妻子，　随意诸眷属，
国土及城邑，　资生诸好物，
欢喜而施与，　心无所恋惜。
头目耳鼻舌，　牙齿及手足，
支节身血肉，　心肝及髓脑，
以此等施人，　犹不以为难，
若得闻正法，　是为最甚难！
假令有一人，　语此菩萨言：
‘汝今若能入，　是大猛火聚，
然后当与汝，　诸佛所说法。’
闻已即欢喜，　自投于火聚：
‘设使大千界，　火聚满其中，
须弥梵世下，　不足以为难。
若为求一句，　诸佛所说法，
救诸苦恼者，　得之甚为难！

He then reasons that this wisdom
can itself only come forth from extensive learning.
Having assessed the matter in this way,
he diligently seeks to acquire the dharma of extensive learning,

becoming ever vigorous both day and night
in tirelessly listening to and absorbing the teachings,
and in studying, reciting, cherishing, and delighting in the Dharma,
taking only the Dharma as worthy of being esteemed as valuable. {14}

Thus, desiring to pursue his quest to acquire the Dharma,
he bestows gifts of the various sorts of precious jewels and such,
as well as his dearly beloved wife and children,
while also freely granting the services of his retinue,

his country, its cities,
and all the fine possessions useful to supporting one's life.
He joyfully presents all of these as gifts
with a mind free of anything it affectionately cherishes. {15}

Hence, no matter whether it be his head, eyes, ears, nose, tongue,
teeth, his hands, or his feet,
and no matter whether it be his limbs or body, his flesh or blood,
his heart, liver, marrow, or brain,

he is able to give all such things away to others
while still not taking this to be particularly difficult.
Rather, he considers the ability to hear right Dharma
as what is the most supremely difficult thing to encounter. {16}

Supposing that there was a person
who told this bodhisattva,
"If you are now able to plunge into
this immense and fiercely blazing bonfire,

then, after you have done that, I will bestow on you
Dharma that has been spoken by the Buddhas,"
having heard this, he would immediately be filled with delight
and would throw himself into that bonfire. {17}

Even if there was a bonfire entirely filling up
a great chiliocosm into which
he had to leap from the heights of Sumeru or the Brahma Worlds,
he would still not see that as sufficient to be seen as difficult

if, in doing so, it was in order to seek a single sentence
of the Dharma proclaimed by the Buddhas
with which he might rescue those embroiled in suffering,
for it is obtaining that which he would see as extremely difficult. {18}

正體字

509a26║ 始從初發心　乃至成佛道
509a27║ 我於其中間　盡此諸劫數
509a28║ 為欲求諸法　備受阿鼻苦
509a29║ 何況於人間　小小諸苦惱 {19}
509b01║ 以聽法因緣　能得正憶念
509b02║ 正憶念因緣　能生諸禪定
509b03║ 深妙等三昧　及五神通事
509b04║ 次第皆能起　自在不隨生 {20}
509b05║ 菩薩住是地　能以決定心
509b06║ 多供養諸佛　聽受所說法
509b07║ 斷邪[受>愛]恚等　餘煩惱微薄
509b08║ 猶如成鍊金　調和得其所 {21}
509b09║ 菩薩住是地　[3]功德藏充滿
509b10║ 多作忉利王　自在化婬欲
509b11║ 愛佛功德故　化導無量眾
509b12║ 悉能令得住　無上佛道中 {22}
509b13║ 菩薩住是地　能以柔軟心
509b14║ 勤行於精進　得百千三昧
509b15║ 悉得見諸佛　相好莊嚴身
509b16║ 其心轉猛利　願力[4]者殊勝 {23}

简体字

始从初发心，　乃至成佛道，
我于其中间，　尽此诸劫数，
为欲求诸法，　备受阿鼻苦，
何况于人间，　小小诸苦恼！
以听法因缘，　能得正忆念，
正忆念因缘，　能生诸禅定，
深妙等三昧，　及五神通事，
次第皆能起，　自在不随生。
菩萨住是地，　能以决定心，
多供养诸佛，　听受所说法，
断邪爱恚等，　余烦恼微薄，
犹如成炼金，　调和得其所。
菩萨住是地，　功德藏充满，
多作忉利王，　自在化淫欲，
爱佛功德故，　化导无量众，
悉能令得住，　无上佛道中。
菩萨住是地，　能以柔软心，
勤行于精进，　得百千三昧，
悉得见诸佛，　相好庄严身，
其心转猛利，　愿力者殊胜，

He thinks, "For the sake of fulfilling my quest to acquire all dharmas,
I would even endure all of the sufferings occurring in the Avīci Hells
beginning from the time I first brought forth the resolve
and continuing on until I reach the realization of buddhahood,

undergoing it to the very end of all these kalpas
that transpire during the intervening time,
how much the more so would I take on such minor sufferings
as are endured within the human realm?" {19}

On account of having heard the Dharma,
he becomes able to develop right mindfulness.
Due to developing right mindfulness,
he becomes able to bring forth the *dhyāna* absorptions,

the profoundly marvelous equally-regarding samādhis,[115] and
the phenomena associated with the five spiritual superknowledges.
He is able to bring them all forth in sequence with sovereign mastery,
so does not acquiesce in their power to determine one's rebirths. {20}

The bodhisattva dwelling on this ground
is able with decisive resolve
to present many offerings to the Buddhas,
hear and accept the Dharma they explain,

cut off all wrongly generated desire, hatred, and such,
and reduce residual afflictions to the point that they are but feeble,
doing so in a manner comparable to refining gold
so that it is evenly purified, thereby reaching its ideal state. {21}

The bodhisattva dwelling on this ground
is possessed of an entirely full treasury of meritorious qualities,
often becomes the Trāyastriṃśa Heaven King
who freely offers instruction in the abandonment of sensual desire

and who, because he cherishes the qualities of the Buddha,
teaches and leads forth an immeasurably vast assembly of devas
in a manner whereby they all succeed in coming to abide
within the unsurpassably superior path of the Buddha. {22}

The bodhisattva dwelling on this ground
who is able to employ a pliant mind
in the diligent application of vigor
will gain realization of a hundred thousand samādhis

and will become able to see the Buddhas
with bodies graced by the major marks and subsidiary signs.
For one whose resolve is even more intensely strong,
the results of his vow power are especially superb. {23}

正體字

509b17‖ 常為諸眾生　勤求好事者
509b18‖ 分別解說此　第三明地已 {24} [5]◎

简体字

常为诸众生，　勤求好事者。
分别解说此，　第三明地已。”

In this, he always diligently strives
to bring about whatever is best for all beings.
This concludes the differentiating explanation
of this third ground, the Ground of Shining Light. {24}

End of Chapter Three

正體字

509b19║ ◎[6]焰地第四
509b20║ 諸佛子聞說　如是地相義
509b21║ 深妙無有量　心皆大歡喜
509b22║ 散眾名花香　供養於如來 {1}
509b23║ 地及大海水　悉皆大震動
509b24║ 天諸婇女等　於上虛空中
509b25║ 同以微妙音　歌頌此上法 {2}
509b26║ 他化自在王　聞[7]以大歡喜
509b27║ 雨摩尼珠寶　以散於佛上
509b28║ 踊躍稱讚言　善哉佛出世
509b29║ 功德藏流布　利益於我等 {3}
509c01║ 我今聞說此　菩薩地相義
509c02║ 是事百千劫　難聞而得聞 {4}
509c03║ 願更說後地　利益諸天人
509c04║ 僉皆喜欲聞　得地諸行相 {5}
509c05║ 解脫月菩薩　重請金剛藏
509c06║ 願為諸菩薩　說至四地行 {6}

简体字

十住经卷第三 焰地第四

诸佛子闻说，　如是地相义，
深妙无有量，　心皆大欢喜，
散众名华香，　供养于如来，
地及大海水，　悉皆大震动。
天诸婇女等，　于上虚空中，
同以微妙音，　歌颂此上法。
他化自在王，　闻以大欢喜，
雨摩尼珠宝，　以散于佛上，
踊跃称赞言：“善哉佛出世！
功德藏流布，　利益于我等。
我今闻说此，　菩萨地相义，
是事百千劫，　难闻而得闻。
愿更说后地，　利益诸天人，
佥皆喜欲闻，　得地诸行相。”
解脱月菩萨，　重请金刚藏：
“愿为诸菩萨，　说至四地行。”

Chapter Four
The Blazing Brilliance Ground

D. The Fourth Ground: The Blazing Brilliance Ground

1. The Fourth Ground's Introductory Verses and Dharma Request

When those Buddha's Sons had finished listening to this explanation
of such aspects and meanings associated with this ground,
so deep, sublime, and immeasurable,
their minds were all filled with joyous delight.
They then scattered the many sorts of fine flowers and incense
as offerings to the Tathāgata. {1}

Thereupon the entire earth was gripped with strong tremors,
all waters of the great seas were roiled,
and the celestial nymphs and others,
high in the air above,
joined their subtle and sublime voices
in singing the praises of this supreme Dharma. {2}

The King of the Transformation of Others' Bliss Heaven,
immensely joyful at hearing this,
rained down *maṇi* pearl jewels
that sprinkled on down to the Buddha from on high.

He then arose and uttered praises, declaring:
"Good indeed! The Buddha has come forth into the world.
His treasury of meritorious qualities is here distributed
in order to benefit us all. {3}

"I have just now been able to hear this teaching
on the characteristics and meanings of this bodhisattva ground.
This event is one that, even in a hundred thousand kalpas,
would be a rarity to hear, and yet I have been able to hear it here. {4}

"We only pray that you will explain the ground that follows
in order to be of benefit to both devas and humans.
Everyone here would delight in it and hence we wish to hear
of the aspects of the practices involved in reaching this ground." {5}

Liberation Moon Bodhisattva
then once again presented a request to Vajragarbha, saying:
"We pray that, for the sake of all bodhisattvas,
you will explain the practices used in reaching the fourth ground." {6}

正體字

509c07‖ {A}爾時金剛藏菩薩摩訶薩。語解脫月菩薩言。
509c08‖ 佛子。諸菩薩摩訶薩。具足清淨行第三地已。
509c09‖ 欲得第四地者。當以十法明門。得入[8]此四地。
509c10‖ 何等為十。一思量眾生性。二思量法性。三思
509c11‖ 量世界性。四思量虛空性。五思量識性。六思
509c12‖ 量欲界性。七思量色界性。八思量無色界性。
509c13‖ 九思量快信解性。十思量大心性。諸佛子。
509c14‖ [9]菩薩。以此十法明門。能從三地。入第四地。
509c15‖ {B}諸佛子。菩薩摩訶薩。若得第四菩薩焰地。即
509c16‖ 於如來家。轉有勢力。得內法故。有十種智。何
509c17‖ 等為十。一不退轉心。二於三寶中得不壞信清
509c18‖ 淨畢竟智。三修習觀生滅。四修習諸法本來
509c19‖ 不生。五常修習轉還世間行。

简体字

尔时，金刚藏菩萨摩诃萨，语解脱月菩萨言："佛子，诸菩萨摩诃萨，具足清净行第三地已，欲得第四地者，当以十法明门，得入此四地。何等为十？一、思量众生性，二、思量法性，三、思量世界性，四、思量虚空性，五、思量识性，六、思量欲界性，七、思量色界性，八、思量无色界性，九、思量快信解性，十、思量大心性。诸佛子，菩萨，以此十法明门，能从三地，入第四地。

"诸佛子，菩萨摩诃萨，若得第四菩萨焰地，即于如来家转有势力，得内法故，有十种智。何等为十？一、不退转心，二、于三宝中得不坏信清净毕竟智，三、修习观生灭，四、修习诸法本来不生，五、常修习转还世间行，

2. Vajragarbha Commences the Fourth Ground's Explanation

{A} At that time, Vajragarbha Bodhisattva Mahāsattva informed Liberation Moon Bodhisattva, saying:

3. 10 Gateways to Dharma Light as Bases for Entering the 4th Ground

O Son of the Buddha, those bodhisattva *mahāsattvas* who have completed the purifying cultivation of the third ground and then wish to reach the fourth ground should avail themselves of ten gateways to the light of Dharma[116] in order to gain entry into this fourth ground. What then are these ten? They are:

First, contemplation of the realms of beings;
Second, contemplation of the Dharma realm;
Third, contemplation of the realms of the worlds;
Fourth, contemplation of the realms of empty space;
Fifth, contemplation of the realms of consciousness;
Sixth, contemplation of the desire realm;
Seventh, contemplation of the form realm;
Eighth, contemplation of the formless realm;
Ninth, contemplation of the realms of happy [resolute intentions and] resolute convictions;[117]
Tenth, contemplation of the realms of magnanimous resolute intentions [and resolute convictions].[118]

Sons of the Buddha, by employing these ten gateways to the light of Dharma, the bodhisattva is able to advance from the third ground into the fourth ground.

4. 10 Knowledge-Maturing Dharmas for Birth in the Buddhas' Clan

{B} Sons of the Buddha, if the bodhisattva *mahāsattva* reaches the fourth ground, the Ground of Blazing Brilliance, he immediately acquires ever more strength in the clan of the Tathāgatas and then, due to acquiring its inner dharmas,[119] he comes to possess ten kinds of knowledge [maturing dharmas].[120] What then are these ten? They are:

First, non-retreating resolve;
Second, the knowledge associated with acquiring indestructible and ultimately pure faith in the Three Jewels;
Third, cultivation of the contemplation of production and extinction;
Fourth, cultivation of understanding all dharmas as originally unproduced;
Fifth, constant cultivation of understanding the actions involved in the generation and dissolution of worlds;

正體字

六修習知業因
509c20‖ 緣故有生。七修習分別生死涅槃門差別。八
509c21‖ 修習眾生業差別。九修習前際後際差別。十
509c22‖ 修習現在常滅不住行。是十智心。則生佛家。
509c23‖ 轉得勢力。{C}復次佛子。菩薩摩訶薩。住是菩薩
509c24‖ 第四地。觀內身循身觀。精勤一心。除世間貪
509c25‖ 憂。觀外身循身觀。精勤一心。除世間貪憂。觀
509c26‖ 內外身循身觀。精勤一心。除世間貪憂。觀內
509c27‖ 受外受內外受。內心外心內外心。內法外法
509c28‖ 內外法。循法觀。精勤一心。除世間貪憂。

简体字

六、修习知业因缘故有生，七、修习分别生死涅槃门差别，八、修习众生业差别，九、修习前际后际差别，十、修习现在常灭不住行。是十智心，则生佛家转得势力。

“复次，佛子，菩萨摩诃萨住是菩萨第四地，观内身循身观，精勤一心除世间贪忧；观外身循身观，精勤一心除世间贪忧；观内外身循身观，精勤一心除世间贪忧；观内受、外受、内外受，内心、外心、内外心，内法、外法、内外法，循法观，精勤一心除世间贪忧。

Sixth, cultivation of an understanding of how birth occurs due to karmic actions' causes and conditions;

Seventh, cultivation of the gateway of discerning the different factors involved in *saṃsāra* and nirvāṇa;

Eighth, cultivation of understanding the different factors involved in beings' karma;

Ninth, cultivation of understanding the different factors associated with the past and the future;

Tenth, cultivation of the practice of understanding [all phenomena's] constant destruction and non-abiding in this very moment.

It is through cultivation of these knowledge-maturing intentional practices that one is born into the clan of the Buddhas and develops ever more strength within it.

5. The Bodhisattva's Practice of the 37 Enlightenment Factors

a. The Four Stations of Mindfulness

{C} Then again, O Sons of the Buddha, the bodhisattva *mahāsattva* dwelling on this fourth ground carries on the body-examining contemplation in regard to his own body and, through energetically diligent single-mindedness in this, succeeds in ridding himself of desires and distress associated with the world.

He carries on as well the body-examining contemplation in regard to the bodies of others, and, through energetically diligent single-mindedness in this, succeeds in ridding himself of desires and distress associated with the world.

So too does he carry on the body-examining contemplation in regard to both his own and others' bodies, and, through energetically diligent single-mindedness in this, succeeds in ridding himself of desires and distress associated with the world.

So too, he contemplates his own feelings, the feelings of others, and the feelings experienced by both himself and others, contemplates his own mind, the minds of others, and the minds of both himself and others, and, using the dharma-examining contemplation, contemplates subjectively associated dharmas, objectively-associated dharmas, and dharmas that are both subjectively associated and objectively associated, thereby bringing energetic and diligent single-mindedness to bear in ridding himself of desire and distress associated with the world.[121]

正體字

是
509c29‖ 菩薩。未生惡不善法。為不生故。欲生勤精進。
510a01‖ 發心正斷。已生諸惡不善法。為斷故。欲生勤
510a02‖ 精進。發心正斷。未生諸善法。為生故。欲生勤
510a03‖ 精進。發心正行。已生諸善法。為住不失。[1]修
510a04‖ 增廣故。欲生勤精進。發心正行。是菩薩。修行
510a05‖ 四如意分。欲定斷行成就。修如意分。依止厭。
510a06‖ 依止離。依止滅。迴向於捨。精進定斷行成就
510a07‖ 修如意分。心定斷行成就。修如意分。思惟定
510a08‖ 斷行成就。修如意分。依止厭離滅。迴向於捨。
510a09‖ 是菩薩。修行信根。依止厭離滅。迴向於捨。精
510a10‖ 進根念根定根。修行慧根。依止厭離滅。迴向
510a11‖ 於捨。是菩薩。修行信力。依止厭離滅。

简体字

是菩萨未生恶不善法为不生故，欲生勤精进发心正断；已生诸恶不善法为断故，欲生勤精进发心正断；未生诸善法为生故，欲生勤精进发心正行；已生诸善法为住不失，修增广故，欲生勤精进发心正行。是菩萨修行四如意分，欲定断行成就修如意分，依止厌、依止离、依止灭，回向于舍；精进定断行成就修如意分，心定断行成就修如意分，思惟定断行成就修如意分，依止厌、离、灭，回向于舍。是菩萨修行信根，依止厌、离、灭，回向于舍；精进根、念根、定根，修行慧根，依止厌、离、灭，回向于舍。是菩萨修行信力，依止厌、离、灭，

b. The Four Right Efforts

This bodhisattva strives to bring forth diligently applied vigor and resolves to rightly cut off any not yet arisen evil and unwholesome dharmas, doing so for the sake of preventing their arising.

He strives to bring forth diligently applied vigor and resolves to rightly cut off any already arisen evil and unwholesome dharmas, doing so for the sake of cutting them off.

He strives to bring forth diligently applied vigor and resolves to carry out right practice of any not yet arisen good dharmas, doing so in order to ensure their arising.

And he also strives to bring forth diligently applied vigor and resolves to carry out that right practice by which one cultivates, increases, and broadens any already arisen good dharmas for the sake of ensuring that they will continue and not be lost.[122]

c. The Four Bases of Psychic Power

This bodhisattva also cultivates the four bases of psychic power. In his cultivation of the bases of psychic power, his establishment of the severance practice associated with zeal-based concentration is done based upon detachment, based upon dispassion, based upon cessation, and directed toward relinquishment.[123] So too is this true of his establishment of the severance practice associated with vigor-based concentration as he cultivates the bases of psychic power, his establishment of the severance practice associated with mind-based concentration as he cultivates the bases of psychic power, and his establishment of the severance practice associated with contemplation-based concentration as he cultivates the bases of psychic power, for they all are done based upon detachment, based upon dispassion, based upon cessation, and directed toward relinquishment.[124]

d. The Five Roots

This bodhisattva's cultivation of the root-faculty of faith is done based upon detachment, based upon dispassion, based upon cessation, and directed toward relinquishment. So too, his cultivation of the root-faculty of vigor, the root-faculty of mindfulness, the root-faculty of concentration, and the root-faculty of wisdom is done based upon detachment, based upon dispassion, based upon cessation, and directed toward relinquishment. [125]

e. The Five Powers

This bodhisattva's cultivation of the power of faith is done based upon detachment, based upon dispassion, based upon cessation,

正體字

迴向於
510a12‖ 捨。精進力念力定力。修行慧力。依止厭離
510a13‖ 滅。迴向於捨。是菩薩。修行念覺分。依止厭
510a14‖ 離滅。迴向於捨。擇法覺分。精進覺分。喜覺
510a15‖ 分除覺分定覺分。修行捨覺分。依止厭離滅。
510a16‖ 迴向於捨。是菩薩。修行正見。依止厭離滅。迴
510a17‖ 向於捨。正思惟正語。正業正命。正精進正念。
510a18‖ 修行正定。依止厭離滅。迴向於捨。{D}是菩薩。以
510a19‖ 不捨眾生心故行。以本願力故。大悲為首。大
510a20‖ 慈合行。為攝一切智。為莊嚴佛國。為具佛
510a21‖ 諸力[2]無畏。不共法。三十二相。八十種好。具
510a22‖ 足音聲。為隨順佛深解脫。為思惟大智慧方
510a23‖ 便故行。

简体字

回向于舍；精进力、念力、定力，修行慧力，依止厌、离、灭，回向于舍。是菩萨修行念觉分，依止厌、离、灭，回向于舍；择法觉分、精进觉分、喜觉分、除觉分、定觉分，修行舍觉分，依止厌、离、灭，回向于舍。是菩萨修行正见，依止厌、离、灭，回向于舍；正思惟、正语、正业、正命、正精进、正念，修行正定，依止厌、离、灭，回向于舍。是菩萨以不舍众生心故行，以本愿力故，大悲为首，大慈合行，为摄一切智，为庄严佛国，为具佛诸力、无畏、不共法、三十二相、八十种好、具足音声，为随顺佛深解脱，为思惟大智慧方便故行。

and directed toward relinquishment. So too, his cultivation of the power of vigor, the power of mindfulness, the power of concentration, and the power of wisdom is done based upon detachment, based upon dispassion, based upon cessation, and directed toward relinquishment.[126]

f. The Seven Limbs of Enlightenment

This bodhisattva's cultivation of the mindfulness limb of enlightenment is done based upon detachment, based upon dispassion, based upon cessation, and directed toward relinquishment. So too, his cultivation of the dharma-selection limb of enlightenment, the vigor limb of enlightenment, the joyfulness limb of enlightenment, the pliancy limb of enlightenment, the concentration limb of enlightenment, and the even-mindedness limb of enlightenment is done based upon detachment, based upon dispassion, based upon cessation, and directed toward relinquishment.[127]

g. The Eightfold Path

This bodhisattva's cultivation of right views is done based upon detachment, based upon dispassion, based upon cessation, and directed toward relinquishment. So too, his cultivation of right thought, right speech, right action, right livelihood, right effort, right mindfulness, and right concentration is done based upon detachment, based upon dispassion, based upon cessation, and directed toward relinquishment.[128]

h. The Bodhisattva's Ten Aims Underlying His 37 Factors Practice

{D} The bodhisattva engages in these practices:

Due to his resolve to refrain from forsaking beings;
Due to the power of his original vows;
In order to take the great compassion as what is foremost;
In order to combine his practice with the great kindness;
In order to accumulate all-knowledge;
In order to engage in the adornment of buddha lands;
In order to become completely equipped with the Buddha's powers, fearlessnesses, dharmas exclusive to the Buddhas, thirty-two marks, and eighty subsidiary signs;
In order to become perfectly endowed with his voice;[129]
In order to accord with the Buddha's profoundly deep liberation;
And in order to reflect upon great wisdom and skillful means.

正體字

{E}諸佛子。諸菩薩摩訶薩。住菩薩焰地。
510a24‖ 所有身見[3]著等。著我。著眾生。著人壽者。知
510a25‖ 者見者。著五陰十二入十八界。所起屈伸卷
510a26‖ 舒出沒。推求心所行。愛著寶重所見。為歸為
510a27‖ 洲。皆悉斷滅。{F*},{G}是菩薩。轉倍精進。慧方便所生
510a28‖ 助道法。隨所修行。心轉柔和。堪任有用。心無
510a29‖ 疲惓。轉求上法。增益智慧。救一切世間。隨順
510b01‖ 諸師。恭敬受教。如所說行。{H}是菩薩。爾時知恩
510b02‖ 知報恩。心轉和善。同止安樂。直心軟心。無有
510b03‖ 邪曲。

简体字

“诸佛子，诸菩萨摩诃萨住菩萨焰地，所有身见著等，著我、著众生，著人、寿者、知者、见者，著五阴、十二入、十八界，所起屈伸卷舒出没，推求心所行爱著宝重所见，为归为洲，皆悉断灭。是菩萨转倍精进，慧方便所生助道法，随所修行，心转柔和堪任有用，心无疲惓转求上法，增益智慧救一切世间，随顺诸师，恭敬受教，如所说行。是菩萨尔时知恩知报恩，心转和善，同止安乐，直心、软心，无有邪曲

6. The Bodhisattva's Leaving of Wrong Views, Attachments, and Actions

{E} Sons of the Buddha, the bodhisattva *mahāsattvas* dwelling on the Ground of Blazing Brilliance confront all of the attachments related to the view imputing the existence of a true self in association with the body. These include the attachment to the existence of self, the attachment to the existence of a being, and the attachments to the existence of a person, an entity possessed of a lifespan, a knower, a perceiver in association with clinging to the five aggregates, the twelve sense bases, or the eighteen sense realms.

They observe that whatever arises in this connection, including whatsoever is contracted or extended, is withdrawn or set forth, or is caused to emerge or sink away is all carried forth by discursive thought's perception of something deemed to be a refuge or an individual territory worthy of affectionate attachment or something worthy of being valued as precious. Consequently they completely sever all of these attachments.[130]

7. Mental & Personal Qualities Gained in Path Cultivation

{F}, {G} This bodhisattva then redoubles his vigor in the dharmas constituting provisions for the path[131] that are developed through wisdom and skillful means. In accordance with what he cultivates his mind becomes ever more:[132]

Gentle;
Harmonious;
Tractable to use;
Mentally inexhaustible;
Inclined to seek increasingly superior dharmas;
Possessed of increased wisdom;
Devoted to rescuing everyone in the world;
Compliant with teachers;
Respectful in receiving teachings;
And compliant in practice with what has been taught.

{H} At this time, this bodhisattva:[133]

Is cognizant of kindnesses received;
Knows to repay kindnesses;
Has a mind that becomes ever more inclined to congeniality and goodness;
Dwells happily together with others;
Is possessed of a straight mind;
Is possessed of a pliant mind;
Is free of any form of deviousness;

正體字

行正定行。無有憍慢。則易與語。隨順
510b04‖ 教誨。得說者意。如是具足善心軟心。寂滅心
510b05‖ 忍辱心。淨地諸法。思惟修行。{I}是菩薩。爾時
510b06‖ 成不轉精進者。不捨精進。不壞精進。不厭精
510b07‖ 進。不惓精進。廣大精進。無邊精進。猛利精進。
510b08‖ 無等等精進。救一切眾生精進。分別是道非
510b09‖ 道精進。{J}是菩薩。心志清淨。不失深心。信解
510b10‖ 明利。諸善根增長。遠離世間垢濁。不信疑悔
510b11‖ 等。皆已滅盡。無疑無悔。現前具足。於一切
510b12‖ 佛大信解事中。不厭不捨。自然習樂。無量之
510b13‖ 心。常現在前。{K}菩薩住是第四焰地。能見諸佛
510b14‖ 數百數千數千萬億那由他佛。

简体字

行正定行，无有憍慢则易与语，随顺教诲得说者意，如是具足善心、软心、寂灭心、忍辱心，净地诸法思惟修行。是菩萨尔时成不转精进者，不舍精进，不坏精进，不厌精进，不惓精进，广大精进，无边精进，猛利精进，无等等精进，救一切众生精进，分别是道非道精进。是菩萨心志清净，不失深心，信解明利，诸善根增长，远离世间垢浊，不信疑悔等皆已灭尽，无疑无悔现前具足，于一切佛大信解事中，不厌不舍自然习乐，无量之心常现在前。

“菩萨住是第四焰地，能见诸佛数百、数千、数千万亿那由他佛，

Implements the practice of right meditative concentration;
Is free of arrogance and is consequently easy to engage in discussion;
Complies with teaching instructions;
And realizes the intent of those who speak to him.

It is in just such a manner as this that he becomes completely equipped with the good mind, the pliant mind, the quiescent mind, and the patient mind, purifies the dharmas associated with the grounds, and proceeds with well-considered cultivation.

8. The Bodhisattva's Acquisition of Ten Kinds of Vigor

{I} At this time, as this bodhisattva perfects non-retreating vigor he becomes possessed of:[134]

Vigor that is never forsaken;
Indestructible vigor;
Insatiable vigor;
Tireless vigor;
Vast vigor;
Boundless vigor;
Fiercely intense vigor;
Utterly matchless vigor;
Vigor that pursues the rescue of all beings;
And vigor that distinguishes what is and is not the path.

9. Other Qualities Developed in the Bodhisattva's 4th Ground Practice

{J} This bodhisattva's aspirations have become purified, he never loses his resolute intentions, and his resolute convictions are bright and sharp. His roots of goodness increase, and he abandons worldly defilements. He has already utterly extinguished disbelief, doubtfulness and regretfulness, and other such factors. His freedom from doubtfulness and regretfulness are manifestly complete. He never grows weary of or abandons any of the endeavors associated with his great resolute faith in all buddhas and he naturally practices and delights in them. His resolute intentions in relation to the immeasurable minds[135] are always directly and presently manifest.

10. The Bodhisattva's Seeing and Serving of Countless Buddhas

{K} The bodhisattva dwelling on this fourth ground, the Ground of Blazing Brilliance, becomes able to see the Buddhas, seeing up to many hundreds, many thousands, and on up to many thousands of myriads of *koṭis* of *nayutas* of buddhas to all of whom he

正體字

供養恭敬。尊
510b15‖ 重讚歎。衣服飲食。臥具醫藥。親近諸佛。一心
510b16‖ 聽法。聽受法已。能信奉持。多於佛所。出家修
510b17‖ 道。是菩薩。樂心深心。清淨信解平等。轉更明
510b18‖ 了。住壽多劫。若干百千。萬億那由他劫。善
510b19‖ 根轉勝明利。諸佛子。如上真金。以為莊嚴。餘
510b20‖ 金不及。如是諸菩薩摩訶薩。住此菩薩焰地。
510b21‖ 諸善根轉增明利。下地菩薩。所不能及。譬如
510b22‖ 摩尼珠。光明清淨。能照四方。餘寶不及。雨漬
510b23‖ 水澆。光明不滅。菩薩住焰地中。下地菩薩所
510b24‖ 不能及。一切諸魔。及諸煩惱。皆不能壞其智
510b25‖ 慧。諸佛子。是名略說諸菩薩摩訶薩第四焰
510b26‖ 地。菩薩摩訶薩。住是地中。多作須夜[4]磨天
510b27‖ 王。

简体字

供养恭敬，尊重赞叹，衣服、饮食、卧具、医药，亲近诸佛，一心听法；听受法已，能信奉持，多于佛所出家修道。是菩萨乐心、深心清净，信解平等转更明了，住寿多劫，若干百千万亿那由他劫，善根转胜明利。诸佛子，如上真金以为庄严，余金不及；如是诸菩萨摩诃萨，住此菩萨焰地，诸善根转增明利，下地菩萨所不能及。譬如摩尼珠，光明清净能照四方，余宝不及；雨渍水浇，光明不灭。菩萨住焰地中，下地菩萨所不能及；一切诸魔及诸烦恼，皆不能坏其智慧。

“诸佛子，是名略说诸菩萨摩诃萨第四焰地。菩萨摩诃萨住是地中，多作须夜摩天王，

then makes offerings and demonstrates his reverence, venerating them, praising them, and presenting offerings to them of robes, food and drink, bedding, and medicines. He draws close to all of these buddhas, listens single-mindedly to their teachings on Dharma, and, having listened to and accepted the Dharma, he is then able to have faith in it and uphold it in practice, often leaving behind the home life to cultivate the path in the presence of buddhas.

11. The Bodhisattva's Purification & Its Comparison to Refining Gold

This bodhisattva's higher aspirations and resolute intentions as well as his purified resolute faith and equal regard for others[136] shine forth ever more brightly. He abides here for a span of many kalpas, for indefinably many hundreds of thousands of myriads of *koṭis* of *nayutas* of kalpas during which his roots of goodness become ever more supremely bright and sharp.

Sons of the Buddha, this is comparable to the use of the best real gold in the making of objects of adornment that all other lesser grades of gold cannot match. So too it is with the bodhisattva *mahāsattvas* who dwell on this bodhisattva's Ground of Blazing Brilliance. Their roots of goodness shine forth with ever more brilliance and sharpness that could never be matched by those of the bodhisattvas abiding on lower grounds.

12. The Radiance of This Bodhisattva's Roots Like That of a Maṇi jewel

This is analogous to the pure and radiant light of the *maṇi* jewel that is able to illuminate the four directions and cannot be matched in this by any other sort of jewel and cannot be dimmed in the brilliance of its radiance even by the soaking of rains or immersion by floods. So too it is with the bodhisattva dwelling on the Ground of Blazing Brilliance. He cannot be matched by any bodhisattva dwelling on a lower ground and none of the *māras* or any of the afflictions are able to overcome his wisdom.

13. Vajragarbha's Final Statements About the 4th Ground Bodhisattva

Sons of the Buddha, this has been a concise explanation of what constitutes the bodhisattva *mahāsattva*'s fourth ground, the Ground of Blazing Brilliance.

a. The Bodhisattva's Station and Dharma Practice

The bodhisattva *mahāsattva* dwelling on this ground often becomes a Suyāma Heaven King who is extensively devoted to instructing beings in doing away with the conception of a truly existent self.[137]

正體字

多教化眾生。破於我心。所作善業。若布施
510b28‖ 若愛語。若利益若同事。皆不離念佛。不離念
510b29‖ 法。不離念諸菩薩摩訶薩為伴。乃至不離念
510c01‖ 具足一切種智。常生是心。我當何時於一切
510c02‖ 眾生中。為首為尊。乃至於一切眾生中。為依
510c03‖ 止者。是菩薩摩訶薩。若欲如是勤行精進。須
510c04‖ 臾之間。得百億三昧。乃至示現百億菩薩。以
510c05‖ 為眷屬。若以願力。自在示現。過於此數。若干
510c06‖ 百千萬億那由他不可計劫。爾時金剛藏菩
510c07‖ 薩。欲重明此義。而說偈言
510c08‖ 諸菩薩具足　修治明地已
510c09‖ 觀諸眾生性　法性世間性
510c10‖ 虛空性識性　三界性信解
510c11‖ 深心清淨故　得入第四地 {7}
510c12‖ 即於如來家　增長得勢力

简体字

多教化众生破于我心。所作善业，若布施、若爱语、若利益、若同事，皆不离念佛、不离念法、不离念诸菩萨摩诃萨为伴，乃至不离念具足一切种智，常生是心：‘我当何时，于一切众生中为首为尊，乃至于一切众生中为依止者？’是菩萨摩诃萨，若欲如是勤行精进，须臾之间得百亿三昧，乃至示现百亿菩萨以为眷属；若以愿力，自在示现过于此数，若干百千万亿那由他不可计劫。”

尔时，金刚藏菩萨欲重明此义，而说偈言：

“诸菩萨具足，　修治明地已，
观诸众生性，　法性世间性，
虚空性识性，　三界性信解，
深心清净故，　得入第四地。
即于如来家，　增长得势力，

b. The Bodhisattva's Mindfulness

In all of the good karmic works that he does, whether in the sphere of giving, pleasing words, beneficial actions, or joint endeavors, he never departs from his mindfulness of the Buddha, never departs from his mindfulness of the Dharma, never departs from his mindfulness of his companions among the bodhisattva *mahāsattvas* and so forth until we come to his never departing from his mindfulness of his quest to achieve complete fulfillment of the knowledge of all modes.

c. The Bodhisattva's Aspiration to Serve Beings

He always brings to mind this thought: "Oh, when will I finally be able to become one who serves all beings as a leader, one worthy of veneration?" and so forth until we come to his thinking, "Oh, when will I finally be able to become one upon whom all beings can rely?"

d. The Consequences of the Bodhisattva's Application of Vigor

If this bodhisattva *mahāsattva* wishes to bring diligent vigor to bear, then, in but a moment, he will become able to acquire a hundred *koṭis* of samādhis, and so forth until we come to his becoming able to manifest a hundred *koṭis* of bodhisattvas. Were he to avail himself of the power of vows, he could freely manifest these phenomena in even greater numbers so large that one could never count them even in however many hundreds of thousands of myriads of *koṭis* of *nayutas* of kalpas one might attempt to do so.

14. Vajragarbha Bodhisattva's Summarizing Verses

At that time, Vajragarbha Bodhisattva, wishing to once again clarify his meaning, thereupon uttered verses, saying:

"Bodhisattvas, having already completely
cultivated the Ground of Shining Light,
then contemplate the realms of beings,
the Dharma realm, the realms of the worlds,

the realms of empty space, the realms of consciousness,
the three realms, and [the realms of] resolute intentions and
resolute convictions.[138] Then, due to having purified
[the previous ground], they are able to enter the fourth ground.[139] {7}

They immediately acquire increasing strength
within the clan of the Tathāgatas
through irreversible [resolute intentions] in the path to buddhahood,
indestructible faith in the Three Jewels,
contemplation of production and extinction, and non-production, {8}

正體字

510c13‖ 不退於佛道　三寶不壞信
510c14‖ 觀生滅無作 {8} 知世間轉行
510c15‖ 從業而有生　生死涅槃異
510c16‖ 知眾生諸業　觀法先後際
510c17‖ 不住常滅相　佛家生勢力 {9}
510c18‖ 諸大菩薩等　得如是法已
510c19‖ 憐愍諸眾生　習身受心法
510c20‖ 內外四念處 {10} 依止於厭離
510c21‖ 亦依止寂滅　迴向於涅槃
510c22‖ 除滅惡法故　善法得增長
510c23‖ 習行四正法　修四如意分
510c24‖ 習行於五根　及以修五力
510c25‖ 修習七覺意　行於八聖道 {11}
510c26‖ 修習如是法　皆為眾生故
510c27‖ 本願之所助　慈悲心為首
510c28‖ 求覓一切智　為淨諸佛土
510c29‖ 成十力功德 {12} 無畏不共法
511a01‖ 諸音聲言說　甚深妙道法
511a02‖ 及無礙解脫　大智慧方便 {13}
511a03‖ 從身見為首　六十二見等

简体字

不退于佛道，　三宝不坏信。
观生灭无作，　知世间转行，
从业而有生，　生死涅槃异。
知众生诸业，　观法先后际，
不住常灭相，　佛家生势力。
诸大菩萨等，　得如是法已，
怜愍诸众生，　习身受心法，
内外四念处，　依止于厌离，
亦依止寂灭，　回向于涅槃。
除灭恶法故，　善法得增长，
习行四正法，　修四如意分，
习行于五根，　及以修五力，
修习七觉意，　行于八圣道，
修习如是法，　皆为众生故。
本愿之所助，　慈悲心为首，
求觅一切智，　为净诸佛土，
成十力功德，　无畏不共法，
诸音声言说，　甚深妙道法，
及无碍解脱，　大智慧方便。
从身见为首，　六十二见等，

understanding of the actions involved in worlds' transformations,
understanding that it is due to karmic actions that birth exists,
understanding of the distinctions involved in *saṃsāra* and nirvāṇa,
understanding of all the karmic actions of beings,
contemplation of dharmas' past and future, and understanding
their characteristics of non-abiding and constant destruction.
Thereby born into Buddha's clan, they develop strength within it.[140] {9}

When great bodhisattvas and such
have successfully acquired such dharmas as these,
they feel kindly pity for all beings,
practice the contemplation of body, feelings, mind, and dharmas
in inward and outward focus on the four stations of mindfulness, {10}

and, in this, rely upon detachment and rely upon dispassion
while also relying upon quiescence,[141]
dedicating this then to the realization of nirvāṇa.
Through ridding themselves of bad dharmas,
good dharmas then successfully increase and grow,
this through practice of the four dharmas of the right efforts.

They cultivate the four factors essential to psychic powers,
cultivate the five root-faculties,
also use them in cultivating the five powers,
cultivate the seven limbs of bodhi,
and practice the eightfold path of the Āryas.[142] {11}

Their cultivation of all such dharmas,
is done entirely for the sake of beings,
in order to be assisted by their original vows, in order to
practice kindness and keep the mind of compassion foremost,
in order to facilitate their quest to acquire all-knowledge,
in order to engage in purification of the buddha lands,
in order to develop the meritorious qualities of the ten powers, {12}

the fearlessnesses, the dharmas exclusive to the Buddhas,
their voices and modes of speech,
and the dharmas of the extremely profound and sublime path,
as well as in order to accord with their unimpeded liberations, and
to further contemplation of their great wisdom and skillful means.[143] {13}

With the view imputing an existent self associated with the body
as chief among the sixty-two views that include
views conceiving existence of beings and existence of persons,
and views conceiving of the existence of a lifespan and a knower,
as well as all the bases of attachment

正體字

511a04‖ 眾生見人見　命者知者見
511a05‖ 於諸陰界入　之所貪著處
511a06‖ 得是第四地　皆悉已除斷 {14}
511a07‖ 隨斷煩惱業　其心亦隨淨
511a08‖ 諸所作善業　皆為救世間 {15}
511a09‖ 菩薩柔軟心　常不為放逸
511a10‖ 堪用心直心　求利眾生心
511a11‖ 如此所求事　皆為無上道
511a12‖ 大智慧職位　利益世間故 {16}
511a13‖ 深心敬養師　如說樂修行
511a14‖ 知恩報恩者　易化無瞋恨
511a15‖ 無有邪曲心　柔和同止樂
511a16‖ 修習如是法　精進不退轉 {17}
511a17‖ 菩薩住是地　深心及直心
511a18‖ 淨心與信解　皆轉得明淨
511a19‖ 增長諸善根　垢濁疑悔法
511a20‖ 如是等諸事　皆悉得除滅 {18}
511a21‖ 諸菩薩住是　第四焰地中
511a22‖ 得值無量佛　諮受所說法
511a23‖ 於是諸佛所　出家難沮壞

简体字

众生见人见，　命者知者见，
于诸阴界入，　之所贪著处，
得是第四地，　皆悉已除断。
随断烦恼业，　其心亦随净，
诸所作善业，　皆为救世间。
菩萨柔软心，　常不为放逸，
堪用心直心，　求利众生心，
如此所求事，　皆为无上道，
大智慧职位，　利益世间故。
深心敬养师，　如说乐修行，
知恩报恩者，　易化无瞋恨，
无有邪曲心，　柔和同止乐，
修习如是法，　精进不退转。
菩萨住是地，　深心及直心，
净心与信解，　皆转得明净，
增长诸善根，　垢浊疑悔法，
如是等诸事，　皆悉得除灭。
诸菩萨住是，　第四焰地中，
得值无量佛，　咨受所说法，
于是诸佛所，　出家难沮坏，

within the aggregates, sense realms and sense bases—
Upon acquiring entry into this fourth ground,
all of them are entirely cut off and done away with. {14}

As karmic actions associated with the afflictions are cut off,
their minds become correspondingly more purified.
All the good karmic actions in which they then engage
are done entirely for the sake of rescuing inhabitants of the world. {15}

The bodhisattva possesses a gentle mind
that is never allowed to fall into negligence,
the mind tractable to use, the straight mind,
and the mind that strives to be of benefit to beings.

All such matters that he strives to accomplish
are done in order to acquire the unsurpassable path's
station of consecration wherein one is possessed of great wisdom
and in order to be of benefit to those in the world. {16}

He acts with a deep mind in revering and supporting his teachers,
delights in cultivating in the manner he is taught,
is cognizant of kindnesses received, knows to repay kindnesses,
is easy to teach, is free of hatred or enmity,

is free of any sort of devious motivation,
is gently congenial, dwells happily together with others,
and cultivates such dharmas as these
vigorously and without retreating from them. {17}

As for the resolute intentions and higher aspirations
of the bodhisattva dwelling on this ground,
he purifies his intentions and resolute faith to the point that
that they all become ever more brightly shining in their purity.

He increases all his roots of goodness
while entirely ridding himself
of defiling turbidity, the dharmas of doubt and regret,
and all other such matters. {18}

The bodhisattvas who abide here
on the fourth ground, the Ground of Blazing Brilliance,
are able to encounter countlessly many buddhas
and inquire into and receive the Dharma that they teach.

In all the places where these buddhas dwell,
they leave the home life and become difficult to impede,
and, in this, they are comparable to true gold used in adornments
that is such that no other sort of gold can match it. {19}

The meritorious qualities, resolute intentions,

正體字

511a24║ 如真金莊嚴　餘金所不及 {19}
511a25║ 菩薩住是地　諸功德深心
511a26║ 智慧及方便　所行清淨道
511a27║ 乃至千億魔　皆所不能壞
511a28║ 如真妙明珠　不為水雨敗 {20}
511a29║ 菩薩住是地　天人所供養
511b01║ 多作夜摩王　能轉諸邪見
511b02║ 所作諸善業　皆為佛智慧
511b03║ 其心常堅固　不可得動轉 {21}
511b04║ 若勤行精進　得百億三昧
511b05║ 能見百億佛　願力則過是 {22}
511b06║ 如是第四地　清淨名為焰
511b07║ 無量福慧者　今已解說竟 {23}

简体字

如真金庄严，　余金所不及。
菩萨住是地，　诸功德深心，
智慧及方便，　所行清净道，
乃至千亿魔，　皆所不能坏，
如真妙明珠，　不为水雨败。
菩萨住是地，　天人所供养，
多作夜摩王，　能转诸邪见，
所作诸善业，　皆为佛智慧，
其心常坚固，　不可得动转。
若勤行精进，　得百亿三昧，
能见百亿佛，　愿力则过是。
如是第四地，　清净名为焰，
无量福慧者，　今已解说竟。”

wisdom, and skillful means
involved in the pure path coursed in
by the bodhisattva who dwells on this ground

are such that even a thousand *koṭis* of *māras*
all assailing him in unison could not destroy.
He becomes like a marvelously radiant pearl
that cannot be ruined even by floods or rains. {20}

The bodhisattva dwelling on this ground
is one to whom both devas and humans present offerings.
He often becomes a Suyāma Heaven king
well able to overturn any of the wrong views.

All the good karmic deeds he carries out
are done for the sake of gaining the Buddha's wisdom.
His resolve is forever solid
and such that it cannot be shaken or turned back. {21}

If he devotes himself to the diligent practice of vigor,
he succeeds in acquiring a hundred *koṭis* of samādhis,
becomes able to see a hundred *koṭis* of buddhas,
and, if resorting to the power of vows, can exceed even this. {22}

We now come here to the end
of this explanatory discussion of the fourth ground
which, practiced by one with measureless merit and wisdom,
is pure and renowned as "the ground of Blazing Brilliance." {23}

The End of Chapter Four

正體字

511b08║ [1]難勝地第五
511b09║ 諸菩薩聞是　第四地行法
511b10║ 心皆大歡喜　踊躍無有量
511b11║ 雨天眾寶花　雰雰如[2]雪下
511b12║ 咸讚言善哉　金剛藏大士 {1}
511b13║ 他化自在王　與諸眷屬等
511b14║ 於上虛空中　心皆大歡喜 {2}
511b15║ 放眾妙光明　作天諸伎樂
511b16║ 歌歎佛功德　并及菩薩眾
511b17║ 天諸婇女等　各以清妙音
511b18║ 同聲[3]稱讚佛　而說如是言 {3}
511b19║ 世尊久遠來　勤苦所求願
511b20║ 無上正真道　於今始乃得
511b21║ 利益天人者　久乃今得[4]見
511b22║ 釋迦牟尼佛　今至於天宮 {4}
511b23║ 從久遠已來　今始異相動
511b24║ 久遠世已來　今始放妙光

简体字

难胜地第五

诸菩萨闻是，　第四地行法，
心皆大欢喜，　踊跃无有量，
雨天众宝华，　雰雰如雪下，
咸赞言善哉！　金刚藏大士，
他化自在王，　与诸眷属等，
于上虚空中，　心皆大欢喜，
放众妙光明，　作天诸伎乐，
歌叹佛功德。　并及菩萨众，
天诸婇女等，　各以清妙音，
同声称赞佛，　而说如是言：
“世尊久远来，　勤苦所求愿，
无上正真道，　于今始乃得！
利益天人者，　久乃今得见！
释迦牟尼佛，　今至于天宫，
从久远已来，　今始异相动！
久远世已来，　今始放妙光！

Chapter Five
The Difficult-to-Conquer Ground

E. The Fifth Ground: The Difficult-to-Conquer Ground

1. The Fifth Ground's Introductory Verses and Dharma Request

When all the bodhisattvas there came to the end of hearing this
teaching on the fourth ground's practice dharmas,
their minds were all so filled with great joyfulness,
that they were moved to boundless exultation.

There rained down the devas' many sorts of jewels and blossoms
that floated softly down like falling snow.
They all then uttered praises in unison: "It is good indeed,
Vajragarbha, O Greatly Eminent One." {1}

The Paranirmita Vaśavartin Heaven King
together with his entire retinue and others,
abiding above in space,
all felt immense joyous delight, {2}

emanated a multitude of marvelously radiant light rays,
created all manner of celestial music,
and sang praises of the meritorious qualities of the Buddha
and that assembly of bodhisattvas.

The celestial nymphs and others,
each with a clear and sublime voice,
united their voices in praising the Buddha,
and thereupon uttered these words: {3}

"That which the Bhagavat has so assiduously and arduously sought
and vowed to bring about from long ago until the present,
namely, realization of the unsurpassable genuine path,
now, for the first time, has finally been obtained.

"This benefactor of devas and men,
after so long, we have now been able to see:
Śākyamuni buddha
has now arrived here in this celestial palace. {4}

"What from long ago in the past till the present, is unprecedented,
we now for the first time meet as the stirring of extraordinary signs.
What from long ago in the past till the present, is unprecedented,
we now for the first time meet as the emanation of marvelous light.

正體字

511b25‖ 眾生從久來　今始得安樂
511b26‖ 久[5]來方得聞　大慈悲德音 {5}
511b27‖ 度諸功德岸　久遠今乃值
511b28‖ 聖王能悉破　憍慢我心等 {6}
511b29‖ 無比可供養　而今得供養
511c01‖ 能開諸天道　使得一切智 {7}
511c02‖ 世尊甚清淨　無量如虛空
511c03‖ 不染於世法　如蓮花在水
511c04‖ 處世最高大　猶如大海中
511c05‖ 須彌金山王　是故歡喜禮 {8}
511c06‖ 如是諸天女　各以眾妙音
511c07‖ 敬心歌頌已　默然而觀佛 {9}
511c08‖ 解脫月菩薩　請金剛藏言
511c09‖ 菩薩得五地　相貌之因緣 {10}
511c10‖ {A}金剛藏菩薩摩訶薩。語解脫月菩薩言。佛子。
511c11‖ 諸菩薩摩訶薩。已具足第四地。欲得第五地。
511c12‖ 以十平等心。能入第五地。何等為十。一過去
511c13‖ 佛法平等。

简体字

众生从久来，　今始得安乐！
久来方得闻，　大慈悲德音，
度诸功德岸，　久远今乃值！
圣王能悉破，　憍慢我心等，
无比可供养，　而今得供养，
能开诸天道，　使得一切智！
世尊甚清净，　无量如虚空，
不染于世法，　如莲华在水；
处世最高大，　犹如大海中，
须弥金山王，　是故欢喜礼！”
如是诸天女，　各以众妙音，
敬心歌颂已，　默然而观佛。
解脱月菩萨，　请金刚藏言：
“菩萨得五地，　相貌之因缘？”

金刚藏菩萨摩诃萨，语解脱月菩萨言：“佛子，诸菩萨摩诃萨已具足第四地，欲得第五地，以十平等心，能入第五地。何等为十？一、过去佛法平等，

"What beings have not had from long ago on up to the present,
they now first acquire as such peace and happiness.
What they have not heard from long ago onward, they now hear
as this sound of the great kindness and the great compassion. {5}

"The crossing on over to the far shore of meritorious qualities,
from long ago till now, never reached, they now are able to reach,
including what the King of Āryas has been able to entirely demolish,
namely, arrogance, conception of the existence of a self, and such. {6}

"The one incomparable as an object of offerings,
we have now become able here to present with offerings,
It is he who is able to open forth the path to the heavens
and bring about the realization of all-knowledge. {7}

"The Bhagavat's profound purity
is so immeasurably vast as to be comparable to empty space.
He remains undefiled by any of the dharmas of the world, and,
in this, he is comparable to a lotus blossom residing atop the water.

"He abides in the world as the one who is the most lofty and great,
and, in this, compares to Mount Sumeru, king of golden mountains,
that abides in the middle of the great sea.
Thus it is that we now, so filled with joy, bow here in reverence." {8}

Thus it was that these celestial maidens,
each with a multitude of marvelous sounds,
and with reverent minds, having finished their songs of praise,
then fell silent and thereupon gazed up at the Buddha. {9}

Liberation Moon bodhisattva
then presented a request to Vajragarbha, asking
about the causes and conditions of the characteristic features
of the bodhisattva's acquisition of the fifth ground. {10}

2. Vajragarbha Begins the Fifth Ground's Explanation

{A} Vajragarbha Bodhisattva Mahāsattva then informed Liberation Moon Bodhisattva, saying:

3. Ten Impartial Resolute Intentions Enabling Fifth Ground Access

O, Son of the Buddha, those bodhisattva *mahāsattvas* who have already completely fulfilled their practice on the fourth ground and then wish to be able to enter the fifth ground then employ ten types of equally regarding resolute intentions[144] to enable entry into the fifth ground. What then are those ten? They are:

First, equally regarding resolute intentions toward the Dharma of the buddhas of the past.

正體字

二未來佛法平等。三現在佛法平
511c14‖ 等。四戒淨平等。五心淨平等。六除見疑悔淨
511c15‖ 平等。七知道非道淨平等。八行知見淨平等。
511c16‖ 九諸菩提分法轉勝淨平等。十等化眾生淨
511c17‖ 平等。諸佛子。諸菩薩摩訶薩。以是十平等淨
511c18‖ 心。具[6]足得入於五地。{B}善修菩提法故。深心
511c19‖ 清淨故。求轉勝道故。則能得佛道。是菩薩。
511c20‖ 得大願力。以慈悲心。不捨於一切。以得念慧
511c21‖ 心道理之勢力。修習於福慧。不捨起方便。欲
511c22‖ 得轉勝道上地。明觀法受諸佛神力所護。生
511c23‖ 定不退心。{C}如[7]實知是苦聖諦。是苦集諦。是

简体字

二、未来佛法平等，三、现在佛法平等，四、戒净平等，五、心净平等，六、除见疑悔净平等，七、知道非道净平等，八、行知见净平等，九、诸菩提分法转胜净平等，十、等化众生净平等。

“诸佛子，诸菩萨摩诃萨以是十平等净心，具足得入于五地。善修菩提法故，深心清净故，求转胜道故，则能得佛道。是菩萨得大愿力，以慈悲心不舍于一切，以得念慧心道理之势力，修习于福慧，不舍起方便，欲得转胜道上地，明观法受，诸佛神力所护，生定不退心，如实知是苦圣谛、是苦集谛、

Second, equally regarding resolute intentions toward the Dharma of the buddhas of the future.

Third, equally regarding resolute intentions toward the Dharma of the buddhas of the present.

Fourth, pure equally regarding resolute intentions toward the moral precepts.

Fifth, pure equally regarding resolute intentions toward the mind.[145]

Sixth, pure equally regarding resolute intentions toward ridding oneself of views, doubts, and regretfulness.

Seventh, pure equally regarding resolute intentions toward the knowledge of what is and is not the path.

Eighth, pure equally regarding resolute intentions toward the knowledge and vision associated with the practices.

Ninth, pure equally regarding resolute intentions toward achieving ever increasing supremacy in [the practice of] the dharmas constituting the limbs of bodhi.

And tenth, pure equally regarding resolute intentions toward the equal teaching of beings.

Sons of the Buddha, it is through these ten types of equally regarding pure resolute intentions that the bodhisattva *mahāsattvas* become fully able to enter the fifth ground.

4. The Bodhisattvas' Bases for Buddhahood and Irreversible Resolve

{B} It is due to thorough cultivation of the dharmas assisting realization of bodhi, due to purification of resolute intentions,[146] and due to striving for ever more superior progress on the path that they succeed in achieving buddhahood.

It is due to acquiring the power of great vows, due to relying on the mind of kindness and compassion to never forsake anyone, due to acquiring the power of the mindful and wise mind's reasoning, due to cultivating merit and knowledge; due to never relinquishing the creation of skillful means; due to striving to acquire the ever more superior path's dharmas enabling illumination and contemplation of higher grounds, and due to receiving the protection of the Buddhas' spiritual powers that this bodhisattva then brings forth the definite and irreversible resolve.

5. The Bodhisattva's Knowledge of the Truths

{C} He knows in accordance with reality: "This is the Āryas' truth of suffering, this is the truth of the accumulation of suffering, this

正體字

511c24‖ 苦滅諦。是至[8]滅苦道諦。是菩薩。善知世諦。
511c25‖ 善知第一義諦。善知相諦。善知差別諦。善知
511c26‖ 示成諦。善知事諦。善知生起諦。善知盡無生
511c27‖ 諦。善知令入道諦。次第成菩薩諸地故。善知
511c28‖ 習如來智諦。爾時菩薩。常在一乘[9]故。善知
511c29‖ 第一義諦。隨眾生意。令歡喜故。知世諦。分別
512a01‖ 諸法自相故。知相諦。諸法各異故。知差別諦。
512a02‖ 分別諸陰界入故。知示成諦。以身心苦惱故。
512a03‖ 知苦諦。諸道生相續故。知集諦。畢竟滅一切
512a04‖ 惱熱故。知滅諦。起不二法故。知道諦。以一切
512a05‖ 種智。知一切法次第。成一切菩薩地故。善知
512a06‖ 習如來智諦。以信解力故。知非得無盡諦智。

简体字

是苦灭谛、是至灭苦道谛。是菩萨善知世谛，善知第一义谛，善知相谛，善知差别谛，善知示成谛，善知事谛，善知生起谛，善知尽无生谛，善知令入道谛，次第成菩萨诸地故，善知习如来智谛。尔时菩萨常在一乘故，善知第一义谛，随众生意令欢喜故知世谛；分别诸法自相故，知相谛；诸法各异故，知差别谛；分别诸阴、界、入故，知示成谛；以身心苦恼故，知苦谛；诸道生相续故，知集谛；毕竟灭一切恼热故，知灭谛；起不二法故，知道谛；以一切种智，知一切法次第，成一切菩萨地故，善知习如来智谛；以信解力故，知非得无尽谛智。

is the truth of the cessation of suffering, and this is the truth of the path to the cessation of suffering." This bodhisattva:

Knows well worldly truth;[147]

Knows well the truth of the supreme meaning;[148]

Knows well the truth of characteristic signs;[149]

Knows well the truth of differentiating distinctions;[150]

Knows well the truth of the manifestation of establishment;[151]

Knows well the truth of phenomena;[152]

Knows well the truth of production;[153]

Knows well the truth of cessation with no further production;[154]

Knows well the truth of the causation for entering the path;[155]

And, by sequentially successful establishment in all of the grounds of the bodhisattva, he knows well the truth associated with the cultivation of the Tathāgata's knowledge.[156]

At this time, the bodhisattva:

Knows well the truth of the supreme meaning through always residing within the One Vehicle;[157]

Knows worldly truth through adapting to beings' mental intentions and thereby causing them to be delighted;[158]

Knows the truth of characteristic signs through distinguishing dharmas' individual characteristic signs;[159]

Knows the truth of differentiating distinctions through knowing the individual differences between dharmas;[160]

Knows the truth of the manifestation of establishment through distinguishing the aggregates, sense realms, and sense bases;[161]

Knows the truth of suffering through the suffering and anguish associated with body and mind;[162]

Knows the truth of accumulation through the continuities in rebirths in all the paths of rebirth;[163]

Knows the truth of cessation through the ultimate extinguishing of all the heat of the afflictions;[164]

Knows the truth of the path through bringing forth the dharma of non-duality;[165]

And knows well the truth associated with cultivating the Tathāgata's knowledge through using the knowledge of all modes to know the sequence involved in all dharmas and in perfection of all the bodhisattva grounds.[166]

It is because of the power of resolute faith[167] that he achieves such a knowing awareness, for this is not a case of his having acquired the inexhaustibly complete knowledge of these truths.

正體字

512a07‖ {D}菩薩如是。以此諸諦智。如實知一切有為法。
512a08‖ 虛偽誑詐。敗壞相。假住須臾。誑惑凡[1]夫人。
512a09‖ 菩薩爾時。於眾生中。大悲轉勝。而現在前。能
512a10‖ 生大慈光明。{E}得如是智慧力。不捨一切眾生。
512a11‖ 常求佛智慧。如實觀一切有為法。先際後際。
512a12‖ 知眾生從先際。無明有愛故。生流轉生死。於
512a13‖ 五陰歸處。不能動發。增大苦惱聚。是中無我
512a14‖ 無我所。無眾生無人。無知者無壽命者。後際
512a15‖ 亦如是。如是無所有。而愚癡貪著不斷。不知
512a16‖ 無邊有出無出。{F}爾時作是念。凡夫眾生。甚為
512a17‖ 可怪。無明癡故。有無量無邊阿僧祇身。已滅
512a18‖ 今滅當滅。如是常受生死。不能於身生厭離
512a19‖ 想。轉更增長機關苦身。常為生死水漂。不能
512a20‖ 得返歸五陰舍。不能捨離。不畏四大毒蛇。不
512a21‖ 能拔出憍慢見箭。不能滅除貪恚癡焰。不能
512a22‖ 破壞無明愚闇。

简体字

菩萨如是以此诸谛智，如实知一切有为法虚伪诳诈、败坏相、假住须臾，诳惑凡夫人。

“菩萨尔时于众生中，大悲转胜而现在前，能生大慈光明，得如是智慧力，不舍一切众生，常求佛智慧。如实观一切有为法先际、后际：知众生从先际，无明有爱故生，流转生死，于五阴归处不能动发，增大苦恼聚，是中无我、无我所、无众生、无人、无知者、无寿命者；后际亦如是，如是无所有，而愚痴贪著不断，不知无边有出无出。尔时作是念：‘凡夫众生甚为可怪！无明痴故，有无量无边阿僧祇身已灭、今灭、当灭。如是常受生死，不能于身生厌离想，转更增长机关苦身，常为生死水漂不能得返，归五阴舍不能舍离，不畏四大毒蛇，不能拔出憍慢见箭，不能灭除贪恚痴焰，不能破坏无明愚闇，

6. The Bodhisattva's Resultant Generation of Compassion & Kindness

{D} So it is that the bodhisattva, through the knowledge associated with these truths, knows all conditioned dharmas as false and deceptive, as characterized by ruination, as merely conventionally and momentarily abiding, and as conducive to the deception and delusion of the common person.

At this time, the bodhisattva's great compassion for beings becomes ever more supreme and directly manifest and he is then able to bring forth the light of great kindness.

7. The Bodhisattva's Contemplation of the Causality of Beings' Plight

{E} Having acquired the power of knowledge such as this, he never forsakes any being and always strives to acquire the Buddha's knowledge. He contemplates all past and future conditioned dharmas in accordance with reality and thereby knows that it is from previous ignorance, becoming, and craving that beings produce their flowing along in cyclic births and deaths wherein they are unable to move to escape from their place of refuge within the five aggregates and thus increase their great accumulation of suffering and anguish. He knows that, within this, there is no self, nothing belonging to a self, no being, no person, no agent of knowing, and no entity possessed of a lifespan. He knows this is also just so in the future and also knows whether or not there is any escape to be had from this ceaseless deluded covetous attachment and boundless ignorance.

{F} He then thinks:

> Common people and other beings are all so very strange. Because of their ignorance and delusion, they take on a countless and unbounded number of *asaṃkhyeyas*[168] of bodies that have been destroyed, are now being destroyed, and will be destroyed in the future. In this way, they are forever subject to births and deaths. They are unable to bring forth thoughts of renunciation for the body, but rather ever increase the mechanisms for producing bodies subject to suffering.
>
> They are always swept along in the waters of the stream of cyclic births and deaths wherein they are unable to go against its current. They take refuge in the abode of the five aggregates and are unable to abandon it. They do not fear the poisonous snakes of the four great elements and are unable to extricate the arrows of their own pride and views. They are unable to extinguish the blazing fire of their desire, hatred, and delusion, are unable to destroy the darkness of ignorance and delusion, and

正體字

不能乾竭愛著大海。不求十
512a23‖ 力大聖導師。常隨魔意。於生死城中。多為諸
512a24‖ 惡覺觀所轉。{G}如是苦惱孤窮眾生。無有救者。
512a25‖ 無有舍者。無有究竟道者。唯我一人。獨無等
512a26‖ 侶。修集福德智慧。以是資糧。令此一切眾生。
512a27‖ 得住畢竟清淨。乃至使得一切法中。佛無礙智
512a28‖ 力。{H}如是思惟。從正觀生於智力。發願所作。一
512a29‖ 切善根。皆為度諸眾生故。為一切眾生求好
512b01‖ 事故。求安樂故。為利益一切眾生故。為解脫
512b02‖ 一切眾生故。為一切眾生無苦惱故。為一切
512b03‖ 眾生無麁惡故。為一切眾生心清淨故。為調伏
512b04‖ 一切眾生故。為滅一切眾生諸憂惱苦滿其願
512b05‖ 故。{I}是菩薩。爾時住此第五難勝地中。不忘諸
512b06‖ 法故。名為念者。決定智慧故名為智者。知經
512b07‖ 書意。次第故。名為有道者。

简体字

不能干竭爱著大海，不求十力大圣导师，常随魔意，于生死城中多为诸恶觉观所转。如是苦恼孤穷众生，无有救者，无有舍者，无有究竟道者。唯我一人，独无等侣，修集福德智慧。以是资粮，令此一切众生得住毕竟清净，乃至使得一切法中佛无碍智力。’如是思惟，从正观生于智力，发愿所作一切善根，皆为度诸众生故，为一切众生求好事故，求安乐故，为利益一切众生故，为解脱一切众生故，为一切众生无苦恼故，为一切众生无粗恶故，为一切众生心清净故，为调伏一切众生故，为灭一切众生诸忧恼苦满其愿故。

“是菩萨尔时住此第五难胜地中，不忘诸法故，名为念者；决定智慧故，名为智者；知经书意次第故，名为有道者；

are unable to dry up the great sea of their cravings and attachments.

They do not seek to encounter the great *ārya* and guide who possesses the ten powers. They always follow along with resolute intentions influenced by *māras*[169] and, within the city of cyclic births and deaths, they are for the most part diverted by bad ideation and mental discursion.[170]

{G} Such suffering, solitary, and poverty-stricken beings have no one to rescue them, no one to shelter them, and no one possessed of the ultimate path. There is only myself, this one person, who, with no comparable companions, will proceed to cultivate and accumulate merit and wisdom. I will then use these provisions to cause all these beings to dwell in a state of utmost purity and then continue on in this until they are caused to acquire the Buddha's unimpeded power of wisdom with respect to all dharmas.

8. The Bodhisattva's Compassionate Dedication of Roots of Goodness

{H} He also contemplates thus: "It is through right contemplation that one is able to develop the power of knowledge." He vows that he will devote all the roots of goodness he accumulates to the liberation of beings, doing so for the sake of:[171]

Rescuing all beings;
Seeking the best circumstances for all beings;
Seeking happiness for all beings;
Benefiting all beings;
Bringing about the liberation of all beings;
Causing all beings to have no more suffering or anguish;
Causing all beings to leave behind all coarse and evil endeavors;
Causing the purification of all beings' minds;
Causing all beings to adopt the training;
And causing the extinguishing of all beings' misery and suffering while also bringing about the fulfillment of their wishes.

9. The Fifth Ground Bodhisattva's Qualities and Their Bases

{I} As for this bodhisattva dwelling on this fifth ground, the Difficult-to-Conquer Ground:

Through never forgetting any dharma, he becomes one possessed of mindfulness;
Through resolute and definite wisdom, he becomes one who is wise;
Through understanding the intent of the scriptural texts and their correct sequence, he becomes one possessed of the path;

正體字

自護護彼故。名為
512b08‖ 有慚愧者。不捨持戒故。名為堅心者。善思惟
512b09‖ 是處非處故。名為覺者。不隨他故。名為隨智
512b10‖ 者。善分別諸法章句義故。名為隨慧者。善修
512b11‖ 禪定故。名為得神通者。隨世間法行故。名為
512b12‖ 方便者。[1]善集福德資糧故。名為無厭足者。常
512b13‖ 求智慧因緣故。名為不捨者。集大慈大悲因
512b14‖ 緣故。名為無疲惓者。常正憶念故。名為遠離
512b15‖ 破戒者。深心求佛十力四無所畏十八不共法
512b16‖ 故。名為常念佛法者。常令眾生離惡修善故。
512b17‖ 名為莊嚴佛國者。種諸福德莊嚴三十二相
512b18‖ 八十種好故。名為行種種善業者。求莊嚴佛
512b19‖ 身口意故。名為常行精進者。供養一切說法
512b20‖ 菩薩故。名為樂大恭敬者。

简体字

自护护彼故，名为有惭愧者；不舍持戒故，名为坚心者；善思惟是处非处故，名为觉者；不随他故，名为随智者；善分别诸法章句义故，名为随慧者；善修禅定故，名为得神通者；随世间法行故，名为方便者；善集福德资粮故，名为无厌足者；常求智慧因缘故，名为不舍者；集大慈大悲因缘故，名为无疲惓者；常正忆念故，名为远离破戒者；深心求佛十力、四无所畏、十八不共法故，名为常念佛法者；常令众生离恶修善故，名为庄严佛国者；种诸福德庄严三十二相、八十种好故，名为行种种善业者；求庄严佛身口意故，名为常行精进者；供养一切说法菩萨故，名为乐大恭敬者；

Through his attention to guarding both himself and others, he becomes one possessed of a sense of shame and dread of blame;

Through never relinquishing his upholding of the moral precepts, he becomes one who possesses solidity of mind;

Through skill in contemplative assessment of what constitute correct and incorrect bases, he becomes one possessed of awakened awareness;[172]

Through not according with anything else, he becomes one who accords with knowledge;[173]

Through his ability to skillfully distinguish the intended meanings implicit in all Dharma compositions and statements, he becomes one who accords with wisdom;[174]

Through skillful cultivation of the *dhyāna* absorptions, he becomes one possessed of the spiritual superknowledges;

Through adapting to worldly dharmas in his practice, he becomes one possessed of skillful means;

{J} Through thoroughly accumulating the provision of merit,[175] he becomes one who is insatiable;

Through always seeking to acquire the causes and conditions for wisdom,[176] he becomes one who never abandons his quest;

Through his accumulation of the causes and conditions for great kindness and great compassion,[177] he becomes one who is tireless;

Through always practicing right mindfulness, he becomes one who utterly abandons the breaking of moral precepts;

Through his deep resolve in seeking to acquire the Buddha's ten powers, four fearlessnesses, and eighteen dharmas exclusive to the Buddhas, he become one who is ever mindful of the Buddha's Dharma;

Through always causing of beings to abandon what is bad and cultivate what is good, he becomes one who adorns buddha lands;

Through planting the merit for acquiring the adornments of the thirty-two major marks and eighty subsidiary signs, he becomes one who practices the many different sorts of good karmic deeds;

Through seeking to acquire the physical, verbal, and mental qualities adorning the Buddha, he becomes one who always practices vigor;

Through making offerings to all Dharma-teaching bodhisattvas, he becomes one who delights in great reverence;

正體字

一切菩薩。諸世間
512b21‖ 方便中。心無瞋礙故。名為心無礙者。常樂教
512b22‖ 化眾生故。名為晝夜遠離餘心者。{K}菩薩如是
512b23‖ 行時布施。亦教化眾生。愛語利益同事。亦教
512b24‖ 化眾生。又以色身示現。亦教化眾生。亦以說
512b25‖ 法。教化眾生。亦示菩薩行事。教化眾生。亦示
512b26‖ 諸佛大事。教化眾生。亦示生死過惡。教化眾
512b27‖ 生。亦示諸佛智慧利益。教化眾生。菩薩如是
512b28‖ 修習。以大神力種種因緣方便道。教化眾生。
512b29‖ 是菩薩。雖種種因緣方便心常在佛智。而不
512c01‖ 退失善根。{L}又復常求轉勝利益眾生法。是人
512c02‖ 利益眾生故。世間所有經書伎藝。文章算數。
512c03‖ [2]名性經書。治病醫方。所謂。治乾[3]消病。小兒
512c04‖ 病。鬼著病。蠱毒病。癩病等。伎樂歌舞。戲笑
512c05‖ 歡娛經書。

简体字

一切菩萨诸世间方便中心无瞋碍故，名为心无碍者；常乐教化众生故，名为昼夜远离余心者。菩萨如是行时布施，亦教化众生；爱语、利益、同事，亦教化众生；又以色身示现，亦教化众生；亦以说法教化众生，亦示菩萨行事教化众生，亦示诸佛大事教化众生，亦示生死过恶教化众生，亦示诸佛智慧利益教化众生。菩萨如是修习，以大神力种种因缘方便道教化众生。是菩萨虽种种因缘方便，心常在佛智，而不退失善根，又复常求转胜利益众生法。是人利益众生故，世间所有经书伎艺、文章算数、名性经书、治病医方，所谓治干消病、小儿病、鬼著病、蛊毒病、癞病等，伎乐歌舞，戏笑欢娱经书，

Through having a mind unimpeded by aversion for the expedient means all bodhisattvas resort to in the world, he becomes one whose mind is unimpeded;

And through always delighting in teaching beings, he becomes one who, both day and night, abandons any other sorts of intentions.

10. The Methods Used by the Bodhisattva in his Teaching of Beings

{K} While the bodhisattva engages in such practices as these:

He also practices giving as a means of teaching beings;

He also uses pleasing words, beneficial actions, and joint endeavors as means of teaching beings;

He also uses the manifestation of form bodies as a means of teaching beings;

He also uses the speaking of Dharma to teach beings;

He also manifests the endeavors associated with the bodhisattva practices to teach beings;

He also manifests the great endeavors of all buddhas to teach beings;

He also reveals the transgressions associated with *saṃsāra* to teach beings;

He also reveals the benefits of all buddhas' wisdom to teach beings;

And, as the bodhisattva cultivates in this manner, he uses the path that involves great spiritual powers as well as skillful means employing all different sorts of causes and conditions to teach beings.

Although this bodhisattva uses skillful means involving many different sorts of causes and conditions, his resolve always remains intent upon the knowledge of the Buddha. Thus he never retreats from or loses his roots of goodness.

11. The Bodhisattva's Adoption of an Array of Means to Benefit Beings

{L} Additionally, he always seeks ever more supreme dharmas with which to benefit beings. In order to be of benefit to beings, he becomes adept in all of the classics, skills, and cultural arts of the world, including writing, mathematical calculation, classical works on the nature of stones,[178] and medical procedures for the treating of diseases such as wasting diseases, children's diseases, diseases involving possession by ghosts, diseases involving poisoning by sorcerers, leprosy, and other such disorders.

He acquires knowledge of the classics devoted to such arts as music , singing, dance, humor, and entertainment while also

正體字

國土城[4]郭。聚落室宅。園觀池泉。
512c06‖ 華果藥草林樹。金銀摩尼珠。琉璃珊瑚虎魄。
512c07‖ 車磲馬碯。示諸寶聚。日月五星。二十八宿。占
512c08‖ 相吉凶。地動夢書怪相。身中諸相布施持戒。
512c09‖ 攝伏其心。禪定神通。四禪四無量心。四無色
512c10‖ 定。凡諸不惱眾生事。安樂眾生事。憐愍眾生
512c11‖ 故。[5]出令入諸佛無上之法。(M)菩薩住是難勝地。
512c12‖ 值數百數千數萬億佛。供養尊重讚歎。衣服
512c13‖ 飲食。臥具醫藥。親近聽法。聽法已出家。出家
512c14‖ 已。於諸佛所。聽受經法。而為法師。說法利益。
512c15‖ 得轉勝多聞[6]積三昧。乃至過百千萬億劫。不
512c16‖ 忘此事。是菩薩。爾時一切福德善根。轉勝明
512c17‖ 淨。

简体字

国土城郭、聚落室宅、园观池泉、华果、药草、林树，金、银、摩尼珠、琉璃、珊瑚、琥珀、砗磲、玛瑙，示诸宝聚，日月、五星、二十八宿，占相吉凶，地动梦书怪相，身中诸相，布施、持戒摄伏其心，禅定、神通、四禅、四无量心、四无色定。凡诸不恼众生事，安乐众生事，怜愍众生故，出令入诸佛无上之法。

“菩萨住是难胜地，值数百、数千、数万亿佛，供养尊重赞叹，衣服、饮食、卧具、医药，亲近听法，听法已出家；出家已，于诸佛所听受经法，而为法师说法利益，得转胜多闻诸三昧，乃至过百千万亿劫不忘此事。是菩萨尔时，一切福德善根转胜明净。

becoming knowledgeable in matters regarding the state, cities, regions beyond the city walls, villages, buildings and homes, parks, viewing terraces, ponds, springs, flowers, fruit, medicinal herbs, and trees.

He becomes knowledgeable about gold, silver, *maṇi* pearls, lapis lazuli, coral, amber, mother-of-pearl, carnelian, the discovery of jewel deposits, the courses of the sun, moon, five stars, and twenty-eight constellations, and the interpretation of the relative auspiciousness of signs including the strange signs appearing in association with earthquakes, dreams, and writings, and all signs appearing on a person's body.

So, too, he becomes knowledgeable regarding the practice of giving, the observance of moral precepts, the focusing of one's mind, the *dhyāna* absorptions, the spiritual superknowledges, the four *dhyānas*, the four immeasurable minds, the four formless absorptions, whatever other matters that would cause no distress to beings, and whatever matters would bring happiness to beings.

Then, out of kindly pity for beings, he brings forth these dharmas[179] in order to influence beings to enter the unsurpassed Dharma of all buddhas.

12. The Bodhisattva's Seeing and Serving of Countless Buddhas

{M} The Bodhisattva dwelling on this Difficult-to-Conquer Ground encounters many hundreds, many thousands, or many myriads of *koṭis* of buddhas to whom he makes offerings, expresses his veneration, makes praises, and presents offerings of robes, food and drink, bedding, and medicines. He draws close to them, listens to their teaching of Dharma, and, having received those teachings on Dharma, he leaves behind the home life. Having left behind the home life, he listens to and accepts the Dharma of the Sutras in the presence of those buddhas and becomes a teacher of the Dharma who proclaims the benefits of the Dharma.

13. The Bodhisattva's Purification of Qualities and Roots of Goodness

He ever increases the supremacy of his extensive learning and accumulation of samādhis up to the point where he is able to carry on such activities beyond a period of even hundreds of thousands of myriads of *koṭis* of kalpas during which he never neglects these endeavors. During this time, the meritorious qualities and roots of goodness of this bodhisattva shine forth ever more brightly in their purity.

正體字

佛子。譬如成鍊真金。以車磲磨瑩。其光轉
512c18‖ 勝。菩薩住是地中。方便智慧力故。功德善根。
512c19‖ 轉淨明勝。下地所不及。又如日月星宿。諸天
512c20‖ 宮殿。風持令去。不失法度。如是佛子。菩薩住
512c21‖ 難勝地。以方便思惟故。福德善根。轉倍明淨。
512c22‖ 而不取證。亦不疾至佛道。諸佛子。是名諸菩
512c23‖ 薩摩訶薩難勝地。[7]今已略說。菩薩摩訶薩。
512c24‖ 住是地中。多[8]作兜率陀天王。諸根猛利。能
512c25‖ 摧伏一切外道。有所作業。若布施愛語。利益
512c26‖ 同事。皆不離念佛念法。[9]念菩[10]薩伴。乃至不
512c27‖ 離念具足一切種智。我當何時。於眾生中。為
512c28‖ 首為尊。乃至於一切眾生中。為依止者。

简体字

佛子，譬如成炼真金，以砗磲磨莹，其光转胜；菩萨住是地中，方便智慧力故，功德善根转净明胜，下地所不及。又如日月星宿、诸天宫殿，风持令去，不失法度；如是，佛子，菩萨住难胜地，以方便思惟故，福德善根转倍明净，而不取证，亦不疾至佛道。

“诸佛子，是名诸菩萨摩诃萨难胜地，今已略说。菩萨摩诃萨住是地中，多作兜率陀天王，诸根猛利，能摧伏一切外道。有所作业，若布施、爱语、利益、同事，皆不离念佛、念法、念菩萨伴，乃至不离念具足一切种智：‘我当何时，于众生中为首为尊，乃至于一切众生中为依止者？’

14. Good Roots Purification Like Refining Gold & Celestial Phenomena

Sons of the Buddha, this circumstance is analogous to the refining of real gold that, when polished to a luster with *musāragalva*,[180] shines ever more supremely in its brightness. Because of the power of his skillful means and wisdom, the meritorious qualities and roots of goodness of this bodhisattva who dwells on this ground shine forth ever more supremely in their purity, doing so to a degree that those on lower grounds cannot even approach. He also becomes comparable to the sun, moon, stars, constellations, and heavenly palaces that wind-like forces support and propel along in their courses in such a way that they never depart from the normal course of things.

For such a son of the Buddha who is a bodhisattva dwelling on the Difficult-to-Conquer Ground, because of his skillful means and contemplative thought, his meritorious qualities and roots of goodness shine forth ever more brightly in their purity. Even so, he still refrains from seizing on the ultimate realization and also refrains from swiftly reaching the culmination of the path to buddhahood.

15. Vajragarbha's Final Statements About the 5th Ground Bodhisattva

Sons of the Buddha, this has been a general explanation of all bodhisattva *mahāsattvas'* Difficult-to-Conquer Ground.

a. The Bodhisattva's Station and Dharma Practice

The bodhisattva *mahāsattva* who dwells on this ground often becomes a Tuṣita Heaven king possessed of fiercely sharp faculties who is able to utterly defeat in debate the proponents of all non-Buddhist traditions.

b. The Bodhisattva's Mindfulness

In whatsoever endeavors he takes up, whether that be the practice of giving, pleasing words, beneficial actions, or joint endeavors, he never departs from his mindfulness of the Buddha, mindfulness of the Dharma, mindfulness of his bodhisattva companions, and so forth until we come to his never departing from mindfulness of his quest to achieve the perfect acquisition of the knowledge of all modes.

c. The Bodhisattva's Aspiration to Serve Beings

He thinks: "Oh, when will I finally become able to serve beings as a leader, as one worthy of veneration?," and so forth until we come to his thinking, "Oh, when will I be able to become one upon whom all beings can rely?"

正體字

諸佛
512c29║ 子。是菩薩若欲如是勤行精進。須臾之間。能
513a01║ 得千億三昧。乃至示千億菩薩。以為眷屬。若
513a02║ 以願力。神力自在復過是數。若干百千萬億
513a03║ 不可得知。爾時金剛藏菩薩欲明此義故。[1]重
513a04║ 說偈言
513a05║ 諸菩薩具足　四地行法已
513a06║ 思惟三世佛　戒等心亦等
513a07║ 除見疑悔等　道非道行等
513a08║ 觀諸平等已　得入第五地 {11}
513a09║ 四念處為弓　諸根為利箭
513a10║ 四正勤為馬　四如意為車
513a11║ 五力以為鎧　破諸煩惱賊
513a12║ 勇健不退轉　直入第五地 {12}
513a13║ 慚愧無垢衣　淨戒以為香
513a14║ 七覺為華鬘　禪定為塗香
513a15║ 智慧與方便　種種念莊嚴
513a16║ 如是得入諸　陀羅尼園林 {13}
513a17║ 四如意為足　正念為頭[2]項

简体字

诸佛子，是菩萨若欲如是勤行精进，须臾之间，能得千亿三昧，乃至示千亿菩萨以为眷属；若以愿力神力，自在复过是数，若干百千万亿不可得知。”

尔时，金刚藏菩萨欲明此义故，重说偈言：

“诸菩萨具足，　四地行法已，
思惟三世佛，　戒等心亦等，
除见疑悔等，　道非道行等，
观诸平等已，　得入第五地。
四念处为弓，　诸根为利箭，
四正勤为马，　四如意为车，
五力以为铠，　破诸烦恼贼，
勇健不退转，　直入第五地。
惭愧无垢衣，　净戒以为香，
七觉为华鬘，　禅定为涂香，
智慧与方便，　种种念庄严，
如是得入诸，　陀罗尼园林。
四如意为足，　正念为头项，

d. The Consequences of the Bodhisattva's Vigor and Vows

If this bodhisattva wishes to bring to bear just such diligence in the practice of vigor, in but a moment, he becomes able to acquire a thousand *koṭis* of samādhis and able to manifest up to a thousand *koṭis* of transformation bodhisattvas to serve as his retinue. Were he to avail himself of the power of vows, through sovereign mastery in the spiritual powers, he could manifest these phenomena in even greater numbers so large that one could never count them even in however many hundreds of thousands of myriads of *koṭis* of *nayutas* of kalpas one might attempt to do so.[181]

16. Vajragarbha Bodhisattva's Summarizing Verses

At this time, Vajragarbha Bodhisattva, wishing to clarify his meaning, then reiterated it in verses, saying:

After the bodhisattvas complete
the practice dharmas associated with the fourth ground,
they equally contemplate the Buddhas of the three periods of time,
the precepts, also equally contemplate the mind itself,

equally contemplate riddance of views, doubts, and regrets,
equally contemplate what practices are and are not the path,
and, having engaged in these equally regarding contemplations,
they become able to enter the fifth ground. {11}

They employ the four stations of mindfulness as bow,
the root faculties as their sharp arrows,
the four right efforts as their steed,
the four bases of psychic power as their vehicle,

the five powers as their sturdy armor,
and are thus able to crush the insurgent afflictions.
They are heroically brave and non-retreating
and thereby directly enter the fifth ground. {12}

They are cloaked in the stainlessness of a sense of shame and blame.
Purity in the moral precepts serves them as fragrant incense,
the seven limbs of enlightenment serve as a floral garland,
and the *dhyāna* absorptions serve them as perfume.

All of their different sorts of thought involving
wisdom together with skillful means serve as adornments.
Thus it is that they succeed in entering
into the parks and groves of the *dhāraṇīs*. {13}

The four bases of psychic power serve as their feet,
right mindfulness as the crown of their heads,

正體字

513a18║ 慈悲明淨眼　利智慧為牙
513a19║ 以空無我吼　破諸煩惱賊
513a20║ 如是人師子　能入第五地 {14}
513a21║ 是菩薩得至　住於第五地
513a22║ 轉修勝淨法　皆為佛道故
513a23║ 常行慈悲心　未曾有厭惓
513a24║ 但為修習此　第五地行法 {15}
513a25║ 深集二資糧　福德及智慧
513a26║ 種種方便力　欲得上明觀
513a27║ 常為佛所護　得成於念慧
513a28║ 次第能善觀　如實知諸諦 {16}
513a29║ 第一諦世諦　差別諦成諦
513b01║ 事生滅道諦　至無障礙諦 {17}
513b02║ 如是觀諸諦　心微妙清淨
513b03║ 雖為未能得　無障礙解脫
513b04║ 以能有智慧　及與信力故
513b05║ 得勝於一切　世間諸智慧 {18}
513b06║ 如是觀諸諦　悉知有為法
513b07║ 虛妄[3]偽詐誑　無有一堅實
513b08║ 能得於諸佛　慈悲光明分

简体字

慈悲明净眼，　利智慧为牙，
以空无我吼，　破诸烦恼贼，
如是人师子，　能入第五地。
是菩萨得至，　住于第五地，
转修胜净法，　皆为佛道故，
常行慈悲心，　未曾有厌惓，
但为修习此，　第五地行法。
深集二资粮，　福德及智慧，
种种方便力，　欲得上明观。
常为佛所护，　得成于念慧。
次第能善观，　如实知诸谛，
第一谛世谛，　差别谛成谛，
事生灭道谛，　至无障碍谛。
如是观诸谛，　心微妙清净，
虽为未能得，　无障碍解脱，
以能有智慧，　及与信力故，
得胜于一切，　世间诸智慧。
如是观诸谛，　悉知有为法，
虚妄伪诈诳，　无有一坚实，
能得于诸佛，　慈悲光明分，

kindness and compassion as their bright and pure eyes,
while it is sharp wisdom that serves as their teeth.

With the roar of emptiness and non-existence of self,
he scatters the insurgent afflictions.
Thus it is that the lion among men
becomes able to enter the fifth ground. {14}

When this bodhisattva succeeds in reaching
and then dwelling within the fifth ground,
he increasingly cultivates the dharmas of supreme purity,
all for the sake of success in the path to buddhahood.

He always implements the minds of kindness and compassion,
is never overcome by disaffection or weariness,
and has as his sole aim the cultivation
of the fifth ground's practice dharmas. {15}

He deeply cultivates the accumulation of the two types of provisions
consisting of merit and wisdom,
implements the power of all different sorts of skillful means,
and aspires to acquire the highest clarity in contemplation.

He is always protected by the Buddha,
succeeds in perfecting mindfulness and wisdom,
and is able to sequentially engage in skillful contemplation
of the truths in accordance with their reality, {16}

namely the truth of the supreme meaning, worldly truth,
the truth of differentiating distinctions, the truth of establishment,
the truths regarding phenomena, arising, cessation, and the path,
on through to the truth associated with what is unimpeded.[182] {17}

Thus it is that he contemplates the truths
with a mind that is subtle, sublime, and pure.
Although he has not yet been able to acquire
the unimpeded liberation,

through his ability to possess wisdom
together with the power of faith,
his succeeds in being that which is supreme over all
of the types of wisdom anywhere in the entire world. {18}

Contemplating the truths in this way,
he is able to entirely realize that conditioned dharmas
are false, artificial, deceptive,
and entirely devoid of any aspect that is substantially real.

He is able to acquire from that radiance possessed by the Buddhas,
a portion of the radiant light of their kindness and compassion

正體字

513b09║ 為諸眾生故　專心求佛慧 {19}
513b10║ 知有為先後　眾生甚可愍
513b11║ 墮在無明闇　愛因緣所繫
513b12║ 是菩薩能拔　世間之苦惱
513b13║ 知法無壽者　猶如草木等 {20}
513b14║ 眾生常以二　煩惱因緣故
513b15║ 從於先世來　後世亦如是
513b16║ 相續不斷絕　不能盡苦邊
513b17║ 於此生愍傷　我當度脫之 {21}
513b18║ 不出五陰舍　不畏四大害
513b19║ 不拔諸邪箭　不滅三毒[4]焰
513b20║ 不破無明闇　墮在大愛海
513b21║ 無有智慧[5]明　離大導師故 {22}
513b22║ 知如是事已　轉加勤精進
513b23║ 有所作起業　皆為度眾生
513b24║ 常[6]念正念慧　修道有慚愧
513b25║ 堅心與智慧　轉更令增益 {23}
513b26║ 修福慧無厭　持戒不羸弱
513b27║ 求多聞無倦　正修淨佛土

简体字

为诸众生故，　专心求佛慧。
知有为先后，　众生甚可愍，
堕在无明闇，　爱因缘所系。
是菩萨能拔，　世间之苦恼，
知法无寿者，　犹如草木等。
众生常以二，　烦恼因缘故，
从于先世来，　后世亦如是，
相续不断绝，　不能尽苦边，
于此生愍伤，　我当度脱之。
不出五阴舍，　不畏四大害，
不拔诸邪箭，　不灭三毒焰，
不破无明闇，　堕在大爱海，
无有智慧明，　离大导师故。
知如是事已，　转加勤精进，
有所作起业，　皆为度众生，
常念正念慧，　修道有惭愧，
坚心与智慧，　转更令增益。
修福慧无厌，　持戒不羸弱，
求多闻无倦，　正修净佛土，

and, for the sake of all beings,
focuses his mind on his quest to acquire the wisdom of the Buddha. {19}

He knows the nature of prior and later aspects of the conditioned,
realizes that beings are extremely pitiable,
that they have fallen into the darkness of ignorance, and
that they are tied up by the bonds of craving's causes and conditions.

This bodhisattva becomes able to extricate
inhabitants of the world from their suffering and anguish.
He realizes dharmas are devoid of any entity possessed of a lifespan
and that, in this sense, they are analogous to grass, trees, and so forth. {20}

He realizes too, because beings are always beset by two types
of afflictions and their associated causes and conditions,
just as they have come forth from earlier lives to the present,
so too shall they proceed in the same way on to their future lives,

continuing on without cease,
never being able to find the end of suffering's bounds.
He feels pity and sadness for these beings
and thinks, "I should see to their liberation." {21}

"They never escape from the house of the five aggregates,
do not fear the injury wrought by the four great elements,
fail to ever extricate the arrow of the wrong views,
and never extinguish the blazing flames of the three poisons.

"They fail to dispel the darkness of ignorance,
fall down into the great sea of desire,
and remain bereft of the light of wisdom
due to having abandoned their great guiding teacher." {22}

Having come to know these matters,
he ever increases his application of diligence in the practice of vigor.
Whatsoever endeavors he initiates
are all done for the sake of liberating beings.

He always bears in mind right mindfulness and wisdom.
In cultivating the path he possesses the senses of shame and blame.
Utilizing solid resolve together with wisdom,
he causes them to increase even more. {23}

He is insatiable in the cultivation of merit and wisdom,
upholds the moral precepts so that they are not allowed to weaken,
tirelessly strives to develop extensive learning,
and rightly cultivates the practices that purify the buddha lands.

正體字

513b28‖ 種相好音聲　因緣無厭足
513b29‖ 所作諸善業　皆為利眾生 {24}
513c01‖ 為利世間故　造立經書等
513c02‖ [7]名姓鬼病方 {25} 歌舞戲笑等
513c03‖ 堂閣園林法　衣服諸飲食
513c04‖ 示種種寶聚　令眾得歡喜 {26}
513c05‖ 占日月五星　二十八宿等
513c06‖ 地動吉凶相　夢書諸怪事
513c07‖ 布施持戒等　離欲修禪定
513c08‖ 四無量神通　安樂世間故 {27}
513c09‖ 大智慧菩薩　得此難勝地
513c10‖ 供養數億佛　從佛而聽法
513c11‖ [8]而修諸善根　皆悉得明淨 {28}
513c12‖ 猶如車磲寶　瑩磨於真金
513c13‖ 譬如寶宮殿　隨風不失法
513c14‖ 世法利不染　如蓮華在水 {29}
513c15‖ 菩薩住是地　多作兜率王
513c16‖ 諸根轉猛利　破諸外道見
513c17‖ 所作諸善業　皆為佛智慧
513c18‖ 得佛力無畏　能度諸眾生 {30}

简体字

种相好音声，　因缘无厌足，
所作诸善业，　皆为利众生。
为利世间故，　造立经书等，
名姓鬼病方，　歌舞戏笑等，
堂阁园林法，　衣服诸饮食，
示种种宝聚，　令众得欢喜。
占日月五星，　二十八宿等，
地动吉凶相，　梦书诸怪事，
布施持戒等，　离欲修禅定，
四无量神通，　安乐世间故。
大智慧菩萨，　得此难胜地，
供养数亿佛，　从佛而听法，
而修诸善根，　皆悉得明净；
犹如砗磲宝，　莹磨于真金，
譬如宝宫殿，　随风不失法，
世法利不染，　如莲华在水。
菩萨住是地，　多作兜率王，
诸根转猛利，　破诸外道见，
所作诸善业，　皆为佛智慧，
得佛力无畏，　能度诸众生。

He is insatiable in planting the causes and conditions
for acquiring a buddha's major marks, subsidiary signs, and voice,
and devotes all of the good works he does
for the purpose of benefiting beings. {24}

For the sake of serving the benefit of the inhabitants of the world,
he sees to the production and establishment of classic texts and such,
learns the nature of stones,[183] ghost-possession, medical formulae, {25}
song, dance, humor, and other such topics

such as methods for establishing halls, towers, gardens, and groves,
and methods for making clothing as well as food and drink.
He shows others where to find deposits of all sorts of precious gems.
Thus it is that he causes the many to be filled with joyous delight. {26}

He is able to interpret signs associated with the sun, moon, five stars,
the twenty-eight constellations, and so forth,
is able to interpret omens of earthquakes, good and bad fortune,
dream writings, and the various sorts of strange events.

He practices giving, observance of the moral precepts, and the rest,
abandons desire, cultivates the *dhyāna* absorptions,
the four immeasurables, and the spiritual superknowledges,
doing so in order to bring happiness to inhabitants of the world. {27}

The bodhisattva possessed of great wisdom
who succeeds in reaching this Difficult-to-Conquer Ground
then makes offerings to many *koṭis* of buddhas
and listens to Dharma taught by those buddhas.

The roots of goodness he thus cultivates
are all brought to a state of shining purity,
just as when, using precious *musāragalva,*
one is able thereby to polish real gold to lustrousness. {28}

Just as the bejeweled celestial palaces, that,
accordant with wind-like forces, never depart their normal course,
even amidst worldly dharmas, he bestows benefit, yet is not defiled.
Thus, in this, he is also like a lotus blossom floating atop the water. {29}

The bodhisattva who dwells on this ground
often becomes a Tuṣita Heaven King
whose faculties become ever more fiercely sharp
such that he is able to utterly refute the views of the non-Buddhists.

All of the good works he does
are done for the sake of acquiring the wisdom of the Buddha
and in order to acquire the Buddha's powers and fearlessnesses
with which to be able to liberate beings. {30}

正體字

513c19║ 是菩薩勤修　轉勝精進力
513c20║ 能得千萬億　諸深妙三昧
513c21║ 供養千億佛　能動千世界
513c22║ 隨其所願力　過是數無量 {31}
513c23║ 如是第五地　種種諸方便
513c24║ 上智慧大人　如法解說竟[9]◎ {32}
513c25║ 十住經卷第二

简体字

是菩萨勤修，　转胜精进力，
能得千万亿，　诸深妙三昧；
供养千亿佛，　能动千世界，
随其所愿力，　过是数无量。
如是第五地，　种种诸方便，
上智慧大人，　如法解说竟。”

If this bodhisattva diligently cultivates
and thus grows ever more supreme in his power of vigor,
he becomes able to acquire a thousand myriads of *koṭis*
of every sort of deep and marvelous samādhi.

He makes offerings to a thousand *koṭis* of buddhas,
becomes able to cause a thousand worlds to tremble,
and, commensurate with the power of vows he brings to bear,
may go well beyond such numbers to the point of immeasurability. {31}

And so it is that we reach the end
of this Dharma-accordant explanation
of the fifth ground and the supremely wise eminence there
who is equipped with many different sorts of skillful means. {32}

The End of Chapter Five

正體字

514a02║ 十住經卷第三 514a03║
514a04║ [*]後秦[*]三藏鳩摩羅什[*]譯
514a05║ ◎[1]現前地第六
514a06║ 諸菩薩聞說　上地之行相
514a07║ 在於虛空中　雨眾妙珍寶
514a08║ 放清淨光明　供養於世尊
514a09║ 咸讚言善哉　善哉金剛藏 {1}
514a10║ 時有無量億　諸天皆歡喜
514a11║ 於上虛空中　雨眾寶末香
514a12║ 光明相綺錯　微妙甚可樂
514a13║ 眾香華瓔珞　幡蓋雨佛上 {2}
514a14║ 他化自在王　與諸眷屬等
514a15║ 雨眾妙寶物　雰雰如[2]雲下
514a16║ 歌頌供養佛　稱歎金剛藏
514a17║ 咸讚言善哉　善哉快說此 {3}
514a18║ 千萬億天女　於上虛空中
514a19║ 作眾天音樂　歌歎佛功德
514a20║ 咸作如是言　如來之所說
514a21║ 微妙無有量　能滅諸煩惱 {4}

简体字

现前地第六

诸菩萨闻说，　上地之行相，
在于虚空中，　雨众妙珍宝，
放清净光明，　供养于世尊，
咸赞言善哉，　善哉金刚藏！
时有无量亿，　诸天皆欢喜，
于上虚空中，　雨众宝末香，
光明相绮错，　微妙甚可乐，
众香华璎珞，　幡盖雨佛上。
他化自在王，　与诸眷属等，
雨众妙宝物，　雰雰如云下，
歌颂供养佛，　称叹金刚藏，
咸赞言善哉，　善哉快说此！
千万亿天女，　于上虚空中，
作众天音乐，　歌叹佛功德，
咸作如是言：“如来之所说，
微妙无有量，　能灭诸烦恼。

Chapter Six
The Direct Presence Ground

F. The Sixth Ground: The Direct Presence Ground

1. The Sixth Ground's Introductory Verses and Dharma Request

When the bodhisattvas had heard the explanation
of the characteristic features of this supreme ground's practices,
they showered down many sorts of marvelous and precious jewels
from the midst of the skies above,

that, emitting pure and radiant light,
they presented there as offerings to the Bhagavat.
Everyone then uttered praises, saying, "This is good indeed,
good indeed, Vajragarbha Bodhisattva." {1}

There were at that time countlessly many *koṭis*
of devas there who all rejoiced and,
from up above in space,
showered down many sorts of precious powdered incense.

The rays of light wove together in an elegantly patterned array
that was subtle, marvelous, and utterly pleasing
as the many sorts of incense, flowers, necklaces,
and canopies showered down to the Buddha from above. {2}

The King of the Paranirmita Vaśavartin Heaven,
together with his retinue and others,
rained down many sorts of marvelous and precious objects
that sprinkled gently down, as if descending in a cloud.

They sang forth verses as offerings to the Buddha
and as praises to Vajragarbha,
all in unison proclaiming, "How good indeed.
This is good indeed. May you soon explain these matters." {3}

A thousand myriads of *koṭis* of celestial nymphs,
from where they were abiding in space above,
sent forth many sorts of heavenly musical sounds
singing forth their praises of the Buddha's meritorious qualities

and all in unison uttered these words:
"That which the Tathāgata has proclaimed
is subtle, sublime, and possessed of incalculable import,
for it is able to extinguish all afflictions, {4}

正體字

514a22║ 諸法本性空　無有毫末相
514a23║ 空無有分別　同若如虛空
514a24║ 無有去住相　亦無有戲論
514a25║ 本來常清淨　如如無分別 {5}
514a26║ 若人能通達　一切諸法性
514a27║ 於有於無中　其心不動搖
514a28║ 但以大悲心　為度諸眾生
514a29║ 是名諸佛子　從佛口法生 {6}
514b01║ 常行於布施　利益諸眾生
514b02║ 本來雖善淨　持戒而堅心
514b03║ 雖知法無傷　而行於忍辱
514b04║ 雖知法性離　而行於精進 {7}
514b05║ 雖先滅煩惱　而入於諸禪
514b06║ 雖先解法空　而選擇諸法
514b07║ 寂滅智雖多　而求利世間
514b08║ 能滅諸惡者　名之為大人 {8}
514b09║ 如是諸天女　百千種妙音
514b10║ 稱讚歌頌已　皆默然觀佛 {9}
514b11║ 解脫月菩薩　請金剛藏言
514b12║ 當以何相貌　得成第六地 {10}

简体字

诸法本性空，　无有毫末相，
空无有分别，　同若如虚空。
无有去住相，　亦无有戏论，
本来常清净，　如如无分别。
若人能通达，　一切诸法性，
于有于无中，　其心不动摇，
但以大悲心，　为度诸众生。
是名诸佛子，　从佛口法生，
常行于布施，　利益诸众生；
本来虽善净，　持戒而坚心；
虽知法无伤，　而行于忍辱；
虽知法性离，　而行于精进；
虽先灭烦恼，　而入于诸禅；
虽先解法空，　而选择诸法；
寂灭智虽多，　而求利世间，
能灭诸恶者，　名之为大人。”
如是诸天女，　百千种妙音，
称赞歌颂已，　皆默然观佛。
解脱月菩萨，　请金刚藏言：
“当以何相貌，　得成第六地？”

reveals all dharmas as, in their fundamental nature, empty,
as devoid of any mark even so small as the point of a tiny hair,
as, in their emptiness, beyond the range of discriminations,
as analogous in this to empty space itself,

as devoid of any mark of either coming forth or abiding,
as beyond the range of frivolous theoretical ideation,
as fundamentally eternally pure,
as in a state of true suchness, and as beyond discriminating thought. {5}

If one is able to reach a penetrating comprehension
of the nature of all dharmas,
his mind remains unshaken
with respect to what exists or what does not exist.

His sole priority is to use the mind of great compassion
for the sake of liberating beings.
One such as this is a son of the Buddhas
born from the Dharma proclaimed by the Buddha. {6}

He is always devoted to the practice of giving
and to bestowing benefit on beings.
Having already become thoroughly pure,
he thus upholds the moral precepts, doing so with solid resolve.

Knowing the dharmas as free of any basis for harming,
he is thus devoted to the practice of patience.
Knowing dharmas are by nature transcendent,[184]
he thus courses in the practice of vigor. {7}

Having previously extinguished the afflictions,
he thus enters all the *dhyānas*.
Having previously comprehended the emptiness of dharmas,
he thus selectively distinguishes dharmas.

Though his knowledge of quiescent cessation is extensive,
he still strives to be of benefit to those abiding in the world.
Whosoever is thus able to extinguish every form of evil
is one who qualifies as great person." {8}

After the celestial nymphs had thus employed
a hundred thousand sublime sounds
in singing forth verses in praise,
they all fell silent and quietly gazed up at the Buddha. {9}

Liberation Moon Bodhisattva
then posed a request to Vajragarbha Bodhisattva, inquiring:
"Availing oneself of which characteristic attributes
might one then succeed in gaining the sixth ground?" {10}

正體字

514b13‖ {A}金剛藏菩薩言。諸佛子。菩薩摩訶薩。已能具
514b14‖ 足五地行。欲入六地。當以十平等法。得入於
514b15‖ 六地。何等為十。一以無[3]性故。一切法平等。
514b16‖ 二以無想故。一切法平等。三以無生故。一切
514b17‖ 法平等。四以無滅故。一切法平等。五以本來
514b18‖ 清淨故。一切法平等。六以無戲論故。一切法
514b19‖ 平等。七以不取不捨故。一切法平等。八以離
514b20‖ 故。一切法平等。九以幻夢影響水中月鏡像
514b21‖ 焰化故。一切法平等。十以有無不二故。一切
514b22‖ 法平等。諸佛子。諸菩薩摩訶薩。具足五地行。
514b23‖ 以是十平等法。能入第六地。諸佛子。若菩薩
514b24‖ 摩訶薩。能如是觀一切法性。能忍隨順得[4]第
514b25‖ 六地。無生法忍。雖未現前。心已明利。成就順
514b26‖ 忍。

简体字

金刚藏菩萨言："诸佛子，菩萨摩诃萨已能具足五地行，欲入六地，当以十平等法，得入于六地。何等为十？一、以无性故，一切法平等；二、以无想故，一切法平等；三、以无生故，一切法平等；四、以无灭故，一切法平等；五、以本来清净故，一切法平等；六、以无戏论故，一切法平等；七、以不取不舍故，一切法平等；八、以离故，一切法平等；九、以幻梦、影响、水中月、镜像、焰化故，一切法平等；十、以有无不二故，一切法平等。

"诸佛子，诸菩萨摩诃萨具足五地行，以是十平等法，能入第六地。诸佛子，若菩萨摩诃萨能如是观一切法性，能忍随顺得第六地，无生法忍虽未现前，心已明利，成就顺忍。

2. Vajragarbha Commences the Fifth Ground's Explanation

{A} Vajragarbha Bodhisattva then replied:

3. The Ten Dharmas of Identity Enabling Access to the Sixth Ground

O Sons of the Buddha, the bodhisattva *mahāsattva* who, having already completely fulfilled the fifth ground's practices, then wishes to enter the sixth ground, should take up the cultivation of ten dharmas of identity[185] to succeed in entering the sixth ground. What then are these ten? They are as follows:[186]

First, all dharmas are the same due to their absence of any inherent nature;

Second, all dharmas are the same due to their signlessness;[187]

Third, all dharmas are the same due to being unproduced;

Fourth, all dharmas are the same due to being undestroyed;

Fifth, all dharmas are the same due to being fundamentally pure;

Sixth, all dharmas are the same due to being beyond frivolous theoretical ideation;

Seventh, all dharmas are the same due to being beyond either grasping or relinquishing;

Eighth, all dharmas are the same due to being entirely transcendent;

Ninth, all dharmas are the same due to being like a conjured illusion, like a dream, like a shadow, like an echo, like the moon reflected on water, like an image in a mirror, like a mirage, and like a magical transformation;[188]

Tenth, all dharmas are the same due to the inherent non-duality in their existence and non-existence.

4. 6th Ground Entry, Acquiescent Patience, and Primacy of Compassion

Sons of the Buddha, the bodhisattva *mahāsattvas* who have already completely fulfilled the fifth ground's practices and who then employ these ten dharmas of identity become able thereby to achieve entry into the sixth ground.

Sons of the Buddha, when the bodhisattva *mahāsattva* becomes able to contemplate the nature of all dharmas in this way he becomes able to employ patience that is acquiescent and gains the sixth ground. Although the unproduced-dharmas patience has not yet become directly manifest, his mind will then have already acquired clarity and acuity and he thus then successfully develops the acquiescent patience.[189]

正體字

{B}是菩薩。觀一切法如是相。大悲為首。增長
514b27‖ 具足。{C}更以勝觀[5]觀世間生滅相。故作是念。
514b28‖ 世間所有。受身生處。皆以貪著我故。若離著
514b29‖ 我。則無世間生處。諸凡夫人。愚癡所盲。貪
514c01‖ 著於我。常樂求有。恒隨邪念。行邪妄道。習起
514c02‖ 三行罪行。福行。不動行。以是行故。起熱心
514c03‖ 種子。有漏有取心故。起生死身。所謂。業為地。
514c04‖ 識為種子。無明覆蔽愛水為潤。我心溉灌。種
514c05‖ 種諸見。令得增長。生名色[6]牙。因名色故。生
514c06‖ 諸根。諸根合故。有觸生。從觸生受。樂受故。
514c07‖ 生渴愛。渴愛增長故。有四取。四取因緣故。起
514c08‖ 業。於有起五陰身。名為生。

简体字

是菩萨观一切法如是相，大悲为首增长具足。更以胜观观世间生灭相，故作是念：‘世间所有受身生处，皆以贪著我故。若离著我，则无世间生处。诸凡夫人愚痴所盲，贪著于我常乐求有，恒随邪念行邪妄道，习起三行罪行、福行、不动行；以是行故，起热心种子；有漏有取心故，起生死身。所谓：业为地，识为种子，无明覆蔽爱水为润，我心溉灌，种种诸见令得增长，生名色芽；因名色故，生诸根；诸根合故，有触生；从触生受；乐受故，生渴爱；渴爱增长故，有四取；四取因缘故，起业。于有起五阴身，名为生；

{B} When this bodhisattva contemplates all dharmas as characterized in these ways, he takes the great compassion as what is foremost and progressively extends the degree to which he completely develops it.

5. The Bodhisattva's Contemplation of Causality in Cyclic Existence[190]

{C} He additionally employs a superior contemplation through which he contemplates the signs of production and cessation in the world.

As a consequence, he reflects thus:[191]

> In all circumstances throughout the entire world wherein one takes on physical rebirth, it occurs due to attachment to a self. Were one to abandon all attachment to a self, then there would be no further circumstance in which one would take rebirth in the world.

a. Contemplation of the Sequential Continuity of Causal Factors

> All common people are blinded by delusion and hence are attached to the existence of a self. They always delight in pursuit of existence and always follow the course of erroneous conceptions. Thus they pursue deviant and false paths and habitually bring forth three sorts of actions: actions involving karmic offenses, actions productive of karmic merit, and imperturbable actions.[192] Through these sorts of actions, they instigate the germination of seeds within the mind. Due to thought characterized by the contaminants and *grasping*, they instigate the birth of a body subject to *birth* and *death* in a circumstance wherein *volitional actions* are the soil, *consciousness* is the seed, *ignorance* is what keeps it covered over, the water of *craving* is what moistens it, the thought conceiving of the existence of a "self" keeps it irrigated, and the generation of all the different sorts of views promotes its growth and gives birth to the sprout of *name-and-form*.
>
> It is due to *name-and-form* that the growth of the *sense faculties* occurs.
>
> It is due to the impingement [of the sense objects] on the *sense faculties* that *contact* is then generated.
>
> It is from *contact* that one then generates *feeling*.
>
> Through delighting in *feeling*, one generates *craving*.
>
> It is due to the growth in *craving* that the four-fold *grasping*[193] occurs.
>
> It is due to the causes and conditions constituted by the four-fold *grasping* that one thus generates *actions*.
>
> Through *becoming*, one generates the five-aggregate body. This is what constitutes *birth*.

正體字

五陰衰變。名為
514c09‖ 老。衰變滅。名為死。老死因緣。有憂悲熱惱眾
514c10‖ 苦聚集。是十二因緣。無有集者。自然而集。無
514c11‖ 有散者。自然而散。因緣合則有。因緣散則
514c12‖ 無。菩薩摩訶薩。如是於六地中。隨順觀十二
514c13‖ 因緣。{D}又作是念。不如實知諸諦第一義故。有
514c14‖ 無明覆心。無明業果。是名諸行。依諸行。有初
514c15‖ 識。與識共生。有四取陰。依止取陰。有名色。
514c16‖ 名色成就。有六入。諸根行塵故。有識。從是
514c17‖ 和合。生有漏觸。觸共生。有受。貪樂於受。名
514c18‖ 為愛。愛增長。名為取。從取起有漏業。

简体字

五阴衰变，名为老；衰变灭，名为死；老死因缘，有忧悲热恼众苦聚集。是十二因缘，无有集者，自然而集；无有散者，自然而散；因缘合则有，因缘散则无。’

“菩萨摩诃萨如是于六地中，随顺观十二因缘，又作是念：‘不如实知诸谛第一义故，有无明覆心；无明业果，是名诸行；依诸行，有初识；与识共生，有四取阴；依止取阴，有名色；名色成就，有六入；诸根行尘故，有识；从是和合，生有漏触；触共生，有受；贪乐于受，名为爱；爱增长，名为取；从取起有漏业，

> The subsequent deterioration occurring in the five aggregates constitutes *aging.*
>
> The culmination of that deterioration in destruction constitutes *death.*
>
> Because of the causes and conditions constituted by *aging* and *death, worry, lamentation,* intense *torment,* and the many sorts of *suffering* then accumulate. Now, within these twelve causes and conditions, there is no entity that accumulates, and yet these naturally accumulate. There is no entity that becomes scattered, and yet scattering naturally occurs. When the causes and conditions come together, then these things exist. When the causes and conditions scatter, then they become nonexistent.

So it is that the bodhisattva *mahāsattva* on the sixth ground carries on the progressive contemplation of the twelve causes and conditions.

b. The Bodhisattva Contemplates the Definitions of Causal Links

{D} He also reflects in this manner:

> It is because of failing to know the ultimate meaning of the truths in accordance with reality that one comes to have *ignorance* covering over the mind.
>
> The karmic effect of *ignorance* is what constitutes *volitional actions.*
>
> It is based on *volitional actions* that there occurs the initial arising of *consciousness.*
>
> The four appropriated aggregates arise together with *consciousness.*
>
> It is based on the appropriated aggregates that *name-and-form* exist.
>
> With development of *name-and-form,* there exist *the six sense faculties.*
>
> Due to *the sense faculties'* interactions with the sense objects, there exist *consciousnesses.*
>
> From the coming together of these factors, there then develops *contact* characterized by the contaminants.
>
> Arising together with *contact* there then exists *feeling.*
>
> It is the desire for and delight in *feelings* that constitute *craving.*
>
> The increase and development of *craving* is what constitutes *grasping.*
>
> From *grasping,* there then arise *volitional actions* characterized by the presence of the contaminants.

正體字

有業有
514c19‖ 果報五陰。名為生。五陰熟名為老[7]熟。五陰
514c20‖ 壞名為死。死別離時。愚人貪著心熱。名為憂
514c21‖ 悲。發聲啼哭五識。名為苦。意識名憂。憂苦轉
514c22‖ 多名為惱。如是但生大苦樹大苦聚。如是十
514c23‖ 二因緣苦聚。無我無我所。無作者無使作者。
514c24‖ 菩薩作是念。若有作者。則有作事。若無作者。
514c25‖ 則無作事。第一義中。無作者無作事。{E}又作是
514c26‖ 念。三界虛妄。但是心作。{F}如來說。所有十二因
514c27‖ 緣分。是皆依心。所以者何。隨事生貪欲心。是
514c28‖ 心即是識。事是行。行誑心故。名無明。識所依
514c29‖ 處名名色。以入生貪心。

简体字

有业有果报五阴，名为生；五阴熟，名为老熟；五阴坏，名为死；死别离时，愚人贪著心热，名为忧悲；发声啼哭五识，名为苦；意识名忧；忧苦转多，名为恼，如是但生大苦树大苦聚。如是十二因缘苦聚，无我无我所，无作者无使作者。’菩萨作是念：‘若有作者，则有作事。若无作者，则无作事。第一义中，无作者无作事。’又作是念：‘三界虚妄，但是心作。如来说所有十二因缘分，是皆依心。所以者何？随事生贪欲心，是心即是识事是行，行诳心故，名无明；识所依处，名名色；以入生贪心，

With the existence of *volitional actions,* there develops the resultant retributive effect of *becoming* occurring in the form of the five aggregates that then constitutes *birth.*

The maturation of the five aggregates is what constitutes *aging.*

It is the destruction of the five aggregates that constitutes *death.*

With the separation occurring at the time of *death,* the agitation arising in the clinging mind of the foolish person brings about *worry* and *lamentation* together with wailing and weeping.

This experience as it occurs in association with the five sense consciousnesses is what constitutes *suffering* here, whereas it is that of the intellectual mind consciousness that is associated with *worry.*

As *worry* and *suffering* become increasingly great, they constitute *torment.*

In a circumstance such as this, there can only be the growth of a great tree of suffering, a great mass of suffering.

Yet, in such a mass of suffering associated with the twelve-fold chain of causes and conditions, there does not exist either any "self" or anything belonging to a self. There is no agent of actions or any entity that directs the performance of actions, either.

The bodhisattva continues to reflect in this manner:

If an agent of actions existed, then there would also be endeavors that it would perform. If no agent of actions existed, then there would be no such endeavors performed. From the standpoint of ultimate truth, no agent of actions exists, nor do there exist any endeavors that are performed.

c. The Bodhisattva's Contemplation of Mind as the Basis of Existence

{E} He additionally thinks:

The three realms of existence themselves are false, for they are mere creations of the mind. {F} The Tathāgata has stated that all of the factors constituting the twelve causes and conditions depend entirely on the mind. And why? It is in accordance with particular circumstances that a thought of desire arises. This thought is identical with *consciousness,* whereas the particular circumstances themselves constitute the basis of *volitional actions.* The delusion of the mind in the context of the *volitional actions* is what constitutes *ignorance.* The location upon which the *consciousness* depends is *name-and-form.* It is in reliance upon the sense bases that a thought of desire is generated. This is an

正體字

名六入。三事和合有
515a01‖ 觸。觸共生名受。貪著所受。名為渴愛。渴愛不
515a02‖ 捨。名為取。是和合故。名為有。此有更有有相
515a03‖ 續。名為生。生變熟名為老。老壞名[1]為死。{G}此
515a04‖ 中無明有二種作。一者緣中癡。二者為生諸
515a05‖ 行因。行亦有二種作。一者生未來世果報。二
515a06‖ 者與識作因。識亦有二種作。一者能令有相
515a07‖ 續。二者與名色作因。名色亦有二種作。一者
515a08‖ 互相助成。二者與六入作因。六入亦有二種
515a09‖ 作。一者能緣六塵。二者能與觸作因。觸亦有
515a10‖ 二種作。一者能觸所緣。二者能與受作因。受
515a11‖ 亦有二種作。一者覺憎愛事。二者與愛作因。
515a12‖ 愛亦有二種作。一者所可染中生貪心。二者
515a13‖ 與取作因。取亦有二種作。一者能增長煩惱。
515a14‖ 二者與有作因。有亦有二種作。一者能於餘
515a15‖ 道中生。二者與生作因。

简体字

名六入；三事和合有触；触共生名受；贪著所受，名为渴爱；渴爱不舍，名为取；是和合故，名为有；此有更有有相续，名为生；生变熟名为老；老坏名为死。’

“此中无明有二种作：一者、缘中痴，二者、为生诸行因。行亦有二种作：一者、生未来世果报，二者、与识作因。识亦有二种作：一者、能令有相续，二者、与名色作因。名色亦有二种作：一者、互相助成，二者、与六入作因。六入亦有二种作：一者、能缘六尘，二者、能与触作因。触亦有二种作：一者、能触所缘，二者、能与受作因。受亦有二种作：一者、觉憎爱事，二者、与爱作因。爱亦有二种作：一者、所可染中生贪心，二者、与取作因。取亦有二种作：一者、能增长烦恼，二者、与有作因。有亦有二种作：一者、能于余道中生，二者、与生作因。

emblematic characteristic of *the six sense bases*. It is through the conjunction of the three factors that there exists *contact*. That which arises in conjunction with *contact* is *feeling*. It is the desire-based attachment for that which is experienced as *feeling* that constitutes *craving*. When *craving* is not relinquished, then this is what constitutes the basis of *grasping*. It is on account of the coming together associated with this that *becoming* then occurs. The additional existence continuing forth from this is what then brings about *birth*. It is the maturation unfolding after *birth* that constitutes *aging*. The destruction that comes about with aging is what constitutes *death*.

d. The Contemplation of 2 Functions of Each Causal Chain Link

{G} Among these, *ignorance* has two functions: First, it constitutes the delusion operative in the midst of conditions. Second, it serves as the cause for the generation of *volitional actions*.

Volitional actions also have two functions: First, they generate future retribution. Second, they serve as the cause of *consciousness*.

Consciousness also has two functions: First, it is able to cause the occurrence of continuity. Second, it serves as the cause of *name-and-form*.

Name-and-form also have two functions: First, they are mutually cooperative in their establishment. Second, they serve as the cause of *the six sense bases*.

The six sense bases also have two functions: First, they are able to take the six sense objects as objective conditions. Second, they serve as the cause of *contact*.

Contact also has two functions: First, it is able to contact objective conditions. Second, it serves as the cause of *feeling*.

Feeling also has two functions: First, it manifests an awareness of circumstances that are either detested or loved. Second, it serves as the cause of *craving*.

Craving also has two functions: First, it generates thoughts of desire toward what may cause defilement. Second, it serves as the cause of *grasping*.

Grasping also has two functions: First, it is able to bring about an increase in the afflictions. Second, it serves as the cause of *becoming*.

Becoming also has two functions: First, it is able to bring about *birth* within other destinies of rebirth. Second, it serves as the cause of *birth*.

正體字

生亦有二種作。一者
515a16‖ 能起五陰。二者與老作因。老亦有二種作。一
515a17‖ 者令諸根熟。二者與死作因。死亦有二種作。
515a18‖ 一者壞五陰身。二者以不見[2]知故。而令相續
515a19‖ 不絕。{H}是中無明緣諸行者。無明令行不斷。助
515a20‖ 成行故。行緣識者。令識不斷。助成識故。識緣
515a21‖ 名色[3]者。令名色不斷。助成名色故。乃至生
515a22‖ 緣老死憂悲苦惱。生不斷。相[4]續助成故。無
515a23‖ 明滅故。則諸行滅。乃至老死憂悲苦惱。亦如
515a24‖ 是。是中無明若無。諸行亦無。因滅。[5]則果滅
515a25‖ 餘分亦如是。{I}是中無明愛取。是三分。不斷煩
515a26‖ 惱道。諸行及有。不斷業道。餘因緣分。不斷苦
515a27‖ 道。

简体字

生亦有二种作：一者、能起五阴，二者、与老作因。老亦有二种作：一者、令诸根熟，二者、与死作因。死亦有二种作：一者、坏五阴身，二者、以不见知故，而令相续不绝。是中无明缘诸行者，无明令行不断，助成行故；行缘识者，令识不断，助成识故；识缘名色者，令名色不断，助成名色故；乃至生缘老死忧悲苦恼，生不断，相续助成故。无明灭故，则诸行灭，乃至老死忧悲苦恼亦如是。是中无明若无，诸行亦无；因灭，则果灭，余分亦如是。是中无明、爱、取，是三分不断烦恼道；诸行及有，不断业道；余因缘分，不断苦道。

Birth also has two functions: First, it is able to bring about the arising of the five aggregates. Second, it serves as the cause of *aging*.

Aging also has two functions: First, it causes the maturation of all of the sense faculties. Second, it serves as the cause of *death*.

Death also has two functions: First, it brings about the destruction of the five-aggregate body. Second, because there is then no conscious awareness, it thus allows this process to continue on and not be cut off.

e. The Contemplation of Causal Chain Production and Destruction

{H} In this context, where *ignorance* serves as a condition for *volitional actions*, it is because *ignorance* causes *volitional actions* to continue on without cease and because it facilitates the establishment of *volitional actions*.

Where *volitional actions* serve as a condition for *consciousness*, it is because *volitional actions* cause *consciousness* to continue on without cease and because they facilitate the establishment of *consciousness*.

Where *consciousness* serves as a condition for *name-and-form*, it is because *consciousness* causes *name-and-form* to continue on without cease and because it facilitates the establishment of *name-and-form*.

[So too does this principle hold true] on through to *birth's* serving as a condition for *aging, death,* worry, lamentation, suffering, and torment. *Birth* then is ceaseless, this because it continuously facilitates the establishment of *name-and-form*.

f. Contemplation of The 12 Links' association with inseparability.

[So too does this same principle hold true where,] if *ignorance* ceases, then *volitional actions* cease, and so forth on through to *aging, death,* worry, lamentation, suffering, and torment.

In this context, if *ignorance* becomes nonexistent, then *volitional actions* also become nonexistent. If the cause is destroyed, then the effect is destroyed. This also holds true for the remaining factors as well.

g. The Twelve Links As Constituents of Three Paths

{I} Among these factors, it is the three factors of *ignorance, craving,* and *grasping* that constitute the ceaseless *path of afflictions*. The factors extending from *volitional actions* on through to *becoming* constitute the ceaseless *path of karmic volitional actions*. The remaining factors in the chain of causes and conditions constitute the ceaseless *path of suffering*.

正體字

先際後際。相續不斷故。是三道不斷。是三
515a28‖ 道。離我我所。而有生滅。如二竹相對而住。
515a29‖ 不堅似堅。{J}無明因緣諸行者。即是過去世事。
515b01‖ 識名色六入觸受。是現在事。愛取有生老死。
515b02‖ 是未來世事。於是有三[6]世出。無明滅故諸行
515b03‖ 滅。名為斷相續說。{K}十二因緣。說名三苦。無明
515b04‖ 行識名色六入。名為行苦。觸受名為苦苦。愛
515b05‖ 取有[7]生死憂悲苦惱。名為壞苦。無明滅故。
515b06‖ 諸行滅。乃至老[8]死。名為斷三苦相續說。{L}因
515b07‖ 無明。諸行生。餘亦如是。無明滅。諸行滅。以
515b08‖ 諸行體性空故。餘亦如是。

简体字

先际、后际相续不断故，是三道不断。是三道离我、我所而有生灭，如二竹相对而住，不坚似坚。无明因缘诸行者，即是过去世事；识、名色、六入、触、受，是现在事；爱、取、有、生、老死，是未来世事，于是有三世出。无明灭故诸行灭，名为断相续说。十二因缘说名三苦：无明、行、识、名色、六入，名为行苦；触、受，名为苦苦；爱、取、生、死忧悲苦恼，名为坏苦。无明灭故，诸行灭；乃至老死，名为断三苦相续说。因无明，诸行生，余亦如是；无明灭，诸行灭，以诸行体性空故，余亦如是。

Because of the ceaseless prior and subsequent continuity involved in these, these three paths themselves are ceaseless. These three paths' constituents exist apart from any self or possessions of a self and yet still undergo a process of production and extinction wherein they are analogous to two stalks of bamboo that, by virtue of their leaning one against the other, they are thus able to remain standing.[194] By themselves, they are not solidly established and yet they are thus able [in this manner] to exist in a manner resembling a state of being solidly established.

h. The Twelve Links' Correlation With the Three Periods of Time

{J} Where *ignorance* serves as a cause and condition for *volitional actions,* this refers to past circumstances. *Consciousness, name-and-form, the six sense bases, contact,* and *feeling* are circumstances associated with the present. *Craving, grasping, becoming, birth, aging,* and *death* are circumstances associated with the future.

There is in these factors a progression going forth through the three periods of time. Where it is stated that, with the extinguishing of *ignorance, volitional actions* are then consequently extinguished, this constitutes an explanation of how continuity is severed.

i. The Twelve Links' Correlation With the Three Kinds of Suffering

{K} This twelve-fold chain of causes and conditions describes *the three sufferings. Ignorance, volitional actions, consciousness, name-and-form,* and *the six sense bases* collectively constitute *the suffering associated with the karmic formative factors.*[195] *Contact* and *feeling* constitute *the suffering of suffering.*[196] *Craving, grasping, becoming, birth, death,* worry, lamentation, suffering, and torment constitute *the suffering of deterioration.*[197]

j. Contemplation of their Arising & Ceasing by Causes and Conditions

Where it is stated that, because *ignorance* is extinguished, *volitional actions* are then consequently extinguished, and so forth on through to *birth* and *death,* this constitutes an explanation of how continuity in *the three sufferings* is severed.

{L} With *ignorance* as the cause, *volitional actions* are then consequently produced. So too it is with the remaining factors. With the extinguishing of *ignorance, volitional actions* are then consequently extinguished. Because *volitional actions* are devoid of any inherently essential nature, the same follows for all of the remaining factors as well.

正體字

無明因緣。諸行以
515b09‖ 生縛說。餘亦如是。無明滅故。諸行滅。以滅縛
515b10‖ 說。餘亦如是。無明因緣諸行。是隨順無所有
515b11‖ 觀說。無明滅諸行滅。是隨順盡觀說。餘亦如
515b12‖ 是。{M}如是逆順十種。觀十二因緣法。所謂。因緣
515b13‖ 分次第。身心所攝。自助成法。不相捨離。隨三
515b14‖ 道行。分別先後際故。三苦差別故。從因緣起
515b15‖ 生滅縛故。無所有盡觀故。{N}爾時菩薩。隨十二
515b16‖ 因緣。[9]觀

简体字

无明因缘诸行，以生缚说，余亦如是；无明灭故，诸行灭，以灭缚说，余亦如是。无明因缘诸行，是随顺无所有观说；无明灭，诸行灭，是随顺尽观说，余亦如是。如是逆顺十种观十二因缘法，所谓：因缘分次第，身心所摄，自助成法，不相舍离，随三道行，分别先后际故，三苦差别故，从因缘起，生灭缚故，无所有尽观故。尔时菩萨随十二因缘，观

k. Contemplation of their Creation and Destruction of the Bonds

Where it is stated that *ignorance* serves as a cause and condition for the generation of *volitional actions,* this corresponds to the explanation of how the development of the bonds develops. Where it is stated that, because *ignorance* is extinguished, *volitional actions* are thus consequently extinguished, this corresponds to the explanation of how the bonds are destroyed. This same principle applies to the remaining factors as well.

l. Contemplation of "Utter Nonexistence" & "Utter Cessation"

Where it is stated that *ignorance* serves as a cause and condition for *volitional actions,* this is a statement accordant with the "utter nonexistence" contemplation.

Where it is stated that, because *ignorance* is extinguished, *volitional actions* are thus consequently extinguished, this is a statement accordant with the "utter cessation" contemplation. This same principle applies to the remaining factors as well.

m. A Summary Listing of 10 Contemplations of the 12 Causal Factors

{M} It is in this manner that one engages in ten types of sequential and counter-sequential contemplations of the dharma of the twelve-fold chain of causes and conditions.[198] Specifically, they are:[199]

Contemplation of the sequential continuity of the causal factors;
Contemplation of their reducibility to body and mind;[200]
Contemplation of it as a dharma wherein each factor assists in its establishment;
Contemplation of their inseparability;
Contemplation of their conforming to proceeding along in the three paths;[201]
Contemplation distinguishing their associations with the past and the future;
Contemplation distinguishing their associations with the three types of suffering;
Contemplation of their arising based on causes and conditions;
Contemplation of their association with the creation and destruction of the bonds;
Contemplation in terms of "utter nonexistence" and "utter cessation."

6. The Bodhisattva's Acquisition of the Three Gates to Liberation

{N} At this time, pursuant to his reflections on the twelve-fold chain of causes and conditions, the bodhisattva contemplates and

正體字

無我無眾生。無壽命者。無人性空。
515b17‖ 離作者使作者。無主屬眾。因緣無所有。如是
515b18‖ 觀時。空解脫門現在前。滅此事。餘不相續故。
515b19‖ 名無相解脫門現在前。知此二種。更不樂生。
515b20‖ [10]唯除大悲心。教化眾生。無願解脫門現在
515b21‖ 前。菩薩修行是三解脫門。離彼我相。離作者
515b22‖ 受者相。離有無相。悲心轉增。{O}以重悲心故。勤
515b23‖ 行精進。未滿助菩提法。欲令滿足。菩薩作是
515b24‖ 念。有為和合故增。離散則滅。眾緣具故增。
515b25‖ 不具故滅。我今知有為法多過故。不應具和
515b26‖ 合因緣。亦不畢竟滅有為法。為教化眾生故。

简体字

无我、无众生、无寿命者、无人性空，离作者、使作者，无主属众，因缘无所有。如是观时，空解脱门现在前；灭此事，余不相续故，名无相解脱门现在前；知此二种，更不乐生，唯除大悲心教化众生，无愿解脱门现在前。

“菩萨修行是三解脱门，离彼、我相，离作者、受者相，离有无相，悲心转增。以重悲心故，勤行精进，未满助菩提法欲令满足，菩萨作是念：‘有为和合故增，离散则灭。众缘具故增，不具故灭。我今知有为法多过故，不应具和合因缘，亦不毕竟灭有为法，为教化众生故。’

observes the nonexistence of self, the nonexistence of beings, the non-existence of any entity possessed of a life, the nonexistence of any person, the absence of any inherently existent nature, and the transcendence of any agent of actions, any director of actions, or any subjective entity, he observes that, because they belong to a multiplicity of subsidiary causes and conditions, they are devoid of anything at all that exists. When he contemplates in this manner, he then acquires the direct manifestation of *the emptiness gate to liberation*.[202]

Due to perceiving the cessation of these phenomena so that they no longer demonstrate any continuity of existence, he acquires what is known as the direct manifestation of *the signlessness gate to liberation*.[203]

Having realized both of these things, he then no longer feels any pleasure in taking on rebirths with the sole exception of doing so to implement the mind of great compassion in the transformative teaching of beings. He then acquires the direct manifestation of *the wishlessness gate to liberation*.[204]

When the bodhisattva cultivates these *three gates to liberation*, he abandons any mark of others or a self, abandons any mark of any agent of actions or anyone who undergoes experiences, and abandons any mark of either existence or nonexistence.

7. The Bodhisattva's Compassionate Reluctance to Enter Final Nirvāṇa

{O} His mind of compassion thus progressively increases. As a consequence of his emphasis on the importance of the mind of compassion, he becomes diligent in the practice of vigor. Thus, whichever dharmas facilitating bodhi he has not yet brought to complete fulfillment, he then wishes to bring to complete fulfillment. Hence the bodhisattva then reflects thus:

> It is due to a circumstance involving a conjunction of factors that conditioned entities continue on. When those factors scatter, they are then destroyed. It is because a multiplicity of conditions are completely present that they continue on and it is because of their becoming incomplete that they are then destroyed.
>
> Because I am now aware of the many faults of conditioned dharmas, I should not indulge the complete fulfillment of such conjunctions of causes and conditions. However, in order to carry on the transformative teaching of beings, I should still refrain from bringing about the ultimate destruction of conditioned dharmas.

正體字

515b27‖ 諸佛子。菩薩如是。知有為法。多過無性。離堅
515b28‖ 固相。無生無滅。與大慈悲和合。不捨眾生。即
515b29‖ 時得無障礙。般若波羅蜜。光明現在前。得如
515c01‖ 是智慧。具足修集。取阿耨多羅三藐三菩提
515c02‖ 因緣。而不與有為法共住。觀有為法性寂滅
515c03‖ 相。亦不住其中。欲具足無上菩提分故。{P}菩薩
515c04‖ 住現前地中。得[11]快空三昧。性空三昧。第一
515c05‖ 義空三昧。第一空三昧。大空三昧。合空三昧。
515c06‖ 生空三昧。如實不分別空三昧。攝空三昧。離
515c07‖ 不離空三昧。如是等。萬空三昧門現在前。無
515c08‖ 相無願三昧。亦如是。{Q}是菩薩。住現前地中。志
515c09‖ 心決定心。妙心深心。不轉心

简体字

诸佛子，菩萨如是知有为法，多过无性，离坚固相，无生无灭，与大慈悲和合不舍众生，即时得无障碍般若波罗蜜光明现在前。得如是智慧，具足修集取阿耨多罗三藐三菩提因缘，而不与有为法共住；观有为法性寂灭相，亦不住其中，欲具足无上菩提分故。

“菩萨住现前地中，得快空三昧、性空三昧、第一义空三昧、第一空三昧、大空三昧、合空三昧、生空三昧、如实不分别空三昧、摄空三昧、离不离空三昧，如是等万空三昧门现在前，无相、无愿三昧亦如是。是菩萨住现前地中，志心、决定心、妙心、深心、不转心、

Sons of the Buddha, so it is that the bodhisattva realizes the manifold faults of conditioned dharmas and realizes that they are devoid of any inherently existent nature, that they exist apart from any characteristic of solidly established durability, and that they are neither produced nor destroyed. Even so, he becomes conjoined with the great kindness and great compassion, refrains from forsaking beings, and then immediately acquires the direct manifestation of the light of unimpeded *prajñāpāramitā*.

Having acquired just such wisdom, he proceeds to completely perfect the cultivation and gathering together of the causes and conditions for acquiring *anuttarasamyaksaṃbodhi*, and yet, even in doing so, refrains from abiding in the midst of conditioned dharmas. He contemplates the nature of conditioned dharmas as characterized by quiescent cessation and yet refrains from abiding in this either. This is because he wishes to completely perfect the factors leading to the unsurpassable bodhi.

8. The Bodhisattva's Samādhis Related to the Three Gates to Liberation

{P} The bodhisattva abiding on the Ground of Direct Presence acquires:[205]

The penetration of emptiness samādhi;
The emptiness of any inherently existent nature samādhi;
The emptiness of the supreme meaning samādhi;
The foremost emptiness samādhi;
The great emptiness samādhi;
The emptiness of unities samādhi;
The emptiness of production samādhi;
The reality-accordant non-discriminating emptiness samādhi;
The all-embracing emptiness samādhi;
And the transcendent yet not transcendent emptiness samādhi.

He acquires the direct manifestation of a myriad such emptiness samādhis. So too does this occur in the same manner with the signlessness samādhis and the wishlessness samādhis.

9. The Bodhisattva's Ten Types of Resolute intentions

{Q} This bodhisattva who abides on the Ground of Direct Presence develops:[206]

The determined resolute intention;[207]
The definitely certain resolute intention;
The sublime resolute intention;[208]
The profound resolute intention;
The non-retreating resolute intention;

正體字

不捨心。廣心。無
515c10‖ 邊心。樂智心慧方便和合心。{R}如是等心。轉勝
515c11‖ 增長故。隨順阿耨多羅三藐三菩提。一切外
515c12‖ 道論師。不能傾動。入於智地。轉聲聞辟支佛。
515c13‖ 決定向佛智。一切眾魔。及諸煩惱。所不能制。
515c14‖ 安住菩薩智慧明中。善修應空無相無願解
515c15‖ 脫門。專以慧方便。行助菩提法。{S}是菩薩。住現
515c16‖ 前地。於般若波羅蜜中。得轉勝行。得第三上
515c17‖ 順忍。以順是法。無有違逆故。菩薩住是現前
515c18‖ 地中。得見數百數千佛。乃至數百千萬億佛。
515c19‖ 供養恭敬。尊重讚歎。衣服飲食。臥具醫藥。親
515c20‖ 近諸佛。於諸佛所。聽法。聽法已。如實隨智慧
515c21‖ 光明故。如所說行。

简体字

不舍心、广心、无边心、乐智心、慧方便和合心，如是等心转胜增长故，随顺阿耨多罗三藐三菩提，一切外道论师不能倾动，入于智地，转声闻、辟支佛，决定向佛智，一切众魔及诸烦恼所不能制，安住菩萨智慧明中，善修应空、无相、无愿解脱门，专以慧方便行助菩提法。是菩萨住现前地，于般若波罗蜜中得转胜行，得第三上顺忍，以顺是法无有违逆故。

“菩萨住是现前地中，得见数百、数千佛，乃至数百千万亿佛，供养恭敬，尊重赞叹，衣服、饮食、卧具、医药，亲近诸佛，于诸佛所听法；听法已，如实随智慧光明故，如所说行，

The unrelenting resolute intention;
The vast resolute intention;
The boundless resolute intention;
The resolute intention that delights in knowledge;
And the resolute intention joining wisdom and skillful means.

10. 10 Consequences of the Bodhisattva's 10 Types of Resolute intentions

{R} Because he brings such resolute intentions as these to ever more supreme degrees of development, he:

Accords with *anuttarasamyaksaṃbodhi;*
Becomes one that none of the treatise masters of other traditions can cause to quaver in the slightest;
Enters the grounds of knowledge;
Turns away from the Śrāvaka-disciples and the Pratyekabuddhas;
Progresses resolutely toward the knowledge of the Buddha;
Becomes invulnerable to being controlled by any of the many sorts of *māras* or afflictions;
Becomes securely established in the light of the bodhisattva's wisdom;
Skillfully cultivates the emptiness, signlessness, and wishlessness gates to liberation;
Devotes himself to the employment of wisdom conjoined to skillful means;
And practices the dharmas assisting the realization of bodhi.

11. The Bodhisattva's Prajñāpāramitā Practice and Patience Acquisition

{S} This bodhisattva who dwells on the Ground of Direct Presence develops ever more supreme practice of *prajñāpāramitā* and acquires the third of the patiences, the supremely acquiescent patience,[209] this due to acting in accordance with and never contrary to this dharma.

12. The Bodhisattva's Seeing and Serving of Countless Buddhas

The bodhisattva dwelling on this Ground of Direct Presence succeeds in being able to see many hundreds of buddhas, many thousands of buddhas, and so forth on up to many hundreds of thousands of myriads of *koṭis* of buddhas, making offerings to them, paying reverence to them, venerating them, praising them, and presenting them with robes, food and drink, bedding, and medicines. He draws close to the Buddhas and listens to the teaching of the Dharma in the presence of the Buddhas. Having heard their teachings on Dharma, he employs the light of reality-concordant wisdom to implement those teachings in practice in a manner

正體字

令諸佛歡喜。是人轉勝。知
515c22║ 諸佛法藏。乃至無量百千萬億劫。諸善根轉
515c23║ 妙明淨。諸佛子。譬如真金。以琉璃磨瑩。光色
515c24║ 轉勝。菩薩住此現前地。以慧方便故。善根轉
515c25║ 勝。明淨寂滅。餘地所不及。諸佛子。譬如月
515c26║ 明。能令眾生。身得清[12]淨。四種風吹。不能遏
515c27║ 絕。菩薩摩訶薩。住是現前地。善根轉勝。能滅
515c28║ 無量眾生煩惱之火。四種惡魔。所不能壞。諸
515c29║ 佛子。是名諸菩薩摩訶薩現前地。菩薩住是
516a01║ 地中。多作善化自在天王智慧猛利。能破一
516a02║ 切增上慢者。聲聞問難。不能窮盡。有所施作。
516a03║ 布施愛語。利益同事。皆不離念佛。念法

简体字

令诸佛欢喜。是人转胜，知诸佛法藏，乃至无量百千万亿劫，诸善根转妙明净。诸佛子，譬如真金，以琉璃磨莹，光色转胜；菩萨住此现前地，以慧方便故，善根转胜，明净寂灭，余地所不及。诸佛子，譬如月明，能令众生身得清净，四种风吹不能遏绝；菩萨摩诃萨住是现前地，善根转胜，能灭无量众生烦恼之火，四种恶魔所不能坏。

“诸佛子，是名诸菩萨摩诃萨现前地。菩萨住是地中，多作善化自在天王，智慧猛利，能破一切增上慢者，声闻问难不能穷尽。有所施作，布施、爱语、利益、同事，皆不离念佛、念法、

accordant with the way they were taught, doing so in a manner that delights all buddhas.

This person becomes ever more superior in his knowledge of the Dharma treasury of the Buddhas, continuing in this way for a time extending even up to countlessly many hundreds of thousands of myriads of *koṭis* of kalpas during which his roots of goodness become ever more marvelous in the shining brilliance of their purity.

13. Purifying Good Roots Like Polishing Gold & Moonlight's Coolness

Sons of the Buddha, this is analogous to that circumstance wherein one uses a lapis lazuli jewel in polishing real gold to such lustrousness that its brilliant appearance becomes ever more supremely radiant. So too, the bodhisattva who abides on this Ground of Direct Presence, through employing wisdom together with skillful means, develops roots of goodness that become ever more supreme in the radiance, purity, and quiescence through which they become unapproachable by the roots of goodness of those abiding on other grounds.

Sons of the Buddha, in this, their radiance is analogous to the light of the moon that is able to cause the bodies of beings to experience a sense of pristine purity that not even the blowing of the four kinds of winds could diminish. The roots of goodness of the bodhisattva *mahāsattva* dwelling on this Ground of Direct Presence increase in their supremacy to the point that they can extinguish the fires of the afflictions of countlessly many beings while also becoming invulnerable to destruction even by any of the four kinds of evil *māras*.

14. Vajragarbha's Final Statements About the 6th Ground Bodhisattva

Sons of the Buddha, this has been a description of the bodhisattva *mahāsattva*'s Ground of Direct Presence.

a. The Bodhisattva's Station and Dharma Practice

The bodhisattva who abides on this ground often becomes a king of the Fine Transformations Heaven[210] possessed of fiercely sharp wisdom that is able to demolish anyone's overweening pride and that can never be exhausted by the challenging questions of any *śrāvaka*-disciple.

b. The Bodhisattva's Mindfulness

In all endeavors he takes up, he employs giving, pleasing words, beneficial actions, and joint endeavors and never departs from mindfulness of the Buddha, mindfulness of the Dharma,

正體字

念諸
516a04‖ 菩薩伴。乃至不離念一切種智。常發願言。我
516a05‖ 於一切眾生。為首為尊。乃至於一切眾生。為
516a06‖ 依止者。是菩薩。[1]若欲勤[2]行精進。於須臾間。
516a07‖ 得十萬億三昧。乃至能示十萬億菩薩眷屬。
516a08‖ 若以願力。能過是數。不可稱計。若干百千萬
516a09‖ 億劫。爾時金剛藏菩薩。欲令此義明了故。而
516a10‖ 說偈言
516a11‖ 諸菩薩已得　具足行五地
516a12‖ 知諸法無[3]相　無相無生滅
516a13‖ 本來常清淨　無有諸戲論
516a14‖ 修[4]集如是智　得入第六地 {11}
516a15‖ 諸法常離相　不取亦不捨
516a16‖ 性空猶如幻　離二無分別
516a17‖ 若能順如是　微妙之理趣
516a18‖ 心無有違逆　得入第六地 {12}

简体字

念诸菩萨伴，乃至不离念一切种智，常发愿言：‘我于一切众生为首为尊，乃至于一切众生为依止者。’是菩萨若欲勤行精进，于须臾间，得十万亿三昧，乃至能示十万亿菩萨眷属；若以愿力，能过是数不可称计，若干百千万亿劫。”

尔时，金刚藏菩萨欲令此义明了故，而说偈言：

“诸菩萨已得，　具足行五地，
知诸法无相，　无相无生灭，
本来常清净，　无有诸戏论，
修集如是智，　得入第六地。
诸法常离相，　不取亦不舍，
性空犹如幻，　离二无分别；
若能顺如是，　微妙之理趣，
心无有违逆，　得入第六地。

mindfulness of his bodhisattva companions, and so forth until we come to his never departing from mindfulness of the knowledge of all modes.

c. The Bodhisattva's Aspiration to Serve Beings

He always brings forth a vow in which he states, "I shall become one who serves as a leader for beings, one worthy of veneration..." and so forth until we come to his thinking, "I shall become one upon whom all beings can rely."

d. The Consequences of the Bodhisattva's Vigor and Vows

If this bodhisattva wishes to bring forth the diligent practice of vigor, then, in but an instant, he becomes able to acquire tens of myriads of *koṭis* of samādhis and so forth until we come to his ability to manifest tens of myriads of *koṭis* of bodhisattvas to serve him as a retinue. Were he to avail himself of the power of vows, he could manifest these phenomena in even greater numbers so large that one could never calculate them even in however many hundreds of thousands of myriads of *koṭis* of *nayutas* of kalpas one might attempt to do so.

15. Vajragarbha Bodhisattva's Summarizing Verses

At that time, Vajragarbha Bodhisattva, wishing to further clarify the meaning of this discourse, thereupon uttered verses, saying:

When bodhisattvas have already succeeded
in completely fulfilling the fifth ground's practices,
realizing dharmas' sameness through absence of inherent nature,[211]
signless, unproduced, undestroyed,

originally and always pure,
and beyond frivolous theoretical ideation—
through cultivation and accumulation of knowledge such as this—
they then succeed in entering the sixth ground. {11}

So too with dharmas' sameness due to always transcending signs,
due to being beyond either grasping or relinquishing,
due to being empty by nature and like mere conjurations,
due to transcending duality, and due to being beyond discrimination.

If they are able to accord with such
a subtle and sublime import
so that their minds refrain from opposing it,
they may then succeed in entering the sixth ground. {12}

正體字

516a19‖ 住於利順忍　智慧得力故
516a20‖ 觀察於一切　世間生滅相
516a21‖ 悉知諸世間　皆從癡闇出
516a22‖ 癡闇若滅者　則無諸世間 {13}
516a23‖ 觀擇因緣法　隨順第一義
516a24‖ 而不壞緣報　所作及假名
516a25‖ 如實無作者　亦無有受者
516a26‖ 如是觀有為　如雲無實事 {14}
516a27‖ 不知真諦義　名之為無明
516a28‖ 從是則生思　身口行得報
516a29‖ 從行故有識　即生於名色
516b01‖ 如是生世間　至生死苦聚 {15}
516b02‖ 了知於三界　但從心而有
516b03‖ 知十二因緣　在於一心中
516b04‖ 如是則生死　但從心而出
516b05‖ 心若得滅者　生死則亦滅 {16}
516b06‖ 無明二種作　作癡作於業
516b07‖ 乃至於老死　破散壞五陰
516b08‖ 從於此事邊　具出於苦惱 {17}
516b09‖ 是事若盡者　苦惱則亦盡

简体字

住于利顺忍，　智慧得力故，
观察于一切，　世间生灭相，
悉知诸世间，　皆从痴闇出，
痴闇若灭者，　则无诸世间。
观择因缘法，　随顺第一义，
而不坏缘报，　所作及假名，
如实无作者，　亦无有受者，
如是观有为，　如云无实事。
不知真谛义，　名之为无明，
从是则生思，　身口行得报，
从行故有识，　即生于名色，
如是生世间，　至生死苦聚。
了知于三界，　但从心而有，
知十二因缘，　在于一心中，
如是则生死，　但从心而出，
心若得灭者，　生死则亦灭。
无明二种作，　作痴作于业，
乃至于老死，　破散坏五阴，
从于此事边，　具出于苦恼，
是事若尽者，　苦恼则亦尽。

Through abiding in clarity and acquiescent patience
and through the development of strength in wisdom,
they contemplate all
characteristic signs of production and destruction in the world

and thus realize that the entire world
in all cases comes forth from the darkness of delusion
and that, were the darkness of delusion to be destroyed,
then the entire world could no longer exist. {13}

Contemplatively investigating the dharma of causes and conditions,
they observe its accordance with the ultimate meaning
even as it does not contradict karmic conditions, retribution,
actions, or conventional designations,

observing too that, in reality, no agent of actions exists at all,
and observing that no entity undergoing experience exists, either.
They contemplate all that is conditioned in just this way,
seeing it all as like clouds wherein nothing substantial exists. {14}

Failure to realize meaning in accordance with ultimate truth
is what constitutes *ignorance.*
It is from this that one generates thought
and pursues physical and verbal *actions* that engender retributions.

It is from *actions* that there exists *consciousness*
and then the immediate development of *name-and-form.*
It is in this manner that one comes to be born into the world,
arriving then amidst birth, death, and a mass of suffering. {15}

If one utterly realizes that the three realms of existence
all exist entirely from the mind
and realizes too that the twelve causes and conditions
reside entirely within the purview of a single thought—

if one develops this realization, then one sees birth and death
as coming forth solely from the mind
and sees that, if one but succeeds in extinguishing this thought,
birth and death will then become extinguished as well. {16}

The two functions of *ignorance*
whereby it serves to produce delusion and instigate actions,
and so forth on through to *aging-and-death's*
destructive ruination of the five aggregates—
it is from the sphere of these very factors
that one entirely brings forth all of this suffering and affliction. {17}

But if these factors were to all be brought to an end,
then this suffering and affliction would also be brought to an end.

正體字

516b10‖ 無明若具足　相續則不斷
516b11‖ 因緣若不具　則斷於相續
516b12‖ 無明及愛取　即是煩惱道
516b13‖ 行有是業道　餘則是苦道 {18}
516b14‖ 癡至於六入　是名為行苦
516b15‖ 觸受是苦苦　餘分是壞苦
516b16‖ 滅三苦相續　則更無有我 {19}
516b17‖ 無明及諸行　則是過去世
516b18‖ 識[5]與及於受　是則為現在
516b19‖ 從愛而生苦　則是未來世
516b20‖ 無明若滅者　是則無有苦 {20}
516b21‖ 癡從眾緣生　則生於諸縛
516b22‖ 眾緣若滅者　則滅於諸縛
516b23‖ 從因而生果　因滅則果滅
516b24‖ 如是觀諸法　自性則皆空 {21}
516b25‖ 隨順於無明　則有世間出
516b26‖ 若逆於無明　是則斷於有
516b27‖ 從是則有是　是無則無是
516b28‖ 如是十種觀　甚深因緣法
516b29‖ 觀因緣相續　去來及現在 {22}

简体字

无明若具足，　相续则不断，
因缘若不具，　则断于相续；
无明及爱取，　即是烦恼道，
行有是业道，　余则是苦道。
痴至于六入，　是名为行苦，
触受是苦苦，　余分是坏苦，
灭三苦相续，　则更无有我。
无明及诸行，　则是过去世；
识与及于受，　是则为现在；
从爱而生苦，　则是未来世；
无明若灭者，　是则无有苦。
痴从众缘生，　则生于诸缚；
众缘若灭者，　则灭于诸缚。
从因而生果，　因灭则果灭，
如是观诸法，　自性则皆空。
随顺于无明，　则有世间出，
若逆于无明，　是则断于有。
从是则有是，　是无则无是，
如是十种观，　甚深因缘法。
观因缘相续，　去来及现在，

So long as *ignorance* is fully present,
then the continuity of this process will not be cut off.

However, if these causes and conditions are not fully present,
then one may thereby cut off this very continuity.
Ignorance on through to *craving* and *grasping*
are synonymous with *the path of afflictions.*
Actions and *becoming* comprise *the path of karmic deeds.*
The remaining factors then are what constitute *the path of suffering.* {18}

Ignorance on through to the *six sense bases*
constitute *the suffering associated with the karmic formative factors.*
Contact and *feeling* constitute *the suffering of suffering.*
The remaining factors are what constitute *the suffering of deterioration.*
If one extinguishes the continuities underlying *the three sufferings,*
then the self itself will no longer exist. {19}

Ignorance as well as *actions*
are associated with the past.
Consciousness on through to *feeling*—
these are associated with the present.

It is on the basis of *craving* that one then generates suffering.
These then are associated with the future.
If one extinguishes *ignorance,*
with this, one then will become free of suffering. {20}

This delusion arises from multiple conditions
and then generates the fetters.
If the multiple conditions are destroyed,
then one thereby destroys the fetters.

It is on the basis of causes that one then generates effects.
If the cause is destroyed, then the effect is destroyed.
Through contemplating all dharmas in this manner,
one observes that they are empty of any inherently existent nature. {21}

It is through following the course of *ignorance*
that the entire world emerges.
"If one acts in a manner that counteracts *ignorance,*
this being the case, then one thereby cuts off *becoming.*"

"It is from having this factor that one then has this other factor,"
"If this factor does not exist, then this other factor no longer exists."
In just this manner, one carries out *the ten kinds of contemplations*
regarding this extremely profound dharma of causes and conditions,
contemplating the continuity of causes and conditions
as they occur in the past, in the future, and in the present. {22}

正體字

516c01‖ 不離一心中　分別有三道
516c02‖ 從三種苦觀　及以生滅法
516c03‖ 無所有而盡　能行逆順觀 {23}
516c04‖ 菩薩如是入　十二因緣法
516c05‖ 知空猶如幻　如夢亦如影
516c06‖ 如焰亦如化　虛誑無作者 {24}
516c07‖ 亦無有受者　但誑於愚人
516c08‖ 如是觀因緣　智者所修空
516c09‖ 無緣則無相　知此二虛假
516c10‖ 其諸一切有　於中無所願
516c11‖ 但以大悲心　愍度眾生故 {25}
516c12‖ 如是諸大士　修習解脫門
516c13‖ 悲心愛樂佛　無量諸功德
516c14‖ 知諸有為法　皆從和合有 {26}
516c15‖ 即得萬空定　無相願亦爾
516c16‖ 智慧轉增進　入於上順忍
516c17‖ 得於諸菩薩　無為智解脫
516c18‖ 如是諸善根　轉勝明淨利 {27}
516c19‖ 供養無量佛　諸佛所稱讚
516c20‖ 常於諸佛所　出家學佛道

简体字

不离一心中，　分别有三道。
从三种苦观，　及以生灭法，
无所有而尽，　能行逆顺观。
菩萨如是入，　十二因缘法，
知空犹如幻，　如梦亦如影，
如焰亦如化，　虚诳无作者，
亦无有受者，　但诳于愚人。
如是观因缘，　智者所修空，
无缘则无相，　知此二虚假，
其诸一切有，　于中无所愿，
但以大悲心，　愍度众生故。
如是诸大士，　修习解脱门，
悲心爱乐佛，　无量诸功德。
知诸有为法，　皆从和合有，
即得万空定，　无相愿亦尔。
智慧转增进，　入于上顺忍，
得于诸菩萨，　无为智解脱。
如是诸善根，　转胜明净利，
供养无量佛，　诸佛所称赞。
常于诸佛所，　出家学佛道，

Not apart from their presence within a single thought,
one distinguishes *the three paths,*
pursuing the contemplation of *the three kinds of suffering*
as well as that of the dharma of production and destruction,
that of "utter nonexistence," and that of "utter cessation,"
being able to carry out both reversed and sequential contemplations. {23}

So it is that the bodhisattva enters into
the dharma of the twelve causes and conditions.
Thus he realizes that dharmas are analogous to mere conjurations,
that they are like a dream, like shadows,
like a mirage, like magical transformations,
and that they are false, deceptive, and devoid of any agent of actions. {24}

So too, he realizes that they are devoid of any recipient of experiences
and that they only deceive foolish people.
It is in this manner that he contemplates causes and conditions
and emptiness as cultivated by the wise, observing that,
if the conditions do not exist, then their associated signs do not exist.

Realizing that these two phenomena are themselves empty and false,
he then becomes free of anything he might wish for
within all that exists among them.
His sole aspiration then is to use the mind of great compassion
in order to liberate beings with kindness. {25}

It is in this way that the greatly eminent masters
cultivate the gates to liberation.
With a mind suffused with compassion, he cherishes the Buddha's countless meritorious qualities
and realizes that conditioned dharmas
all exist due to the conjoining of factors. {26}

He then immediately acquires a myriad emptiness absorptions
and also gains the same number for signlessness and wishlessness.
His wisdom progressively increases,
culminating in his acquisition of the supremely acquiescent patience.

He gains the bodhisattvas' realizations
of the unconditioned, wisdom, and liberation.
Such roots of goodness as these
become increasingly superior in their radiant purity and acuity. {27}

He makes offerings to countlessly many buddhas,
is praised by all buddhas,
and always, wherever buddhas dwell,
leaves the home life to pursue study of the Buddha's path.

正體字

516c21‖ 到諸佛法藏　善根轉增長
516c22‖ 猶[6]以琉璃寶　瑩磨於真金
516c23‖ 光明轉清淨　其喻亦如是 {28}
516c24‖ 如於虛空中　滿月光清淨
516c25‖ 四種風所吹　不能令遏絕
516c26‖ 菩薩智慧光　滅諸煩惱熱
516c27‖ 四魔不能制　其喻亦如是 {29}
516c28‖ 菩薩住是地　多作善化王
516c29‖ 諸根悉猛利　能破增上慢
517a01‖ 所作諸[1]善業　皆隨順智慧
517a02‖ 聲聞諸問難　不能得窮盡 {30}
517a03‖ 是佛子若欲　如是勤精進
517a04‖ 能得於百千　億數諸三昧
517a05‖ 得見於百千　億數十方佛
517a06‖ 如春清了時　日光明[2]則淨 {31}
517a07‖ 如是第六地　深妙難知見
517a08‖ 聲聞所不了　大士略說竟[3]◎ {32}

简体字

到诸佛法藏，　善根转增长；
犹以琉璃宝，　莹磨于真金，
光明转清净，　其喻亦如是。
如于虚空中，　满月光清净，
四种风所吹，　不能令遏绝；
菩萨智慧光，　灭诸烦恼热，
四魔不能制，　其喻亦如是。
菩萨住是地，　多作善化王，
诸根悉猛利，　能破增上慢，
所作诸善业，　皆随顺智慧，
声闻诸问难，　不能得穷尽。
是佛子若欲，　如是勤精进，
能得于百千，　亿数诸三昧，
得见于百千，　亿数十方佛，
如春清了时，　日光明则净。
如是第六地，　深妙难知见，
声闻所不了，　大士略说竟。”

Arriving within the treasury of the Buddha's Dharma,
his roots of goodness continually develop
until they become like real gold
when polished with a lapis lazuli jewel,
the radiance of which then grows ever more pristine.
Just so is the simile most fitting for this. {28}

Just as the purity of the full moon's light
as it hangs in the middle of an empty sky
is invulnerable then to the blowing of the four winds
that remain unable to cause it to diminish or cease,

so too, the light of the bodhisattva's wisdom
in its extinguishing of the heat of all afflictions
is such that not even the four types of *māras* can subdue it.
Just so is the simile most fitting for this. {29}

The bodhisattva abiding on this ground
often becomes a king of the Skillful Transformations Heaven
who, possessed of faculties that are fiercely sharp,
is thus well able to dispel anyone's overweening pride.

All the good works that he does
in every case conform to guidance by wisdom
of a sort that the challenging questions of *śrāvaka*-disciples
still remain unable to ever exhaust. {30}

Should this son of the Buddha wish
to bring to bear such diligent application of vigor,
he becomes able then to acquire hundreds of thousands
of *koṭis* of samādhis,

and becomes able as well to see hundreds of thousands
of *koṭis* of buddhas abiding throughout the ten directions
just as, on a clear spring day,
the sun's light shines forth with pure brightness. {31}

So it is that this sixth ground
has such profound sublimity that it is so difficult to know or see
that no *śrāvaka*-disciple could ever completely fathom it.
Thus ends this general description of such greatly eminent masters.
{32}

End of Chapter Six

正體字

517a09║ ◎[4]遠行地第七
517a10║ 爾時諸天眾　在於虛空中
517a11║ 雨香花珍寶　如雲散佛上
517a12║ 踊躍發妙音　咸讚言 {1} 善哉
517a13║ 善哉金剛藏　善知第一義
517a14║ 無量功德聚　人中之蓮花
517a15║ 說此上妙行　利益諸世間 {2}
517a16║ 他化自在王　雨光明華香
517a17║ 雰雰而供養　除憂煩惱者 {3}
517a18║ 諸天及天王　發妙音聲言
517a19║ 若聞此地義　則為得大利 {4}
517a20║ 時作百千種　上妙諸伎樂
517a21║ 諸天女[5]善歌　承佛神力故 {5}
517a22║ 佛是最寂滅　能令惡為善
517a23║ 一切諸世間　皆所共恭敬 {6}
517a24║ 雖出過世間　[6]而示世間法
517a25║ 知身同實相　而示種種身

简体字

十住经卷第四　远行地第七

尔时诸天众，　在于虚空中，
雨香华珍宝，　如云散佛上，
踊跃发妙音，　咸赞言善哉：
“善哉金刚藏，　善知第一义，
无量功德聚，　人中之莲华，
说此上妙行，　利益诸世间！”
他化自在王，　雨光明华香，
雰雰而供养，　除忧烦恼者，
诸天及天王，　发妙音声言：
“若闻此地义，　则为得大利！”
时作百千种，　上妙诸伎乐，
诸天女善歌，　承佛神力故：
“佛是最寂灭，　能令恶为善，
一切诸世间，　皆所共恭敬。
虽出过世间，　而示世间法，
知身同实相，　而示种种身。

Chapter Seven
The Far-Reaching Ground

G. The Seventh Ground: The Far-Reaching Ground

1. The Seventh Ground's Introductory Verses and Dharma Request

At that time, the congregation of devas
abiding above in space
rained down incense, flowers, and precious jewels
that, resembling clouds, spread about above the Buddha.
Exultant with delight and making sublimely wonderful music,
they all sang praises, saying: {1}

"It is good indeed, good indeed, O Vajragarbha,
that you possess such excellent awareness of the ultimate meaning,
possess such an aggregation of countless meritorious qualities,
and are a lotus blossom among men
who expounds on these supremely marvelous practices,
thereby bestowing such benefit on the entire world." {2}

The King of the Paranirmita Vaśavartin Heaven
then rained down light, flowers, and incense
that gently floated down as offerings
to he who dispels worries and afflictions. {3}

The devas there along with that king of the devas
then chorused forth sublime voicings in which they said:
"If one but hears of the meaning of this ground,
he will thereby be able to garner great benefit." {4}

They then created a hundred thousand varieties
of supremely marvelous music wherein,
by availing themselves of the Buddha's spiritual powers,
those celestial nymphs sang this splendid song: {5}

"The Buddha is possessed of the most supreme quiescence
and he is able to influence those who are evil to become good.
He is one for whom those in all worlds
all join in expressing their reverence. {6}

"Although he has entirely transcended the world,
he nonetheless manifests in the midst of worldly dharmas.
He knows the body as identical to dharmas' true character,
and so manifests many different types of bodies.

正體字

517a26‖ 雖以諸言音　演說寂滅法
517a27‖ 而知於語言　無有音聲相 {7}
517a28‖ 能過百千土　上妙供諸佛
517a29‖ 知身佛國土　捨相智自在 {8}
517b01‖ 雖教化眾生　而無彼我想
517b02‖ 廣集大功德　不於中起著 {9}
517b03‖ 以見取相故　三毒火然世
517b04‖ 不取一切相　慈悲起精進 {10}
517b05‖ 諸天及天女　歡喜設供養
517b06‖ 如是讚歎已　默然而觀佛 {11}
517b07‖ 爾時解脫月　請金剛藏言
517b08‖ 大眾皆清淨　願說七地相 {12}
517b09‖ {A}金剛藏菩薩言。諸佛子。菩薩摩訶薩。已具足
517b10‖ 第六地行。若欲入第七菩薩地者。從方便慧。
517b11‖ 起十妙行。何等為十。是菩薩善修空無相無
517b12‖ 願。而以慈悲心。處在眾生。隨諸佛平等法。而
517b13‖ 不捨供養諸佛。

简体字

虽以诸言音，　演说寂灭法，
而知于语言，　无有音声相。
能过百千土，　上妙供诸佛，
知身佛国土，　舍相智自在。
虽教化众生，　而无彼我想，
广集大功德，　不于中起著。
以见取相故，　三毒火然世，
不取一切相，　慈悲起精进。”
诸天及天女，　欢喜设供养，
如是赞叹已，　默然而观佛。
尔时解脱月，　请金刚藏言：
“大众皆清净，　愿说七地相！”

金刚藏菩萨言：“诸佛子，菩萨摩诃萨已具足第六地行，若欲入第七菩萨地者，从方便慧起十妙行。何等为十？是菩萨善修空无相无愿，而以慈悲心处在众生；随诸佛平等法，而不舍供养诸佛；

Although he uses all manner of words and speech
to proclaim the dharma of quiescent cessation,
he still realizes that all speech
is devoid of any of the signs associated with its sounds. {7}

"He is able to travel beyond a hundred thousand lands
to present the most supremely marvelous offerings to all buddhas,
even while knowing the body, buddhas, and lands
with sovereign mastery in the knowledge that relinquishes signs. {8}

"Although he engages in the teaching of beings,
he still remains free of any conception of either 'others' or 'self.'
He pursues extensive accumulation of great meritorious qualities,
yet does not indulge in any attachment for them, {9}

"for he perceives that it is because of seizing upon signs
that the fire of the three poisons burns up the entire world.
He refrains from seizing on any signs whatsoever, and yet
raises forth vigor in implementing kindness and compassion." {10}

Then all of the devas and the celestial nymphs,
filled with delight, presented offerings,
and, having finished their singing of praises,
they fell silent and gazed up at the Buddha. {11}

At that time, Liberation Moon Bodhisattva
extended a request to Vajragarbha Bodhisattva, saying:
"Everyone in this entire assembly is pure.
They wish you will now explain the features of the seventh ground."
{12}

2. Vajragarbha Commences the Seventh Ground's Explanation

Vajragarbha Bodhisattva then said:

3. Ten Types of Sublime Practice Enabling Seventh Ground Access

{A} Sons of the Buddha, where there is a bodhisattva *mahāsattva* who has already completely fulfilled the sixth ground's practices and who then wishes to gain entry into the seventh bodhisattva ground, he should draw upon skillful means and wisdom[212] to bring forth ten types of sublime practice. What then are these ten? They are:

Although this bodhisattva thoroughly cultivates emptiness, signlessness and wishlessness, he still uses the mind of kindness and compassion as he resides among beings;

Although he complies with all buddhas' dharma of uniform equality, he still never relinquishes his practice of presenting offerings to all buddhas;

正體字

常樂思惟空智門。而廣修集
517b14‖ 福德資糧。遠離三界。而能莊嚴三界。畢竟寂
517b15‖ 滅諸煩惱焰。而能為眾生。起滅貪恚癡煩惱
517b16‖ 焰法。隨順諸法。如幻如夢。如影如響。如化如
517b17‖ 水中月。鏡中像不二相。而起分別種種煩惱。
517b18‖ 及不失業果報。知一切佛國土。空如虛空。諸
517b19‖ 國土皆是離相。而起淨佛國土行。知一切佛。
517b20‖ 法身無身。而起色身。三十二相。八十種好。以
517b21‖ 自莊嚴。知諸佛音聲不可說相。信解如來音
517b22‖ 聲本來寂滅相。而隨一切眾生。起種種莊嚴
517b23‖ 音聲。知諸佛於一念頃。通達三世事。而知種
517b24‖ 種相種種時種種劫。得阿耨多羅三藐三菩
517b25‖ 提。隨眾生心信解故。作如是說。諸佛子。是名
517b26‖ 從慧方便。生十妙行。菩薩摩訶薩。具足六地
517b27‖ 行已。

简体字

常乐思惟空智门，而广修集福德资粮；远离三界，而能庄严三界；毕竟寂灭诸烦恼焰，而能为众生起灭贪恚痴烦恼焰法；随顺诸法，如幻、如梦、如影、如响、如化、如水中月、镜中像不二相，而起分别种种烦恼，及不失业果报；知一切佛国土空如虚空，诸国土皆是离相，而起净佛国土行；知一切佛法身无身，而起色身三十二相、八十种好以自庄严；知诸佛音声不可说相，信解如来音声本来寂灭相，而随一切众生起种种庄严音声；知诸佛于一念顷通达三世事，而知种种相、种种时、种种劫，得阿耨多罗三藐三菩提，随众生心信解故，作如是说。诸佛子，是名从慧方便生十妙行。菩萨摩诃萨具足六地行已，

Although he always delights in the gateway to wisdom of contemplating emptiness, he still engages in extensive cultivation and accumulation of the provision of merit;[213]

Although he has become detached from the three realms of existence, he is still able to engage in the adornment of the three realms of existence;

Although he has achieved the final extinguishing of the flames of all afflictions, he still brings forth for beings the dharmas for extinguishing the flames of their afflictions of greed, hatred, and delusion;

Although he accords with his realization that all dharmas are like conjurations, like dreams, like shadows, like echoes, like magical transformations, like the moon reflected on the water, and like images in a mirror, and also accords with his realization that they are characterized by non-duality, he still brings forth distinctions in the many different sorts of afflictions and also never errs in his understanding of karmic actions' resulting retributions;

Although he realizes that, due to their emptiness, all buddha lands are like empty space, and although he also realizes that all lands transcend their characteristic signs, he still brings forth the practices by which one purifies buddha lands;

Although he realizes that all buddhas' Dharma body free of any "body," he still brings forth as self-adornment the form body's thirty-two marks and eighty subsidiary signs;

Although he realizes that the voice of all buddhas is characterized by ineffability and although he has a resolute conviction that the Tathāgata's voice is fundamentally characterized by quiescence, he still accords with all beings by bringing forth for them many different sorts of well-adorned voices;

And although he knows that, in but a single mind-moment, all buddhas achieve a penetrating comprehension of all phenomena throughout the three periods of time, he still acquires the knowledge of the many different appearances, many different temporal circumstances, and many different types of kalpas in which buddhas' realize *anuttarasamyaksaṃbodhi*. Then, in order to adapt to beings' minds and resolute beliefs, he provides them with teachings accordant with this.

Sons of the Buddha, this is what is meant by generating ten kinds of sublime practice from wisdom and skillful means. The bodhisattva *mahāsattva* who has already completely fulfilled the sixth

正體字

修[7]此妙行。得[8]入[9]七地。諸佛子。如是
517b28‖ 方便慧現前。故名為入七地。{B}是菩薩。住七地
517b29‖ 中。入無量眾生性。入無量諸佛教化眾生法。
517c01‖ 入無量世間性。入諸佛無量清淨國土。入無
517c02‖ 量諸[10]法差[11]別。入無量諸佛智得無上道。入
517c03‖ 無量諸劫算數。入無量諸佛通達三世。入無
517c04‖ 量眾生信樂差別。入無量諸佛色身別異。入
517c05‖ 無量諸佛眾生志行[12]根差別。入無量諸佛音
517c06‖ 聲語言令眾生歡喜。入諸佛無量眾生心心
517c07‖ 所行差別。入無量諸佛隨智慧行。

简体字

修此妙行得入七地。

“诸佛子，如是方便慧现前故名为入七地。是菩萨住七地中，入无量众生性，入无量诸佛教化众生法，入无量世间性，入诸佛无量清净国土，入无量诸法差别，入无量诸佛智得无上道，入无量诸劫算数，入无量诸佛通达三世，入无量众生信乐差别，入无量诸佛色身别异，无量诸佛众生志行根差别，入无量诸佛音声语言令众生欢喜，入诸佛无量众生心心所行差别，入无量诸佛随智慧行，

ground's practices cultivates these sublime practices and thereby succeeds in entering the seventh ground.

Sons of the Buddha, it is on the basis of the direct manifestation of just such skillful means and wisdom that one achieves entry into the seventh ground.

4. The Bodhisattva's Twenty Kinds of Penetrating Comprehension

{B} When this bodhisattva abides on the seventh ground:

He acquires a penetrating comprehension of the measurelessly many realms of beings;

He acquires a penetrating comprehension of the measurelessly many dharmas used by the Buddhas in their teaching of beings;

He acquires a penetrating comprehension of the measurelessly many world realms;

He acquires a penetrating comprehension of the Buddhas' measurelessly many pure lands;

He acquires a penetrating comprehension of the differences in the measurelessly many dharmas;

He acquires a penetrating comprehension of the Buddhas' measureless knowledge associated with their realization of the unsurpassable path;[214]

He acquires a penetrating comprehension of the calculation of the measurelessly many kalpas;

He acquires a penetrating comprehension of the Buddhas' measureless fathoming of the three periods of time;

He acquires a penetrating comprehension of the differences in beings' measurelessly many different resolute convictions;

He acquires a penetrating comprehension of the particular differences in the Buddhas' measurelessly many form bodies;[215]

He acquires a penetrating comprehension of the Buddhas' [knowledge of] the measurelessly many differences in beings' mental dispositions and faculties;[216]

He acquires a penetrating comprehension of the measurelessly many voices and languages through which the Buddhas inspire delight in beings;

He acquires a penetrating comprehension of the Buddhas' [knowledge of] beings' measurelessly many different minds and courses of thought;[217]

He acquires a penetrating comprehension of the Buddhas' measurelessly many wisdom-concordant actions;

正體字

入示無量
517c08‖ 聲聞乘信解。入諸佛無量說道因緣令眾生信
517c09‖ 解。入無量辟支佛智慧習成。入諸佛無量甚
517c10‖ 深智慧所說。入諸菩薩無量所行道。入[13]諸佛
517c11‖ 無量所說大乘集成事。令眾生得入。{C}諸菩薩。
517c12‖ 作是念。如是諸佛世尊。有無量無邊大勢力。
517c13‖ 不可以若干百千萬億劫算數所知。如是諸
517c14‖ 佛勢力。我皆應集。不以強分別此彼得成。以
517c15‖ 不分別不取相故成。{D}此菩薩如是智慧。善思
517c16‖ 惟。常修習大方便慧。令其安[14]住佛道智中。
517c17‖ 以不動法故。若欲常起種種度眾生道。無有
517c18‖ 障礙。來時亦起。去時亦起。坐臥[15]住立。皆能
517c19‖ 起道。度脫眾生。離諸陰蓋。住諸威儀。常不離
517c20‖ 如是想念。

简体字

入示无量声闻乘信解，入诸佛无量说道因缘令众生信解，入无量辟支佛智慧习成，入诸佛无量甚深智慧所说，入诸菩萨无量所行道，入诸佛无量所说大乘集成事令众生得入。诸菩萨作是念：‘如是诸佛世尊，有无量无边大势力，不可以若干百千万亿劫算数所知。如是诸佛势力，我皆应集，不以强分别此彼得成，以不分别、不取相故成。’此菩萨如是智慧善思惟，常修习大方便慧，令其安住佛道智中。以不动法故，若欲常起种种度众生道，无有障碍。来时亦起，去时亦起，坐卧住立皆能起道，度脱众生，离诸阴盖，住诸威仪，常不离如是想念。

He acquires a penetrating comprehension of the measurelessly many sorts of resolute convictions of adherents of the Śrāvaka-disciple Vehicle;

He acquires a penetrating comprehension of the measurelessly many sorts of proclamations of the causes and conditions of the path set forth by the Buddhas in inspiring beings' resolute faith;

He acquires a penetrating comprehension of *pratyekabuddhas* measurelessly many sorts of practice and wisdom development;

He acquires a penetrating comprehension of the measurelessly many sorts of extremely profound wisdom proclaimed by the Buddhas;

He acquires a penetrating comprehension of the measurelessly many sorts of paths coursed in by bodhisattvas;

And he acquires a penetrating comprehension of the measurelessly many works accumulated and accomplished in the Great Vehicle that, when described by the Buddhas, then influence beings to succeed in entering them.

5. His Adoption of Non-Discriminating Mind & Meditative Practice

{C} The bodhisattvas reflect in this manner:

Such measureless, boundless, and immense powers as these could never be known even through calculations performed across the course of however many hundreds of thousands of myriads of *koṭis* of kalpas. I should accumulate all such powers of the Buddhas as these, however I shall not succeed in this through the forced distinguishing of this from that, but rather shall succeed in this through refraining from making discriminating distinctions and through refraining from seizing on signs.

{D} Availing himself of wisdom such as this, this bodhisattva applies himself to skillful meditative contemplations and always cultivates great wisdom and skillful means whereby he is caused to become well established in the wisdom of the path to buddhahood. By resort to the dharma of immovability, whenever he wishes to engage in the constant implementation of the many different courses of action that liberate beings, he remains so utterly unimpeded in his efforts that he is able to bring forth these courses of action that liberate beings when coming, when going, and when sitting, lying down, or standing. In doing so, he remains free of the hindrances, abides in the awesome deportment, and never abandons thought such as this.

正體字

是菩薩。於念念中。具足菩薩十波
517c21‖ 羅蜜及菩薩十地。何以故。是菩薩摩訶薩。於
517c22‖ 念念中。以大悲心為首。修習一切佛法。皆迴
517c23‖ 向如來智慧故。十波羅蜜者。以菩薩求佛道
517c24‖ 所修善根。與一切眾生故。是檀波羅蜜。能滅
517c25‖ 一切煩惱熱。是尸羅波羅蜜。慈悲為首。於一
517c26‖ 切眾生中。無所傷。是羼提波羅蜜。求轉勝善
517c27‖ 根。無厭足。是毘梨耶波羅蜜。修道心。不馳散。
517c28‖ 常向一切智。是禪波羅蜜。忍諸法先來不生
517c29‖ 門。是般若波羅蜜。能起無量智門。是方便波
518a01‖ 羅蜜。期轉勝智慧。是願波羅蜜。一切外道諸
518a02‖ 魔。不能沮壞。是力波羅蜜。於一切法相。如實
518a03‖ 成故。是智波羅蜜。

简体字

“是菩萨于念念中，具足菩萨十波罗蜜及菩萨十地。何以故？是菩萨摩诃萨，于念念中，以大悲心为首，修习一切佛法，皆回向如来智慧故。十波罗蜜者，以菩萨求佛道所修善根，与一切众生故，是檀波罗蜜；能灭一切烦恼热，是尸罗波罗蜜；慈悲为首，于一切众生中无所伤，是羼提波罗蜜；求转胜善根无厌足，是毗梨耶波罗蜜；修道心不驰散，常向一切智，是禅波罗蜜；忍诸法先来不生门，是般若波罗蜜；能起无量智门，是方便波罗蜜；期转胜智慧，是愿波罗蜜；一切外道诸魔不能沮坏，是力波罗蜜；于一切法相如实成故，是智波罗蜜。

6. His Practice of Ten Pāramitās & Other Dharmas Leading to Bodhi

In each successive mind-moment, this bodhisattva achieves complete fulfillment of the bodhisattva's ten *pāramitās* and the ten grounds' practices. And how is this the case? This is because, in each successive mind-moment, this bodhisattva *mahāsattva* takes the great compassion as what is foremost and it is also because, as he cultivates all of the dharmas of the Buddha, he directs all of this to the realization of the Tathāgata's knowledge.

As for the ten *pāramitās*:

The bodhisattva's bestowal on all beings of all roots of goodness he cultivates in pursuing the path to buddhahood constitutes *dāna pāramitā;*

His ability to extinguish all heat associated with the afflictions constitutes *śīla pāramitā;*

His taking of kindness and compassion as foremost and his refraining from harming any being are what constitute *kṣānti pāramitā;*

His insatiable striving to acquire ever more supreme roots of goodness constitutes *vīrya pāramitā;*

His preventing the path-cultivating mind from becoming scattered as he always progresses toward all-knowledge constitutes *dhyāna pāramitā;*

His acquiescent patience in the originally and perpetually unproduced nature of all dharmas constitutes *prajñā pāramitā;*

His ability to bringing forth countless gateways to knowledge constitutes the *pāramitā* of skillful means;

His aspiration to ever more superior wisdom constitutes the *pāramitā* of vows;

His ability to remain invulnerable to obstruction or ruination by any followers of non-Buddhist paths or by any of the *māras* constitutes the *pāramitā* of the powers;

His accomplishment of knowing the characteristic aspects of all dharmas in accordance with reality constitutes the *pāramitā* of knowledge.

It is in this way that, in each successive mind-moment, he completely fulfills the ten *pāramitās*. Even as this bodhisattva perfects the ten *pāramitās* in each successive mind-moment, he also perfects the four means of attraction, the dharma of the thirty-seven factors facilitating realization of bodhi, and the three gates to liberation. To state the essential point, he perfects all of the dharmas conducing to *anuttarasamyaksaṃbodhi* in each successive mind-moment.

正體字

如是念念中。具足十波羅
518a04‖ 蜜。是菩薩。具足十波羅蜜時。念念中亦具足
518a05‖ 四攝法。三十七[1]菩提分法。三解脫門。舉要
518a06‖ 言之。一切助阿耨多羅三藐三菩提法。於念
518a07‖ 念中。皆悉具足。{E}爾時解脫月菩薩。問金剛藏
518a08‖ 菩薩言。佛子。菩薩摩訶薩。但於七地中。具足
518a09‖ 助菩提法。一切諸地中。亦具足。[2]金剛藏菩
518a10‖ 薩言。佛子。菩薩摩訶薩。[3]於十地中。悉具足
518a11‖ 助菩提法。但第七地勝故得名。何以故。諸菩
518a12‖ 薩摩訶薩。於七地中。功[4]行具足。入智慧神
518a13‖ 通道故。佛子。菩薩於初地中。發願緣一切佛
518a14‖ 法故。具足助菩提法。第二地中。除心惡垢故。
518a15‖ 具足助菩提法。第三地中。願轉增長。得法明
518a16‖ 故。具足助菩提法。第四地中。得入道故。具足
518a17‖ 助菩提法。第五地中。隨順行世間法故。具足
518a18‖ 助菩提法。第六地中。入甚深法門故。具足助
518a19‖ 菩提法。

简体字

如是念念中，具足十波罗蜜。是菩萨具足十波罗蜜时，念念中亦具足四摄法、三十七菩提分法、三解脱门。举要言之，一切助阿耨多罗三藐三菩提法，于念念中皆悉具足。”

尔时，解脱月菩萨，问金刚藏菩萨言：“佛子，菩萨摩诃萨，但于七地中具足助菩提法，一切诸地中亦具足？”

金刚藏菩萨言：“佛子，菩萨摩诃萨于十地中，悉具足助菩提法，但第七地胜故得名。何以故？诸菩萨摩诃萨，于七地中功行具足，入智慧神通道故。佛子，菩萨于初地中，发愿缘一切佛法故，具足助菩提法。第二地中，除心恶垢故，具足助菩提法。第三地中，愿转增长得法明故，具足助菩提法。第四地中，得入道故，具足助菩提法。第五地中，随顺行世间法故，具足助菩提法。第六地中，入甚深法门故，具足助菩提法。

7. Vimukticandra Asks About the Perfection of Bodhyaṅga Dharmas

{E} At that time, Liberation Moon Bodhisattva inquired of Vajragarbha Bodhisattva: "O Son of the Buddha, does the bodhisattva *mahāsattva* only perfect the dharmas facilitating realization of bodhi on the seventh ground or can he perfect them on all of the grounds?"

8. Vajragarbha on the Perfection of Bodhyaṅgas on All Grounds

Vajragarbha Bodhisattva replied:

O Son of the Buddha, the bodhisattva *mahāsattva* may perfect all of the dharmas facilitating realization of bodhi on all ten of the grounds. It is only because they become supremely well implemented on the seventh ground that the seventh ground is accorded this particular designation. How does this come to be the case? It is because the bodhisattva *mahāsattvas'* implementation of effortful preparatory practice[218] reaches complete fullness on this seventh ground and then enables their entry into the path of wisdom and spiritual superknowledges.[219]

Son of the Buddha, on the first ground, it is through generation of the vow taking all dharmas of buddhahood as its objective focus that the bodhisattva perfects the dharmas facilitating realization of bodhi.

On the second ground, it is through ridding himself of defilements of mind that he perfects the dharmas facilitating realization of bodhi.

On the third ground, it is through increased development in implementation of vows and through acquisition of the radiant brilliance associated with the Dharma that he perfects the dharmas facilitating realization of bodhi.

On the fourth ground, it is through success in entering the path that he perfects the dharmas facilitating realization of bodhi.

On the fifth ground, it is through adapting his practice to the ways of the world that he perfects the dharmas facilitating realization of bodhi.

On the sixth ground, it is through entering extremely profound Dharma gateways that he perfects the dharmas facilitating realization of bodhi.

正體字

此第七地中。起一切佛法故。具足助
518a20‖ 菩提法。(F)何以故。諸佛子。菩薩摩訶薩。於此地
518a21‖ 中。得諸智慧所[5]得道。以是力故。第八地自
518a22‖ 然得成。佛子。譬如二三千大千世界。一定清
518a23‖ 淨。一定垢穢。是二中間。難可得過。但以大精
518a24‖ 進力。大神通力。大願力故。[6]乃能[7]過諸佛子。
518a25‖ 諸菩薩如是。行於雜道。難可得過。但以大願
518a26‖ 力。大智慧力。大方便力故。乃可得過。解脫月
518a27‖ 菩薩言。第七菩薩地。為是淨行。為是垢行。金
518a28‖ 剛藏菩薩言。從初歡喜地來。菩薩所行。皆離
518a29‖ 煩惱罪業。何以故。迴向阿耨多羅三藐三菩
518b01‖ 提故。隨地所行清淨。不名為過。佛子。譬如轉
518b02‖ 輪聖王。乘大寶象。遊四天下。知有貧窮苦惱
518b03‖ 者。而過不在王。然王未免人身。若捨王身。生

简体字

此第七地中，起一切佛法故，具足助菩提法。何以故？诸佛子，菩萨摩诃萨于此地中，得诸智慧所得道，以是力故，第八地自然得成。佛子，譬如二三千大千世界，一定清净，一定垢秽，是二中间难可得过，但以大精进力、大神通力、大愿力故乃能过。诸佛子，诸菩萨如是，行于杂道难可得过，但以大愿力、大智慧力、大方便力故，乃可得过。”

解脱月菩萨言：“第七菩萨地，为是净行？为是垢行？”

金刚藏菩萨言：“从初欢喜地来，菩萨所行，皆离烦恼罪业。何以故？回向阿耨多罗三藐三菩提故，随地所行清净，不名为过。佛子，譬如转轮圣王，乘大宝象游四天下，知有贫穷苦恼者，而过不在王。然王未免人身，若舍王身

On this seventh ground, it is through bringing forth all Buddha dharmas that he perfects the dharmas assisting realization of bodhi.

{F} And how is this so? Sons of the Buddha, it is on this ground that the bodhisattva *mahāsattva* acquires all paths reached through wisdom. Due to the power arising from this, he naturally succeeds in reaching the eighth ground.

Sons of the Buddha, it is as if there were two great trichiliocosms of which one is definitely pure and the other is definitely defiled and it is so difficult to pass from one to the other that it is only by resort to the power of great vigor, the power of great spiritual superknowledges, and the power of great vows that one may then successfully pass from one to the other.

Sons of the Buddha, just so it is for the bodhisattvas who pursue a mixed path and thus find it difficult to successfully pass beyond it. It is only by resort to the power of great vows, the power of great wisdom, and the power of great skillful means that they then succeed in passing beyond it.

9. Vimukticandra Asks About Transcendence of Afflictions

Liberation Moon Bodhisattva then inquired, "Is the seventh ground characterized by pure practices or by defiled practices?"

10. Vajragarbha Explains the Transcendence of Afflictions

Vajragarbha Bodhisattva replied:

Beginning with the first ground, the Ground of Joyfulness, and continuing on forward from there, whatever the bodhisattva practices is devoted to abandoning actions involving afflictions and karmic offenses. How is this the case? This is because all that he does is dedicated to realization of *anuttarasamyaksaṃbodhi*. However, because the purity of what he practices corresponds to that of the particular ground on which he abides, this circumstance cannot yet be referred to as one in which he has gone entirely beyond such actions.

11. Vajragarbha's Cakravartin Sage King Analogy

Sons of the Buddha, this circumstance is analogous to that of a wheel-turning sage king who roams the four continents mounted on his precious elephant. In so doing, he becomes well aware that there are those beset by poverty, suffering, and afflictions. Still, the fault in that circumstance does not lie with the King. Rather this is simply due to the King's having not yet avoided rebirth in a human body. However, if he were to relinquish his king's body

正體字

518b04‖ 於梵世。住梵天宮。遊行[8]千世界。示梵王威
518b05‖ 力。爾時[9]乃離人身。諸佛子。菩薩亦如是。從
518b06‖ 初地來。在諸波羅蜜乘。知一切眾生心所行
518b07‖ 事。及煩惱垢。而不為煩惱垢之所污。以乘善
518b08‖ 道故。而不名為過。若菩薩。[10]捨一切所修功行
518b09‖ 道。[11]從七地。[12]入八地。爾時名為乘菩薩清淨
518b10‖ 乘。悉知一切世間諸煩惱垢。而不為諸煩惱
518b11‖ 所污。亦名為過。諸佛子。菩薩住是七地。多過
518b12‖ 貪欲等諸煩惱。[13]眾在此七地。不名有煩惱者。
518b13‖ 不名無煩惱者。何以故。一切煩惱。不發起故。
518b14‖ 不名有煩惱者。貪求如來智慧。未滿願故。不
518b15‖ 名無煩惱者。{G}菩薩住是七地。成就深淨身業。
518b16‖ [14]深淨口業。深淨意業是菩薩。所有不善業
518b17‖ 道。[15]諸佛所呵。隨煩惱垢者。如是諸業。悉已
518b18‖ 得過。所有善業道。諸佛所讚。是則常行。又世
518b19‖ 間經書伎藝。如五地中說。自然而得。於三千
518b20‖ 大千世界中。最為希有。

简体字

生于梵世，住梵天宫，游行千世界，示梵王威力，尔时乃离人身。诸佛子，菩萨亦如是，从初地来，在诸波罗蜜乘，知一切众生心所行事及烦恼垢，而不为烦恼垢之所污，以乘善道故，而不名为过。若菩萨舍一切所修功行道，从七地入八地，尔时名为乘菩萨清净乘，悉知一切世间诸烦恼垢，而不为诸烦恼所污亦名为过。

“诸佛子，菩萨住是七地，多过贪欲等诸烦恼，众生在此七地，不名有烦恼者，不名无烦恼者。何以故？一切烦恼不发起故，不名有烦恼者；贪求如来智慧，未满愿故，不名无烦恼者。菩萨住是七地，成就深净身业，深净口业，深净意业。是菩萨所有不善业道，诸佛所呵，随烦恼垢者，如是诸业悉已得过；所有善业道，诸佛所赞，是则常行。又世间经书伎艺，如五地中说，自然而得。于三千大千世界中，最为希有，

and take rebirth in the Brahma World, he could then dwell in a Brahma Heaven deva's palace wherein he could roam the chiliocosm's worlds displaying a Brahma Heaven king's awesome powers. In that case, he would have then abandoned the circumstances attendant upon having a human body.

Sons of the Buddha, so too it is with the bodhisattva. From the first ground onward, as he abides in the vehicle of the *pāramitās,* he becomes aware of the actions of all beings' minds and their affliction-related defilements. Even so, he remains unsullied by such affliction-related defilements because he abides in the courses of good karmic action. Still, he does not yet qualify as having gone entirely beyond such circumstances.

If the bodhisattva leaves behind the path involving cultivation of all of the deliberately effortful preliminary practices, he then advances from the seventh ground into the eighth ground. At that time, he becomes one who abides in the bodhisattva's pure vehicle wherein he is entirely cognizant of all worlds' affliction-related defilements even as he remains unsullied by those afflictions. At that point, he too qualifies as having gone beyond them.

Sons of the Buddha, the bodhisattva abiding on this seventh ground has for the most part gone beyond the multitudes beset by desire and the other afflictions. One who resides on the seventh ground is not designated as possessed of afflictions nor is he designated as entirely free of the afflictions. Why is this so? It is because he does not generate any of the afflictions that he is not designated as possessed of the afflictions. However, because he desires to acquire the Tathāgata's knowledge and he has not yet fulfilled his aspirations, he is not yet designated as entirely free of afflictions, either.

{G} The bodhisattva abiding on this seventh ground perfects deeply purified physical karmic actions, deeply purified verbal karmic actions, and deeply purified mental karmic actions. As for all bad courses of karmic action censured by all Buddhas and all of the defilements associated with the secondary afflictions, this bodhisattva has already passed beyond all such karmic actions. And as for whatever all Buddhas have praised, these are the actions that he always practices.

Additionally, as for the world's classics, texts, skills, and cultural arts, his actions here are as described earlier in relation to the fifth ground. Here, his knowledge of these is naturally acquired. He is the most rare of any who reside anywhere in all the worlds of the great trichiliocosm. He succeeds in becoming a

正體字

得為大師。[*]唯除如
518b21‖ 來入八地菩薩。無有眾生。深心妙行。能與等
518b22‖ 者。是菩薩。所有禪定。神通解脫三昧。雖未得
518b23‖ 果報。所[16]生而隨意自在。菩薩住是遠行地。
518b24‖ 於念念中。具足修[*]集方便慧力。及一切助菩
518b25‖ 提法。轉勝具足。{H}住是遠行地中。能入善擇菩
518b26‖ 薩三昧。善思[17]義三昧。益意三昧。分別義藏
518b27‖ 三昧。如實擇法三昧。堅根安住三昧。[18]知神
518b28‖ 通門三昧。法[19]性三昧。如來利三昧。種種義
518b29‖ 藏三昧。不向生死涅槃三昧。如是具足百萬
518c01‖ 菩薩三昧。能淨治此地。{I}是菩薩。得是三昧。
518c02‖ 智慧方便。善清淨故。深得大悲力故。名為過
518c03‖ 聲聞辟支佛地。趣佛智地。

简体字

得为大师。唯除如来，入八地菩萨，无有众生深心妙行能与等者。是菩萨所有禅定、神通、解脱三昧，虽未得果报，所生而随意自在。菩萨住是远行地，于念念中，具足修集方便慧力，及一切助菩提法转胜具足。住是远行地中，能入善择菩萨三昧、善思义三昧、益意三昧、分别义藏三昧、如实择法三昧、坚根安住三昧、知神通门三昧、法性三昧、如来利三昧、种种义藏三昧、不向生死涅槃三昧。如是具足百万菩萨三昧，能净治此地。是菩萨得是三昧，智慧方便，善清净故，深得大悲力故，名为过声闻、辟支佛地，趣佛智地。

greatly eminent teacher whose resolute intentions and marvelous practices cannot be rivaled by any being with the sole exception of a *tathāgata* or those bodhisattvas who have entered the eighth ground.

Although this bodhisattva has not yet reached the point wherein all of his *dhyāna* concentrations, spiritual superknowledges, liberations, and samādhis are spontaneously produced as a matter of karmic reward, he is still freely able to invoke them at will. In each successive mind-moment, the bodhisattva who abides on this Far-reaching Ground completely implements his cultivation and accumulation of the power of skillful means and wisdom as well as all dharmas assisting realization of bodhi, all of which become ever more supremely fulfilled herein.

12. The Conquest of Samādhis & Unproduced-Dharmas Patience

(H) As he abides on the Far-Reaching Ground, he becomes able to enter:[220]

The bodhisattva's samādhi of skillful investigative contemplation;
The skillful consideration of meanings samādhi;
The mind-augmenting samādhi;
The distinguishing of the treasury of meanings samādhi;
The selection of dharmas in accordance with reality samādhi;
The secure abiding in solidly established roots samādhi;
The gateway to knowledge[221] and spiritual superknowledges samādhi;
The Dharma realm samādhi;
The Tathāgata's benefit samādhi;
The treasury of many different meanings samādhi;
And the samādhi leading neither toward *saṃsāra* nor toward nirvāṇa.[222]

In this way, he completely acquires hundreds of myriads of bodhisattva samādhis whereby he is able to carry out the purifying cultivation of this ground.

(I) Having acquired these samādhis, due to thoroughly purifying wisdom and skillful means and due to deep realization of the great compassion's power, this bodhisattva then becomes one who has passed beyond the grounds of *śrāvaka*-disciples and *pratyekabuddhas* and progressed toward the ground of the Buddha's wisdom.[223]

正體字

{J}是菩薩。住[20]是地。
518c04‖ 無量身業無相行。無量口業無相行。無量意
518c05‖ 業無相行。是菩薩清淨行故。顯照無生法忍。
518c06‖ 解脫月菩薩言。佛子。[21]若菩薩住初地。有無
518c07‖ 量身業。無量口業。無量意業。已能過一切聲
518c08‖ 聞辟支佛地。金剛藏菩薩言。緣大法故。能過。
518c09‖ 非是實行力。此第七地。自實行力故。一切聲
518c10‖ 聞辟支佛。所不能壞。佛子。譬如生在王家。即
518c11‖ 勝一切群臣百官。何以故。豪尊力故。身既長
518c12‖ 大。智慧成立。真實得勝。諸佛子。菩薩摩訶
518c13‖ 薩。初發心時。已勝一切聲聞辟支佛。以發大
518c14‖ 願。深心清淨故。今住此地。自以智力故勝。
518c15‖ {K}諸佛子。菩薩住在七地。得甚深遠離無行。身
518c16‖ 口意業。

简体字

是菩萨住是地，无量身业无相行，无量口业无相行，无量意业无相行。是菩萨清净行故，显照无生法忍。”

解脱月菩萨言：“佛子，若菩萨住初地，有无量身业、无量口业、无量意业，已能过一切声闻、辟支佛地？”

金刚藏菩萨言：“缘大法故能过，非是实行力。此第七地，自实行力故，一切声闻、辟支佛所不能坏。佛子，譬如生在王家，即胜一切群臣百官。何以故？豪尊力故。身既长大，智慧成立，真实得胜。诸佛子，菩萨摩诃萨初发心时，已胜一切声闻、辟支佛，以发大愿深心清净故；今住此地，自以智力故胜。诸佛子，菩萨住在七地，得甚深远离无行，身口意业

{J} The bodhisattva dwelling on this ground engages in countless signlessness practices related to physical karma, countless signlessness practices related to verbal karma, and countless signlessness practices related to mental karma. Due to his purification of these practices, this bodhisattva then manifests the illumination of the unproduced-dharmas patience.

13. Vimukticandra: "Doesn't the 1st Ground Surpass the Two Vehicles?"

Liberation Moon Bodhisattva then asked, "O Son of the Buddha, is it not the case that the measurelessly many physical deeds, measurelessly many verbal deeds, and measurelessly many mental deeds of the bodhisattva dwelling on the first ground are already able at that point to surpass the practices characteristic of the *śrāvaka*-disciple and *pratyekabuddha* grounds?"

14. Vajragarbha: "In Aspiration, Yes. By Virtue of Practice, Not Yet"

Vajragarbha Bodhisattva then replied, "Because they take the great Dharma as their objective, they are able to surpass them, but they have not yet done so through the power of their actual practice. However, on this seventh ground, it is because of the power of their actual practice that they cannot be overcome by any *śrāvaka*-disciple or *pratyekabuddha*.

15. Vajragarbha's Analogy of a Prince Not Yet Ascended to Power

Son of the Buddha, this circumstance is analogous to that of someone born as a prince in a royal family who thereby immediately achieves supremacy over even the many ministers and the hundred officials. Why does this occur? It is due to the power of his power as one of aristocratic and venerable birth. Once he has grown to adulthood and his wisdom has become fully established, he then truly acquires supremacy.

Sons of the Buddha, when the bodhisattva *mahāsattva* first brings forth his resolve, he has right then already achieved supremacy over all *śrāvaka*-disciples and *pratyekabuddhas*. This is due to having already brought forth the great vow with pure resolute intentions. Now, however, on this ground, he achieves superiority due to the power of his own knowledge.

16. This Bodhisattva's Unique Practice & Restraint From Final Nirvāṇa

{K} Sons of the Buddha, the bodhisattva dwelling on the seventh ground acquires the ability to engage in extremely profound and secluded non-practice even as, in his actions of body, speech, and mind, he strives ever more to acquire the supreme Dharma and

正體字

轉求勝法。而不捨離。以是轉勝心故。
518c17‖ 雖行實際。而不證實際。{L}解脫月言。佛子。菩薩
518c18‖ 摩訶薩。從何地來。能入寂滅。金剛藏言。菩薩
518c19‖ 摩訶薩。從第六地來。能入寂滅。今住此地。於
518c20‖ 念念中。能入寂滅。而不證寂滅。是名菩薩。成
518c21‖ 就不可思議。身口意業。行實際而不證實際。
518c22‖ 佛子。譬如有人。乘船入於大海。善為行法。善
518c23‖ 知水相。不為水患所害。如是菩薩摩訶薩。住
518c24‖ 此七地。乘諸波羅蜜船。能行實際。而不證實
518c25‖ 際。{M}菩薩如是。以大願力故。得智慧力故。從
518c26‖ 禪定智慧。生大方便力故。雖深愛涅槃。而現
518c27‖ 身生死。雖眷屬圍繞。而心常遠離

简体字

转求胜法而不舍离。以是转胜心故，虽行实际，而不证实际。”

解脱月言：“佛子，菩萨摩诃萨，从何地来能入寂灭？”

金刚藏言：“菩萨摩诃萨，从第六地来能入寂灭。今住此地，于念念中能入寂灭，而不证寂灭，是名菩萨成就不可思议身口意业，行实际而不证实际。佛子，譬如有人乘船入于大海，善为行法，善知水相，不为水患所害；如是菩萨摩诃萨住此七地，乘诸波罗蜜船，能行实际，而不证实际。菩萨如是以大愿力故，得智慧力故，从禅定智慧生大方便力故，虽深爱涅槃，而现身生死；虽眷属围绕，而心常远离；

thereby refrains from abandoning that quest. It is because of this intention to reach what is ever more superior that, although he practices in accordance with ultimate reality, he still refrains from bringing about the complete realization of ultimate reality.[224]

17. Vimukticandra: "When Can One Enter The Cessation Samādhi?"

{L} Liberation Moon Bodhisattva then inquired, "O Son of the Buddha, beginning with which of the grounds is the bodhisattva *mahāsattva* able to enter into quiescent cessation?"

18. Vajragarbha: "From 6th Ground On; Now He Enters & Arises at Will"

Vajragarbha Bodhisattva then replied:

It is beginning with the sixth ground that the bodhisattva *mahāsattva* has the ability to enter quiescent cessation. Now, even as he abides on this ground, he is able, even in each successive thought, to enter into quiescent cessation while nonetheless still refraining from entering absolute realization of quiescent cessation. This is what is known as the bodhisattva's perfection of the inconceivable karma of body, speech, and mind wherein he courses in the sphere of ultimate reality and yet still refrains from entering the absolute realization of ultimate reality.

19. Vajragarbha Likens Practice To Sailing on the Open Ocean

Son of the Buddha, this circumstance is analogous to that of a person who has set sail in a boat out into the great ocean and who, well versed in the methods of such travel, is skillful in recognizing the signs occurring on the water so that he is thereby able to avoid injury through a calamity at sea. In this same way, the bodhisattva *mahāsattva* dwelling on this ground who has set sail in the ship of the *pāramitās*, is able to travel along in the sphere of ultimate reality and yet refrain from absolute realization of ultimate reality.

20. 10 Paradoxical Aspects of the 7th Ground Bodhisattva's Practice

{M} Because of the power of his great vows, because he has acquired the power of wisdom, and because he brings forth the power of skillful means from his *dhyāna* absorptions and wisdom:

Although he has a deep fondness for nirvāṇa, he still manifests bodies in *saṃsāra*;

Although he may be surrounded by a retinue of followers, his mind is still always detached;

正體字

以願力受
518c28‖ 生三界。而不為世法所污。心常善寂。以方便
518c29‖ 力故。而還熾然。雖[22]然不燒。隨行佛智。轉聲
519a01‖ 聞辟支佛地。得至諸佛法藏。而現於魔界。雖
519a02‖ 過四魔道。而現行魔行。雖現諸外道行。而深
519a03‖ 心不捨佛法。雖現身一切世間。而心常在出
519a04‖ 世間法。所有莊嚴之事。勝諸天龍夜叉乾闥
519a05‖ 婆阿修羅迦樓羅緊那羅摩睺羅伽人非[1]人。
519a06‖ 四天王。釋提桓因。梵天王。而不捨樂法愛法。
519a07‖ {N}菩薩成就如是智慧。住是遠行地中。值百千
519a08‖ [2]億萬那由他諸佛。供養恭敬。尊重讚歎。衣
519a09‖ 服飲食。臥具醫藥。供養諸佛已。護持諸佛法。
519a10‖ 諸聲聞辟支佛。智慧問難。所不能壞。是菩薩
519a11‖ 憐愍眾生故。法忍轉得清淨。是菩薩。無量百
519a12‖ 千萬億那由他劫。善根轉勝清淨。

简体字

以愿力受生三界，而不为世法所污；心常善寂，以方便力故而还炽然，虽炽不烧；随行佛智，转声闻、辟支佛地；得至诸佛法藏，而现于魔界；虽过四魔道，而现行魔行；虽现诸外道行，而深心不舍佛法；虽现身一切世间，而心常在出世间法；所有庄严之事，胜诸天、龙、夜叉、乾闼婆、阿修罗、迦楼罗、紧那罗、摩睺罗伽、人非人、四天王、释提桓因、梵天王，而不舍乐法爱法。

“菩萨成就如是智慧，住是远行地中，值百千亿万那由他诸佛，供养恭敬，尊重赞叹，衣服、饮食、卧具、医药，供养诸佛已，护持诸佛法，诸声闻、辟支佛智慧问难，所不能坏。是菩萨怜愍众生故，法忍转得清净。是菩萨无量百千万亿那由他劫，善根转胜清净。

Although, employing the power of vows, he takes on births within the three realms of existence, he still remains undefiled by worldly dharmas;

Although his mind is always thoroughly quiescent, through the power of skillful means, he may appear as if ablaze even as, although ablaze, he is not burned;

Although he practices in accordance with the knowledge of the Buddha, he still manifests transformations on the grounds of the Śrāvaka-disciples and the Pratyekabuddhas;

Although he succeeds in acquiring the Dharma treasury of the Buddhas,[225] he still manifests within the realms of *māras*.

Although he has already stepped beyond the paths of the four types of *māras*,[226] he may still manifest as practicing the *māras'* practices;

Although he may manifest practices characteristic of non-Buddhist traditions, his resolute intentions still never relinquishes the Dharma of the Buddha;

Although he manifests bodies in all worlds, his mind still always abides in the world-transcending Dharma.

And although all of his adorning phenomena are superior to those of the devas, dragons, *yakṣas*, *gandharvas*, *asuras*, *garuḍas*, *kinnaras*, *mahoragas*, humans, non-humans, the Four Heavenly Kings, Śakra Devānām Indra, or the Brahma Heaven King, he still never relinquishes his delight in the Dharma or his cherishing of the Dharma.[227]

21. The Bodhisattva's Seeing and Serving of Countless Buddhas

{N} Having completely developed wisdom such as this, the bodhisattva dwelling on this Far-Reaching Ground encounters hundreds of thousands of *koṭis* of myriads of *nayutas* of buddhas, making offerings to them, paying reverence to them, venerating them, praising them, and presenting them with robes, food and drink, bedding, and medicines. Having made offerings to all those buddhas, he then guards and sustains the Dharma of the Buddhas and becomes one who can never be overcome by the wisdom or challenging questions of any *śrāvaka*-disciple or *pratyekabuddha*.

Because of this bodhisattva's kindly pity for beings, his patience with respect to dharmas becomes ever more purified. The roots of goodness of this bodhisattva become increasingly supreme in their purification across the course of countless hundreds of thousands of myriads of *koṭis* of *nayutas* of kalpas.

正體字

佛子。譬如
519a13‖ 成鍊真金。以諸好寶。莊[3]飾間錯。轉勝明好。
519a14‖ 餘寶不及。諸佛子。菩薩亦如是。住菩薩遠行
519a15‖ 地中。諸善根。從方便智慧生。轉勝明淨。無能
519a16‖ 壞者。佛子。譬如日光。一切星宿月光。所不能
519a17‖ 及。閻浮提內。所有泥水。悉能乾竭。菩薩亦如
519a18‖ 是。住遠行地。善根轉勝。一切聲聞辟支佛。
519a19‖ 所不能及。又能乾竭眾生煩惱污泥。諸佛子。
519a20‖ 是名菩薩摩訶薩。第七遠行地。菩薩摩訶薩。
519a21‖ 住是地中。多作他化自在天王。諸根猛利。能
519a22‖ 發眾生。悟道[4]善緣。所作善業。若布施若愛
519a23‖ 語。若利益若同事。皆不離念佛。不離念法。不
519a24‖ 離念諸菩薩摩訶薩伴。乃至不離念具足一
519a25‖ 切種智。常生是心。我何時。當於一切眾生中。
519a26‖ 為首為尊。

简体字

佛子，譬如成炼真金，以诸好宝庄饰间错，转胜明好，余宝不及。诸佛子，菩萨亦如是，住菩萨远行地中，诸善根从方便智慧生，转胜明净，无能坏者。佛子，譬如日光，一切星宿月光所不能及，阎浮提内所有泥水悉能干竭；菩萨亦如是，住远行地，善根转胜，一切声闻、辟支佛所不能及，又能干竭众生烦恼污泥。

"诸佛子，是名菩萨摩诃萨第七远行地。菩萨摩诃萨住是地中，多作他化自在天王，诸根猛利，能发众生悟道善缘。所作善业，若布施、若爱语、若利益、若同事，皆不离念佛，不离念法，不离念诸菩萨摩诃萨伴，乃至不离念具足一切种智。常生是心：'我何时当于一切众生中为首为尊？

22. Good Roots Purification Likened to Gold Inlay and Sunlight

Sons of the Buddha, this circumstance is comparable to when, in fashioning adornments of real gold, one inlays it with fine jewels, thus making it ever more supremely fine in its radiance so that it cannot be rivaled in its beauty by any other sort of jewelry. Sons of the Buddha, so too it is with the bodhisattva dwelling on the bodhisattva's Far-Reaching Ground whose roots of goodness born from skillful means and wisdom become ever more supremely bright in their radiance so that they then remain invulnerable to ruin by anyone.

Sons of the Buddha, this circumstance is comparable to the sun's radiance that cannot even be approached by the light of stars, constellations, or the moon in its ability to dry up all of the muddy waters throughout the entire continent of Jambudvīpa. So too it is with the bodhisattva dwelling on this Far-Reaching Ground whose roots of goodness become so developed in their supremacy that no *śrāvaka*-disciple or *pratyekabuddha* can ever rival them in their ability to dry up the defiling mud of beings' afflictions.

23. Vajragarbha's Final Statements About the 7th Ground Bodhisattva

Sons of the Buddha, this has been a description of the bodhisattva *mahāsattva*'s seventh ground, the Far-Reaching Ground.

a. The Bodhisattva's Station and Dharma Practice

The bodhisattva *mahāsattva* dwelling on this ground often becomes a king of the Paranirmita Vaśavartin Heaven, one whose faculties are so fiercely sharp that he is able to bring forth those wholesome causes[228] and conditions facilitating beings' awakening to the path.

b. The Bodhisattva's Mindfulness

In all of the good karmic deeds that he carries out, whether they be done with the aid of giving, pleasing words, beneficial actions, or joint endeavors, he never departs from his mindfulness of the Buddha, never departs from his mindfulness of the Dharma, never departs from his mindfulness of all of his companions among the bodhisattva *mahāsattvas* and so forth until we come to his never departing from his mindfulness of his quest to reach perfect fulfillment of the knowledge of all modes.

c. The Bodhisattva's Aspiration to Serve Beings

He always brings forth this thought: "Oh, when will I be able to finally become one who can serve as a leader for beings, one

正體字

乃至於一切眾[5]生。為依止者。是
519a27‖ 菩薩若欲如是勤行精進。於須臾間。得百千
519a28‖ 億那由他三昧。乃至能示現百[6]千億那由他。
519a29‖ 菩薩眷屬。[7]菩薩若以願力。自在示現。過於
519b01‖ 此數。百千萬億那由他[8]劫不可計知。爾時金
519b02‖ 剛藏菩薩。欲重明此義。而說偈言
519b03‖ 深智慧定心　具行六地已
519b04‖ 一時生方便　智慧入七地 {13}
519b05‖ 行空無相願　而修慈悲心
519b06‖ 順佛平等法　而供養諸佛
519b07‖ 雖以智觀空　而修福無厭
519b08‖ 然後能得入　第七遠行地 {14}
519b09‖ 雖能嚴三界　而心樂遠離
519b10‖ 雖心常寂滅　而滅煩惱者
519b11‖ 行空不二法　如幻如夢等
519b12‖ 而行慈悲心　得入第七地 {15}
519b13‖ 雖觀一切土　空若如虛空

简体字

乃至于一切众生为依止者？’是菩萨若欲如是勤行精进，于须臾间，得百千亿那由他三昧，乃至能示现百千亿那由他菩萨眷属；菩萨若以愿力，自在示现过于此数，百千万亿那由他劫不可计知。”

尔时，金刚藏菩萨欲重明此义，而说偈言：

“深智慧定心，　具行六地已，
一时生方便，　智慧入七地，
行空无相愿，　而修慈悲心，
顺佛平等法，　而供养诸佛。
虽以智观空，　而修福无厌，
然后能得入，　第七远行地。
虽能严三界，　而心乐远离；
虽心常寂灭，　而灭烦恼者；
行空不二法，　如幻如梦等，
而行慈悲心，　得入第七地。
虽观一切土，　空若如虚空，

worthy of their veneration, and one who serves them in other such ways up to and including being able to serve them as one upon whom all beings can rely?"

d. The Consequences of the Bodhisattva's Vigor and Vows

If this bodhisattva wishes to bring the diligent practice of vigor to bear in this, in but a moment, he becomes able to acquire hundreds of thousands of *koṭis* of *nayutas* of samādhis, and so forth until we come to his becoming able to manifest hundreds of thousands of *koṭis* of *nayutas* of bodhisattvas serving him as a retinue. Were he to avail himself of the power of vows, this bodhisattva could freely manifest these phenomena in even greater numbers so large that one could never calculate them even in however many hundreds of thousands of myriads of *koṭis* of *nayutas* of kalpas one might attempt to do so.

24. Vajragarbha Bodhisattva's Summarizing Verses

At that time, Vajragarbha Bodhisattva, wishing to once again clarify the meaning of his discourse, thereupon uttered verses, saying:

When, with deep wisdom and concentrated mind,
he has already completed the practice of the sixth ground,
he simultaneously brings forth skillful means
together with wisdom and then enters the seventh ground. {13}

Although he practices emptiness, signlessness, and wishlessness,
he still cultivates the minds of kindness and compassion.
Though he complies with the Buddha's dharma of uniform equality,
he still makes offerings to all buddhas.

Although availing himself of knowledge in contemplating emptiness,
he is still insatiable in his cultivation of merit.
As a consequence, he then becomes able to enter
the seventh ground, the Far-Reaching Ground. {14}

Although he is able to carry on the adornment of the three realms,
his mind still delights in detachment from them.
Though his own mind is always quiescent,
he still facilitates the extinguishing of others' afflictions.

Although he practices emptiness and perceives dharmas as non-dual,
as like mere conjurations, as like a dream, and so forth,
he still implements the minds of kindness and compassion
and thus succeeds in entering the seventh ground. {15}

Although, through contemplation, he observes all lands
as empty and as comparable to empty space,

正體字

519b14‖ 而能善莊嚴　清淨諸佛土
519b15‖ 雖知諸佛身　同法相無相
519b16‖ 而種三十二　八十諸相好
519b17‖ 雖知於諸[9]佛　不可言說相
519b18‖ 而嚴佛音聲　令世歡喜故
519b19‖ 雖知於諸佛　一念中成道
519b20‖ 而示時劫[10]數　引導諸眾生 {16}
519b21‖ 如是知於法　則得法照明
519b22‖ 菩薩如是者　即入第七地
519b23‖ 住是地能觀　無量眾生行
519b24‖ 亦知於諸佛　勢力亦無量 {17}
519b25‖ 世間及劫數　法性皆無量
519b26‖ 又知諸眾生　所欲之所樂
519b27‖ 知說三乘法　皆悉是無量
519b28‖ 我當應教化　成就是眾生 {18}
519b29‖ 以如是思惟　方便慧和合
519c01‖ 於四威儀中　常行如是道
519c02‖ 於一一念中　能具助菩提
519c03‖ 所謂是十種　波羅蜜等法 {19}

简体字

而能善庄严，　清净诸佛土。
虽知诸佛身，　同法相无相，
而种三十二，　八十诸相好。
虽知于诸佛，　不可言说相，
而严佛音声，　令世欢喜故。
虽知于诸佛，　一念中成道，
而示时劫数，　引导诸众生。
如是知于法，　则得法照明，
菩萨如是者，　即入第七地。
住是地能观，　无量众生行，
亦知于诸佛，　势力亦无量，
世间及劫数，　法性皆无量。
又知诸众生，　所欲之所乐，
知说三乘法，　皆悉是无量，
‘我当应教化，　成就是众生。’
以如是思惟，　方便慧和合，
于四威仪中，　常行如是道。
于一一念中，　能具助菩提，
所谓是十种，　波罗蜜等法。

he is still able to carry forth skillful adorning practices
whereby he pursues the purification of all buddha lands.

Although he realizes that the bodies of all buddhas are
identical to dharmas' aspects in their signlessness,
he still plants the causes for acquiring the thirty-two marks
and all of the eighty subsidiary signs.

Although he realizes that, as it is present in all buddhas,
it is characterized by its ineffability,
he still avails himself of the adornments of the Buddha's voice
to cause delight in the inhabitants of the world.

Although he knows that as it occurs among all buddhas,
realization of the path takes place in but a single mind-moment,
he still appears in all periods of time and all enumerations of kalpas
in order to provide guidance to all beings. {16}

If one possesses just such knowing awareness of Dharma as this,
then one succeeds in acquiring the radiant illumination of Dharma.
The bodhisattva who has become of this sort
immediately succeeds in entering the seventh ground.

One who abides on this ground becomes able to contemplate
the measurelessly many beings and their actions
while also comprehending the Buddhas'
powers that are themselves so immeasurably extensive. {17}

He also comprehends the worlds, the kalpas,
and the realms of dharmas, all of which are measureless,
while also comprehending what all beings
desire and what they delight in.

He comprehends and proclaims the dharmas of the Three Vehicles,
all of which are measureless,
reflecting, "I should engage in such teaching
to bring about the complete development of these beings." {18}

Utilizing contemplative reflection such as this
along with the combination of skillful means and wisdom,
he always practices a path such as this
in the midst of all four of the awesome deportments.

Even in each successive thought,
he is able to perfectly implement the bodhi-realization factors,
in particular the ten types
of *pāramitās* and the other such associated dharmas. {19}

正體字

519c04║ 如是諸菩薩 所修之福德
519c05║ 皆與諸眾生 名檀波羅蜜
519c06║ 滅除心惡垢 名尸波羅蜜
519c07║ 不為六塵傷 羼提波羅蜜
519c08║ 能起轉勝法 精進波羅蜜
519c09║ 於是道不動 名禪波羅蜜 {20}
519c10║ 無生忍是名 般若波羅蜜
519c11║ 迴向佛道名 方便波羅蜜
519c12║ 求於轉勝法 名願波羅蜜
519c13║ 無有能壞者 名力波羅蜜
519c14║ 能解如實說 名智波羅蜜
519c15║ 是助菩提法 念念皆能攝 {21}
519c16║ 發於廣大願 緣於大事故
519c17║ 初地中功德 名之為具足
519c18║ 第二地名為 除諸心[11]惡垢
519c19║ 第三願增明 第四地住道
519c20║ 第五隨世行 第六入深法
519c21║ 得無生相分 漸漸而增長 {22}
519c22║ 第七集一切 具菩提分法
519c23║ 能起諸功德 及以一切願

简体字

如是诸菩萨， 所修之福德，
皆与诸众生， 名檀波罗蜜；
灭除心恶垢， 名尸波罗蜜；
不为六尘伤， 羼提波罗蜜；
能起转胜法， 精进波罗蜜；
于是道不动， 名禅波罗蜜；
无生忍是名， 般若波罗蜜；
回向佛道名， 方便波罗蜜；
求于转胜法， 名愿波罗蜜；
无有能坏者， 名力波罗蜜；
能解如实说， 名智波罗蜜。
是助菩提法， 念念皆能摄，
发于广大愿， 缘于大事故，
初地中功德， 名之为具足；
第二地名为， 除诸心恶垢；
第三愿增明； 第四地住道；
第五随世行； 第六入深法，
得无生相分， 渐渐而增长；
第七集一切， 具菩提分法，
能起诸功德， 及以一切愿。

Bodhisattvas such as these
take the merit arising from what they cultivate
and bestow all of it on beings.
It is this that constitutes the perfection of *dāna pāramitā.*

It is the utter extinguishing of mental defilements
that constitutes the perfection of *śīla pāramitā.*
Refraining from harm inflicted for the sake of the six sense objects
is what constitutes the perfection of *kṣānti pāramitā.*

His ability to bring forth increasingly superior dharmas
is what constitutes the perfection of the vigor *pāramitā.*
It is remaining unmoving even as one pursues the path
that constitutes the perfection of *dhyāna pāramitā.* {20}

It is realization of the unproduced-dharmas patience that defines
the perfection of *prajñāpāramitā.*
It is dedication of one's endeavors to realization of the buddha path
that constitutes the perfection of the skillful means *pāramitā.*

It is the pursuit of ever more supreme dharmas
that defines the perfection of the *pāramitā* of vows.
Becoming one who cannot be overcome by anyone
is what constitutes the perfection of the powers *pāramitā.*

The ability to comprehend discourse accordant with reality
is what constitutes the perfection of the knowledge *pāramitā.*
He is able in each successive mind-moment
to subsume all of these dharmas assisting the realization of bodhi. {21}

It is because he brings forth the vast and magnificent vow
taking the great endeavor as the object of his resolve
that his meritorious qualities as possessed on the very first ground
qualify then as fully implemented.

On the second ground, this qualification is defined
by his ridding the mind of evil's defilements.
On the third ground, it is through his vow's increasing brilliance.
On the fourth ground, it is through his then abiding in the path.

On the fifth, this is defined by practice adapted to those in the world.
On the sixth, this is defined by entry into deep dharmas
through partial acquisition of aspects of the unproduced's realization
that then gradually develop thereafter. {22}

On the seventh ground, he accumulates all
dharmas conducing to realization of bodhi,
and becomes able to develop all of the meritorious qualities
while also availing himself of all of the vows.

正體字

519c24‖ 如是諸功德　令後八地中
519c25‖ 一切諸所行　自然得清淨 {23}
519c26‖ 遠行地難過　大智力所[12]能
519c27‖ 如二國中間　難可得過度
519c28‖ 在於七地中　不污如聖王
519c29‖ 住於此道中　不名一切過 {24}
520a01‖ 若到於第八　菩薩智慧地
520a02‖ 爾時過意界　住於智業中
520a03‖ 如梵王觀世　不得名為人
520a04‖ 菩薩罪不污　如蓮花在水 {25}
520a05‖ 菩薩住是地　過種種煩惱
520a06‖ 不名有煩惱　不名盡煩惱
520a07‖ 入是正道中　無有諸煩惱
520a08‖ 願求佛道故　不名盡煩惱 {26}
520a09‖ 於諸世間中　經書伎藝事
520a10‖ 文頌呪術等　自然能了知
520a11‖ 修習諸禪定　及諸神通等
520a12‖ 無量心利世　是事皆能起 {27}
520a13‖ 爾時此菩薩　過於二乘行
520a14‖ 安住第七地　菩薩諸行中

简体字

如是诸功德，　令后八地中，
一切诸所行，　自然得清净。
远行地难过，　大智力所能，
如二国中间，　难可得过度。
在于七地中，　不污如圣王，
住于此道中，　不名一切过。
若到于第八，　菩萨智慧地，
尔时过意界，　住于智业中。
如梵王观世，　不得名为人，
菩萨罪不污，　如莲华在水。
菩萨住是地，　过种种烦恼，
不名有烦恼，　不名尽烦恼。
入是正道中，　无有诸烦恼；
愿求佛道故，　不名尽烦恼。
于诸世间中，　经书伎艺事，
文颂咒术等，　自然能了知。
修习诸禅定，　及诸神通等，
无量心利世，　是事皆能起。
尔时此菩萨，　过于二乘行，
安住第七地，　菩萨诸行中。

Such meritorious qualities as these
cause the development of that circumstance on the eighth ground
wherein everything that he practices
is then naturally characterized by purity. {23}

The Far-Reaching Ground is difficult to pass beyond.
Those possessed of the power of great wisdom are able to do so.
This circumstance is analogous to one wherein there are two lands
in which it is difficult to be able to pass from one into the other.

On the seventh ground,
his avoidance of defilements is comparable to that of the sage king,
for, while he still abides in these paths,
he cannot yet qualify as having passed on beyond them all. {24}

In that circumstance where he reaches the eighth
bodhisattva wisdom ground,
he then passes beyond the sphere of deliberately intentional practice
and then abides in karmic deeds arising from knowledge.

This circumstance is comparable to that of the Brahma Heaven King
who, as he observes the world, no longer qualifies as merely human.
This bodhisattva is unsullied by any karmic offenses and,
in this, he is analogous to the lotus blossom resting on the water. {25}

The bodhisattva dwelling on this ground
has himself passed beyond the various sorts of afflictions.
Thus he cannot be designated as one possessed of afflictions.
Still, he has not yet entirely exhausted all of the afflictions.

Having entered into this right path,
he does not possess any of the afflictions.
Nonetheless, having vowed to continue on the path to buddhahood,
he is not one who puts a complete end to the afflictions. {26}

He is one who is naturally able to entirely fathom
all of those matters in the world
that are associated with the classics, texts, technical skills, arts,
literature, poetry, proficiency in the use of mantras, and such.

He cultivates and practices all of the *dhyāna* absorptions
as well as all of the spiritual superknowledges and such.
Employing the immeasurable minds, he strives to benefit the world.
Thus he is able to bring forth all of these endeavors. {27}

It is at this point in time that this bodhisattva
passes beyond the practices associated with the Two Vehicles
and becomes securely established in the bodhisattva practices
associated with the seventh ground.

正體字

520a15‖ 以初發心時　大願力故勝
520a16‖ 今於此地中　智慧力故勝
520a17‖ 猶如國王子　小時豪[1]性勝
520a18‖ 後以功[2]德成　於諸人中勝 {28}
520a19‖ 住此得深智　轉發勝精進
520a20‖ 念念入寂滅　而亦不取證
520a21‖ 猶如人乘船　入於大海中
520a22‖ 雖行深水難　不為水所害 {29}
520a23‖ 菩薩行轉勝　方便智慧故
520a24‖ 功德悉備足　諸世所難知
520a25‖ 供養無量佛　其心清淨故
520a26‖ 如真金雜寶　間錯而莊嚴 {30}
520a27‖ 得佛智慧光　乾諸愛水潤
520a28‖ 猶如日光明　消涸於泥潦
520a29‖ 菩薩住是地　他化自在王
520b01‖ 諸根悉猛利　通達諸道果 {31}
520b02‖ 若欲勤精進　見十萬千億
520b03‖ 那由他諸佛　願力過是數 {32}
520b04‖ [3]七地智慧淨　一切世二乘
520b05‖ 皆所共難知　今已略說竟 {33}

简体字

以初发心时，　大愿力故胜；
今于此地中，　智慧力故胜。
犹如国王子，　小时豪姓胜；
后以功德成，　于诸人中胜。
住此得深智，　转发胜精进，
念念入寂灭，　而亦不取证。
犹如人乘船，　入于大海中，
虽行深水难，　不为水所害。
菩萨行转胜，　方便智慧故，
功德悉备足，　诸世所难知。
供养无量佛，　其心清净故，
如真金杂宝，　间错而庄严。
得佛智慧光，　干诸爱水润，
犹如日光明，　消涸于泥潦。
菩萨住是地，　他化自在王，
诸根悉猛利，　通达诸道果。
若欲勤精进，　见十万千亿，
那由他诸佛，　愿力过是数。
七地智慧净，　一切世二乘，
皆所共难知，　今已略说竟。”

He first acquires this supremacy due to the power of his great vow
brought forth at the time of bringing forth the initial resolve.
Now, in abiding on this ground,
it is due to the power of wisdom that he is established in supremacy.

This circumstance is analogous to that of a son born to a king
who, even when young, is superior by virtue of aristocratic caste,
but who later, due to accomplishment in meritorious service,
indeed becomes, among all the people, the one who is supreme. {28}

Abiding herein, he acquires profoundly deep wisdom
and increasingly brings forth the supreme practice of vigor.
In each successive moment, he is immersed in quiescent cessation
and yet still refrains from opting for its absolute realization.

This circumstance is like that of a person setting sail in a ship who,
having ventured out onto the great sea
is able to avoid being brought to harm by the waves
even though he may encounter difficult conditions in deep waters. {29}

The practice of the bodhisattva becomes increasingly supreme
due to skillful means and wisdom.
His acquisition of meritorious qualities becomes entirely complete
and such that it would be difficult to fathom by anyone in the world.

He makes offerings to countlessly many buddhas
and, due to the purification of his mind,
he becomes comparable to real gold wherein the various jewels
have been inlaid in order to adorn it. {30}

He acquires the brilliant light of the Buddha's wisdom
whereby he becomes able to dry up the waters of the desires
just as the light of the sun
dries up the pools of muddy water.

The bodhisattva who abides on this ground
may become a king of the Paranirmita Vaśavartin Heaven
who, possessed of faculties that are all fiercely sharp,
acquires a penetrating comprehension of the fruits of the path. {31}

If he wishes to avail himself of the diligent application of vigor,
he becomes able to see tens of thousands of myriads of *koṭis*
of *nayutas* of buddhas.
By resort to the power of his vows, the number exceeds even this. {32}

The purification of the wisdom characteristic of the seventh ground
is such that even all inhabitants of the world and the Two Vehicles
combined would find difficult to completely fathom.
Here we now conclude a brief explanation of the seventh ground. {33}

End of Chapter Seven

正體字

520b06║ [4]不動地第八
520b07║ 他化自在王　諸天及菩薩
520b08║ 聞說此上行　心皆大歡喜
520b09║ 供養佛[5]佛子{1}雨上妙華香
520b10║ 瓔珞眾幡蓋　末香諸寶衣
520b11║ 真妙摩尼珠　莊嚴身諸物
520b12║ 如雲空中下　散佛及大眾{2}
520b13║ 天女於空中　作種種伎樂
520b14║ 供養於如來　并及諸菩薩
520b15║ 同以微妙音　歌頌諸功德{3}
520b16║ 一切智慧者　眾生中最尊
520b17║ 憐愍世間故　佛現神通力
520b18║ 華香珍寶等　皆出如是音{4}
520b19║ 所有毛塵沙　各示那由他
520b20║ 無量數諸佛　於中而說法{5}
520b21║ 於一毛頭中　見無量佛國
520b22║ 須彌鐵圍海　世間不迫隘{6}

简体字

不动地第八

他化自在王，　诸天及菩萨，
闻说此上行，　心皆大欢喜。
供养佛弟子，　雨上妙华香，
璎珞众幡盖，　末香诸宝衣。
真妙摩尼珠，　庄严身诸物，
如云空中下，　散佛及大众。
天女于空中，　作种种伎乐，
供养于如来，　并及诸菩萨，
同以微妙音，　歌颂诸功德：
“一切智慧者，　众生中最尊！”
怜愍世间故，　佛现神通力，
华香珍宝等，　皆出如是音。
所有毛尘沙，　各示那由他，
无量数诸佛，　于中而说法。
于一毛头中，　见无量佛国，
须弥铁围海，　世间不迫隘。

Chapter Eight
The Immovability Ground

H. The Eighth Ground: The Immovability Ground

1. The Eighth Ground's Introductory Verses and Dharma Request

The Paranirmita Vaśavartin Deva King
along with all the devas and bodhisattvas,
on hearing the explanation of these superior practices,
were all moved to feelings of great exultation.
Presenting offerings to the Buddha and those sons of the Buddha, {1}

they then showered down supremely marvelous blossoms, incenses,
jeweled necklaces, many sorts of banners and canopies,
powdered scents, robes embroidered with gems,
real and wondrous *maṇi* jewels,
and all manner of other bodily adornments,
all of them descending like a cloud from space above,
sprinkling down on the Buddha and that immense congregation. {2}

Then, from their place in the space above, the celestial nymphs
made many and various sorts of music
as their offering to the Tathāgata
and to all of the bodhisattvas as well,
while also uniting in a chorusing of sublime voices
in which they sang forth verses praising their meritorious qualities: {3}

"He who is possessed of all-knowledge
and who, among all beings, is the most revered,
Because of his kindly pity for the inhabitants of the world,
the Buddha manifests the power of his spiritual superknowledges,
thereby causing these blossoms, incenses, jewels, and other such gifts
to also send forth these very same sounds. {4}

Within every point of hair, mote of dust, or grain of sand,
there are manifest *nayutas*
of countlessly many buddhas,
who are proclaiming the Dharma therein. {5}

Even in the tip of but a single hair,
one sees countlessly many buddha lands,
Sumerus, Iron Ring Mountains, and seas,
even as those worlds all reside therein without any constriction. {6}

正體字

520b23|| 於一毛頭中 [6]具有三惡道
520b24|| 天人阿修羅 各各受業報 {7}
520b25|| 見諸佛國中 一切佛妙音
520b26|| 轉無上法輪 隨起眾生念 {8}
520b27|| 諸佛世界中 眾生身種種
520b28|| 國有眾生身 眾生身有國
520b29|| 一切諸天人 悉皆離共住
520c01|| 佛先觀察已 然後為說法 {9}
520c02|| 微塵中國土 眾生心想細
520c03|| 以國土麁故 眾生心[7]想麁
520c04|| 佛現如是等 種種神通力
520c05|| 若為眾生說 是事不可盡 {10}
520c06|| 如是以妙音 稱歎於世尊
520c07|| 心皆大歡喜 默然而觀佛
520c08|| 解脫月菩薩 請金剛藏言
520c09|| 佛子今可說 入於八地相 {11}
520c10|| {A}金剛藏菩薩言。佛子。諸菩薩摩訶薩。已習七
520c11|| 地微妙行。慧方便道。

简体字

于一毛头中，　具有三恶道，
天人阿修罗，　各各受业报。
见诸佛国中，　一切佛妙音，
转无上法轮，　随起众生念。
诸佛世界中，　众生身种种，
国有众生身，　众生身有国。
一切诸天人，　悉皆离共住，
佛先观察已，　然后为说法。
微尘中国土，　众生心想细，
以国土粗故，　众生心想粗。
佛现如是等，　种种神通力，
若为众生说，　是事不可尽。
如是以妙音，　称叹于世尊，
心皆大欢喜，　默然而观佛。
解脱月菩萨，　请金刚藏言：
“佛子今可说，　入于八地相。”

金刚藏菩萨言：“佛子，诸菩萨摩诃萨已习七地微妙行，慧方便道，

Even within the tip of but a single hair,
There exist in their entirety the three wretched destinies,
the devas, the humans, and the *asuras*, in each and every one of which
there is the undergoing of their karmic retributions therein. {7}

One sees in all of these buddha lands
all buddhas holding forth with their marvelous voices,
turning the wheel of the unsurpassable Dharma
in accordance with the thoughts arising in the minds of beings. {8}

Within the lands of the Buddhas,
the bodies of the beings therein are of all different sorts.
These lands contain the bodies of these beings
and these beings' bodies themselves contain lands as well.

All of the devas and humans therein
in every case dwell separately from each other.
After first closely contemplating them, the Buddhas
afterward speak the Dharma for their sakes. {9}

In those lands residing within even the finest atoms,
it is in correspondence to beings' thoughts that they appear minute,
whereas, in the case of lands that manifest as large,
it is in correspondence to beings' thoughts that they appear large.[229]

The Buddhas manifest such phenomena as these as a function of
the power of their many different sorts of spiritual superknowledges.
Even if all beings at once attempted to describe them all, their
narration of such phenomena could never be brought to an end." {10}

It was in this way that they used such sublime sounds
to set forth the praises of the Bhagavat.
The minds of everyone there were filled with immense delight
as they then became silent and gazed up at the Buddha.

Liberation Moon Bodhisattva
then set forth the request to Vajragarbha Bodhisattva, saying:
"O Son of the Buddha, could it be that you will now explain
the characteristic features of the eighth ground?" {11}

2. Vajragarbha Commences the Eighth Ground's Explanation

{A} Vajragarbha Bodhisattva then replied, saying:

3. 10 Accomplishments Associated With Entering the 8th Ground

O Son of the Buddha, here we have those bodhisattva *mahāsattvas* who, on seven grounds:

Have already implemented sublime practices;
Have followed the path of wisdom and skillful means;

正體字

淨善集助道法。大願力
520c12‖ 故。心住不滅。諸佛神力所護。善根得力。常念
520c13‖ 隨順如來力無畏。不共法。樂心深心。善淨成
520c14‖ 就。福德智力。大慈悲心故。不捨一切眾生。
520c15‖ 修行無量智道。{B}能入諸法本來。無生無滅。無
520c16‖ 相不出。不失不去。不還無所有性。初中後平
520c17‖ 等。不異如來。無分別智。一切心意識。憶想
520c18‖ 分別。無所貪著。入一切法。如虛空性。{C}是名菩
520c19‖ 薩得無生法忍入第八地。即時得是第八不
520c20‖ 動地。名為深行菩薩。難可得知。無能分別。離
520c21‖ 一切相。離一切想。[8]一切貪著。

简体字

净善集助道法，大愿力故，心住不灭，诸佛神力所护，善根得力，常念随顺如来力、无畏、不共法，乐心深心，善净成就，福德智力大慈悲心故，不舍一切众生，修行无量智道，能入诸法本来无生无灭无相、不出不失、不去不还无所有性，初中后平等，不异如来无分别智，一切心意识忆想分别无所贪著，入一切法如虚空性，是名菩萨得无生法忍入第八地。即时得是第八不动地，名为深行菩萨，难可得知，无能分别，离一切相，离一切想、一切贪著，

Have, with purity, well accumulated the dharmas assisting realization of the path;

Have, due to the power of their great vows, caused their resolve to endure and never cease;[230]

Have become protected by the spiritual powers of the Buddhas;[231]

Have acquired the power arising from their roots of goodness;[232]

Have remained ever mindful of and compliant with the Tathāgata's powers, fearlessnesses, and exclusive dharmas;[233]

Have well purified their higher aspirations and intentions;[234]

Have completely developed the power of merit and wisdom;[235]

And, by resort to the greatly kind and compassionate mind, have refrained from ever forsaking any being. So it is that they cultivate the path of measureless knowledge.[236]

4. 10 Types of Comprehension Associated With 8th Ground Access

{B} They have become able to penetratingly comprehend all dharmas:[237]

As originally unproduced;

As undestroyed;

As signless;

As neither coming forth into existence nor being lost;

As neither going nor coming;

As, by nature, devoid of any inherent existence;

As the same in the past, the present, and the future;

As not differing when penetrated by the Tathāgata's non-discriminating cognition;

As beyond any covetous grasping by the mind and mental consciousness's discriminations;

And they penetratingly comprehend all dharmas as, by nature, like empty space.

{C} This is what defines the bodhisattvas' acquisition of the unproduced-dharmas patience and marks their entry into eighth ground.

5. The Unproduced Dharmas Patience Basis of "Profound Practice"

It is on this basis that they immediately gain this eighth ground, the Ground of Immovability, and become known as "profound practice" bodhisattvas, those who have achieved a state that is difficult to know, one impenetrable by anyone's discriminating thought, one that has transcended all characteristic signs, one that has left behind all conceptual thought and all covetous attachment, one that is measureless, boundless, inconceivable,

正體字

無量無邊。不
520c22‖ 可思議。一切聲聞辟支佛。所不能壞。深大遠
520c23‖ 離。而現在前。諸佛子。譬如比丘。得於神通。
520c24‖ 心得自在。次第乃入滅盡定。一切動心。憶想
520c25‖ 分別。心所行事。皆悉盡滅。菩薩亦如是。住
520c26‖ 是遠行地。即時一切忽務都滅。得無身口意
520c27‖ 務。住大遠離。諸佛子。如人夢中。欲渡深水。
520c28‖ 是人爾時。發大精進。施大方便。欲渡此水。未
520c29‖ 渡之間。[9]廓然便覺。所渡方便。[10]乃忽遽事。即
521a01‖ 皆放捨。諸佛子。菩薩摩訶薩。亦如是。從初已
521a02‖ 來。發大精進。廣修行道。至不動地。一切遽
521a03‖ 事。[1]皆悉放捨。不行二心。諸所憶想。不復現
521a04‖ 前。譬如生梵世者。欲界煩惱。不現在前。如是
521a05‖ 諸佛子。菩薩住是不動地。一切心意識。不現
521a06‖ 在前。

简体字

无量无边，不可思议，一切声闻、辟支佛所不能坏，深大远离而现在前。

“诸佛子，譬如比丘得于神通，心得自在，次第乃入灭尽定，一切动心忆想分别、心所行事皆悉尽灭。菩萨亦如是，住是远行地，即时一切匆务都灭，得无身口意务，住大远离。诸佛子，如人梦中，欲渡深水，是人尔时发大精进，施大方便欲渡此水；未渡之间，廓然便觉，所渡方便乃匆遽事，即皆放舍。诸佛子，菩萨摩诃萨亦如是，从初已来发大精进，广修行道至不动地，一切遽事皆悉放舍，不行二心，诸所忆想不复现前。譬如生梵世者，欲界烦恼不现在前。如是，诸佛子，菩萨住是不动地，一切心意识不现在前，

insurmountable by any *śrāvaka*-disciple or *pratyekabuddha,* and one in which deep and vast transcendence is directly manifest.

6. "Profound Practice" Like a Monk with Superknowledges & Dhyānas

Sons of the Buddha, this circumstance is comparable to that of a bhikshu who has acquired the spiritual superknowledges, whose mind has achieved sovereign mastery, and who has sequentially pursued the acquisition of the absorptions to the point of entering the absorption of complete cessation wherein all movement of mind, all recollective thought, all discriminations, and all endeavors carried out by the mind have become entirely extinguished. So too it is with this bodhisattva who, dwelling on this Far-Reaching Ground, suddenly extinguishes all of his urgent involvements and thereby reaches a state entirely free of physical, verbal, and mental undertakings wherein he abides in a state of great detachment.

7. 8th Ground Likened to Awakening from a River-Fording Dream

Sons of the Buddha, his situation is like that of a man in the midst of a dream in which he is striving to get across a deep river. This man then exerts intensely vigorous effort in pursuing some great means to cross over this river. When he has still not gotten all the way across, beset by distress, he wakes up, whereupon he immediately entirely abandons his urgently pursued efforts.

Sons of the Buddha, so too it is with the bodhisattva *mahāsattva* who from the very beginning on forth to the present, has been engaged in exerting himself with great vigor, applying himself in the vast endeavor of cultivating the path. On arriving at the Ground of Immovability, all urgent endeavors are entirely relinquished. He does not course in duality-based thought. There is no longer any present manifestation of any sort of recollective thought.

8. 8th Ground Likened to the Brahma World's Absence of Afflictions

This circumstance is comparable to that of someone reborn into the Brahma World Heavens wherein none of the desire realm afflictions any longer manifest in him. So it is, O Sons of the Buddha, with this bodhisattva dwelling on the Ground of Immovability. None of the mental activity associated with the intellectual mind consciousness is any longer presently manifest in him. He does not even bring forth any further manifestation of thought associated with buddhahood, thought associated with bodhi, or thought

正體字

乃至佛心。菩提心涅槃心。尚不現前。
521a07‖ 何況當生世間心。諸佛子。是菩薩摩訶薩。隨
521a08‖ 順是地。以本願力故。又諸佛。為現其身。住
521a09‖ 在諸地。法流水中。如來智[2]慧。為作因緣。{D}諸
521a10‖ 佛皆作是言。善哉善哉。善男子。汝得是第一
521a11‖ 忍。順一切諸佛法。善男子。我有佛十力。四無
521a12‖ 所畏。十八不共法。汝今未得。當為得是諸功
521a13‖ 德故。加勤精進。亦莫捨此忍門。{E}善男子。汝
521a14‖ 雖得此第一甚深寂滅解脫。凡夫眾生。不善
521a15‖ 非寂滅。常發種種煩惱。為種種覺觀所害。汝
521a16‖ 當愍此眾生。{F}又善男子。汝應念本所願。欲大
521a17‖ 利益眾生。欲得不可思議智慧門。{G}又善男子。
521a18‖ 一切法性。一切法相。若有佛若無佛。常住
521a19‖ 不異。諸如來不以得此法故說名為佛。聲
521a20‖ 聞辟支佛。亦能得此寂滅無分別法。{H}善男
521a21‖ 子。汝觀我等無量清淨身相。無量智慧。無
521a22‖ 量清淨國土。

简体字

乃至佛心、菩提心、涅槃心，尚不现前，何况当生世间心？

“诸佛子，是菩萨摩诃萨随顺是地，以本愿力故，又诸佛为现其身，住在诸地法流水中，如来智慧为作因缘。诸佛皆作是言：‘善哉！善哉！善男子，汝得是第一忍，顺一切诸佛法。善男子，我有佛十力、四无所畏、十八不共法，汝今未得。当为得是诸功德故，加勤精进，亦莫舍此忍门。善男子，汝虽得此第一甚深寂灭解脱；凡夫众生不善非寂灭，常发种种烦恼，为种种觉观所害。汝当愍此众生！又善男子，汝应念本所愿，欲大利益众生，欲得不可思议智慧门。又善男子，一切法性，一切法相，若有佛、若无佛，常住不异。诸如来不以得此法故说名为佛，声闻、辟支佛亦能得此寂灭无分别法。善男子，汝观我等无量清净身相、无量智慧、无量清净国土，

associated with nirvāṇa, how much the less might he bring forth any sorts of worldly thoughts.

9. The Buddhas' Manifestation Before the 8th Ground Bodhisattva

Sons of the Buddha, as this bodhisattva *mahāsattva* follow along in accordance with this ground, he does so in reliance upon the power of his original vows. Additionally, the Buddhas manifest their bodies before him so that, as he abides on the grounds, he abides within the flow of the Dharma wherein the wisdom of the Tathāgatas serves for him as a cause and condition.

10. The Buddhas' Praise & Instructions for the 8th Ground Bodhisattva

{D} The Buddhas then say to him:

It is good indeed, good indeed, Son of Good Family, that you have acquired the foremost form of patience through which you accord with the Dharma of all buddhas. Son of Good Family. We are possessed of the ten powers of the Buddhas, the four fearlessness, and the eighteen dharmas exclusive to the Buddhas. You, however, have now still not acquired them. For the sake of acquiring these very qualities, you should bring diligence and vigor to bear even while you must still not allow yourself to relinquish this gateway of patience.

{E} Son of Good Family. Although you have acquired this foremost and extremely profound quiescent liberation, still, the common people and the other beings are not skilled in this and thus have not achieved this quiescence. They always bring forth all manner of afflictions and are injured by the many different sorts of ideation and discursive thought. You should extend your kindly pity to these beings.

{F} Furthermore, Son of Good Family. You should recall what you originally vowed to do in aspiring to bestow great benefit on beings and in aspiring to bring about their successful entry into the gateway of inconceivable wisdom.

{G} Additionally, Son of Good Family. Whether buddhas are present or buddhas are not present, the nature of all dharmas and the character of all dharmas always abide no differently. It is not on the basis of acquiring this dharma that the Tathāgatas are referred to as buddhas. Both *śrāvaka*-disciples and *pratyekabuddhas* are also able to acquire this dharma of quiescence and non-discrimination.

{H} Son of Good Family. Regard our measureless pure physical signs, our measureless wisdom, our measureless pure lands, our generation of measureless wisdom and measureless skillful means, our measureless light auras,[238] and our measureless

正體字

起無量智慧無量方便。無量
521a23‖ 圓光無量淨音。汝今應起如是等事。{I}又善男
521a24‖ 子。汝今適得此一法明。所謂。一切法寂滅。
521a25‖ 無有分別。無生法明。我等所得。無量無邊。
521a26‖ 若干億劫。算數所不能知。汝為得此故。應起
521a27‖ 此法。{J}[3]善男子。汝觀十方無量國土。無量眾
521a28‖ 生。無量諸法差別。汝應如實通達是事。隨順
521a29‖ 如是智。是菩薩。諸佛與如是等無量無邊。起
521b01‖ 智慧因緣門。以此無量門故。是菩薩。能起無
521b02‖ 量智差別業。皆悉成就。{K}諸佛子。我今為汝說。
521b03‖ 若諸佛。不令此菩薩住如是智慧門者。是菩
521b04‖ 薩。爾時畢竟則取涅槃。捨利益一切眾生。以
521b05‖ 諸佛與此菩薩如是無量無邊起智慧因緣
521b06‖ 故。於一念中。所生智慧。比從初地已來。乃至
521b07‖ 竟。第七地。百分不及一。千萬億分。百千萬億
521b08‖ 那由他。乃至無量無邊。阿僧祇分。不及一。乃

简体字

起无量智慧、无量方便、无量圆光、无量净音，汝今应起如是等事。又善男子，汝今适得此一法明，所谓一切法寂灭无有分别无生法明。我等所得，无量无边，若干亿劫算数所不能知。汝为得此故，应起此法。善男子，汝观十方无量国土、无量众生、无量诸法差别，汝应如实通达是事，随顺如是智。’是菩萨，诸佛与如是等无量无边起智慧因缘门。以此无量门故，是菩萨能起无量智差别业，皆悉成就。

“诸佛子，我今为汝说，若诸佛不令此菩萨住如是智慧门者，是菩萨尔时毕竟则取涅槃，舍利益一切众生。以诸佛与此菩萨如是无量无边起智慧因缘故，于一念中所生智慧，比从初地已来，乃至竟第七地，百分不及一，千万亿分、百千万亿那由他，乃至无量无边、阿僧祇分不及一，

pure voices. You should now bring forth these very phenomena yourself.

{I} Also, Son of Good Family. You have now acquired this one Dharma light,[239] namely the quiescence and absence of differentiating distinctions of all dharmas.[240] The light of the dharma of non-production that we have already acquired is such that it could never be known through calculations carried on across the course of an immeasurable and boundless number of however many *koṭis* of kalpas. It is for the sake of acquiring just such light as this that you should raise forth dharmas such as these.

{J} Son of Good Family. As you contemplate all the countlessly many lands, all the countlessly many beings, and all the countlessly many dharmas throughout the ten directions so possessed as they are of their distinct differences, you should develop an utterly penetrating reality-based comprehension of these phenomena that accords with knowledge such as this.

The Buddhas bestow upon this bodhisattva just so very countlessly and boundlessly many gateways into the generation of the causes and conditions associated with the development of wisdom. It is through employing these countlessly many gateways that this bodhisattva becomes able to generate countlessly many different wise karmic works and then bring them to complete realization.

11. The Importance of Buddhas' Appearing to 8th Ground Bodhisattvas

{K} Sons of the Buddha, I shall now explain this for your sakes. If the Buddhas did not cause this bodhisattva to dwell within gateways to wisdom such as these, this bodhisattva would then choose to enter into the absolute and final nirvāṇa, thereby abandoning his devotion to benefiting all beings. It is because the Buddhas bestow upon this bodhisattva just so countlessly and boundlessly many causes and conditions associated with the generation of wisdom that the wisdom he is then able to generate in but a single moment becomes such that all of that already produced from the first ground on through to the end of the seventh ground could not constitute even a single part in a hundred parts, a single part in a thousand myriads of *koṭis* of parts, a single part in a hundred thousand myriads of *koṭis* of *nayutas* of parts, and so forth until we come to its not being able to equal even a single part in countlessly and boundlessly many *asaṃkhyeyas* of parts, and its being unable to equal even a single part in a number of parts describable only by calculation or analogy.

正體字

521b09‖ 至算數譬喻。所不能及。所以者何。先以一身
521b10‖ 行道。修集功德。今此地中。得無量身。修菩薩
521b11‖ 道。以無量音聲。以無量智慧。無量生處。無
521b12‖ 量清淨國土。無量教化眾生。供養給侍無量
521b13‖ 諸佛故。隨順無量佛法故。無量神通力故。無
521b14‖ 量大會差別故。無量身口意業。集一切菩薩
521b15‖ 所行道。以不動法故。佛子。譬如乘船。欲入大
521b16‖ 海。未得大海。多用功力。或以手力。若至大
521b17‖ 海。不復用力。但以風力而去。若本功力。於
521b18‖ 大海中。一日之行。於百千歲。不能得及。諸佛
521b19‖ 子。諸菩薩摩訶薩。亦如是。多集善根資糧。乘
521b20‖ 大乘船。到菩薩所行大智慧海。於須臾間。不
521b21‖ 施功力。

简体字

乃至算数譬喻所不能及。所以者何？先以一身行道修集功德，今此地中，得无量身修菩萨道，以无量音声，以无量智慧、无量生处、无量清净国土、无量教化众生，供养给侍无量诸佛故，随顺无量佛法故，无量神通力故，无量大会差别故，无量身口意业，集一切菩萨所行道，以不动法故。

“佛子，譬如乘船欲入大海，未得大海，多用功力，或以手力；若至大海，不复用力，但以风力而去。若本功力，于大海中一日之行，于百千岁不能得及。诸佛子，诸菩萨摩诃萨亦如是，多集善根资粮，乘大乘船，到菩萨所行大智慧海，于须臾间，不施功力，

12. The Reasons 8th Ground Bodhisattva Practices Are So Measureless

And why is this the case? This is because all of the meritorious qualities cultivated and accumulated so far have been the product of but a single body's progression along the path. Now, beginning with this ground, he acquires countlessly many bodies in which he cultivates the bodhisattva path, employing as he does so countlessly many voices and countlessly many expressions of wisdom in countlessly many places of rebirth, and in countlessly many pure lands wherein, in all such circumstances, he engages in teaching countlessly many beings and in making offerings to, providing for, and serving countlessly many buddhas.

This is because, in doing so, he accords with the Dharma of countlessly many Buddhas and avails himself of the power of countlessly many sorts of spiritual superknowledges. It is because he engages in these practices in the context of countlessly many different sorts of congregations and carries forth countlessly many physical, verbal, and mental deeds in accumulating the path practices engaged in by all bodhisattvas, doing so in reliance upon the dharma of immovability.

13. This Bodhisattva's Practices Likened to Sailing out onto the Ocean

Sons of the Buddha, in this, he is comparable to someone embarking on a boat, aspiring to set sail on the great ocean. Before he can even succeed in setting sail on the great ocean, he must first devote a great deal of effort, perhaps even having to use the strength of his own arms to set forth. If he does indeed succeed in reaching the great ocean, only then may he desist from further exertion, for he then requires only the power of the wind to continue traveling. Were one to compare all of the effortful exertion initially required in reaching the ocean to that required after successfully launching out onto the great ocean, the distance travelled in a single day at sea could not be matched by even a hundred thousand years of his previous types of effort.

Sons of the Buddha, so too it is with the bodhisattva *mahāsattva*. He must first assemble abundant provisions in the form of his roots of goodness, whereupon he then boards the ship of the Great Vehicle. Having reached the great ocean of wisdom coursed in by the bodhisattvas, in the course of but a single instant during which he does not devote any effortful application of his powers, he is then able to draw near to that wisdom that is employed by all buddhas. All of those accumulated efforts that he originally devoted to this could not even approach his current capacities

正體字

能近一切諸佛智慧。本所施功。若一
521b22‖ 劫。若百千萬劫。不能得及。{L}諸佛子。菩薩摩
521b23‖ 訶薩。得至第八地。從[4]本方便慧。生無功用
521b24‖ 心。在菩薩道。思惟諸佛智慧勢力。所謂。知世
521b25‖ 界生。世界滅。世界壞。世界成。知以何業因緣
521b26‖ 滅故世界壞。知以何業因緣集故世界成。是
521b27‖ 菩薩。知地性小相。知地性大相。知地性無量
521b28‖ 相。知地性差別相。知水火風性。小相大相。
521b29‖ 無量相。差別相。知微塵細相。知微塵差別相。
521c01‖ 於一世界中。所有微塵差別。皆悉能知。此一
521c02‖ 世界所有地。若干微塵。皆悉能知。若[5]干水
521c03‖ [6]火風微塵。皆悉能知。[7]知若干寶物。斤兩微
521c04‖ 塵。

简体字

能近一切诸佛智慧。本所施功，若一劫、若百千万劫，不能得及。

“诸佛子，菩萨摩诃萨得至第八地，从本方便慧生无功用心，在菩萨道思惟诸佛智慧势力，所谓：知世界生、世界灭、世界坏、世界成，知以何业因缘灭故世界坏，知以何业因缘集故世界成。是菩萨知地性小相，知地性大相，知地性无量相，知地性差别相，知水、火、风性小相、大相、无量相、差别相。知微尘细相，知微尘差别相，于一世界中所有微尘差别，皆悉能知。此一世界所有地，若干微尘，皆悉能知；若干水、火、风微尘，皆悉能知。知若干宝物斤两微尘，

even if they were similarly employed for an entire kalpa or even if they were employed for a hundred thousand myriads of kalpas.

14. The Bodhisattva's Contemplation of Buddha's All-Knowledge

{L} Sons of the Buddha, the bodhisattva *mahāsattva* who has reached the eighth ground gives birth to effortless functioning of mind arising from great[241] skillful means and knowledge. Then, as he abides on the bodhisattva path, he contemplates the power of all buddhas' wisdom.

15. His Knowledge of Worlds' Arising, Deterioration, & Destruction

In particular, he thereby knows of the production of worlds, the destruction of worlds, the deterioration of worlds, and the creation of worlds. He knows on account of the cessation of which karmic causes and conditions worlds then deteriorate and he knows on account of the aggregation of which karmic causes and conditions worlds are then created.

16. His Knowledge of the Four Elemental Phases

This bodhisattva knows with respect to the earth element its character when small, knows with respect to the earth element its character when large, knows with respect to the earth element its character when manifest on an immeasurable scale, knows with respect to the earth element its character in its different manifestations, and knows too with respect to the water, fire, and wind elements, their character when small, their character when large, their character when manifest on an immeasurable scale, and their character in their different manifestations.

17. His Knowledge of Atoms' Manifestations in Worlds and Beings

He knows too with respect to atoms their character when minute and knows with respect to atoms their character in their different manifestations. He is able to completely know with respect to a single world system all of the different manifestations of the atoms contained within it, is able to completely know with respect to the earth element within this single world system precisely how many atoms are contained within it, and is able to completely know with respect to the water, fire, and wind element, precisely how many atoms are associated with each of them.

He knows however many precious things are contained therein, knows the volume and weight of atoms contained therein, knows the number of atoms contained in the beings therein, and knows with respect to the myriad things within that world system all of differences in the atoms comprising them.

正體字

若干眾生身微塵。世界中萬物。微塵差別。
521c05‖ 分別眾生。麁身細身。從若干微塵。生地獄身。
521c06‖ 從若干微塵。生畜生身。以若干微塵。生餓鬼
521c07‖ 身。以若干微塵。生阿修羅身。以若干微塵。生
521c08‖ 天身。以若干微塵。生人身。皆悉了知。是菩
521c09‖ 薩。入如是分別微塵智中。知欲界壞。知欲界
521c10‖ 成。知色界壞。知色界成。知無色界壞。知無色
521c11‖ 界成。知欲界色界無色界成壞。知欲界小相。
521c12‖ 知欲界大相。知欲界無量相。知欲界差別相。
521c13‖ 知色界無色界。小相大相。無量相差別相。如
521c14‖ 是知三界。

简体字

若干众生身微尘，世界中万物微尘差别。分别众生粗身、细身，从若干微尘生地狱身，从若干微尘生畜生身，以若干微尘生饿鬼身，以若干微尘生阿修罗身，以若干微尘生天身，以若干微尘生人身，皆悉了知。是菩萨入如是分别微尘智中，知欲界坏，知欲界成；知色界坏，知色界成；知无色界坏，知无色界成；知欲界、色界、无色界成坏；知欲界小相，知欲界大相，知欲界无量相，知欲界差别相；知色界、无色界小相、大相、无量相、差别相。如是知三界，

He is able to distinguish with respect to the beings therein the character of their bodies when large and the character of their bodies when minute, knows how many atoms comprise the bodies of those born into the hell realms, knows how many atoms comprise the bodies of those born into the animal realms, knows how many atoms comprise the bodies of those born into the hungry ghost realms, knows how many atoms comprise bodies of those born into the celestial realms, and knows how many atoms comprise bodies of those born into the human realm. He completely knows all of these things. This bodhisattva accesses such forms of knowledge as are capable of distinguishing these manifestations of the atoms contained therein.

18. His Knowledge of the Three Realms of Existence

He knows too with respect to the desire realm the character of destruction as it takes place therein, knows with respect to the desire realm the character of creation as it takes place therein, knows with respect to the form realm the character of destruction as it take place therein, knows with respect to the form realm the character of creation as it takes place therein, knows with respect to the formless realm the character of destruction as it takes place therein, and knows with respect to the formless realm the character of creation as it takes place therein. So it is that he knows with respect to the desire realm, form realm, and formless realm the character of creation and destruction as they take place therein.

He knows with respect to the desire realm the character of phenomena when they are small, knows with respect to the desire realm the character of phenomena when they are large, knows with respect to the desire realm the character of phenomena when they are manifest to an immeasurably vast extent, and knows with respect to the desire realm the character of phenomena in their various different manifestations.

He knows too with respect to form realm and formless realm phenomena their character when small, their character when large, their character when manifest to an immeasurably vast extent, and their character in their different manifestations. Just so is the character of his knowing of the three realms of existence.

正體字

是名菩薩教化眾生助智明分。善
521c15‖ 知分別眾生身。善觀所應生處。隨眾生生處。
521c16‖ 隨眾生身。而為受身。是菩薩。現身遍滿三千
521c17‖ 大千世界。隨眾生身。各各差別。如日於一切
521c18‖ 水。皆現其像。若二三千大千世界。三四五。十
521c19‖ 二十三十四十五十百。三千大千世界。若千
521c20‖ 若萬。若百萬若千萬。若億若百千萬億。那由
521c21‖ 他世界。身遍其中。乃至無量無邊。不可思議。
521c22‖ 不可說。三千大千世界。身遍滿其中。隨眾生
521c23‖ 身差別。而為受身。是菩薩。成就如是智慧。於
521c24‖ 一世界。身不動搖。乃至不可說諸佛世界。隨
521c25‖ 眾生身。隨所信樂。於諸佛大會。而現身像。{M}若
521c26‖ 於沙門會中。示沙門形色婆羅門眾中。示婆
521c27‖ 羅門形色。剎利眾中。示剎利形色。居士眾中。
521c28‖ 示居士形色。四天王眾中。帝釋眾中。魔眾
521c29‖ 中。梵天眾中。

简体字

是名菩萨教化众生助智明分，善知分别众生身，善观所应生处，随众生生处，随众生身而为受身。是菩萨现身遍满三千大千世界，随众生身各各差别，如日于一切水皆现其像，若二三千大千世界，三、四、五、十、二十、三十、四十、五十、百、三千大千世界，若千、若万、若百万、若千万、若亿、若百千万亿那由他世界，身遍其中；乃至无量无边、不可思议、不可说三千大千世界，身遍满其中，随众生身差别而为受身。是菩萨成就如是智慧，于一世界身不动摇，乃至不可说诸佛世界，随众生身，随所信乐，于诸佛大会而现身像。若于沙门会中，示沙门形色。婆罗门众中，示婆罗门形色。刹利众中，示刹利形色。居士众中，示居士形色。四天王众中，帝释众中，魔众中，梵天众中，

19. His Application of Knowledge in Adaptive Births To Teach Beings

These factors constitute aspects contributing to the bodhisattva's light of knowledge used in teaching beings. He thoroughly assesses the differences in the various bodies of beings and thoroughly contemplates into which circumstances he should take on rebirth. He accords with the circumstances into which beings are born and adapts to the types of bodies into which beings are born and thereby takes on bodies for their benefit.

This bodhisattva manifests bodies filling all places everywhere throughout the worlds of a great trichiliocosm that adapt to the types of bodies into which beings are born, adapting to each and every one of their different types. In this, he is comparable to the sun that manifests its reflected image in every single body of water. Whether it is in the worlds of two great trichiliocosms, of three, four, or five great trichiliocosms, of twenty, thirty, forty, fifty, or a hundred great trichiliocosms, in the worlds of a thousand, a myriad, a hundred myriad, a thousand myriad, a *koṭi,* a hundred thousand myriad *koṭis,* or even in the worlds of a *nayuta* of great trichiliocosms, his bodies go forth everywhere within them. So too does this continue to be the case even on up to the point where, in the worlds of countlessly many, boundlessly many, inconceivably many, and ineffably many great trichiliocosms, his bodies go forth everywhere within them as, in each case, he takes on incarnations that adapt to the different variations in the bodies of the beings residing therein.

Having perfected wisdom such as this, even as this bodhisattva abides in but a single world in a body that remains utterly motionless, he manifests physical appearances within the great congregations of the buddhas residing in even up to an indescribably great number of buddha worlds, adapting to the types of physical incarnations taken on by beings there and adapting, too, to those beings' resolute convictions.

{M} If a being amenable to liberation abides within an assembly of *śramaṇas,* he manifests in the form of a *śramaṇa,* if within a congregation of brahmins, he manifests in the form of a brahmin, if within a congregation of *kṣatriyas,* he manifests in the form of a *kṣatriya,* and if within a congregation of the laity, he then manifests in the form of a layman. So, too, if a being abides within a congregation associated with the Four Heavenly Kings, in a congregation associated with Śakra Devānām Indra, in a congregation of *māras,* or in a congregation associated with the Brahma Heaven King, then he manifests in forms appropriate to those

正體字

示梵天形色。乃至阿迦貳吒天
522a01‖ 眾中。示阿迦貳[1]吒形色。以聲聞乘度者。
522a02‖ 示聲聞形色。以辟支佛乘度者。示辟支佛
522a03‖ 形色。以菩薩乘度者。示菩薩形色。以佛身
522a04‖ 度者。示佛身形色。諸佛子。所有不可說。諸
522a05‖ 佛[2]國中。隨眾生身。信樂差別。現為受身。{N}而
522a06‖ 實遠離身相差別。常住諸身平等。是菩薩。
522a07‖ 知眾生身。知國土身。知業報身。知聲聞身。
522a08‖ 知辟支佛身。知菩薩身。知如來身。知智身。
522a09‖ 知法身。知虛空身。[3]菩薩如是。知眾生深心
522a10‖ 所樂。若於眾生身。作己身。若於眾生身。作
522a11‖ 國土身。

简体字

示梵天形色；乃至阿迦贰吒天众中，示阿迦贰吒形色。以声闻乘度者，示声闻形色。以辟支佛乘度者，示辟支佛形色。以菩萨乘度者，示菩萨形色。以佛身度者，示佛身形色。

“诸佛子，所有不可说诸佛国中，随众生身信乐差别现为受身，而实远离身相差别，常住诸身平等。是菩萨知众生身，知国土身，知业报身，知声闻身，知辟支佛身，知菩萨身，知如来身，知智身，知法身，知虚空身。菩萨如是知众生深心所乐，若于众生身作己身，若于众生身作国土身、

circumstances up to and including the circumstance where he manifests within a Brahma Heaven congregation. And so it goes all the way on up to that circumstance of a being amenable to liberation abiding in an Akaniṣṭha Heaven congregation whereupon he manifests in the form of a resident of the Akaniṣṭha Heaven.

Where there are those who would most readily achieve liberation through the Śrāvaka-disciple Vehicle, he then manifests in the form of a *śrāvaka*-disciple. Where someone would most readily achieve liberation through the Pratyekabuddha Vehicle, he then manifests in the form of a *pratyekabuddha.* Where someone would most readily achieve liberation through the Bodhisattva Vehicle, he then manifests in the form of a bodhisattva. And for someone who would most readily achieve liberation through the appearance of a buddha's body, he then manifests in the form of a buddha's body.

20. His Transcendence of Discriminations & Knowledge of 10 Body Types

Sons of the Buddha, he manifests in this manner in all of the ineffable numbers of buddha lands, manifesting rebirth in bodies adapting to the different physical forms of beings and adapting too to their different resolute dispositions. {N} Even so, he has actually completely abandoned any such discriminations regarding the distinctions in beings' characteristic physical features, for he always abides in the recognition of the uniformly equal character of all physical forms. This bodhisattva:

Knows beings' bodies;
Knows the physical bodies of lands;
Knows those bodies received as karmic retribution;
Knows the bodies of *śrāvaka*-disciples;
Knows the bodies of *pratyekabuddhas;*
Knows the bodies of bodhisattvas;
Knows the bodies of *tathāgatas;*
Knows the body of knowledge;
Knows the Dharma body;
And knows empty space bodies.

a. The Bodhisattva's Manifestation of Different Bodies for Beings

So it is that the bodhisattva, knowing a being's resolute convictions, may make the body of a being into his own body. So too, he may cause a being's body:

To become the body of a land;

正體字

業報身。聲聞身。辟支佛身。菩薩身。
522a12‖ 如來身。智身法身。虛空身。若於國土身。作
522a13‖ 己身。業報身。乃至虛空身。若於業報身作己
522a14‖ 身。乃至虛空身。若於己身。作眾生身。國土
522a15‖ 身。業報身。聲聞身辟支佛身。菩薩身如來
522a16‖ 身。智身法身虛空身。是菩薩。知眾生集業身。
522a17‖ 報身。煩惱身。色身無色身。諸佛國土。小相大
522a18‖ 相。垢相淨相。無量相。

简体字

业报身、声闻身、辟支佛身、菩萨身、如来身、智身、法身、虚空身，若于国土身作己身、业报身乃至虚空身，若于业报身作己身乃至虚空身，若于己身作众生身、国土身、业报身、声闻身、辟支佛身、菩萨身、如来身、智身、法身、虚空身。是菩萨知众生集业身、报身、烦恼身、色身、无色身，诸佛国土小相、大相、垢相、净相、无量相、

To become a karmic retribution body;
To become the body of a *śrāvaka*-disciple;
To become the body of a *pratyekabuddha;*
To become the body of a bodhisattva;
To become the body of a *tathāgata;*
To become a knowledge body;
To become the Dharma body;
Or to become an empty space body.

So too may he turn the physical body of a land into his own body, into a body received as karmic retribution, and so forth on through to his turning of that physical body into an empty space body.

So too may he turn a body received as karmic retribution into his own body, and so forth on through to his doing this with all of the other sorts of bodies on up to and including an empty space body.

So too may he turn his own body into:

The body of a being;
The body of a land;
The body received as karmic retribution;
The body of a *śrāvaka*-disciple;
The body of a *pratyekabuddha;*
The body of a bodhisattva;
The body of a *tathāgata;*
The knowledge body;
The Dharma body;
Or an empty space body.

b. The Bodhisattva's Knowledge of Beings' Bodies

This bodhisattva knows beings' bodies associated with the accumulation of karmic deeds, their karmic retribution bodies, their bodies associated with the afflictions, their form-realm bodies, and their formless-realm bodies.

c. The Bodhisattva's Knowledge of the Bodies of Lands

He also knows with regard to the lands of buddhas:

Their characteristics when small;
Their characteristics when large;
Their characteristics when defiled;
Their characteristics when pure;
Their characteristics when immeasurable;

正體字

廣相倒相。平相曲相。
522a19‖ 方相方差別相。知業報身假名差別。聲聞身
522a20‖ 假名差別。辟支佛身假名差別。菩薩身假名
522a21‖ 差別。如來身差別。菩提身願身。化身受神力
522a22‖ 身。相好莊嚴身。勢力身意生身。福德身智身
522a23‖ 法身。善分別。如實[4]說諸身相。知諸法身平
522a24‖ 等不壞相。知虛空身。無量相周遍相無形相。
522a25‖ {O}是菩薩。善知起如是諸身。

简体字

广相、倒相、平相、曲相、方相、方差别相，知业报身假名差别、声闻身假名差别、辟支佛身假名差别、菩萨身假名差别、如来身差别，菩提身、愿身、化身、受神力身、相好庄严身、势力身、意生身、福德身、智身、法身善分别。如实说诸身相，知诸法身平等不坏相，知虚空身无量相、周遍相、无形相。是菩萨善知起如是诸身，

Their characteristics when vast;
Their characteristics when inverted;
Their characteristics when flat;
Their characteristics when curved;
Their characteristics when associated with a particular spatial direction;
And their characteristics when associated with different spatial directions.

d. His Knowledge of Retribution, 2-Vehicles, and Bodhisattva Bodies

He knows with respect to karmic retribution bodies the distinctions in the conventional names applied to them, knows with respect to the bodies of *śrāvaka*-disciples the distinctions in the conventional names applied to them, knows with respect to the bodies of *pratyekabuddhas* the distinctions in the conventional names applied to them, and knows with respect to the bodies of bodhisattvas the distinctions in the conventional names applied to them.

e. The Bodhisattva's Knowledge of Tathāgatas' Bodies

So, too, he knows with respect to the bodies of *tathāgatas* the distinctions associated with them. Thus he knows their possession of:

Bodhi bodies;
Bodies associated with vows;
Transformationally produced bodies;
Bodies sustained with spiritual powers;
Bodies graced with the major marks and subsidiary signs;
Bodies possessed of strength;
Mind-generated bodies;
Merit bodies;
The knowledge body;
And the Dharma body.

He skillfully distinguishes and discourses in accordance with reality on the characteristic features of all of these bodies. He knows with respect to the Dharma body its characteristics of uniform equality and indestructibility and knows with respect to empty space bodies their quality of immeasurability, their quality of universal pervasion, and their quality of formlessness.

21. The Bodhisattva's Acquisition of Ten Kinds of Sovereign Mastery

{O} Having developed a skillful knowing with regard to the arising of all of these bodies, this bodhisattva then acquires:

正體字

則得命自在心自
522a26‖ 在。財物自在業自在。生自在願自在。信解
522a27‖ 自在如意自在。智自在法自在。{P}是菩薩。得
522a28‖ 是菩薩十自在。即時為不可思議智者。無
522a29‖ 量智者。廣智者。不可壞智者。菩薩隨如是智
522a30‖ 慧。畢竟常淨。起無罪身業口業意業。身業隨
522b01‖ 智行。口業隨智行。意業隨智行。般若波羅蜜
522b02‖ 為增上。大悲為首。善修方便。善起諸願。善為
522b03‖ 諸佛神通所護。常不捨行利益眾生智。悉知
522b04‖ 無邊世界中差別事。諸佛子。舉要言之。菩薩
522b05‖ 住無動地。身口意業所作。皆能集一切佛法。

简体字

则得命自在、心自在、财物自在、业自在、生自在、愿自在、信解自在、如意自在、智自在、法自在。是菩萨得是菩萨十自在，即时为不可思议智者、无量智者、广智者、不可坏智者。菩萨随如是智慧毕竟常净，起无罪身业、口业、意业，身业随智行，口业随智行，意业随智行，般若波罗蜜为增上，大悲为首，善修方便，善起诸愿，善为诸佛神通所护，常不舍行利益众生智，悉知无边世界中差别事。

“诸佛子，举要言之，菩萨住无动地，身口意业所作，皆能集一切佛法。

Sovereign mastery in lifespan;
Sovereign mastery of mind;
Sovereign mastery in wealth;
Sovereign mastery in karmic deeds;
Sovereign mastery in births;
Sovereign mastery in vows;
Sovereign mastery in resolute faith;
Sovereign mastery in psychic power;
Sovereign mastery in knowledge;
And sovereign mastery in Dharma.

{P} Having acquired these ten types of bodhisattva sovereign mastery, this bodhisattva then immediately becomes one whose knowledge is inconceivable, one whose knowledge is measureless, one whose knowledge is vast, and one whose knowledge is invincible.

22. Ten Characteristic Aspects of this Eighth Ground Bodhisattva

According with just such wisdom as this, the bodhisattva thereby becomes:

One who remains ultimately and always pure;
One who remains entirely free of karmic transgressions in his physical karmic deeds, verbal karmic deeds, and mental karmic deeds;
One in whom his physical karmic deeds are carried forth in accordance with knowledge, his verbal karmic deeds are carried forth in accordance with knowledge, and his mental karmic deeds are carried forth in accordance with knowledge;
One in whom the *prajñāpāramitā* is dominant;
One who takes the great compassion as what is foremost;
One who skillfully cultivates expedient means;
One who skillfully brings forth the vows;
One who is well protected by the spiritual superknowledges of all buddhas;
One who never abandons his practice of that knowledge through which he carries on the practice of benefiting beings;
And one who completely knows the different phenomena occurring within all the boundlessly many worlds.

Sons of the Buddha, to state this in terms of the most essential point, this bodhisattva dwelling on the Ground of Immovability is able to gather all dharmas of the Buddha in all that he accomplishes through his physical, verbal, and mental deeds.

正體字

522b06‖ 是菩薩。到此地中。離一切煩惱故善住淨心
522b07‖ 力中。心常不離道故善住深心力中。不捨眾
522b08‖ 生故善住大悲力中。救一切世間故善住大
522b09‖ 慈力中。不忘所聞法故善住陀羅尼力中。分
522b10‖ 別選擇一切佛法故善住一切樂說力中。行
522b11‖ 無邊差別世界故善住神通力中。不捨一切
522b12‖ 菩薩所行故善住願力中。修集一切佛法故
522b13‖ 安住波羅蜜力中。善起一切種智故安住如
522b14‖ 來力中。是菩薩。得如是智力。示一切所作無
522b15‖ 有過咎。{Q}諸佛子。諸菩薩摩訶薩。此地不可壞
522b16‖ 故。名為不動地。智慧不轉故。名為不轉地。一
522b17‖ 切世間。難測知故。名威德地。無家過故。名王
522b18‖ 子地。隨意自在故。名菩薩生地。

简体字

是菩萨到此地中，离一切烦恼故善住净心力中，心常不离道故善住深心力中，不舍众生故善住大悲力中，救一切世间故善住大慈力中，不忘所闻法故善住陀罗尼力中，分别选择一切佛法故善住一切乐说力中，行无边差别世界故善住神通力中，不舍一切菩萨所行故善住愿力中，修集一切佛法故安住波罗蜜力中，善起一切种智故安住如来力中。是菩萨得如是智力，示一切所作无有过咎。

“诸佛子，诸菩萨摩诃萨，此地不可坏故，名为不动地。智慧不转故，名为不转地。一切世间难测知故，名威德地。无家过故，名王子地。随意自在故，名菩萨生地。

23. Ten Types of Power in Which This Bodhisattva Is Well Established

Having reached this ground, this bodhisattva:

Is well established in the power of the pure mind through abandoning all afflictions;

Is well established in the power of the resolute intentions[242] through his mind's never departing from the path;

Is well established in the power of the great compassion through never forsaking beings.

Is well established in the power of the great kindness through rescuing the inhabitants of all worlds;

Is well established in the power of the *dhāraṇīs* through never forgetting Dharma he has heard;

Is well established in the power of eloquence through distinguishing and selectively choosing from among all dharmas of the Buddha;

Is well established in the power of the spiritual superknowledges through coursing in boundlessly many different worlds;

Is well established in the power of vows through never abandoning anything practiced by bodhisattvas;

Is well established in the power of the *pāramitās* through cultivating and accumulating all dharmas of the Buddha;

And is well established in the sustaining power of the Tathāgata[243] through his skillful development of the knowledge of all modes.

Because this bodhisattva has acquired powers of knowledge such as these, he remains free of fault in any of the endeavors that he brings forth.

24. The Ten Names of this Eighth Bodhisattva Ground

{Q} Sons of the Buddha, regarding this ground:

Because the bodhisattva *mahāsattvas* dwelling on this ground are invincible, it is known as the Ground of Immovability;

Because they are irreversible in their wisdom it is known as the ground of irreversibility;

Because no one in the entire world can fathom it, it is known as the ground of awe-inspiring qualities;

Because it is free of the faults associated with the home life, it is known as the ground of the prince;[244]

Because they possess sovereign mastery in accomplishing everything they turn their mind to, it is known as the ground of the bodhisattva's birth;

正體字

更不作故。名
522b19‖ 為成地。善擇[5]知故。名為究竟地。善發大願
522b20‖ 故。名為變化地。不[6]懷諸法故。名為勝處地。
522b21‖ 善修起先道故。名為無功力地。{R}諸佛子。諸菩
522b22‖ 薩摩訶薩。得如是智慧。名為得入佛境界。名
522b23‖ 為佛功德所照明。名為隨佛威儀行。趣向佛
522b24‖ 法。常為諸佛神力善護。常為四天王。釋提桓
522b25‖ 因。梵天王等所奉迎。常為密迹金剛神之所
522b26‖ 侍衛。善能生諸[7]深禪定。常能作無量諸身
522b27‖ 差別。於諸身中。皆有勢力。得大果報神通力。
522b28‖ 於無邊三昧中。得自在。能受無量記。隨眾
522b29‖ 生成就處。示成阿耨多羅三藐三菩提。是菩
522c01‖ 薩。入如是大智慧。善通達諸法。常放大慧
522c02‖ 光明。度無障礙法性道。善知世間[8]法道差
522c03‖ 別。能示一切諸功德。隨意自在。善解先際後
522c04‖ 際。

简体字

更不作故，名为成地。善择知故，名为究竟地。善发大愿故，名为变化地。不怀诸法故，名为胜处地。善修起先道故，名为无功力地。诸佛子，诸菩萨摩诃萨得如是智慧，名为得入佛境界，名为佛功德所照明，名为随佛威仪行趣向佛法，常为诸佛神力善护，常为四天王、释提桓因、梵天王等所奉迎，常为密迹金刚神之所侍卫，善能生诸深禅定，常能作无量诸身差别，于诸身中皆有势力，得大果报神通力，于无边三昧中得自在，能受无量记，随众生成就处，示成阿耨多罗三藐三菩提。是菩萨入如是大智慧，善通达诸法，常放大慧光明，度无障碍法性道，善知世间法道差别，能示一切诸功德随意自在，善解先际后际，

Because there is nothing more to be done, it is known as the ground of completion;
Because they are skillful in investigation with knowledge, it is known as the ultimate ground;
Because they are skillful in bringing forth great vows, it is known as the ground of transformations;
Because they are invincible in all dharmas, this ground is known as the place of victory;[245]
And because they have skillfully cultivated and developed the earlier phases of the path, it is known as the power of effortlessness ground.

25. Additional 8th Ground Bodhisattva Qualities and Practice Aspects

{R} Sons of the Buddha, when the bodhisattva *mahāsattvas* acquire wisdom such as this, they are said to thereby gain entry into the realms of the Buddhas, are said to become illuminated by the light of the Buddha's meritorious qualities, and are said to become accordant in their practice with the awe-inspiring deportment of the Buddha. They then progress toward the Dharma of buddhahood, are always well protected by the spiritual power of all buddhas, and are respectfully received by the Four Heavenly Kings, Śakra Devānām Indra, the Brahma Heaven King, and others of this sort while also always being surrounded and served by a protective coterie of traceless vajra-wielding guardian spirits.

They are well able then to generate all of the deep *dhyāna* absorptions and are well able to create countless different bodies, all of which bodies are then invested with powerful capacities, all of which acquire the power of superknowledges as karmically generated effects, all of which achieve sovereign mastery in boundlessly many samādhis, all of which become able to receive the bestowal of countless predictions, and all of which manifest the achievement of *anuttarasamyaksaṃbodhi* in circumstances adapted to the beings wherever this facilitates their complete development.

Having entered into such great wisdom as this, this bodhisattva skillfully achieves a penetrating comprehension of all dharmas, always sends forth the light of great wisdom, and moves along a path of unimpeded movement throughout the Dharma realm. He knows well the distinctions in the destinies associated with the worldly dharmas, is able to manifest all of the meritorious qualities, has sovereign mastery in whatever he directs his mind to, well understands both the past and the future, is able

正體字

能入迴轉魔道智中。入如來所行境界中。
522c05‖ 能於無邊世界。行菩薩道。以不轉相故。是故
522c06‖ 此地名為不動。{S}諸佛子。諸菩薩摩訶薩。在不
522c07‖ 動地。善生禪定力故。常不離[9]見無邊諸佛。
522c08‖ 而不捨麁[10]供養。供給諸佛。是菩薩。於一一
522c09‖ [11]劫。一[12]切世界中。見數百千萬億那由他無
522c10‖ 量無邊阿僧祇佛。供養恭敬。尊重讚歎。具一
522c11‖ 切供養事。而用供養。親近諸佛。從諸佛。受世
522c12‖ 間別異等諸法明。是人轉深入如來法藏。問
522c13‖ 世間性差別事中。無能盡者。乃至百千萬億
522c14‖ 劫。說不可盡。又諸善根。轉勝明淨。譬如成
522c15‖ 鍊真金。巧匠雜寶。作瓔珞已。繫四天下主
522c16‖ [13]頸。閻浮提人。無能奪者。諸佛子。菩薩摩訶
522c17‖ 薩。亦如是。住是無動地。諸善根轉勝明淨。一
522c18‖ 切聲聞辟支佛。

简体字

能入回转魔道智中，入如来所行境界中，能于无边世界行菩萨道。以不转相故，是故此地名为不动。

“诸佛子，诸菩萨摩诃萨在不动地，善生禅定力故，常不离见无边诸佛，而不舍粗现供具供给诸佛。是菩萨于一一劫，一切世界中，见数百千万亿那由他无量无边阿僧祇佛，供养恭敬，尊重赞叹，具一切供养事而用供养，亲近诸佛，从诸佛受世间别异等诸法明。是人转深入如来法藏，问世间性差别事中无能尽者，乃至百千万亿劫说不可尽。又诸善根转胜明净，譬如成炼真金，巧匠杂宝作璎珞已，系四天下主颈，阎浮提人无能夺者。诸佛子，菩萨摩诃萨亦如是，住是无动地，诸善根转胜明净，一切声闻、辟支佛，

to enter into the knowledge that turns back those ensconced in the paths of the *māras,* enters the realms in which the Tathāgata courses, and is able to practice the bodhisattva path in boundlessly many worlds. Because it is characterized by irreversibility, this ground is referred to as the Ground of Immovability.

26. The Bodhisattva's Seeing and Serving of Countless Buddhas

(S) Sons of the Buddha, because the bodhisattva *mahāsattvas* dwelling on the Ground of Immovability skillfully bring forth the power of *dhyāna* absorptions, they never depart from their viewing of all of the boundlessly many buddhas even as they never abandon their practice of making gifts of material offerings and providing sustaining support to the Buddhas.

In each and every kalpa and in all worlds, this bodhisattva sees many hundreds of thousands of myriads of *koṭis* of *nayutas* of incalculably and boundlessly many *asaṃkhyeyas* of buddhas. He makes offerings to them, pays them reverence, venerates them, and praises them. He acquires everything used as offerings and then uses them to present offerings to them.

27. The Bodhisattva's Further Acquisition of Buddhas' Dharma Light

He draws close to all buddhas and receives from all buddhas the light with which to illuminate the differences among worlds and other such dharmas. This person enters ever more deeply into the Dharma treasury of the Tathāgata. In this, he becomes such that no one questioning him on matters related to the differences in world realms could ever come to the end of his understanding, for it could never be exhaustively narrated even in hundreds of thousands of myriads of *koṭis* of kalpas.

28. The Radiance of Good Roots Likened to a Sage King's Adornments

Additionally, his roots of goodness become ever more supreme in their radiance and purity in the same way that occurs with the smelting of real gold and its skillful inlaying with various gems. After it has been made into a precious strand of jewels to be worn around the neck of the lord of the four continents, it becomes a precious object of a sort that none owned by anyone else on the continent of Jambudvīpa could ever rival its brilliance.

Sons of the Buddha, so too it is with this bodhisattva *mahāsattva* for, as he dwells on this Ground of Immovability, his roots of goodness become ever more superior in their radiance and purity, becoming such that *śrāvaka*-disciples, *pratyekabuddhas,* and even seventh-ground bodhisattvas cannot surpass them. Because the

正體字

乃至七地菩薩。所不能壞。菩
522c19‖ 薩住是地。以善分別智門故。智慧光明。滅眾
522c20‖ 生惱熱。[14]譬如佛子若千世界主。大梵天王。
522c21‖ 能於一時。流布慈心。滿千世界。亦能放光。
522c22‖ 遍照其中。諸佛子。菩薩摩訶薩。亦如是住無
522c23‖ 動地中。能放身光。照十萬三千大千世界微
522c24‖ 塵數等世界眾生。次能滅諸惱熱。令得清涼
522c25‖ 諸佛子。是名略說菩薩摩訶薩不動地。若廣
522c26‖ 說者。無量劫數。所不能盡。菩薩住是地中。多
522c27‖ 作大梵天王。主千世界。諸根猛利。與諸眾生。
522c28‖ 聲聞辟支佛菩薩。波羅蜜道因緣。無有窮盡。
522c29‖ 說世間性差別中。無能壞者。所作善業。若布
523a01‖ 施若愛語。若利益若同事。皆不離念佛念法
523a02‖ 念諸菩薩伴。乃至不離念一切種智。

简体字

乃至七地菩萨，所不能坏。菩萨住是地，以善分别智门故，智慧光明灭众生恼热。譬如，佛子，若千世界主大梵天王，能于一时流布慈心，满千世界，亦能放光遍照其中。诸佛子，菩萨摩诃萨亦如是，住无动地中，能放身光，照十万三千大千世界微尘数等世界众生；次能灭诸恼热，令得清凉。

“诸佛子，是名略说菩萨摩诃萨不动地。若广说者，无量劫数所不能尽。菩萨住是地中，多作大梵天王，主千世界，诸根猛利，与诸众生、声闻、辟支佛、菩萨波罗蜜道因缘，无有穷尽。说世间性差别中，无能坏者。所作善业，若布施、若爱语、若利益、若同事，皆不离念佛、念法、念诸菩萨伴，乃至不离念一切种智。

bodhisattva dwelling on this ground skillfully distinguishes the gateways to knowledge, the light of his wisdom extinguishes the fevers of beings' afflictions.

29. This Bodhisattva's Radiance Like That of a Brahma Heaven King

Sons of the Buddha, he is comparable in this to the king of the Great Brahma Heaven, the lord of a thousand worlds, who is able in but a moment to stream forth his thoughts of compassion in a way that causes them to entirely fill all of those thousand worlds even as he is also able to send forth light to entirely illuminate all places therein.

Sons of the Buddha, so too it is with this bodhisattva *mahāsattva* who abides on the Ground of Immovability, for he is able to send forth light from his body that illuminates beings in worlds as numerous as the atoms in the worlds of ten myriads of trichiliocosms which is then able to extinguish the fevers of all their afflictions and cause them to experience clarity and coolness.

30. Vajragarbha's Final Statements About the 8th Ground Bodhisattva

Sons of the Buddha, this has been a summary explanation of the bodhisattva *mahāsattva*'s Ground of Immovability. Were one to describe it extensively, one could never reach the end of that presentation even by continuing it for measurelessly many kalpas.

a. The Bodhisattva's Station and Dharma Practice

The bodhisattva dwelling on this ground often serves as a king of the Great Brahma Heaven, the lord over a thousand worlds. There, equipped with acutely sharp faculties, he endlessly bestows teachings on beings including *śrāvaka*-disciples and *pratyekabuddhas,* teachings on the causes and conditions of the path of the *pāramitās*. No one is able to prevail over him in discussions on the distinctions among world realms.

b. The Bodhisattva's Mindfulness

In all of the good karmic works that he pursues, whether it be through giving, pleasing words, beneficial actions, or joint endeavors, he never departs from mindfulness of the Buddha, mindfulness of the Dharma, mindfulness of his bodhisattva companions, and so forth until we come to his never departing from mindfulness of his quest to acquire the knowledge of all modes.

正體字

常生是
523a03‖ 心。我當何時於眾生中。為首為尊。乃至於一
523a04‖ 切眾[1]生。為依止者。是菩薩。若欲勤行精進。
523a05‖ 於須臾間。得百萬三千大千世界微塵數諸
523a06‖ 三昧。乃至能示百萬三千大千世界微塵數
523a07‖ 菩薩眷屬。{T}若以願力。神通自在。能過是數。若
523a08‖ 干百千萬億劫。不可稱計。爾時金剛藏菩薩。
523a09‖ 欲重明此義。而說偈言
523a10‖ 菩薩住七地 慧方便已[2]得
523a11‖ 善集助道法 大願之所繫
523a12‖ 諸佛神力護 善根悉成就
523a13‖ 求於勝智故 能入第八地 {12}
523a14‖ 善集於福[3]德 而有深慈悲
523a15‖ 離諸有量心 心同如虛空
523a16‖ 如所說法中 心得決定力
523a17‖ 如是得寂滅 微妙無生忍 {13}

简体字

常生是心：‘我当何时于众生中为首为尊？乃至于一切众生为依止者？’是菩萨若欲勤行精进，于须臾间，得百万三千大千世界微尘数诸三昧，乃至能示百万三千大千世界微尘数菩萨眷属；若以愿力神通自在，能过是数，若干百千万亿劫不可称计。”

尔时，金刚藏菩萨欲重明此义，而说偈言：

“菩萨住七地， 慧方便已得，
善集助道法， 大愿之所系。
诸佛神力护， 善根悉成就，
求于胜智故， 能入第八地。
善集于福德， 而有深慈悲，
离诸有量心， 心同如虚空。
如所说法中， 心得决定力，
如是得寂灭， 微妙无生忍。

c. The Bodhisattva's Aspiration to Serve Beings

He always reflects, "Oh, when will I finally become able to serve beings as a leader, as one who, in this, becomes worthy of veneration?" and so forth until we come to his thinking, "Oh, when will I finally become one upon whom all beings can rely?"

d. The Consequences of the Bodhisattva's Vigor and Vows

If this bodhisattva wishes to apply himself to the diligent practice of vigor, then, in but a moment, he acquires samādhis as numerous as the atoms in the worlds within hundreds of myriads of trichiliocosms, and so forth on up to his ability to manifest bodhisattvas in his retinue as numerous as the atoms in the worlds existing within hundreds of myriads of trichiliocosms.

{T} Were he to avail himself of the power of vows, through sovereign mastery in the spiritual superknowledges, he could manifest these phenomena in numbers even greater that this so large that one could never calculate them even in however many hundreds of thousands of myriads of *koṭis* of *nayutas* of kalpas one might attempt to do so.

31. Vajragarbha Bodhisattva's Summarizing Verses

At that time, Vajragarbha Bodhisattva, wishing to once again make clear these meanings, thereupon uttered verses, saying:

The bodhisattva dwelling on the seventh ground
who has already acquired skillful means and wisdom,
who has thoroughly gathered the dharmas assisting the path,
who is bound by great vows,

who is under the protection of all buddhas' spiritual powers,
and whose roots of goodness have all become completely developed,
because he seeks to acquire the supreme knowledge,
he then becomes able to enter the eighth ground. {12}

He skillfully accumulates merit and knowledge[246]
while also being possessed of deep kindness and compassion.
He transcends entirely the range of merely measurable thought
through the possession of a mind like empty space.

His mind reaches decisive and resolute power
accordant with the Dharma as it was actually proclaimed.
Thus he achieves realization of the quiescent
and sublime unproduced-dharmas patience. {13}

正體字

523a18║ 諸法從本來 無生亦無滅
523a19║ 無相亦無出 不失亦不行
523a20║ 諸法初中後 與如無分別
523a21║ 無有心意行 同若如虛空 {14}
523a22║ 成就如是忍 無有諸戲論
523a23║ 得是不動地 甚深寂滅行
523a24║ 一切諸世間 不能得測量
523a25║ 一切諸心相 皆悉已壞盡 {15}
523a26║ 菩薩住是地 心識無分別
523a27║ 如入滅盡定 無念想分別
523a28║ 猶如人夢中 [4]遽欲行渡水
523a29║ 覺則[5]心廓然 自知無所作
523b01║ 得是深忍已 一切想念滅
523b02║ 亦如諸梵[6]王 無欲界煩惱 {16}
523b03║ 先以願力護 諸佛[7]今勸言
523b04║ 如是第一忍 是諸佛職位
523b05║ 我等深智力 無畏不共法
523b06║ 汝既無有此 當加勤精進 {17}
523b07║ 汝今雖得滅 一切煩惱火
523b08║ 當觀諸世間 煩惱常熾然

简体字

诸法从本来，无生亦无灭，
无相亦无出，不失亦不行。
诸法初中后，与如无分别，
无有心意行，同若如虚空。
成就如是忍，无有诸戏论，
得是不动地，甚深寂灭行，
一切诸世间，不能得测量；
一切诸心相，皆悉已坏尽。
菩萨住是地，心识无分别，
如入灭尽定，无念想分别。
犹如人梦中，遽欲行渡水，
觉则心廓然，自知无所作。
得是深忍已，一切想念灭，
亦如诸梵王，无欲界烦恼。
先以愿力护，诸佛今劝言：
'如是第一忍，是诸佛职位！
我等深智力，无畏不共法；
汝既无有此，当加勤精进。
汝今虽得灭，一切烦恼火，
当观诸世间，烦恼常炽然。

He knows that all dharmas, from their very origin onward,
are neither produced nor destroyed,
are signless and uncreated,
and are neither lost nor continuing onward.

He knows all dharmas as, in the beginning, middle, and end,
indistinguishable from suchness.
He is free of any activity of the intellectual mind
and, in this, he is like empty space. {14}

Having perfected patience such as this,
he becomes free of any sort of frivolous theoretical ideation
and acquires this Ground of Immovability
and the practice of its extremely deep quiescence

that no one in the entire world
could ever fathom,
for he has already utterly destroyed
all characteristic features of thought. {15}

The bodhisattva abiding on this ground
is free of the mind consciousness's discriminations and in this is
just like one who has entered the complete cessation absorption
who thereby becomes free of recollective thought's discriminations.

He is like someone immersed in a dream wherein,
with fearful urgency, he is striving to finish fording a river.
When awakened from this, his mind experiences immense relief,
realizing then that there is really nothing at all that needs be done.

Once he has acquired this profoundly deep patience,
all thinking then becomes extinguished in him.
With this, he then becomes comparable to a Brahma Heaven king
who has become entirely free of the desire realm's afflictions. {16}

From the very beginning, he is protected by the power of his vows.
The Buddhas now manifest to him and encourage him, saying:
"It is this very patience, the foremost among them all,
that is a position assumed by all buddhas.

Our deep knowledge and powers,
our fearlessnesses, and our dharmas exclusive to the Buddhas—
given that you do not yet possess these yourself,
you must bring forth diligence and vigor to acquire them. {17}

Although you have now succeeded in extinguishing
all fires originating with the afflictions,
you should nonetheless contemplate that, in all worlds,
the fires of the afflictions still always blaze on fiercely.

正體字

523b09‖ 當念本所願　欲利諸眾生
523b10‖ 悉遍知諸法　廣度於一切 {18}
523b11‖ 諸法實性相　常住無變異
523b12‖ 二乘亦得此　不以得名佛
523b13‖ 但以得無礙　甚深微妙智
523b14‖ 通達三世故　乃得名為佛 {19}
523b15‖ 是諸無等等　天人所恭敬
523b16‖ 開是眾智門　令入諸佛法
523b17‖ 成就無邊底　無量妙智慧
523b18‖ 先所行諸法　不及今一念 {20}
523b19‖ 如是諸菩薩　得妙智慧地
523b20‖ 能在一念中　身遍於十方
523b21‖ 入是智慧門　行道疾無[8]礙
523b22‖ 如行於大海　風力令去疾 {21}
523b23‖ 離諸功用心　但在於智業
523b24‖ 觀十方世界　成壞及與住
523b25‖ 能知四大一　亦知種種異
523b26‖ 小大無量相　種種諸差別 {22}
523b27‖ 能數知三千　大千界微塵
523b28‖ 亦知眾生身　四大微塵數

简体字

当念本所愿，　欲利诸众生，
悉遍知诸法，　广度于一切。
诸法实性相，　常住无变异，
二乘亦得此，　不以得名佛。
但以得无碍，　甚深微妙智，
通达三世故，　乃得名为佛。
是诸无等等，　天人所恭敬，
开是众智门，　令入诸佛法。
成就无边底，　无量妙智慧，
先所行诸法，　不及今一念。 ，
如是诸菩萨，　得妙智慧地，
能在一念中，　身遍于十方。
入是智慧门，　行道疾无碍，
如行于大海，　风力令去疾。
离诸功用心，　但在于智业，
观十方世界，　成坏及与住。
能知四大一，　亦知种种异，
小大无量相，　种种诸差别。
能数知三千，　大千界微尘，
亦知众生身，　四大微尘数。

You should call to mind the vows you originally brought forth
in which you aspired to serve the benefit of all beings,
vowed to acquire the universal knowing of all dharmas,
and vowed to engage then in the vast work of liberating everyone. {18}

The actual character of the nature of dharmas
is that it is eternally abiding and unchanging.
Even followers of the Two Vehicles succeed in realizing this.
Thus being known as a buddha is not due merely to achieving this.

It is solely due to having acquired their unimpeded,
extremely profound, and sublime knowledge along with their
utterly penetrating comprehension of the three periods of time
that one can then be known as a buddha. {19}

It is these eminences who are the equal of even the unequaled
and who are those revered by both devas and humans
who have opened these many gateways to knowledge,
thereby allowing them to enter the Dharma of the Buddhas

and completely develop the boundless, bottomless,
immeasurable, and sublime wisdom.
With this, the entirety of all of his earlier practice of dharmas
cannot match a single instant of that in which he now courses. {20}

It is in this way that the bodhisattvas
succeed in reaching the ground of sublime wisdom
and become able in but a single instant,
to send forth their bodies everywhere throughout the ten directions.

They thereby enter the gate of wisdom
and progress on the path with unimpeded swiftness
just as when, as one sails along across the great sea,
the power of the wind causes one to move forth rapidly. {21}

He then entirely abandons all deliberately effortful thought,
resides solely within karmic works guided by knowledge,
and contemplates the worlds of the ten directions,
observing their creation, their destruction, and their abiding.

He is able to know the unity of the four elements
while also knowing all of the differences therein,
their characteristics when small, when large, and when measureless,
as well as all their different sorts of differentiating aspects. {22}

He is able even to calculate all of the atoms comprising
the worlds within a great trichiliocosm
while also being able to know of all of those beings' bodies
and, of the four great elements, the number of atoms therein.

正體字

523b29‖ 諸天身眾寶　微塵數差別
523c01‖ 皆悉遍照了　餘亦如是知 {23}
523c02‖ 智慧因緣故　心轉得調柔
523c03‖ 為利諸眾生　遍諸世界身
523c04‖ 能於眾生身　而自作己身
523c05‖ 及諸佛世界　諸餘種種身 {24}
523c06‖ 如日月隨風　影現一切水
523c07‖ 菩薩亦如是　隨順智慧風
523c08‖ 常住於法性　湛然不移動
523c09‖ 於淨心眾生　各現其身像 {25}
523c10‖ 隨諸心所樂　而現為受生
523c11‖ 於諸人天會　悉皆示其身
523c12‖ 菩薩於因緣　和合中自在
523c13‖ 乃至能隨意　而為現佛身 {26}
523c14‖ 眾生國土身　業報賢聖身
523c15‖ 智身與法身　[*]知皆同平等
523c16‖ 以是因緣故　得如意神通
523c17‖ 為令世歡喜　而現種種身 {27}
523c18‖ 能得於十種　妙大自在智
523c19‖ 所作隨智行　順於慈悲心

简体字

诸天身众宝，　微尘数差别，
皆悉遍照了，　余亦如是知。
智慧因缘故，　心转得调柔，
为利诸众生，　遍诸世界身。
能于众生身，　而自作己身，
及诸佛世界，　诸余种种身。
如日月随风，　影现一切水，
菩萨亦如是，　随顺智慧风，
常住于法性，　湛然不移动，
于净心众生，　各现其身像。
随诸心所乐，　而现为受生，
于诸人天会，　悉皆示其身。
菩萨于因缘，　和合中自在，
乃至能随意，　而为现佛身，
众生国土身，　业报贤圣身，
智身与法身，　知皆同平等。
以是因缘故，　得如意神通，
为令世欢喜，　而现种种身。
能得于十种，　妙大自在智，
所作随智行，　顺于慈悲心。

The bodies of all devas, the many jewels,
and the varying number of atoms comprising each type—
He entirely and everywhere illuminates all of these factors,
and also knows all other such factors as well. {23}

Due to the causes and conditions associated with wisdom,
his mind becomes ever more subdued and pliant.
In order to serve the benefit of all beings,
he everywhere manifests bodies in all worlds.

He is able to appear in the body of a being
and thereby make it into his own body,
doing so as well in the lands of all buddhas
in which he manifests all of the other different sorts of bodies. {24}

Just as the sun and moon, following the cosmic winds,
display their reflections on the surface of all waters,
so too the bodhisattva,
following the breeze of wisdom,

always abides in the Dharma realm,
completely clear and motionlessness,
and, for beings with pure minds,
manifests for each of them the appearance of his body. {25}

Adapting to their minds' predilections,[247]
he thus presents the appearance of taking on births
and, within all congregations of men and devas,
he manifests his bodies there.

The bodhisattva exercises sovereign mastery in this
wherever the causes and conditions come together,
even to the point of being able, in accordance with his wishes,
to manifest the body of a buddha for them. {26}

He manifests bodies of beings, physical bodies of lands,
karmic retribution bodies, bodies of worthies and *āryas*,
the knowledge body, and the Dharma body, doing so
while knowing that they are all of the same uniform equality.

Availing himself of these causes and conditions,
he is able at will to implement spiritual superknowledges
to inspire joyous delight among the inhabitants of the world
by thus manifesting for them many different sorts of bodies. {27}

He is able to acquire ten varieties
of sublime and great sovereign mastery of knowledge.
Whatever he does is carried forth in accordance with knowledge
and in compliance with the minds of kindness and compassion.

正體字

523c20‖ 諸佛所有法 皆能善修習
523c21‖ 住三淨業中 不動如須彌 {28}
523c22‖ 能得大菩薩 所有十種力
523c23‖ 一切諸魔眾 皆所不能轉
523c24‖ 常為諸佛護 釋梵所敬禮
523c25‖ 密迹金剛神 常隨而侍衛 {29}
523c26‖ 菩薩得是地 功德無有量
523c27‖ 百千萬億劫 說之不可盡
523c28‖ 得近無數佛 增益諸善根
523c29‖ 如真金雜寶 莊嚴在王頸 {30}
524a01‖ 菩薩在是地 多作大梵王
524a02‖ 典領千國土 功德富無量
524a03‖ 能以三乘教 而無有窮盡
524a04‖ 慈心光普照 破諸煩惱熱 {31}
524a05‖ 若欲於須臾 能得百三千
524a06‖ 大千世界數 微塵諸三昧
524a07‖ 能見十方佛 其數亦如是
524a08‖ 若以其願力 過是無有量 {32}
524a09‖ 今已略解說 第八地妙相
524a10‖ 若廣演說者 千億劫不盡 {33}

简体字

诸佛所有法， 皆能善修习，
住三净业中， 不动如须弥。
能得大菩萨， 所有十种力，
一切诸魔众， 皆所不能转。
常为诸佛护， 释梵所敬礼，
密迹金刚神， 常随而侍卫。
菩萨得是地， 功德无有量，
百千万亿劫， 说之不可尽。
得近无数佛， 增益诸善根，
如真金杂宝， 庄严在王颈。
菩萨在是地， 多作大梵王，
典领千国土， 功德富无量。
能以三乘教， 而无有穷尽，
慈心光普照， 破诸烦恼热。
若欲于须臾， 能得百三千，
大千世界数， 微尘诸三昧，
能见十方佛， 其数亦如是；
若以其愿力， 过是无有量。
今已略解说， 第八地妙相，
若广演说者， 千亿劫不尽。”

He is able to skillfully cultivate and implement
all dharmas of all buddhas
as he abides within the three types of pure karmic actions,
remaining as unmoving in doing so as Mount Sumeru itself. {28}

He is able to acquire all ten of the powers
possessed by the great bodhisattvas
and becomes one whom none of Māra's hordes
could ever cause to turn back in retreat.

He is always protected by all buddhas,
receives the reverential obeisance of Śakra and Brahmā,
and is always followed, served, and guarded
by traceless vajra-wielding spirits. {29}

The bodhisattva who has reached this ground
acquires so countlessly many meritorious qualities that,
even in hundreds of thousands of myriads of *koṭis* of kalpas,
one could never finish describing them.

He becomes able to draw close to countless buddhas,
and so increase his roots of goodness that their radiance
becomes like that of the real gold inlaid with various jewels
that adorns the neck of a king. {30}

The bodhisattva dwelling on this ground
often becomes a king of the Great Brahma Heaven
who rules over a thousand lands,
one who is possessed of immeasurably vast merit and wealth

and who is able to deploy the teachings of the Three Vehicles,
doing so with an inexhaustible capacity to explain their meanings.
The light from his mind of kindness everywhere illuminates
and dispels the fever of all beings' afflictions. {31}

Should he wish to do so, he is able,
in but a single moment, to acquire samādhis
as numerous as the atoms contained in
the worlds within a hundred great trichiliocosms.

He is also able to see buddhas throughout the ten directions
in equally great numbers as this, and,
should he wish to avail himself of the power of his vows,
the numbers would extend beyond this, becoming immeasurable. {32}

We have now come to the conclusion of this summary explanation
of the eighth ground's marvelous aspects.
Were one to carry forth with a vast proclamation of this,
one could never finish it even in a thousand *koṭis* of kalpas. {33}

End of Chapter Eight

正體字

524a14‖ 十住經卷[2]第四
524a16‖ [3]後秦三[4]藏鳩摩羅[5]什譯
524a17‖ 妙善地第九
524a18‖ 佛子演說此　八地妙義時
524a19‖ 以佛神力故　震動無量國 {1}
524a20‖ 一切智身出　無量微妙光
524a21‖ 遍照十方界　眾生得安樂 {2}
524a22‖ 千萬數菩薩　住於虛空中
524a23‖ 設眾妙供養　諸天所無有 {3}
524a24‖ 大自在天王　并及他化王
524a25‖ 歡喜眾妙供　大海功德佛 {4}
524a26‖ 天女數千萬　恭敬咸歡喜
524a27‖ 同以微妙音　[6]歌歎佛功德 {5}
524a28‖ 以佛神力故　出如是妙法 {6}
524a29‖ 善行寂滅者　無有諸惡心
524b01‖ 各在於其地　善修菩薩行
524b02‖ 利益世間故　遍遊於十方
524b03‖ 示眾以佛道　心同空無礙 {7}

简体字

十住经卷第五
妙善地第九

佛子演说此，　八地妙义时，
以佛神力故，　震动无量国。
一切智身出，　无量微妙光，
遍照十方界，　众生得安乐。
千万数菩萨，　住于虚空中，
设众妙供养，　诸天所无有。
大自在天王，　并及他化王，
欢喜众妙供，　大海功德佛。
天女数千万，　恭敬咸欢喜，
同以微妙音，　歌叹佛功德：
“以佛神力故，　出如是妙法！
善行寂灭者，　无有诸恶心，
各在于其地，　善修菩萨行。
利益世间故，　遍游于十方，
示众以佛道，　心同空无碍。

Chapter Nine
The Sublime Goodness Ground[248]

I. The Ninth Ground: The Sublime Goodness Ground

1. The Ninth Ground's Introductory Verses and Dharma Request

Once that son of the Buddha had finished holding forth on this
eighth ground's sublime meaning,
through the spiritual powers of the Buddha,
the countless lands were then caused to tremble. {1}

The body of the Omniscient One emanated
countless subtle and marvelous rays of light
entirely illuminating worlds through the ten directions,
whereupon the beings therein were filled with happiness. {2}

A thousand myriads of bodhisattvas
standing up amidst the sky above
then presented a multitude of marvelous offerings
of a sort that not even the devas possessed. {3}

The Maheśvara Heaven King
together with the kings of the Paranirmita Vaśavartin Heavens—
all were filled with joyous delight and presented wondrous offerings
in reverence to the Buddha, the great ocean of meritorious qualities. {4}

Celestial nymphs numbering in the thousands of myriads
paid reverence as all of them, filled with joyous delight,
united with sublimely wondrous voices
in singing praises of the Buddha's meritorious qualities. {5}

Due to the spiritual powers of the Buddha,
they brought forth marvelous dharmas such as these: {6}

"Those who skillfully practice quiescence
are entirely free of any sorts of evil thoughts.
Each of them, abiding on his respective ground,
skillfully cultivates the bodhisattva practices.

In order to benefit those in the world,
they roams everywhere throughout the ten directions,
instructing the multitudes in the path to buddhahood,
even as their minds, like empty space, remain entirely unimpeded. {7}

正體字

524b04‖ 諸菩薩神力　上妙供養具
524b05‖ 勝十方人天　福德之所致
524b06‖ 佛子樂智者　以此示佛力 {8}
524b07‖ 於一國不動　而現一切處
524b08‖ 利益於世間　如滿月明淨
524b09‖ 滅一切音聲　語言諸想念
524b10‖ 而以諸音聲　說法猶如響 {9}
524b11‖ 隨眾生下劣　其心厭沒者
524b12‖ 示說聲聞道　令出於眾苦
524b13‖ 隨所有眾生　諸根少利者
524b14‖ 樂於因緣法　為說辟支佛 {10}
524b15‖ 隨所有利根　利益眾生者
524b16‖ 有大慈悲心　為說菩薩[7]法
524b17‖ 若無上大心　決定樂大事
524b18‖ 為示於佛身　說無量佛法 {11}
524b19‖ 譬如幻化師　示種種身色
524b20‖ 如是諸身相　皆無有實事
524b21‖ 如是諸佛子　善知智慧術
524b22‖ 能示一切行　心離於有無 {12}

简体字

诸菩萨神力，　上妙供养具，
胜十方人天，　福德之所致。
佛子乐智者，　以此示佛力，
于一国不动，　而现一切处，
利益于世间，　如满月明净。
灭一切音声，　语言诸想念，
而以诸音声，　说法犹如响。
随众生下劣，　其心厌没者，
示说声闻道，　令出于众苦。
随所有众生，　诸根少利者，
乐于因缘法，　为说辟支佛。
随所有利根，　利益众生者，
有大慈悲心，　为说菩萨法。
若无上大心，　决定乐大事，
为示于佛身，　说无量佛法。
譬如幻化师，　示种种身色，
如是诸身相，　皆无有实事。
如是诸佛子，　善知智慧术，
能示一切行，　心离于有无。’

"Through their spiritual powers, the bodhisattvas
offered up marvelous offering gifts
superior to those that the merit of any of humans or devas
throughout the ten directions could ever bring forth.
Those sons of the Buddha that delight in wisdom,
by such phenomena as these, reveal the powers of the Buddha. {8}

"Even as they reside in a single land, unmoving,
they still manifest their presence in all places,
benefiting those in the world,
doing so in a way that is like the light and purity of the full moon.

"Even though their voices, speech,
and conceptual thought have all become quiescent,[249]
they still avail themselves of all manner of voices
that resound like echoes as they discourse on the Dharma. {9}

"Adapting to those beings of lesser capacity
whose minds have sunken into renunciation,
he reveals the path of *śrāvaka*-disciples,
thereby allowing them to succeed in escaping the many sufferings.

Where there are those beings
whose faculties are possessed of a minor degree of acuity
and who delight in the dharmas of causes and conditions,
he explains for them the way of the *pratyekabudddha.* {10}

"Adapting to those who are possessed of sharp faculties,
who are devoted to benefiting beings,
and who are possessed of the great kindness and great compassion,
he explains for them the Dharma of the bodhisattva.

For those who possess the unsurpassably great resolve
resolutely fixed in its fondness for the great endeavor,
he reveals to them the body of the Buddha
and explains for them the Buddha's measureless Dharma. {11}

"In this he is like a master conjurer
who manifests appearances of all different sorts of physical forms
even as all such physical appearances
are devoid of any genuine phenomena.

In this same way, all of these sons of the Buddha
well know wisdom's stratagems
whereby they are able to display all manner of actions
even as their minds have transcended existence and nonexistence." {12}

正體字

524b23‖ 諸天女千萬 微妙音歌歎
524b24‖ 如是歌歎已 默然而[8]視佛
524b25‖ 又解脫月言 佛子大會淨
524b26‖ 一心願樂聞 過八地正行 {13}
524b27‖ {A} [9]金剛藏菩薩言。佛子。諸菩薩摩訶薩。以如
524b28‖ 是無量[10]智善觀佛道。欲更求轉勝深寂滅解
524b29‖ 脫。欲轉勝思惟如來智慧。欲入如來深密法
524c01‖ 中。欲選擇取不可思議大智慧。欲選擇諸陀
524c02‖ 羅尼三昧重令清淨。欲令諸神通廣大。欲隨
524c03‖ 順世間差別行。[11]欲修諸力無畏佛不共法。無
524c04‖ 能壞者。[*]欲順行諸佛轉法輪力。[*]欲不捨所
524c05‖ 受大悲大願。得入第九地。{B} 諸菩薩。住此地中。
524c06‖ 如實知

简体字

诸天女千万，　微妙音歌叹，
如是歌叹已，　默然而视佛。
又解脱月言：“佛子大会净，
一心愿乐闻，　过八地正行。”

金刚藏菩萨言：“佛子，诸菩萨摩诃萨，以如是无量智善观佛道，欲更求转胜深寂灭解脱，欲转胜思惟如来智慧，欲入如来深密法中，欲选择取不可思议大智慧，欲选择诸陀罗尼三昧重令清净，欲令诸神通广大，欲随顺世间差别行，欲修诸力、无畏、佛不共法无能坏者，欲顺行诸佛转法轮力，欲不舍所受大悲大愿，得入第九地。诸菩萨住此地中，如实知

Those celestial nymphs employed there a thousand myriads
of sublime and wondrous sounds in singing forth praises.
Having finished the singing of praises such as these,
they then became silent and gazed up at the Buddha.

Once again Liberation Moon said:
"O Son of the Buddha, those in this Great Assembly are pure.
They single-mindedly wish to delight in hearing
of right practice as it occurs beyond the eighth ground." {13}

2. Vajragarbha Commences the Ninth Ground's Explanation

{A} Vajragarbha Bodhisattva then said:

3. Ten Earnestly Pursued Endeavors Enabling Ninth Ground Access

O Son of the Buddha, here we have the bodhisattva *mahāsattvas* who, resorting to such immeasurably vast knowledge as this, have focused skillful meditative contemplation on the path to buddhahood, and:

Have additionally sought to seek ever more superior depth of realization in quiescent liberation;
Have sought to achieve ever more supremely deep reflection upon the wisdom of the Tathāgata;
Have sought to achieve entry into the Tathāgata's profound and esoteric Dharma;
Have sought to selectively contemplate and acquire inconceivably great wisdom;
Have sought to selectively contemplate the *dhāraṇīs* and samādhis and cause them to become doubly purified;
Have sought to cause their spiritual superknowledges to become vast;
Have sought to adapt to the world's different practices;
Have sought to cultivate the powers, fearlessnesses, and dharmas exclusive to the Buddhas to the point where they are invulnerable to destructive interference by anyone at all;
Have sought to accord with the power of the Buddhas' turning of the wheel of the Dharma;
And have sought to never relinquish the greatly compassionate great vows that they have taken on.

It is they who then succeed in entering the ninth ground.

4. This Bodhisattva's 10 Types of Reality-Based Knowledge of Karma

{B} The bodhisattvas dwelling on this ground also know in accordance with reality:

正體字

起善不善無記法行。知有漏無漏法
524c07‖ 行。世間出世間法行。思議不可思議法行。定
524c08‖ 不定法行。聲[12]聞辟支佛法行。菩薩道法行。
524c09‖ 如來地法行。有為[13]法無為法[14]行。{C}隨順如是
524c10‖ 智慧。如實知菩提心所行難。知諸煩惱難。業
524c11‖ 難諸根難。[15]願樂難性難。志心難深心難。生
524c12‖ 難殘氣難。三聚差別難。{D}知眾生諸心差別相。
524c13‖ 心雜相。心輕轉相。

简体字

起善、不善、无记法行，知有漏无漏法行、世间出世间法行、思议不可思议法行、定不定法行、声闻辟支佛法行、菩萨道法行、如来地法行、有为法无为法行，随顺如是智慧，如实知菩提心所行难，知诸烦恼难、业难、诸根难、愿乐难、性难、志心难、深心难、生难、残气难、三聚差别难，知众生诸心差别相、心杂相、心轻转相、

The effects of practicing[250] good dharmas, bad dharmas, or karmically neutral dharmas;
The effects of practicing dharmas either associated with or free of the contaminants;
The effects of practicing worldly dharmas and world-transcending dharmas;
The effects of practicing conceivable dharmas and inconceivable dharmas;
The effects of practicing dharmas that are definite or dharmas that are indefinite;
The effects of practicing the dharmas associated with *śrāvaka*-disciples and *pratyekabuddhas;*
The effects of practicing the dharmas of the bodhisattva path;
The effects of practicing the dharmas of the Tathāgata's ground;
The effects of practicing conditioned dharmas;
And the effects of practicing unconditioned dharmas.

5. Ten Types of Reality-Based Knowledge of Entangling Difficulties

{C} Pursuant to such knowledge, they know in accordance with reality the entangling difficulties[251] associated with implementing the bodhi resolve, specifically knowing:[252]

The entangling difficulties associated with the afflictions;
The entangling difficulties associated with karmic actions;
The entangling difficulties associated with the faculties;
The entangling difficulties associated with resolute beliefs;[253]
The entangling difficulties associated with sense realms;[254]
The entangling difficulties associated with the mind's resolute intentions;[255]
The entangling difficulties associated with latent tendencies;[256]
The entangling difficulties associated with births;[257]
The entangling difficulties associated with residual karmic propensities;[258]
And the entangling difficulties associated with the differences in the three groups of beings.[259]

6. Ten Types of Reality-Based Knowledge of Beings' Mental Aspects

{D} So too do they know with regard to beings the different characteristics of their minds, specifically knowing:

The mind's characteristic of manifesting in diverse ways;
The mind's characteristic of ready transformation;

正體字

心壞不壞相。心無形相。心
524c14‖ 無邊遍自在相。心清淨差別相。心垢相。心無
524c15‖ 垢相。心縛相。心解相。心諂曲相。心質直相。
524c16‖ 心隨道相。皆如實知。{E}是菩薩。知煩惱深相。知
524c17‖ 淺相。知煩惱心伴相不離相。知使纏差別相。
524c18‖ 知是心相應不相應相。[16]知是生時得果報相。
524c19‖ 知是三界中差別相。知愛癡見深入如箭相。
524c20‖ 知憍慢癡重罪相。知是三業因緣不斷相。略
524c21‖ 說乃至如實知入八萬四千煩惱行差別相。

简体字

心坏不坏相、心无形相、心无边遍自在相、心清净差别相、心垢相、心无垢相、心缚相、心解相、心谄曲相、心质直相、心随道相，皆如实知。是菩萨知烦恼深相，知浅相，知烦恼心伴相、不离相，知使缠差别相，知是心相应不相应相，知是生时得果报相，知是三界中差别相，知爱痴见深入如箭相，知憍慢痴重罪相，知是三业因缘不断相，略说乃至如实知入八万四千烦恼行差别相。

The mind's characteristic of being either destroyed or undestroyed;
The mind's characteristic of having no physical form;[260]
The mind's characteristic of being boundless and independent;[261]
The mind's characteristic of having different degrees of purity;
The mind's characteristic of being either defiled or free of defilement;[262]
The mind's characteristic of being either held in bondage or liberated;[263]
The mind's characteristic of being either deceptive or straightforward;[264]
And the mind's characteristic of following along in accordance with the destinies of rebirth.

They know in accordance with reality all such characteristics as these.

7. His Reality-Based Knowledge of the Afflictions' Characteristics

{E} So too in the case of the afflictions, wherein this bodhisattva:

Knows their characteristics when they have gone deep;
Knows their characteristics when they are but shallow;
Knows their characteristic of accompanying the mind;
Knows their characteristic of not being abandoned;
Knows their different characteristics when latent and when one is entangled with them;
Knows they are characterized of being either associated with mind or disassociated from mind;
Knows they are characterized by conducing to the undergoing of resulting retributions when one is reborn;
Knows they are characterized by differences in each of the three realms;
Knows that craving, ignorance, and views are characterized by being like arrows in the depth of their penetration;
Knows that pride and delusion are characterized by association with grave karmic offenses;
And knows they are characterized by ceaselessly serving as causes and conditions of the three types of karmic deeds.

To state it briefly, he knows and fathoms in accordance with reality even up to eighty-four thousand different characteristics associated with the action of the afflictions.

正體字

524c22‖ (F)是菩薩。知諸業善不善無記相。分別未分別
524c23‖ 相。心伴相不離相自然盡相。行道盡相。種相
524c24‖ 集相。不失果報相。次第相。有報相無報相。黑
524c25‖ 黑報相。白白報相。黑白黑白報相。非黑非白
524c26‖ 能盡業相。知業起處相。受業法別異相。知無
524c27‖ 量因緣起業相。知世間業出世間業差別相。
524c28‖ 現報相生報相後報相。

简体字

是菩萨知诸业善不善无记相、分别未分别相、心伴相、不离相、自然尽相、行道尽相、种相、集相、不失果报相、次第相、有报相、无报相、黑黑报相、白白报相、黑白黑白报相、非黑非白能尽业相，知业起处相、受业法别异相，知无量因缘起业相，知世间业、出世间业差别相、现报相、生报相、后报相、

8. His Reality-Based Knowledge of Characteristics of Karmic Actions

{F} So too does this bodhisattva know with respect to karmic actions:

Their characteristic of being good, bad, or karmically neutral;
Their characteristic of being either distinguishable or not yet distinguishable;
Their characteristic of occurring in association with mind;
Their characteristic of not arising apart from mind;
Their characteristic of naturally coming to an end;
Their characteristic of being ended through practice of the path;
Their characteristic of serving as seeds;
Their characteristic of accumulating;
Their characteristic of never failing to culminate in karmic retribution;
Their characteristic of being sequential;
Their characteristic of having brought forth karmic retributions or not yet having brought forth karmic retributions;
Their characteristic of rewarding black actions with black retributions;[265]
Their characteristic of rewarding white actions with white retributions;
Their characteristic of rewarding a combination of black and white actions with a combination of black and white retributions;
Their characteristic of being amenable to ending through actions that are neither black nor white;
He knows the characteristic of karmic actions to have [corresponding] stations of existence wherein [their retribution] arises;
He knows their characteristic of involving differing means through which their karmic [retribution] is undergone;
He knows karmic actions' characteristic of involving countless causes and conditions in their arising;[266]
He knows the characteristic of worldly karmic actions and world-transcending karmic actions to differ [in their corresponding retributions];
He knows the characteristics of karmic actions when bound to generate their effects in the present life;
He knows the characteristics of karmic actions when bound to generate their effects in the immediately ensuing incarnation;

正體字

隨諸[17]業定相不定相。
524c29|| 略說。乃至如實知八萬四千諸業差別相。{G}是
525a01|| 菩薩。知諸根軟中利差別相。知先際後際別
525a02|| 異[1]相不別異相。知上中下相。知煩惱伴相。
525a03|| 不相離相。隨諸乘定相不定相。淳熟相未淳
525a04|| 熟相。隨心行相。易壞相。深取相。增上相。不
525a05|| 可壞相。轉相。不轉相。三世差別相。深隱共生
525a06|| 差別相。略說。[2]乃至如實知八萬四千諸根差
525a07|| 別相。

简体字

随诸业定相不定相，略说乃至如实知八万四千诸业差别相。是菩萨知诸根软中利差别相，知先际、后际别异相、不别异相，知上中下相，知烦恼伴相、不相离相，随诸乘定相、不定相、淳熟相未淳熟相，随心行相、易坏相、深取相、增上相、不可坏相、转相、不转相、三世差别相、深隐共生差别相，略说乃至如实知八万四千诸根差别相。

He knows the characteristics of karmic actions when bound to generate their effects in yet more distantly subsequent incarnations;

The characteristics of karmic actions when fixed in their karmic effects;

And he knows the characteristics of karmic actions when unfixed in their karmic effects.

To state it briefly, he knows in accordance with reality even up to eighty-four thousand different characteristics associated with karmic actions.

9. His Reality-Based Knowledge of Characteristics of Beings' Faculties

{G} This bodhisattva knows the characteristics associated with the faculties, specifically knowing:

Their characteristic of possessing distinct differences associated with being either weak, middling, or sharp;

Their characteristic of either possessing or not possessing distinct differences in the past and future;

Their characteristic of being either superior, middling, or inferior;

Their characteristic of being accompanied by and inseparable from the afflictions;

Their characteristic of involving either fixed or unfixed results as a function of being associated with particular vehicles;

Their characteristic of having become either completely matured or not yet completely matured;

Their characteristic of according with the actions of the mind;

Their characteristic when vulnerable to easy ruination;

Their characteristic when being deeply rooted;

Their characteristic when especially superior;

Their characteristic when invulnerable to ruination;

Their characteristic when reversible;

Their characteristic when irreversible;

Their characteristic of becoming different across the course of the three periods of time;

And their characteristic of being deeply hidden and different in the manner in which they accompany one in their arising.

To state it briefly, he knows in accordance with reality even up to eighty-four thousand different characteristics associated with the faculties.

正體字

是菩薩。知眾生諸欲樂軟中利相。略說。
525a08‖ 乃至如實知八萬四千欲樂差別相。是菩薩。
525a09‖ 知諸性軟中利相。略說。乃至如實知八萬四
525a10‖ 千諸性差別相。是菩薩。知深心軟中利相。略
525a11‖ 說。乃至如實知八萬四千深心差別相。{H}是菩
525a12‖ 薩。分別知諸結使有伴。共心生不共心生心
525a13‖ 相應心不相應。深[3]入相。無始來隨惱眾生
525a14‖ 相。與一切禪定。解脱神通相違。堅繫縛。三
525a15‖ 界繫。無量心。而不現前。開諸業門。而無所
525a16‖ 知。可[4]對治相。無所有相。無定事相。

简体字

是菩萨知众生诸欲乐软中利相，略说乃至如实知八万四千欲乐差别相。是菩萨知诸性软中利相，略说乃至如实知八万四千诸性差别相。是菩萨知深心软中利相，略说乃至如实知八万四千深心差别相。是菩萨分别知诸结使有伴，共心生、不共心生，心相应、心不相应，深入相，无始来随恼众生相；与一切禅定解脱神通相违，坚系缚，三界系，无量心而不现前，开诸业门而无所知，可对治相、无所有相、无定事相、

10. His Knowledge of Beliefs, Sense Realms, and Resolute Intentions

This bodhisattva also knows the characteristic of beings' resolute beliefs[267] to be either weak, middling, or sharp. Briefly stated, he knows in accordance with reality even up to eighty-four thousand distinctions associated with beings' resolute beliefs.

This bodhisattva also knows the characteristic of beings' sense realms[268] to be either weak, middling, or sharp. Briefly stated, he knows in accordance with reality even up to eighty-four thousand distinctions associated with beings' sense realms.

This bodhisattva also knows the characteristic of beings' resolute intentions[269] to be either weak, middling, or supremely sharp. Briefly stated, he knows in accordance with reality even up to eighty-four thousand distinctions associated with beings' resolute intentions.

11. His Knowledge of Latent Tendencies' Characteristics

{H} This bodhisattva also distinguishes and knows the characteristics of the latent tendencies[270] when in an associative role, knowing:

Their characteristics when arising with thought and when not arising with thought;
Their characteristics when concomitant with mind and when not concomitant with mind;
Their characteristic of deep penetration;
Their characteristic of following and tormenting beings from the beginningless past onward;
Their characteristic of running counter to the realization of any of the *dhyāna* absorptions, liberations, or spiritual superknowledges;
Their characteristic of holding one tightly in bondage;
Their characteristic of binding one to existence within the three realms;
Their characteristic of involvement in countless mind states even as they do not directly manifest their presence;
Their characteristic of opening the gates to every sort of karmic circumstance, even as one remains unaware of them;
Their characteristic of amenability to counteraction;
Their characteristic of being devoid of anything that exists;
Their characteristic of being devoid of any fixed circumstances;

正體字

不異聖
525a17‖ 道相。滅動相。{I}是菩薩。如實知[5]諸生差別相。
525a18‖ 所謂。地獄畜生餓鬼阿修羅人天差別。色界
525a19‖ 無色界差別。有想無想差別。業是田。愛是水。
525a20‖ 無明是黑闇。覆識是種子。後身是生[6]牙。名
525a21‖ 色共生。而不相離。有癡愛相續相。欲生欲作
525a22‖ 欲[7]愛。不離樂眾生相。分別三界差別相。三
525a23‖ 有相續相。皆如實知。{J}是菩薩。如實知諸習氣。
525a24‖ 若有餘若無餘。隨所生處有習氣。隨共眾生
525a25‖ 住有習氣。隨業煩惱有習氣。

简体字

不异圣道相、灭动相。是菩萨如实知诸生差别相，所谓地狱、畜生、饿鬼、阿修罗、人、天差别，色界、无色界差别，有想、无想差别；业是田，爱是水，无明是黑闇，覆识是种子，后身是生芽，名色共生而不相离，有痴爱相续相，欲生欲作欲爱，不离乐众生相，分别三界差别相，三有相续相，皆如实知。是菩萨如实知诸习气，若有余若无余，随所生处有习气，随共众生住有习气，随业烦恼有习气，

And their characteristic of being invulnerable to the extinguishing of their activity through any means other than the path of the Āryas.

12. His Knowledge of Characteristics Associated With Births

(I) This bodhisattva also knows in accordance with reality the characteristics associated with different rebirth circumstances, specifically knowing:

The characteristics associated with differences between hell realm, animal realm, hungry ghost realm, *asura* realm, human realm, and celestial realm rebirths;

The characteristics associated with differences between form realm and formless realm rebirths;

The characteristics associated with the difference between rebirths with perception and rebirths without perception;

The characteristics associated with karmic action acting as a field, cravings as water, ignorance as sheltering darkness, consciousness as seed, and the subsequent body as sprout;

The characteristics of simultaneous arising and inseparability of name and form;

The characteristic of delusion and craving to instigate continuity of existence;

The characteristics of beings whereby they desire birth, desire actions, desire feeling,[271] and desire to never be apart from pleasure;

The characteristics associated with distinguishing the differences in the three realms of existence;

And the characteristics associated with the continuity of the three realms of existence.

He knows all of these characteristics in accordance with reality.

13. His Knowledge of Characteristics of Habitual Karmic Propensities

(J) This bodhisattva also knows in accordance with reality the characteristics associated with the habitual karmic propensities,[272] specifically knowing:

Whether they have residual aspects or do not having residual aspects;

That there are habitual karmic propensities that follow one into the rebirth destiny where one is reborn;

That there are habitual karmic propensities that accompany beings wherever they abide;

That there are habitual karmic propensities that accord with karmic actions and afflictions;

正體字

[8]善不善無記有
525a26‖ 習氣。離欲有習氣。隨後身有習氣。次第隨逐
525a27‖ 有習氣。深入道斷相。持煩惱相。離則無法。皆
525a28‖ 如實知。{K}是菩薩。如實知眾生定不定相。正定
525a29‖ 相邪定相。不定相。邪見中邪定相。正見中正
525b01‖ 定相。離此[9]二無定相。一一五逆。是邪定相。
525b02‖ 五根是正定相。邪位是[10]邪定。正[11]位是[12]正
525b03‖ 定。更不作故。離此二位。是不定相。深入邪
525b04‖ 聚。有難[13]得轉相。

简体字

善、不善、无记有习气，离欲有习气，随后身有习气，次第随逐有习气，深入道断相，持烦恼相，离则无法，皆如实知。是菩萨如实知众生定不定相、正定相、邪定相、不定相、邪见中邪定相、正见中正定相，离此二无定相。一一五逆是邪定相，五根是正定相；邪位是邪定，正位是正定，更不作故，离此二位，是不定相。深入邪聚有难得转相，

That there are habitual karmic propensities that are good, bad, or neutral;
That there are habitual karmic propensities associated with abandoning desire;
That there are habitual karmic propensities that follow one into subsequent incarnations;
That there are habitual karmic propensities that manifest sequentially as they follow along in pursuit;
That they are characterized by deep penetration and are severed by the path;
That they are characterized by sustenance of afflictions;
And that, if they are abandoned, they then become nonexistent dharmas.

He knows all such things in accordance with reality.

14. His Knowledge of Those Fixed in Right, in Wrong, or Unfixed

{K} This bodhisattva also knows in accordance with reality beings' fixed and unfixed characteristics, specifically knowing:[273]

The characteristic of being fixed in adherence to what is right;
The characteristic of being fixed in adherence to what is wrong;
The characteristic of being unfixed in these regards;
The characteristic of being fixed in what is wrong through possession of wrong views;
The characteristic of being fixed in what is right through possession of right views;
The characteristic of being unfixed through dissociation from both;
The characteristic of being fixed in what is wrong through committing each of the five heinous karmic offenses.[274]
The characteristic of being fixed in what is right through the five root faculties;
The characteristic of being fixed in what is wrong through dwelling in stations associated with what is wrong;
The characteristic of being fixed in what is right through dwelling in stations associated with what is right;
The characteristic of being unfixed [in either what is right or what is wrong] through separating from these two;
The characteristic of being difficult to turn back through deeply entering into the class [of beings][275] inclined toward what is wrong;

正體字

令修無上道因緣相。不定
525b05‖ 聚。邪定聚。眾生守護相。皆如實知。{L}佛子。諸
525b06‖ 菩薩摩訶薩。隨如是智。名為安住妙善地。菩
525b07‖ 薩住是[14]地。知眾生如是諸行差別相。隨其解
525b08‖ 脫。而與因緣。是菩薩。知化眾生法。知度眾
525b09‖ 生法。如實知而為說法。聲聞乘相。辟支佛乘
525b10‖ 相。菩薩乘相。如來地相。如實知隨眾生因
525b11‖ 緣。而為說法。隨心隨根。隨欲樂差別。而為說
525b12‖ 法。又隨行處。隨智慧處。而為說法。知一切
525b13‖ 行處。隨而說法。隨眾生性。深入難處。而為
525b14‖ 說法。隨道隨生。隨煩惱隨習氣轉故說法。隨
525b15‖ [15]乘令解脫故說法。

简体字

令修无上道因缘相，不定聚、邪定聚众生守护相，皆如实知。

“佛子，诸菩萨摩诃萨随如是智，名为安住妙善地。菩萨住是地，知众生如是诸行差别相，随其解脱而与因缘。是菩萨知化众生法，知度众生法，如实知而为说法。声闻乘相、辟支佛乘相、菩萨乘相、如来地相如实知，随众生因缘而为说法，随心、随根、随欲乐差别而为说法，又随行处、随智慧处而为说法，知一切行处随而说法，随众生性深入难处而为说法，随道、随生、随烦恼、随习气转故说法，随乘令解脱故说法。

And the characteristic of having causes and conditions making one amenable to being caused to cultivate the unsurpassable path.

These characteristics of the group that is unfixed, the group that is fixed in what is wrong, and [the group] of beings preserving [what is right]—he knows them all in accordance with reality.

15. His Knowledge-Based Adaptive Teaching and Liberation of Beings

{L} Son of the Buddha, the bodhisattva *mahāsattvas* who accord with knowledge such as this are said to dwell securely on the Ground of Sublime Goodness. The bodhisattva dwelling on this ground knows all such characteristics in beings' different practices and, adapting to what will cause them to gain liberation, then provides them with the corresponding causes and conditions.

This bodhisattva knows those dharmas appropriate to the teaching of beings, knows those dharmas conducing to the liberation of beings, and, knowing these in accordance with reality, he then teaches the Dharma for their sakes.

He knows in accordance with reality the characteristics of those with affinity for the Śrāvaka-disciple Vehicle, the characteristics of those with affinity for the Pratyekabuddha Vehicle, the characteristics of those with affinity for the Bodhisattva Vehicle, and the characteristics of those with affinity for the ground of the Tathāgata. He then adapts to the causes and conditions of these beings and teaches the Dharma for their sakes.

He adapts to the differences in their minds, adapts to the differences in their faculties, and adapts to the differences in their predilections, and then teaches the Dharma for their sakes.

So too, he adapts to their bases in practice and their bases in wisdom and then explains the Dharma for their sakes. He knows the bases for all courses of action and, adapting specifically to those, he teaches the Dharma accordingly.

He adapts to beings' sense realms[276] and the particular entangling difficulties[277] they have deeply entered and teaches Dharma for them accordingly.

He adapts to their rebirth destinies, adapts to the births they have taken on, adapts to their afflictions, and adapts to the permutations in their habitual karmic propensities and therefore teaches Dharma accordingly.

He adapts to whichever vehicle would conduce to liberation and therefore teaches Dharma accordingly.

正體字

{M}是菩薩。住此地中。為大
525b16‖ 法師。守護諸佛法藏。{N}墮在大法師深妙義中。
525b17‖ 用無量慧方便。四無礙智。起菩薩言辭說法。
525b18‖ 是菩薩。常隨四無礙智。而不分別。何等為四。
525b19‖ 一法無礙。二義無礙。三辭無礙。四樂說無礙。
525b20‖ {O}是菩薩。用法無礙智。知諸法自相。以義無礙
525b21‖ 智。知諸法差別。以辭無礙智。知無分別說諸
525b22‖ 法。以樂說無礙智。知諸法次第不斷。{P}復次以
525b23‖ 法無礙智。知諸法無體性。以義無礙智。知諸
525b24‖ 法生滅相。以辭無礙智。知諸法假名。而不斷
525b25‖ 假名說。以樂說無礙智。隨假名不壞無邊說。
525b26‖ {Q}復次以法無礙智。知現在諸法差別相。以義
525b27‖ 無礙智。知過去未來諸法差別相。以辭無礙
525b28‖ 智。知過去未來現在諸法。

简体字

是菩萨住此地中，为大法师，守护诸佛法藏，堕在大法师深妙义中，用无量慧、方便、四无碍智，起菩萨言辞说法。是菩萨常随四无碍智而不分别。何等为四？一、法无碍，二、义无碍，三、辞无碍，四、乐说无碍。是菩萨用法无碍智，知诸法自相；以义无碍智，知诸法差别；以辞无碍智，知无分别说诸法；以乐说无碍智，知诸法次第不断。复次，以法无碍智，知诸法无体性；以义无碍智，知诸法生灭相；以辞无碍智，知诸法假名，而不断假名说；以乐说无碍智，随假名不坏无边说。复次，以法无碍智，知现在诸法差别相；以义无碍智，知过去、未来诸法差别相；以辞无碍智，知过去、未来、现在诸法，

16. The Bodhisattva's Command of Four Types of Unimpeded Knowledge

{M} This bodhisattva dwelling on this ground becomes a great expounder of the Dharma[278] who preserves and protects the Dharma treasury of the Buddhas.

{N} He thereby becomes one who is well equipped with the profound and sublime meaning understood by a great expounder of the Dharma. Consequently he employs measurelessly many wise skillful means and the four types of unimpeded knowledge in bringing forth the bodhisattva's command of phrasing as he explains the Dharma.

This bodhisattva always accords with the four types of unimpeded knowledge[279] and never abandons them. What then are these four? They are:

First, unimpeded knowledge of Dharma.
Second, unimpeded knowledge of meaning.
Third, unimpeded knowledge of language.
Fourth, unimpeded knowledge of eloquence.

a. Ten Permutations of Expertise in the Four Unimpeded Knowledges

{O} It is through unimpeded knowledge of Dharma that this bodhisattva knows the individual characteristics of any given dharma, through unimpeded knowledge of meaning that he knows the different characteristics by which dharmas differ, through unimpeded knowledge of language that he knows how to discourse on dharmas in a manner free of discriminations, and through unimpeded knowledge of eloquence that his knowledge of all dharmas is presented as sequential and uninterrupted discourse.

{P} Additionally, it is through unimpeded knowledge of Dharma that he knows the insubstantial nature of all dharmas, through unimpeded knowledge of meaning that he knows the production and destruction of dharmas, through unimpeded knowledge of language that he knows all dharmas' conventional designations and presents uninterrupted explanations incorporating these conventional designations, and through unimpeded knowledge of eloquence that he presents boundless explanations that accord with and do no violence to these conventional designations.

{Q} Furthermore, it is through unimpeded knowledge of Dharma that he knows the different characteristics of dharmas of the present. It is through unimpeded knowledge of meaning that he knows the different characteristics of dharmas of the past and future. It is through unimpeded knowledge of language that, knowing all dharmas of the past, future, and present, he

正體字

以無分別說。以樂
525b29‖ 說無礙[16]智。於一一世。得無邊法[17]相故說。{R}復
525c01‖ 次以法無礙智。知諸法差別。以義無礙智。知
525c02‖ 諸法義差別。以辭無礙[*]智。隨諸言音。而為
525c03‖ 說法。以樂說無礙智。隨所樂解。而為說法。
525c04‖ {S}復次以法無礙智。以法智知諸法差別。以方
525c05‖ 便知諸法無差別。以義無礙智。以比智如實
525c06‖ 知諸法差別。以辭無礙智。以世[*]智說諸法差
525c07‖ 別。以樂說無礙[18]智。知善說第一義。{T}復次以
525c08‖ 法無礙智。知諸法一相不壞。以義無礙智。善
525c09‖ 入陰入界諦因緣法。以辭無礙智。一切世間
525c10‖ 之所歸趣。以微妙音故。以樂說無礙。[*]智所說
525c11‖ 轉勝。能令眾生得無邊法明。{U}復次以法無礙
525c12‖ 智。知諸法無有分別。攝在一乘。以義無礙
525c13‖ [*]智。入分別諸法差別門。以辭無礙智。能說
525c14‖ 諸乘。無分別義。以樂說無礙智。以一法門。說
525c15‖ 無邊法明。

简体字

以无分别说；以乐说无碍智，于一一世得无边法相故说。复次，以法无碍智，知诸法差别；以义无碍智，知诸法义差别；以辞无碍智，随诸言音而为说法；以乐说无碍智，随所乐解而为说法。复次，以法无碍智，以法智知诸法差别，以方便知诸法无差别；以义无碍智，以比智如实知诸法差别；以辞无碍智，以世智说诸法差别；以乐说无碍智，知善说第一义。复次，以法无碍智，知诸法一相不坏；以义无碍智，善入阴入界谛因缘法；以辞无碍智，一切世间之所归趣，以微妙音故；以乐说无碍，智所说转胜，能令众生得无边法明。复次，以法无碍智，知诸法无有分别摄在一乘；以义无碍智，入分别诸法差别门；以辞无碍智，能说诸乘无分别义；以乐说无碍智，以一法门说无边法明。

discourses on them in a manner free of discriminations. And it is through unimpeded knowledge of eloquence that he is therefore able to discourse with boundless Dharma light on each of the periods of time.[280]

{R} Additionally, it is through unimpeded knowledge of Dharma that he knows the differences in dharmas, through unimpeded knowledge of meaning that he knows the differences in dharmas' meanings, through unimpeded knowledge of language that he is able to accord with all languages in discoursing on Dharma for others, and through unimpeded knowledge of eloquence that, in discoursing on Dharma for others, he adapts to their predilections and understandings.

{S} Then again, it is through unimpeded knowledge of Dharma that he uses Dharma knowledge to know dharmas' differentiating aspects even as he uses skillful means to know dharmas' non-differentiating aspects. It is through unimpeded knowledge of meaning that he uses comparative knowledge to know the distinctions among dharmas, through unimpeded knowledge of language that he uses worldly knowledge to discourse on dharmas' distinctions, and through unimpeded knowledge of eloquence that he knows how to discourse skillfully on ultimate truth.

{T} Additionally, it is through unimpeded knowledge of Dharma that he knows all dharmas' singular and indestructible character. It is through unimpeded knowledge of meaning that he thoroughly fathoms the dharmas of the aggregates, sense bases, sense realms, truths, and causes and conditions. It is through unimpeded knowledge of language that he employs such a subtle and wondrous voice in his discourse that all inhabitants of the world are able to understand its import. And it is through unimpeded knowledge of eloquence that whatever he discourses upon becomes ever more supremely able to cause beings to acquire the boundless light of Dharma.

{U} Then again, it is through unimpeded knowledge of Dharma that he knows the absence of differentiating distinctions among all dharmas and knows them to be entirely subsumed within the One Vehicle. It is through unimpeded knowledge of meaning that he enters the gateway of the distinctions between dharmas. It is through unimpeded knowledge of language that he is able to discourse on the meaning of the nonexistence of distinctions between the vehicles. And it is through unimpeded knowledge of eloquence that, employing but a single Dharma gateway, he discourses with boundless Dharma radiance.

正體字

{V}復次以法無礙智。能入一切菩薩
525c16‖ 行。智行法行隨智行。以義無礙智。能分別說
525c17‖ 十地義差別。以辭無礙智。不分別說隨順諸
525c18‖ 地道。以樂說無礙智。[19]說一切行無邊相。{W}復
525c19‖ 次以法無礙智。知一切佛。於一念中。得菩提。
525c20‖ 以義無礙智。知種種時處差別。以辭無礙。[*]智
525c21‖ 隨諸佛得道事差別說。以樂說無礙[*]智。於一
525c22‖ 句法無邊[20]劫。說而不窮盡。{X}復次以法無礙
525c23‖ 智。知一切佛[21]說。一切佛力。無所畏不共法。
525c24‖ 大慈大悲。無礙智轉法輪等。隨順一切智。以
525c25‖ 義無礙[*]智。隨如來音聲。出八萬四千。隨眾
525c26‖ 生心。隨根隨欲樂差別。以辭無礙智以如來
525c27‖ 音聲。不分[22]別說一切諸行。以樂說無礙[*]智。
525c28‖ 以諸佛智慧力。隨眾生所樂音聲說。{Y}諸佛子。
525c29‖ 菩薩摩訶薩。如是善知無礙智。安住第九地。
526a01‖ 名為得諸佛法藏。

简体字

复次，以法无碍智，能入一切菩萨行、智行、法行、随智行；以义无碍智，能分别说十地义差别；以辞无碍智，不分别说随顺诸地道；以乐说无碍智，说一切行无边相。复次，以法无碍智，知一切佛于一念中得菩提；以义无碍智，知种种时处差别；以辞无碍智，随诸佛得道事差别说；以乐说无碍智，于一句法无边劫说而不穷尽。复次，以法无碍智，知一切佛语、一切佛力、无所畏、不共法、大慈大悲、无碍智、转法轮等，随顺一切智；以义无碍智，随如来音声，出八万四千，随众生心、随根、随欲乐差别；以辞无碍智，以如来音声，不分别说一切诸行；以乐说无碍智，以诸佛智慧力，随众生所乐音声说。

“诸佛子，菩萨摩诃萨如是善知无碍智，安住第九地，名为得诸佛法藏，

{V} Additionally, it is through unimpeded knowledge of Dharma that he is able to enter the practices of all bodhisattvas, the practice of knowledge, the practice of the Dharma, and the practices following from knowledge. It is through unimpeded knowledge of meaning that he is able to distinguish and explain the differentiating aspects in meaning contained within the ten grounds. It is through unimpeded knowledge of language that he discourses without discrimination on progressing along the path of the grounds. And it is through unimpeded knowledge of eloquence that he discourses on the boundless aspects of all practices.

{W} Also, it is through unimpeded knowledge of Dharma that he knows all buddhas' realization of bodhi in but a single mind-moment, through unimpeded knowledge of meaning that he knows all of the distinctions among all different sorts of times and places, through unimpeded knowledge of language that he discourses on different matters related to all buddhas' realization of the path, and through unimpeded knowledge of eloquence that he may discourse on but a single sentence of Dharma for boundlessly many kalpas and still not come to the end of it.

{X} Furthermore, it is through unimpeded knowledge of Dharma that he knows all buddhas' proclamations as well as all buddhas' powers, fearlessnesses, dharmas exclusive to buddhas, great kindness, great compassion, unimpeded knowledges, turning of the Dharma wheel, and other such matters that follow from and accord with their all-knowledge. It is through unimpeded knowledge of meaning that he knows the manner in which the voice of the Tathāgata is brought forth in eighty-four thousand different ways adapted to beings resolute intentions,[281] adapted to their faculties, and adapted to their different resolute convictions.[282] It is through unimpeded knowledge of language that in he employs the Tathāgata's voice to discourse on all of the practices without making discriminations. And it is through unimpeded knowledge of eloquence that he employs the power of all buddhas' wisdom to discourse with a voice adapted to beings' resolute convictions.[283]

17. His Acquisition of Dhāraṇīs & Further Receipt of Buddhas' Dharma

{Y} Sons of the Buddha, the bodhisattva *mahāsattva* who thoroughly knows the unimpeded knowledges in these ways dwells securely on the ninth ground wherein he is known as one who has acquired the Dharma treasury of all buddhas. He is able to become a great master of the Dharma who acquires the manifold

正體字

能為大法師。得眾義陀羅
526a02‖ 尼。眾法陀羅尼。起智陀羅尼。眾明陀羅尼。善
526a03‖ 意陀羅尼。眾財陀羅尼。名聞陀羅尼。威德陀
526a04‖ 羅尼。無礙陀羅尼。無邊旋陀羅尼。雜義藏陀
526a05‖ 羅尼。得如是等百萬阿僧祇陀羅尼。隨應方
526a06‖ 便說。如是無量樂說差別門演法。是菩薩。得
526a07‖ 如是無量陀羅尼門。能於無量諸佛所聽法。
526a08‖ 聞已不忘。如所聞法能以無量差別門。為人
526a09‖ 演說。{Z}是菩薩。於一佛所。以百萬阿僧祇陀羅
526a10‖ 尼。聽受法。如從一佛聽法。餘無量無邊諸佛。
526a11‖ 亦如是。是菩薩。於禮敬佛時。所聞法明門。非
526a12‖ 多學聲聞得陀羅尼力。於十萬劫。所能受持。
526a13‖ 是菩薩。得如是陀羅尼力。諸無礙智。樂說力。
526a14‖ 以說法故。在於法座。遍三千大千世界眾生。
526a15‖ 隨意說法。是菩薩。在法座上。[1]唯除諸佛及
526a16‖ 受職菩薩。於一切中。最為殊勝。心中得無量
526a17‖ 法明。是菩薩。處於法座。

简体字

能为大法师，得众义陀罗尼、众法陀罗尼、起智陀罗尼、众明陀罗尼、善意陀罗尼、众财陀罗尼、名闻陀罗尼、威德陀罗尼、无碍陀罗尼、无边旋陀罗尼、杂义藏陀罗尼，得如是等百万阿僧祇陀罗尼，随应方便说，如是无量乐说差别门演法。是菩萨得如是无量陀罗尼门，能于无量诸佛所听法，闻已不忘；如所闻法能以无量差别门，为人演说。是菩萨于一佛所，以百万阿僧祇陀罗尼听受法，如从一佛听法，余无量无边诸佛亦如是。是菩萨于礼敬佛时，所闻法明门，非多学声闻得陀罗尼力，于十万劫所能受持。是菩萨得如是陀罗尼力、诸无碍智乐说力，以说法故，在于法座，遍三千大千世界众生，随意说法。是菩萨在法座上，唯除诸佛及受职菩萨，于一切中最为殊胜，心中得无量法明。是菩萨处于法座，

meanings *dhāraṇī*, the manifold dharmas *dhāraṇī*, the arising of wisdom *dhāraṇī*, the manifold illuminations *dhāraṇī*, the good intelligence *dhāraṇī*, the manifold wealth *dhāraṇī*, the *dhāraṇī* of wide renown, the awe-inspiring virtue *dhāraṇī*, the unobstructed *dhāraṇī*, the boundless *dhāraṇī*, and the treasury of various meanings *dhāraṇī*, acquiring thus a hundred myriads of *asaṃkhyeyas* of such *dhāraṇīs*. Adapting to what is appropriate to the circumstances, he employs skillful means in his discourse. In this way, as he expounds on the Dharma, he utilizes measurelessly many different gateways of eloquence.

Having acquired such an immeasurably great number of *dhāraṇī* gateways as these, he is able then to listen to the Dharma in the presence of all buddhas and, having heard it, he does not then forget it. According with the way that he has heard the Dharma spoken, he is able then to use measurelessly many different gateways in expounding for others.

{Z} Just as this bodhisattva employs a hundred myriads of *asaṃkhyeyas* of *dhāraṇīs* in listening to and taking in the Dharma in the presence of a single buddha, so too does he also do so in the presence of all of the other immeasurably and boundlessly many buddhas. When this bodhisattva goes forth and pays reverence to a Buddha, the gateways of Dharma light that he then learns are so extensive that, even in a hundred thousand kalpas, a greatly learned *śrāvaka*-disciple possessed of *dhāraṇī* powers could never succeed in absorbing and retaining them.

18. His Expounding on Dharma Throughout a Great Trichiliocosm

Having acquired such *dhāraṇī* power, unimpeded knowledges, and powers of eloquence as these, when this bodhisattva discourses on Dharma, even as he resides there on the Dharma throne, he speaks on Dharma throughout the worlds of a great trichiliocosm in a manner adapted to the mental dispositions[284] of the beings therein. As he holds forth from the Dharma throne, the Dharma light acquired in the mind of this bodhisattva is paramount in its supremacy over everyone with the sole exception of buddhas and those bodhisattvas who have already received the consecration.

19. This Bodhisattva's Various Voice-Like Expressions in Teaching Beings

When this bodhisattva sits on the Dharma throne:

He may employ but a single utterance of his voice to influence everyone in an entire great assembly to gain complete

正體字

或以一音。令一切
526a18‖ 大眾悉得解了。即得解了。或以種種音聲。令
526a19‖ 一切大眾。各得開解。即得開解。或以默然。但
526a20‖ 放光明。令一切大眾。各得解法。即得解法。
526a21‖ [2]或一切毛孔。皆出法音。或三千大千世界。
526a22‖ 所有色無色物。皆出法音。或以一音。周滿
526a23‖ [3]世性。悉令得解。是菩薩。三千大千世界。所
526a24‖ 有眾生。一時問難。[4]一眾生。以無量無邊音
526a25‖ 聲差別問難。如一人所問。餘者異問。是菩薩。
526a26‖ 於一念中。悉受如是問難。但以一音。皆令開
526a27‖ 解。如是二三千大千世界。三四五十二十三
526a28‖ 十四十五十。若百三千大千世界。若千三千
526a29‖ 大千世界。若萬十萬百萬。若億三千大千世
526b01‖ 界。若十億百千萬億那由他。乃至不可說不
526b02‖ 可說。三千大千世界。滿中眾生。廣為說法時。
526b03‖ 承佛神力。能為眾生廣作佛事。

简体字

或以一音，令一切大众悉得解了；即得解了，或以种种音声，令一切大众各得开解；即得开解，或以默然，但放光明，令一切大众各得解法；即得解法，或一切毛孔皆出法音，或三千大千世界所有色无色物皆出法音，或以一音周满世性悉令得解。是菩萨，三千大千世界所有众生一时问难，一一众生以无量无边音声差别问难，如一人所问，余者异问；是菩萨于一念中，悉受如是问难，但以一音皆令开解。如是二三千大千世界，三、四、五、十、二十、三十、四十、五十、若百三千大千世界、若千三千大千世界，若万、十万、百万、若亿三千大千世界，若十亿、百千万亿那由他，乃至不可说不可说三千大千世界，满中众生，广为说法时，承佛神力，能为众生广作佛事，

comprehension, whereupon they immediately succeed in acquiring complete comprehension.

Or he may employ many different sorts of voices to cause everyone in a great assembly to develop an understanding, whereupon they immediately develop an understanding.

Or he may remain silent and only emanate radiant light in order to cause everyone in an entire great assembly to acquire an understanding of Dharma, whereupon they immediately acquire an understanding of Dharma.

Or he may cause all of his hair pores to put forth the sounds of Dharma, or he may cause all things both with and without form throughout an entire great trichiliocosm to put forth the sounds of Dharma, or else he may cause a single sound to everywhere fill up the world, thereby causing everyone therein to gain an understanding.

20. His Independent Command of Countless Simultaneous Voices

Even if all beings in a great trichiliocosm's worlds were to simultaneously present questions to this bodhisattva while each of those beings employed a measureless and boundless number of voices that each presented different questions to him, and even as this was so for each single being, so too did all the other beings also pose entirely different questions, this bodhisattva would still be able in but a single mind-moment to absorb all such questions and then, employing but a single voice, he would be able to cause all those beings to acquire understandings corresponding to their particular questions.

So too would this be the case in a circumstance involving two great trichiliocosms filled with such beings, in a circumstance involving three, four, five, ten, twenty, thirty, forty, or fifty great trichiliocosms, in a circumstance involving a hundred trichiliocosms, in a circumstance involving a thousand great trichiliocosms, or in a circumstance involving a myriad, ten myriads, a hundred myriads, a *koṭi,* or even ten *koṭis* of great trichiliocosms, a hundred, a thousand, or even a myriad *koṭis* of *nayutas* of trichiliocosms, and so forth on up to an ineffable[285] number of ineffably many great trichiliocosms, all of them filled with such beings. As he expounds the Dharma for them on such a vast scale, he is augmented by the spiritual power of the Buddha. Thus he is able then to engage on a vast scale in performing the works of the Buddha for the sake of all these beings.

正體字

倍復精勤。攝
526b04‖ 取如是智明。若於一毫末中。有不可說不可
526b05‖ 說世界微塵數大會。佛在此中。而為說法。佛
526b06‖ 隨若干眾生心說法。令一一眾生。心中得若
526b07‖ 干無量諸法。如一佛。一切佛在大會中說法。
526b08‖ 皆亦如是。如一毛頭。一切十方世界。皆亦如
526b09‖ 是。於是中。應生大憶念力。於一念中。從一切
526b10‖ 佛所。受一切法明。而不失一句。如上大會滿
526b11‖ 中眾生聽法。[5]或於是中。以決定清淨法明演
526b12‖ 說。令得開解。於一念中。令爾所眾生。皆得歡
526b13‖ 喜。何況若[6]干世界中眾生。是菩薩。住是地
526b14‖ 中。善根轉勝。晝夜更無餘念。深入諸佛行處。
526b15‖ 常與一切佛會。深入菩薩解脫。菩薩隨順。如
526b16‖ 是智。常見諸佛。而於一一劫中。無量無邊百
526b17‖ 千萬億。[7]以[8]妙供具。供養諸佛。

简体字

倍复精勤，摄取如是智明。若于一毫末中，有不可说不可说世界微尘数大会，佛在此中而为说法，佛随若干众生心说法，令一一众生心中得若干无量诸法。如一佛，一切佛在大会中说法，皆亦如是。如一毛头，一切十方世界，皆亦如是。于是中应生大忆念力，于一念中从一切佛所，受一切法明而不失一句。如上大会满中众生听法，或于是中，以决定清净法明演说，令得开解。于一念中，令尔所众生皆得欢喜，何况若干世界中众生！是菩萨住是地中，善根转胜，昼夜更无余念，深入诸佛行处，常与一切佛会，深入菩萨解脱。菩萨随顺如是智，常见诸佛，而于一一劫中，无量无边百千万亿，以妙供具供养诸佛，

21. The Bodhisattva's Vigor in Quest of the Light of Knowledge

He redoubles the intensity of his vigor in acquisition of the light of knowledge such as this even to this degree: Suppose that on the tip of a single hair there existed great assemblies as numerous as the atoms in an ineffable number of ineffably many world systems wherein buddhas residing in the midst of each of those assemblies were expounding Dharma for beings' sakes. Suppose as well that each buddha therein adapted his discourse on Dharma to the minds of however many beings were present therein, thereby causing each and every one of those beings to acquire in his own mind however countlessly many dharmas he was setting forth. Suppose also that, just as this circumstance held for any one of those buddhas, so too did it also hold for all the buddhas residing in all of those great assemblies discoursing on Dharma. And suppose too that, just as this circumstance obtained on this one single hair point, so too did it also hold for all such places throughout the worlds of all the ten directions. Even in a circumstance such as this, he is accordingly able to bring forth just such a commensurately immense power of recall that, in but a single mind-moment, he is able to absorb all of the Dharma light received from all those buddhas and still not forget even a single sentence.

In circumstances such as the above described great assemblies full of beings listening to the Dharma, he may even be present therein employing the absolutely pure light of Dharma to expound it in such a way that they are caused to understand it. He is thus able in but a single mind-moment to cause however many beings are present therein to all become filled with delight. How much the more so is he able to accomplish this for the sake of the beings in any particular number of worlds.

The roots of goodness of this bodhisattva dwelling on this ground become ever more supreme. Whether it be day or night, he has no other thought aside from his aspiration to deeply enter the realm in which the Buddhas course.[286] Abiding within the assemblies of all buddhas, he always deeply penetrates into the bodhisattva's liberations.

22. The Bodhisattva's Seeing and Serving of Countless Buddhas

As he continues along in his compliance with knowledge such as this, this bodhisattva always sees all buddhas such that, in each and every kalpa, he sees incalculably and boundlessly many hundreds of thousands of myriads of *koṭis* of buddhas and then presents offerings of marvelous gifts to all those buddhas. In the

正體字

於諸佛所。種
526b18‖ 種問難。通達諸陀羅尼。是菩薩。善根轉勝明
526b19‖ 淨。如是佛子。如成鍊金。具足莊嚴。轉輪聖王
526b20‖ 寶冠。若在瓔珞。一切小王。四天下人。無能奪
526b21‖ 者。諸佛子。菩薩摩訶薩。亦如是。住此妙善地
526b22‖ 中。諸善根。轉勝明淨。無能壞者。聲聞辟支
526b23‖ 佛。及諸地菩薩。所不能壞。是菩薩善根轉明。
526b24‖ 能照眾生煩惱難處。照已還攝。佛子。譬如大
526b25‖ 梵王。三千大千世界。一切所有難處。皆悉能
526b26‖ 照。菩薩亦如是。住是菩薩妙善地中。善根明
526b27‖ 淨照眾生煩惱難處。照已還攝。諸佛子。是名
526b28‖ 略說菩薩摩訶薩第九菩薩妙善地。若廣說。
526b29‖ 則無量無邊劫。不可得盡。

简体字

于诸佛所种种问难，通达诸陀罗尼。是菩萨善根转胜明净！

“如是，佛子，如成炼金具足庄严，转轮圣王宝冠、若在璎珞，一切小王、四天下人，无能夺者。诸佛子，菩萨摩诃萨亦如是，住此妙善地中，诸善根转胜明净，无能坏者；声闻、辟支佛，及诸地菩萨，所不能坏。是菩萨善根转明，能照众生烦恼难处，照已还摄。佛子，譬如大梵王，三千大千世界一切所有难处，皆悉能照。菩萨亦如是，住是菩萨妙善地中，善根明净，照众生烦恼难处，照已还摄。

“诸佛子，是名略说菩萨摩诃萨第九菩萨妙善地。若广说，则无量无边劫不可得尽。

presence of all those buddhas, he poses all different sorts of queries to them on difficult topics and develops a penetrating comprehension of all of the *dhāraṇīs.*

23. His Good Roots' Purity Like the Gold of a Cakravartin's Crown

The roots of goodness of this bodhisattva become ever more supremely radiant in their purity. In the case of such sons of the Buddha as this, that purity is comparable to when one refines gold to the point where it becomes sufficiently pure to serve in adornments like the jeweled crown of a wheel-turning sage king. In such a circumstance, that crown's radiance becomes such that the necklaces of any of the lesser kings or residents of the four continents could never outshine it.

Sons of the Buddha, so too it is with this bodhisattva *mahāsattva.* As he abides on this Ground of Sublime Goodness, his roots of goodness become ever more supremely radiant in their purity, so much so that they cannot be rivaled by anyone at all. They cannot be rivaled by any *śrāvaka*-disciple, by any *pratyekabuddha,* or by any bodhisattva residing on any of the [lower][287] grounds.

The roots of goodness of this bodhisattva so increase in their brightness that they become able to illuminate beings' affliction-related entangling difficulties[288] and, having illuminated them, they then recede.

24. His Good Roots' Purity Like a Brahma Heaven King's Radiance

Sons of the Buddha, this circumstance is analogous to that of the Great Brahma Heaven King who is able to illuminate all of the entangling difficulties existing anywhere throughout the entire great trichiliocosm. So too it is in the case of this bodhisattva who, as he abides on this bodhisattva ground, the Ground of Sublime Goodness, he develops such radiant purity in his roots of goodness that he is able to illuminate beings' affliction-related entangling difficulties and, having once illuminated them, they then recede.

25. Vajragarbha's Final Statements About the 9th Ground Bodhisattva

Sons of the Buddha, this constitutes a summary explanation of the bodhisattva *mahāsattva*'s ninth bodhisattva ground, the Ground of Sublime Goodness. Were one to engage in an extensive discussion of it, then one could never come to the end of it even in incalculably many kalpas.

正體字

菩薩摩訶薩住是
526c01‖ 地中。多作大梵王。典領三千大千世界。無有
526c02‖ 能勝。如實解義者。於自在中。而得自在。善能
526c03‖ 宣說聲聞辟支佛。菩薩波羅蜜。眾生問難。無
526c04‖ 能窮盡。所作善業。若布施若愛語。若利益若
526c05‖ 同事。皆不離念佛念法念菩薩伴。乃至不離
526c06‖ 念一切種智。常生是心。我當何時於眾生中。
526c07‖ 為首為尊。乃至於一切眾生中。為依止者。是
526c08‖ 菩薩。若欲如是勤行精進。於一念中。得百萬
526c09‖ 阿僧祇三千大千世界微塵數三昧。乃至能
526c10‖ 示百萬阿僧祇三千大千世界微塵數菩薩眷
526c11‖ 屬。若以願力。神通自在。復過是數。百千萬億
526c12‖ 那由他劫。不可稱說。爾時金剛藏菩薩。欲重
526c13‖ 明此義。而說偈言

简体字

菩萨摩诃萨住是地中，多作大梵王，典领三千大千世界，无有能胜。如实解义者，于自在中而得自在，善能宣说声闻、辟支佛、菩萨波罗蜜，众生问难无能穷尽。所作善业，若布施、若爱语、若利益、若同事，皆不离念佛、念法、念菩萨伴，乃至不离念一切种智。常生是心：‘我当何时于众生中为首为尊？乃至于一切众生中为依止者？’是菩萨若欲如是勤行精进，于一念中，得百万阿僧祇三千大千世界微尘数三昧，乃至能示百万阿僧祇三千大千世界微尘数菩萨眷属；若以愿力神通自在，复过是数，百千万亿那由他劫不可称说。”

尔时，金刚藏菩萨欲重明此义，而说偈言：

a. The Bodhisattva's Station and Dharma Practice

The bodhisattva dwelling on this ground often serves as a Great Brahma Heaven king in which capacity he serves as the leader overseeing a great trichiliocosm, one over whom no one can establish supremacy, one who explains principles in accordance with reality, and one who acts with sovereign mastery wherever such mastery may be exercised. He is well able to proclaim the teachings of *śrāvaka*-disciples and *pratyekabuddhas* as well as the *pāramitās* of the bodhisattvas. Should any being pose a challenging question to him, no one is able to exhaust his ability to completely respond.

b. The Bodhisattva's Mindfulness

In all of the good works to which he devotes himself, whether they be in the sphere of giving, pleasing words, beneficial actions, or joint endeavors, he never departs from mindfulness of the Buddha, mindfulness of the Dharma, mindfulness of his bodhisattva companions, and so forth until we come to his never departing from mindfulness of the knowledge of all modes.

c. The Bodhisattva's Aspiration to Serve Beings

He always brings forth this thought: "Oh, when will I be able to finally become one who can serve as a leader for beings, one worthy of their veneration?," and so forth until we come to his thinking, "Oh, when will I be able to become one upon whom all beings can rely?"

d. The Consequences of the Bodhisattva's Vigor and Vows

If this bodhisattva wishes to devote himself to the diligent application of vigor, then in but a single mind-moment, he succeeds in acquiring samādhis as numerous as the atoms in a hundred myriad *asaṃkhyeyas* of trichiliocosms, and so forth until we come to his becoming able to manifest a hundred myriads of *asaṃkhyeyas* of bodhisattvas serving him as a retinue. Were he to avail himself of the power of vows, through sovereign mastery in the spiritual superknowledges, he could manifest these phenomena in even greater numbers so large that one could never describe them even in however many hundreds of thousands of myriads of *koṭis* of *nayutas* of kalpas one might attempt to do so.

26. Vajragarbha Bodhisattva's Summarizing Verses

At that time, Vajragarbha Bodhisattva, wishing to once again clarify his meaning, thereupon uttered verses, saying:

正體字

526c14‖ 諸菩薩隨順　無量深智力
526c15‖ 第一最微妙　一切世難知
526c16‖ 利益眾生者　能至第九地 {14}
526c17‖ 得入於諸佛　祕密之藏處
526c18‖ 得微妙最上　三昧陀羅尼
526c19‖ 廣大神通力　善入世間相
526c20‖ 智慧力決定　能觀諸佛法
526c21‖ 大願悲心淨　得入第九地 {15}
526c22‖ 順行此上地　持諸佛藏者
526c23‖ 即能通諸法　善不善無記
526c24‖ 是有漏無漏　世間出世間
526c25‖ 是[9]則可思議　是不可思議 {16}
526c26‖ 知法定[10]不定　三乘具足相
526c27‖ 思惟分別此　有為無為相
526c28‖ 起知如是法　破諸無明闇 {17}
526c29‖ 隨順是智心　則為第一妙
527a01‖ 悉知諸眾生　嶮難諸雜心
527a02‖ 輕躁易轉心　無邊自在心 {18}
527a03‖ 煩惱深淺相　心伴不離心
527a04‖ 又知使纏相　隨順相續有

简体字

“诸菩萨随顺，　无量深智力，
第一最微妙，　一切世难知，
利益众生者，　能至第九地，
得入于诸佛，　秘密之藏处。
得微妙最上，　三昧陀罗尼，
广大神通力，　善入世间相。
智慧力决定，　能观诸佛法，
大愿悲心净，　得入第九地。
顺行此上地，　持诸佛藏者，
即能通诸法，　善不善无记，
是有漏无漏，　世间出世间，
是则可思议，　是不可思议。
知法定不定，　三乘具足相，
思惟分别此，　有为无为相，
起知如是法，　破诸无明闇，
随顺是智心，　则为第一妙。
悉知诸众生，　崄难诸杂心，
轻躁易转心，　无边自在心，
烦恼深浅相，　心伴不离心，
又知使缠相，　随顺相续有。

The bodhisattvas who accord
with the power of that immeasurably profound wisdom
that is the most sublimely subtle
and difficult for anyone in the world to know
and who pursue the benefit of beings
become able to reach to the ninth ground. (14)

They succeed in entering the Buddha's
treasury of secrets
and become able to acquire the most supremely subtle and sublime
samādhis and *dhāraṇīs*.

Employing immense powers of spiritual superknowledges,
they skillfully penetrate the characteristic aspects of the world.
With decisive power of wisdom,
they are able to contemplate the dharmas of the Buddha
and, with great vows and compassionate resolve that is pure,
they succeed in entering the ninth ground. (15)

One practicing in accordance with this superior ground
who preserves the treasury of the buddhas
immediately becomes able to penetratingly understand all dharmas
whether they are good, unwholesome, or neutral,

whether they are associated with or free of the contaminants,
associated with the world or transcendent of the world,
and whether they are conceivable
or they are inconceivable. (16)

He knows of dharmas whether they are definite or indefinite
and knows the characteristic features comprising the Three Vehicles.
He contemplates and distinguishes these.
As for the characteristics of the conditioned and the unconditioned,
he brings forth a knowledge of dharmas such as these
and dispels all darkness of ignorance. (17)

As for his mind in its accordance with knowledge such as this,
it reaches the foremost level of subtlety.
He completely knows with respect to all beings their
hazardous entangling difficulties, their minds' diverse manifestations,
their readily agitated and easily turned minds,
and their boundless and independent minds. (18)

He knows their afflictions' deep and superficial aspects
and their accompanying and never existing apart from the mind.
He also knows the signs of entanglement with the latent tendencies
in the coursing along through continuous existences.

正體字

527a05║ 知業種種雜　各各差別相
527a06║ 因滅果不失　通達如是事 {19}
527a07║ 又知於眾生　諸根軟中利
527a08║ 廣大差別等　先際後際相
527a09║ 上中下差別　及諸欲樂等
527a10║ 乃至能悉知　八萬四千種 {20}
527a11║ 世間性亦爾　煩惱見難處
527a12║ 無始來不斷　諸心一切使
527a13║ 皆與心共行　縛心難可斷 {21}
527a14║ 知諸結使等　但妄想分別
527a15║ 無有方處所　亦無定事相
527a16║ 亦不離於身　又亦難得知
527a17║ 禪定力能遮　金剛道能斷 {22}
527a18║ 又能知[1]眾生　入六道差別
527a19║ 愛水癡闇覆　業田識是種
527a20║ 生於後身[＊]牙　名色共增長
527a21║ 無始生死來　相續在三界 {23}
527a22║ 及知天龍等　煩惱諸業心
527a23║ 若離於[2]心者　是則無所有

简体字

知业种种杂，　各各差别相，
因灭果不失，　通达如是事。
又知于众生，　诸根软中利，
广大差别等，　先际后际相，
上中下差别，　及诸欲乐等，
乃至能悉知，　八万四千种。
世间性亦尔，　烦恼见难处，
无始来不断，　诸心一切使，
皆与心共行，　缚心难可断，
知诸结使等，　但妄想分别，
无有方处所，　亦无定事相，
亦不离于身，　又亦难得知，
禅定力能遮，　金刚道能断。
又能知众生，　入六道差别，
爱水痴闇覆，　业田识是种，
生于后身芽，　名色共增长，
无始生死来，　相续在三界。
及知天龙等，　烦恼诸业心，
若离于心者，　是则无所有。

He knows all the different sorts of variations in their karma,
knows each and every one of its different characteristics,
knows that, even with destruction of causes, their effects are not lost,
and thus has a penetrating comprehension of such matters as these. {19}

He also knows with respect to beings
all their various faculties, whether weak, middling, or sharp,
as well as the vast number of other such distinctions
including their characteristics in both the past and the future,

their distinct differences when superior, middling, or inferior,
as well as all of their various aspirations, predilections, and such,
even up to the point that he is able to completely know
their eighty-four thousand different varieties. {20}

He knows the sense realms[289] of those in the world in this same way,
knows their entangling difficulties connected to afflictions and views,
knows they remain unsevered from the beginningless past onward,
knows their mental intentions and all their latent tendencies,
all of which act together with the mind,
and knows that they tie up the mind and are difficult to sever. {21}

He knows all of their latent tendencies and such,
knows they are but discriminations arising with discursive thinking,
knows that they are devoid of any place wherein they abide,
knows that they are also devoid of fixed phenomenal characteristics,

that they do not exist apart from the body,
that they are also difficult to become aware of,
that one is able to block them through the power of *dhyāna* samādhi,
and knows that one becomes able to sever them on the vajra path. {22}

He is also able to know with respect to beings
the differences in their entry into the six rebirth destinies, knows that
cravings serve as water, ignorance serves as darkness that covers,
karmic actions are the field, and consciousness is the seed

that gives rise to its sprout as the subsequent life's body
wherein name-and-form develop and grow together, and that,
throughout beginningless births and deaths up to the present,
this continues on within the three realms of existence. {23}

He knows too with respect to the devas, the dragons, and all the rest,
their afflicted actions and mental propensities,
knows that, if they were to leave behind such mental propensities,
then none of these births would occur at all,

正體字

527a24‖ 一切諸眾生　皆在三聚中
527a25‖ 或沒諸邪見　或在於智道 {24}
527a26‖ 菩薩住是地　悉知眾生心
527a27‖ 諸根及欲樂　種種差別等
527a28‖ 深心善思惟　隨宜而說法
527a29‖ 通達無礙智　善以言辭說 {25}
527b01‖ 菩薩為法師　猶如師子王
527b02‖ 牛王如山王　安住無所畏
527b03‖ 普於諸世界　雨美甘露味
527b04‖ 猶如大龍王　能雨滿大海 {26}
527b05‖ 是菩薩善知　法義辭無礙
527b06‖ 善能隨順行　具足樂說力
527b07‖ 能得於百萬　阿僧祇總持
527b08‖ 能受諸佛法　如海受龍雨 {27}
527b09‖ 菩薩得如是　諸深妙清淨
527b10‖ 無量陀羅尼　諸三昧力故
527b11‖ 能於一念中　得見無量佛
527b12‖ 聞已淨梵音　演說妙法寶 {28}
527b13‖ 是菩薩或教　大千界眾生
527b14‖ 隨心根所好　說法令歡喜 {29}

简体字

一切诸众生，　皆在三聚中，
或没诸邪见，　或在于智道。
菩萨住是地，　悉知众生心，
诸根及欲乐，　种种差别等；
深心善思惟，　随宜而说法，
通达无碍智，　善以言辞说。
菩萨为法师，　犹如师子王，
牛王如山王，　安住无所畏；
普于诸世界，　雨美甘露味，
犹如大龙王，　能雨满大海。
是菩萨善知，　法义辞无碍，
善能随顺行，　具足乐说力；
能得于百万，　阿僧祇总持；
能受诸佛法，　如海受龙雨。
菩萨得如是，　诸深妙清净，
无量陀罗尼，　诸三昧力故，
能于一念中，　得见无量佛，
闻已净梵音，　演说妙法宝。
是菩萨或教，　大千界众生，
随心根所好，　说法令欢喜。

and knows too that all beings,
in every case reside within the three categorical types of beings[290]
that may be either submerged in wrong views
or else abiding on the path of knowledge. {24}

The bodhisattva dwelling on this ground
knows entirely the mental dispositions of beings,
their faculties, their resolute beliefs,
and so forth in all their different variations.

Through profound thought and skillful contemplation,
he adapts to what is appropriate and then teaches them the Dharma.
Through penetrating comprehension of the unimpeded knowledges,
he is skillful in the use of language as he speaks. {25}

In his serving as a master of the Dharma, this bodhisattva
is like the king of the lions,
like the king of the bulls, and like the king of the mountains,
for he abides established in fearlessness,

everywhere raining down in all worlds
the flavor of the finest sweet-dew elixir.
In this, he is like the great king of the dragons
who is able to send down the rains that fill the great oceans. {26}

This bodhisattva thoroughly knows
the unimpeded knowledges of Dharma, meaning, and language
and is well able to adaptively implement
the fully accomplished power of eloquence.

He is able to acquire a hundred myriads
of *asaṃkhyeyas* of comprehensive-retention *dhāraṇīs*
through which he is able to take in the dharmas of all buddhas
just as the ocean takes in the rains sent down by the dragons. {27}

This bodhisattva acquires just such
profoundly marvelous and pure
dhāraṇīs, countless in number, and,
through the power associated with all of his samādhis,

he becomes able in just the space of a single mind-moment
to see incalculably many buddhas.
Having heard their teachings, with a pure Brahman voice,
he then expounds upon those marvelous Dharma jewels. {28}

This bodhisattva may provide instruction
to the beings inhabiting a great trichiliocosm,
adapting in this to their minds' faculties and mental dispositions,
speaking the Dharma in a way that causes them to be delighted. {29}

正體字

527b15║ 如是等無量　三千大千國
527b16║ 轉深勤精進　而作是思惟
527b17║ 或於一毛頭　無量佛說法
527b18║ 佛為種種人　演說於妙法
527b19║ 是菩薩皆受　如地受諸種 {30}
527b20║ 復作如是願　十方諸所有
527b21║ 國土中眾生　皆合為一會
527b22║ 應於一念中　皆悉知其心
527b23║ 以一音說法　悉令斷疑網 {31}
527b24║ 菩薩住是地　人天中法王
527b25║ 為大說法師　隨順眾生心
527b26║ 常於日夜中　與諸佛共會
527b27║ 能住甚深妙　寂滅智解脫 {32}
527b28║ 供養無量佛　善根轉明淨
527b29║ 猶如轉輪王　真金嚴寶冠
527c01║ 光明照眾生　煩惱嶮難處
527c02║ 如梵王光明　照於大千界 {33}
527c03║ 菩薩住是地　作三千大千
527c04║ 世界大梵王　諸根悉猛利

简体字

如是等无量，　三千大千国，
转深勤精进，　而作是思惟。
或于一毛头，　无量佛说法，
佛为种种人，　演说于妙法。
是菩萨皆受，　如地受诸种，
复作如是愿：　十方诸所有，
国土中众生，　皆合为一会，
应于一念中，　皆悉知其心，
以一音说法，　悉令断疑网。
菩萨住是地，　人天中法王，
为大说法师，　随顺众生心。
常于日夜中，　与诸佛共会，
能住甚深妙，　寂灭智解脱。
供养无量佛，　善根转明净，
犹如转轮王，　真金严宝冠。
光明照众生，　烦恼崄难处，
如梵王光明，　照于大千界。
菩萨住是地，　作三千大千，
世界大梵王，　诸根悉猛利。

In a manner such as this, even in the lands throughout
an incalculable number of great trichiliocosms,
he becomes ever more intensely diligent in his application of vigor
in a manner that one could contemplate in this way:

Suppose that on the tip of a single hair
there are measurelessly many buddhas speaking Dharma
wherein, for the sake of all different sorts of people, those buddhas
are expounding on the sublime Dharma.
In such a case, this bodhisattva is able to take it all in
in a manner comparable to the earth's taking in of all seeds. {30}

Additionally, he makes a vow such as this:
"Supposing all of the beings existing
in all lands throughout the ten directions
all came together as a single assembly,

I should, in but a single mind-moment,
completely know the thoughts in all their minds
and then, employing but a single voice, proclaim the Dharma
in a manner that causes all of their nets of doubts to be cut away." {31}

The bodhisattva dwelling on this ground
serves as a king of the Dharma for both humans and devas
among whom he becomes a great Dharma proclaiming master
who adapts his teachings to accord with the minds of beings

and always, throughout both day and night,
gathers together with all buddhas and
is able to abide in the extremely profound and sublime
quiescent knowledge and liberation. {32}

As he presents offerings to countlessly many buddhas
and as his roots of goodness become so increasingly radiant in purity
that they become comparable in their radiance to that of the real gold
adorning the crown of the Wheel-Turning King,

his light illuminates beings'
hazardous difficulties linked to their afflictions
just as the light of the Brahma Heaven King
illuminates the worlds of the great trichiliocosm. {33}

The bodhisattva dwelling on this ground
serves the worlds of a great trichiliocosm
as a great Brahma Heaven king
whose faculties are all acutely sharp

正體字

527c05‖ 善以三乘法　示悟諸眾生
527c06‖ 所作諸善業　皆順於正念 {34}
527c07‖ 能在一念中　而得於無量
527c08‖ 世界微塵數　諸深妙三昧
527c09‖ 得見十方佛　微妙音說法
527c10‖ 見佛大神力　更發無量願 {35}
527c11‖ 如是第九地　大智所行處
527c12‖ 深妙難知見　今已略說竟 {36}

简体字

善以三乘法，　示悟诸众生，
所作诸善业，　皆顺于正念。
能在一念中，　而得于无量，
世界微尘数，　诸深妙三昧。
得见十方佛，　微妙音说法，
见佛大神力，　更发无量愿。
如是第九地，　大智所行处，
深妙难知见，　今已略说竟。”

and who is skillful in using the Dharma of the Three Vehicles
to instruct and awaken all of those beings residing therein.
The good karmic works to which he devotes himself
are all done in a manner accordant with right mindfulness. {34}

He becomes able, in but a single mind-moment,
to acquire deep and sublime samādhis
as numerous as the atoms
in measurelessly many worlds.

He is able to see the buddhas of the ten directions
speaking the Dharma with their sublimely marvelous voices.
The buddhas he sees and the power of his great superknowledges
increase through his additional generation of immeasurable vows. {35}

We hereby now conclude this summary explanation
of such aspects as these of the practice of great knowledge
as it is carried forth on the ninth ground
in profoundly marvelous way that is difficult to know or see. {36}

End of Chapter Nine

正體字

527c13‖ [3]法雲地第[4]十
527c14‖ 說諸大菩薩　所行無上事
527c15‖ 無數那由他　首陀會諸天
527c16‖ 於上虛空中　心皆大歡喜
527c17‖ 咸以恭敬心　眾妙供養佛 {1}
527c18‖ 那由他菩薩　歡悅無有量
527c19‖ 燒諸奇妙香　滅除諸煩惱 {2}
527c20‖ 他化自在王　與諸天[5]大眾
527c21‖ 住在虛空中　心皆大歡喜
527c22‖ 咸以恭敬心　種種設供養
527c23‖ 各散眾寶衣　空中旋轉下 {3}
527c24‖ 無量億天女　諸根欣悅豫
527c25‖ 於上虛空中　敬心供養佛
527c26‖ 同作無量億　那由他伎樂
527c27‖ 於諸眾物中　皆出如是音 {4}
527c28‖ 佛坐於此處　悉遍於一切
527c29‖ 十方國土中　皆亦有佛現

简体字

法云地第十上

说诸大菩萨，　所行无上事，
无数那由他，　首陀会诸天，
于上虚空中，　心皆大欢喜，
咸以恭敬心，　众妙供养佛。
那由他菩萨，　欢悦无有量，
烧诸奇妙香，　灭除诸烦恼。
他化自在王，　与诸天大众，
住在虚空中，　心皆大欢喜，
咸以恭敬心，　种种设供养，
各散众宝衣，　空中旋转下。
无量亿天女，　诸根欣悦豫，
于上虚空中，　敬心供养佛，
同作无量亿，　那由他伎乐，
于诸众物中，　皆出如是音：
“佛坐于此处，　悉遍于一切，
十方国土中，　皆亦有佛现。

Chapter Ten
The Dharma Cloud Ground

J. The Tenth Ground: The Dharma Cloud Ground

1. The Tenth Ground's Introductory Verses and Dharma Request

When these unsurpassably excellent endeavors
practiced by the great bodhisattvas had been described,
the countless *nayutas*
of devas from the Śuddhāvāsa Heaven,

witnessing this from high in the sky,
felt great delight in mind
and then, with thoughts imbued with reverence,
they presented a multitude of marvelous offerings to the Buddha. {1}

The *nayutas* of bodhisattvas,
having felt immeasurably great delight,
then lit all manner of exotic and sublime incenses
that had the effect of extinguishing all afflictions. {2}

The Paranirmita Vaśavartin Heaven King
as well as that great assembly of devas
that stood there in the sky
all felt great delight in their minds.

With thoughts imbued with reverence,
they all presented all different sorts of gifts as offerings
as they each scattered down raiment adorned with many jewels
that swirled down, descending from the sky. {3}

Incalculably many *koṭis* of celestial nymphs,
with all their faculties suffused with happiness,
from on high where they stood in the sky,
with reverential minds, presented offerings to the Buddha.

They all then joined in creating measurelessly many *koṭis*
of *nayutas* of skillful musical offerings
as from all of their many gifts
there came forth voicings such as these: {4}

"The Buddha sits here in this place
while everywhere pervading all
of the lands throughout the ten directions wherein,
in all of them, there are also manifestations of the Buddha

正體字

528a01║ 無量億種種　相好莊嚴身
528a02║ 姝妙無有比　充滿於世界 {5}
528a03║ 於一毛孔中　出無量光明
528a04║ 滅除於一切　世間煩惱火
528a05║ 十方微塵數　不可得計量
528a06║ 一毛孔光明　亦復不可盡 {6}
528a07║ 各見有佛身　以三十二相
528a08║ 八十好莊嚴　轉於無上輪
528a09║ 或見佛種種　為眾而說法 {7}
528a10║ 或見在兜率　教化於諸天
528a11║ 或見從兜率　來下處胞胎
528a12║ 或見初生時　或見夜出家 {8}
528a13║ 或見坐道場　而成無上道
528a14║ 或見轉法輪　或見入涅槃 {9}
528a15║ 於無量國土　種種而示現
528a16║ 欲度眾生故　皆有如是事
528a17║ 譬如巧幻師　善知於幻術
528a18║ 多示諸眾生　種種諸異身
528a19║ 如是佛慧中　善巧於示現
528a20║ 變化一切身　周遍諸世間 {10}

简体字

无量亿种种，　相好庄严身，
姝妙无有比，　充满于世界。
于一毛孔中，　出无量光明，
灭除于一切，　世间烦恼火。
十方微尘数，　不可得计量，
一毛孔光明，　亦复不可尽。
各见有佛身，　以三十二相，
八十好庄严，　转于无上轮；
或见佛种种，　为众而说法；
或见在兜率，　教化于诸天；
或见从兜率，　来下处胞胎；
或见初生时；　或见夜出家；
或见坐道场，　而成无上道；
或见转法轮；　或见入涅槃，
于无量国土，　种种而示现，
欲度众生故，　皆有如是事。
譬如巧幻师，　善知于幻术，
多示诸众生，　种种诸异身；
如是佛慧中，　善巧于示现，
变化一切身，　周遍诸世间。

of many different sorts that are countless *koṭis* in number,
all with the major marks and subsidiary signs adorning their bodies
that, in their incomparably refined sublimity,
completely fill up the worlds. {5}

Even from within a single hair pore,
there are sent forth incalculably many rays of light
that extinguish all
of the world's fires of affliction.

The number of atoms throughout the ten directions
is such as one could never calculate.
The number of light rays sent forth from but a single hair pore
are also such that one could never exhaustively count them. {6}

In each of them, one sees that there are Buddha bodies
adorned with the thirty-two major marks
and the eighty subsidiary signs,
turning the unsurpassable wheel.
One may see there all the different circumstances wherein
the Buddha expounds on Dharma for beings' sakes. {7}

One may see his residing in the Tuṣita Heaven,
teaching all the devas,
may see him descending from the Tuṣita Heaven,
coming down to reside in the womb,
may see him when he is first born,
and may see him in the night, leaving behind the home life. {8}

One may see him sitting in the *bodhimaṇḍa*
whereupon he then achieves the unsurpassable enlightenment,
may see him turning the wheel of Dharma,
or may see him entering nirvāṇa. {9}

Throughout incalculably many lands,
he brings forth all different kinds of manifestations.
It is because he wishes to bring about the liberation of beings
that, in all such cases, there come to be such circumstances as these.

In this, he is comparable to a master conjurer
who knows well the arts of conjuration
and thus presents many such displays to beings
of all different sorts of different bodies.

From the midst of such wisdom of the Buddha as this,
he is skillful in presenting manifestations
wherein he transformationally creates all manner of bodies
that manifest everywhere throughout all worlds. {10}

正體字

528a21‖ 如諸法空寂　先來無性相
528a22‖ 同若如虛空　大師亦如是
528a23‖ 得入第一義　微妙之性相
528a24‖ 隨於法性相　示佛大神力 {11}
528a25‖ 諸佛所行性　一切諸眾生
528a26‖ 皆在是性中　相可相同相
528a27‖ 一切諸法等　入在於第一
528a28‖ 寂滅義趣中　悉皆無有相 {12}
528a29‖ 若欲得佛智　應離諸想念
528b01‖ 有無[1]俱通達　疾[2]作天人師 {13}
528b02‖ 諸天婇女眾　皆出如是等
528b03‖ 千萬種妙音　寂然而觀佛 {14}
528b04‖ 解脫月菩薩　見眾皆寂然
528b05‖ 請金剛藏言　大名稱佛子 {15}
528b06‖ 菩薩從九地　至於第十地
528b07‖ 諸大神通力　願今為略說 {16}
528b08‖ {A} 爾時金剛藏菩薩言。佛子。諸菩薩摩訶薩。如
528b09‖ 是無量智慧。善修行佛道。乃至九地。

简体字

如诸法空寂，　先来无性相，
同若如虚空，　大师亦如是。
得入第一义，　微妙之性相，
随于法性相，　示佛大神力。
诸佛所行性，　一切诸众生，
皆在是性中，　相可相同相。
一切诸法等，　入在于第一，
寂灭义趣中，　悉皆无有相。
若欲得佛智，　应离诸想念，
有无俱通达，　疾作天人师。”
诸天婇女众，　皆出如是等，
千万种妙音，　寂然而观佛。
解脱月菩萨，　见众皆寂然，
请金刚藏言：“大名称佛子，
菩萨从九地，　至于第十地，
诸大神通力，　愿今为略说！”

尔时，金刚藏菩萨言：“佛子，诸菩萨摩诃萨如是无量智慧，善修行佛道，乃至九地，

Just as all dharmas are empty, quiescent,
and, from their origin onward, devoid of nature or marks
and identically comparable to empty space,
so too it is with the Great Teacher.

Having achieved entry into the ultimate truth's
sublime nature and characteristics,
he accords with dharmas' nature and characteristics
in manifesting the Buddha's great spiritual powers. {11}

As for the very nature of that in which the Buddhas course,
all beings themselves
in every case abide within this nature wherein signs
and whatever can be vested with signs are of the same character.

All dharmas equally
enter and abide in the ultimate truth's
meaning and purport of quiescence
wherein, in every case, they are all entirely signless. {12}

If one wishes to acquire the knowledge of the Buddha,
one should abandon all conceptual thought,
penetratingly comprehend both existents and non-existents,
and swiftly become a teacher of both devas and men." {13}

Having all sung forth
a thousand myriad sorts of marvelous voicings such as these,
that assemblage of celestial nymphs
then fell silent and gazed up at the Buddha. {14}

Seeing that the assembled congregation had become entirely silent,
Liberation Moon Bodhisattva
then set forth a request to Vajragarbha Bodhisattva, saying:
"O Greatly Eminent Son of the Buddha." {15}

"We pray that you will now present a general explanation
of all the powers of great spiritual superknowledges involved in
the bodhisattva's going forth from the ninth ground
to then arrive on the tenth ground." {16}

2. Vajragarbha Commences the Tenth Ground's Explanation

{A} At that time, Vajragarbha Bodhisattva then said:

3. The Categories of Practice Before Entering the Tenth Ground

O Son of the Buddha, having employed such measureless wisdom as this in skillful cultivation of the path to buddhahood on through to the ninth ground, the bodhisattva *mahāsattvas*:[291]

正體字

善集諸
528b10‖ 白法。集無量助道法。大功德智慧所護。廣行
528b11‖ 大悲。深知分別世間性差別。深入眾生難處。
528b12‖ 至諸如來行處。念隨順如來寂滅行處。趣向
528b13‖ 諸佛力無所畏。不共法等。堅持不捨。得至一
528b14‖ 切智慧位。{B}諸佛子。菩薩摩訶薩。隨行如是智。
528b15‖ 近佛位地。則得菩薩離垢三昧。而現在前。又
528b16‖ 入法性差別三昧。莊嚴道場三昧。雨一切世
528b17‖ 間華光三昧。海藏三昧。海印三昧。虛空廣三
528b18‖ 昧。觀擇一切法性三昧。隨一切眾生心行三
528b19‖ 昧。如實擇一切法三昧。得如來智信三昧。如
528b20‖ 是等百萬阿僧祇三昧。皆現在前。是菩薩悉
528b21‖ 入此三昧。善知其中功用差別。最後三昧。名
528b22‖ 益一切智位。

简体字

善集诸白法，集无量助道法，大功德智慧所护，广行大悲，深知分别世间性差别，深入众生难处，至诸如来行处，念随顺如来寂灭行处，趣向诸佛力、无所畏、不共法等坚持不舍，得至一切智慧位。诸佛子，菩萨摩诃萨随行如是智，近佛位地，则得菩萨离垢三昧而现在前；又入法性差别三昧、庄严道场三昧、雨一切世间华光三昧、海藏三昧、海印三昧、虚空广三昧、观择一切法性三昧、随一切众生心行三昧、如实择一切法三昧、得如来智信三昧，如是等百万阿僧祇三昧皆现在前。是菩萨悉入此三昧，善知其中功用差别。最后三昧，名益一切智位。

Thoroughly accumulate every sort of white dharma;
Accumulate the measurelessly many dharmas constituting the provisions for the path;
Become protected by immense merit and wisdom;
Practice the great compassion on a vast scale;
Deeply know and distinguish the differences between worlds;
Deeply penetrate beings' entangling difficulties;[292]
Reach the Tathāgatas' domains of practice;
Carry forth mindfulness in a manner concordant with the Tathāgata's stations of quiescent practice;
And progress toward the powers, fearlessnesses, exclusive dharmas, and other such attainments of the Buddhas.

Firmly maintaining and never relinquishing these [practices], they thereby succeed in reaching the station [wherein they receive the consecration of imminent realization] of all-knowledge.

4. This Bodhisattva's Subsequent Acquisition of Samādhis

{B} Sons of the Buddha, it is through practicing in accord with knowledge such as this that the bodhisattva *mahāsattva* nearing the ground of buddhahood then acquires the direct manifestation of the bodhisattva's stainless samādhi. He then additionally enters:[293]

The distinctions within the Dharma realm samādhi;
The adornment of the *bodhimaṇḍa* samādhi;
The showering of all worlds with floral radiance samādhi;
The oceanic treasury samādhi;
The oceanic reflection samādhi;
The vastness of empty space samādhi;
The contemplative investigation of the nature of all dharmas samādhi;
The adaptation to the minds and actions of all beings samādhi;
The selection of all dharmas in accordance with reality samādhi;
And the acquisition of the Tathāgata's knowledge and reliability samādhi.

Hundreds of myriads of *asaṃkhyeyas* of samādhis such as these all manifest directly before him. This bodhisattva enters all of these samādhis and thoroughly knows the differences in their functions. Among them, the very last samādhi is known as "enhancement of the station of all-knowledge."

正體字

{C}是三昧現在前時。大寶蓮花王
528b23‖ 出。周圓如百萬三千大千世界。一切眾寶。間
528b24‖ 錯莊嚴。過一切世間所有。出世間善根所生。
528b25‖ 行諸法如幻。性空慧所成。光明能照一切世
528b26‖ 界。大寶琉璃為莖。勝一切諸天所有。不可[3]量
528b27‖ 栴檀王為臺。大馬瑙寶為鬚。閻浮檀金光為
528b28‖ [4]葉。中有無量光明。一切妙寶。皆在其內。寶
528b29‖ 網覆上。滿十三千大千世界微塵數蓮花為
528c01‖ 眷屬。爾時菩薩。其身[妹>姝]妙。稱可華座。是菩
528c02‖ 薩。得益一切智位三昧力故。身現在大蓮華
528c03‖ 座上。即時諸眷屬蓮華上。皆有菩薩圍遶之。
528c04‖ 一一菩薩。坐蓮華上。即得百萬三昧。皆一心
528c05‖ 恭敬。瞻仰大菩薩。{D}是菩薩。昇蓮華座時。十方
528c06‖ 現在。一切世界。皆大震動。一切惡道。皆悉休
528c07‖ 息。光明普照十方世界。一切世界。皆悉嚴淨。
528c08‖ 皆得見聞一切諸佛大會。何以故。是菩薩。坐
528c09‖ 大蓮華座上。即時足下。出百萬阿僧祇光明。

简体字

是三昧现在前时，大宝莲华王出，周圆如百万三千大千世界，一切众宝间错庄严，过一切世间所有，出世间善根所生，行诸法如幻性空慧所成，光明能照一切世界。大宝琉璃为茎，胜一切诸天所有，不可量栴檀王为台，大玛瑙宝为须，阎浮檀金光为叶，中有无量光明，一切妙宝皆在其内，宝网覆上，满十三千大千世界微尘数莲华为眷属。

“尔时，菩萨其身姝妙，称可华座。是菩萨得益一切智位三昧力故，身现在大莲华座上。即时诸眷属莲华上，皆有菩萨围绕之。一一菩萨坐莲华上，即得百万三昧，皆一心恭敬瞻仰大菩萨。是菩萨升莲华座时，十方现在一切世界皆大震动，一切恶道皆悉休息。光明普照十方世界，一切世界皆悉严净，皆得见闻一切诸佛大会。何以故？是菩萨坐大莲华座上，即时足下出百万阿僧祇光明，

5. The Final Samādhi's Manifestation of an Immense Radiant Lotus

{C} When this samādhi manifests directly before him, there then emerges an immense bejeweled king of lotus blossoms with a circumference comparable to that of a hundred myriad great trichiliocosms. It is adorned by and inlaid with all of the many sorts of precious gems and surpasses any other that exists anywhere in any world. It comes forth from his roots of world-transcending goodness and is perfected by his practice of the wisdom that fathoms all dharmas as like mere illusions and as devoid of any inherently existent nature.

Its radiant light is able to illuminate all worlds. Its stem is composed of immense jewels and beryl that is superior to any existing anywhere in the heavens. A measurelessly immense king of *candana* incenses composes its central dais and huge emerald gems form its floral pistils. Radiant *jambūnada* gold forms its petals. There is measureless light shining forth from its center and every sort of marvelous gem resides there within it. It is covered over by a bejeweled net canopy and it is attended by a retinue of lotus blossoms as numerous as the atoms in ten great trichiliocosms.

6. This Bodhisattva Sits Atop a Lotus Encircled by Retinue Bodhisattvas

At that time, this bodhisattva's body, especially beautiful in its marvelousness, matches the scale of that flower throne. Because he has acquired the power of the samādhi of "enhancement of the station of all-knowledge," his body then appears atop that great lotus blossom throne. Then, on all of the lotus blossoms forming its retinue, bodhisattvas immediately appear and encircle it with each and every one of those bodhisattvas sitting atop a lotus blossom. Each of them then immediately acquires a hundred myriad samādhis and they all abide there in single-minded reverence, gazing up at that great bodhisattva.

{D} When this bodhisattva ascends that lotus blossom throne, all of the present-era worlds throughout the ten directions undergo an immense quaking, whereupon everything occurring in the wretched destinies ceases. Those light rays everywhere illuminate the worlds of the ten directions, whereupon they all become adorned and purified and everyone is able to see and hear what is transpiring in the Buddha's great assembly.

7. His Body Emanates Light Illuminating Ten Realms of Beings

How is it that this takes place? As this bodhisattva sits atop the throne on that immense lotus blossom, from the bottom of his feet, he suddenly puts forth a hundred myriads of *asaṃkhyeyas* of

正體字

528c10‖ [5]照[6]十方阿鼻地獄等。[7]滅眾生[8]苦惱。兩膝
528c11‖ 上。放若干光明。[9]悉照十方一切畜生。滅除
528c12‖ 苦惱。臍放若干光明。照十方一切餓鬼。滅除
528c13‖ 苦惱。左右脇。放若干光明。照十方[10]人身。安
528c14‖ 隱快樂。兩手放若干光明。照十方諸天阿修
528c15‖ 羅宮殿。兩[11]肩放若干光明。照十方聲聞人。
528c16‖ 項放若干光明。照十方辟支佛。口放若干光
528c17‖ 明。照十方世界諸菩薩身乃至住九地者。白
528c18‖ 毫放若干光明。照十方得位菩薩身。一切魔
528c19‖ 宮。隱蔽不現。頂上放百萬阿僧祇三千大千
528c20‖ 世界微塵數光明。照十方諸佛大會。圍遶世
528c21‖ 界十匝。住於虛空。成光明網。高大明淨。供養
528c22‖ 諸佛。如是供養。從初發心。乃至九地。菩薩所
528c23‖ 作供養。

简体字

照十方阿鼻地狱等，灭众生苦恼。两膝上放若干光明，悉照十方一切畜生，灭除苦恼。脐放若干光明，照十方一切饿鬼，灭除苦恼。左右胁，放若干光明，照十方人身，安隐快乐。两手放若干光明，照十方诸天阿修罗宫殿。两肩放若干光明，照十方声闻人。项放若干光明，照十方辟支佛。口放若干光明，照十方世界诸菩萨身，乃至住九地者。白毫放若干光明，照十方得位菩萨身。一切魔宫隐蔽不现。顶上放百万阿僧祇三千大千世界微尘数光明，照十方诸佛大会，围绕世界十匝，住于虚空成光明网，高大明净，供养诸佛。如是供养，从初发心乃至九地菩萨所作供养，

light rays that, throughout the ten directions, illuminate the Avīci Hells as well as the rest of the hells, thus extinguishing the sufferings of the beings dwelling in them.

From his two knees, he releases just such a number of light rays that, throughout the ten directions, entirely illuminate the animal realms, thus extinguishing their sufferings. From his navel, he releases just such a number of light rays that, throughout the ten directions, illuminate the realms of hungry ghosts, thus extinguishing their sufferings.

From his right and left sides, he releases just such a number of light rays that, throughout the ten directions, illuminate the bodies of all of those in the human realms, thereby causing them to feel secure and happy. From his two hands, he releases just such a number of light rays that, throughout the ten directions, illuminate the palaces of all the devas and *asuras.*

From his two shoulders, he then releases just such a number of light rays that, throughout the ten directions, illuminate those persons who are *śrāvaka*-disciples. From his neck, he then releases just such a number of light rays that, throughout the ten directions, illuminate those who are *pratyekabuddhas.*

From his mouth, he then releases just such a number of light rays that, throughout the ten directions, illuminate the bodies of the bodhisattvas, inclusive of all of those who have reached the ninth ground.

From the white hair mark between his eyebrows, he then releases just such a number of light rays that, throughout the ten directions, illuminate the bodies of all those bodhisattvas who have reached the consecration stage and thus so cast shade on the palaces of all the *māras* that they no longer appear.

From the crown of his head, he then releases a number of light rays as numerous as the atoms in a hundred myriads of *asaṃkhyeyas* of great trichiliocosms that, throughout the ten directions, illuminate the great assemblies attending upon all buddhas.

8. The Light Rays Form a Canopy That Makes Offerings to All Buddhas

They then circle ten times around those worlds, dwell up in space, and then form a net-like canopy that, high above, shines with greatly radiant purity, sending forth offerings to all those buddhas.

Those offerings are so numerous that the offerings made by all the bodhisattvas, from those who have newly brought forth the resolve on through to those who have reached the ninth ground

正體字

百分不及一。乃至百千萬億分不及
528c24‖ 一。乃至算數譬喻。所不能及。是大光明網。勝
528c25‖ 十方世界所有華香末香。燒香塗香。衣服幡
528c26‖ 蓋。眾寶瓔珞。摩尼寶珠。供養之具。以從出
528c27‖ 世善根生故。一一佛大會上。皆雨眾寶。狀如
528c28‖ 大雲。若有眾生。覺知如是供養者。當知皆是
528c29‖ 必定無上大道。如是諸光。雨大供養已。還繞
529a01‖ 諸佛大會十匝。入諸佛足下。爾時諸佛。及大
529a02‖ 菩薩。知[1]某世界中。某甲菩薩摩訶薩。行如
529a03‖ 是道。成就受職。諸佛子。即時十方無邊菩薩。
529a04‖ 乃至住九地者。皆來圍遶。設大供養。一心恭
529a05‖ 敬瞻[2]禮各得萬三昧。諸得職菩薩摩訶薩。於
529a06‖ 金剛莊嚴胸。出一大光。名破魔賊。有無量百
529a07‖ 千萬光。以為眷屬。照十方世界。示無量神力。
529a08‖ 亦來入是

简体字

百分不及一，乃至百千万亿分不及一，乃至算数譬喻所不能及。是大光明网，胜十方世界所有华香、末香、烧香、涂香、衣服、幡盖、众宝璎珞、摩尼宝珠供养之具，以从出世善根生故。一一佛大会上，皆雨众宝，状如大云。若有众生，觉知如是供养者，当知皆是必定无上大道。如是诸光，雨大供养已，还绕诸佛大会十匝，入诸佛足下。尔时，诸佛及大菩萨，知某世界中，某甲菩萨摩诃萨，行如是道，成就受职。

“诸佛子，即时十方无边菩萨，乃至住九地者，皆来围绕，设大供养，一心恭敬瞻礼各得万三昧。诸得职菩萨摩诃萨，于金刚庄严胸出一大光，名破魔贼，有无量百千万光以为眷属，照十方世界，示无量神力，亦来入是

could not compare to even a hundredth part and so forth until we come to their inability to compare to even a single part in a hundred thousand myriads of *koṭis* of parts and their inability to compare at all, even by resort to calculation or analogy.

The offerings rained down by this immense net-like canopy of light are superior to all offering gifts made anywhere throughout the worlds of the ten directions, including all floral, powdered, burnable, and unguent incenses, all raiment, banners, canopies, many-jeweled necklaces, precious *maṇi* jewels, and other such offerings. This is because they issue from world-transcending roots of goodness. This canopy that rains down the many sorts of precious treasures into each and every one of the Buddhas' great assemblies has the appearance of an immense cloud.

If any being were to even become aware that such offerings as this were taking place, one should realize that these are all beings who have already become definitely bound to succeed in realizing the unsurpassable great path.

9. The Light Rays Circle Around All Buddhas and Enter Their Feet

After these light rays rain down all their great offerings, they again circle ten times around those buddhas and their great assemblies and then enter the feet of all those buddhas.

At that time, all the buddhas and the great bodhisattvas become aware that in such-and-such a world, there is such-and-such a bodhisattva *mahāsattva* who has traveled this path to the point where he has succeeded in reaching the stage of consecration.

10. The 10 Regions' Bodhisattvas Come, Make Offerings & Enter Samādhi

Sons of the Buddha, at that time, all bodhisattvas throughout the ten directions inclusive of those who dwell on the ninth ground immediately come, surround him, present grand offerings, single-mindedly and respectfully gaze up at him, and pay reverence to him, whereupon each of them acquires a myriad samādhis.

11. They Emanate Light from Their Chests That Enters His Chest

Then all of those bodhisattva *mahāsattvas* who have reached the consecration stage emanate a single large beam of light from the vajra adornment symbol on their chests. This light named "destroyer of Māra's thieves" is attended by a retinue of countlessly many hundreds of thousands of myriads of light rays that illuminate the worlds of the ten directions, reveal measurelessly many spiritual powers, and then also arrive and enter this great

正體字

大菩薩胸。此光明滅已。是菩薩。即
529a09‖ 時得大勢力。神通智慧。百千萬倍。(E)諸佛子。爾
529a10‖ 時諸佛。出眉間白毫相光。名益一切智[3]位。
529a11‖ 有無量無邊光明眷屬。照一切十方世界。無
529a12‖ 有遺餘。十匝圍遶一切世界。示於諸佛大神
529a13‖ 通力。勸進無量無邊百千萬億諸菩薩。一切
529a14‖ 十方世界。六種震動。滅除一切惡道苦惱。一
529a15‖ 切魔宮。皆蔽不現。示一切諸佛得道之處。示
529a16‖ 一切諸佛大會莊嚴事。廣大如[4]法性。究竟如
529a17‖ 虛空。照明一切世界已。集在虛空。右遶。示大
529a18‖ 神通莊嚴之事。入是菩薩頂上。其諸眷屬光
529a19‖ 明。入諸眷屬蓮華菩薩頂上。即時諸菩薩。各
529a20‖ 得先所未得十千三昧。是光明入此菩薩頂。
529a21‖ 如一佛光。一切佛光。皆亦如是。一切十方佛
529a22‖ 光明。入是菩薩頂時。名為得職。名為入諸佛
529a23‖ [5]境界。為具佛十力。當墮在佛數。

简体字

大菩萨胸。此光明灭已，是菩萨即时得大势力，神通智慧百千万倍。诸佛子，尔时诸佛出眉间白毫相光，名益一切智位，有无量无边光明眷属，照一切十方世界无有遗余。十匝围绕一切世界，示于诸佛大神通力，劝进无量无边百千万亿诸菩萨。一切十方世界六种震动，灭除一切恶道苦恼，一切魔宫皆蔽不现，示一切诸佛得道之处，示一切诸佛大会庄严事，广大如法性，究竟如虚空。照明一切世界已，集在虚空，右绕示大神通庄严之事，入是菩萨顶上。其诸眷属光明，入诸眷属莲华菩萨顶上。即时诸菩萨，各得先所未得十千三昧。是光明入此菩萨顶，如一佛光，一切佛光皆亦如是。一切十方佛光明，入是菩萨顶时，名为得职，名为入诸佛境界，为具佛十力，当堕在佛数。

bodhisattva's chest. After this light disappears, this bodhisattva immediately acquires great powers, spiritual superknowledges, and wisdom that then increase a hundred thousand myriad fold.

12. All Buddhas Send Forth Light That Enters This Bodhisattva's Crown

{E} Sons of the Buddha, at that time, the Buddhas put forth a beam of light from the white hair mark between their eyebrows, one known as "enhancer of all-knowledge"[294] that is attended by a retinue of measurelessly and boundlessly many light rays that illuminate all worlds of the ten directions without exception. It circles ten times around all those worlds, displaying the immense spiritual powers of all buddhas, encourages the progress of countlessly and boundlessly many hundreds of thousands of myriads of *koṭis* of bodhisattvas, causes all worlds throughout the ten directions to shake in six ways, extinguishes all the sufferings in the wretched destinies, obscures the palaces of the *māras* so they no longer appear, displays all those places in which buddhas achieved realization of the path, and reveals all the adorning phenomena in the great assemblies of all buddhas that are as vast as the Dharma realm and as extensive as empty space.

After those light rays have illuminated all worlds, they then gather together in the midst of space and circle around in a rightward direction, thus revealing the adornments produced by great spiritual powers, whereupon that beam of light enters the crown of this bodhisattva's head as all of its retinue light rays enter the crowns of the heads of those retinue bodhisattvas that are present there atop their own lotus blossoms.

13. This Bodhisattva Acquires Samādhis and All Buddhas' Consecration

At that point, these bodhisattvas each immediately acquire a myriad samādhis they had never previously acquired. Just as this beam of light sent out by this one buddha enters this bodhisattva's crown, so too does this occur in this very same way in the case of the beams of light sent forth by all buddhas. Just when all those beams of light sent forth from all buddhas of the ten directions enter the crown of this bodhisattva's head, he becomes known as one who has received the consecration and becomes known as one who has entered the realm of the Buddhas wherein, having completely developed the Buddha's ten powers, he is then bound to join the ranks of the Buddhas.

正體字

諸佛子。譬
529a24‖ 如轉輪聖王長子。[6]大夫人所生。成就轉輪王
529a25‖ 相。轉輪聖王。令子在白象寶閻浮檀金座上。
529a26‖ 取四大海水。上張羅[7]幔。種種莊嚴。幢幡伎
529a27‖ 樂。執金鍾香水。灌子頂上。即名為灌頂。大王
529a28‖ 具足。轉十善道故。得名轉輪聖王。諸佛子。菩
529a29‖ 薩摩訶薩。亦如是。受職時。諸佛以智水。灌是
529b01‖ 菩薩頂。名灌頂法王。具足佛十力故。墮在佛
529b02‖ 數。諸佛子。是名諸菩薩摩訶薩大智慧[8]職。
529b03‖ 以是職故。諸菩薩摩訶薩。受無量百千億萬
529b04‖ 苦行難事。是菩薩。得是職已。住菩薩法雲地。
529b05‖ 無量功德。智慧轉增。{F}諸佛子。菩薩住是法雲
529b06‖ 地。如實知集欲界。集色界。集無色界。如實知
529b07‖ 集世間性。集眾生性。集識性。集有為性。

简体字

“诸佛子，譬如转轮圣王长子，大夫人所生，成就转轮王相。转轮圣王，令子在白象宝阎浮檀金座上，取四大海水，上张罗幔种种庄严，幢幡伎乐，执金钟香水灌子顶上，即名为灌顶。大王具足转十善道故，得名转轮圣王。诸佛子，菩萨摩诃萨亦如是，受职时，诸佛以智水灌是菩萨顶，名灌顶法王，具足佛十力故，堕在佛数。诸佛子，是名诸菩萨摩诃萨大智慧职。以是职故，诸菩萨摩诃萨，受无量百千亿万苦行难事。是菩萨得是职已，住菩萨法云地，无量功德智慧转增。诸佛子，菩萨住是法云地，如实知集欲界、集色界、集无色界，如实知集世间性、集众生性、集识性、集有为性、

14. The Simile of the Consecration of the Wheel Turning Sage King's Son

Sons of the Buddha, this circumstance is analogous to that of the eldest son of a wheel-turning sage king who, born to his primary wife, is replete with the marks of the wheel-turning king. That wheel-turning sage king orders his son to mount the throne of *jambūnada* gold atop his precious white elephant treasure, whereupon he takes water from each of the four great seas and, after having raised up a canopy with all different sorts of adornments, banners, and music, he takes up that gold vase of perfumed waters and pours it over the crown of his son's head, whereupon he is henceforth known as one who has received the consecration and is thereby completely invested with the status of a great king. Because he then turns the wheel of the ten courses of good karmic action, he is then able to be known as a wheel-turning sage king.

Sons of the Buddha, so too it is with the bodhisattva *mahāsattva*. At that time when he receives his consecration, the Buddhas pour the waters of knowledge onto the crown of this bodhisattva's head whereupon he becomes known as a consecrated Dharma king. Through complete development of the Buddha's ten powers he joins the ranks of the Buddhas.

15. The Capacities Arising From This Bodhisattva's Consecration

Sons of the Buddha, this is what is known as all bodhisattva *mahāsattvas'* great wisdom consecration. It is by means of this consecration that all bodhisattva *mahāsattvas* are able to take on countlessly-many hundreds of thousands of myriads of *koṭis* of austere practices and difficult endeavors. After this bodhisattva acquires this consecration, he thereupon dwells on the Dharma Cloud Ground wherein he brings about ever increasing growth in incalculably many forms of merit and wisdom.

16. This Bodhisattva's Knowledge of Attainments

{F} Sons of the Buddha, the bodhisattva dwelling on this Dharma Cloud Ground knows in accordance with reality:

Attainment as it takes place within the desire realm;[295]
Attainment as it takes place within the form realm;
And attainment as it takes place within the formless realm;

He knows in accordance with reality:

Attainment as it takes place within the worldly realms;
Attainment as it takes place within the realm of beings;
Attainment as it takes place within the realms of consciousness;
Attainment as it takes place within the realm of the conditioned;

正體字

集無
529b08‖ 為性。集虛空性。集法性。集涅槃性。集邪見諸
529b09‖ 煩惱性。如實知諸世間行法還法。[9]如實知集
529b10‖ 聲聞道。集辟支佛道。集菩薩道。集諸佛力無
529b11‖ 畏。不共法。集色身法身。集一切智慧。如是集
529b12‖ 得佛道。集轉法輪。集示滅度。舉要言之。如實
529b13‖ 知示集一切法差別。是菩薩。以[10]如是智慧。
529b14‖ 隨順菩提行。[11]如實轉深入。知眾生化。業化
529b15‖ 煩惱化。[12]諸見化世性化。法性化。聲聞化。

简体字

集无为性、集虚空性、集法性、集涅槃性、集邪见诸烦恼性，如实知诸世间行法还法，如实知集声闻道、集辟支佛道、集菩萨道、集诸佛力无畏不共法、集色身法身、集一切智慧，如是集得佛道、集转法轮、集示灭度。举要言之，如实知示集一切法差别。是菩萨以如是智慧，随顺菩提行，如实转深入，知众生化、业化、烦恼化、诸见化、世性化、法性化、声闻化、

Attainment as it takes place within the realm of the unconditioned;
Attainment as it takes place within the realm of empty space;
Attainment as it takes place within the Dharma realm;
Attainment as it takes place within the realm of nirvāṇa;
And attainment as it takes place in the realm of the afflictions associated with erroneous views.

He knows in accordance with reality [attainment] as it takes place in all worlds' dharmas of enactment and dharmas of returning [to dissolution][296] and also knows in accordance with reality:

Attainment as it takes place on the path of *śrāvaka* disciples;
Attainment as it takes place on the path of *pratyekabuddhas;*
Attainment as it takes place on the path of bodhisattvas;
Attainment as it takes place with a buddha's powers, fearlessnesses, and exclusive dharmas;
Attainment as it takes place with form bodies and the Dharma body;
And attainment as it takes place with the cognition of all-knowledge.

In this same manner, he knows:

Attainment as it takes place in realization of the path to buddhahood;
Attainment as it takes place in the turning of the Dharma wheel;
And attainment as it takes place in the manifestation of crossing into a state of cessation.

To speak of what is essential, he knows in accordance with reality the distinctions occurring in attainment as it takes place in relation to all dharmas.

17. This Bodhisattva's Knowledge of Transformation

This bodhisattva employs wisdom such as this that accords with the bodhi practices, penetrates ever more deeply, and knows in accordance with reality:

Transformation as it takes place in beings;
Transformation as it takes place in karmic actions;
Transformation as it takes place among the afflictions;
Transformation as it takes place in the views;
Transformation as it takes place in worldly realms;
Transformation as it takes place in the Dharma realm;
Transformation as it takes place among *śrāvaka*-disciples;

正體字

辟
529b16‖ 支佛化菩薩化。如來化一切化。[13]分別無分別
529b17‖ 化。皆如實入。是菩薩。爾時如實知[14]佛力所
529b18‖ 持。如實知法處持。如實知業持。煩惱持。時
529b19‖ 持願持。先世持行持。[15]劫[16]壽持智持。是菩薩。
529b20‖ 住十地中。諸佛所有。微細行智。所謂。細微生
529b21‖ 死智。細微世智。細微出家智。細微得道智。細
529b22‖ 微神力自在智。細微轉法輪智。細微持壽命
529b23‖ 智。

简体字

辟支佛化、菩萨化、如来化、一切化、分别无分别化，皆如实入。是菩萨尔时如实知佛力所持，如实知法处持，如实知业持、烦恼持、时持、愿持、先世持、行持、劫寿持、智持。是菩萨住十地中，诸佛所有微细行智，所谓细微生死智、细微世智、细微出家智、细微得道智、细微神力自在智、细微转法轮智、细微持寿命智、

Transformation as it takes place among *pratyekabuddhas;*
Transformation as it takes place among bodhisattvas;
Transformation as it takes place among *tathāgatas;*
And transformation as it occurs in the presence and absence of differences.

He penetrates into all of these in a way that accords with reality.

18. This Bodhisattva's Knowledge of Sustaining Bases

At that time, this bodhisattva:

Knows in accordance with reality the sustaining bases[297] of a buddha's powers;
Knows in accordance with reality the sustaining bases of the Dharma's abiding;
And knows in accordance with reality the sustaining bases of karmic deeds.

So, too, he knows in accordance with reality:

The sustaining bases of the afflictions;
The sustaining bases of time;
The sustaining bases of vows;
The sustaining bases of prior lifetimes;
The sustaining bases of practices;
The sustaining bases of kalpas' duration;
And the sustaining bases of knowledge.

19. This Bodhisattva's Knowledge of Subtleties of Practice

This bodhisattva dwells in all buddhas' knowledge regarding the subtleties of practice on the ten grounds, specifically including:

Their knowledge regarding the subtleties involved in births and deaths;
Their knowledge regarding the subtleties involved in worlds;
Their knowledge regarding the subtleties involved in abandoning the home life;
Their knowledge regarding the subtleties involved in achieving realization of the path;
Their knowledge regarding the subtleties involved in sovereign mastery in the exercise of the spiritual powers;
Their knowledge regarding the subtleties involved in turning the Dharma wheel;
Their knowledge regarding the subtleties involved in the sustaining of a lifespan;

正體字

細微示涅槃智。細微法久住智。如是等細
529b24‖ 微智。皆如實知。又諸佛密處。所謂身密口密
529b25‖ 意密。[17]籌量時非時密。與[18]菩薩[19]受記密。攝
529b26‖ 伏眾生[20]密。諸乘差別密。八萬四千諸根差別
529b27‖ 密。業如實所作密。行密。得菩提密。如是等
529b28‖ 密。皆如實知。是菩薩。諸佛所有入劫智。所
529b29‖ 謂。一劫攝阿僧祇劫。阿僧祇劫攝一劫。有數
529c01‖ 攝無數。無數攝有數。一念攝無量世。無量世
529c02‖ 攝一念。

简体字

细微示涅槃智、细微法久住智，如是等细微智皆如实知。又诸佛密处，所谓身密、口密、意密、筹量时非时密、与菩萨受记密、摄伏众生密、诸乘差别密，八万四千诸根差别密、业如实所作密、行密、得菩提密，如是等密皆如实知。是菩萨诸佛所有入劫智，所谓一劫摄阿僧祇劫，阿僧祇劫摄一劫，有数摄无数，无数摄有数，一念摄无量世，无量世摄一念，

Their knowledge regarding the subtleties involved in manifesting the appearance of entering nirvāṇa;
And their knowledge regarding the subtleties involved in the long endurance of the Dharma.

He knows in accordance with reality all of the other such sorts of knowledge with regard to subtleties.

20. This Bodhisattva's Knowledge of the Tathāgatas' Secrets

So too does he know in accordance with reality the secret circumstances of all buddhas, specifically including:

Their secrets associated with the body;
Their secrets associated with the mouth;
Their secrets associated with the mind;
Their secrets associated with the assessment of what is and is not the right time;
Their secrets associated with bestowing predictions on bodhisattvas;
Their secrets associated with the attraction and training of beings;
Their secrets associated with the distinctions among vehicles;
Their secrets associated with the eighty-four thousand sorts of different root faculties;
Their secrets associated with the doing of karmic deeds in accordance with reality;
Their secrets associated with actions;
And their secrets associated with the realization of bodhi.

He knows all such secrets in accordance with reality.

21. This Bodhisattva's Knowledge of the Interpenetration of Kalpas

This bodhisattva fathoms all of the knowledge of the Buddhas with regard to the interpenetration of kalpas [and other such measures of time], specifically knowing:

How a single kalpa may subsume an *asaṃkhyeya* of kalpas;
How an *asaṃkhyeya* of kalpas may subsume a single kalpa;
How an enumerated number of kalpas may subsume innumerable kalpas;
How innumerable kalpas may subsume an enumerated number of kalpas;
How a single mind-moment may subsume an incalculably long period of time;
How an incalculably long period of time may subsume a single mind-moment;

正體字

劫攝非劫。非劫攝劫。有佛劫攝無佛
529c03‖ 劫。無佛劫攝有佛劫。過去未來劫攝現在劫。
529c04‖ 現在劫攝過去未來劫。未來過去劫攝現在
529c05‖ 劫。現在劫攝未來過去劫。長劫攝短劫。短
529c06‖ 劫攝長劫。諸劫攝[21]想。皆如實知。是菩薩。諸
529c07‖ 佛所入毛道智。若入微塵智。若國土智。身[22]心
529c08‖ 智。得道智。若眾生身心得道智。若眾生行智。
529c09‖ 得道智。遍行佛道智。順行示智。逆行示智。不
529c10‖ 可思議智。世間能知。聲聞能知。辟支佛能知。
529c11‖ 菩薩能知。有不能知。但如來能知。皆如實入。

简体字

劫摄非劫。非劫摄劫，有佛劫摄无佛劫，无佛劫摄有佛劫，过去、未来劫摄现在劫，现在劫摄过去、未来劫，未来、过去劫摄现在劫，现在劫摄未来、过去劫，长劫摄短劫，短劫摄长劫，诸劫摄想，皆如实知。是菩萨诸佛所入毛道智，若入微尘智，若国土智、身心智、得道智，若众生身心得道智，若众生行智、得道智、遍行佛道智、顺行示智、逆行示智、不可思议智，世间能知、声闻能知、辟支佛能知、菩萨能知，有不能知但如来能知，皆如实入。

How a kalpa may subsume what does not constitute a kalpa;
How what does not constitute a kalpa may subsume a kalpa;
How a kalpa in which there is a buddha subsumes a kalpa in which there is no buddha;
How a kalpa with no buddha subsumes a kalpa in which there is a buddha;
How past and future kalpas subsume the present kalpa;
How the present kalpa subsumes past and future kalpas;
How future and past kalpas subsume the present kalpa;
How the present kalpa subsumes future and past kalpas;
How long kalpas subsume short kalpas;
And how short kalpas subsume long kalpas.

So, too, he knows in accordance with reality all the other characteristic features of how kalpas [and other such measures of time] may mutually subsume each other.[298]

22. This Bodhisattva's Knowing of the Buddha's Penetrating Knowledge

This bodhisattva [knows in accordance with reality]:

The Buddhas' penetrating knowledge[299] that knows ordinary common people;[300]
The penetrating knowledge that knows atoms;
The penetrating knowledge that knows [the bodies of buddha] lands;[301]
The penetrating knowledge that knows bodies and minds;
The types of enlightened penetrating knowledge such as the enlightened penetrating knowledge that knows beings' bodies and minds, the enlightened penetrating knowledge that knows beings' actions, or the enlightened penetrating knowledge that knows universally pervasive practices;
The penetrating knowledge that knows the manifestation of adaptive practices;
The penetrating knowledge that knows the manifestation of contrary practices;
The penetrating knowledge that knows what is inconceivable;
The penetrating knowledge that knows what beings of the world, *śrāvaka*-disciples, *pratyekabuddhas*, and bodhisattvas are capable of knowing;
And the penetrating knowledge that knows what no one else is capable of knowing for only a *tathāgata* is capable of knowing it.

He penetratingly comprehends all of these in accordance with reality.

正體字

529c12‖ 諸佛子。諸佛智廣大。無量無邊。菩薩住是地。
529c13‖ 則能得入如是智慧。{G}諸佛子。是菩薩摩訶薩。
529c14‖ 隨是地行。得菩薩不可思議解脫。得菩薩無
529c15‖ 礙解脫。淨行解脫。普門明解脫。如來藏解脫。
529c16‖ 隨無礙論解脫。入三世解脫。法性藏解脫。解
529c17‖ 脫明解脫。離差別解脫。諸佛子。是菩薩。十
529c18‖ 解脫為首。如是等無量無邊百千萬億阿僧
529c19‖ 祇解脫。皆於此地。得[23]得百千萬無量阿僧祇
529c20‖ 三昧。百千萬無量阿僧祇陀羅尼。百千萬無
529c21‖ 量阿僧祇神通。亦復如是。{H}是菩薩。成就如是
529c22‖ [24]智慧。隨順於菩提。成就無量念力。能於一
529c23‖ 念頃。至十方無量佛所。受無量法明。無量法
529c24‖ 雨。皆能受持。譬如娑伽羅龍王。所[25]澍大雨。
529c25‖ 唯除大海。

简体字

“诸佛子，诸佛智广大无量无边，菩萨住是地，则能得入如是智慧。诸佛子，是菩萨摩诃萨随是地行，得菩萨不可思议解脱，得菩萨无碍解脱、净行解脱、普门明解脱、如来藏解脱、随无碍论解脱、入三世解脱、法性藏解脱、解脱明解脱、离差别解脱。诸佛子，是菩萨十解脱为首，如是等无量无边百千万亿阿僧祇解脱皆于此地得，得百千万无量阿僧祇三昧、百千万无量阿僧祇陀罗尼、百千万无量阿僧祇神通，亦复如是。是菩萨成就如是智慧，随顺于菩提，成就无量念力，能于一念顷至十方无量佛所，受无量法明、无量法雨，皆能受持。譬如娑伽罗龙王，所澍大雨，唯除大海，

Sons of the Buddha, the knowledge of all buddhas is vast, measureless, and boundless. If one is a bodhisattva dwelling on this ground, then one is able to have a penetrating knowledge of wisdom such as this.

23. This Bodhisattva's Acquisition of Countless Liberations

{G} Sons of the Buddha, as this bodhisattva *mahāsattva* engages in the practices associated with this ground, he acquires:

The bodhisattva's inconceivable liberation;
The bodhisattva's unimpeded liberation;
The pure practice liberation;
The light of the universal gateway liberation;
The *tathāgata* treasury liberation;
The accordance with the unimpeded wheel liberation;[302]
The penetration of the three periods of time liberation;
The Dharma realm treasury liberation;
The liberation light liberation;
The transcendence of differences liberation.

Sons of the Buddha, these ten liberations are chief among those acquired by this bodhisattva. It is on this ground that he acquires all of the measurelessly and boundlessly many hundreds of thousands of myriads of *koṭis* of *asaṃkhyeyas* of liberations such as these.

24. This Bodhisattva's Samādhis, Dhāraṇīs, and Superknowledges

In this very same manner, he acquires hundreds of thousands of myriads of measureless *asaṃkhyeyas* of samādhis, acquires hundreds of thousands of myriads of measureless *asaṃkhyeyas* of *dhāraṇīs*, and acquires hundreds of thousands of myriads of measureless *asaṃkhyeyas* of spiritual superknowledges.

25. This Bodhisattva's Limitless Memory Power

{H} In this bodhisattva's complete development of bodhi-concordant wisdom such as this, he completely develops measureless memory power. He is able in but a single mind-moment to go to the dwelling places of the measurelessly many buddhas throughout the ten directions, receiving illumination in measurelessly many dharmas and taking in the rain of measurelessly many dharmas. In every case, he is able to take in and retain all of these.

26. His Limitless Memory Compared to the Ocean's Limitless Capacity

Just as, with the sole exception of the great ocean, all other land is unable to take in the great rains poured down by Sāgara, the

正體字

餘地不能堪受。諸佛子。菩薩摩訶
529c26‖ 薩。亦如是。受大法雨故。能入如來密處。是大
529c27‖ 法雨。一切眾生聲聞辟支佛。皆不能受。從初
529c28‖ 地乃至九地菩薩。亦不能受持。唯此菩薩摩
529c29‖ 訶薩。住法雲地。悉能受持。諸佛子。譬如大海
530a01‖ 一龍王。起大雲雨。皆能堪受。若二龍王。三四
530a02‖ 五十二十三十四十五十。若百龍王。若千若
530a03‖ 萬。若億若百億。[1]若千萬億那由他龍王。乃
530a04‖ 至無量無邊大龍王。起雲所雨。一時澍下。
530a05‖ 皆能受持。所以者何。大海是無量器故。諸佛
530a06‖ 子。菩薩摩訶薩。亦如是。住法雲地。於一佛
530a07‖ 所。能受大法明雨二佛[2]三[3]四五十百千萬
530a08‖ 億。乃至無量無邊。不可稱不可說。無有限過
530a09‖ 諸算數。於一念中。皆能堪受如是諸佛大法
530a10‖ 雲雨。是故此地。名法雲地。問言佛子。是菩
530a11‖ 薩。於一念中。為能堪受幾所佛法明大雨。答
530a12‖ 言。

简体字

余地不能堪受。诸佛子，菩萨摩诃萨亦如是，受大法雨故，能入如来密处。是大法雨，一切众生声闻、辟支佛皆不能受，从初地乃至九地菩萨亦不能受持，唯此菩萨摩诃萨住法云地，悉能受持。诸佛子，譬如大海，一龙王起大云雨，皆能堪受。若二龙王，三、四、五、十、二十、三十、四十、五十、若百龙王，若千、若万、若亿、若百亿、若千万亿那由他龙王，乃至无量无边大龙王起云所雨，一时澍下，皆能受持。所以者何？大海是无量器故。诸佛子，菩萨摩诃萨亦如是，住法云地，于一佛所，能受大法明雨；二佛、三、四、五十、百千万亿，乃至无量无边、不可称、不可说、无有限、过诸算数，于一念中，皆能堪受如是诸佛大法云雨，是故此地名法云地。”

问言：“佛子，是菩萨于一念中，为能堪受几所佛法明大雨？”

答言：

dragon king, so too, O Sons of the Buddha, is this also the case for this bodhisattva *mahāsattva*. Because he is able to take in the great Dharma rains, he becomes able to enter into the Tathāgata's secret places. This Dharma rain is such that all beings including *śrāvaka*-disciples and *pratyekabuddhas* are in every case unable to take it in. Even all bodhisattvas from the first ground on through the ninth ground are also unable to take it in and retain it. It is only this bodhisattva *mahāsattva* who dwells on the Dharma Cloud Ground who is able to take it all in and retain it.

Sons of the Buddha, this circumstance is comparable to that of the great ocean. It is always able to take in all the rain sent down from the great clouds created by a single dragon king. So, too, even if the rain sent down from the clouds created by two dragon kings, three, four, five, ten, twenty, thirty, forty, fifty, a hundred, a thousand, a myriad, a *koṭi*, a hundred *koṭis*, a thousand myriads of *koṭis* of *nayutas* of dragon kings, or even up to countlessly and boundlessly many dragon kings who were to all simultaneously pour down their rains, the great ocean would still be able to take it all in and retain it. How is this the case? This is because the great ocean is a vessel possessed of incalculably great capacity.

Sons of the Buddha, so too it is with this bodhisattva *mahāsattva*. As he dwells on the Dharma Cloud Ground in the abode of but a single buddha, his capacity to take in the great rain of Dharma illumination is such that, whether it be the rain which is rained down by two buddhas, three, four, five, ten, a hundred, a thousand, a myriad, a *koṭi*, and so forth up to all the rain that is rained down by countlessly and boundlessly many buddhas, so many buddhas that their number is indescribable and ineffable, beyond limits, and beyond calculation, he is always able even then to take in all of the rain poured down from their great Dharma clouds, doing so in but a single mind-moment. It is for this very reason that this ground is known as the Dharma Cloud Ground.

27. Vimukticandra Asks About the Limits of This Bodhisattva's Memory

[Liberation Moon Bodhisattva] then asked, "Son of the Buddha, from how many buddhas is this bodhisattva *mahāsattva* able in but a single mind-moment to take in their great rain of Dharma illumination?"

28. Vajragarbha's Analogy to Describe This Bodhisattva's Memory Power

[Vajragarbha Bodhisattva] then replied:

正體字

不可以算數所知。但以譬喻可說。諸佛子。
530a13‖ 譬如十方所有不可說百千萬億那由他世界
530a14‖ 中微塵。爾所微塵世界中眾生。假使皆得聞
530a15‖ 持陀羅尼。為佛侍者。為大聲聞。多聞第一。譬
530a16‖ 如金剛蓮花上佛。有大擇比丘。多聞第一。其
530a17‖ 一眾生。成就如是多聞之力。餘若干眾生。皆
530a18‖ 亦如是。其一人所受法。第二人不重受。如是
530a19‖ 一切。各各不同。諸佛子。於意云何。是一切
530a20‖ 眾生。受持多聞力。為多不。答言無[4]量。諸佛
530a21‖ 子。我今當為汝說。是菩薩住此法雲地。於一
530a22‖ 念一時。於一[5]佛所。能堪受三世法性藏。名
530a23‖ 曰大法明雨。上一切眾生多聞之力。比此百
530a24‖ 分不及一。千分萬分。千萬億那由他。乃至算
530a25‖ 數譬喻。所不能及。如一佛所聞。十方若干世
530a26‖ 界。所有微塵諸佛。皆能堪受大法明雨。

简体字

“不可以算数所知，但以譬喻可说。”

“诸佛子，譬如十方所有不可说百千万亿那由他世界中微尘，尔所微尘世界中众生，假使皆得闻持陀罗尼，为佛侍者，为大声闻，多闻第一。譬如金刚莲华上佛，有大择比丘，多闻第一。其一众生，成就如是多闻之力，余若干众生皆亦如是。其一人所受法，第二人不重受，如是一切各各不同。诸佛子，于意云何？是一切众生，受持多闻力，为多不？”

答言：“无量。”

“诸佛子，我今当为汝说。是菩萨住此法云地，于一念一时，于一佛所，能堪受三世法性藏，名曰大法明雨；上一切众生多闻之力，比此百分不及一，千分、万分、千万亿那由他，乃至算数譬喻，所不能及。如一佛所闻，十方若干世界所有微尘诸佛，皆能堪受大法明雨。

This is something that one could not know even through numerical calculations. It could only be described by resort to analogy. Sons of the Buddha, suppose for instance that all the beings in worlds as numerous as the atoms in all the ineffably many hundreds of thousands of myriads of *koṭis* of *nayutas* of worlds of the ten directions had each acquired the "hearing-and-retaining" *dhāraṇī,* had each become the attendant of a buddha, had each become foremost in learning among all of the *śrāvaka*-disciples, and had each become the likes of Great Differentiation Bhikshu,[303] foremost in learning among the disciples of Vajra Lotus Blossom Supremacy Buddha.[304] Suppose too that, just as one of these beings had perfected just such power of extensive learning, so too had all of those other beings also done so in the same manner. Suppose as well that the Dharma acquired by any one of them was not duplicated in that received by the second and that this was also true of all the rest of them so that the Dharma received by every one of them was in each and every case different.

Sons of the Buddha, what do you think? Would all of that which is taken in and retained by all these beings through their powers of extensive learning be a great amount, or not?

[Liberation Moon Bodhisattva] replied, "It would be incalculably so."

[Vajragarbha Bodhisattva] then said:

Sons of the Buddha, I should now inform you that, in but a single mind-moment, all at the same time, in the abode of but a single Buddha, this bodhisattva dwelling on this Dharma Cloud Ground is able to take in the entire Dharma realm's Dharma treasury of all three periods of time, that which is known as "the great rain of Dharma light."

When compared with the extensive learning power of this bodhisattva, the extensive-learning power of all those beings described above would not even amount to a hundredth part, would not even amount to a thousandth part or one part in a myriad parts, would not amount to even a single part in a thousand myriads of *koṭis* of *nayutas* of parts, and so forth until we come to its inability to become comparable even by resort to numerical calculation or analogy.

And just as this is the case regarding what he hears from one single buddha, so too is he also able in every case to simultaneously take in the great rain of Dharma light rained down by all the buddhas as numerous as the atoms in however many worlds there are throughout the ten directions.

正體字

復能
530a27‖ 過此。無量無邊。於一念一時。悉能堪受大法
530a28‖ 明雨。是故名為法雲地[6]◎
530a29‖ ◎[7]復次佛子。菩薩摩訶薩。住是大法雲地。自
530b01‖ 從願力。生大慈悲。放大法雷音。諸通明無
530b02‖ 畏。以為電光。發大智慧。以為疾風。大福德
530b03‖ 善根。以為密雲。現種種身色。為雜色雲。說
530b04‖ 法降魔。以為雷音。一念一時。能於上所說
530b05‖ 微塵世界。皆悉周普。無有遺餘。復過此數。以
530b06‖ 雨善法甘露法雨故。滅眾生隨心所樂。無明
530b07‖ 所起。煩惱塵焰是故名為法雲地。復次諸佛
530b08‖ 子。菩薩摩訶薩。住是法雲地。於一世界中。從
530b09‖ 兜率天上來下。乃至示大涅槃。一切佛事。隨
530b10‖ 所度眾生。皆現神力。若二三千世界。乃至
530b11‖ 如上微塵數世界。又復過是百千萬億阿僧
530b12‖ 祇世界。從兜率來下。乃至示[8]大涅槃。一切
530b13‖ 佛事。隨所度眾生。皆現神力。

简体字

复能过此，无量无边，于一念一时，悉能堪受大法明雨，是故名为法云地。

十住经卷第六

法云地第十下

“复次，佛子，菩萨摩诃萨住是大法云地，自从愿力生大慈悲，放大法雷音，诸通明无畏以为电光，发大智慧以为疾风，大福德善根以为密云，现种种身色为杂色云，说法降魔以为雷音，一念一时，能于上所说微尘世界，皆悉周普无有遗余，复过此数，以雨善法甘露法雨故，灭众生随心所乐、无明所起烦恼尘焰，是故名为法云地。复次，诸佛子，菩萨摩诃萨住是法云地，于一世界中，从兜率天上来下，乃至示大涅槃一切佛事，随所度众生皆现神力。若二三千世界，乃至如上微尘数世界，又复过是百千万亿阿僧祇世界，从兜率来下，乃至示大涅槃一切佛事，随所度众生皆现神力。

Furthermore, he is even able in every case to take in simultaneously and in but a single mind-moment the entire great rain of Dharma light sent down by incalculably and boundlessly many more buddhas than this.

29. The Dharma Cloud Bodhisattva's Great Dharma Rain

Additionally, O Son of the Buddha, through the power of his vows, the bodhisattva *mahāsattva* dwelling on this Dharma Cloud Ground brings forth the great kindness and compassion, thus setting loose the great Dharma thunder. His superknowledges, clarities, and fearlessnesses are the radiance of his lightning, his bringing forth of great wisdom is the blowing of his swift winds, his immense merit and roots of goodness are his dense clouds, his manifestation of all the different sorts of form bodies are his variously colored clouds, and his defeat of the *māras* through the proclamation of the Dharma is the sound of his thunder.

He is able, simultaneously and in but a single mind-moment, to reach everywhere without exception throughout all those worlds as numerous as or even greater than the above-described number of atoms and, in accordance with beings' dispositions, he rains down the sweet-dew Dharma rain of the good Dharma, extinguishing the smoke and flames of beings' ignorance-generated afflictions. It is for this reason that this is known as the Dharma Cloud Ground.

Additionally, O Sons of the Buddha, from the time this bodhisattva *mahāsattva* who dwells on the Dharma Cloud Ground descends from a world's Tuṣita Heaven on through to the time he manifests entry into *mahāparinirvāṇa,* in carrying out all the buddha works that he does, he adapts to the beings that he brings to liberation, using the power of spiritual superknowledges in every case. He also does this in the worlds contained within two great trichiliocosms and so forth on up to worlds as numerous as the atoms described above and additionally does this in a number of worlds exceeding even this, doing so even in a hundred thousand myriads of *koṭis* of *asaṃkhyeyas* of additional worlds wherein, from the time he descends from the Tuṣita Heaven to the time that he manifests entry into *mahāparinirvāṇa,* in carrying out all the buddha works that he does, he adapts to the beings that he brings to liberation, using the power of spiritual superknowledges in every case.

正體字

[1] 是菩薩。住在
530b14‖ 此地。於智慧中。得上自在力。善擇大智慧。
530b15‖ 或以狹國為廣。廣國為狹。或以垢國為[9]淨。
530b16‖ 如是。一切世間性。皆有神力。是菩薩。或於
530b17‖ 一微塵中。有一三千大千世界鐵圍山川。而
530b18‖ 不迫隘。或二三四五十二十三十四十五十。
530b19‖ 若百若千。萬億無量。不可說不可說世界。
530b20‖ 諸莊嚴事。皆示入一微塵。若以一世界莊嚴
530b21‖ 事。示不可說不可說世界。或以乃至不可說
530b22‖ 不可說世界眾生。置一世界中。亦不迫隘。或
530b23‖ 以一世界眾生。置不可說不可說世界中。或
530b24‖ 以不可說不可說世界。示著一毛頭。而不惱
530b25‖ 眾生。或於一毛中。示一切佛神通力莊嚴之
530b26‖ 事。或以十方所有不可說不可說世界微塵。
530b27‖ 於一念中。現如是等身。於一身中。示若干無
530b28‖ 量手。以此手。勤心供養十方諸佛。以一一手。
530b29‖ 捉恒河沙等蓮華。聚以散諸佛。塗香雜香。末

简体字

是菩萨住在此地，于智慧中得上自在力，善择大智慧，或以狭国为广、广国为狭，或以垢国为净，如是一切世间性皆有神力。是菩萨或于一微尘中，有一三千大千世界铁围山川而不迫隘；或二、三、四、五、十、二十、三十、四十、五十、若百、若千、万亿无量，不可说不可说世界诸庄严事，皆示入一微尘。若以一世界庄严事，示不可说不可说世界。或以乃至不可说不可说世界众生，置一世界中亦不迫隘。或以一世界众生，置不可说不可说世界中。或以不可说不可说世界，示著一毛头而不恼众生。或于一毛中，示一切佛神通力庄严之事。或以十方所有不可说不可说世界微尘，于一念中现如是等身。于一身中示若干无量手，以此手勤心供养十方诸佛，以一一手捉恒河沙等莲华聚以散诸佛，涂香、杂香、

30. This Bodhisattva's Use of Spiritual Powers in Transforming Worlds

{I} In using his wisdom, this bodhisattva who dwells on this ground acquires the power of supreme sovereign mastery. Through skillful selectivity in the application of his great wisdom, he may transform a narrow land into a broad one, a broad land into narrow one, or a defiled land into a pure one. In this manner, throughout all worldly realms, he is in every case possessed of spiritual powers such as these.

Or this bodhisattva may bring it about that an entire great trichiliocosm together with its Iron Ring Mountains and rivers is placed within a single atom even without there being any constriction occurring therein as a result of this.

Or he may manifest the entry into a single atom of all the adornments in two, three, four, five, ten, twenty, thirty, forty, fifty worlds, a hundred or a thousand worlds, a myriad *koṭis* of worlds, or measurelessly many ineffable numbers of ineffably many worlds.

Or he may manifest within the adornments associated with a single world those associated with an ineffably large number of worlds.

Or he may see to the placement into but a single world all the beings contained within up to an ineffably large number of worlds, in all such cases being able to do so without there being any constriction occurring therein.

Or it may be that he sees to the placement of the beings contained in a single world into an ineffably large number of worlds.

Or it may be that he sees to the placement onto the tip of a single hair an ineffably large number of worlds, doing so even without causing any disturbance to the beings contained within them.

Or he may manifest within but a single hair all of the adornments associated with all buddhas' spiritual powers.

31. His Use of Powers in Manifesting Bodies & Supernatural Phenomena

Or it may be that, in but a single mind-moment, he manifests bodies as numerous as the atoms in an ineffably large number of worlds while also manifesting for each and every one of those bodies just such an incalculably great number of hands that proceed with diligent mind to make offerings to all buddhas of the ten directions. Each and every one of those hands then takes up a number of lotus blossoms as numerous as the sands of the Ganges, gathers them together, and scatters them down as offerings to the Buddhas. In the same manner, they gather up perfumes, blends

正體字

530b30║ 香衣服。幡蓋寶物。亦復如是。一切莊嚴之具。
530c01║ 皆以手執供養諸佛。於一一身。皆亦如是。又
530c02║ 一一身。化有爾所塵數頭。於一一頭。有爾所
530c03║ 塵數舌。以是神力。讚歎諸佛。如是等事。於念
530c04║ 念中。遍滿十方。於念念中。以神通力。[10]於無
530c05║ 量世界。示得佛道。轉於法輪。乃至大般涅槃。
530c06║ 於三世中。以神通力。示現無量身。於自身中。
530c07║ 現[11]佛無量無邊。佛土莊嚴事。於自身中。示
530c08║ 一切世界成壞事。或令一切諸風皆於一毛
530c09║ 孔出。而不惱眾生。或欲以無量無邊世界。為
530c10║ 一海水。此海水中。作大蓮華。形色光明。遍
530c11║ [12]照無量無邊世界。於中示得菩提莊嚴妙事。
530c12║ 乃至示得一切種智。自身中所有一[13]方光明。
530c13║ 摩尼寶珠。電光日月。星宿諸光明。乃至十方
530c14║ 世界。所有光明諸物。皆於身中現。以口噓氣。
530c15║ 能令一切十方無量無邊世界震動。而不令
530c16║ 眾生。有驚畏想。

简体字

末香、衣服、幡盖宝物，亦复如是。一切庄严之具，皆以手执供养诸佛，于一一身皆亦如是。又一一身化有尔所尘数头，于一一头有尔所尘数舌，以是神力赞叹诸佛。如是等事，于念念中遍满十方，于念念中以神通力，于无量世界示得佛道，转于法轮，乃至大般涅槃。于三世中，以神通力示现无量身。于自身中，现佛无量无边佛土庄严事。于自身中，示一切世界成坏事。或令一切诸风皆于一毛孔出，而不恼众生。或欲以无量无边世界为一海水，此海水中作大莲华，形色光明，遍照无量无边世界，于中示得菩提庄严妙事，乃至示得一切种智。自身中所有一切光明，摩尼宝珠、电光、日、月、星宿诸光明，乃至十方世界所有光明诸物，皆于身中现。以口嘘气，能令一切十方无量无边世界震动，而不令众生有惊畏想。

of various scents, powdered incenses, raiment, banners, canopies, and precious things to present as offerings to the Buddhas.

Additionally, for each and every one of those bodies, he may transformationally manifest a number of heads as numerous as all those atoms. For each and every one of those heads he may manifest tongues as numerous as all those atoms from each and every one of which, through the exercise of his spiritual powers, there then resound his praises of all buddhas.

In each succeeding mind-moment, he may fill up the ten directions with phenomena such as these and, in each succeeding mind-moment, he may then employ his spiritual superknowledges to manifest in countless worlds the appearances of realizing the path to buddhahood, turning the wheel of the Dharma, and so forth on through to his manifestation of entering *mahāparinirvāṇa.*

Using the powers of his spiritual superknowledges, he manifests throughout the three periods of time countless bodies while manifesting within his bodies the appearance of the Buddhas' measurelessly and boundlessly numerous adornments of buddha lands while also manifesting within his bodies the appearance of the phenomena occurring during the creation and destruction of all worlds.

He may cause all the various sorts of winds to blow forth from a single one of his hair pores while still not disturbing any being, or he may wish to form measurelessly and boundlessly many worlds into the waters of a single sea in which sea he then creates a great lotus blossom the form, color and brilliant light of which illuminate everywhere throughout measurelessly and boundlessly many worlds even as it manifests within itself the appearances of the marvelous adornments associated with the realization of bodhi, and so forth up to and including the appearances associated with acquiring the knowledge of all modes.

He may manifest within his bodies all the different sorts of light including that of precious *maṇi* pearls, lightning, the light of the sun, moon, and stars, and so forth, including all the radiant phenomena throughout the worlds of the ten directions, manifesting the appearance of all such things within his bodies.

Or it may be that, with the breath from his mouth, he is able to cause all the measurelessly and boundlessly many worlds of the ten directions to tremor while nonetheless not causing any of their beings to be seized with thoughts of terror.

正體字

示十方世界。水劫盡[14]風[15]劫
530c17‖ [16]火劫盡。而眾生身。隨意莊嚴。或欲於自身。
530c18‖ 示作如來身。如來身作自身。如來身作己佛
530c19‖ 國。己佛國。作如來身。諸佛子。菩薩摩訶薩。
530c20‖ 在此菩薩法雲地。神變如是。又餘無量神力
530c21‖ 自在。奇異[17]示現。{J}爾時會中。有諸菩薩。天龍
530c22‖ 夜叉。乾闥婆阿修羅。迦樓羅緊那羅。摩睺羅
530c23‖ 伽。釋提桓因。梵天王。四天王。自在天子。淨
530c24‖ 居天等。各作是念。若菩薩神通[18]力。智慧力。
530c25‖ 如是無量無邊。佛復云何。爾時解脫月菩薩
530c26‖ 摩訶薩。知大眾心所念。問金剛藏菩薩言。佛
530c27‖ 子。今諸大眾。皆有所疑。聞是菩薩大神通智
530c28‖ 慧力。墮在疑網。汝今當斷一切疑惑。示菩薩
530c29‖ 神通莊嚴妙事。即時金剛藏菩薩。入一切佛
531a01‖ 國體性三昧。時諸大眾。天龍夜叉。乾闥婆阿
531a02‖ 修羅。迦樓羅緊那羅。摩睺羅伽。釋提桓因。梵
531a03‖ 天王。

简体字

示十方世界水劫尽、风劫尽、火劫尽，而众生身随意庄严。或欲于自身示作如来身，如来身作自身，如来身作己佛国，己佛国作如来身。诸佛子，菩萨摩诃萨在此菩萨法云地，神变如是，又余无量神力自在奇异示现。”

尔时，会中有诸菩萨，天、龙、夜叉、乾闼婆、阿修罗、迦楼罗、紧那罗、摩睺罗伽、释提桓因、梵天王、四天王、自在天子、净居天等，各作是念：“若菩萨神通力、智慧力，如是无量无边，佛复云何？”

尔时，解脱月菩萨摩诃萨知大众心所念，问金刚藏菩萨言：“佛子，今诸大众皆有所疑，闻是菩萨大神通智慧力，堕在疑网。汝今当断一切疑惑，示菩萨神通庄严妙事。”

即时金刚藏菩萨，入一切佛国体性三昧。时诸大众，天、龙、夜叉、乾闼婆、阿修罗、迦楼罗、紧那罗、摩睺罗伽、释提桓因、梵天王、

Or it may be that he manifests the appearances of the kalpa-ending water disasters and kalpa-ending wind and fire disasters taking place in the worlds of the ten directions.

Or in this same way, he may manifest adornments of a being's body that accord with beings' predilections. He may wish to manifest within his own body the body of a *tathāgata,* manifest his own body within that of a *tathāgata,* manifest his own buddha land within the body of a *tathāgata,* or manifest the body of a *tathāgata* within his own buddha land.

Sons of the Buddha, the bodhisattva *mahāsattva* dwelling on this Dharma Cloud Ground may carry out just such transformations of spiritual powers as these as well as measurelessly many other sorts of extraordinary appearances produced through his sovereign mastery of the spiritual powers.

32. The Congregants Wonder: "What More Could Even a Buddha Do?"

{J} At that time, there were bodhisattvas, devas, dragons, *yakṣas, gandharvas, asuras, garuḍas, kinnaras,* and *mahoragas* as well as Śakra Devānām Indra, the Brahma Heaven devas, the Four Heavenly Kings, the devas' sons of the Maheśvara Heavens, and the devas of the Pure Dwelling Heaven who each had this thought: "If the powers of spiritual superknowledges and wisdom powers of this bodhisattva are so measurelessly and boundlessly great as this, what more in addition to that could be done even by a buddha?"

33. Liberation Moon Asks Vajragarbha for an Explanation

At that time, Liberation Moon Bodhisattva Mahāsattva himself well aware of the thoughts in the minds of those in that great assembly, then posed a question to Vajragarbha Bodhisattva, saying: "O Son of the Buddha, those in the great assembly all have that about which they are now beset with doubts. Having heard about this bodhisattva's great powers of spiritual penetration and wisdom, they have fallen into a net of doubts. You should now cut off all their doubting delusions by revealing the marvelous phenomena associated with this bodhisattva's spiritual superknowledges and adornments."

34. Vajragarbha Enters "The Nature of All Buddha Lands Samādhi"

Vajragarbha Bodhisattva then immediately entered "the nature of the physical form of all buddha lands samādhi."[305] The devas, dragons, *yakṣas, gandharvas, asuras, garuḍas,* and *mahoragas* as well as Śakra Devānām Indra, the Brahma Heaven devas, the World-protecting Heavenly Kings, the devas' sons of the Maheśvara

正體字

護世天王。自在天子。淨居天等大眾。皆
531a04‖ 自見知入金剛藏菩薩身中。於其身內。見有
531a05‖ 三千大千世界莊嚴眾事。若滿一劫。說不可
531a06‖ 盡於中見佛道場樹。其莖周圍。十萬三千大
531a07‖ 千世界。高百萬三千大千世界。覆蔭三千億
531a08‖ 三千大千世界。稱樹高廣。有師子座。其座上
531a09‖ 有佛。號一切智王如來。一切大眾。咸皆見佛
531a10‖ 坐在座上。其中所有莊嚴上妙供養之具。滿
531a11‖ 一劫說。亦不可盡。金剛藏菩薩。示現如是大
531a12‖ 神力已。還令大眾各在本處。爾時一切眾會。
531a13‖ 生希有想。默然一心。觀金剛藏菩薩。爾時解
531a14‖ 脫月菩薩。問金剛藏菩薩言。佛子。甚為希有。
531a15‖ 是三昧。有大勢力。是三昧者。名為何等。答言。
531a16‖ 是三昧者。名為一切佛國體[1]性。問言。是三
531a17‖ 昧。所有勢力為齊幾所。答言。佛子。若菩薩摩
531a18‖ 訶薩。善修成是三昧力者。能以如是無量恒
531a19‖ 河沙世界微塵數三千大千世界。於身中現。
531a20‖ 復過是數。佛子。菩薩摩訶薩。

简体字

护世天王、自在天子、净居天等大众，皆自见知入金刚藏菩萨身中。于其身内，见有三千大千世界庄严众事，若满一劫说不可尽。于中见佛道场树，其茎周围十万三千大千世界，高百万三千大千世界，覆荫三千亿三千大千世界，称树高广。有师子座，其座上有佛，号一切智王如来。一切大众，咸皆见佛坐在座上。其中所有庄严上妙供养之具，满一劫说亦不可尽。金刚藏菩萨示现如是大神力已，还令大众各在本处。尔时，一切众会生希有想，默然一心观金刚藏菩萨。

尔时，解脱月菩萨问金刚藏菩萨言："佛子，甚为希有！是三昧有大势力。是三昧者，名为何等？"

答言："是三昧者，名为一切佛国体性。"

问言："是三昧所有势力，为齐几所？"

答言："佛子，若菩萨摩诃萨善修成是三昧力者，能以如是无量恒河沙世界微尘数三千大千世界，于身中现，复过是数。佛子，菩萨摩诃萨

Heavens, and the devas of the Pure Dwelling Heaven all observed their own bodies enter into the body of Vajragarbha Bodhisattva wherein they saw the multitude of adorning phenomena transpiring throughout a great trichiliocosm that were such that, even were they to spend an entire kalpa attempting to describe them all, they could never come to the end of them.

They observed therein a buddha's bodhi tree within the *bodhimaṇḍa*. It had a trunk ten myriads of trichiliocosms in circumference that was a hundred myriads of trichiliocosms in height and that shaded an area of three thousand *koṭis* of trichiliocosms. Beneath it, there was a lion throne matching in scale the height and breadth of that tree upon which sat a buddha named All-Knowledge King Tathāgata.[306] Everyone in that great assembly observed that buddha seated upon his throne along with all the supremely marvelous offerings that, even were one to try to describe them for an entire kalpa, one could still never finish.

After Vajragarbha Bodhisattva had manifested such great spiritual powers, he caused everyone in that great assembly to return once again to their original circumstance. Then the entire great assembly had thoughts of amazement at the rarity of what they had experienced, whereupon they fell silent and single-mindedly gazed up at Vajragarbha Bodhisattva.

35. Liberation Moon Asks About This Samādhi's Name and Capacity

Liberation Moon Bodhisattva then inquired of Vajragarbha Bodhisattva, asking, "O Son of the Buddha, this is the most profoundly rare of circumstances. This samādhi is possessed of such immense power. What then is the name of this samādhi?"

Vajragarbha Bodhisattva then replied, "This samādhi is known as "the nature of the physical form of all buddha lands samādhi."

Liberation Moon Bodhisattva then inquired, "To how many places is the power of this samādhi able to extend?"

Vajragarbha Bodhisattva then replied:

> O Son of the Buddha, were a bodhisattva *mahāsattva* to well cultivate and develop the power of this samādhi, he would thus be able in this way to manifest within his own body great trichiliocosms in number as the atoms in measurelessly many Ganges' sands of worlds and would in fact be able to exceed even this number. O Son of the Buddha, the bodhisattva *mahāsattva* dwelling on this Dharma Cloud Ground acquires measurelessly and boundlessly

正體字

在此法雲地。得
531a21‖ 如是諸菩薩三昧。無量無邊百千萬億。以是
531a22‖ 故。此菩薩。住是地中。身身業。難可測知。口
531a23‖ 口業。難可測知。意意業。難可測知。神力自
531a24‖ 在。難可測知。觀三世法。難可測知。諸三昧
531a25‖ 行入。難可測知。智力。難可測知。遊[2]戲諸解
531a26‖ 脫。難可測知。變化所作。神力所作。勢力所
531a27‖ 作。難可測知。略說。乃至舉足下足。乃至小
531a28‖ 王子菩薩。住妙善地者。不能測知。諸佛子。
531a29‖ 菩薩法雲地。如是無量。今已略說。若廣說者。
531b01‖ 無量無邊阿僧祇劫。不能得盡。問言佛子。若
531b02‖ 菩薩。行處力神通力如是者。佛行處力神通
531b03‖ 力。復云何。答言佛子。譬如有人取四天下中
531b04‖ 二三塊土。作是言。無邊世界地性。為多此耶。
531b05‖ 汝所問者。我謂如是。

简体字

在此法云地，得如是诸菩萨三昧，无量无边百千万亿。以是故，此菩萨住是地中，身身业，难可测知；口口业，难可测知；意意业，难可测知；神力自在，难可测知；观三世法，难可测知；诸三昧行入，难可测知；智力，难可测知；游戏诸解脱，难可测知；变化所作，神力所作，势力所作，难可测知，略说乃至举足下足，乃至小王子菩萨，住妙善地者，不能测知。诸佛子，菩萨法云地，如是无量，今已略说。若广说者，无量无边阿僧祇劫，不能得尽。”

问言：“佛子，若菩萨行处力神通力如是者，佛行处力、神通力复云何？”

答言：“佛子，譬如有人取四天下中二三块土，作是言：‘无边世界地性，为多此耶？’汝所问者，我谓如是。

many hundreds of thousands of myriads of *koṭis* of such bodhisattva samādhis.

Hence the body and physical deeds of this bodhisattva dwelling on this ground are difficult to fathom. His speech and verbal deeds are difficult to fathom. His mind and mental deeds are difficult to fathom. His sovereign mastery of the spiritual powers is difficult to fathom. His ability to contemplate the dharmas of the three periods of time is difficult to fathom. The samādhis he practices and enters are difficult to fathom. The power of his knowledge is difficult to fathom. His roaming and sporting in the liberations is difficult to fathom. And as for what he accomplishes through transformations, what he accomplishes through spiritual powers, and what he accomplishes through his strength, these are all difficult for anyone to fathom. To state it briefly, all that this bodhisattva does even up to and including when he raises up and sets down his feet cannot be fathomed by any bodhisattva even up to and including one who dwells in the position of the Dharma Prince on the Ground of Sublime Goodness.

Sons of the Buddha, I have now concluded this summary explanation of such incalculable circumstances as pertain to the this bodhisattva dwelling on the Dharma Cloud Ground. Were one to attempt an extensive explanation of it, one could never finish it even in measurelessly and boundlessly many *asaṃkhyeyas* of kalpas.

36. He Asks: "What More Might a Buddha's Powers Accomplish?"

[Liberation Moon Bodhisattva] then inquired, "O Son of the Buddha, if the powers of the practice domain and powers of spiritual superknowledges possessed by this bodhisattva are of this sort, then what additional factors must characterize the powers of the practice domain and powers of spiritual superknowledges as possessed by a buddha?"

37. Vajragarbha Contrasts a Few Clumps of Soil to All Worlds

[Vajragarbha Bodhisattva] replied:

O Son of the Buddha, by way of comparison, suppose there was someone who picked up two or three clumps of earth from somewhere on the four continents and then asked, 'Is the quantity of earth element contained in all of the boundlessly many worlds of even greater quantity than this?' As I see it, the question you have just asked is of this very sort. How could it be that one might

正體字

如來無量智慧。云何以
531b06‖ 菩薩智慧。而欲測量。諸佛子。如人取四天下
531b07‖ 中少地性。餘在極多。諸菩薩法雲地。於無量
531b08‖ 劫。但可說[3]耳。何況如來地。諸佛子。我今[4]唱
531b09‖ 說。令汝知之。佛現在為證。如一一方。無量無
531b10‖ 邊世界微塵等諸佛世界。十地菩薩皆滿其
531b11‖ 中。譬如稻麻叢林。是諸菩薩。有無量無邊業。
531b12‖ 修習菩薩功德智慧禪定。於如來功德智慧
531b13‖ 力。百分不及一。百千萬億分不及一。乃至算
531b14‖ 數譬喻。所不能及。諸佛子。是菩薩。隨如是智
531b15‖ 慧。順如來身口意。亦不捨諸菩薩三昧。而勤
531b16‖ 心供養諸佛。於一一劫。[5]以一切[6]麁現[7](丹本微妙)
531b17‖ 供養具。供養無量無邊諸佛。而能具受諸佛
531b18‖ 神力。轉復明勝。是菩薩。於法性問難。無能勝
531b19‖ 者。

简体字

如来无量智慧，云何以菩萨智慧而欲测量？诸佛子，如人取四天下中少地性，余在极多；诸菩萨法云地，于无量劫但可说耳，何况如来地！诸佛子，我今唱说，令汝知之，佛现在为证。如一一方，无量无边世界微尘等诸佛世界，十地菩萨皆满其中，譬如稻麻丛林。是诸菩萨有无量无边业，修习菩萨功德智慧禅定，于如来功德智慧力，百分不及一，百千万亿分不及一，乃至算数譬喻所不能及。诸佛子，是菩萨随如是智慧，顺如来身口意，亦不舍诸菩萨三昧，而勤心供养诸佛，于一一劫以一切粗现供养具，供养无量无边诸佛，而能具受诸佛神力，转复明胜。是菩萨于法性问难，无能胜者，

employ the wisdom of a bodhisattva as a basis for seeking to fathom the measureless wisdom of the Tathāgata?

Sons of the Buddha, if one were to pick up a small amount of earth from somewhere on the four continents, what remains would exceed it by the most extremely great amount. If it would take measurelessly many kalpas to merely describe a minor portion of the circumstances of those bodhisattvas dwelling on the Dharma Cloud Ground, how much the less could one succeed in describing the circumstances associated with one who dwells on the ground of the Tathāgata?

38. Vajragarbha Compares Many Bodhisattvas' Wisdom to One Buddha's

Sons of the Buddha, I shall now describe this matter, causing you to understand it in a manner to which the Buddha will now attest. Suppose for example that there existed in each and every one of the directions a number of buddha worlds as numerous as the atoms in a measurelessly and boundlessly great number of world systems, all of which were filled as densely as paddy rice or thick forests with bodhisattvas dwelling on the tenth ground who had performed measurelessly and boundlessly many deeds in cultivation of a bodhisattva's meritorious qualities, wisdom, and *dhyāna* absorptions. Even so, when compared with the power of a single *tathāgata*'s merit and wisdom, theirs could not amount even to a hundredth part, could not amount even to one part in a hundred thousand myriad *koṭis* of parts, and so forth until we come to its inability to achieve comparability even by resort to numerical calculation or analogy.

39. The Nature of This Bodhisattva's Practice and Wisdom Light

Sons of the Buddha, employing wisdom such as this, this bodhisattva accords with the physical, verbal, and mental actions of the Tathāgata himself even while never relinquishing any of his bodhisattva samādhis. Thus he continues in each and every kalpa to diligently make offerings of material gifts to all buddhas, thereby making offerings to countlessly and boundlessly many buddhas even while being able to completely take on the spiritual powers of all buddhas. So it is that he becomes ever more supreme in his illumination.

There is no one anywhere throughout the entire Dharma realm who, challenging him with difficult questions, would ever be able to prevail over this bodhisattva even if they were to pursue such challenges for hundreds of thousands of myriads of *koṭis* of kalpas.

正體字

乃至無量無邊百千萬億劫不可窮盡。佛
531b20‖ 子。譬如[8]大金[9]師。善治此金。為莊嚴物。以無
531b21‖ 上摩尼寶珠。間錯其中。安置自在天王頸上。
531b22‖ 其餘諸天。無能奪者。又諸天人莊嚴之具。無
531b23‖ 能及者。諸佛子。菩薩住十地中。智慧功德善
531b24‖ 根。從初地至九地。諸菩薩摩訶薩。所不能及。
531b25‖ 菩薩住是地中。得大智照明故。能隨順一切
531b26‖ 智慧。其餘智慧之明。所不能壞。[10]譬如佛子。
531b27‖ 大自在天王光明。一切生處。眾生光明。所不
531b28‖ 能及。能令眾生。身心涼冷。諸佛子。菩薩摩
531b29‖ 訶薩。亦如是。住是法雲地中。智慧光明。一切
531c01‖ 聲聞。辟支佛。所不能及。從初地乃至九地菩
531c02‖ 薩摩訶薩。亦不能及。是菩薩。住是地中。能令
531c03‖ 無量眾生。住一切智道。諸佛子。菩薩摩訶薩。
531c04‖ 住是地中。諸十方佛。為說智慧。令通達三世。
531c05‖ 正知法性相。以智普覆一切世[11]間。照一切世
531c06‖ 間性。[12]大悲大慈。普覆一切眾生。正遍見知一
531c07‖ 切諸法。

简体字

乃至无量无边百千万亿劫不可穷尽。

“佛子，譬如大金师，善治此金为庄严物，以无上摩尼宝珠间错其中，安置自在天王颈上。其余诸天，无能夺者。又诸天人庄严之具，无能及者。诸佛子，菩萨住十地中，智慧功德善根，从初地至九地，诸菩萨摩诃萨所不能及。菩萨住是地中，得大智照明故，能随顺一切智慧，其余智慧之明所不能坏。譬如，佛子，大自在天王光明，一切生处众生光明所不能及，能令众生身心凉冷。诸佛子，菩萨摩诃萨亦如是，住是法云地中智慧光明，一切声闻、辟支佛所不能及，从初地乃至九地菩萨摩诃萨亦不能及。是菩萨住是地中，能令无量众生住一切智道。

“诸佛子，菩萨摩诃萨住是地中，诸十方佛为说智慧，令通达三世正知法性相，以智普覆一切世间，照一切世间性，大悲大慈普覆一切众生，正遍见知一切诸法。

40. The Light of His Wisdom, Merit, and Good Roots Compared to Gold

Sons of the Buddha, it is as if there were a great master goldsmith who was skilled in refining gold to make adornments inlaid with precious *maṇi* pearls, adornments to be worn about the neck of the Vaśavartin Heaven King[307] that are so superior that such adornments cannot be outshone [by the radiance of] any of the other devas and cannot be rivaled by any other deva's adornments.

Sons of the Buddha, the wisdom, meritorious qualities, and roots of goodness of this bodhisattva dwelling on the tenth ground could never be rivaled by that of all the bodhisattva *mahāsattvas* dwelling on the first ground through the ninth ground. Because the bodhisattva dwelling on this ground has acquired the illuminating light of great wisdom, it is able to accord with all-knowledge. Hence it is such that the wisdom light of the others cannot outshine it.

41. The Radiance of This Bodhisattva's Wisdom Compared to Gold

Sons of the Buddha, this is analogous to the light of the Maheśvara Heaven King[308] that cannot be rivaled by the light of any being in any other station of rebirth. It has the capacity to cause beings' bodies and minds to feel clear and cool.

Sons of the Buddha, so too it is with this bodhisattva *mahāsattva*. As he dwells on this Dharma Cloud Ground, his wisdom light cannot be rivaled by that of any *śrāvaka*-disciple or *pratyekabuddha*. So too, that of bodhisattva *mahāsattvas* dwelling on the first ground through the ninth ground is also unable to rival it. The bodhisattva dwelling on this ground is able to influence incalculably many beings to abide in the path to the realization of all-knowledge.

42. The Buddhas' Ongoing Teaching of This Bodhisattva

Sons of the Buddha, all buddhas of the ten directions expound on wisdom for the bodhisattva *mahāsattva* who dwells on this ground, thereby causing him to achieve a penetrating comprehension of the three periods of time, causing him to rightly know the characteristic features of the Dharma realm, causing him to everywhere cover all worlds with his knowledge, causing him to illuminate all worldly realms, causing him to everywhere cover all beings with great compassion and great kindness, and causing him to rightly and universally see and know all dharmas. To speak of what is essential, they completely explain the path to all-knowledge for his sake.

正體字

舉要言之。具足為說。至一切智道。佛
531c08‖ 子。是名菩薩摩訶薩第十菩薩法雲地。菩薩
531c09‖ 摩訶薩。住是地中。多作摩醯首羅天王。智慧
531c10‖ 明達。善說聲聞辟支佛。菩薩波羅蜜。於法性
531c11‖ 中。有問難者。無能令盡。所作善業。若布施若
531c12‖ 愛語。若利益若同事。皆不離念佛念法念菩
531c13‖ 薩伴。念菩薩行。念諸波羅蜜。念諸地行。不離
531c14‖ 念十力。念無所畏。念不共法。乃至不離念具
531c15‖ 足一切種智。常作是念。我當何時於眾生中。
531c16‖ 為首為勝。為大為妙。為上為無上為導為將。
531c17‖ 為師為尊。乃至於一切眾生中。為依止者。若
531c18‖ 欲如是勤行精進。於一念中。得無量百千萬
531c19‖ 億那由他不可說不可說世界微塵數三昧。

简体字

举要言之，具足为说，至一切智道。佛子，是名菩萨摩诃萨第十菩萨法云地。菩萨摩诃萨住是地中，多作摩醯首罗天王，智慧明达，善说声闻、辟支佛、菩萨波罗蜜，于法性中有问难者，无能令尽。所作善业，若布施、若爱语、若利益、若同事，皆不离念佛、念法、念菩萨伴、念菩萨行、念诸波罗蜜、念诸地行，不离念十力、念无所畏、念不共法，乃至不离念具足一切种智。常作是念：‘我当何时于众生中为首、为胜、为大、为妙、为上、为无上、为导、为将、为师、为尊？乃至于一切众生中为依止者？’若欲如是勤行精进，于一念中，得无量百千万亿那由他不可说不可说世界微尘数三昧，

43. Vajragarbha's Final Statements About a 10th Ground Bodhisattva

Sons of the Buddha, this has been the presentation on the bodhisattva *mahāsattva*'s tenth ground, the Dharma Cloud Ground.

a. The Bodhisattva's Station and Dharma Practice

Dwelling on this ground, he most often becomes a Maheśvara Heaven King endowed with the penetrating light of wisdom with which he skillfully expounds on *śrāvaka*-disciple and *pratyekabuddha* practice as well as on the bodhisattva's *pāramitās*. Even if challenged with any of the difficult questions posed by anyone in the Dharma realm, there would still be no one who could exhaust his ability to answer.

b. The Bodhisattva's Mindfulness

In all of the good works that he pursues, no matter whether it be in his practice of giving, pleasing words, beneficial actions, or joint endeavors, he never departs from his mindfulness of the Buddha, his mindfulness of the Dharma, his mindfulness of his bodhisattva companions, his mindfulness of the bodhisattva practices, his mindfulness of the *pāramitās*, and his mindfulness of all the practices associated with the grounds. He never departs from his mindfulness of the ten powers, his mindfulness of the fearlessnesses, his mindfulness of the exclusive dharmas, and so forth until we come to his never departing from his mindfulness of his quest to achieve complete fulfillment of the knowledge of all modes.

c. The Bodhisattva's Aspiration to Serve Beings

He always thinks, "Oh when will I become able to serve these beings as a leader, one who is supremely excellent, one who is great, one who is marvelous, one who is superior, one who is insuperable, one who serves them as guide, one who serves them as a general, one who serves them as a mentor, one who is worthy of their veneration?," and so forth on up to "...one upon whom all beings can rely?"

d. The Consequences of the Bodhisattva's Vigor and Vows

If he wishes in this way to devote himself to the diligent practice of vigor, then, in but a single mind-moment, he succeeds in acquiring samādhis as numerous as the atoms in immeasurably many hundreds of thousands of myriads of *koṭis* of *nayutas* of ineffable numbers of ineffably many worlds and becomes able to manifest a bodhisattva retinue as numerous as just so very many atoms.

正體字

531c20‖ 乃至[13]示爾所微塵數。菩薩眷屬。若以願力。
531c21‖ 神通自在。復過是數。所謂諸行上妙供具。信
531c22‖ 解起業若身若口。若光明若諸根。若如意若
531c23‖ 音聲。若行處。乃至若干百千萬億劫。不可稱
531c24‖ 數。{A}諸佛子。是名菩薩摩訶薩地次第順[14]行趣
531c25‖ 向一切種智。佛子。譬如從阿耨達池。四河流
531c26‖ 出。滿足四天下。轉增無有窮盡。乃入大海。諸
531c27‖ 佛子。菩薩摩訶薩。亦如是。從菩薩出於善根
531c28‖ 大願之水。以四攝法。滿足眾生。而不窮盡。
531c29‖ 轉更增長乃至一切種智。{B}諸佛子。是諸菩薩
532a01‖ 十地。因佛智故。而有差別。譬如因大地故。有
532a02‖ 十大山王。何等為十。所謂。雪山王。香山王。
532a03‖ 軻梨羅山王。仙聖山王。由乾陀羅山王。馬耳
532a04‖ 山王。尼民陀羅山王。斫迦婆羅山王。眾相山
532a05‖ 王。須彌山王。

简体字

乃至示尔所微尘数菩萨眷属；若以愿力神通自在，复过是数，所谓诸行上妙供具，信解起业若身、若口、若光明、若诸根、若如意、若音声、若行处，乃至若干百千万亿劫不可称数。

"诸佛子，是名菩萨摩诃萨地次第顺行趣向一切种智。佛子，譬如从阿耨达池，四河流出，满足四天下，转增无有穷尽，乃入大海。诸佛子，菩萨摩诃萨亦如是，从菩萨出于善根大愿之水，以四摄法满足众生而不穷尽，转更增长乃至一切种智。诸佛子，是诸菩萨十地，因佛智故而有差别。譬如因大地故有十大山王。何等为十？所谓雪山王、香山王、轲梨罗山王、仙圣山王、由乾陀罗山王、马耳山王、尼民陀罗山王、斫迦婆罗山王、众相山王、须弥山王。

Were he to avail himself of the power of vows, through sovereign mastery in the spiritual superknowledges, he could freely manifest these phenomena in even greater numbers so large that, no matter whether we speak of his practices, of his supremely marvelous offerings, of his resolute faith, of the physical or verbal karma that he generates, of his radiance, of his faculties, of his employment of psychic powers, of his voice, or of his domains of practice, one could never enumerate them even in however many hundreds of thousands of myriads of *koṭis* of *nayutas* of kalpas one might attempt to do so.

III. The Final Summarizing Discussion of the Ten Grounds[309]

A. His Eventual All-Knowledge Likened to Rivers' Flow Into the Sea

{A} Sons of the Buddha, this is what is known as the bodhisattva *mahāsattva*'s sequential progression through the grounds as he moves toward acquisition of the knowledge of all modes.

Sons of the Buddha, this circumstance is analogous to that of Lake Anavatapta from which the four rivers flow forth and completely fill the four continents' waterways, progressively increasing without ever being exhausted until they finally flow into the great ocean.

Sons of the Buddha, so too it is with the bodhisattva *mahāsattva*. The waters of roots of goodness and great vows flow forth from the bodhisattva. Employing the four means of attraction, he becomes inexhaustible in his complete satisfaction of beings' needs and continually increases in this until he finally reaches the knowledge of all modes.

B. The 10 Grounds' Differences Likened to Those of 10 Mountain Kings

{B} Sons of the Buddha, these ten bodhisattva grounds each have distinct differences that all originate in the Buddha's knowledge. This is just as it is with the ten great mountain kings the existence of which originates in the great earth. What then are these ten? They are: the Snow Mountain King, the Fragrance Mountain King, the Khadira Mountain King, the Rishis-and-Āryas Mountain King, the Yugaṃdhara Mountain King, the Horse Ear Mountain King, the Nimindhara Mountain King, the Cakravāḍa Mountain King, the Manifold Features Mountain King, and the Sumeru Mountain King.

1. The First Ground Compared to the Snow Mountain King

Sons of the Buddha, just as the Snow Mountain King has all the various sorts of herbs gathered thereon so abundantly that one

正體字

佛子。如雪山王。一切藥草。集
532a06‖ 在其中。取不可盡。諸佛子。菩薩摩訶薩。亦如
532a07‖ 是。住在菩薩歡喜地。一切世間。經書伎藝。文
532a08‖ 頌呪術。集在其中。無有窮盡。諸佛子。如香山
532a09‖ 王。一切諸香。聚在其中。而不可盡。菩薩摩訶
532a10‖ 薩。亦如是。住菩薩離垢地中。持戒頭陀。威儀
532a11‖ 助法。集在其中。無有窮盡。[1]諸佛子。如軻梨
532a12‖ 羅[2]伽山王。但以寶成。集諸妙華。取不可盡。
532a13‖ 諸佛子。菩薩亦如是。住於明地。集一切世間。
532a14‖ 禪定神通。解脱三昧[3]門不可盡。諸佛子。如
532a15‖ 仙聖山王。但以寶成。多有五神通聖人。不可
532a16‖ 窮盡。[4]諸佛子。菩薩摩訶薩。亦如是。住菩薩
532a17‖ [5]焰地中。集令眾生。入道因緣。種種問難。不
532a18‖ 可窮盡。諸佛子。如由乾陀羅山王。但以寶成。
532a19‖ 集夜叉大神。

简体字

佛子，如雪山王，一切药草集在其中，取不可尽。诸佛子，菩萨摩诃萨亦如是，住在菩萨欢喜地，一切世间经书伎艺、文颂咒术集在其中，无有穷尽。诸佛子，如香山王，一切诸香聚在其中，而不可尽。菩萨摩诃萨亦如是，住菩萨离垢地中，持戒头陀威仪助法集在其中，无有穷尽。诸佛子，如轲梨罗伽山王，但以宝成，集诸妙华，取不可尽。诸佛子，菩萨亦如是，住于明地，集一切世间禅定、神通、解脱三昧门不可尽。诸佛子，如仙圣山王，但以宝成，多有五神通圣人，不可穷尽。诸佛子，菩萨摩诃萨亦如是，住菩萨焰地中，集令众生入道因缘，种种问难，不可穷尽。诸佛子，如由乾陀罗山王，但以宝成，集夜叉大神、

could never harvest them all, so too is this the case, O Sons of the Buddha, for the bodhisattva *mahāsattva* who dwells on the bodhisattva's Ground of Joyfulness, for the world's classical texts, cultural arts, literature, verse, mantras, and occult techniques are all so completely gathered together in him there that one could never come to the end of them all.

2. The Second Ground Compared to the Fragrance Mountain King

Sons of the Buddha, just as on the Fragrance Mountain King, all of the various sorts of incenses are all so abundantly gathered together there that they are endless, so too it is with the bodhisattva *mahāsattva* who dwells on the Ground of Stainlessness, for the moral precept observances, *dhūta* practices, awe-inspiring deportments, and supportive dharmas are all so completely gathered together in him there that one could never come to the end of them all.

3. The Third Ground Compared to the Khadira Mountain King

Sons of the Buddha, just as the Khadira Mountain King composed solely of jewels has all the marvelous flowers so abundantly gathered together on it that one could never harvest them all, so too it is for the bodhisattva who dwells on the Ground of Shining Light, for the world's *dhyāna* absorptions, spiritual superknowledges, and samādhi gateways are all so completely gathered together in him there that one could never come to the end of them all.

4. The 4th Ground Compared to the Rishis-and-Āryas Mountain King

Sons of the Buddha, just as on the Rishis-and-Āryas Mountain King composed solely of jewels there are endlessly many *āryas* possessed of the five spiritual superknowledges, so too it is, O Sons of the Buddha, with the bodhisattva *mahāsattva* dwelling on the Ground of Blazing Brilliance, for the causes and conditions by which beings are caused to enter the path along with his facility in responding to the many different sorts of related challenging questions are so completely gathered together in him there that one could never come to the end of them all.

5. The Fifth Ground Compared to the Yugaṃdhara Mountain King

Sons of the Buddha, just as on the Yugaṃdhara Mountain King composed solely of jewels, there are gathered together there so many *yakṣas,* those great spirits, that the aggregation of *yakṣas* and *rākṣasas* is endlessly abundant, so too it is, O Sons of the Buddha, with the bodhisattva dwelling on the bodhisattva's Difficult-to-Conquer Ground, for the sovereign masteries, psychic powers, and

正體字

夜叉羅剎[6]眾不可窮盡。諸佛
532a20‖ 子。菩薩亦如是。住菩薩難勝地中。集一切自
532a21‖ 在。如意神通。說不可盡。諸佛子。如馬耳山
532a22‖ 王。但以寶成。集眾妙果。取不可盡。諸佛子。
532a23‖ 菩薩摩訶薩。亦如是。住現前地中。集深因緣
532a24‖ 法。說聲聞果。不可窮盡。諸佛子。如尼民陀羅
532a25‖ 山王。但以寶成。集諸一切大力龍神。不可窮
532a26‖ 盡。諸佛子。菩薩摩訶薩。亦如是。住菩薩遠行
532a27‖ 地中。集種種方便智慧。說辟支佛道。不可窮
532a28‖ 盡。諸佛子。如斫迦婆羅山王。但以寶成。集心
532a29‖ 自在者。不可窮盡。諸佛子。菩薩摩訶薩。亦如
532b01‖ 是。住無動地。集一切菩薩自在道。說世間性。
532b02‖ 不可窮盡。諸佛子。如眾相山王。但以寶成。集
532b03‖ 大神力。諸阿修羅。無有窮盡。諸佛子。菩薩亦
532b04‖ 如是。

简体字

夜叉罗刹众不可穷尽。诸佛子，菩萨亦如是，住菩萨难胜地中，集一切自在如意神通，说不可尽。诸佛子，如马耳山王，但以宝成，集众妙果，取不可尽。诸佛子，菩萨摩诃萨亦如是，住现前地中，集深因缘法，说声闻果，不可穷尽。诸佛子，如尼民陀罗山王，但以宝成，集诸一切大力龙神，不可穷尽。诸佛子，菩萨摩诃萨亦如是，住菩萨远行地中，集种种方便智慧，说辟支佛道，不可穷尽。诸佛子，如斫迦婆罗山王，但以宝成，集心自在者，不可穷尽。诸佛子，菩萨摩诃萨亦如是，住无动地，集一切菩萨自在道，说世间性，不可穷尽。诸佛子，如众相山王，但以宝成，集大神力诸阿修罗，无有穷尽。诸佛子，菩萨亦如是，

spiritual superknowledges are so completely gathered together in him there that one could never describe them all.

6. The Sixth Ground Compared to the Horse Ear Mountain King

Sons of the Buddha, just as on the Horse Ear Mountain King composed solely of jewels, the many kinds of marvelous fruits are gathered there in such abundance that one could never harvest them all, so too it is, O Sons of the Buddha, with the bodhisattva *mahāsattva* dwelling on the Ground of Direct Presence, for the profound dharmas of causes and conditions and the facility to discourse on *śrāvaka*-disciples' fruits of the path are so completely gathered together in him there that one could never come to the end of them all.

7. The Seventh Ground Compared to the Nimindhara Mountain King

Sons of the Buddha, just as on the Nimindhara Mountain King composed solely of jewels all of the greatly powerful dragon spirits are so abundantly gathered together there that one could never come to the end of them, so too it is, O Sons of the Buddha, with the bodhisattva *mahāsattva* dwelling on the Far-Reaching Ground, for the many different skillful means and wisdom as well as his facility to discourse on a *pratyekabuddha*'s path are so completely gathered together in him there that one could never come to the end of them all.

8. The Eighth Ground Compared to the Cakravāḍa Mountain King

Sons of the Buddha, just as on the Cakravāḍa Mountain King composed solely of jewels, those whose minds have achieved sovereign mastery are so abundantly gathered together there that one could never come to the end of them, so too it is, O Sons of the Buddha, with the bodhisattva *mahāsattva* dwelling on the Ground of Immovability, for all bodhisattvas' paths of sovereign mastery and their abilities to discourse on the world's realms are so completely gathered together in him there that one could never come to the end of them all.

9. The Ninth Ground Compared to the Manifold Signs Mountain King

Sons of the Buddha, just as on the Manifold Signs Mountain King composed solely of jewels, all the *asuras* possessed of great spiritual powers are so abundantly present there that one could never come to the end of them, so too it is, O Sons of the Buddha, in the case of the bodhisattva dwelling on the bodhisattva's Ground of Sublime Goodness, for the practices and knowledge by which one transforms beings and discourses on the world's aspects are so

正體字

住菩薩妙善地中。集轉眾生行智。說世
532b05‖ 間相。不可窮盡。諸佛子。如須彌山王。但以寶
532b06‖ 成。集諸天神。無有窮盡。諸佛子。菩薩亦如
532b07‖ 是。住法雲地中。集如來十力。四無所畏。說
532b08‖ 諸佛法。不可窮盡。諸佛子。是十寶山。同在大
532b09‖ 海。因大海水。有差別相。諸菩薩摩訶薩十
532b10‖ 地。亦如是。同在佛智。因一切智故。有差別
532b11‖ 相。(C)諸佛子。譬如大海。以十相故。數名大海。
532b12‖ 無有能壞。何等為十。一漸次深。二不共死屍
532b13‖ 宿。三餘水失本名。四一味。五多寶聚。六極深
532b14‖ 難入。七廣大無量。八多有大身眾生依住。九
532b15‖ 不過常限。十能受一切大雨無有盈溢。諸佛
532b16‖ 子。諸菩薩行。亦如是。以十因緣故。得名無有
532b17‖ 能壞。

简体字

住菩萨妙善地中，集转众生行智，说世间相，不可穷尽。诸佛子，如须弥山王，但以宝成，集诸天神，无有穷尽。诸佛子，菩萨亦如是，住法云地中，集如来十力、四无所畏，说诸佛法，不可穷尽。诸佛子，是十宝山同在大海，因大海水有差别相。诸菩萨摩诃萨十地亦如是，同在佛智，因一切智故有差别相。

“诸佛子，譬如大海，以十相故数名大海，无有能坏。何等为十？一、渐次深，二、不共死尸宿，三、余水失本名，四、一味，五、多宝聚，六、极深难入，七、广大无量，八、多有大身众生依住，九、不过常限，十、能受一切大雨无有盈溢。诸佛子，诸菩萨行亦如是，以十因缘故，得名无有能坏。

completely gathered together in him there that one could never come to the end of them all.

10. The Tenth Ground Compared to the Sumeru Mountain King

Sons of the Buddha, just as on the Sumeru Mountain King, there are endlessly gathered together all of the devas and spirits, so too it is, O Sons of the Buddha, in the case of the bodhisattva dwelling on the Dharma Cloud Ground, for the Tathāgata's ten powers, four fearlessnesses, and proclamations of the Dharma of all buddhas are so completely gathered together in him there that one could never come to the end of them all.

11. The 10 Grounds in All-Knowledge Likened to Mountains in the Sea

Sons of the Buddha, just as these ten jeweled mountains all abide in the midst of the great sea and possess their distinctive features based on the waters of that great sea, so too it is with the bodhisattva *mahāsattva*'s ten grounds that all reside within the knowledge of the Buddha and possess their distinctive aspects in reliance upon all-knowledge.

C. The Ten Grounds Compared to Ten Aspects of the Great Ocean

{C} Sons of the Buddha, [these ten bodhisattva grounds] are comparable to the great ocean that, because of ten characteristic features, is inalterably referred to as "the great ocean."[310] What then are those ten features? They are:

First, it progresses gradually from its shallows to its depths;
Second, it refuses to remain together with dead bodies;
Third, all other waters lose their names on flowing into it;
Fourth, it is of a single flavor;
Fifth, it is a place in which an abundance of precious jewels are found;
Sixth, it is the most extremely deep and difficult to fathom;
Seventh, it is incalculably vast;
Eighth, it is a place in which beings with huge bodies reside;
Ninth, it does not move beyond its long-established boundaries;
Tenth, it is able to take in all the great rains without ever overflowing.

Sons of the Buddha, so too it is with the bodhisattva practices that on the basis of ten causes and conditions acquire the inalterably exclusive designation "bodhisattva practices." What then are those ten? They are:

正體字

何等為十。歡喜地中。漸次生堅固願。
532b18‖ 離垢地中。不與破戒者共宿。明地中。捨諸世
532b19‖ 間假名。[*]焰地中。於佛所得一心不壞信淨。
532b20‖ 難勝地中。生世間無量方便神通。起世間事。
532b21‖ 現前地中。觀甚深因緣法。遠行地中。以[7]廣
532b22‖ 大心。善擇諸法。無動地中。能起大莊嚴事示
532b23‖ 現。妙善地中。能得深解脫。通達世間行。如實
532b24‖ 不過。法雲地中。能受一切諸佛大法明雨。諸
532b25‖ 佛子。{D}譬如大摩尼寶珠。有十事。能與眾生一
532b26‖ 切寶物。何等為十。一出大海。二巧匠加治。三
532b27‖ 轉精細。四除其垢穢。五以火鍊治。六眾寶莊
532b28‖ 嚴。七貫以寶縷。八置在琉璃高柱。九光明四
532b29‖ 照。十隨王意雨眾寶物。

简体字

何等为十？欢喜地中，渐次生坚固愿；离垢地中，不与破戒者共宿；明地中，舍诸世间假名；焰地中，于佛所得一心不坏信净；难胜地中，生世间无量方便神通，起世间事；现前地中，观甚深因缘法；远行地中，以广大心善择诸法；无动地中，能起大庄严事示现；妙善地中，能得深解脱，通达世间行，如实不过；法云地中，能受一切诸佛大法明雨。

“诸佛子，譬如大摩尼宝珠，有十事能与众生一切宝物。何等为十？一、出大海，二、巧匠加治，三、转精细，四、除其垢秽，五、以火炼治，六、众宝庄严，七、贯以宝缕，八、置在琉璃高柱，九、光明四照，十、随王意雨众宝物。

On the Ground of Joyfulness one gradually and sequentially develops increasingly solid vows;

On the Ground of Stainlessness one does not abide in company with those who break the moral precepts;

On the Ground of Shining Light one relinquishes the world's false designations;

On the Ground of Blazing Brilliance one acquires a single-minded and indestructible pure faith in the Buddha;

On the Difficult-to-Conquer Ground one develops incalculably many skillful means and spiritual superknowledges and initiates endeavors within the world;

On the Ground of Direct Presence one contemplates the extremely profound dharmas of causes and conditions;

On the Far-Reaching Ground one employs a vast mind in skillful examination and selection of dharmas;

On the Ground of Immovability one becomes able to initiate the manifestation of immense works of adornment;

On the Ground of Sublime Goodness one becomes able to acquire profound liberations and reach a penetrating comprehension of practice in the world that accords with reality and never goes beyond it;

On the Dharma Cloud Ground one becomes able to take in all buddhas' great rain of Dharma light.

D. The Ten Grounds Compared to a Large Maṇi Jewel

{D} Sons of the Buddha, this circumstance is analogous to that of a large and precious *maṇi* jewel that by virtue of possessing ten characteristic aspects is able to bestow all manner of precious things on beings. What then are those ten? They are:

First, it comes forth from the great sea;

Second, it is enhanced by the refinements of a skillful artisan;

Third, it is made ever more refined;

Fourth, it is rid of defilements;

Fifth, fire is used in its refinement;

Sixth, it is adorned with a multitude of precious jewels;

Seventh, it is strung with precious thread;

Eighth, it is placed atop a tall pillar composed of lapis lazuli;

Ninth, its light rays radiate in the four directions;

Tenth, it rains down the many sorts of precious things in response to the King's wishes.

正體字

諸佛子。菩薩摩訶薩。
532c01‖ 發菩提心寶。亦有十事。何等為十。一初發心
532c02‖ 布施離慳。二修持戒頭陀苦行。三以諸禪定
532c03‖ 解脫三昧令轉精妙。四以道行清淨。五練以
532c04‖ 方便神通。六以深因緣法莊嚴。七以種種深
532c05‖ 方便智慧貫穿。八置以神通自在幢上。九觀
532c06‖ 眾生行放多聞智慧光明。十諸佛授智職。爾
532c07‖ 時於一切眾生。能為佛事。墮在薩婆若數。{E}諸
532c08‖ 佛子。是諸菩薩所行。集一切智慧功德法門
532c09‖ 品。若不深種善根者。不能得聞。問言。若得聞
532c10‖ 者。是人為得幾許福。答言。隨諸佛所有智慧
532c11‖ [8]慧力。

简体字

诸佛子，菩萨摩诃萨发菩提心宝，亦有十事。何等为十？一、初发心布施离悭，二、修持戒头陀苦行，三、以诸禅定解脱三昧令转精妙，四、以道行清净，五、练以方便神通，六、以深因缘法庄严，七、以种种深方便智慧贯穿，八、置以神通自在幢上，九、观众生行放多闻智慧光明，十、诸佛授智职，尔时于一切众生能为佛事，堕在萨婆若数。诸佛子，是诸菩萨所行，集一切智慧功德法门品，若不深种善根者，不能得闻。”

问言：“若得闻者，是人为得几许福？”

答言：“随诸佛所有智慧慧力，

Sons of the Buddha, in his bringing forth the precious jewel of the resolve to realize bodhi, the bodhisattva *mahāsattva* is also possessed of ten characteristic aspects. What then are those ten? They are:

First, from the point of bringing forth that resolve, he pursues the practice of giving and abandons miserliness;

Second, he cultivates the observance of the moral precepts and practices the *dhūta* austerities;

Third, through the *dhyāna* absorptions, liberations, and samādhis, he is caused to become increasingly refined in his marvelousness;

Fourth, he brings forth purity in his path practices;

Fifth, he trains himself in skillful means and spiritual superknowledges;

Sixth, he creates adornments based on the profound dharma of causes and conditions;

Seventh, whatever he does is strung together with all the different sorts of profound skillful means and wisdom;

Eighth, he is placed high atop the pillar of the spiritual superknowledges and sovereign masteries;

Ninth, he contemplates the actions of beings and then emanates the light of extensive learning and wisdom;

Tenth, all buddhas bestow on him their consecration of his knowledge at which time he becomes able to carry out for all beings the works of a buddha and then falls in among those counted as possessed of all-knowledge.

E. The Prerequisite Conditions for Hearing The Ten Grounds Teachings

{E} Sons of the Buddha, as for this chapter on all bodhisattvas' practice of the Dharma gateways to the attainment of all-knowledge and the meritorious qualities, if one had not already deeply planted roots of goodness, one would be unable even to obtain a hearing of it.

F. Liberation Moon Asks: "How Much Merit by Hearing This Teaching?

Liberation Moon Bodhisattva then asked, "If one does succeed in hearing it, how much merit does such a person thereby acquire?"

G. Vajragarbha Explains Merit and Importance of 10 Grounds Teaching

[Vajragarbha Bodhisattva] replied, saying, "This corresponds to the merit associated with the power of all buddhas' omniscient wisdom. Thus the merit acquired from this person's hearing of these Dharma gateways is equivalent to the merit associated with

正體字

如是發薩婆若心。所緣攝福德。是人
532c12‖ 得聞此法門。所得福德。亦復如是。何以故。若
532c13‖ 無菩薩心。聞是法門。不能信解受持。何況以
532c14‖ 身修習。能成是事。諸佛子。以是故當知。是人
532c15‖ 隨順一切種智。得聞信解受持修行。說是經
532c16‖ 時。以佛神力。十方世界。十億佛國。微塵數世
532c17‖ 界。六種十八相動。又法應震動。諸天雨華。如
532c18‖ 雲而下。雨諸香瓔珞。天寶衣。天幡蓋。天寶
532c19‖ 物。天莊嚴身具。雨天伎樂歌頌。而下更有大
532c20‖ 音。讚歎十地殊勝之事。此他化自在天王宮。
532c21‖ 四天下中。如是十方一切世界周[9]遍。皆說十
532c22‖ 地經。以佛神力故。十方過十億佛國微塵數
532c23‖ 世界。有十億佛國微塵數諸菩薩來。遍滿十
532c24‖ 方虛空。皆作是言。善哉善哉。金剛藏。佛子。
532c25‖ 善說諸菩薩摩訶薩住諸地相。

简体字

如是发萨婆若心，所缘摄福德；是人得闻此法门，所得福德亦复如是。何以故？若无菩萨心，闻是法门，不能信解受持，何况以身修习能成是事？诸佛子，以是故当知，是人随顺一切种智，得闻信解受持修行。”

说是经时，以佛神力，十方世界十亿佛国微尘数世界，六种十八相动，又法应震动。诸天雨华，如云而下，雨诸香、瓔珞、天宝衣、天幡盖、天宝物、天庄严身具，雨天伎乐歌颂。而下更有大音，赞叹十地殊胜之事。此他化自在天王宫，四天下中，如是十方一切世界周遍，皆说十地经。

以佛神力故，十方过十亿佛国微尘数世界，有十亿佛国微尘数诸菩萨来，遍满十方虚空，皆作是言：“善哉！善哉！金刚藏。佛子，善说诸菩萨摩诃萨住诸地相。

the goal sought when bringing forth the resolve to gain all-knowledge.

"How could this be? If one did not possess the bodhisattva's resolve, then, on hearing this Dharma gateway, one would not have resolute faith in it, would not accept it, and would not uphold it. How much the less might one be able to actually personally carry forth its cultivation and achieve success in this endeavor?

"Sons of the Buddha, therefore one should realize that this person's pursuit of the knowledge of all modes occurs because of having been able to hear this, because of having resolute faith in it, because of accepting it, and because of maintaining it in his cultivation of the practices."

H. The Auspicious Signs That Occurred When This Sutra's Teaching Ended

On finishing the proclamation of this sutra, because of the spiritual powers of the Buddha, worlds throughout the ten directions as numerous as the atoms in ten *koṭis* of buddha lands underwent the six types and eighteen varieties of characteristic movements. Additionally, it was because of the very nature of the Dharma that such quaking occurred. The heavens then all rained down flowers that, like a cloud, floated on down. They also rained down all manner of incenses, necklaces, precious heavenly raiment, heavenly banners and canopies, precious things from the heavens, and heavenly physical adornments while also raining down celestial music, songs, and verses. As they descended, there arose even greater sounds of praises to the extraordinarily supreme matter of the ten grounds.

I. The Ten Directions' Bodhisattvas Attest to the Teaching's Universality

Just as the proclamation of this sutra on the ten grounds was taking place in the Paranirmita Vaśavartin Heaven associated with these four continents, so too did this also occur everywhere throughout all worlds of the ten directions. Because of the Buddha's spiritual powers, from a number of worlds throughout the ten directions greater than the number of atoms in ten *koṭis* of buddha lands, bodhisattvas in numbers equal to the atoms in ten *koṭis* of buddha lands all came there and, completely filling up the space of the ten directions, they all spoke thus:

> It is good indeed, good indeed, Vajragarbha, O Son of the Buddha, that you have so well proclaimed the characteristic features of the grounds in which all bodhisattva *mahāsattvas* dwell.

正體字

佛子。我等皆
532c26‖ 亦名金剛藏。從金剛德世界。金剛憧佛所來。
532c27‖ 所經歷處。皆說是經。眾會亦如是。言辭亦如
532c28‖ 是。義趣亦如是。不增不減。佛子。我等以佛力
532c29‖ 故。到此大眾。來證是事。諸佛子。如我等來至
533a01‖ 此眾。如是十方一切世界。一一世間種性。四
533a02‖ 天下上他化自在天王宮摩尼寶殿。皆有十
533a03‖ 億佛國微塵數菩薩。[1]往為作證。爾時金剛藏
533a04‖ 菩薩觀察十方。觀一切大眾。觀深法性。讚歎
533a05‖ 助發薩婆若心。示眾生菩薩大力。欲淨諸菩
533a06‖ 薩行攝一切眾生。隨順薩婆若。除一切世間
533a07‖ 之垢。與諸眾生一切種智因緣。示不可思議
533a08‖ 智慧莊嚴妙事。說一切菩薩功德差別相。欲
533a09‖ 令此義轉勝明顯示眾生故。承佛神力。而說
533a10‖ 偈言
533a11‖ 諸菩薩所行　樂於善寂滅
533a12‖ 其心無所著　猶若如虛空

简体字

佛子，我等皆亦名金刚藏，从金刚德世界，金刚憧佛所来。所经历处皆说是经，众会亦如是，言辞亦如是，义趣亦如是，不增不减。佛子，我等以佛力故，到此大众，来证是事。诸佛子，如我等来至此众，如是十方一切世界，一一世间种性，四天下上他化自在天王宫摩尼宝殿，皆有十亿佛国微尘数菩萨，往为作证。”

尔时，金刚藏菩萨观察十方，观一切大众，观深法性，赞叹助发萨婆若心，示众生菩萨大力，欲净诸菩萨行，摄一切众生，随顺萨婆若，除一切世间之垢，与诸众生一切种智因缘，示不可思议智慧庄严妙事，说一切菩萨功德差别相，欲令此义转胜明显示众生故，承佛神力，而说偈言：

“诸菩萨所行，　乐于善寂灭，
其心无所著，　犹若如虚空。

Son of the Buddha, we too have all identically been given the name "Vajragarbha." We come here from a land called "Vajra Qualities," from that place in which Vajra Banner Buddha resides. In all those places through which we passed in coming here, there was this proclamation of this sutra.

The assembled congregations were also of this very sort. So too were the words and phrases spoken also of this very sort. And so too were their meanings of this very sort, being neither enhanced nor reduced by comparison.

O Son of the Buddha, it is because of the power of the Buddha that we have arrived here in this great assembly, offering this certifying corroboration regarding these circumstances.

Son of the Buddha, just as we have come here to this assembled congregation, so too do bodhisattvas as numerous as the atoms in ten *koṭis* of buddha lands also go forth throughout all worlds of the ten directions to each and every one of the types of world realms, proceeding then to offer this certifying corroboration in all the Maṇi Jewel Palaces of the Paranirmita Vaśavartin Heaven Kings above their four-continent worlds.

J. Vajragarbha's Summarizing Verses Augmented by the Buddha's Powers

At that time, Vajragarbha Bodhisattva contemplated the ten directions, contemplated that entire great assembly, and contemplated the deep Dharma realm, and, in order to offer praises to the generation of the resolve to gain all-knowledge, in order to reveal to beings the great power of the bodhisattvas, wishing to purify all the bodhisattva practices, wishing to draw in all beings, wishing to hold forth on the pursuit of all-knowledge, wishing to do away with all forms of worldly defilement, wishing to bestow upon all beings the causes and conditions associated with the knowledge of all modes, wishing to reveal the marvelous adorning phenomena associated with inconceivable wisdom, wishing to explain the differentiating aspects in the meritorious qualities possessed by all bodhisattvas, and wishing to cause the meaning of this to become ever more supremely and brightly manifest to beings, he took on the augmentation of the spiritual powers of the Buddha and then uttered verses, saying:

In all that bodhisattvas practice,
they delight in skillfully achieved quiescence
wherein their minds are free of any sort of attachment
and, in this, are like empty space.

正體字

533a13‖ 除貪恚癡垢　安住道智中
533a14‖ 如是無上行　願樂欲聽聞 {17}
533a15‖ 如是諸菩薩　在於無量劫
533a16‖ 勤心常修習　萬億種善根
533a17‖ 供養無量佛　辟支阿羅漢
533a18‖ 為利眾生故　乃生菩提心 {18}
533a19‖ [2]精勤持戒行　頭陀除罪垢
533a20‖ 修善忍轉妙　慚愧威德滿
533a21‖ 福慧因緣故　高勝心明淨
533a22‖ 深樂於佛智　同佛生菩提 {19}
533a23‖ 供養於一切　十方三世佛
533a24‖ 如虛空等國　悉皆令清淨
533a25‖ 一切法平等　善悉通達故
533a26‖ 為度一切眾　生於菩提心 {20}
533a27‖ 諸菩薩如是　生是無量心
533a28‖ 至於歡喜地　息惡樂布施
533a29‖ 得諸本願力　慈悲心偏多
533b01‖ 深行十善道　能到離垢地
533b02‖ 戒聞功德富　慈心愍世間
533b03‖ 永離諸垢穢　深心常清淨

简体字

除贪恚痴垢，　安住道智中，
如是无上行，　愿乐欲听闻。
如是诸菩萨，　在于无量劫，
勤心常修习，　万亿种善根，
供养无量佛，　辟支阿罗汉，
为利众生故，　乃生菩提心。
精勤持戒行，　头陀除罪垢，
修善忍转妙，　惭愧威德满，
福慧因缘故，　高胜心明净，
深乐于佛智，　同佛生菩提。
供养于一切，　十方三世佛，
如虚空等国，　悉皆令清净，
一切法平等，　善悉通达故，
为度一切众，　生于菩提心。
诸菩萨如是，　生是无量心，
至于欢喜地，　息恶乐布施。
得诸本愿力，　慈悲心偏多，
深行十善道，　能到离垢地。
戒闻功德富，　慈心愍世间，
永离诸垢秽，　深心常清净，

They are rid of the defilements of covetousness, hatred, and delusion
and abide securely in the knowledge of the path.
Such unsurpassable practices as these
are such that one should wish to listen to them. {17}

It is in this way that bodhisattvas
throughout incalculably many kalpas
persevere with diligent minds in always cultivating
myriads of *koṭis* of types of roots of goodness,

in making offerings to countless buddhas,
pratyekabuddhas, and arhats,
and, for the sake of benefiting beings,
then bring forth the bodhi resolve. {18}

They are intensely diligent in upholding moral precept practice,
in *dhūta* austerities, and in eliminating the defilement of offenses.
Their cultivation of goodness and patience are ever more sublime.
Sensible to shame and blame, they are replete in awesome virtue.

Due to the causes and conditions provided by merit and knowledge,
they have lofty and supreme minds that are bright and pure.
They deeply delight in the knowledge of the Buddha and,
to become the same as Buddha, they generate the bodhi resolve. {19}

They present offerings to all buddhas
throughout the ten directions and the three periods of time,
bringing about the complete purification of so many lands
that they are commensurate with the expanse of empty space.

Due to skillfulness in the completely penetrating comprehension
of the uniform equality of all dharmas,
and for the sake of bringing about the liberation of all beings,
they bring forth the bodhi resolve.[311] {20}

In this manner, all bodhisattvas
bring forth this incalculably vast resolve
and, on reaching the Ground of Joyfulness,
put evils to rest and delight in the practice of giving.

They acquire the power of their original vows
and give greater devotion to practicing kindness and compassion.
They institute the profound practice of the ten good karmic paths
and thereby become able to reach the Ground of Stainlessness.

Through moral precepts and learning, they develop a wealth of merit
and, with a mind imbued with kindness, they feel pity for the world.
They eternally abandon every form of defilement
and thus possess a profound mind that is always pure.

正體字

533b04║ 普觀諸世間　三毒火熾然
533b05║ 如是之大士　能入三明地
533b06║ 觀三界皆空　無常亦如病
533b07║ 如癰如瘡箭　百種苦常然
533b08║ 見諸有為過　貪著佛功德
533b09║ 得佛智明焰　得入於焰地
533b10║ 成就於念慧　得至道智中
533b11║ 在此地供養　百千種諸佛
533b12║ 常能思惟念　[3]諸佛無量德
533b13║ 得入於一切　世間難勝地
533b14║ 能以慧方便　種種而示現
533b15║ 諸有所為作　以利於世間
533b16║ 供養於諸佛　作益眾生事
533b17║ 無生法在前　得入現前地
533b18║ 菩薩諸所行　一切世難知
533b19║ 常無有我心　離有亦離無
533b20║ 諸法先空[4]寂　十二緣故行
533b21║ 善了此微細　能入遠行地
533b22║ 行慧方便等　得法寂滅相
533b23║ 如是之大士　難知難可及

简体字

普观诸世间，　三毒火炽然，
如是之大士，　能入三明地。
观三界皆空，　无常亦如病，
如痈如疮箭，　百种苦常然，
见诸有为过，　贪著佛功德，
得佛智明焰，　得入于焰地。
成就于念慧，　得至道智中，
在此地供养，　百千种诸佛，
常能思惟念，　诸佛无量德，
得入于一切，　世间难胜地。
能以慧方便，　种种而示现，
诸有所为作，　以利于世间，
供养于诸佛，　作益众生事，
无生法在前，　得入现前地。
菩萨诸所行，　一切世难知，
常无有我心，　离有亦离无，
诸法先空寂，　十二缘故行，
善了此微细，　能入远行地。
行慧方便等，　得法寂灭相，
如是之大士，　难知难可及，

They everywhere contemplate in all worlds
the blazing fires of the three poisons.
Great eminences of this sort
are then able to enter the third ground, the Ground of Shining Light.

They contemplate the three realms as entirely empty,
as impermanent, as like a disease,
as like a boil, like an open sore shot with an arrow,
and as constantly aflame with the hundred varieties of suffering.

Observing all the faults of conditioned existence,
they have a desire to acquire a buddha's meritorious qualities,
develop the radiant flaming of a buddha's wisdom,
and then succeed in entering the Ground of Blazing Brilliance.

They perfect mindfulness and wisdom
and thus succeed in arriving in the knowledge of the path.
As they abide on this ground, they present offerings
of a hundred thousand varieties to all buddhas,

and are always able to deliberate with mindfulness
on the measureless qualities of the Buddhas.
They then succeed in entering what in all worlds
is known as the Difficult-to-Conquer Ground.

They are able to employ wisdom and skillful means
that they manifest in all different ways.
Everything to which they devote themselves
is done for the sake of benefiting those in the world.

They present offerings to all buddhas,
pursue endeavors that benefit beings,
and, keeping the dharma of the unproduced directly before them,
then enter the Ground of Direct Presence.

All that these bodhisattvas engage in
is such that everyone in the world would find difficult to know.
They are always free of any thought conceiving of a "self,"
while also having abandoned "existence" and "nonexistence" as well.

From their origin onward, all dharmas are empty and quiescent,
and function as they do because of the twelve-fold chain of causation.
They skillfully and completely fathom these subtleties
and become able then to enter the Far-Reaching Ground.

Practicing wisdom, skillful means, and such,
they realize that dharmas are characterized by quiescent cessation.
A great eminence of this sort
is someone who is difficult to fathom and difficult to rival.

正體字

533b24║ 為欲令世間　得善寂滅故
533b25║ 還起修諸行　種種福德事
533b26║ 普入於眾生　種種心行處
533b27║ 如是能得入　等空不動地
533b28║ 大智諸菩薩　悉善能具[5]行
533b29║ 種種[6]諸智業　得十自在力
533c01║ 能以無有量　無邊限諸身
533c02║ 普現十方界　而為說妙法
533c03║ 善達世間性　及諸眾生性
533c04║ 如是大慈悲　能入妙善地
533c05║ 第一妙淨智　善觀諸世間
533c06║ 縷練煩惱業　深曲險難處
533c07║ 為度是等故　得諸佛法藏
533c08║ 善說第一義　悉無所違錯
533c09║ 如是次第行　具足諸善法
533c10║ 乃至到九地　所修集福[7]慧
533c11║ 欲得諸佛力　第一深妙利
533c12║ 乃於一切佛　能得受智職
533c13║ 先得無數定　智行極廣大
533c14║ 末後得難壞　諸智職三昧

简体字

为欲令世间，　得善寂灭故，
还起修诸行，　种种福德事，
普入于众生，　种种心行处，
如是能得入，　等空不动地。
大智诸菩萨，　悉善能具行，
种种诸智业，　得十自在力，
能以无有量，　无边限诸身，
普现十方界，　而为说妙法，
善达世间性，　及诸众生性，
如是大慈悲，　能入妙善地。
第一妙净智，　善观诸世间，
缕练烦恼业，　深曲险难处，
为度是等故，　得诸佛法藏，
善说第一义，　悉无所违错。
如是次第行，　具足诸善法，
乃至到九地，　所修集福慧，
欲得诸佛力，　第一深妙利，
乃于一切佛，　能得受智职。
先得无数定，　智行极广大，
末后得难坏，　诸智职三昧。

Out of a desire to cause those in the world
to achieve skillful realization of quiescent cessation,
he returns to bring forth his cultivation of all of the practices
and engages in the various sorts of merit-generating endeavors.

He acquires a universally penetrating understanding
of the bases of all beings' different sorts of mental actions
and, in this manner, becomes able to enter
that ground comparable to empty space, the Ground of Immovability.

All of these bodhisattvas possessed of great wisdom
are completely able to embody the practice
of all the different sorts of wise endeavors
and acquire the power of the ten types of sovereign mastery.

Availing themselves of incalculably
and boundlessly many bodies, they are able
to manifest everywhere throughout the realms of the ten directions
and thereby expound on the sublime Dharma for others' sakes.

They have a skillful penetrating comprehension of all worldly realms
as well as of all realms of beings,
and, possessed of such great kindness and compassion as this,
they are then able to enter the Ground of Sublime Goodness.

Employing the foremost sort of marvelous and pure wisdom,
they skillfully contemplate the continuously-woven
fabric of karma and afflictions of the world's beings,
their deeply entangling and hazardous difficulties.

In order to bring beings such as these to liberation,
they acquire all buddhas' Dharma treasury
and skillfully discourse on the supreme meaning
while always remaining free of contradiction and error.

In this manner, they carry forth the sequential practice
and become completely equipped with all good dharmas,
thus progressing on to acquire the merit and wisdom
cultivated and accumulated on the ninth ground.

Wishing to acquire all buddhas' powers
and their foremost profound and marvelous benefit,
they then become able to receive the wisdom consecration
that is bestowed on them by all buddhas.

They first acquire countless meditative absorptions
with knowledge and practices that are the most ultimately vast.
At the very last, they acquire the indestructible
samādhi of the consecration of all-knowledge.

正體字

533c15║ 若能得如是　一切職三昧
533c16║ 一切寶莊嚴　大蓮花即出
533c17║ 菩薩稱蓮花　現身坐其上
533c18║ 餘花諸菩薩　咸共一心視
533c19║ 爾時大菩薩　從身放無量
533c20║ 百千億光明　滅諸世間苦
533c21║ 然後頂上出　百千億光明
533c22║ 普照十方界　[8]諸佛大[9]會眾
533c23║ 於上虛空中　化成光明網
533c24║ 供養諸佛已　入諸佛足下
533c25║ 時諸一切佛　及諸大菩薩
533c26║ 各知[10]其菩薩　得受於智職
533c27║ 如是一切佛　報以眉間光
533c28║ 名曰一切職　入此菩薩頂
533c29║ 一切無量佛　與此菩薩職
534a01║ 猶如轉輪王　假[1]授太子位
534a02║ 時諸十方界　普皆大震動
534a03║ 乃至阿鼻等　諸苦皆除滅
534a04║ 菩薩為一切　智慧得是職
534a05║ 如是名為到　無上法雲地

简体字

若能得如是，　一切职三昧，
一切宝庄严，　大莲华即出。
菩萨称莲华，　现身坐其上，
余华诸菩萨，　咸共一心视。
尔时大菩萨，　从身放无量，
百千亿光明，　灭诸世间苦。
然后顶上出，　百千亿光明，
普照十方界，　诸佛大会众。
于上虚空中，　化成光明网，
供养诸佛已，　入诸佛足下。
时诸一切佛，　及诸大菩萨，
各知其菩萨，　得受于智职。
如是一切佛，　报以眉间光，
名曰一切职，　入此菩萨顶。
一切无量佛，　与此菩萨职，
犹如转轮王，　假授太子位。
时诸十方界，　普皆大震动，
乃至阿鼻等，　诸苦皆除灭。
菩萨为一切，　智慧得是职，
如是名为到，　无上法云地。

In this case where one becomes able to achieve realization
of just such a samādhi of all-knowledge consecration as this,
an immense lotus blossom immediately emerges,
adorned with all sorts of precious jewels.

The bodhisattva, matching the scale of that lotus blossom,
manifests his body as sitting on it
with the other bodhisattvas, each sitting on his own lotus,
all together gazing single-mindedly up at him.

At that time, that great bodhisattva,
emanates from his body countlessly many
hundreds of thousands of *koṭis* of light rays
that extinguish all the world's sufferings

and then, afterward, emanates from the crown of his head
hundreds of thousands of *koṭis* of light rays
that everywhere illuminate the great assemblies
of all buddhas throughout the ten directions.

Those rays then transform into a net-like canopy of light
dwell in space up above them.
After having then made offerings to all buddhas,
those rays then enter the bottoms of all buddhas' feet.

At that time, all buddhas
as well as all great bodhisattvas
each know that this bodhisattva
has succeeded in acquiring the consecration of his knowledge.

After this occurs in this way, all buddhas then respond
with a beam of light sent forth from between their eyebrows
known as "[enhancer of] the station of all-knowledge"
that then enters the crown of this bodhisattva's head.

The bestowal on this bodhisattva of the consecration
by all the incalculably many buddhas
is analogous to that of a wheel turning king
when he bequeaths his position to his crown prince.

At that time, the worlds throughout the ten directions
are everywhere beset with a great quaking movement that,
reaching all the way down to the Avīci Hells and other such places,
entirely extinguishes all of their sufferings.

It is for the sake of consummating all-knowledge
that this bodhisattva acquires this consecration.
It is in this way that he then becomes one who has reached
the Dharma Cloud Ground.

正體字

534a06║ 住於是地中　智慧無邊限
534a07║ 善知度一切　世間諸因緣
534a08║ 入色無色法　欲色無色界
534a09║ 能知眾生性　國土性法性
534a10║ 又能入可數　不可數法中
534a11║ 乃至能觀擇　虛空無量性
534a12║ [2]入此地悉具　菩薩變化事
534a13║ 諸佛威神力　微細智密事
534a14║ 又能悉通達　一切諸劫數
534a15║ 於一毛端中　觀見世間性
534a16║ 一切諸如來　於此無上地
534a17║ 初生及出家　得道轉法輪
534a18║ 示入於涅槃　皆隨順於智
534a19║ 寂滅妙解脫　悉於此地得
534a20║ 此地諸大士　憶念力大故
534a21║ 諸佛大法雨　皆悉能受持
534a22║ 譬如大海水　能持龍王雨
534a23║ 諸佛大法雨　菩薩受亦爾
534a24║ 若於一佛所　一時聽受法
534a25║ 十方無量土　微塵數眾生

简体字

住于是地中，　智慧无边限，
善知度一切，　世间诸因缘。
入色无色法，　欲色无色界，
能知众生性，　国土性法性。
又能入可数，　不可数法中，
乃至能观择，　虚空无量性。
入此地悉具，　菩萨变化事，
诸佛威神力，　微细智密事。
又能悉通达，　一切诸劫数，
于一毛端中，　观见世间性。
一切诸如来，　于此无上地，
初生及出家，　得道转法轮，
示入于涅槃，　皆随顺于智，
寂灭妙解脱，　悉于此地得。
此地诸大士，　忆念力大故，
诸佛大法雨，　皆悉能受持。
譬如大海水，　能持龙王雨，
诸佛大法雨，　菩萨受亦尔。
若于一佛所，　一时听受法；
十方无量土，　微尘数众生，

Dwelling on this ground,
his wisdom then becomes boundless.
He then thoroughly knows those causes and conditions
by which to bring about the liberation of everyone in all worlds.

He gains a penetrating knowledge of form and formless dharmas,
the desire realm, the form realm, and the formless realm,
is able to know the realms of beings,
the realms of lands, and the Dharma realm,

and is able as well to penetratingly fathom the enumerated dharmas,
the innumerable dharmas,
and so forth, on up to his ability to employ meditative contemplation
in fathoming the countless other realms throughout empty space.

On entering this ground, he becomes entirely replete
with all of the bodhisattva's transformative capacities,
the awesome spiritual powers of the Buddhas,
their subtle knowledge, and their secret matters as well.

He is also able then to wield an utterly penetrating comprehension
of all enumerations of kalpas,
while also being able to contemplate the realms of worlds
residing even on the point of a single hair.

All of the Tathāgatas,
when dwelling on this unsurpassable ground,
whether it be in their first taking on birth, their leaving the home life,
their gaining right enlightenment, their turning the Dharma wheel,

or their manifesting the appearance of entering nirvāṇa—
this is all done entirely in accordance with wisdom.
The wondrous liberation of quiescent cessation
is brought to complete realization on this ground.

Due to the immensity of their powers of recollection,
those great eminences who dwell on this ground
are able to entirely take in and retain
the great Dharma rain of all buddhas.

This circumstance is analogous to that of the waters of the great sea
that are able to retain all rains sent down by the dragon kings.
This bodhisattva's taking in of all of the great Dharma rains
sent down by the Buddhas is just the same as this.

If one compared the Dharma he simultaneously hears and absorbs
in the abode of but a single buddha
to that acquired by beings as numerous as the dusts
in the incalculably many ten directions lands

正體字

534a26‖ 皆得聞總持　成於聲聞乘
534a27‖ 不如是菩薩　算數所不及
534a28‖ 大智慧力故　及[3]生大願力
534a29‖ 能於一念中　遍滿無量國
534b01‖ 雨甘露法水　滅諸煩惱火
534b02‖ 是故諸佛名　此地為法雲
534b03‖ 大士住此地　供養諸佛具
534b04‖ 過諸天所有　普示大神力
534b05‖ 示眾轉勝力　過是數無量
534b06‖ 若人欲思量　迷悶不能解
534b07‖ 大智住此地　舉足下足事
534b08‖ 及餘諸菩薩　乃至於九地
534b09‖ 皆悉不能知　何況餘眾生
534b10‖ 三世諸聲聞　及與辟支佛
534b11‖ 住此諸佛示　一切智慧事
534b12‖ 亦與令通達　三世無礙智
534b13‖ 亦示法性寂　亦示種種變
534b14‖ 一切諸世界　所有眾生類
534b15‖ 所行一切法　深微隱妙事
534b16‖ 一切佛功德　次第示令知

简体字

皆得闻总持，　成于声闻乘，
不如是菩萨，　算数所不及。
大智慧力故，　及生大愿力，
能于一念中，　遍满无量国，
雨甘露法水，　灭诸烦恼火，
是故诸佛名，　此地为法云。
大士住此地，　供养诸佛具，
过诸天所有，　普示大神力。
示众转胜力，　过是数无量；
若人欲思量，　迷闷不能解。
大智住此地，　举足下足事，
及余诸菩萨，　乃至于九地，
皆悉不能知，　何况余众生，
三世诸声闻，　及与辟支佛？
住此诸佛示，　一切智慧事，
亦与令通达，　三世无碍智，
亦示法性寂，　亦示种种变。
一切诸世界，　所有众生类，
所行一切法，　深微隐妙事，
一切佛功德，　次第示令知。

who had all acquired hearing-and-retention *dhāraṇīs*
and had achieved the realization of the Śrāvaka Disciple Vehicle,
that of the latter could never match that gained by this bodhisattva,
and could never be made to compare even by numerical calculation.

Through the power of his great wisdom
as well as through the power of his previous[312] great vows,
he is able in the space of but a single mind-moment to go forth and
appear throughout the incalculably many lands of the ten directions.

He sends down the sweet-dew elixir of the Dharma rain
and thereby extinguishes the fires of the afflictions.
It is for this reason that all buddhas
refer to this as "the Dharma Cloud Ground."

The number of gifts bestowed as offerings on all buddhas
by the great eminence who dwells on this ground
surpasses that of all gifts presented by the devas.
His manifesting great spiritual powers everywhere

to appear before the many is so much more superior in its power that
it exceeds them by orders of magnitude so incalculably many times,
if one wished to calculate this through pondering it, one would then
become confused and discouraged and unable to comprehend it.

The works done by the greatly wise ones dwelling on this ground
as they raise up and set down each step
are such that not even any of the other bodhisattvas
dwelling on the ninth ground

could ever be able to fathom them.
How much the less might they be known by any other being,
including even any other *śrāvaka*-disciple or *pratyekabuddha*
throughout the three periods of time.

As he dwells herein, all buddhas reveal to him
the phenomena associated with all-knowledge
and cause him to possess a penetrating comprehension
and unobstructed knowledge of the three periods of time.

They reveal to him the quiescence of the Dharma realm,
and reveal too all of their different sorts of transformations
throughout all worlds
in the midst of all types of beings

wherein all the dharmas practiced
involve profound, subtle, hidden, and sublime phenomena.
It is in this way that all of the Buddha's meritorious qualities
are sequentially revealed to him so that he is caused to know them.

正體字

534b17‖	菩薩住此地	能以大供具
534b18‖	供養十方佛	遍滿一切方
534b19‖	一切諸世間	所有眾生類
534b20‖	其餘諸供具	皆所不能及
534b21‖	智者住此地	皆能破一切
534b22‖	無明諸闇冥	開示以佛道
534b23‖	如自在天王	光滅[4]眾熱惱
534b24‖	佛子智光明	滅眾惱亦爾
534b25‖	住是地[5]皆作	三界自在王
534b26‖	通達諸智慧	善以三乘化
534b27‖	能於一念中	得無量三昧
534b28‖	能見十方佛	其數亦如是
534b29‖	金剛藏菩薩	告諸大士言
534c01‖	我今略解說	十地妙行已
534c02‖	若廣演說者	千億劫不盡
534c03‖	是則名清淨	諸大菩薩地
534c04‖	為得佛智故	住於此地中
534c05‖	安住不[6]移動	猶如大山王
534c06‖	初地具一切	經書諸[7]伎術
534c07‖	猶如雪山[8]王	積聚眾藥草

简体字

菩萨住此地，	能以大供具，
供养十方佛，	遍满一切方；
一切诸世间，	所有众生类，
其余诸供具，	皆所不能及。
智者住此地，	皆能破一切，
无明诸闇冥，	开示以佛道。
如自在天王，	光灭众热恼，
佛子智光明，	灭众恼亦尔。
住是地皆作，	三界自在王，
通达诸智慧，	善以三乘化，
能于一念中，	得无量三昧，
能见十方佛，	其数亦如是。”
金刚藏菩萨，	告诸大士言：
“我今略解说，	十地妙行已；
若广演说者，	千亿劫不尽！
是则名清净，	诸大菩萨地。
为得佛智故，	住于此地中，
安住不移动，	犹如大山王。
初地具一切，	经书诸伎术，
犹如雪山王，	积聚众药草。

The bodhisattva dwelling on this ground
is able, using grand gifts presented as offerings,
to go everywhere throughout all of the directions,
making offerings to the Buddhas of the ten directions,

presenting such gifts in offering
that all of the other gifts presented by any type of being
in any world
remain entirely unable to rival them.

The wise one who dwells on this ground
is in every case able to dispel
the darkness of every sort of ignorance
while offering instruction in the path of the Buddha.

In this, he is comparable to the Maheśvara Heaven King
whose radiance extinguishes the afflictions of the multitudes,
for the extinguishing of the many sorts of afflictions
by the wisdom light of this son of the Buddha is much the same.

Those dwelling on this ground may all become
sovereignly independent kings within the three realms of existence
who, possessed of deeply penetrating wisdom,
are skilled in using the Three Vehicles in their teaching.

They are able in the space of but a single mind-moment
to acquire incalculably many samādhis
and are able to see the buddhas of the ten directions
in just as many numbers.

Vajragarbha Bodhisattva
informed all of those great eminences, saying,
"I have now concluded this general explanation
of the marvelous practices that take place on these ten grounds.

Were one to attempt an expansive explanation,
one could never finish it even in a thousand *koṭis* of kalpas.
These then are what constitute
the pure grounds of all of the great bodhisattvas.

In order to acquire the wisdom of the Buddha,
one dwells on these grounds,
securely abiding there, unmoving,
like the great king of mountains.

On the first ground, one becomes completely equipped
with the classical texts and all of the culture's skills and arts,
and, in this, one is comparable to the Snow Mountain King
on which all of the many types of herbs grow in abundance.

正體字

534c08‖ 持戒及多聞　在於二地中
534c09‖ 猶如香山[*]王　集諸一切香
534c10‖ 如軻梨羅山　多積諸寶花
534c11‖ 明地集聞智　其喻亦如是
534c12‖ 焰地多積[9]聚　道法寶不壞
534c13‖ 如仙聖山中　善寂人不少
534c14‖ 五地諸神通　無能得及者
534c15‖ 如由乾陀[10]山　夜叉神不少
534c16‖ 六地善分別　諸果無窮盡
534c17‖ 猶如馬耳山　諸果無有量
534c18‖ 七地中大慧　無有能及者
534c19‖ 如尼民陀山　諸龍王不少
534c20‖ 住於八地中　自在智無量
534c21‖ 如斫迦羅山　多心自在者
534c22‖ 九地心清淨　說法無障礙
534c23‖ 猶如眾相山　阿修羅不少
534c24‖ 十地中諸佛　功德無窮盡
534c25‖ 如須彌山王　多諸天神眾
534c26‖ 又復初地中　發於廣大願
534c27‖ 二地持戒品　三地行功德

简体字

持戒及多闻，　在于二地中，
犹如香山王，　集诸一切香。
如轲梨罗山，　多积诸宝华，
明地集闻智，　其喻亦如是。
焰地多积聚，　道法宝不坏，
如仙圣山中，　善寂人不少。
五地诸神通，　无能得及者，
如由乾陀山，　夜叉神不少。
六地善分别，　诸果无穷尽，
犹如马耳山，　诸果无有量。
七地中大慧，　无有能及者，
如尼民陀山，　诸龙王不少。
住于八地中，　自在智无量，
如斫迦罗山，　多心自在者。
九地心清净，　说法无障碍，
犹如众相山，　阿修罗不少。
十地中诸佛，　功德无穷尽，
如须弥山王，　多诸天神众。
又复初地中，　发于广大愿；
二地持戒品；　三地行功德；

In one's observance of moral precepts and in one's extensive learning,
one abides on the second ground
in a way comparable to the Fragrance Mountain King
on which all varieties of incenses are found gathered together there.

And just as on the Khadira Mountain King,
the many sorts of precious flowers are found abundantly together,
on the Blazing Brilliance Ground, one gathers learning and wisdom
in a way that is comparable to this.

On the Ground of Blazing Brilliance, one extensively gathers together
the indestructible Dharma jewels of the path
and becomes comparable there to the Mountain of Rishis and Āryas
where those skilled in realization of quiescence are never rare.

On the fifth ground, one's spiritual superknowledges
become of a sort that no one is able to rival
and such that make one compare to the Yugaṃdhara Mountain King
wherein the *yakṣas* and spirits are never rare.

On the sixth ground, one becomes skillful in distinguishing
all of the endless number of fruitions
and, in this, one becomes comparable to the Horse Ear Mountain
whereon all the varieties of fruits are found in countless numbers.

On the seventh ground, one's great wisdom
becomes such that no one is able to rival them
and, in this, one becomes comparable to Nimindhara Mountain
whereon the dragon kings are never rare.

When dwelling on the eighth ground,
one's sovereign masteries and knowledge become incalculable
and one becomes comparable then to Cakravāda Mountain whereon
there are many whose minds are possessed of sovereign mastery.

On the ninth ground, one's mind is purified
and one becomes unimpeded in expounding on Dharma
in a manner comparable to Manifold Features Mountain
whereon the *asuras* dwelling there are never rare.

The meritorious qualities of buddhas
acquired by one dwelling on the tenth ground are inexhaustible
and comparable then to Sumeru Mountain King
whereon there is a congregation of many deva spirits.

Moreover, on the first ground,
one brings forth the vast vows.
On the second, one upholds all classes of moral precepts.
On the third ground, one cultivates the meritorious qualities.

正體字

534c28‖ 第四地專一　五地眾妙事
534c29‖ 六地甚深相　七地廣大心
535a01‖ 八地中種種　莊嚴諸神通
535a02‖ 九地思妙智　能過一切世
535a03‖ 十地能受持　諸佛大法雨
535a04‖ 菩薩行大海　難動不可盡
535a05‖ 發心出世間　得入於初地
535a06‖ 二地淨持戒　三地修諸禪
535a07‖ 四地道行淨　五練方便慧
535a08‖ 六因緣莊嚴　七深方便慧
535a09‖ 八到琉璃幢　九地行眾生
535a10‖ 一切險難處　智慧光普照
535a11‖ 十地受智職　猶如國王許
535a12‖ 如是次第淨　菩提心妙寶
535a13‖ 十方諸世界　所有微塵數
535a14‖ 可於一念中　計知其多少
535a15‖ 可以一毛頭　數知於虛空
535a16‖ 諸佛大功德　無量不可盡

简体字

第四地专一；　五地众妙事；
六地甚深相；　七地广大心；
八地中种种，　庄严诸神通；
九地思妙智，　能过一切世；
十地能受持，　诸佛大法雨。
菩萨行大海，　难动不可尽，
发心出世间，　得入于初地；
二地净持戒；　三地修诸禅；
四地道行净；　五练方便慧；
六因缘庄严；　七深方便慧；
八到琉璃幢；　九地行众生；
一切险难处，　智慧光普照，
十地受智职，　犹如国王许。
如是次第净，　菩提心妙宝，
十方诸世界，　所有微尘数，
可于一念中，　计知其多少，
可以一毛头，　数知于虚空。
诸佛大功德，　无量不可尽！”

On the fourth ground, one develops singular focus.
On the fifth ground, one accomplishes many marvelous works.
On the sixth ground, it is characterized by extreme profundity.
On the seventh ground, one is possessed of the vast mind.

On the eighth ground, one practices all manner of adornments
and brings forth the spiritual superknowledges.
On the ninth ground, one's thought possesses such sublime wisdom
that it exceeds that present anywhere in the world.

On the tenth ground, one becomes able to take in and retain
the great Dharma rain sent down by all buddhas.
Hence the great sea of this bodhisattva's practices
is unshakeable and inexhaustible.

When one brings forth the initial resolve and transcends the world,
one succeeds then in entering the first ground.
On the second ground, one upholds the moral precepts purely.
On the third ground, one cultivates the *dhyāna* absorptions.

On the fourth ground, one's path practices become purified.
On the fifth, one trains in skillful means and wisdom.
On the sixth, one uses causes and conditions in adorning practice.
On the seventh, one employs profound skillful means and wisdom.

On the eighth, one reaches the top of the lapis lazuli pillar.
On the ninth ground one's practice is with regard to beings wherein
one addresses all of their hazardous entangling difficulties
and the light of one's wisdom shines forth everywhere.

On the tenth, one receives the consecration of one's knowledge
comparable to the certifying endorsement bestowed by the King.
In this way, one sequentially purifies
the marvelous jewel of one's bodhi resolve.

Even if, in the space of but a single thought,
one might be able to calculate and know the number
of all the atoms
throughout all worlds of the ten directions,

and even if, using the point of but a single hair,
one could measure all of empty space, one would still find
that the vast number of all buddhas' meritorious qualities herein
are so measurelessly numerous as to be utterly inexhaustible.

正體字

535a17‖ 說是十住經時。自在天王。及諸天眾。解脫月
535a18‖ 菩薩。及諸菩薩。一切世間。皆大歡喜。信受奉
535a19‖ 行
535a20‖ 十住經卷[1]第四

简体字

说是十住经时，自在天王，及诸天众，解脱月菩萨及诸菩萨，一切世间皆大欢喜，信受奉行。

乾隆大藏经・大乘华严部・十住经

Once this Ten Grounds Sutra had been completely expounded, the Maheśvara Heaven King, that entire assembly of devas, Liberation Moon Bodhisattva, all of the other bodhisattvas, and those residing in the all worlds were all filled with great and joyous delight, and, imbued with faith, they accepted and upheld its teachings in practice.

The End of the Ten Grounds Sutra

Translation Endnotes

1. The Later Qin (384-417) was a state of the Qiang ethnicity of the Sixteen Kingdoms during the Chinese Jin dynasty (265-420). It has been referred to as one of a number of "barbarian" dynasties because it was founded by an ethnic Qiang ruler who took on a Chinese dynastic name to describe his 33-year reign over a portion of northern China.
2. Kumārajīva (344-413 CE).
3. Kucha was an ancient Silk Road Buddhist kingdom on the northern edge of the Taklamakan Desert. Its location corresponds to Aksu Prefecture in China's Xinjiang Province.
4. *"pramuditā bhūmi."*
5. Although the Chinese references "wisdom" (*zhihui* / 智慧) in two places in this passage, DSBC references "knowledge" (*jñāna*): *"sarvab odhisattvajñānaviṣayagocarapratilabdhavihāribhiḥ, sarvatathāgatajñānaviṣ ayapraveśāvatārāpratiprasrabdhagocaraiḥ."*
6. "Clear knowledges" refers here to the "three knowledges" (*trividyā*): 1) The remembrance of previous lives (*pūrvavanivāsānusmṛti*); 2) Knowledge of beings' rebirth destinies (*cyutyupapattijñāna*); and 3) Knowledge of the destruction of the contaminants or "taints" (*āsravakṣaya*).
7. The four bases of psychic power (*catvāra ṛddhi-pāda*) are: zeal (*chanda*); vigor (*vīrya*); [concentration of] mind/thought (*citta*); and reflective or investigative consideration, examination, or imagination (*mīmāṃsā*).
8. The "wheel of Dharma" or "Dharma wheel" (*dharmacakra*) refers to the eight-spoked wheel emblematic of the Buddha's teaching of the eight-fold path of the Āryas or "Noble Ones" consisting of right views, right thought or intention, right speech, right physical action, right livelihood, right effort, right mindfulness, and right meditative absorption (*samādhi*).
9. A *mahāsattva* is a "great bodhisattva," one who has practiced the bodhisattva path for countless kalpas.
10. Per DSBC, the Sanskrit names of these bodhisattva *mahāsattvas*, (37 in BB and KB, 38 in BR, 39 in SA, SD and the Sanskrit) are:

    Vajragarbha, Ratnagarbha, Padmagarbha, Śrīgarbha, Padmaśrīgarbha, Ādityagarbha, Sūryagarbha, Kṣitigarbha, Śaśivimalagarbha, Sarvavyūhālaṃkārapratibhāsasaṃdarśanagarbha, Jñānavairocanagarbha, Ruciraśrīgarbha, Candanaśrīgarbha, Puṣpaśrīgarbha, Kusumaśrīgarbha, Utpalaśrīgarbha, Devaśrīgarbha, Puṇyaśrīgarbha,

Anāvaraṇajñānaviśuddhigarbha, Guṇaśrīgarbha, Nārāyaṇaśrīgarbha, Amalagarbha, Vimalagarbha, Vicitrapratibhānālaṃkāragarbha, Mahāraśmijālāvabhāsagarbha, Vimalaprabhāsaśrītejorājagarbha, Sarvalakṣaṇapratimaṇḍita-viśuddhiśrīgarbha, Vajrārciḥśrīvatsālaṃkāragarbha, Jyotirjvalanārciḥśrīgarbha, Nakṣatrarājaprabhāvabhāsagarbha, Gaganakośānāvaraṇajñānagarbha, Anāvaraṇasvaramaṇḍala-madhuranirghoṣagarbha, Dhāraṇīmukhasarvajagatpraṇidhi-saṃdhāraṇagarbha, Sāgaravyūhagarbha, Meruśrīgarbha, Sarvaguṇaviśuddhigarbha, Tathāgataśrīgarbha, Buddhaśrīgarbha, and Vimukticandra.

11. Although the Chinese specifies "wisdom" (*zhihui* / 智慧) here, DSBC references "knowledge" (*jñāna*): "***jñāna****vairocanagarbha*."

12. The numerical descriptors: "measureless" (*aparimāṇa* = 106th level), "boundless" (*aparyanta* = 108th level), "inconceivable" (*acintya* = 116th level), and "indescribable" (*atulya* = 114th level) represent a specific nearly unimaginably large number described in Chapter Thirty, "Asaṃkhyeyas," of the Flower Adornment Sutra wherein each of those numbers is defined as being the square of the immediately previous number the first of which is a *lakṣa* (100,000).

13. Although the Sanskrit refers to this samādhi as "the bodhisattva samādhi known as 'the light of the Great Vehicle' (*mahāyānaprabhāsaṃ nāma bodhisattvasamādhiṃ*)," this may be a later textual modification of the text, for both KB and SA refer to it as "the great wisdom light samādhi."

14. A *koṭi* is a number that is defined in the Flower Adornment Sutra Chapter Thirty as the product of multiplying a *lakṣa* (100,000) by a *lakṣa*. Hence it equals 10,000,000, i.e. ten million.

15. "Rocana" is the name exclusively used to refer to Śākyamuni Buddha's "reward body" (*saṃboghakāya*). Both the DSBC Sanskrit and SA refer instead here to "Vairocana," a name that is sometimes used to refer to Śākyamuni Buddha's reward body, but is also used to refer to his "Dharma body" (*dharmakāya*).

16. Although the Chinese specifies "wisdom" here (*zhihui* / 智慧)," DSBC references not *prajñā*, but rather the word more commonly rendered as "knowledge" (*jñāna*): "*puṇya****jñāna****viśeṣeṇa*."

17. As above, DSBC specifies not *prajñā*, but rather *jñāna*: "*jñānabhūmyavatāraṇāya*."

18. "Contaminants" here translates the slightly ambiguous pre-Buddhist Jain term *āsrava*, translated into Chinese as "flows" (漏). The allusion is to the defiling influence (read "influents") of either three or four factors, as follows: 1) sensual desire (*kāma*); 2) [craving for] becoming

(*bhāva*), i.e. the craving for continued existence; 3) ignorance (*avidyā*), i.e. delusion; 4) views (*dṛṣṭi*) This fourth type is not included in some listings. Often-encountered alternate translations include "taints," "outflows," "influxes," and "fluxes."

19. In some texts including this one, the KJ and KB translation teams very often or nearly always used *xing* (性), usually translated as "nature," to translate the Sanskrit *dhātu*, "realm." This is just such a case. This fact is easily deduced by comparisons of their translations into Chinese with the surviving Sanskrit materials and the many parallel translations by other translators.

20. This is another instance in which the KB translation team chose to use *xing* (性), usually translated as "nature," to translate the Sanskrit *dhātu*, "realm." DSBC has "*dharmadhātusuparyavadāpanāya*."

    As a Buddhist technical term, "Dharma realm" or "dharma realm," *dharma-dhātu*, has at least several levels of meaning, of which this endnoted instance refers to the second of the three listed below:

    1) At the most granular level, "dharma realm" refers to one of the eighteen sense realms, dharmas as "objects of mind" (*dharma-āyatana*);
    2) In the most cosmically and metaphysically vast sense, "Dharma realm" refers in aggregate to all conventionally-existent phenomena and the universally pervasive noumenal "true suchness" (*tathatā*) that underlies and characterizes all of those phenomena. In this sense, it is identical with the "Dharma body" (*dharma-kāya*);
    3) As a classifying term, "dharma realm" is used to distinguish realms of existence (as in the ten dharma realms consisting of the realms of buddhas, bodhisattvas, *śrāvaka* disciples, *pratyekabuddhas*, devas, *asuras*, humans, animals, hungry ghosts, hell-dwellers) or metaphysical modes of existence (as in the "four dharma realms" of the Huayan hermeneutic tradition that speaks of: a] the dharma realm of the "noumenal" [synonymous with emptiness or *śūnyatā*]; b] the dharma realm of the "phenomenal"; c] the dharma realm of the unimpeded interpenetration of the phenomenal and the noumenal; and d] the dharma realm of the unimpeded interpenetration of all phenomena with all other phenomena in a manner that resonates somewhat with quantum entanglement and non-locality).

21. I emend the Taisho text here to correct an apparent graphic-similarity scribal error, doing so by substituting the clearly intended *yu* (與) character found in most other editions for the obviously erroneous *shi* (示) character found in the Taisho edition of the KB text. BB, BR, SA, SD, and the DSBC Sanskrit are unanimous in corroborating

the first component in this list of ten enhancements bestowed on Vajragarbha by the Buddhas of the ten directions as the bestowal of an unsurpassable body. Absent this emendation, KB would be completely out of step with all of the Sanskrit and Chinese analogue editions of this ten grounds text, none of which support its reading here.

22. Although the Chinese references "wisdom" here (*zhihui* / 智慧)," DSBC references not *prajñā*, but rather the word more commonly rendered as "knowledge" (*jñāna*): *"suviśobhitajñānavibhaktipraveśatāṃ ca."*
23. *"suviniścitamatikauśalyatāṃ."*
24. *"tathāgatavaiśāradyānavalīnatāṃ."*
25. The DSBC Sanskrit (*pratisaṃvid*) makes it clear that "unimpeded knowledges" is intended to refer to the four types of unimpeded knowledge discussed at great length later in the text in the explanation of the ninth ground. Briefly, they are unimpeded knowledge of Dharma, meaning, language, and eloquence.
26. DSBC: *"supariśodhitādhyāśayatayā ca,"* i.e. "has well purified his *higher* resolute intentions (or 'higher aspirations')."
27. Although the Chinese references "wisdom" here (*zhihui* / 智慧)," DSBC references not *prajñā*, but rather the word more commonly rendered as "knowledge" (*jñāna*): *"svavadātajñānamaṇḍalatayā ca."*
28. *"susaṃbhṛtasaṃbhāratayā ca."*
29. "Resolute faith," *xinjie* (信解), which corresponds to the Sanskrit *adhimukti* is a term that generally refers to confidently held, rationally based inclinations toward wholesome objective conditions or path-associated endeavors. That said, this term is *also* used to refer to sentient beings' strongly held habitual interests or predilections toward the whole range of wholesome, unwholesome, or karmically neutral objective conditions or endeavors, hence it is incumbent on the teaching bodhisattva to be comprehensively cognizant of all of these different types of "resolute dispositions" along with the most skillful teaching stratagems to adopt in teaching the beings who possess them.
30. "Dhāraṇīs" refers primarily to formulae that constitute a kind of pronunciation-dependent Sanskrit code language consisting of Sanskrit syllables which may or may not have a translatable meaning but which can never be translated into another language without destroying their primary functions which are of primarily two types: a) to facilitate the remembrance and comprehensive retention of teachings and their meanings even for many lifetimes; and b) when more-or-less equivalent to mantras, to protect the practitioner

or other vulnerable beings from danger, the manifestation of karmic obstacles, and demonic influences.

Dhāraṇīs may also facilitate the bodhisattva's unproduced-dharmas patience through which he can remain in *saṃsāra* for countless kalpas as he continues to work for the spiritual liberation of all other beings. They may also be used to invoke the manifestation of beneficial supernormal powers either in conjunction with or independent of *mudras* (hand postures) and/or visualizations.

31. *"dharmadhātujñānamudrāsumudritatayā ca."*

32. Per DSBC, the names of the *bhūmis* are: *pramuditā; vimalā; prabhākarī; arciṣmatī; sudurjayā; abhimukhī; dūraṃgamā; acalā; sādhumatī; dharmameghā.*

33. This is the only place in the KB translation that the translation of the name of the ninth ground is "the Excellent Intelligence Ground" (善慧地). Everywhere else, it is rendered as "the Sublime Goodness Ground" (妙善地).

34. Although the Chinese references "wisdom" here (*zhihui* / 智慧)," DSBC references not *prajñā*, but rather the word more commonly rendered as "knowledge" (*jñāna*): *"acintyamidaṃ bhavanto jinaputrāḥ sthānaṃ yadidaṃ bhūmijñānamiti."*

35. For the most part, throughout the text, in the introductory and reiterative verses for this and most other grounds, for each four-line Sanskrit gatha, the KB Chinese translation team employs as few as two or as many as six, eight, or even more verse lines to translate the ideas contained in each gatha. In any case, it is not always possible to precisely map the Chinese line-by-line onto the much later and somewhat "evolved" gathas found in the extant Sanskrit editions. Although the ideas are mostly all present in both editions, the exact content and sequencing often differ somewhat. To aid correlation with the Sanskrit edition, I have appended the verse number of the DSBC Sanskrit (in reduced font bold curly braces) to the last line of each equivalent KB verse.

36. Again, although the Chinese references "wisdom" here (*zhihui* / 智慧)," DSBC records not *prajñā*, but rather the word more commonly rendered as "knowledge" (*jñāna*): *"buddhajñānaṃ."*

37. "Resolute intentions" (otherwise rendered simply as "intentions") here translates the Chinese *shenxin* (深心), one of KB's translations of the Sanskrit *āśaya*.

38. The "provisions for the realization of the path" (*bodhisaṃbhāra*) are the requisites for realization of buddhahood. These are often explained

as consisting of karmic merit on the one hand (*puṇya*) and "knowledge" or "wisdom" (*jñāna*) on the other.

39. "*mātṛkā*."

40. An *asaṃkhyeya* is an exceedingly large number the definition for which varies so widely in Buddhist texts that I have seen definitions ranging between 10 to the fifty-first power and 10 to a power the exponent for which is transcribed with 35 placeholders (i.e. exponent = 74,436,000,000,000,000,000,000,000,000,000,000).

41. Vasubandhu explains the comparison of the Buddha to empty space thus: "Again, as for 'like empty space,' [just as empty space cannot be stained by anything at all, so too, the Buddha] cannot be stained by worldly dharmas, this because all habitual karmic propensities associated with ignorance and afflictions have been extinguished." (復如虛空世間法不能染。無明煩惱習氣滅故。[131c05-06])

42. Again, although the Chinese references "wisdom" here (*zhihui* / 智慧)," DSBC references not *prajñā*, but rather the word more commonly rendered as "knowledge" (*jñāna*): "*jñānābhinirhāramunīndraveditam*."

43. DR, SA, BR, SD, and DSBC (*śakuna*) all specify "bird." (BB follows KB exactly).

44. This is another reference to the provisions required for the realization of bodhi (*bodhisaṃbhāra*) usually explained as consisting primarily of merit and knowledge or wisdom. DSBC: "*susaṃbhṛtasaṃbhārāṇāṃ*."

45. "*udārādhimuktisamanvāgatānāṃ*."

46. It appears that the two factors reflected here in the KB translation are "*adhyāśaya*" (直心) and "*āśaya*" (深心), presented in reversed order from what we now find in DSBC: "*āśayādhyāśayopastabdhaṃ*."

47. DSBC: "*svayaṃbhūjñānānukūlaṃ*."

48. KB and BB identically only retain nine factors here whereas most other analogue editions have ten. DSBC gives: "*pramuditāyāṃ bodhisattvabhūmau sthito bodhisattvaḥ prāmodyabahulo bhavati prasādabahulaḥ prītibahula utplāvanābahula udagrībahula utsībahula utsāhabahulo 'saṃrambhabahulo 'vihiṃsābahulo 'krodhabahulo bhavati*."

49. Again, although the Chinese references "wisdom" here (*zhihui* / 智慧)," DSBC references not *prajñā*, but rather the word more commonly rendered as "knowledge" (*jñāna*): "*sarvatathāgatajñānapraveśa*."

50. Although the Chinese references "wisdom" here (*zhihui* / 智慧)," DSBC references the word more commonly rendered as "knowledge" (*jñāna*): "*jñānabhūmeḥ*."

51. Bhikkhu Bodhi points out that this same list appears in the Pali (albeit in slightly different order and with mild differences in

the interpretation of two of the five points). See his translation of *Numerical Discourses* 9:5, p. 1255. The most exhaustive of all treatments of this list appears to be Nāgārjuna's discussion of it in his Ten Grounds Sutra commentary, for which see my complete translation of that entire text under separate cover.

52. "Perception of a self" here reflects the extant DSBC Sanskrit: *"ātmasaṃjñā."* (The Chinese Buddhist canon in general and perhaps the KB translation team in particular often employ 相, "sign," as an abbreviation for the graphically similar 想, "perception," sometimes leading to confusion in the works of translators unaware of this fact.

53. Ibid.

54. *"prasādabahulatayā."* BHSD lists "faith" as the primary definition, although MW doesn't mention it at all and prefers definitions along the lines of "purity" and "tranquility" reflected here, hence the apparent discrepancy between KB and SA translations. BB follows KB precisely here, whilst SD similarly prefers "abundant realization of purity" (多證淨) and Bodhiruci falls somewhat farther afield with "abundant reverence" (多恭敬).

55. *"adhimuktiviśuddhyā."*

56. I emend the reading of the text here by preferring the variant reading in other editions and parallel texts, thereby correcting an obvious scribal error that inserted an echoed 觀 ("to contemplate") where there should be 聞 ("to learn" or "to hear").

57. To correct a fairly definite graphic-similarity scribal error, I emend the reading of the *Taisho* text here by preferring the Gong edition's *bao* (寶), "jewel," to the *Taisho* edition's *shi* (實), "real." The DSBC Sanskrit (*ratnopamacittotpādātṛptābhinirhāratayā*) corroborates the correctness of this emendation.

58. In his Treatise on the Ten Grounds Sutra, (*Daśabhūmika-vibhāṣā* / 十住毘婆沙論 [T no. 1521]), Nāgārjuna devotes all of Chapter Five (T26n1521_p30b10-35a21) to an extensive explanation of the following ten vows, for an English translation of which see my translation of this entire treatise.

59. DSBC (*sarvajñajñānapratiṣṭhāpanāya*) is more like "...to become established in the cognition of all-knowledge."

60. To correct an apparent scribal error, I emend the reading of the *Taisho* text here by preferring the SYMG editions' *jin* (盡), "complete, entire" to the *Taisho* edition's *jing* (淨), "pure." (None of the other editions of this text or its analogues in BB or SA support the Taisho reading here.)

61. DSBC doesn't specify "'wise' beings" so much as "beings possessed of knowledge": *"apramāṇajñānākarasattva."*
62. DSBC doesn't specify "wisdom," but rather "knowledge": *"sahaghoṣo dāhārajñānānugamāya."*
63. Again, DSBC specifies "knowledge" rather than "wisdom": *"mahājñāna."*
64. Again, DSBC specifies "knowledge" rather than "wisdom": *"mahājñānābhijñābhinirhārāya."*
65. DSBC specifies "knowledge" (*jñāna*) rather than "wisdom."
66. DSBC specifies "knowledge" (*jñāna*) rather than "wisdom."
67. DSBC specifies "knowledge" (*jñāna*) rather than "wisdom."
68. DSBC specifies "knowledge" (*jñāna*) rather than "wisdom."
69. The following list of ten mental qualities is present with minor variations in BB, SA, and KB, but is missing seven of these mental qualities in SD and eight of these mental qualities in BR and the (very late) surviving Sanskrit editions of the Ten Grounds Sutra.
70. DSBC lists these expressions of faith as follows:

    "tathāgatānām arhatāṃ samyaksaṃbuddhānāṃ pūrvāntacaryābhinirhārapraveśaṃ pāramitāsamudāgamaṃ bhūmipariniṣpattiṃ vaiśeṣikatāṃ balapariniṣpattiṃ vaiśāradyaparipūrim āveṇikabuddhadharmāsaṃhāryatām acintyāṃ buddhadharmatām anantamadhyaṃ tathāgataviṣayābhinirhāram aparimāṇajñānānugataṃ tathāgatagocarānupraveśaṃ phalapariniṣpattim abhiśraddadhāti."
71. DSBC specifies "knowledge" (*jñāna*) rather than "wisdom."
72. This is a reference to the four inverted views (*viparyāsa*):
    1) Viewing as pleasurable what is in fact conducive to suffering;
    2) Viewing as permanent what is in fact impermanent;
    3) Viewing as lovely what is in fact unlovely by virtue of its impurity;
    4) Viewing as "self" what is in fact devoid of anything constituting an inherently and enduringly existent self.
73. These are collectively referred to as "the four floods" (*ogha*).
74. "Name-and-form" is a reference to the five aggregates of mentality and physicality that are generally construed by unenlightened beings to constitute an inherently existent "self." Specifically, they are: form, feeling, perception, karmic formative factors (*saṃskāras*), and consciousness.
75. "The six sense bases" is a reference to the six sense faculties: eye, ear, nose, tongue, body, and intellectual mind faculty. They are

commonly metaphorically referred to as a village wherein beings falsely impute the existence of an inherently existent self.

76. DSBC specifies "knowledge" (*jñāna*) rather than "wisdom."

77. Where KB has this "intensely diligent cultivation of irreversible resolve" (精勤修行。心不懈退。), SA has "Diligently cultivates irreversible renunciaton" (勤修出離。不退不轉。) The DSBC Sanskrit has "*naiṣkramyacārī avivartya*" for which BHSD foregrounds as definitions for "*naiṣkramya*": "departure from the world, renunciation of worldly things," and "renunciation as regards desires (lusts)" whilst Conze's MDPL has: "leaving home."

78. DSBC gives this entire list as: "*tadyathā - śraddhā karuṇā maitrī tyāgaḥ khedasahiṣṇutā śāstrajñatā lokajñatā hryapatrāpyaṃ dhṛtibalādhānaṃ tathāgatapūjopasthānamiti.*"

79. Although the phrasing of the Chinese text might lead one to think these are two separate dharmas, I follow QLSC in combining these two subcomponents as a single grounds-purifying dharma. The surviving Sanskrit for this tenth member of the list (per DSBC) is: "*tathāgatapūjopasthānamiti.*"

80. The remaining two means of attraction are "beneficial actions and joint endeavors."

81. DSBC specifies "knowledge" (*jñāna*) rather than "wisdom" in both places in this sentence.

82. DSBC specifies "knowledge" (*jñāna*) rather than "wisdom."

83. DSBC specifies "knowledge" (*jñāna*) rather than "wisdom."

84. DSBC makes no mention of "wisdom" here, but rather only specifies "the great city of all-knowledge" (*sarvajñatāmahānagara*).

85. To correct an apparent graphic-similarity scribal error, I emend the reading of the *Taisho* text here by preferring the SYMG editions' *da* ( ), "great," to the *Taisho* edition's *bu* ( ), "bestow," SD, BR, and the DSBC Sanskrit (*mahātyāgena*) all support the emendation.

86. I emend the text with the addition of "kalpas" based on the evidence provided by the numerous analogue editions of this text (including the Sanskrit) from which it is clear that the KB text is either corrupted or else the presence of the word was intended to be understood as implicit in this passage as it occurs in the descriptions of the first, second, and fifth ground. The other editions of this ten grounds text (both in sutras [BB and SA] and independently-circulating editions [Bodhiruci, etc.]) clarify that "any number of hundreds of thousands of myriads of *koṭis* of *nayutas*" is intended to refer to the number of kalpas one might exhaust in fruitlessly attempting to count the

number of manifestations the bodhisattva might bring forth when resorting to the power of vows.

87. To correct an apparent graphic-similarity scribal error, I emend the reading of the *Taisho* text here by preferring the Gong edition's *bao* (寶), "jewel," to the *Taisho* edition's *shi* (實), "genuine." SD, the DSBC Sanskrit (*sahajāticittaratanaṃ*), BB, and SA all support the emendation.

88. DSBC specifies "knowledge" (*jñāna*) rather than "wisdom."

89. I insert "paths" here because the last character in this reiterative verse line, "variations" (種) is most definitely intended to echo this entire line in the prose section: "Tenth, the varieties of worldly paths, the varieties of Dharma paths, and the varieties of paths of knowledge cannot end." (十世間道種法道種智慧道種不可盡。[501c24-25])

90. DSBC specifies "knowledge" (*jñāna*) rather than "wisdom."

91. "... should bring forth ten types of resolute intentions" = DSBC: "*tasya daśa cittāśayāḥ pravartante.*"

92. For these ten "resolute intentions" (*cittāśaya*), DSBC gives: *ṛjvāśaya* (= *ārjava?*), *mṛdvāśaya, karmaṇyāśaya, damāśaya, śamāśaya, kalyāṇāśaya, asaṃsṛṣṭāśaya, anapekṣāśaya, udārāśaya, māhātmyāśaya.*

93. Although it might seem that KB is somewhat anomalous in rendering *udāra* as "happy" (*kuai*快) here, Śiladharma gives us much the same thing with his "sublimely happy" (*miao yile*妙意樂), so, even though dictionaries don't seem to directly reflect this nuance for *udāra*, it may well have been one of its peripheral connotations in the Sanskrit Buddhist literature of the time. What's more, a sort of spontaneous, elevated, and broadly inclusive happiness is indeed a state of mind that often accompanies most of the connotations otherwise associated with *udāra*, which, per MW, includes such attributes as: "high, lofty, exalted, noble, generous, liberal, gentle, munificent, etc."

94. This refers to the avoidance of the ten courses of bad karmic action, namely: killing; taking what is not given; sexual misconduct; false speech; divisive speech; harsh speech; frivolous speech; covetousness; ill will; wrong views.

95. I emend the text here, accepting the variant found in three other editions (直) in place of the default Taisho reading (隨), this because the latter can only be made minimally sensible through forced interpretation.

96. "Frivolous speech" (*saṃbhinna-pralāpa*) refers to idle chatter, lewd speech, etc.

97. For these ten kinds of minds, DSBC gives: "...*hitacittatām utpādayati / sukhacittatāṃ maitracittatāṃ kṛpācittatāṃ dayācittatām anugrahacittatām ārakṣācittatāṃ samacittatām acāryacittatāṃ śāstṛcittatām utpādayati.*"

98. There are four types of *māras* (*catur-māra*) that are often translated elsewhere as "demons" when not directly referencing the celestial *māras*. Those four types of *māras* are: affliction *māras* (*kleśa-māra*), the *māras* of the aggregates (*skandha-māra*), the *māras* of death (*mṛtya-māra*), and celestial *māras* (*deva-putra-māra*).

99. "The view imputing the existence of a true self in association with one's body" corresponds to the Sanskrit *satkāya-dṛṣṭi*.

100. The SA Chinese gives "礬石," the modern translation of which is "aluminite." This does not correspond to the DSBC Sanskrit which specifies "*kāsīsa*," a type of iron oxide. Hence I am compelled to prefer the Sanskrit antecedent term.

101. Again (as explained with respect to this passage as it occurs in the first ground's text), I emend this passage by adding the word "kalpas" based on abundant evidence that its absence in the Chinese is either due to textual corruption or to the assumption that its presence here should be understood as implicit.

102. As with the previous *bhūmi*, DSBC shows "*citta āśaya*" as the antecedent for "resolute intentions" (心).

103. For these ten "resolute intentions" (*cittāśaya*), DSBC gives: *śuddha-cittāśaya, sthira-cittāśaya, nirvic-cittāśaya, avirāga-cittāśaya, avinivarta-cittāśaya, dṛḍha-cittāśaya, uttapta-cittāśaya, atṛpta-cittāśaya, udāra-cittāśaya*, and *māhātmya-cittāśaya*. (The last two correspond precisely to the last two listed for the second *bhūmi*.)

104. It appears that the KB edition is missing one element, perhaps "unequaled" (*atulya*)? DSBC gives this tenfold list as: *acintya, atulya, aprameya, durāsada, asaṃspṛṣṭa, nirupadrava, nirupāyāsa, abhayapuragamanīya, apunarāvṛtti, bahujanaparitrāṇa*.

105. Again, DSBC has "*cittāśaya*" for these ten.

106. DSBC lists these as:

anāthātrāṇāpratiśaraṇacittāśaya;
nityadaridrapratiśaraṇacittāśaya;
rāgadveṣamohāgnisaṃpradīptapratiśaraṇacittāśaya;
bhavacārakāvaruddhapratiśaraṇacittāśaya;
satatasamitaklaśagahenāvṛtaprasuptapratiśaraṇacittāśaya;
vilokanasamarthapratiśaraṇacittāśaya;
kuśaladharmacchandarahitapratiśaraṇacittāśaya;
buddhadharmapramuṣitapratiśaraṇacittāśaya;
saṃsārasrotonuvāhipratiśaraṇacittāśaya;

mokṣopāyapraṇaṣṭapratiśaraṇacittāśaya.

107. DSBC seems to leave out part of this list, but it is complete in Rahder (herein bracketed): "...*paritrātavyāḥ parimocayitavyāḥ [pariśodhayitavyā uttārayitavyā niveśayitavyāḥ pratiṣṭhāpayitavyāḥ] paritoṣayitavyāḥ saṃropayitavyā vinetavyāḥ parinirvāpayitavyā*...." The KB rendering is somewhat variant.

108. Both the BB and KB editions appear to dispense with "non-production" here. (It is retained in SA, BR, SD, and the Sanskrit.) DSBC: "*sa ca sarvadharmayathāvadavabodho nānyatra apracārānutpādacāriṇyāḥ prajñāyāḥ.*"

109. DSBC lists these ten as: "...*dharmārāmo dharmarato dharmapratiśaraṇo dharmanimno dharmapravaṇo dharmaprāgbhāro dharmaparāyaṇo dharmalayano dharmatrāṇo dharmānudharmacārī.*"

110. Here and in four additional instances in the next two paragraphs, I emend the Taisho scribal error (相) to accord with the obviously intended character (想), this in accordance with four alternate editions of the text as well as the very precise testimony of the Indian Buddhist descriptions of these meditation states. (KB's translation team seems at times to use these two characters more or less interchangeably. A particularly obvious case in point is his translation of the Diamond Sutra wherein this idiosyncrasy occurs many times.)

111. DR, BB, SA, SD, and DSBC all indicate that KB's "defilement" and "abandonment of defilement" refer specifically to "desire." For instance DSBC specifies: "*sarāgaṃ cittaṃ sarāgacittamiti yathābhūtaṃ prajānāti | virāgaṃ cittaṃ virāgacittamiti prajānāti.*"

112. The DSBC Sanskrit text clarifies that *xin* (心), otherwise legitimately translated as "minds," in fact refers more specifically to "resolute intentions," "dispositions," "mental intentions," or "inclinations" (*āśaya*).

113. The DSBC Sanskrit, SA, BR, and SD all speak here of only one means of attraction (beneficial action) and only one *pāramitā* (patience). However, BB and KB (the chronologically earlier extant analogue editions) both speak here of two means of attraction (pleasing words and beneficial actions) and two *pāramitās* (patience and vigor).

114. The KB text here leaves out two of the ten types of resolute intention found at the beginning of the third ground's text that this verse is attempting to echo, namely "flourishing brilliance" and "unquenchable zeal" for which it substitutes a single resolute intention not otherwise found on this ground, "the mind capable of withstanding whatever comes." This is a resolute intention that was listed not

on this ground, but rather was listed as the third of the ten resolute intentions set forth at the beginning of the *second* ground.

115. This is a reference to the four immeasurable minds (*apramāṇa-citta*), all of which require identifying with all beings everywhere as equally deserving of kindness, compassion, sympathetic joy, and equanimity.
116. "*dharmālokapraveśa*."
117. KB apparently chose to subsume "resolute intentions" (*āśaya*) within "convictions" (*adhimukti*) in this next to last list component, hence my bracketed emendation. The DSBC Sanskrit text clarifies this ambiguity. It gives us "*udāra-āśaya-adhimukti-dhātu-vicaraṇāloka-praveśena*.")
118. KB here collapses "convictions" (*adhimukti*) into "intentions" (*āśaya*), hence my bracketed emendation. The DSBC Sanskrit text provides the much clearer "*māhātmya-āśaya-adhimukti-dhātu-vicaraṇāloka-praveśena*."
119. "*tadātmakadharma*."
120. "*jñānaparipācakairdharma*."
121. These contemplations are anchored to the four stations of mindfulness focusing on the body, feelings, thought / mind, and dharmas (*catuḥ-smṛty-upasthāna*).
122. This is a summation of the bodhisattva's exercise of the four right efforts (*samyak-pradhāna*).
123. "*vivekaniśritaṃ virāganiśritaṃ nirodhaniśritaṃ vyavasargapariṇataṃ*."
124. This is a summation of the bodhisattva's practice of the four foundations of psychic power.
125. This is a summation of the bodhisattva's practice of the five root faculties.
126. This is a summation of the bodhisattva's practice of the five powers.
127. This is a summation of the bodhisattva's practice of the seven limbs of enlightenment.
128. This is a summation of the bodhisattva's practice of the eight-fold right path, hereby concluding the narration of the bodhisattva's practice of the thirty-seven enlightenment factors.
129. The extant edition of KB's translation of this list follows BB fairly precisely. DR, BB, and KB differ from SA, BR, SD, and the DSBC Sanskrit in their failure to include what constitutes the eighth item in all of those later ten-fold lists: "In order to search for ever more supreme dharmas" (*uttarottara-vaiśeṣika-dharma-parimārgaṇatayā*)."

130. KB and BB do not have a short section found at this point in the text in SA, BR, SD, and the Sanskrit that, per SA reads as follows: "Whenever this bodhisattva observes that there are karmic actions that have been censured by the Tathāgata and are defiled by the afflictions, he entirely relinquishes and abandons them. Whenever he observes that there are karmic actions that accord with the bodhisattva path and have been praised by the Tathāgata, in all such cases he cultivates them." DSBC's corresponding text is:

"sa yānīmāni karmāṇyakaraṇīyāni samyaksaṃbuddhavivarṇitāni saṃkleśopasaṃhitāni, tāni sarveṇa sarvaṃ prajahāti / yāni cemāni karmāṇi karaṇīyāni samyaksaṃbuddhapraśastāni bodhimārgasaṃbhārānukūlāni, tāni samādāya vartate /"

131. *"bodhimārgasaṃbhāra."*

132. KB is virtually identical in this ten-fold list to BB (554a24-26) and somewhat variant from the later mostly similar editions by SA, BR, SD, and the Sanskrit, all of which are mostly mutually consistent as reflected here in DSBC's tenfold list:

"snigdhacittaśca bhavati, maducittaśca karmaṇyacittaśca hitasukhāvahacittaśca aparikliṣṭacittaśca uttarottaraviśeṣaparimārga ṇacittaśca jñānaviśeṣaṇābhilāṣacittaśca sarvajagatparitrāṇacittaśca gurugauravānukūlacittaśca yathāśrutadharmapratipatticittaśca."

133. KB is virtually identical in this list to BB (554a26-29). They both include "implementation of the practice of right concentration." Hence they are somewhat variant from the later mostly similar editions by SA, BR, SD, and the Sanskrit, all of which are quite mutually consistent as reflected here in DSBC's tenfold list:

"... sa kṛtajñaśca bhavati, kṛtavedī ca sūrataśca sukhasaṃvāsaśca ṛjuśca mṛduśca agahanacārī ca nirmāyanirmāṇaśca suvacāśca pradakṣiṇagrāhī ca."

134. The lists of ten types of vigor are generally quite consistent in most of the extant editions with the exception of BB's non-inclusion of the final member of the other lists: "The vigor that distinguishes what is and is not the Path." DSBC gives us:

"aprasrabdhavīryaśca bhavati aparikliṣṭaḥ / apratyudāvartyavīryaśca vipulavīryaśca anantavīryaśca uttaptavīryaśca asamavīryaśca asaṃhāryavīryaśca sarvasattvaparipācanavīryaśca nayānayavibhaktavīryaśca bhavati."

135. *"apramāṇacittāśaya."*

136. *"āśayādhyāśayādhimuktisamatā viśudhyati"* Most editions (BB, KB, DSBC, SD) have not only SA's two-fold "intentions" (*āśaya)* and "resolute faith" (*adhimukti*) but also include "higher aspirations" (*adhyāśaya*) and "impartiality" (*samatā*), thus producing a list of four

elements. BR is slightly ambiguous and appears to include all but "higher aspirations."

137. DSBC: *"satkāyadṛṣṭi."*

138. Here this verse itself and KB even more so radically condense the ninth and tenth members of the ten-fold list opening the discussion of this *bhūmi*: "Ninth, contemplation of the realms of happy [resolute intentions and] resolute convictions; Tenth, contemplation of the realms of magnanimous resolute intentions [and resolute convictions]," the corresponding DSBC Sanskrit for which is:
udārāśayādhimuktidhātu-vicaraṇālokapraveśena ca
māhātmyāśayādhimuktidhātuvicaraṇālokapraveśena.

139. These first two quatrains condense the first ten-fold list ("the ten gateways to Dharma illumination") that opens the initial discussion of this ground.

140. The twelve lines concluding here are a condensation of the second ten-fold list set forth earlier in the discussion of this *bhūmi*, "the ten kinds of knowledge-maturing dharmas."

141. "Relying upon quiescence" here most likely refers to *dhyāna* meditation.

142. The sixteen lines that conclude here summarize the earlier discussion of the bodhisattva's cultivation of the thirty-seven enlightenment factors.

143. The twelve lines concluding here summarize the ten aims behind cultivation of the thirty-seven enlightenment factors that were brought up earlier in the discussion of this fourth ground.

144. *"āśayaviśuddhisamatā."*

145. HH explains this pure and equally regarding mental disposition "toward the mind" as primarily meaning "toward the minds of beings."

146. Although DSBC gives us *"adhyāśaya"* here ("higher aspirations"), this is not supported by any other of the Chinese editions except the very latest one done by Śīladharma in 790 CE who renders this as "especially supreme dispositions / aspirations" (增上意樂). BB, KB, BR, and SA are all clearly translating simply *"āśaya,"* ("resolute intentions" or "intentions").

147. *"saṃvṛtisatya."*

148. *"paramārthasatya."*

149. *"lakṣaṇasatya."*

150. *"vibhāgasatya."*

151. *"nistīraṇasatya."*
152. *"vastusatya."*
153. *"prabhavasatya."*
154. *"kṣayānutpādasatya."*
155. *"mārgajñānāvatārasatya."*
156. *"sarvabodhisattvabhūmikramānusaṃdhiniṣpādanatayā yāvat tathāgatajñānasamudayasatya."*
157. *"ekanayasamavasaraṇātparamārthasatyaṃ prajānāti."*
158. *"sa parasattvānāṃ yathāśayasaṃtoṣaṇātsaṃvṛtisatyaṃ prajānāti."*
159. *"svasāmanyalakṣaṇānubodhāllakṣaṇasatyaṃ prajānāti."*
160. *"dharmavibhāgavyavasthānānubodhādvibhāgasatyaṃ prajānāti."*
161. *"skandhadhātvāyatanavyavasthānānubodhānnistīraṇasatyaṃ prajānāti."*
162. *"cittaśarīraprapīḍanopanipātitatvādvastusatyam."*
163. *"gatisaṃdhisaṃbandhanatvātprabhavasatyam."*
164. *"sarvajvaraparidāhātyantopaśamātkṣayānutpādasatyam."*
165. For this passage, DSBC gives us the following: *"advayānutpādasatyam, advayābhinirhāranmārgajñānāvatārasatyam."*
166. DSBC:

"sarvākārābhisaṃbodhitsarvabodhisattvabhūmikramānusaṃdhiniṣpādanatayā yāvattathāgatajñānasamudayasatyaṃ prajānāti."

167. *"adhimukti."*
168. Although, for easy readability in English, I have herein simplified the manner by which one attempts to represent the particular enumeration given in the text, "countless," "boundless," and *"asaṃkhyeya"* are actually three categories of huge numbers yielding an unimaginably large number arrived at by each of them being used to multiply the immediately following number. These are but three of many Sanskrit numbers defined in the "Asaṃkyeya" chapter of the Floral Adornment Sutra.
169. *"mārāśayagahana."*
170. Although the extant Sanskrit refers here only to a*kuśalavitarka* ("bad initial ideation"), the Chinese texts of most editions (BB, KB, SA, and SD) use the translation for both *vitarka* and *vicāra* ("ideation and mental discursion").
171. All editions seem to vary somewhat, but only slightly. DSBC has:

tatsarvasattvaparitrāṇāyārabhate, sarvasattvahitāya, sarvasattvasukhāya, sarvasattvānukampāyai, sarvasattvānupadravāya, sarvasattvaparimocanāya, sarvasattvānukarṣāya, sarvasattvaprasādanāya, sarvasattvavinayāya, sarvasattvaparinirvāṇāy ārabhate.

172. *"buddhi."*

173. *"jñāna."*

174. *"prajñā."*

175. *"puṇyasaṃbhāra."*

176. *"jñānasaṃbhāra."*

177. *"mahāmaitrīkṛpāsaṃbhāra."*

178. Emendation: 石 in place of 名, this to correct a scribal error involving graphic similarity, the emendation here being supported by four other editions of the KB text (SYMG) as well as by BB, SA, BR, and the dictates of sensibility.

179. Emendation: Following four other editions of the KB text (SYMG), I insert "these dharmas" (此法) after "brings forth" (出).

180. MW defines *musāragalva* as "a kind of coral." Other definitions state that it is a kind of shell or mother-of-pearl.

181. Again (as explained with respect to this passage as it occurs in the first ground's text), I emend this passage by adding the word "kalpas" based on abundant evidence that its absence in the Chinese is either due to textual corruption or to the assumption that its presence here should be understood as implicit.

182. As is often the case with these radically and tersely condensed verse lines, this one can only be made sensible by referring back to information solely available in the main text of this *bhūmi*. For comparison here, we have the following:

    DSBC is equally terse: "... on up to the truth associated with what is unimpeded," (*yāvantanāvaraṇasatya samosaranti* [Rahder footnotes a variant ending the line as *"samāsaranti"*]).

    SA: "...and so on up to the truth of what, for the Tathāgata, is unimpeded," (乃至如來無礙諦). This is clarified as "unimpeded knowledge" by SA's fifth ground text.

    SD: "... on up to truth associated with the unimpeded knowledge of the Buddha," (乃至無礙佛智諦). SD is the only truly clear edition here, for only it can stand on its own without supplementation by information found in the main fifth ground text.

    BB is a complete outlier barely relating in these verse lines to any of the other editions. And of course BR has no verses at all, only the main text of the Sutra itself.

183. Just as in the prose section, so too here in the reiterative verse, I make the following emendation: *shi* (石), "stones," in place of *ming* (名),

"names," this to correct a scribal error involving graphic similarity, the emendation here being supported by four other editions of the KB text as well as by BB, SA, and VB.

184. "Knowing *dharmas are by nature transcendent*" (知法性離) corresponds to DSBC's *"sarvadharmāviviktāḥ"* which infers that all dharmas "are beyond distinctions or discriminations," hence my translation of the Chinese as "transcendent."

185. *"dharmasamatā."*

186. Most extant editions are quite similar but slightly variant in a few list components. The DSBC Sanskrit gives us:

    animitta; alakṣaṇa; anutpāda; ajāta; vivikta; adiviśuddhi; niṣprapañca; anāvyūhānirvyūha; māyāsvapnapratibhāsapratiśrutkodakacandrapratibi mbanirmāṇa; bhāvābhāvādvaya.

187. I emend the text here, substituting *xiang* (相) for the graphically-similar *xiang* (想), this to rectify an obvious scribal error, the emendation being supported here by the reading of the corresponding passage as it appears in BR, SA, and BB. It is, by the way, not the least bit uncommon, in reading the Chinese canon, to find the two characters often employed more-or-less interchangeably with the one as a short-form for the other. This seems to be especially common in translation manuscripts issuing from Kumārajīva's translation bureau.

188. Nāgārjuna provides an extensive discussion of these similes in his Mppu (T25.1509.101c6-105c18 [fasc. 6]).

189. DSBC: *"ānulomikyā kṣāntyā."* (In MDPL, Conze suggests "adaptable patience" for *ānulomikī kṣānti.*)

190. The rather long (6 pages) ensuing discussion of causality more or less follows the listing of "the ten types of sequential and counter-sequential contemplation of the factors involved in conditioned arising" with which the discussion ends.

191. In the following discussion of origination through causes and conditions (*pratitya-samutpāda*), each of the characteristic features associated with the twelve links is italicized to enhance the reader's ease of understanding.

192. DSBC: *"puṇyāpuṇyāneñjyānabhisaṃskāra."* Regarding the third of these three types of actions, in commenting on this phrase in the SA translation, QL interprets "imperturbable actions" as referring to the pure karma of the eight levels of *dhyāna* (which, of course would refer not only to abiding in those levels of meditative absorption, but also would refer to taking rebirth in the corresponding heavens). He also notes that this "pure karma of the eight *dhyānas* also qualifies as being a function of delusion," the rationale for that statement being

that, rarified as these modes of existence are, as an end in themselves, they still do not constitute or conduce to liberation from cyclic existence and hence function as erroneous karmic paths.

193. The four kinds of grasping: desire; views; moral regulations; and ideation rooted in the conception of a self.

194. *Erzhu* (二竹) is a KB attempt to render in terms familiar to Chinese the Sanskrit *naḍa-kalāpa*, standing sheaves of reeds (as, for instance, *Phragmites karka india*), wherein, whether as they grow in naturally-occurring stands, or as they may be deliberately bundled together in the construction of shelters and such in order to remain upright, each reed serves to support the others while simultaneously relying entirely upon the support of the others to keep from collapsing. Hence we have in this phenomenon an analogy for the utter codependence of these three subsets of "links" comprising the twelve-fold chain of serially-unfolding conditioned coproduction. This is of course equally true of the mutually supporting and sustaining nature of all twelve of the links *individually* as well.

Bhikkhu Bodhi points out a scriptural citation for the "sheaves of reeds" causality analogy as *Saṃyutta Nikāya* 12-67: "The Sheaves of Reeds."

195. "Suffering associated with the karmic formative factors" = *xingku* (行苦) = *saṃskāraduḥkhatā*.

196. *Suffering of suffering* = *kuku* (苦苦) = *duḥkhaduḥkhatā*.

197. *Suffering associated with deterioration* = *huaiku* (壞苦) = *pariṇāmaduḥkhatā*.

198. *"sa evaṃ dvādaśākāraṃ pratītyasamutpādaṃ pratyavekṣate 'nulomapratilomaṃ."*

199. Most editions are fairly consistent throughout this list of ten contemplations with the exception of a possible textual corruption in the second contemplation in the KB edition wherein "body" is included where the other editions have only "thought" (or "mind"). DSBC gives the list as follows:

bhavāṅgānusaṃdhitaśca;
ekacittasamavasaraṇataśca;
svakarmāsaṃbhedataśca;
avinirbhāgataśca;
trivartmānuvartanataśca;
pūrvāntapratyutpannāparāntāvekṣaṇataśca;
triduḥkhatāsamudayataśca;
hetupratyayaprabhavataśca;
utpādavyayavinibandhanataśca;
abhāvākṣayatāpratyavekṣaṇataśca.

200. In most other editions this contemplation refers to reducibility to a single thought (or to "the one mind").

201. In commenting on the SA edition, HH identifies these as the three paths discussed earlier in this passage on conditioned origination: the path of afflictions, the path of karmic actions, and the path of suffering.

202. "*śūnyatāvimokṣamukha.*"

203. "*ānimittavimokṣamukha.*"

204. "*apraṇihitavimokṣamukha.*"

205. These ten emptiness samādhis, per DSBC: *avatāraśūnyatā; svabhāvaśūnyatā; paramārthaśūnyatā; paramaśūnyatā; mahāśūnyatā; saṃprayogaśūnyatā; abhinirhāraśūnyatā; yathāvadavikalpaśūnyatā; sāpekṣaśūnyatā; vinirbhāgāvinirbhāgaśūnyatā.*

206. These ten types of resolute intentions per DSBC: *abhedyāśaya; niyatāśaya; kalyāṇāśaya; gambhīrāśaya; apratyudāvartyāśaya; apratiprasrabdhāśaya; vimalāśaya; anantāśaya; jñānābhilāṣāśaya; upāyaprajñāsaṃprayogāśaya.*

207. Context often requires a somewhat adaptive translation of *āśaya* that otherwise may mean "mental intention," "mental disposition," "intent," "resolution," or "mentality." Here I prefer Conze's (MDPL) "resolute intention."

208. DSBC has *kalyāṇāśaya,* "the mental disposition toward goodness."

209. "Acquiescent patience" = *ānulomikī kṣānti.* In his XHYJL, LTX points out that this "acquiescent patience" is the third of "the five types of patience" and the second of "the ten types of patience" and that in both cases, it is the level of patience acquired just before realizing "the unproduced-dharmas patience" (*anutpattika-dharma-kṣānti*). (T36n1739_p0899b7-12)

210. "King of the Fine Transformations Heaven" (善化天王) = *sunirmita-deva-rāja.* Bodhiruci translates this as "King of the Delight in Transformations Heaven" (化樂天王). This is a clear reference to the Nirmāṇarati Heaven, the heaven just above the Tuṣita Heaven within the six desire-realm heavens.

211. In accordance with the other editions as well as BB and SA, I emend the text here to eliminate a clearly accidental repetition of the two-character term referring to "signlessness" (*wuxiang* - 無相), doing so by following the variant editions in replacing the *xiang* (相) in the third line with *xing* (性).

212. None of the Chinese editions (DR, BB, BR, KB, SA, SD) agree with the Sanskrit's inclusion of three instead of two factors here: skillful means, wisdom, and knowledge (*upāyaprajñājñāna*).

213. "Merit" (*puṇya*) is one of the two primary provisions (*bodhisaṃbhāra*) required for realization of the highest enlightenment.

214. "*apramāṇaṃ ca buddhānāṃ bhagavatāṃ jñānābhisaṃbodhimavatarati.*"

215. SA, BR, and SD all specify "name-and-form bodies," whereas BB, KB, and the Sanskrit all refer only to "form bodies" (*rūpakāya*).

216. Only BB and KB mention "buddhas" here at all, and, of the two of them, a strict reading of KB would infer that the bodhisattva penetratingly comprehends such differences in mental dispositions and faculties of both buddhas and beings, a reading which does not comport with buddhas' complete transcendence of such limitations, hence my brackets to correct an apparent corruption or Sanskrit translation error in the transmitted KB editions. The bracketed change here aligns the KB reading with the very clear reading in BB: "He acquires a penetrating comprehension of the Buddhas' knowledge of the measurelessly many differences in beings' mental dispositions and faculties." (入無量諸佛知眾生志行諸根差別.)

217. Only the KB edition mentions "buddhas" here and, again, a strict reading of it would infer that the bodhisattva fathoms the mind of a buddha, a doctrinal impossibility: "He acquires a penetrating comprehension of the Buddhas' and beings' measurelessly many different minds and courses of thought." One can only infer then that, once again, there is either a corruption or translation error in the transmitted text. I believe that my bracketed emendation produces the only doctrinally sensible reading of the text.

218. "*prāyogikacaryā.*"

219. "*jñānābhijñānacaryākramaṇī.*"

220. Most editions are fairly consistent here with the exception that BB and KB list eleven samādhis here, whereas most others collapse the final two list members in BB and KB into a single samādhi. DSBC provides the following list: *suvicitavicayaṃ; suvicintitārthaṃ; viśeṣamatiṃ; prabhedārthakośaṃ; sarvārthavicayaṃ; supratiṣṭhitadṛḍhamūlaṃ; jñānābhijñāmukhaṃ; dharmadhātu(pari)karmaṃ; tathāgatānuśaṃsaṃ; vic itrārthakośasaṃsāranirvāṇamukhaṃ.*

221. I emend the text here per the Sanskrit and four other editions (SYMG) by replacing KB's *zhi* (知), "knowing," with *zhi* (智), "knowledge."

222. The BB edition has: "The samādhi that turns away from *saṃsāra* and toward nirvāṇa." (背生死向涅槃三昧) whereas SA has a single tenth samādhi that joins this samādhi and the immediately previous "treasury of many different meanings samādhi": "The samādhi of the treasury of many different meanings and the gateway to *saṃsāra* and

nirvāṇa." So, too, the Sanskrit: "*vicitrārthakośasaṃsāranirvāṇamukhaṃ ca.*"

223. BB and KB have "progress toward the ground of the Buddha's wisdom" (趣佛智地). DSBC: "*prajñājñānavicāraṇābhūmeḥ.*" ("The ground of contemplating wisdom and knowledge.")

224. The Sanskrit text makes it clear that KB's "ultimate reality" (實際) apparently refers here not to its usual Sanskrit antecedent (*bhūtakoṭi*), but rather to *nirodha,* i.e. to a state of quiescent cessation synonymous with nirvāṇa.

225. "Dharma treasury of the Buddhas corresponds to DSBC's "*buddhajñānaviṣayakośa.*"

226. There are four types of *māras* (*catur-māra*) that are often translated elsewhere as "demons" when not directly referencing the celestial *māras*.The four types of *māras* (*catur-māra*): affliction *māras* (*kleśa-māra*), the *māras* of the aggregates (*skandha-māra*), the *māras* of death (*mṛtya-māra*), celestial *māras* (*deva-putra-māra*).

227. HH clarifies that these "adorning phenomena" refer to the bodhisattva's cultivation and accumulation of many different sorts of roots of goodness and meritorious qualities with which he, figuratively speaking, "adorns" buddha lands: "菩薩以他修積的種種善 根功德，莊嚴佛的國土，無不超過天、龍，及八部神祇、帝釋、梵王、 四大天王等所有的莊嚴之事。"

228. I emend the reading of the text here, inserting the translation of a character missing from the Taisho text (因) that is found in five other editions.

229. Were one to attempt a strictly literal rendering of KB, it would read:

    "In the lands within atomic particles, the thoughts in beings' minds are fine. / Because the lands are coarse the thoughts in beings' minds are coarse."

    Either the Sanskrit text from which the KB team made its translation was very, very different from all other extant editions or else the KB manuscript became corrupted or its translation was terribly incorrect in the first place. Consequently, in producing my translation of these two lines, I had to refer to the other editions and interpolate meanings derived from them to improve the meaning so that it is consistent with the ideas in the text.

    Compare SA who, reflecting the same sensibility as the Sanskrit and SD, has:

    "Large lands, in response to thought, transform, becoming small.
    Small lands, in response to thought, transform, becoming large."

230. Vasubandhu correlates this with the bodhisattva's first ground practice.
231. Vasubandhu correlates this with the bodhisattva's second ground practice.
232. Vasubandhu correlates this with the bodhisattva's third ground practice.
233. Vasubandhu correlates this with the bodhisattva's fourth ground practice.
234. Vasubandhu correlates this with the bodhisattva's fifth ground practice. DSBC: *"supariśodhitādhyāśayasaṃkalpa."*
235. Vasubandhu correlates this with the bodhisattva's sixth ground practice.
236. Vasubandhu correlates this with the bodhisattva's seventh ground practice and also mentions that it is becaue of his encounters with measurelessly many realms of beings that the bodhisattva "enters the path of measureless knowledge."
237. All editions' lists vary somewhat. DSBC has:

    "ajātatāṃ ca; alakṣaṇatāṃ ca; asaṃbhūtatāṃ ca; avināśitāṃ ca; aniṣṭhitatāṃ ca; apravṛttitāṃ ca; anabhinivṛttitāṃ ca; abhāvasvabhāvatāṃ ca; ādimadhyaparyavasānasamatāṃ ca; tathatāvikal pasarvajñajñānapraveśatāṃ ca."
238. BB (圓光), BR (光輪), KB (圓光), SD (光輪), and the Sanskrit (*prabhāmaṇḍala*) all specify "aura."
239. *"dharmāloka."*
240. *"sarvadharmanirvikalpālokaḥ."*
241. I emend the text here to correct an obvious graphic-similarity scribal error, substituting *da* (大) for *ben* (本). The emendation is supported by four other editions of the text (SYMG), the Sanskrit, and Bodhiruci's translation.
242. *"āśayabala."*
243. DSBC: *"tathāgatādhiṣṭhānabala."*
244. *"kumārabhūmi."*
245. I emend the text here to correct an obvious graphic-similarity scribal error arising from graphic similarity, substituting *huai* (壞) for *huai* (懷) in accordance with the superior sensibility of four alternative editions (SYMG).
246. I emend the text here to favor the reading preserved in four other editions, this through substituting *hui* (慧 = "knowledge") for *de* (德 = "merit; qualities; etc.") which apparently must have entered the

text as a scribal error substituting the character for a very common compound for "merit." The content of the earlier prose section here reiterated in verse corroborates the correctness of the emendation. So too with the Sanskrit text (*puṇyajñānupagatāḥ*).

247. "*āśaya.*"

248. There seem to be two distinctly different understandings of the meaning of this ground:

DR, SA, BB, BR, SD, and Prajñā all translate the name of this *bhūmi* as "the Ground of Excellent Intelligence" (善慧地). DR translates that same meaning slightly differently: (善哉意). The Tibetan translation also echoes this interpretation "the Ground of Excellent Insight" (*legs pa'i blo gros*). Strictly speaking, one could infer that these renderings all appear be the result of an error arising from misinterpreting the Sanskrit name (*sādhumatī*) by mistaking a suffix indicating possession (*-mat* modified to agree with the feminine noun *bhūmi* to become *-matī*) for a completely unrelated word that means "intelligence," "intellect," "mind" (*mati*).

Of all of the Chinese and Tibetan translators, it appears that the Kumārajīva-Buddhayaśas translation team may have been the only one to render the name of this *bhūmi* more or less in accordance with the above-referenced "grammatically correct" interpretation of the Sanskrit term as "the Ground of Sublime Goodness" (妙善地). The KB edition only employs the possibly erroneous Chinese and Tibetan default rendering once (in its initial listing of the ten bodhisattva grounds), but otherwise accords with the grammatically strict interpretation of the term throughout its detailed discussion of the ninth *bhūmi* itself.

249. "*praśamita.*"

250. "Effects of practicing" (lit. "actions") = Skt. *abhisaṃskāra*. (BHSD foregrounds "performance," "accomplishment," and "accumulation.") The intended reference here is to this bodhisattva's knowing in accordance with reality the karmic effects of implementing the various categories of dharmas arrayed in this list.

251. "Entangling difficulty" = Skt. *gahana*. SA, BR, and SD all translate this as *choulin* (稠林) which means "thicket."

252. Each of these "entangling difficulties" (*gahana*) is explored in greater detail below in the subsections corresponding to the Sanskrit text's sections "E" through "K."

253. "Resolute beliefs" = Skt. *adhimukti*. There appears to be either a corruption of the KB text or original mistranslation into Chinese of the Sanskrit for list items numbers four, six, and seven (願樂 for *adhimukti*, 志心 for *āśaya*, and 深心 for *anuśaya*.

254. "Sense realms" = Skt. *dhātu*. This refers to the eighteen sense realms: the six sense faculties, the six sense objects, and the six sense consciousnesses.

255. *"āśaya."*

256. "Latent tendencies" = *"anuśaya."*

257. *"upapatti."*

258. *"vāsana anusaṃdhi."*

259. These "three groups" (三聚) refer to:
    1) those fixed in their adherence to what is wrong;
    2) those fixed in their adherence to what is right;
    3) those who are "unfixed" as to their adherence to either what is wrong or what is right.

260. "Devoid of physical form" = Rahder Skt. *aśarīratāṁ*. (There is an error in DSBC which has *śarīratāṁ*.)

261. Bhikkhu Bodhi points out that this is a reference to the Buddha's statements on the boundlessness of consciousness found in DN 11 and MN 49 wherein "consciousness" there may be equated with "mind" as intended here. See *Long Discourses*, Walshe, p. 179 and *The Middle Length Discourses*, Bhikkhus Ñāṇamoli & Bodhi, p. 428.

262. The KB edition splits these opposites into two separate characteristics. I have collapsed them into one to accord with all other Chinese editions and the Sanskrit.

263. Ibid.

264. Ibid.

265. Bhikkhu Bodhi points out that this list item (together with the next three list items) is an allusion to a fourfold classification of karma at AN 4:232-233 for which see *The Numerical Discourses of the Buddha*, Bhikkhu Bodhi, p.601.

266. DR, SA, SD, and the Sanskrit (*karmakṣetrāpramāṇatāṃ ca*) all reference a "farm fields" metaphor with different degrees of conceptual opacity. Of those four editions, DR's translation is the most conceptually penetrable through its mentioning of the types of seeds that are planted, namely "karmic offense and merit," as follows: "[The characteristic of having] farm fields of karmic offense and merit that are measureless" (罪福田地，則無有量).

    KB, BB, and BR all skip the metaphor entirely, preferring a brief explanation of the concept. For instance BR (very similar to KB and BB whose translations here are identical) has: "karmic actions' characteristic of involving measureless causes" (業因無量相).

267. "Resolute beliefs" = *"adhimukti."*

268. "Sense realms" = "*dhātu*."

269. "Resolute intentions" = "*āśaya*."

270. "Latent tendencies" = Skt. *anuśaya*. It is apparent from the Sanskrit as well as from the other analogue texts that KB's Chinese scribes accidentally recorded the Chinese translation for "fetters" here (結使) instead of the obviously intended and nearly identical alternate Chinese rendering for "latent tendencies" (使). This is also made clear by the fact that the order of items in this section of the text is simply discussing in the same order the items originally listed above in the section on the "thickets" or "difficulties" (Skt. *gahana*) at 524c11.

271. I emend the reading here by substituting for愛, this in accordance with four other editions of the text, the demands of sensibility, the testimony of the "Ten Grounds" chapter of the Avataṃsaka Sutra, and the relative obviousness that the reading in Taisho edition of the text reflects a graphic-similarity scribal error.

272. "Habitual karmic propensities" = "*vāsanā*."

273. Again, this listing refers to the "three groups" of beings mentioned above as the last of the "entangling difficulties" in Sanskrit section C above.

274. "Five heinous karmic offenses" refers to patricide, matricide, killing an arhat, spilling the blood of a buddha, and causing a sectarian schism in the monastic community.

275. This refers to the first of these three types: 1) those fixed in their adherence to what is wrong; 2) those fixed in their adherence to what is right; 3) those who are "unfixed" as to their adherence to either what is wrong or what is right.

276. "*dhātu*."

277. "*gahana*," lit. "thickets."

278. "Expounder" = "*dharmabhāṇaka*."

279. "Four unimpeded knowledges" = "*catuḥpratisaṃvid*." These are: *dharmapratisaṃvid*, *arthapratisaṃvid*, *niruktipratisaṃvid*, and pratibhānapratisaṃvid.

280. I emend the Taisho text here, substituting "light" (明) for "characteristic (相) to correct a graphic-similarity scribal error, this in accordance with three other editions of this text (S,Y,M), Bodhiruci, BB, SA, and the DSBC Sanskrit (*pratibhānapratisaṃvidā ekaikamadhvānamārabhya aparyantadharmālokatayā dharmaṃ deśayati*).

281. "*āśaya*."

282. "*adhimukti*."

283. "*adhimukti*."

284. *"āśaya."*

285. An "ineffable"(*anabhilāpya*) is a specific nearly unimaginably large number that is the 120th of 123 numbers described in Chapter Thirty of the Flower Adornment Sutra wherein each of those numbers is defined as being the square of the immediately previous number the first of which is a *lakṣa* (100,000).

286. *"buddhagocara."*

287. The Sanskrit, Bodhiruci, and SD all specify "lower" grounds. Hence, aside from KB, only BB fails to specify this rather obvious point.

288. "Affliction-related entangling difficulties" = *kleśacittagahana*.

289. *"dhātu."*

290. This refers to these three categorical types (三聚):
    1) those fixed in their adherence to what is wrong;
    2) those fixed in their adherence to what is right;
    3) those who are "unfixed" as to their adherence to either what is wrong or what is right.

291. Neither BB nor KB include a first list component (just before "white dharmas") found in the later editions SA, BR, SD, and the Sanskrit that refers to thorough investigation (*suvicitavicayaḥ*). (SA translates it as善思惟修習: "Engages in thorough meditative contemplation on cultivation.")

292. This is clearly a reference to the ten types of "entangling difficulties" (*gahana*) discussed at some length in relation to the ninth ground beginning with their listing at 524c10–12.

293. DR, BB, and KB are identical in their treatment of this acquisition of one preliminary samādhi known as "stainless" immediately followed by the acquisition of ten listed samādhis whereas all other editions simply give a list of ten samādhis beginning with the "stainless samādhi."

294. I emend the Taisho edition of the KB text to correct the scribal error involving an erroneously included "station" (*wei* [位]) that simply echoes the name of the samādhi treated in the previous endnote. The emendation is supported by four other editions as well as by BB, BR, SD, and the Sanskrit. That said, SA, BR, SD, and the Sanskrit are quite different in that they all reference augmentation with the superknowledges associated with all-knowledge. For instance, SA has the name of this light as "the enhancer of all-knowledge's superknowledges" (增益一切智神通) whereas the DSBC Sanskrit has: *"sarvajñatābhijñāvatyo nāma."*

295. Although the entire ensuing section of the Chinese text employs the Chinese character most commonly associated in Buddhist doctrinal discussions with the second of the four truths, i.e. "accumulation" or "origination" of suffering (集 [*ji*] = Skt. *samudaya*), as context demonstrates and the Sanskrit text corroborates, that is *not* the concept intended here. In this instance, the Sanskrit antecedent term is not *samudaya* but rather *samudāgama* which refers instead to "attainment." (MW = "Full or complete knowledge." BHSD = "*approach* [*to*], *arrival* [*of*], *attainment* [*of*], a religious goal, esp. enlightenment, which is to be understood when no goal is specifically named.") This being the case, I translate this character in this context as "attainment."

296. This text's ambiguity in this statement is clarified by reference to both Śikṣānanda and Bodhiruci, both of whom render the Sanskrit of this sentence as "attainment as it applies to the creation and destruction of worlds" (世界成壞集).

297. "Sustaining bases" (持) = *adhiṣṭhāna*. Although this technical term is often translated as "empowerment," that would not be an appropriate rendering here as many of the members of this list may or may not be sustained through empowerments as they are for the most part causally sustained by past karmic actions.

298. I emend the text here, replacing 想 with 相, this to correct an obvious graphic-similarity scribal error. The correctness of the emendation is supported by five other editions of the text.

299. "Knowledge that penetratingly comprehends" = "*avatārajñāna*."

300. "Ordinary common people," on the face of it, might appear to be a mistranslation of the Chinese term recorded here as 毛道, i.e. "hair path." But, as it turns out, this in fact *is* the very literal translation of the Sanskrit *vāla-patha*, lit. "hair path," apparently a traditional Sanskrit corruption of *bāla* that is in turn an abbreviation for *bāla-pṛthagjana*, literally "foolish common person."

301. "*buddhakṣetrakāyābhisaṃbodhyavatārajñānaṃ*."

302. I emend the reading here to correct a fairly obvious scribal error by replacing *lun* (論), "discourse," with *lun* (輪), "wheel." BB and KB, both have *lun* (論), "discourse," whereas all other editions have the graphically very similar *lun* (輪), "wheel" also occurring in one alternate edition of BB. The Sanskrit edition also supports this "wheel" translation (*apratihatacakrānugataṃ*).

303. "*mahāvijayo bhikṣu*."

304. "*vajrapadmottarasya tathāgata*."

305. This samādhi per DSBC: "*sarvabuddhakṣetrakāyasvabhāvasaṃdarśanaṃ nāma bodhisattvasamādhiṃ*."

306. *"sarvābhijñāmatirājaṃ nāma tathāgataṃ."*

307. *"vaśavartino devarāja."*

308. *"maheśvarasya devarājasya."*

309. The DSBC edition of the surviving Sanskrit refers to this final section as the *"parīndanāparivartaḥ"* or "bequest."

310. Bhikkhu Bodhi points out that eight of these ten comparisons are found in Anguttara Nikāya 8:19 (The Simile of the Ocean).

311. From this point on, the verses in the surviving Sanskrit edition diverge entirely from those found in any of the Chinese texts. Because their composition must be of relatively recent origin, there appears to be no clear way to correlate these Sanskrit verses with those of any of the much earlier Chinese texts, whether it be DR, BB, SA, KB, or SD.

312. In accordance with five alternative editions (SYMG and Sen), I emend the reading here to correct an obvious scribal error by substituting *xian* (先), "previous," for *sheng* (生), "to produce, etc."

Variant Readings from Other Chinese Editions

Fascicle One Variant Readings

[0497016] 後＝姚【宋】【元】【明】【宮】
[0497017] 〔龜茲國〕－【宋】【元】【明】【宮】
[0497018] 三藏＋（法師）【宋】【元】【明】【宮】
[0497019] 什＋（共佛陀耶舍）【宋】【元】【明】【宮】
[0497020] 〔界〕－【元】【明】【宮】
[0498001] 閡＝礙【宋】【元】【明】【宮】＊ [＊ 1 2 3 4 5 6 7 8]
[0498002] 智＋（慧）【宋】【元】【明】【宮】
[0498003] 十＝一【宋】【宮】
[0498004] 地＋（故）【宋】【元】【明】【宮】
[0498005] 薩＝提【宋】【元】【明】【宮】
[0498006] 遠＋（行）【宋】【元】【明】【宮】
[0498007] 是＝爾【宋】【元】【明】【宮】
[0498008] （諸）＋菩薩【元】【明】
[0498009] 實法＝寶中【宋】，＝實中【元】【明】【宮】
[0499001] 則＝即【宋】【元】【明】【宮】
[0499002] 深＝法【宮】
[0499003] 月＋（菩薩）【宋】【元】【明】【宮】
[0499004] （諸）＋佛子【宋】【宮】
[0499005] 智＝知【宋】【元】【明】【宮】
[0499006] 餘＝如【宋】【元】【明】【宮】＊ [＊ 1]
[0499007] 已＝以【宮】
[0499008] 唯＝惟【宋】【元】【明】【宮】＊ [＊ 1]
[0499009] 主＝王【宋】【元】【明】【宮】
[0499010] 以＝已【宋】【元】【明】【宮】
[0500001] 渧＝滴【宋】【元】【明】【宮】
[0500002] 〔界〕－【宋】【元】【明】
[0500003] 離＋（一切）【宋】【元】【明】【宮】
[0500004] 止＝上【宋】
[0501001] 觀＝聞【宋】【元】【明】【宮】
[0501002] 實＝寶【宮】
[0501003] 〔決〕－【宋】【元】【明】【宮】
[0501004] 成熟＝成就【宋】【元】【明】【宮】＊
[0501005] 淨＝盡【宋】【元】【明】【宮】
[0501006] 〔以〕－【宋】【元】【明】【宮】
[0501007] 〔通〕－【宮】
[0501008] 自於＝於自【宋】【元】【明】【宮】

[0501009] 世＝際【宋】【元】【明】【宮】＊［＊ 1］
[0501010] 〔所作〕－【宋】【元】【明】
[0502001] 心＝以【宋】【元】【明】【宮】
[0502002] 無明流見流＝見流無明流【宋】【元】【明】【宮】
[0502003] 入＋（與）【宋】【元】【明】【宮】
[0502004] 深＝染【宋】【元】【明】
[0502005] 德＋（得力）【宋】【元】【明】【宮】
[0502006] 以發願故廣見於＝以廣大願故見於【宋】【元】【明】【宮】
[0502007] 成＋（初）【宋】【元】【明】【宮】
[0502008] 厭廢＝疲厭【宋】【元】【明】【宮】
[0502009] 廢＝疲【宋】【元】【明】【宮】
[0502010] 果＝緣【宋】【元】【明】【宮】
[0502011] 相＋（貌）【宋】【元】【明】
[0502012] 地＋（故）【宋】【元】【明】【宮】
[0502013] 住＋（於）【宋】【元】【明】【宮】
[0503001] 衰＝憂【宋】【元】【明】【宮】
[0503002] 布＝大【宋】【元】【明】【宮】
[0503003] 〔是〕－【宋】【元】【明】【宮】
[0503004] 集＝習【宋】【元】【明】【宮】＊［＊ 1］
[0503005] 合＝令【宋】【元】【明】
[0503006] 實＝寶【宮】
[0504001] 卷第一終【宋】【元】【明】
[0504002] 卷第二首[＞【宋】【元】【明】]，（十住經）＋離【宋】【宮】
[0504003] 〔諸〕－【宋】【元】【明】【宮】
[0504004] 杖＝仗【宋】【元】【明】【宮】
[0504005] 隨＝直【宋】【元】【明】
[0504006] （不）＋麁【宋】【元】【明】【宮】
[0504007] [麩-夫+黃]＝獷【宋】【元】【明】【宮】
[0504008] 又＝不【宋】【元】【明】【宮】
[0504009] 愛＝憂【元】【明】
[0504010] 語＝說【明】
[0504011] 作＋（綺語）【明】
[0505001] 廣＝曠【宋】【明】【宮】
[0505002] 鬼＋（道）【明】【宮】
[0505003] 常＝當【明】
[0505004] 於＋（十）【宋】【元】【明】【宮】
[0505005] 住＝置【宮】
[0505006] 住＝在【元】【明】
[0505007] （得）＋一【宋】【元】【明】【宮】
[0505008] 墮＝墜【宋】【元】【明】【宮】

[0505009] 虫=中【宋】【元】【明】【宮】
[0505010] 垢+（則）【宋】【元】【明】【宮】
[0506001] （遠）+離【宋】【元】【明】
[0506002] 師=帥【宮】
[0506003] 千+（佛）【元】【明】
[0506004] 墜=墮【宋】【元】【明】【宮】
[0506005] 世=惡【宋】【宮】
[0506006] 不分卷【宋】【元】【明】

Fascicle Two Variant Readings

[0506007] 後秦=姚秦【宮】*
[0506008] 三藏+（法師）【宮】*
[0506009] （共佛陀耶舍）+譯【宮】*
[0506010] 不分卷【宋】【元】【明】
[0507001] 處=足【宋】【元】【明】【宮】
[0507002] 息=悉【宮】
[0507003] 精進=精勤【宮】
[0507004] 匱=遺【宮】
[0507005] 〔求〕－【元】【明】【宮】
[0507006] 相=想【宋】【元】【明】【宮】* [* 1 2 3 4]
[0508001] 〔無〕－【宋】【元】【明】【宮】
[0508002] （第）+三【宋】【元】【明】【宮】
[0508003] 距=拒【宋】【元】【明】【宮】
[0508004] 淫=婬【宮】
[0508005] 生+（中）【宋】【元】【明】
[0508006] 〔不可計知〕－【宋】【元】【明】【宮】
[0509001] 唯=惟【宋】【元】【明】【宮】* [* 1 2]
[0509002] 身=及【宋】【元】【明】【宮】
[0509003] 功=福【宋】【元】【明】【宮】
[0509004] 者=皆【宋】【元】【明】【宮】
[0509005] 卷第二終【宋】【元】【明】
[0509006] 卷第三首【宋】【元】【明】，（十住經）+焰地【宋】【宮】
[0509007] 以=已【宋】【元】【明】【宮】
[0509008] 此=第【宋】【元】【明】【宮】
[0509009] （諸）+菩【宋】【元】【明】【宮】
[0510001] 修+（滿）【宋】【元】【明】【宮】
[0510002] （四）+無畏【宋】【元】【明】
[0510003] 著=為首【宋】【元】【明】
[0510004] 磨=摩【宋】【元】【明】【宮】
[0511001] （十住經）+難【宋】【宮】

[0511002] 雪=雨【宋】【元】【明】【宮】
[0511003] 稱讚=讚歎【宋】【元】【明】【宮】
[0511004] 見=現【宮】
[0511005] 來=遠【宋】【元】【明】【宮】
[0511006] 足+(第四地)【宋】【元】【明】【宮】
[0511007] 實=寔【宋】【元】【明】【宮】
[0511008] 滅苦=苦滅【宋】【元】【明】【宮】
[0511009] 〔故〕-【宋】【元】【明】【宮】
[0512001] 〔夫〕-【宋】【元】【明】【宮】
[0512002] 名=石【宋】【元】【明】【宮】
[0512003] 消=痟【宋】【元】【明】【宮】
[0512004] 郭+(法)【宋】【元】【明】【宮】
[0512005] 出+(此法)【宋】【元】【明】【宮】
[0512006] 積=諸【宋】【元】【明】【宮】
[0512007] 〔今〕-【宋】【元】【明】【宮】
[0512008] 作+(刪)【宋】【元】【明】【宮】
[0512009] 念+(諸)【宋】【元】【明】
[0512010] 薩+(為)【宋】【元】【明】
[0513001] (而)+重【宋】【元】【明】【宮】
[0513002] 項=頂【宋】【元】【明】【宮】
[0513003] 偽=為【宋】【元】【明】【宮】
[0513004] 焰=火【宋】【元】【明】【宮】
[0513005] 明=眼【宋】【元】【明】【宮】
[0513006] 念=令【元】【明】
[0513007] 名姓=石性【宋】【元】【明】【宮】
[0513008] 而=所【宋】【元】【明】【宮】
[0513009] 次頁[01]不分卷【宋】【元】【明】

Fascicle Three Variant Readings

[0514001] 前頁[09]不分卷【宋】【元】【明】
[0514002] 雲=雪【宋】【元】【明】【宮】
[0514003] 性=相【宋】【元】【明】【宮】
[0514004] 第=入【明】【宮】
[0514005] 〔觀〕-【宋】【元】【明】【宮】
[0514006] 牙=芽【宋】【元】【明】
[0514007] 〔熟〕-【宋】【元】【明】
[0515001] 〔為〕-【宋】【元】【明】【宮】
[0515002] 知=智【宋】【元】【明】【宮】
[0515003] 〔者〕-【宋】【元】【明】【宮】
[0515004] 續+(以)【宋】【元】【明】【宮】

[0515005] 〔則果滅〕－【宋】【元】【明】【宮】
[0515006] 世＋（名）【宋】【元】【明】【宮】
[0515007] 生＋（老）【宋】【元】【明】【宮】
[0515008] 死＋（滅）【宋】【元】【明】【宮】
[0515009] 〔觀〕－【宋】【元】【明】【宮】＊
[0515010] 唯＝惟【宋】【元】【明】【宮】
[0515011] 快＝決定【宋】【元】【明】【宮】
[0515012] 淨＝涼【宋】【元】【明】【宮】
[0516001] 〔若欲〕－【宋】【元】【明】【宮】
[0516002] 〔行〕－【宋】【元】【明】【宮】
[0516003] 相＝性【宋】【元】【明】【宮】
[0516004] 集＝習【宋】【元】【明】【宮】＊ [＊ 1]
[0516005] 與及於受＝乃至於愛【宋】【元】【明】，＝乃至於受【宮】
[0516006] 以＝如【宋】【元】【明】【宮】
[0517001] 善＝上【明】
[0517002] 則淨＝淨好【宋】【元】【明】【宮】
[0517003] 卷第三終【宋】【元】【明】
[0517004] 卷第四首【宋】【元】【明】，（十住經）＋遠【宋】【宮】
[0517005] 善＝喜【宋】【元】【明】【宮】
[0517006] 而示＝知是【宋】【元】【明】【宮】
[0517007] 此＋（十）【宋】【元】【明】
[0517008] 入＋（第）【宋】【元】【明】
[0517009] 七＝八【宋】
[0517010] 法＝佛【宋】【元】【明】【宮】
[0517011] 別＋（法）【宋】【元】【明】
[0517012] （諸）＋根【宋】【元】【明】
[0517013] 諸＝無【宋】
[0517014] 住＋（入）【宋】【元】【明】
[0517015] 住＝位【宮】
[0518001] （助）＋菩【宋】【元】【明】【宮】
[0518002] 〔金剛藏菩薩言〕－【宮】
[0518003] （但）＋於【宋】【元】【明】
[0518004] 行＝德【宋】【元】【明】【宮】
[0518005] 得＝行【宋】【元】【明】【宮】
[0518006] 〔乃〕－【宮】
[0518007] 過＋（耳）【宋】【元】【明】
[0518008] （大）＋千【宋】【元】【明】
[0518009] 乃＋（至）【宋】【元】【明】【宮】
[0518010] 捨＋（於）【宋】【元】【明】
[0518011] 從＋（第）【宋】【元】【明】

[0518012] 入+（於）【宋】【元】【明】
[0518013] 眾+（生）【宋】【元】【明】【宮】
[0518014] 深=清【明】
[0518015] 諸佛=場佛【明】
[0518016] 生+（處）【宋】【元】【明】【宮】
[0518017] 義=議【宋】【元】【明】
[0518018] 知=智【宋】【元】【明】【宮】＊ [＊ 1]
[0518019] 性+（本）【宋】【元】【明】【宮】
[0518020] 是+（七）【宋】【元】【明】
[0518021] 若菩薩=菩薩若【宋】【元】【明】【宮】
[0518022] 然=熾【元】【明】
[0519001] 人+（等）【宋】【元】【明】
[0519002] 億萬=萬億【宋】【元】【明】【宮】
[0519003] 飾=嚴【宋】【元】【明】【宮】
[0519004] 善=因【宋】【元】【明】【宮】
[0519005] 生+（中）【宋】【元】【明】
[0519006] 千+（萬）【宋】【元】【明】
[0519007] 菩薩若=若菩薩【宋】【元】【明】【宮】
[0519008] 劫+（數）【宋】【元】【明】
[0519009] 佛=法【宋】【元】【明】【宮】
[0519010] 數=處【宋】【元】【明】【宮】
[0519011] 惡垢=垢惡【宋】【元】【明】【宮】
[0519012] 能=行【宋】【元】【明】【宮】
[0520001] 性=姓【宋】【元】【明】【宮】
[0520002] 德=行【宋】【元】【明】【宮】
[0520003] 七=十【宋】【元】【明】【宮】
[0520004] （十住經）+不動【宋】【宮】
[0520005] 佛=弟【宋】【元】【明】【宮】
[0520006] 具=見【宋】【元】【明】【宮】
[0520007] 想=相【宋】【元】【明】【宮】
[0520008] （離）+一【宋】【元】【明】
[0520009] 〔廓然〕－【宮】
[0520010] 〔乃忽〕－【宮】
[0521001] 皆悉=悉皆【宋】【元】【明】【宮】
[0521002] 慧+（力）【宋】【元】【明】
[0521003] （又）+善【宋】【元】【明】
[0521004] 本=大【宋】【元】【明】【宮】
[0521005] [于>干]+（大）【宋】【元】【明】【宮】
[0521006] 〔火〕－【宮】
[0521007] 〔知〕－【宋】【元】【明】

[0522001] 吒+（天）【宋】【元】【明】
[0522002] 國中=國土中【宋】【元】【明】，=國土【宮】
[0522003] （是）+菩【宋】【元】【明】【宮】
[0522004] 說=成【宋】【元】【明】【宮】
[0522005] 知=智【宋】【元】【明】
[0522006] 懷=壞【宋】【元】【明】【宮】
[0522007] （甚）+深【宋】【元】【明】【宮】
[0522008] 法=性【宋】【元】【明】【宮】
[0522009] 見+（無量）【宋】【元】【明】
[0522010] 供養=現供具【宋】【元】【明】【宮】
[0522011] 劫+（中）【宋】【元】【明】
[0522012] 切=一【宋】【元】【明】【宮】
[0522013] 頸+（所佩）【宋】【元】【明】
[0522014] 譬如佛子若=佛子譬如若【宋】【元】【宮】，=佛子譬如【明】
[0523001] 生+（中）【宋】【元】【明】
[0523002] 得=淨【宋】【元】【明】【宮】
[0523003] 德=慧【宋】【元】【明】【宮】
[0523004] 遽=懅【宋】【宮】
[0523005] 心=意【宋】【元】【明】【宮】
[0523006] 王=天【宋】【元】【明】【宮】
[0523007] 今=念【宮】
[0523008] 礙=障【明】【宮】
[0524001] 三=四【宋】【元】【明】

Fascicle Four Variant Readings

[0524002] 第四=第五【宋】【元】【明】
[0524003] 後=姚【宋】【元】【明】【宮】
[0524004] 藏+（法師）【宋】【元】【明】【宮】
[0524005] 什+（共佛陀耶舍）【宋】【元】【明】【宮】
[0524006] 歌=讚【宋】
[0524007] 法=道【宋】【元】【明】【宮】
[0524008] 視=觀【宋】【元】【明】
[0524009] （爾時）+金【宋】【元】【明】
[0524010] 智+（慧）【元】【明】
[0524011] 〔欲〕－【宋】【元】【明】【宮】＊ ［＊ 1 2］
[0524012] 聞+（法行）【宋】【元】【明】【宮】
[0524013] 〔法〕－【宋】【元】【明】【宮】
[0524014] 〔行〕－【宮】
[0524015] 願=欲【宋】【元】【明】
[0524016] 知=隨【宋】【宮】

[0524017] 業=乘【宋】【元】【明】【宮】
[0525001] 〔相〕-【宋】【元】【明】【宮】
[0525002] 〔乃至〕-【宮】
[0525003] 入=心【宋】【元】【明】【宮】
[0525004] 〔對〕-【宋】【元】【明】【宮】
[0525005] 諸+(眾)【宋】【元】【明】
[0525006] 牙=芽【宋】【元】【明】【宮】* [* 1]
[0525007] 愛=受【宋】【元】【明】【宮】
[0525008] (隨)+善【宋】【元】【明】
[0525009] 二+(是)【宋】【元】【明】
[0525010] 邪=不【宮】
[0525011] 位=住【宮】
[0525012] 〔正〕-【宮】
[0525013] 〔得〕-【宋】【元】【明】【宮】
[0525014] 地+(已)【宋】【元】【明】
[0525015] 乘=樂【宋】【元】【明】【宮】
[0525016] 智+(知)【宋】*【元】*【明】* [* 1 2 3 4 5 6 7 8]
[0525017] 相=明【宋】【元】【明】
[0525018] 智+(以如實智)【宋】【元】【明】
[0525019] (能)+說【宋】【元】【明】
[0525020] 劫+(中)【宋】【元】【明】
[0525021] 說=語【宋】【元】【明】【宮】
[0525022] 〔別〕-【宋】【宮】
[0526001] 唯=惟【宋】【宮】
[0526002] 或+(以)【宋】【元】【明】
[0526003] 世+(界)【宋】【元】【明】【宮】
[0526004] 一+(十)【宋】【元】【明】
[0526005] 或=我【宋】【元】【明】【宮】
[0526006] 干=千【明】
[0526007] 以+(上)【宋】【元】【明】
[0526008] 妙=麁現【宮】
[0526009] 則=即【宋】【元】【明】【宮】
[0526010] 不=非【宋】【元】【明】【宮】
[0527001] 眾=諸【宮】
[0527002] 心=法【宮】
[0527003] (十住經)+法【宋】【宮】
[0527004] 十+(上)【元】【明】
[0527005] 大=人【宋】【元】【明】【宮】
[0528001] 俱=皆【森】
[0528002] 作=得【森】

[0528003] （稱）＋量【森】
[0528004] 葉＝莖【宮】
[0528005] （悉）＋照【森】
[0528006] 十方＋（一切）【森】
[0528007] 〔滅〕－【森】
[0528008] （滅除）＋苦惱【森】
[0528009] 〔悉〕－【森】
[0528010] （一切）＋人身【森】
[0528011] 肩＝臂【宮】
[0529001] 某＝其【森】
[0529002] 禮＝視【宋】【元】【明】【宮】【森】
[0529003] 〔位〕－【宋】【元】【明】【宮】
[0529004] 法＝世【森】
[0529005] 〔境〕－【宋】【元】【明】【宮】
[0529006] 〔大〕－【森】
[0529007] 幔＝網【森】
[0529008] 職＋（地）【宋】【元】【明】【宮】
[0529009] 〔如實〕－【宋】【元】【明】【宮】
[0529010] 如＝知【森】
[0529011] 如＋（是）【森】
[0529012] 〔諸見化…辟支佛化〕十六字－【森】
[0529013] 分別＋（化）【宮】
[0529014] 佛＋（十）【宋】【元】【明】【宮】
[0529015] （知）＋劫【森】
[0529016] 壽＝辨【明】
[0529017] 籌量＋（密）【森】
[0529018] （諸）＋菩薩【森】
[0529019] 受＝授【宋】【元】【明】【宮】
[0529020] 〔密〕－【森】
[0529021] 想＝相【宋】【元】【明】【宮】【森】
[0529022] 〔心〕－【宮】【森】
[0529023] 〔得〕－【宋】【元】【明】【森】
[0529024] （知）＋智慧【森】
[0529025] 澍＝注【森】*
[0530001] （若千億）＋若千萬億【森】
[0530002] 三＋（佛）【森】
[0530003] 四＋（佛）【森】
[0530004] 量＋（問言）【宋】【元】【明】【森】
[0530005] 佛＋（前）【森】
[0530006] 卷第五終【宋】【元】【明】

[0530007] 卷第六首【宋】【元】【明】，法雲地第十下【元】【明】，宋本缺品題
[0530008] 大＝入【森】
[0530009] 淨＋（淨國為垢）【宋】【元】【明】【宮】
[0530010] 〔於〕－【宋】【元】【明】【宮】
[0530011] 佛＝有【宋】【元】【明】【宮】
[0530012] 〔照〕－【宋】【元】【明】【宮】
[0530013] 方＝切【宋】【元】【明】【宮】
[0530014] 〔風劫火劫盡〕－【森】
[0530015] 劫＋（盡）【宋】【元】【明】
[0530016] 火＝大【宮】
[0530017] 示現＋（無量）【森】
[0530018] 〔力〕－【宋】【元】【明】【宮】
[0531001] 性＋（三昧）【宋】【元】【明】【宮】
[0531002] 〔戲〕－【森】
[0531003] 耳＝聞【宋】【元】【明】【宮】，〔耳〕－【森】
[0531004] 唱＝略【宋】【元】【明】【宮】
[0531005] 〔以〕－【森】
[0531006] 麁現＝微妙【森】
[0531007] 〔丹本微妙〕－【宋】【元】【明】【宮】
[0531008] 大＝天【森】
[0531009] （工）＋師【森】
[0531010] 譬如佛子＝佛子譬如【宋】【元】【明】【宮】
[0531011] 間＋（性）【宋】【元】【明】【宮】【森】
[0531012] 大悲大慈＝大慈大悲【森】
[0531013] 示＝亦【宋】【元】【明】【宮】
[0531014] 〔行〕－【森】
[0532001] 〔諸佛子〕－【宋】【元】【明】【宮】
[0532002] 〔伽〕－【森】
[0532003] 門＝問【宋】【元】【明】【宮】
[0532004] 〔諸佛子〕－【宋】【元】【明】【宮】
[0532005] 焰＋（慧）【宋】＊【元】＊【明】＊ [＊ 1]
[0532006] 眾＋（生）【宋】【元】【明】【宮】
[0532007] 廣大＝大廣【宋】【元】【明】【宮】
[0532008] 慧＝勢【宋】【元】【明】【宮】
[0532009] 遍＝匝【森】
[0533001] 往＝住【宮】
[0533002] 精勤＝精進【宋】【元】【明】【宮】
[0533003] 諸＝念【宋】【元】【明】【宮】
[0533004] 寂＝空【森】
[0533005] 行＝足【森】

[0533006] 諸智＝智慧【森】
[0533007] 慧＝德【宋】【元】【明】【宮】
[0533008] 諸佛大會眾＝諸佛及大會【森】
[0533009] 會眾＝眾會【宋】【元】【明】【宮】
[0533010] 其＝某【宋】【元】【明】【宮】
[0534001] 授＝受【宮】
[0534002] 入＝又【宋】【元】【明】【宮】【森】
[0534003] 生＝先【宋】【元】【明】【宮】【森】
[0534004] 眾＝諸【森】
[0534005] 皆＝亦【宋】【元】【明】【宮】
[0534006] 移動＝動移【宋】【元】【明】【宮】【森】
[0534007] 伎＝技【宮】
[0534008] 王＝中【森】＊［＊ 1］
[0534009] 聚＝集【明】【宮】【森】
[0534010] 山＝中【宋】【元】【明】【宮】
[0535001] 第四＝第六【宋】【元】【明】

Bibliography

Bodhi. (2000). *The Connected Discourses of the Buddha: A New Translation of the Saṃyutta Nikāya* ; translated from the Pāli ; original translation by Bhikkhu Bodhi. (Teachings of the Buddha). Somerville, MA: Wisdom Publications.

Bodhi. (2012). The Numerical Discourses of the Buddha: A Translation of the Aṅguttara Nikāya (Teachings of the Buddha). Boston: Wisdom Publications.

Bodhiruci (c. 508–511 CE). Shidi jing lun (十地經論). T26, no. 1522.

Buddhabhadra (c. 418–20 CE). Dafangguang fo huayan jing (大方廣佛華嚴經). T10, no. 278.

Cleary, T. (1984). The Flower Ornament Scripture: A Translation of the Avatamsaka Sutra. Boulder : [New York]: Shambhala Publications ; Distributed in the U.S. by Random House.

Conze, E., & Suzuki Gakujutsu Zaidan. (1967). Materials for a Dictionary of the Prajñāpāramitā Literature. Tokyo: Suzuki Research Foundation.

Dharmarakṣa (c. 297). Pusa shizhu xingdao pin (菩薩十住行道品). T10, no. 283).

Edgerton, F. (1953). Buddhist Hybrid Sanskrit grammar and dictionary. (William Dwight Whitney linguistic series). New Haven: Yale University Press.

Hirakawa, A. (1997). Buddhist Chinese-Sanskrit Dictionary / Bukkyō Kan-Bon daijiten. Tokyo]; [Tokyo] :: Reiyūkai : Hatsubaimoto Innātorippusha; 霊友会 : 発売元いんなあとりっぷ社.

Kumārajīva and Buddhayaśas (c. 408). Shizhu jing (十住經). T10, no. 286.

Ñāṇamoli, & Bodhi. (1995). The Middle Length Discourses of the Buddha: A New Translation of the Majjhima Nikāya (Teachings of the Buddha). Boston: Wisdom Publications in association with the Barre Center for Buddhist Studies.

Rahder, J. (1928). Glossary of the Sanskrit, Tibetan, Mongolian, and Chinese Versions of the Daśabhūmika-Sūtra. Compiled by J. Rahder. (Buddhica, Documents et Travaux pour l'Étude du Bouddhisme publiés sous la direction de J. Przyluski; Deuxième Série; Documents—Tome I). Paris: Librarie Orientaliste Paul Geuthner, 1928.

Rahder, J., & Vasubandhu. (1926). Daśabhumikasutra. Leuven: J.B. Istas.

Robinson, R. (1967). Early Mādhyamika in India and China. Madison: University of London.

Śīladharma (c. 790 CE) - T 287. Foshuo shidi jing (佛說十地經). T10, no. 287.

Sinor, D., Raghu Vira, Honda, Megumu, & Permanent International Altaistic Conference. (1968). Studies in South, East, and Central Asia: Presented as a memorial volume to the late Professor Raghu Vira (Śata-piṭaka series ; v. 74). New Delhi: International Academy of Indian Culture.

Rahder, J. (1928). Glossary of the Sanskrit, Tibetan, Mongolian, and Chinese Versions of the Daśabhūmika-Sūtra. Compiled by J. Rahder. (Buddhica, Documents et Travaux pour l'Étude du Bouddhisme publiés sous la direction de J. Przyluski; Deuxième Série; Documents—Tome I). Paris: Librarie Orientaliste Paul Geuthner, 1928.

Rahder, J., & Vasubandhu. (1926). Daśabhumikasutra. Leuven: J.B. Istas.

Śikṣānanda (c. 695–699 CE). Dafangguang fo huayan jing (大方廣佛華嚴經). T10, no. 279.

Takakusu, J., & Watanabe, Kaigyoku. (1924). Taishō shinshū Daizōkyō. Tōkyō; 東京 :: Taishō Issaikyō Kankōkai; 大正一切經刊行會.

Vaidya, P. L., ed. Daśabhūmikasūtram. Darbhanga: The Mithila Institute of Post-Graduate Studies and Research in Sanskrit Learning, 1969.

Walshe, M. (2012). The Long Discourses of the Buddha: A Translation of the Dīgha Nikāya (Teachings of the Buddha). Boston: Wisdom Publications.

Williams, M. Monier, Sir. (n.d.). A Sanskrit-English Dictionary. Delhi: Sri Satguru.

Zhonghua dian zi fo dian xie hui. (2004). CBETA dian zi fo dian ji cheng = CBETA Chinese electronic Tripitaka collection (Version 2004. ed.). Taibei; 台北 :: Zhonghua dian zi fo dian xie hui; 中華電子佛典協會.

Appendix: The P.L. Vaidya Sanskrit Text[1]

|| Daśabhūmikasūtram ||

1 pramuditā nāma prathamā bhūmiḥ |

A

evaṃ mayā śrutam | ekasmin samaye bhagavān paranirmitavaśavartiṣu devabhuvaneṣu viharati sma acirābhisaṃbuddho dvitīye saptāhe vaśavartino devarājasya vimāne maṇiratnagarbhe prabhāsvare prāsāde mahatā bodhisattvagaṇena sārdhaṃ sarvairavaivartikairekajātipratibaddhaiḥ | yaduta anuttarāyāṃ samyaksaṃbodhāvanyonyalokadhātusaṃnipatitaiḥ | sarvaiḥ sarvabodhisattvajñānaviṣayagocarapratilabdhavihāribhiḥ sarvatathāgatajñānaviṣayapraveśāvatārāpratiprasrabdhagocaraiḥ sarvajagatparipācanavinayayathākālakṣaṇādhiṣṭhānasarvakriyāsaṃdarśanakuśalaiḥ sarvabodhisattvapraṇidhānābhinirhārāpratiprasrabdhagocaraiḥ kalpārthakṣetracaryāsaṃvāsibhiḥ sarvabodhisattvapuṇyajñānarddhisaṃbhārasuparipūrṇākṣayasarvajagadupajīvyatāpratipannaiḥ sarvabodhisattvaprajñopāyaparamapāramitāprāptaiḥ saṃsāranirvāṇamukhasaṃdarśanakuśalaiḥ bodhisattvacaryopādānāvyavacchinnaiḥ sarvabodhisattvadhyānavimokṣasamādhisamāpatyabhijñājñānavikrī ḍitābhijñāsarvakriyāsaṃdarśanakuśalaiḥ sarvabodhisattvarddhibalavaśitāprāptānabhisaṃskāracittakṣaṇasarvatathāgataparṣanmaṇḍalop asaṃkramaṇapūrvaṃgamakathāpuruṣaiḥ sarvatathāgatadharmacakrasaṃdhāraṇavipulabuddhapūjopasthānābhyutthitaiḥ sarvabodhisattvakarmasamādānasamatāprayogasarvalokadhātukāyapratibhāsaprāptaiḥ sarvadharmadhātvasaṅgasvararutaghoṣānuravitasarvatryadhvāsaṅgacittajñānaviṣayaspharaṇaiḥ sarvabodhisattvaguṇapratipattisuparipūrṇānabhilāpyakalpādhiṣṭhānasaṃprakāśanāparikṣīṇaguṇavarṇanirdeśakaiḥ | yadidamvajragarbheṇa ca bodhisattvena mahāsattvena | ratnagarbheṇa ca | padmagarbheṇa ca | śrīgarbheṇa ca | padmaśrīgarbheṇa ca | ādityagarbheṇa ca | sūryagarbheṇa ca | kṣitigarbheṇa ca | śaśivimalagarbheṇa ca | sarvavyūhālaṃkārapratibhāsasaṃdarśanagarbheṇa ca | jñānavairocanagarbheṇa ca | ruciraśrīgarbheṇa ca | candanaśrīgarbheṇa ca | puṣpaśrīgarbheṇa ca | kusumaśrīgarbheṇa ca | utpalaśrīgarbheṇa ca | devaśrīgarbheṇa ca | puṇyaśrīgarbheṇa ca | anāvaraṇajñānaviśuddhigarbheṇa ca | guṇaśrīgarbheṇa ca | nārāyaṇaśrīgarbheṇa ca |

amalagarbheṇa ca | vimalagarbheṇa ca | vicitrapratibhānālaṃkāragarbheṇa ca | mahāraśmijālāvabhāsagarbheṇa ca | vimalaprabhāsaśrītejorājagarbheṇa ca | sarvalakṣaṇapratimaṇḍitaviśuddhiśrīgarbheṇa ca | vajrārciḥśrīvatsālaṃkāragarbheṇa ca | jyotirjvalanārciḥśrīgarbheṇa ca | nakṣatrarājaprabhāvabhāsagarbheṇa ca | gaganakośānāvaraṇajñānagarbheṇa ca | anāvaraṇasvaramaṇḍalamadhuranirghoṣagarbheṇa ca | dhāraṇīmukhasarvajagatpraṇidhisaṃdhāraṇagarbheṇa ca | sāgaravyūhagarbheṇa ca | meruśrīgarbheṇa ca | sarvaguṇaviśuddhigarbheṇa ca | tathāgataśrīgarbheṇa ca | buddhaśrīgarbheṇa ca | vimukticandreṇa ca bodhisattvena mahāsattvena | evaṃpramukhairaparimāṇāprameyāsaṃkhyeyācintyātulyāmāpyānantāparyantāsīmāprāptānabhilāpyānabhilāpyair bodhisattvairmahāsattvaiḥ sārdhaṃ nānābuddhakṣetrasaṃnipatitairvajragarbhabodhisattvapūrvaṃgamaiḥ ||

B

atha khalu vajragarbho bodhisattvayāṃ velāyāṃ buddhānubhāvena mahāyānaprabhāsaṃ nāma bodhisattvasamādhiṃ samāpadyate sma |

C

samanantarasamāpannaśca vajragarbho bodhisattva imaṃ mahāyānaprabhāsaṃ nāma bodhisattvasamādhim,atha tāvadeva daśasu dikṣu daśabuddhakṣetrakoṭiparamāṇurajaḥsamānāṃ lokadhātūnāmapareṇa daśabuddhakṣetrakoṭiparamāṇurajaḥsamāstathāgatā mukhānyupardaṣayāmāsuṃ yadidaṃ vajragarbhasamanāmakā eva | te cainaṃ buddhā bhagavanta evamūcuḥ-sādhu sādhu bho jinaputra, yastvamimaṃ mahāyānaprabhāsaṃ bodhisattvasamādhiṃ samāpadyase | api tu khalu punastvaṃ kulaputra, amī daśasu dikṣu daśabuddhakṣetrakoṭiparamāṇurajaḥsamānāṃ lokadhātūnāmapareṇa daśabuddhakṣetrakoṭiparamāṇurajaḥsamāstathāgatā adhitiṣṭhanti sarve vajragarbhasamanāmānaḥ asyaiva bhagavato vairocanasya pūrvapraṇidhānādhiṣṭhānena tava ca puṇyajñānaviśeṣeṇa sarvabodhisattvānāṃ ca acintyabuddhadharmālokaprabhāvanājñānabhūmyavatāraṇāya |

D

sarvakuśalamūlasaṃgrahaṇāya | sarvabuddhadharmanirdeśāya | asaṃbhinnajñānavyavadānāya | sarvalokadharmānupalepāya | lokottarakuśalamūlapariśodhanāya | acintyajñānaviṣayādhigamāya

| yāvatsarvajñānaviṣayādhigamāya | yadidaṃ daśānāṃ bodhisattvabhūmīnāmārambhapratilambhāya | yathāvadbodhisattvabhūmivyavasthānanirdeśāya | sarvabuddhadharmādhyālambanāya | anāsravadharmapravibhāgavibhāvanāya | suvicitavicayamahāprajñālokakauśalyāya | sunistīritakauśalyajñānamukhāvatāraṇāya | yathārhasthānāntaraprabhāvanāmandapratibhānālokāya | mahāpratisaṃvidbhūministīraṇāya | bodhicittasmṛtyasaṃpramoṣāya | sarvasattvadhātuparipācanāya | sarvatrānugataviniścayakauśalyapratilambhāya |

E

api tu khalu punaḥ kulaputra pratibhātu te'yaṃ dharmālokamukhaprabhedakauśalyadharmaparyāyo buddhānubhāvena tathāgatajñānālokādhiṣṭhānena svakuśalamūlapariśodhanāya dharmadhātusuparyavadāpanāya sattvadhātvanugrahāya dharmakāyajñānaśārīrāya sarvabuddhābhiṣekasaṃpratīcchanāya sarvalokābhyudgatātmabhāvasaṃdarśanāya sarvalokagatisamatikramāya lokottadharmagatipariśodhanāya sarvajñajñānaparipūraṇāya ||

F

atha khalu te buddhā bhagavanto vajragarbhasya bodhisattvasya anabhibhūtātmabhāvatāṃ copasaṃharanti sma | asaṅgapratibhānanirdeśatāṃ ca suviśobhitajñānavibhaktipraveśatāṃ ca smṛtyasaṃprabhoṣādhiṣṭhānatāṃ ca suviniścitamatikauśalyatāṃ ca sarvatrānugatabuddhyanutsargatāṃ ca samyaksaṃbuddhabalānavamṛdyatāṃ ca tathāgatavaiśāradyānavalīnatāṃ ca sarvajñajñānapratisaṃvidvibhāgadharmanayanistīraṇatāṃ ca sarvatathāgatasuvibhaktakāyavākcittālaṃkārābhinirhāratāṃ copasaṃharanti sma |

G

tatkasmāddhetoḥ? yathāpi nāma asyaiva samādherdharmatāpratilambhena pūrvaṃ praṇidhānābhirhāreṇa ca supariśodhitādhyāśayatayā ca svavadātajñānamaṇḍalatayā ca susaṃbhṛtasaṃbhāratayā ca sukṛtaparikarmatayā ca apramāṇasmṛtibhājanatayā ca prabhāsvarādhimuktiviśodhanatayā ca suprатividvadhāraṇīmukhāsaṃbhedanatayā ca dharmadhātujñānamudrāsumudritatayā ca ||

H

atha khalu te buddhā bhagavantastatrasthā eva ṛddhyanubhāvena dakṣiṇān pāṇīn prasārya vajragarbhasya bodhisattvasya śīrṣaṃ saṃpramārjayanti sma ।

I

samanantaraspṛṣṭaśca vajragarbho bodhisattvastairbuddhairbhagavadbhiḥ, atha tāvadeva samādhestasmād vyutthāya tān bodhisattvānāmantrayate sma - suviniścitamidaṃ bhavanto jinaputrā bodhisattvapraṇidhānamasaṃbhinnamanavalokyaṃ dharmadhātuvipulaṃ ākāśadhātuparyavasānamaparāntakoṭiniṣṭhaṃ sarvasattvadhātuparitrāṇam । yatra hi nāma bhavanto jinaputrā bodhisattvā atītānāmapi buddhānāṃ bhagavatāṃ jñānabhūmimavataranti, anāgatānāmapi buddhānāṃ bhagavatāṃ jñānabhūmimavataranti pratyutpannānāmapi buddhānāṃ bhagavatāṃ jñānabhūmimavataranti, tatra bhavanto jinaputrā daśa bodhisattvabhūmayo buddhānāṃ bhagavatāṃ jñānabhūmimavataranti, tatra bhavanto jinaputrāśca daśa bodhisattvabhūmayo'tītānāgatapratyutpannairbuddhairbhagadbhirbhāṣitāśca bhāṣiṣyante ca bhāṣyante ca, yāḥ saṃdhāya ahaṃ evaṃ vadāmi । katamā daśa ? yaduta pramuditā ca nāma bodhisattvabhūmiḥ । vimalā ca nāma । prabhākarī ca nāma । arciṣmatī ca nāma । sudurjayā ca nāma । abhimukhī ca nāma । dūraṃgamā ca nāma । acalā ca nāma । sādhumatī ca nāma । dharmameghā ca nāma bodhisattvabhūmiḥ । imā bhavanto jinaputrā daśa bodhisattvānāṃ bodhisattvabhūmayaḥ, yā atītānāgatapratyutpannaīrbuddhairbhagavadbhirbhāṣitāśca bhāṣiṣyante ca bhāṣyante ca । nāhaṃ bhavanto jinaputrāstaṃ buddhakṣetraprasaraṃ samanupaśyāmi, yatra tathāgatā imā daśa bodhisattvabhūmīrna prakāśayanti । tatkasya hetoḥ ? sāmutkarṣiko›yaṃ bhavanto jinaputrā bodhisattvānāṃ mahāsattvānāṃ bodhi(sattva)mārgapariśodhanadharmamukhāloko yadidaṃ daśabhūmiprabhedavyavasthānam । acintyamidaṃ bhavanto jinaputrāḥ sthānaṃ yadidaṃ bhūmijñānamiti । ।

K

atha khalu vajragarbho bodhisattva āsāṃ daśānāṃ bodhisattvabhūmīnāṃ nāmadheyamātraṃ parikīrtya tūṣṇīṃ babhūva, na bhūyaḥ prabhedaśo nirdiśati sma । atha khalu sā sarvāvatī bodhisattvaparṣat paritṛṣitā babhūva āsāṃ daśānāṃ bodhisattvabhūmīnāṃ nāmadheyamātraśravaṇena bhūmivibhāgānudīraṇena ca । tasyā etadabhavat-ko nu khalvatra hetuḥ kaśca pratyayaḥ, yadvajragarbho bodhisattva āsāṃ bodhisattvabhūmīnāṃ nāmadheyamātraṃ parikīrtya tūṣṇīṃbhāvena atināmayati, na bhūyaḥ prabhedaśo nirdiśatīti ?

tena khalu punaḥ samayena tasminneva bodhisattvaparṣatsaṃnipāte vimukticandro nāma bodhisattvastasyā bodhisattvaparṣadaścittāśayavicāramājñāya vajragarbhaṃ bodhisattvaṃ gāthābhigītena parigṛcchati sma -

kimarthaṃ śuddhasaṃkalpasmṛtijñānaguṇānvita |
samudīryottamā bhūmīrna prakāśayase vibho || 1 ||

viniścitā ime sarve bodhisattvā mahāyaśaḥ |
kasmādudīrya bhūmīśca(stvaṃ) pravibhāgaṃ na bhāṣase || 2 ||

śrotukāmā ime sarve jinaputrā viśāradāḥ |
vibhajyārthagatiṃ samyaragbhūmīnāṃ samudāhara || 3 ||

parṣadvi viprasanneyaṃ kausīdyāpagatā śubhā |
śuddhā pratiṣṭhitā sāre guṇajñānasamanvitā || 4 ||

nirīkṣamāṇā anyonyaṃ sthitāḥ sarve sagauravāḥ |
kṣaudraṃ hyaneḍakaṃ yadvatkāṅkṣanti tvamṛtopamam || 5 ||

tasya śrutvā mahāprajño vajragarbho viśāradaḥ |
parṣatsaṃtoṣaṇārthaṃ hi bhāṣate sma jinātmajaḥ || 6 ||

duṣkaraṃ paramametadadbhutaṃ
bodhisattvacaritapradarśanam |
bhūmikāraṇavibhāga uttamo
buddhabhāvasamudāgamo yataḥ || 7 ||

sūkṣma durdṛśa vikalpavarjita-
ścittabhūmivigato durāsadaḥ |
gocaro hi viduṣāmanāsravo
yatra muhyati jagacchave sati || 8 ||

vajropamaṃ hṛdayaṃ sthāpayitvā
buddhajñānaṃ paramaṃ cādhimucya ।
anātmānaṃ cittabhūmiṃ viditvā
śakyaṃ śrotuṃ jñānametatsusūkṣmam ।। 9 ।।

antarīkṣa iva raṅgacitraṇā
mārutaḥ khagapathāśrito yathā ।
jñānamevamiha bhāgaśaḥ kṛtaṃ
durdṛśaṃ bhagavatāmanāsravam ।। 10 ।।

tasya me bhavati buddhirīdṛśī
durlabho jagati yo'sya vedakaḥ ।
śraddhadhīta ca ya etaduttamaṃ
na prakāśayitumutsahe yataḥ ।। 11 ।।

L

evamukte vimukticandro bodhisattvo vajragarbhaṃ bodhisattvametadavocat - supariśuddho batāyaṃ bho jinaputra parṣatsaṃnipātaḥ supariśodhitādhyāśayānāṃ bodhisattvānāṃ supariśodhitasaṃkalpānāṃ sucaritacaraṇānāṃ suparyupāsitabahubuddhakoṭiśatasahasrāṇāṃ susaṃbhṛtasaṃbhārāṇāmaparimitaguṇajñānasamanvāgatānāmapagatavimatisaṃdehānāmanaṅgaṇānāṃ supratiṣṭhitādhyāśayādhimuktīnāmaparapratyayānāmeṣu buddhadharmeṣu । tatsādhu bho jinaputra, prabhāṣasva । pratyakṣavihāriṇo hyate bodhisattvā atra sthāne ।।

M

vajragarbha āha - kiṃcāpi bho jinaputra ayaṃ bodhisattvaparṣatsaṃnipātaḥ supariśuddhaḥ । peyālaṃ । atha ca punarye'nye imānyevaṃrūpāṇyacintyāni sthānāni śṛṇuyuḥ, śrutvā ca vimatisaṃdehamutpādayeyuḥ, teṣāṃ tatsyāddīrgharātramanarthāya ahitāya duḥkhāya । iyaṃ me kāruṇyacittatā, yena tūṣṇīṃbhāvamevābhirocayāmi ।।

N

atha khalu vimukticandro bodhisattvaḥ punareva vajragarbhaṃ bodhisattvametamevārthamadhyeṣate sma - tatsādhu bho jinaputra, prabhāṣasva । tathāgatasyaivānubhāvena imānyevaṃrūpāṇyacintyāni sthānāni svārakṣitāni śraddheyāni bhaviṣyanti । taskasya hetoḥ? tathā hi bho jinaputra asmin bhūminirdeśe bhāṣyamāṇe dharmatāpratilambha eṣa yatsarvabuddhasamanvāhāro bhavati I sarve bodhisattvāśca asyā eva jñānabhūmerārakṣārthamautsukyam-āpadyante I tatkasya hetoḥ? eṣā hyādicaryā I eṣa samudāgamo buddhadharmāṇām I tadyathāpi nāma bho jinaputra sarva-lipyakṣarasaṃkhyānirdeśo mātṛkāpūrvaṃgamo mātṛkāpary-avasānaḥ nāsti sa lipyakṣarasaṃkhyānirdeśo yo vinā mātṛkānir-deśam, evameva bho jinaputra sarve buddhadharmā bhūmipūrva-ṃgamāśca caryāpariniṣpattito bhūmiparyavasānāḥ svayaṃbhūjñān-ādhigamatayā I tasmāttarhi bho jinaputra, prabhāṣasva I tathāgatā eva arhantaḥ samyaksaṃbuddhā ārakṣāmadhiṣṭhāsyanti I I

O

atha khalu te sarve bodhisattvā ekasvarasaṃgītena tasyāṃ velāyāṃ vajragarbhaṃ bodhisattvaṃ gāthābhigītenaiva tamartham-adhyeṣante sma -

pravaravaravimalabuddhe svabhidhānānantaghaṭitapratibha I
pravyāhara madhuravarāṃ vācaṃ paramārthasaṃyuktām I I 12 I I

smṛtidhṛtiviśuddhabuddhe daśabalabalalābhamāśayaviśuddhim I
pratisaṃviddaśavicayaṃ bhāṣasva daśottamā bhūmīḥ I I 13 I I

śamaniyamanibhṛtasumanāḥ prahīṇamadamānadṛṣṭisaṃkleśā I
niṣkāṅkṣā parṣadiyaṃ prārthayate bhāṣitāni tava I I 14 I I

tṛṣita iva śītamudakaṃ bubhukṣito'nnaṃ subheṣajamivārtaḥ I
kṣaudramiva sa madhukaragaṇastava vācamudīkṣate parṣat I I 15 I I

tatsādhu vimalabuddhe bhūmiviśeṣān vadasva virajaskān I
daśabalayuktāsaṅgāṃ sugatagatimudīrayannikhilām I I 16 I I

P

atha khalu tasyāṃ velāyāṃ bhagavataḥ śākyamunerūrṇākośād bodhisattvabalāloko nāma raśmirniścacāra asaṃkhyeyāsaṃkhyeya-raśmiparivārā I sā sarvāsu daśasu dikṣu sarvalokadhātupra-sarānavabhāsya sarvāpāyaduḥkhāni pratiprasrabhya sarvamāra-bhavanāni dhyāmīkṛtya aparimitāni buddhaparṣanmaṇḍalāny-avabhāsya acintyaṃ buddhaviṣayākāraprabhāvaṃ nidarśya sarvāsu daśasu dikṣu sarvalokadhātuprasareṣu sarvatathāgataparṣanmaṇḍaleṣu dharmadeśanādhiṣṭhānādhiṣṭhitān bodhisattvān-avabhāsya acintyaṃ buddhavikurvaṇaṃ saṃdarśya uparyantarīkṣe mahāraśmighanābhrajālakūṭāgāraṃ kṛtvā tasthau I teṣāmapi buddhānāṃ bhagavatāmūrṇākośebhya evameva bodhisattvabalālokā nāma raśmayo niśceruḥ I niścarya asaṃkhyeyāsaṃkhyeyaraśmi-parivārāstāḥ sarvāsu....pe...buddhavikurvaṇamādarśya idaṃ bhagavataḥ śākyamuneḥ parṣanmaṇḍalaṃ vajragarbhasya bodhi-sattvasyātmabhāvamavabhāsya uparyantarīkṣe evameva mahāraśmi-ghanābhrajālakūṭāgāraṃ kṛtvā tasthuḥ I iti hi ābhiśca bhagavataḥ śākyamunerūrṇākośaprasṛtābhī raśmibhiste lokadhātavastāni ca buddhaparṣanmaṇḍalāni teṣāṃ ca bodhisattvānāṃ kāyā āsanāni ca sphuṭānyavabhāsitāni saṃdṛśyante sma I teṣāṃ ca aparimāṇeṣu lokadhātuṣu buddhānāṃ bhagavatāmūrṇākośaprasṛtābhī raśmi-bhirayaṃ trisāhasramahāsāhasralokadhāturidaṃ ca bhagavataḥ śākyamuneḥ parṣanmaṇḍalaṃ vajragarbhasya ca bodhisattvasya kāya āsanaṃ sphuṭamavabhāsitaṃ saṃdṛśyante sma I atha khalu tato mahāraśmighanābhrajālakūṭāgārādvuddhānubhāvena ayam-evaṃrūpaḥ śabdo niścarati sma –

asamasamākāśamairdaśabalavṛṣabhairanantamukhyaguṇaiḥ I
śākyakulajasya dharmairdevamanuṣyottamaiḥ kṛtamadhiṣṭhānam I I
17 I I

anubhāvātsugatānāṃ kośaṃ vivṛṇuṣva dharmarājānām I
caryāvarāmudārāṃ prabhedaśo jñānabhūmiṃ ca I I 18 I I

adhiṣṭhitāste sugatairdhāritā bodhisattvaiśca I
yeṣāṃ śrotrapathāgataḥ śreṣṭho yo dharmaparyāyaḥ I I 19 I I

daśa bhūmīrvirajasaḥ pūrayitvānupūrveṇa I
balāni daśa ca prāpya jinatāmarpayiṣyanti I I 20 I I

sāgarajale nimagnāḥ kalpoddāheṣu prakṣiptāḥ I
bhavyāste dharmaparyāyamimaṃ śrotumasaṃdigdhāḥ I I 21 I I

ye tu vimatisaktāḥ saṃśayaiścābhyupetāḥ I
sarvaśo na hi teṣāṃ prāpsyate śrotrametat I I 22 I I

bhūmijñānapathaṃ śreṣṭhaṃ praveśasthānasaṃkramam |
anupūrveṇa bhāṣasva caryāviṣayameva ca || 23 ||
Q
atha khalu vajragarbho bodhisattvo daśa diśo vyavalokya bhūyasyā mātrayā tasyāḥ parṣadaḥ saṃprasādarnārthaṃ tasyāṃ velāyāmimā gāthā abhāṣata -

sūkṣmaṃ durājñeyapadaṃ maharṣiṇā-
makalpakalpāpagataṃ suduḥspṛśam |
anāvilaṃ paṇḍitavijñaveditaṃ
svabhāvaśāntaṃ hyanirodhasaṃbhavam || 24 ||

svabhāvaśūnyaṃ praśamādvayakṣayaṃ
gatyā vimuktaṃ samatāptinirvṛtam |
anantamadhyaṃ vacasānudīritaṃ
triyaghvavimuktaṃ nabhasā samānakam || 25 ||

śāntaṃ praśāntaṃ sugatapraveditaṃ
sarvairudāhārapadaiḥ sudurvacam |
bhūmiśca caryāpi ca tasya tādṛśī
vaktuṃ suduḥkhaḥ kuta eva śrotum || 26 ||

taccintayā cittapathaiśca varjitaṃ
jñānābhinirhāramunīndraveditam |
na skandhadhātvāyatanaprabhāvitaṃ
na cittagamyaṃ na manovicintitam || 27 ||

yathāntarīkṣe śakuneḥ padaṃ budhai-
rvaktuṃ na śakyaṃ na ca darśanopagam |
tathaiva sarvā jinaputra bhūmayo
vaktuṃ na śakyāḥ kuta eva śrotum || 28 ||

pradeśamātraṃ tu tato'bhidhāsye
maitrīkṛpābhyāṃ praṇidhānataśca |
yathānupūrvaṃ na ca cittagocaraṃ
zñānena tāḥ pūrayatāṃ yathāśayam || 29 ||

etādṛśo gocara durdṛśo'sya
vaktuṃ na śakyaḥ sa hi svāśayasthaḥ |
kiṃ tu pravakṣyāmi jinānubhāvataḥ
śṛṇvantu sarve sahitāḥ sagauravāḥ || 30 ||

jñānapraveśaḥ sa hi tādṛśo'sya
vaktuṃ na kalpairapi śakyate yat |
samāsatastacchṛṇuta bravīmyahaṃ
dharmārthatattvaṃ nikhilaṃ yathāsthitam || 31 ||

sagauravāḥ santa(ḥ) sajjā bhavanto
vakṣyāmyahaṃ sādhu jinānubhāvataḥ |
udīrayiṣye varadharmaghoṣaṃ
dṛṣṭāntayuktaṃ sahitaṃ samākṣaram || 32 ||

suduṣkaraṃ tadvacasāpi vaktuṃ
yaścāprameyaḥ sugatānubhāvaḥ |
mayi praviṣṭaḥ sa ca raśmimūrti-
ryasyānubhāvena mamāsti śaktiḥ || 33 ||

R

tatra bhavanto jinaputrāḥ sūpacitakuśalamūlānāṃ sucarita-caraṇānāṃ susaṃbhṛtasaṃbhārāṇāṃ suparyupāsitabuddh-otpādānāṃ suparipiṇḍitaśukladharmāṇāṃ suparigṛhītakalyāṇa-mitrāṇāṃ suviśuddhāśayānāṃ vipulāghyāśayopagatānāṃ udārādhi-muktisamanvāgatānāṃ kṛpākaruṇābhimukhānāṃ (bodhi)sattvānāṃ bodhāya cittamutpādyate |

S

buddhajñānābhilāṣāya daśabalabalādhigamāya mahāvaiśārady-ādhigamāya samatābuddhadharmapratilambhāya sarvajagatpari-trāṇāya mahākṛpākaruṇāviśodhanāya daśadigaśeṣajñānādhigamāya sarvabuddhakṣetrāsaṅgapariśodhanāya tryadhvaikakṣaṇavibodhāya mahādharmacakrapravartanavaiśāradyāya ca taccittamutpadyate bodhisattvānāṃ

T

mahākaruṇāpūrvaṃgamaṃ prajñājñānādhipateyamupāyakauśalya-parigṛhītamāśayādhyāśayopastabdhaṃ tathāgatabalāprameyaṃ sattvabalabuddhibalasuvicitavicayamasaṃbhinnajñānābhimukhaṃ svayaṃbhūjñānānukūlaṃ sarvabuddhadharmaprajñājñānāvavādasaṃpratyeṣakaṃ dharmadhātuparamamākāśadhātusthitakamaparāntakoṭiniṣṭham ǀ

U

yena cittotpādena sahotpannena bodhisattvo'tikrānto bhavati, pṛthagjñānabhūmīmavakrānto bhavati, bodhisattvaniyāmaṃ jāto bhavati, tathāgatakule'navadyo bhavati, sarvajātivādena vyāvṛtto bhavati, sarvalokagatibhyo'vakrānto bhavati, lokottarāṃ gatiṃ sthito bhavati, bodhisattvadharmatāyāṃ suvyavasthito bhavati, bodhisattvāvasthānena samatānugato bhavati, tryaghvatathāgatavaṃśaniyato bhavati saṃbodhiparāyaṇaḥ ǀ evaṃrūpadharmavyavasthito bhavanto jinaputrā bodhisattvaḥ pramuditāyāṃ bodhisattvabhūmau vyavasthito bhavatyacalanayogena ǀǀ

V

atra bhavanto jinaputrāḥ pramuditāyāṃ bodhisattvabhūmau sthito bodhisattvaḥ prāmodyabahulo bhavati prasādabahulaḥ prītibahula utplāvanābahula udagrībahula utsībahula utsāhabahulo'saṃrambhabahulo'vihiṃsābahulo'krodhabahulo bhavati ǀ

W

iti hi bhavanto jinaputrāḥ pramuditāyāṃ bodhisattvabhūmau sthito bodhisattvan pramudito bhavati, buddhān bhagavato›nusmaran buddhadharmān bodhisattvān bodhisattvacaryāḥ pāramitāviśuddhiṃ bodhisattvabhūmiviśeṣān bodhisattvāsaṃhāryatāṃ tathāgatāvavādānuśāsanīṃ sattvārthasaṃprāpaṇam ǀ pramudito bhavati sarvatathāgatajñānapraveśaprayogamanusmaran ǀ bhūyaḥ prāmodyavān bhavati –

X

vyāvṛtto'smi sarvajagadviṣayāt, avatīrṇo'smi buddhabhūmisamīpam, dūrībhūto'smi bālapṛthagjanabhūmeḥ, āsanno'smi jñānabhūmeḥ, vyavacchinno'smi sarvāpāyadurgativinipātāt, pratiśaraṇabhūto'smi sarvasattvānām, āsannadarśano'smi sarvatathāgatānām, saṃbhūto'smi sarvabuddhaviṣaye, sarvabodhisattvasamatām upagato'smi ǀ vigatāni me sarvabhayatrāsacchambhitatvānīti prāmodyamutpādayati ǀ

Y

tatkasya hetoḥ ? tathā hi bhavanto jinaputrā bodhisattvasya asyāḥ pramuditāyā bodhisattvabhūmeḥ sahapratilambhena yānīmāni bhayāni bhavanti - yadidamājīvikābhayaṃ vā aślokabhayaṃ vā maraṇabhayaṃ vā durgatibhayaṃ vā parṣacchāradyabhayaṃ vā, tāni sarvāṇi vyapagatāni bhavanti I tatkasya hetoḥ ? yathāpi idam-ātmasaṃjñāpagamādātmasneho›sya na bhavati, kutaḥ punaḥ sarv-opakaraṇasnehaḥ ? ato'sya ājīvikābhayaṃ na bhavati I na ca kaṃcit-satkāraṃ kasyacitsakāśātpratikāṅkṣati, anyatra mayaiva teṣāṃ sattvānāṃ sarvopakaraṇabāhulyamupanāmayitavyamiti, ato'sya aślokabhayaṃ na bhavati I ātmadṛṣṭivigamācca asyātmasaṃjñā na bhavati, ato'sya maraṇabhayaṃ na bhavati I mṛtasyaiva me niyataṃ buddhabodhisattvairna virahito bhaviṣyāmīti, ato'sya durgati-bhayaṃ na bhavati I nāsti me kaścidāśayena sarvaloke samasamaḥ, kutaḥ punaruttara ityato'sya parṣacchāradyabhayaṃ na bhavati I evaṃ sarvabhayatrāsacchambhitatvaromaharṣāpagataḥ I I

Z

atha khalu punarbhavanto jinaputrā bodhisattvo mahākaruṇāpuras-kṛtatvādanupahatena aprākṛtenādhyāśayena bhūyasyā mātrayā prayujyate sarvakuśalamūlamudāgamāya I

AA

sa śraddhādhipateyatayā prasādabahulatayā adhimuktiviśuddhyā avakalpanābahulatayā kṛpākaruṇābhinirhāratayā mahāmaitry-upetatayā aparikhinnamānasatayā hryapatrāpyālaṃkāratayā kṣāntisauratyopetatayā tathāgatārhatsamyaksaṃbuddhaśāsana-gauravacitrīkaraṇatayā

BB

rātriṃdivātṛptakuśalamūlopacayatayā kalyāṇamitraniṣevaṇatayā dharmārāmābhiratatayā atṛptabāhuśrutyaparyeṣaṇatayā yathāśruta-dharmayoniśaḥpratyavekṣaṇatayā aniketamānasatayā anadhya-vasitalābhasatkāraślokatayā anabhinanditopakaraṇasnehatayā ratn-opamacittotpādātṛptābhinirhāratayā

CC

sarvajñabhūmyabhilāṣaṇatayā tathāgatabalavaiśāradyāveṇika-buddhadharmādhyālambanatayā pāramitāsaṅgaparyeṣaṇatayā māyāśāṭhyaparivarjanatayā yathāvāditathākāritayā satatasamitaṃ satyavacanānurakṣaṇatayā tathāgatakulabhūṣaṇatayā bodhisattva-śikṣānutsarjanatayā mahāśailendrarājopamasarvajñatācittā-prakampanatayā sarvalokakriyānabhilakṣaṇatayā utsargalokottarapathopetatayā atṛptabodhyaṅgasaṃbhāropacayatayā satatasamitamuttarottaraviśeṣaparimārgaṇatayā I evaṃrūpairbhavanto jinaputrā bhūmipariśodhakairdharmaiḥ samanvāgato bodhisattvaḥ supratiṣṭhito bhavati pramuditāyāṃ bodhisattvabhūmau I I

DD

so'syāṃ pramuditāyāṃ bodhisattvabhūmau sthitaḥ san imānyevaṃrūpāṇi mahāpraṇidhānāni mahāvyavasāyān mahābhinirhārānabhinirharati - yaduta aśeṣaniḥśeṣānavaśeṣasarvabuddhapūjopasthāpanāya sarvākāravaropetamudārādhimuktiviśuddhaṃ dharmadhātuvipulamākāśadhātuparyavasānamaparāntakoṭiniṣṭhaṃ sarvakalpasaṃkhyābuddhotpādaṃsaṃkhyāpratiprasrabdhaṃ mahāpūjopasthānāya prathamaṃ mahāpraṇidhānamabhinirharati I

EE

yaduta sarvatathāgatabhāṣitadharmanetrīsaṃdhāraṇāya sarvabuddhabodhisattvasuparigrahāya sarvasamyaksaṃbuddhaśāsanaparirakṣaṇāya....buddhotpādasaddharmaparigrahāya dvitīyam I

FF

yaduta sarvabuddhotpādaniravaśeṣasarvalokadhātuprasareṣu tuṣitabhavanavāsamādiṃ kṛtvā cyavanāsaṃkramaṇagarbhasthitijanmakumārakrīḍāntaḥpuravāsābhiniṣkramaṇaduṣkaracaryābo dhimaṇḍopa-saṃkramaṇamāragharṣaṇābhisaṃbodhyadhyeṣaṇamahādharmacakrapravartanamahāparinirvāṇopasaṃkramaṇāya pūjādharmasaṃgrahaprayogapūrvaṃgamaṃ kṛtvā sarvatraikakālavivartanāya...buddhotpāda....yāvanmahāparinirvāṇopasaṃkramaṇā ya tṛtīyam I

GG

yaduta sarvabodhisattvacaryāvipulamahadgatāpramāṇāsaṃbhinnasarvapāramitāsaṃgṛhītasarvabhūmipariśodhanaṃ sāṅgopāṅganirhārasalakṣaṇasaṃvartavivartasarvabodhisattvacaryābhūtayathāva dbhūmipathopadeśapāramitāparikarmāvavādānuśāsanyanupradāno pastabdhacittotpādābhinirhārāya...caryā...cittotpādābhinirhārāya caturtham I

HH

yaduta niravaśeṣasarvasattvadhāturūpyarūpisaṃjñāsaṃjñinaivasaṃjñināsaṃjñāṇḍajajarāyujasaṃsvedajaupapāduka-... traidhātukaparyāpannaṣaḍgatisamavasṛtasarvopapattiparyāpannanāmarūpasaṃ gṛhītāśeṣasarvasattvadhātuparipācanāya sarvabuddhadharmāvatāraṇāya sarvagatisaṃkhyāvyavacchedanāya sarvajñajñānapratiṣṭhāpanāya...sattvadhātu...sarvasattvadhātuparipācanāya pañcamam I

II

yaduta niravaśeṣasarvalokadhātuvipulasaṃkṣiptamahadgatāpramā ṇa-
sūkṣmaudārikavyatyastāvamūrdhasamatalapraveśasamavarasaraṇā nugatendrajālavibhāgadaśadigaśeṣavimātratāvibhāgapraveśajñānān ugamapratyakṣatāyai...lokadhātu...lokadhātuvaimātryāvatāraṇāya ṣaṣṭham I

JJ

yaduta sarvakṣetraikakṣetraikakṣetrasarvakṣetrasamavasaraṇapariśod hana
mapramāṇabuddhakṣetraprabhāvyūhālaṃkārapratimaṇḍitaṃ sarvakleśāpanayanapariśuddhapathopetamapramāṇajñānākarasattvapari pūrṇamudārabuddhaviṣayasamavasaraṇaṃ yathāśayasarvasattvasaṃdarśanasaṃtoṣaṇāya...buddhakṣetra...sarvabuddhakṣetrapariśod hanāya saptamam I

KK

yaduta sarvabodhisattvaikāśayaprayogatāyai niḥsapatnakuśalamūlopacayāya ekālambanasarvabodhisattvasamatāyai avirahitasatatasamitabuddhabodhisattvasamavadhānāya yatheṣṭabuddhotpādasaṃdarśanāya svacittotpādatathāgataprabhāvajñānānugamāya acyutānugāminyabhijñāpratilambhāya sarvalokadhātvanuvicaraṇāya sarvabuddhaparṣanmaṇḍalapratibhāsaprāptaye sarvopapattisvaśarīrānugamāya acintyamahāyānopetatāyai bodhisattvacaryācaraṇāvyavacchedāya...caryā...mahāyānāvatāraṇāya aṣṭamam I

LL

yaduta avivartyacakrasamārūḍhabodhisattvacaryācaraṇāya amoghakāyavāṅmanaskarmaṇe sahadarśananiyatabuddhadharmatvāya sahaghoṣodāhārajñānānugamāya sahaprasādakleśavinivartanāya mahābhaiṣajyarājopamāśrayapratilambhāya cintāmaṇivatkāyapratilambhāya sarvabodhisattvacaryā-
caraṇāya...caryā...amoghasarvaceṣṭatāyai navamam I

MM

yaduta sarvalokadhātuṣvanuttarasamyaksaṃbodhyabhisaṃbodhāya

ekavālapathāvyativṛttasarvabālapṛthagjanajanmopapatyabhiniṣkram aṇavikurvaṇabodhimaṇḍadharmacakrapravartanamahāparinirvāṇop adarśanāya mahābuddhaviṣayaprabhāvajñānānugamāya sarva-sattvadhātuyathāśayabuddhotpādakṣaṇakṣaṇavibhaṅgavibodhapraś amaprāpaṇasaṃdarśanāya ekābhisaṃbodhisarvadharmanirmāṇa-spharaṇāya ekaghoṣodāhārasarvasattvacittāśayasaṃtoṣaṇāya mahā-parinirvāṇopadarśanacaryābalāvyavacchedāya mahājñānabhūmi-sarvadharmavyavasthāpanasaṃdarśanāya dharmajñānarddhim-āyābhijñāsarvalokadhātuspharaṇāya abhisaṃbodhimahājñānābhijñ-ābhinirhārāya daśamam | iti hi bhavanto jinaputrā imānyevaṃ-rūpāṇi mahāpraṇidhānāni mahāvyavasāyān mahābhinirhārān daśa praṇidhānamukhāni pramukhaṃ kṛtvā paripūrṇāni daśapraṇidhān-āsaṃkhyeyaśatasahasrāṇi yāni bodhisattvaḥ pramuditāyāṃ bodhi-sattvabhūmau sthito'bhinirharati pratilabhate ca ||

NN

tāni ca mahāpraṇidhānāni daśabhirniṣṭhāpadairabhinirharati | katamairdaśabhiḥ? yaduta sattvadhātuniṣṭhayā ca lokadhātuniṣṭhayā ca ākāśadhātuniṣṭhayā ca dharmadhātuniṣṭhayā ca nirvāṇadhātu-niṣṭhayā ca buddhotpādadhātuniṣṭhayā ca tathāgatajñānadhātu-niṣṭhayā ca cittālambanadhātuniṣṭhayā ca buddhaviṣayajñāna-praveśadhātuniṣṭhayāḥ ca lokavartanīdharmavartanījñāna-vartanīdhātuniṣṭhayā ca | iti hi yā niṣṭhā sattvadhātuniṣṭhāyāḥ, sā me niṣṭhā eṣāṃ mahāpraṇidhānānāṃ bhavatu | yā niṣṭhā yāvajjñānavartanīdhātuniṣṭhāyāḥ, sā me niṣṭhā eṣāṃ mahāpraṇi-dhānānāṃ bhavatu | iti hyaniṣṭhā sattvadhātuniṣṭhā | aniṣṭhānīmāni me kuśalamūlāni bhavantu | aniṣṭhā yāvajjñānavartanīdhātuniṣṭhā | aniṣṭhānīmāni me kuśalamūlāni bhavantviti ||

OO

sa evaṃ svabhinihṛrtapraṇidhānaḥ karmaṇyacitto mṛducitto'saṃ-hāryaśraddho bhavati | so'bhiśraddadhāti tathāgatānāmarhatāṃ samyaksaṃbuddhānāṃ pūrvāntacaryābhinirhārapraveśaṃ pāramit-āsamudāgamaṃ bhūmipariniṣpattiṃ vaiśeṣikatāṃ balapariniṣpattiṃ vaiśāradyaparipūrimāveṇikabuddhadharmāsaṃhāryatāmacintyāṃ buddhadharmatāmanantamadhyaṃ tathāgataviṣayābhinirhārama-parimāṇajñānānugataṃ tathāgatagocarānupraveśaṃ phalapari-niṣpattimabhiśraddadhāti | samāsataḥ sarvabodhisattvacaryāṃ yāvattathāgatabhūmijñānanirdeśādhiṣṭhānamabhiśraddadhāti ||

PP

tasyaivaṃ bhavati - evaṃ gambhīrāḥ khalu punarime buddhadharmāḥ evaṃ viviktāḥ evaṃ śāntāḥ evaṃ śūnyāḥ evamānimittāḥ evamapraṇihitāḥ evaṃ nirupalepāḥ evaṃ vipulāḥ evamaparimāṇāḥ evamudārāḥ evaṃ durāsadāśceme buddhadharmāḥ |

QQ

atha ca punarime bālapṛthagjanāḥ kudṛṣṭipatitayā saṃtatyā avidyāndhakārapayarvanaddhamānasena mānadhvajasamucchrittaiḥ saṃkalpaistṛṣṇājālābhilaṣitairmanasikārairmāyāśāṭhyagahanānucarit aiścittāśayairīrṣyāmātsaryasaṃprayuktairgatyupapattiprayogai rāgadveṣamohaparicittaiḥ karmopacayaiḥ krodhopanāhasaṃdhukṣitābhiścittajvālābhirviparyāsasaṃprayuktaiḥ karmakriyābhinirhāraiḥ kāmabhavāvidyāsravānubaddhaiścittamanovijñānabījais

RR

traidhātuke punarbhavāṅkuramabhinirvartayanti yadidaṃ nāmarūpasahajāvinirbhāgagatam | tenaiva ca nāmarūpeṇa vivardhitena eṣāṃ ṣaḍāyatanagrāmaḥ saṃbhavati | saṃbhūteṣvāyataneṣvanyonyasparśanipātato vedanā saṃbhavati | tāmeva vedanāṃ bhūyo bhūyo'bhinandatāṃ tṛṣṇopādānaṃ vivardhate | vivṛddhe tṛṣṇopādāne bhavaḥ saṃbhavati | saṃbhūte ca bhave jātijarāmaraṇaśokaparidevaduḥkhadaurmanasyopāyāsāḥ prādurbhavanti | evameteṣāṃ sattvānāṃ duḥkhaskandho'bhinirvartate ātmātmīyavigato riktastucchaḥ śūnyo nirīho niśceṣṭo jaḍastṛṇakāṣṭhakuḍyavartmapratibhāsopamaḥ | na caivamavabudhyanta iti |

SS

teṣāmevaṃrūpeṇa sattvānāṃ duḥkhaskandhāvipramokṣaṃ dṛṣṭvā sattveṣu mahākaruṇonmiñjaḥ saṃbhavati - ete'smābhiḥ sattvāḥ paritrātavyāḥ parimocayitavyā ato mahāsaṃmohāt, atyantasukhe ca nirvāṇe pratiṣṭhāpayitavyāḥ iti | ato'sya mahāmaitryunmiñjaḥ saṃbhavati ||

TT

evaṃ kṛpāmaitryanugatena khalu punarbhavanto jinaputrā bodhisattvo'dhyāśayena prathamāyāṃ bodhisattvabhūmau vartamānaḥ sarvavastuṣu sāpekṣacittaṃ parivarjya buddhajñāne ca udāraspṛhābhilāṣabuddhirmahātyāgeṣu prayuñjate | sa ya ime tyāgāḥ - yaduta dhanadhānyakośakoṣṭhāgāraparityāgo vā hiraṇyasuvarṇamaṇimuktāvaiḍūryaśaṅkhaśilāpravālajātarūparajataparityāgo vā ratnābharaṇavibhūṣaṇaparityāgo vā hayarathagajapativāhanaparityāgo vā udyānatapovanavihāraparityāgo vā dāsīdāsakarmakarapauruṣeyaparityāgo vā grāmanagaranigamajanapadarāṣṭrarājadhānīparityāgo vā bhāryāputraduhitṛparityāgo vā sarvapriyamanāpavastuparityāgo vā śiraḥkarṇanāsākaracaraṇanayanasvamāṃsaśoṇitāsthimajjāmedaśchavicarmahṛdayasarvātmabhāvaparityāgo vā, teṣvanapekṣo bhūtvā sarvavastuṣu buddhajñāne ca udāraspṛhābhilāṣabuddhiḥ parityajati I evaṃ hyasya prathamāyāṃ bodhisattvabhūmau sthitasya mahātyāgaḥ saṃbhavati I I

UU

sa evaṃ karuṇāmaitrītyāgāśayo bhūtvā sarvasattvaparitrāṇārthaṃ bhūyo bhūyo laukikalokottarānarthān parimārgate parigaveṣate I parimārgamāṇaḥ parigaveṣamāṇaśca aparikhedacittamutpādayati I evamasyāparikhedaḥ saṃbhavati I aparikhinnaśca sarvaśāstraviśārado bhavati I ato'sya śāstrajñatā saṃbhavati I sa evaṃ śāstropetaḥ kriyākriyāvicāritayā buddhyā hīnamadhyapraṇīteṣu sattveṣu tathatvāya pratipadyate yathābalaṃ yathābhajamānam I ato'sya lokajñatā saṃbhavati I lokajñaśca kālavelāmātracārī hryapatrāpyavibhūṣitayā saṃtatyā ātmārthaparārtheṣu prayujyate I ato'sya hryapatrāpyaṃ saṃbhavati I teṣu ca prayogeṣu naiṣkramyacārī avivartyāpratyudāvartyabalādhānaprāpto bhavati I evamasya dhṛtibalādhānamājataṃ bhavati I dhṛtibalādhānaprāptaśca tathāgatapūjopasthāneṣu prayujyate, śāsane ca pratipadyate I evaṃ hyasyeme daśa bhūmipariśodhakā dharmā ājātā bhavanti I tadyathā - śraddhā karuṇā maitrī tyāgaḥ khedasahiṣṇutā śāstrajñatā lokajñatā hryapatrāpyaṃ dhṛtibalādhānaṃ tathāgatapūjopasthānamiti I I

VV

tasya asyāṃ pramuditāyāṃ bodhisattvabhūmau sthitasya bodhisattvasya bahavo buddhā ābhāsamāgacchanti audārikadarśanena praṇidhānabalena ca I bahūni buddhaśatāni bahūni buddhasahasrāṇi bahūni buddhaśatasahasrāṇi bahūni buddhanayutaśatasahasrāṇi bahavo buddhakoṭyo bahūni buddhakoṭīśatāni bahūni buddhakoṭīsahasrāṇi bahūni buddhakoṭīśatasahasrāṇi bahūni buddhakoṭīnayutaśatasahasrāṇyābhāsamāgacchanti audārikadarśanena praṇidhānabalena ca I sa tāṃstathāgatānarhataḥ samyaksaṃbuddhān dṛṣṭvā udārādhyāśayena satkaroti gurukaroti mānayati pūjayati, cīvarapiṇḍapātraśayanāsanaglānapratyayabhaiṣajya-

pariṣkāraiśca pratipādayati | bodhisattvasukhopadhānaṃ copasaṃharati | saṃghagaṇasaṃmānatāṃ ca karoti | tāni ca kuśalamūlānyanuttarāyāṃ samyaksaṃbodhau pariṇāmayati | tāṃśca asya buddhān bhagavataḥ pūjayataḥ sattvaparipāka ājāto bhavati | sa sattvāṃśca paripācayati dānena priyavadyena ca adhimuktibalena ca | asyopari dve arthasaṃgrahavastūnyājāyete na tu khalvaśeṣajñānaprativedhapratilambhena | tasya daśabhyaḥ pāramitābhyo dānapāramitā atiriktatamā bhavati, na ca pariśeṣāsu na samudāgacchati yathābalaṃ yathābhajamānam | sa yathā yathā buddhāṃśca bhagavataḥ pūjayati, sattvaparipākāya ca prayujya tānimān daśa bhūmipariśodhakān dharmān samādāya vartate, tathā tathāsya tāni kuśalamūlāni sarvajñatāpariṇāmitāni bhūyasyā mātrayottapyante, pariśuddhyanti, karmaṇyāni ca bhavanti yathākāmatayā | tadyathāpi nāma bhavanto jinaputrā jātarūpaṃ kuśalena karmāreṇa yathā yathāgnau prakṣipyate, tathā tathā pariśuddhyati karmaṇyaṃ ca bhavati vibhūṣaṇālaṃkāravidhiṣu yathākāmatayā, evameva bhavanto jinaputrā yathā yathā bodhisattvo-
...peyālaṃ...yathākāmatayā ||

WW

punaraparaṃ bhavanto jinaputra bodhisattvena asyāṃ prathamāyāṃ bodhisattvabhūmau sthitena asyā eva prathamāyā bodhisattvabhūmerākārapratilambhaniṣyandāḥ parimārgitavyāḥ parigaveṣitavyāḥ paripraṣṭavyāḥ | buddhabodhisattvānāṃ kalyāṇamitrāṇāṃ ca sakāśādatṛptena ca bhavitavyaṃ bhūmyaṅgapariniṣpādanāya | evaṃ yāvaddaśamyā bodhisattvabhūmeraṅgapariniṣpādanāya | tena bhūmipakṣapratipakṣakuśalena ca bhavitavyaṃ bhūmisaṃvartavivartakuśalena ca bhūmyākāraniṣyandakuśalena ca bhūmipratilambhavibhāvanākuśalena ca bhūmyaṅgapariśodhanakuśalena ca bhūmerbhūmisaṃkramaṇakuśalena ca bhūmibhūmivyavasthānakuśalena ca bhūmibhūmiviśeṣajñānakuśalena ca bhūmibhūmipratilambhāpratyudāvartyakuśalena ca sarvabodhisattvabhūmipariśodhanatayā tathāgatajñānabhūmyākramaṇakuśalena ca bhavitavyam | evaṃ bhūmyākārābhinirhārakuśalasya hi bhavanto jinaputrā bodhisattvasya prathamāyā bodhisattvabhūmerucchalitasya niṣṭhānaṃ na saṃbhavati yāvaddaśabhūmibhūmyākramaṇamiti | mārgādhiṣṭhānāgamena ca bhūmejñānālokena ca buddhajñānālokaṃ prāpnoti | tadyathāpi nāma bhavanto jinaputrāḥ kuśalaḥ sārthavāho mahāsārthaparikarṣaṇābhiprāyo mahānagaramanuprāpayitukāmaḥ ādāveva mārgaguṇāṃśca mārgavivartadoṣāṃśca mārgasthānāntaraviśeṣāṃśca mārgasthānāntaravivartadoṣāṃśca mārgakriyāpathyodanakāryatāṃ ca parimārgayati parigaveṣayate I sa yāvanmahānagarānuprāptaye kuśalo bhavatyanuccalita eva prathamānmārgāntarasthānāt I sa evaṃ jñānavicāritayā buddhyā mahāpathyodanasamṛddhyā anupūrveṇa mahāsārthena sārdhaṃ yāvanmahānagaramanuprāpnoti, na cāṭavīkāntāradoṣaiḥ sārthasya vā ātmano vāsyopaghātaḥ saṃpadyate I evameva bhavanto jinaputrā bodhisattvaḥ kuśalo mahāsārthavāho yadā prathamāyāṃ bodhisattvabhūmau sthito bhavati, tadā bhūmipakṣapratipakṣakuśalo bhavati, bhūmisaṃvartavivartakuśalo bhavati, bhūmyākāraniṣyandakuśalo bhavati, bhūmipratilambhavibhāvanākuśalo bhavati, bhūmyaṅgapariśodhanakuśalo bhavati, bhūmerbhūmisaṃkramaṇakuśalo bhavati, bhūmibhūmivyavasthānakuśalo bhavati, bhūmibhūmiviśeṣajñānakuśalo bhavati, bhūmibhūmipratilambhāpratyudāvartyakuśalo bhavati, sarvabodhisattvabhūmipariśodhanatayā tathāgatajñānabhūmyākramaṇakuśalaśca bhavati I tadā bodhisattvo mahāpuṇyasaṃbhārapathyodanasusaṃgṛhito jñānasaṃbhārasukṛtavicayo mahāsattvasārthaparikarṣaṇābhiprāyaḥ sarvajñatāmahānagaramanuprāpayitukāmaḥ ādāveva bhūmimārgaguṇāṃśca bhūmimārgavivartadoṣāṃśca bhūmimārgasthānāntaraviśeṣāṃśca bhūmimārgasthānāntaravivartadoṣāṃśca mahāpuṇyajñānasaṃbhārapathyadanakriyākāryatāṃ ca parimārgate parigaveṣate buddhānāṃ bhagavatāṃ bodhisattvānāṃ kalyāṇamitrāṇāṃ ca sakāśāt I sa yāvatsarvajñatāmahānagarānuprāptikuśalo bhavatyanuccalita eva prathamānmārgāntarasthānāt I sa evaṃ jñānavicāritayā buddhyā mahāpuṇyajñānasaṃbhārapathyadanasaṃruddhayā mahāntaṃ sattvasārthaṃ yathāparipācitaṃ saṃsārāṭavīkāntāradurgādatikramya yāvatsarvajñatāmahānagaramanuprāpayati I na saṃsāraṭavīkāntāradoṣaiḥ sattvasārthasya vā ātmano vā asyopaghātaḥ saṃpadyate I tasmāttarhi bhavanto jinaputrā bodhisattvena aparikhinnena bhūmiparikarmaparikarmaviśeṣābhiyuktena bhavitavyam I ayaṃ bhavanto jinaputrā bodhisattvasya prathamāyāḥ pramuditāyā bodhisattvabhūmermukhapraveśaḥ samāsato nirdiśyate I I

XX

yo'syāṃ pratiṣṭhito bodhisattvo bhūyastvena jambūdvīpeśvaro bhavati mahaiśvaryādhipatyapratilabdho dharmānurakṣī kṛtī prabhuḥ sattvān mahātyāgena saṃgrahītukuśalaḥ sattvānāṃ mātsaryamalavinivṛttaye'paryanto mahātyāgārambhaiḥ I yacca kiṃcitkarmārabhate dānena vā priyavadyatayā vā arthakriyayā vā samānārthatayā vā, tatsarvamavirahitaṃ buddhamanasikārairdharmamanasikāraiḥ saṃghamanasikārairbodhisattvamanasikārairbodhisattvacaryāmanasikāraiḥ pāramitāmanasikārairbhūmimanasikārairbalamanasikārairvaiśāradyamanasikārairāveṇikabuddhadharmamanasikārairyāvatsarvākāravaropetasarvajñajñānamanasikaraiḥ I kimiti ? sarvasattvānāmagryo bhaveyaṃ śreṣṭho jyeṣṭho varaḥ pravara uttamo'nuttamo nāyako vināyakaḥ pariṇāyako yāvatsarvajñajñānapratiśaraṇo bhaveyam iti I ākāṅkṣaṃśca tathārūpaṃ vīryamārabhate yathārūpeṇa vīryārambheṇa sarvagṛhakalatrabhogānutsṛjya tathāgataśāsane pravrajati I pravrajitaśca san ekakṣaṇalavamuhūrtena samādhiśataṃ ca pratilabhate samāpadyate ca I buddhaśataṃ ca paśyati, teṣāṃ cādhiṣṭhānaṃ saṃjānīte I lokadhātuśataṃ ca kampayati I kṣetraśataṃ cākramati I lokadhātuśataṃ cāvabhāsayati I sattvaśataṃ ca paripācayati I kalpaśataṃ ca tiṣṭhati I kalpaśataṃ ca pūrvāntāparāntataḥ praviśati I dharmamukhaśataṃ ca pravicinoti I kāyaśataṃ cādarśayati I kāyaṃ kāyaṃ ca bodhisattvaśataparivāramādarśayati I

YY

tathā uttare praṇidhānabalikā bodhisattvāḥ praṇidhānaviśeṣikatayā vikurvanti yeṣāṃ na sukarā saṃkhyā kurtuṃ kāyasya vā prabhāyā vā ṛdvervā cakṣuṣo vā gocarasya vā svarasya vā caryāyā vā vyūhasya vā adhiṣṭhānasya vā adhimuktervā abhisaṃskāraṇāṃ vā yāvadevatāvadbhirapi kalpakoṭiniyutaśatasahasrairiti I I

pramuditā nāma prathamā bhūmiḥ I I

[Beginning of first bhūmi's final gathas]

1 pramuditā nāma prathamā bhūmiḥ ।

upakramaḥ ।

te śukladharmupacitāḥ kuśalopapetāḥ
paryupāsitāḥ sugatamaitrakṛpānukūlāḥ ।
adhimuktyudāra kuśalāśaya śuddhabhāvā-
ścittaṃ janenti atulaṃ jinajñānahetoḥ ।। 1 ।।

sarvajñabuddhabalaśodhanavīryasthāmā
jinadharmaniṣpattijagatparitrāyaṇārthāḥ ।
mahākṛpocayavartanadharmacakraṃ
jinakṣetraśodhamupapadyati cittaśreṣṭham ।। 2 ।।

tryadhvaikavīkṣaṇavibuddhananirvikalpā
nānāvidhe jagati kālaviśodhanārtham ।
saṃkṣepasarvaguṇa eṣitu nāyakānām
ākāśatulya samudeti udāracittam ।। 3 ।।

prajñādhipatya kṛpapūrvamupāyayuktam
adhimukti - āśaya - viśuddha - balāpramāṇam ।
āsaṅgatābhimukhatā - aparapraṇeyaṃ
samatopapeta - sugataṃ varacittajātam ।। 4 ।।

sahajāticittaratanaṃ sugatātmajānām
atikrānta bālacari buddhacari hyupetaḥ ।
jātaḥ kule daśabalāna anodyapadyaḥ
samatāṃ jine anugato niyatāgrabodhiḥ ।। 5 ।।

ekasmi citta upapadyati bhūmilābho
bhavate acalyu girirājasamāśayaśca ।
prāmodyaprītibahulaśca prasādavāṃśca
utsāhavegavipulaḥ sadudagracittaḥ ।। 6 ।।

saṃrambhahiṃsavigataśca akrodhanaśca
hrīgauravārjavataraśca susaṃvṛtaśca I
jagatāyanaṃ smarati apratimānajñānaṃ
prītiṃ janetyupagataspṛhameta sthānam I I 7I I

pañcā bhayā apagatāḥ sahabhūmilābho
ājīvikā maraṇa kīrtyatha durgatiśca I
parṣadbhayaṃ ca vigataṃ tatha chambhitatvaṃ
kiṃ kāraṇaṃ tatha hi ātmaniketu nāsti I I 8 I I

te chambhitatvavigatāḥ kṛpamaitrayuktāḥ
śraddhāsagauravahriyopagatā guṇāḍhyāḥ I
rātriṃdivaṃ kuśalapakṣa niṣevamāṇāḥ
satyārtha dharmaniratā na tu kāmabhogaiḥ I I 9 I I

śrutadharmacintakuśalā aniketacittā
lābhādaśīcittagatā uta bodhicittāḥ I
jñānābhilāṣi balaśodhanabuddhadharmā
eṣanti pāramita varjitamāyaśāṭhyāḥ I I 10 I I

yathāvādinastathakriyāḥ sthitasatyavākyā
na tu dūṣaṇā jinakule cari bodhiśikṣām I
lokakriyāya vigatā niratā jagārthaṃ
śuklairatṛpta bhumayottarimārabhante I I 11 I I

te eva dharmaniratā guṇārthayuktā
abhinirharanti praṇidhiṃ jinadarśanāya I
saddharmadhāraṇa upasaṃkramaṇā ṛṣiṇām
abhinirharanti praṇīdhiṃ varacārikāyām I I 12 I I

paripākasattvapariśodhanabuddhakṣetraṃ
te cāsya kṣetra sphuṭikā jinaaurasehi I
ekāśayā jinasutehi amoghatāyāḥ
sarvatra bālapathi buddhiya hetumarthe I I 13 I I

etāṃśca naikapraṇidhīnabhinirharanti
te co anantavipulāya anantatāyai I

ākāśadhātusattvadharmatanirvṛtaṃ ca
loko hyaniṣṭha jinamutpadi jñānabhūmī || 14 ||

cittasya no viṣayajñānapraveśaniṣṭhā
yā vartani trividhaniṣṭha jagatyanantā |
praṇidhānaniṣṭhitu bhavenna mamaivarūpā
yatha eta niṣṭha tatha carya samā labheyam || 15 ||

evaṃ sunirhṛtasumārdavasnigdhacittāḥ
śraddheta buddhaguṇa sattva vilokayantaḥ |
prītyāntulambhupagataḥ kṛpamaitratāṃ ca
paritāyitavya maya sattva dukhārditāni || 16 ||

teṣārthi tyāga vividhaṃ puna ārabhante
rājyaṃ varaṃ vividharatnahayān gajāṃśca |
śirahastapādanayanā svakamātmamāṃsaṃ
sarvaṃ tyajanti na ca dīnamanā bhavanti || 17 ||

eṣanti śāstra vividhānna ca khedamenti |
śāstrajña lokacaritānyanuvartayanti |
lokajñatāmupagatā hriyatā dhṛtiṃ ca
pūjyanti cāpratisamān gurugauraveṇa || 18 ||

eṣābhiyuktavidunā divarātri nityam
uttapyate kuśala svarṇa yathaiva agnau |
so cāpi eva parikarma daśāna bhūmī
kṛtvā asaṅgatamupeti aviṣṭhihantā || 19 ||

yatha sārthavāha mahasārthahitāya yukto
pucchitva mārgaguṇa kṣematamabhyupeti |
emeva bhūmi prathamā sthita bodhisattvaḥ
kṛtaniṣkramo daśabhibodhimupetyasaṅgaḥ || 20 ||

atra sthitā guṇadharā nṛpatī bhavanti
dharmānuśāsaka ahiṃsaka maitrayuktāḥ |
jambudhvajaṃ sakalarājya praśāsayantaḥ
sthāpenti tyāgi janatāṃ varabuddhajñāne || 21 ||

ākāṅkṣamāṇa vṛṣabhā vijahitva rājyaṃ
jinaśāsane upagatāścari ārabhantaḥ ।
labdhvā samādhiśata buddhaśataṃ ca paśyi
kampenti kṣetraśatu bhāsi atikramanti ।। 22 ।।

śodhyanti sattvaśata dharmamukhān viśanti
praviśanti kalpaśatakāyaśataṃ nidarśi ।
pūrṇaṃ śataṃ jinasutāna nidarśayanti
bhūyottari praṇidhiśreṣṭhabalāpramāṇāḥ ।। 23 ।।

ityeṣā prathamā bhūmirnidiṣṭā sugatātmajāḥ ।
sarvalokahitaiṣiṇāṃ bodhisattvānanutamā ।। 24 ।।

[End of first bhūmi's final gathas]

[Beginning of second bhūmi's initial gathas]

2 vimalā nāma dvitīyā bhūmiḥ |

upakramagāthāḥ |

śrutvaitaduttamaṃ sthānaṃ bhūmyāḥ śreṣṭhaṃ manoramam |
prasannamanasaṃkalpaharṣitāḥ sugatātmajāḥ || 1 ||

abhyutthitā āsanebhya abhyudgamya khagapathe |
abhyokiranti kusumaiḥ sādhviti vyāharī girā || 2 ||

sādhu sādhu mahāprājña vajragarbha viśārada |
yannirdiṣṭā tvayā bhūmi bodhisattvāna yā carī || 3 ||

parṣaddhi viprasannā tu vimukticandraḥ pṛcchati |
uttariṃ kīrtiyā bhūmiṃ dvitīyāṃ sugatātmajāḥ || 4 ||

kīdṛśā manasaṃkalpā dvitīyāmabhilakṣataḥ |
pravyāhara mahāprājña śrotukāmā jinātmajāḥ || 5 ||

[End of second bhūmi's initial gathas]

2 vimalā nāma dvitīyā bhūmiḥ I

A

vajragarbho bodhisattva āha–yo'yaṃ bhavanto jinaputrā bodhisattvaḥ prathamāyāṃ bodhisattvabhūmau suparikarmakṛto dvitīyāṃ bodhisattvabhūmimabhilaṣati, tasya daśa cittāśayāḥ pravartante I katame daśa? yaduta ṛjvāśayatā ca mṛdvāśayatā ca karmaṇyāśayatā ca damāśayatā ca śamāśayatā ca kalyāṇāśayatā ca asaṃsṛṣṭāśayatā ca anapekṣāśayatā ca udārāśayatā ca māhātmyāśayatā ca I ime daśa cittāśayāḥ pravartante I tato dvitīyāyāṃ bodhisattvabhūmau vimalāyāṃ pratiṣṭhito bhavati I I

B

tatra bhavanto jinaputrā vimalāyāṃ bodhisattvabhūmau sthito bodhisattvaḥ prakṛtyaiva daśabhiḥ kuśalaiḥ karmapathaiḥ samanvāgato bhavati I katamairdaśabhiḥ? yaduta prāṇātipātātprativirato bhavati I nihatadaṇḍo nihataśastro nihatavairo lajjāvān dayāpannaḥ sarvaprāṇibhūteṣu hitasukhānukampī maitracittaḥ I sa saṃkalpairapi prāṇivihiṃsāṃ na karoti, kaḥ punarvādaḥ parasattveṣu sattvasaṃjñinaḥ saṃcintyaudārikakāyaviheṭhanayā I I

C

adattādānātprativirataḥ khalu punarbhavati svabhogasaṃtuṣṭaḥ parabhogānabhilāṣī anukampakaḥ I sa paraparigṛhītebhyo vastubhyaḥ paraparigṛhītasaṃjñī steyacittamupasthāpya antaśastṛṇaparṇamapi nādattamādātā bhavati, kaḥ punarvādo'nyebhyo jīvitopakaraṇebhyaḥ I I

D

kāmamithyācārātprativirataḥ khalu punarbhavati svadārasaṃtuṣṭaḥ paradārānabhilāṣī I sa paraparigṛhītāsu strīṣu parabhāryāsu gotradhvajadharmarakṣitāsu abhidhyāmapi notpādayati, kaḥ punarvādo dvīndriyasamāpatyā vā anaṅgavijñaptyā vā I I

E

anṛtavacanātprativirataḥ khalu punarbhavati satyavādī bhūtavādī kālavādī, yathāvādī tathākārī I so'ntaśaḥ svapnāntaragato'pi vinidhāya dṛṣṭiṃ kṣāntiṃ ruciṃ matiṃ prekṣāṃ visaṃvādanābhiprāyo nānṛtāṃ vācaṃ niścārayati, kaḥ punarvādaḥ samanvāhṛtya I

F

piśunavacanātprativirataḥ khalu punarbhavati abhedāviheṭhāpratipannaḥ sattvānām I sa netaḥ śrutvā amutrākhyātā bhavatyamīṣāṃ bhedāya I na amutaḥ śrutvā ihākhyātā bhavatyeṣāṃ bhedāya I na saṃhitān bhinatti, na bhinnānāmanupradānaṃ karoti I na vyagrārāmo bhavati na vyagrarato na vyagrakaraṇīṃ vācaṃ bhāṣate sadbhūtāmasadbhūtāṃ vā I I

G

paruṣavacanātprativirataḥ khalu punarbhavati I sa yeyaṃ vāgadeśā karkaśā parakaṭukā parābhisaṃjananī anvakṣānvakṣaprāgbhārā grāmyā pārthagjanakī anelā akarṇasukhā krodharoṣaniścāritā hṛdayaparidahanī manaḥsaṃtāpakarī apriyā amanaāpā amanojñā svasaṃtānaparasaṃtānavināśinī I tathārūpāṃ vācaṃ prahāya yeyaṃ vāk snigdhā mṛdvī manojñā madhurā priyakaraṇī manaāpakaraṇī hitakaraṇī nelā karṇasukhā hṛdayaṃgamā premaṇīyā paurī varṇavispaṣṭā vijñeyā śravaṇīyā niśritā bahujaneṣṭā bahujanakāntā bahujanapriyā bahujanamanaāpā vijñāpannā sarvasattvahitasukhāvahā samāhitā manautplāvanakarī manaḥprahlādanakarī svasaṃtānaparasaṃtānaprasādanakarī tathārūpāṃ vācaṃ niścārayati I I

H

saṃbhinnapralāpātprativirataḥ khalu punarbhavati suparihāryavacanaḥ kālavādī bhūtavādī arthavādī dharmavādī nyāyavādī vinayavādī I sa nidānavatīṃ vācaṃ bhāṣate kālena sāvadānam I sa cāntaśa itihāsapūrvakamapi vacanaṃ parihārya pariharati, kaḥ punarvādo vāgvikṣepeṇa I I

I

anabhidhyāluḥ khalu punarbhavati parasveṣu parakāmeṣu parabhogeṣu paravittopakaraṇeṣu I paraparigṛhīteṣu spṛhāmapi n-otpādayati, kimiti yatpareṣāṃ tannāma syāditi nābhidhyām-utpādayati, na prārthayate na praṇidadhāti, na lobhacittam-utpādayati I I

J

avyāpannacittaḥ khalu punarbhavati I sarvasattveṣu maitracitto hitacitto dayācittaḥ sukhacittaḥ snigdhacittaḥ sarvajagadanugrahacittaḥ sarvabhūtahitānukampācittaḥ I sa yānīmāni krodhopanāhakhilamalavyāpādaparidāhasaṃdhukṣitapratighādyāni tāni prahāya yānīmāni hitopasaṃhitāni maitryupasaṃhitāni sarvasattvahitasukhāya vitarkitavicāritāni, tānyanuvitarkayitā bhavati I I

K

samyagdṛṣṭiḥ khalu punarbhavati samyakpathagataḥ kautukamaṅgalanānāprakārakuśīladṛṣṭivigataṛjudṛṣṭiraśaṭho'māyāvī buddhadharmasaṃghaniyatāśayaḥ I sa imān daśa kuśalān karmapathān satatasamitamanurakṣan

L

evaṃ cittāśayamabhinirharati - yā kācitsattvānāmapāyadurgativinipātaprajñaptiḥ sarvā sā eṣāṃ daśānāmakuśalānāṃ karmapathānāṃ samādānahetoḥ I hanta ahamātmanaiva samyakpratipattisthitaḥ parān samyakpratipattau sthāpayiṣyāmi I tatkasya hetoḥ? asthānametadanavakāśo yadātmā vipratipattisthitaḥ parān samyakpratipattau sthāpayet, naitasthānaṃ vidyata iti I

M

sa evaṃ pravicinoti - eṣāṃ daśānāṃ akuśalānāṃ karmapathānāṃ samādānahetornirayatiryagyoniyamalokagatayaḥ prajñāyante I punaḥ kuśalānāṃ karmapathānāṃ samādānahetormanuṣyopapattimādiṃ kṛtvā yāvadbhavāgramityupapattayaḥ prajñāyante I tata uttaṃra ta eva daśa kuśalāḥ karmapathāṃ prajñākāreṇa paribhāvyamānāḥ prādeśikacittatayā traidhātukottrastamānasatayā mahākaruṇāvikalatayā parataḥ śravaṇānugamena ghoṣānugamena ca śrāvakayānaṃ saṃvartayanti I

N

tata uttarataraṃ pariśodhitā aparapraṇeyatayā svayaṃbhūtvānukūlatayā svayamabhisaṃbodhanatayā parato'parimārgaṇatayā mahākaruṇopāyavikalatayā gambhīredaṃpratyayānubodhanena pratyekabuddhayānaṃ saṃvartayati I

O

tata uttarataraṃ pariśodhitāvipulāpramāṇatayā mahākaruṇopetatayā upāyakauśalasaṃgṛhītatayā saṃbaddhamahāpraṇidhānatayā sarvasattvāparityāgatayā buddhajñānavipuladhyālambanatayā bodhisattvabhūmipariśuddhyai pāramitāpariśuddhyai caryāvipulatvāya saṃvartante I

P

tata uttarataraṃ pariśodhitāḥ sarvākārapariśodhitatvādyāvaddaśabalabalatvāya sarvabuddhadharmāḥ samudāgamāya saṃvartante I tasmāt tarhyasmābhiḥ samābhinirhāre sarvākārapariśodhanābhinirhāra eva yogaḥ karaṇīyaḥ I I

Q

sa bhūyasyā mātrayā evaṃ pratisaṃśikṣate - ime khalu punardaśākuśalāḥ karmapathā adhimātratvādāsevitā bhāvitā bahulīkṛtā nirayaheturmadhyatvāt tiryagyoniheturmṛdutvādyamalokahetuḥ I tatra prāṇātipāto nirayamupanayati tiryagyonimupanayati, yamalokamupanayati I atha cetpunarmanuṣyeṣu upapadyate, dvau vipākāvabhinirvartayati alpāyuṣkatāṃ ca bahuglānyatāṃ ca I adattādanaṃ...peyālaṃ...parīttabhogatāṃ ca sādhāraṇabhogatāṃ ca I kāmamithyācāro...anājāneyaparivāratāṃ ca sasapatnadāratāṃ ca I mṛṣāvādo...abhyākhyānabahulatāṃ ca parairvisaṃvādanatāṃ ca I paiśunyaṃ...bhinnaparivāratāṃ ca hīnaparivāratāṃ ca I pāruṣyaṃ-...amanāpaśravaṇatāṃ ca kalahavacanatāṃ ca I saṃbhinnapralāpo-...anādeyavacanatāṃ ca aniścitapratibhānatāṃ ca I abhidhyā-...asaṃtuṣṭitāṃ ca mahecchatāṃ ca I vyāpādo...ahitaiṣitāṃ ca parotpīḍanatāṃ ca I mityādṛṣṭiḥ...kudṛṣṭipatitaśca bhavati śaṭhaśca māyāvī I evaṃ khalu mahato'parimāṇasya duḥkhaskandhasya ime daśākuśalāḥ karmapathāḥ samudāgamāya saṃvartante I

R

hanta vayaṃ imān daśākuśalān karmapathān vivarjya dharmārāmaratiratā viharāma I

S

sa imān daśākuśalān karmapathān prahāya daśakuśalakarmapathapratiṣṭhitaḥ parāṃsteṣveva pratiṣṭhāpayati I

T

sa bhūyasyā mātrayā sarvasattvānāmantike hitacittatāmutpādayati I sukhacittatāṃ maitracittatāṃ kṛpācittatāṃ dayācittatāmanugrahacittatāmārakṣācittatāṃ samacittatāmacāryacittatāṃ śāstṛcittatāmutpādayati I

U

tasyaivaṃ bhavati - kudṛṣṭipatitā bateme sattvā viṣamamatayo viṣamāśayā utpathagahanacāriṇaḥ I te'smābhirbhūtapathasamyagdṛṣṭimārgayāthātathye pratiṣṭhāpayitavyāḥ I

V

bhinnavigṛhītacittavivādopapannā bateme sattvāḥ satatasamitaṃ krodhopanāhasaṃdhukṣitāḥ I te'smābhiranuttare mahāmaitryupasaṃhāre pratiṣṭhāpayitavyāḥ I

W

atṛptā bateme sattvāḥ paravittābhilāṣiṇo viṣamājīvānucaritāḥ । te'smābhiḥ pariśuddhakāyavāṅmanaskarmāntājīvikāyāṃ pratiṣṭhāpayitavyāḥ ।

X

rāgadveṣamohatrinidānānugatā bateme sattvā vividhakleśāgnijvālābhiḥsatatasamitaṃ pradīptāḥ । na ca tato'tyantaniḥsaraṇopāyaṃ parimārgayanti । te'smābhiḥ sarvakleśapraśame nirupadrave nirvāṇe pratiṣṭhāpayitavyāḥ ।

Y

mahāmohatamastimirapaṭalāvidyāndhakārāvṛtā bateme sattvā mahāndhakāragahanānupraviṣṭāḥ prajñālokasudūrībhūtā mahāndhakārapraskannāḥ kudṛṣṭikāntārasamavasṛtāḥ । teṣāmasmābhiranāvaraṇaṃ prajñācakṣurviśodhayitavyaṃ yathā sarvadharmayāthātathyāparapraṇayatāṃ pratilapsyante ।

Z

mahāsaṃsārāṭavīkāntāramārgaprapannā bateme sattvā ayogakṣemiṇo'nāśvāsaprāptā mahāprapātapatitā nirayatiryagyoniyamalokagatiprapātābhimukhāḥ kudṛṣṭiviṣamajālānuparyavanaddhā mohagahanasaṃchannā mithyāmārgavipathaprayātā jātyandhībhūtāḥ pariṇāyakavikalā aniḥsaraṇe niḥsaraṇasaṃjñino namucipāśabaddhā viṣayataskaropagṛhītāḥ kuśalapariṇāyakavirahitā mārāśayagahanānupraviṣṭā buddhāśayadūrībhūtāḥ । te'smābhirevaṃvidhāt saṃsārāṭavīkāntāradurgāduttārayitavyā abhayapure ca sarvajñatānagare nirupadrave nirupatāpe pratiṣṭhāpayitavyāḥ ।

AA

mahaughormyāmathairnimagnā bateme sattvāḥ kāmabhavāvidyādṛṣṭyoghasamavasṛṣṭāḥ saṃsārasrotonuvāhinastṛṣṇānadīprapannā mahāvegagrastā avilokanasamarthāḥ kāmavyāpādavihiṃsāvitarkapratānānucaritāḥ satkāyadṛṣṭyudakarākṣasagṛhītāḥ kāmagahanāvartānupraviṣṭā nandīrāgamadhyasaṃchannā asmimānasthalotsannā dauḥśīlyaviṣamācārāntaḥputībhūtāḥ ṣaḍāyatanagrāmabhayatīramanuccalitāḥ kuśalasaṃtārakavirahitā anāthā aparāyaṇā aśaraṇāḥ । te'smābhirmahākaruṇākuśalamūlabalenoddhṛtya nirupadrave'rajasi kṣeme śive'bhaye sarvabhayatrāsāpagate sarvajñatāratnadvīpe pratiṣṭhāpayitavyāḥ ।

BB

ruddhā bateme sattvā bahuduḥkhadaurmanasyopāyāsabahule-

'nunayapratighapriyāpriyavinibandhane saśokaparidevānucarite tṛṣṇānigaḍabandhane māyāśāṭhyāvidyāgahanasaṃchanne traidhātukacārake | te'smābhiḥ sarvatraidhātukaviveke sarvaduḥkhopaśame'nāvaraṇanirvāṇe pratiṣṭhāpayitavyāḥ |

CC

ātmātmīyābhiniviṣṭā bateme sattvāḥ skandhālayānuccalitāścaturviparyāsānuprayātāḥ ṣaḍāyatanaśūnyagrāmasaṃniśritāścaturmahābhūtoragābhidrutāḥ skandhavadhakataskarābhighātitā aparimāṇaduḥkhapratisaṃvedinaḥ | te'smābhiḥ paramasukhe sarvaniketavigame pratiṣṭhāpayitavyā yaduta sarvāvaraṇaprahāṇanirvāṇe |

DD

hīnalīnadīnādhimuktā bateme sattvā agryasarvajñajñānacittavikalāḥ sati niḥsaraṇe mahāyāne śrāvakapratyekabuddhayānāvatīrṇamatayaḥ | te'smābhirudārabuddhadharmamativipulādhyālambena sarvajñajñānalocanatayā anuttare mahāyāne pratiṣṭhāpayitavyāḥ ||

iti hi bhavanto jinaputrā evaṃ śīlabalādhānānugatasya bodhisattvasya kṛpākaruṇāmaitryabhinirhārakuśalasya sarvasattvānavadhīṣṭakalyāṇamitrasyāparityaktasarvasattvasya kriyākriyābhinirhārakuśalasya

EE

vimalāyāṃ bodhisattvabhūmau pratiṣṭhitasya bahavo buddhā ābhāsabhāgacchānti...audārika...peyālaṃ...pariṇāmayati | tāṃśca tathāgatānarhataḥ samyaksaṃbuddhān paryupāsate, teṣāṃ ca sakāśebhyo gauraveṇemāneva daśa kuśalān karmapathān pratigṛhṇāti, yathāpratigṛhītāṃśca nāntarā praṇāśayati | so'nekān kalpānanekāni kalpaśatāni anekāni kalpasahasrāṇi anekāni kalpaśatasahasrāṇi anekāni kalpaniyutaśatasahasrāni anekakalpakoṭīranekānikalpakoṭiśatāni anekāni kalpakoṭiśatasahasrāni anekāni kalpakoṭiniyutaśatasahasrāṇi mātsaryadauḥśīlyamalāpanītatayā tyāgaśīlaviśuddhau samudāgacchati | tadyathāpi nāma bhavanto jinaputrāstadeva jātarūpaṃ kāsīsaprakṣiptaṃ bhūyasyā mātrayā sarvamalāpagataṃ bhavati, evameva bhavanto jinaputrāstadeva jātarūpaṃ kāsīsaprakṣiptaṃ bhūyasyā mātrayā sarvamalāpagataṃ bhavati, evameva bhavanto jinaputrā bodhisattvo'syāṃ vimalāyāṃ bodhisattvabhūmau sthito'nekān kalpān yāvadanekāni kalpakoṭiniyutaśatasahasrāṇi mātsaryadauḥśīlyamalāpanītatayā tyāgaśīlaviśudvau samudāgacchati I tasya caturbhyaḥ saṃgrahavastubhyaḥ priyavadyatā atiriktatamā bhavati I daśabhyaḥ pāramitābhyaḥ śīlapāramitā atiriktatamā bhavati I na ca pariśeṣāsu na samudāgacchati yathābalaṃ yathābhajamānam I I

iyaṃ bhavanto jinaputrā bodhisattvasya vimalā nāma dvitīyā bodhisattvabhūmiḥ samāsanirdeśataḥ, yasyāṃ pratiṣṭhito bodhisattvo bhūyastvena rājā bhavati cakravartī caturdvīpādhipatidharmādhipatyapratilabdhaḥ saptaratnasamanvāgataḥ kṛtī prabhuḥ sattvānāṃ dauḥśīlyamalavinivartanāya kuśalaḥ sattvān daśasu kuśaleṣu karmapatheṣu pratiṣṭhāpayitum I yacca kiṃcit karmārabhate...peyālam I I

vimalā nāma dvitīyā bhūmiḥ I I

[Beginning of 2nd bhūmi's final gathas]

upasaṃhāragāthāḥ |

te mārdavārjavamṛdūkarmaṇīyacittāḥ
kalyāṇaāśaya damāśayatābhyupetāḥ |
saṃsargapekṣavigatāśca udārabuddhi
māhātmya āśayavid dvitīyākramanti || 6 ||

atra sthitā guṇadharāḥ kuśalopapetāḥ
prāṇātipātavigatā avihiṃsacittāḥ |
adattadānapagatāḥ paradāratāṃ ca
satyānvitā apiśunaḥ puruṣapradhānāḥ || 7 ||

parabhogabhidyavigatā vidu maitracittāḥ
samyakpathe upagatā aśaṭhajñakāśca |
nirmāṇakāyagrahaṇāśca supeśalāśca
rakṣanti śāstuśaraṇaṃ sada apramattāḥ || 8 ||

duḥkhāni yāni niraye tatha tiryagyonau
yamaśāsane jvalitaāśrayanityupetāḥ |
sarve ti pāpapatitākṣalāḥ prabhonti
hantā vivarjiya upemahi satyadharmam || 9 ||

ādau ca kṛtva manujānupapattimiṣṭāṃ
yāvadbhavāgramaraṇāśayadhyānu śikṣām |
pratyekayānamatha śrāvakabuddhayānaṃ
sarve ito daśabhi śuklapathaiḥ prabhūtam || 10 ||

evaṃ viditva satataṃ vidu apramattāḥ
śīleṣu saṃsthita parānapi sthāpayanti |
bhūyottare karuṇaāśayatābhyupetāḥ
sattvān viditva dukhitān kṛpa saṃjanenti || 11 ||

hanto vidṛṣṭipatitā imi bālabuddhī
krodhopanāhadrutacitta vivādaprāptāḥ |

satataṃ atṛpta viṣaye bhuyu prārthayanti
trinidāna sattva parimocayitavya ete || 12 ||

mahaandhakāratamasāvṛta mohachannāḥ
kāntāramārgapatitā mahadṛṣṭijāle |
saṃsārapañjaragatā ripu dharṣayanti
mokṣāmyahaṃ namucipañjaramadhyaprāptān || 13 ||

kleśormibhihriyata oghacaturnimagnā
traidhātuke dukhaśataiḥ paripīḍyamānāḥ |
skandhālayābhyupagatā vṛtaātmasaṃjñā
teṣārthi yujyami ahaṃ dukhamocanārtham || 14 ||

avasṛjya śreṣṭhapravaraṃ ima buddhajñānaṃ
sati eva niḥsaraṇi hīnamatiṃ janenti |
sthāpemi tān vimalajñāni tathāgatānāṃ
vīryārabhanti atulaṃ vidu bodhihetoḥ || 15 ||

atra sthitā guṇaśatopacitā maharṣi
paśyanti naikasugatānapi pūjayanti |
teṣāṃ śubhaṃ bhuyu uttapyati kalpakoṭyāṃ
kāsīsakāñcanavaraṃ ca yathā nikṣiptam || 16 ||

atra sthitā jinasutā nṛpacakravarti
bhūtvā praṇenti daśabhiḥ kuśalebhi sattvān |
yaccaiva saṃci śubhasaṃcaya saṃcinanti
trātā bhavema jagato daśabhirbalāḍhyaiḥ || 17 ||

ākāṅkṣamāṇa vijahitva ca rajabhogān
pravrajya śāsanavare upagamya dhīrāḥ |
vīryānvitā labhiya śreṣṭhavaraṃ samādhiṃ
buddhā sahasra paripūrṇa kṣeṇe dṛśanti || 18 ||

evaṃvidhā gaṇanayā bhuyu anya nekā
ādarśayanti vṛṣabhī sthita atra bhūmau |
ata uttari praṇidhijñānavarābhyupetā
naikā vikurvitavidhau vinayanti sattvān || 19 ||

ityeṣā dvitiyā bhūmirnirdiṣṭā sugatātmajāḥ |
sarvalokahitaiṣīṇāṃ bodhisattvānanuttamā || 20 ||

[End of 2nd bhūmi's final gathas]

[Beginning of third bhūmi's initial gathas]

3 prabhākarī nāma tṛtīyā bhūmiḥ |

upakramagāthāḥ |

evaṃ śruṇitva caribhūmimuttamāṃ
bodhisattvaviṣaye acintiyām |
harṣita jinasutāḥ sagauravāḥ
puṣpamegha nabhataḥ pramuñciṣuḥ || 1 ||

sādhu sādhu girisārasākaya (?)
deśito viduna śīlasaṃvaraḥ |
sarvasattvakaruṇāya āśayo
bhūmiśreṣṭha dvitiyāya gocaraḥ || 2 ||

bhūtatattva vitathāmananyathā
bodhisasattvacaraṇaṃ manoramam |
sarvalokahitaśaukhyacintanā
deśitaṃ tu paramaprabhāsvaram || 3 ||

bhūyu bhūyu naradevapūjitāṃ
bhūmiśreṣṭha tṛtiyāmudāhara |
dharmajñānakriyamukti sūcaya
yādṛśo'nubhava tādṛ(śo) gocaraḥ || 4 ||

dānaśīlacaraṇaṃ maharṣiṇāṃ
kṣāntivīryaśamaprajñupāyatām |
maitraśreṣṭha karuṇāya mārgaṇaṃ
bhāṣadhvaṃ jinacarīviśodhanam || 5 ||

vimukticandra uvāca vajragarbhaviśāradam |
tṛtīyā saṃkramantānāmāśayaṃ bhaṇa sūraṇa || 6 ||

[End of third bhūmi's initial gathas]

3 prabhākarī nāma tṛtīyā bhūmiḥ ।

A

vajragarbho bodhisattva āha - yo'yaṃ bhavanto jinaputrā bodhisattvo dvitīyāyāṃ bodhisattvabhūmau supariśodhitādhyāśayastṛtīyāṃ bodhisattvabhūmimākramati, sa daśabhiścittāśayamanaskārairākramati । katamairdaśabhiḥ ? yaduta śuddhacittāśayamanaskāreṇa ca sthiracittāśayamanaskāreṇa ca nirviccittāśayamanaskāreṇa ca avirāgacittāśayamanaskāreṇa ca avinivartacittāśayamanaskāreṇa ca dṛḍhacittāśayamanaskāreṇa ca uttaptacittāśayamanaskāreṇa ca atṛptacittāśayamanaskāreṇa ca udāracittāśayamanaskāreṇa ca māhātmyacittāśayamanaskāreṇa ca । ebhirdaśabhiścittāśayamanaskārairākramati ।

B

sa khalu punarbhavanto jinaputrā bodhisattvastṛtīyāyāṃ bodhisattvabhūmau sthito'nityatāṃ ca sarvasaṃskāragatasya yathābhūtaṃ pratyavekṣate, duḥkhatāṃ ca aśubhatāṃ ca anāśvāsikatāṃ ca vipralopatāṃ ca acirasthitikatāṃ ca kṣaṇikotpādanirodhatāṃ ca pūrvantāsaṃbhavatāṃ ca aparāntāsaṃkrāntitāṃ ca pratyutpannāvyavasthitatāṃ ca sarvasaṃskāragatasya pratyavekṣate ।

C

sa evaṃbhūtaṃ sarvasaṃskāragataṃ saṃpaśyannanabhisaraṃ nirākrandaṃ saśokaṃ saparidevaṃ sopāyāsaṃ priyāpriyavinibaddha duḥkhadaurmanasyopāyāsābahulamasaṃnicayabhūtaṃ rāgadveṣamohāgnisaṃpradīptamanekavyādhivivardhitaṃ ca ātmabhāvaṃ saṃpaśyan

D

bhūyasyā mātrayā sarvasaṃskārebhyaścittamuccālayati, tathāgatajñāne ca saṃpreṣayati । sa tathāgatajñānasyācintyatāṃ ca samanupaśyati, atulyatāṃ ca aprameyatāṃ ca durāsadatāṃ ca asaṃspṛṣṭatāṃ ca nirupadravatāṃ ca nirupāyāsatāṃ ca abhayapuragamanīyatāṃ ca apunarāvṛttitāṃ ca bahujanaparitrāṇatāṃ ca samanupaśyati ।

E

sa evamapramāṇatāṃ ca tathāgatajñānasya samanupaśyan evaṃ bahūpadravatāṃ ca sarvasaṃskāragatasya vyupaparīkṣamāṇo bhūyasyā mātrayā sattvānāmantike daśa cittāśayānupasthāpayati ।

katamān daśa? yaduta anāthātrāṇāpratiśaraṇacittāśayatāṃ ca nityadaridrapratiśaraṇacittāśayatāṃ ca rāgadveṣamohāgnisaṃpradīptapratiśaraṇacittāśayatāṃ ca bhavacārakāvaruddhapratiśaraṇacittāśayatāṃ ca satatasamitaklaśagahenāvṛtaprasuptapratiśaraṇacittāśayatāṃ ca vilokanasamarthapratiśaraṇacittāśayatāṃ ca kuśaladharmacchandarahitapratiśaraṇacittāśayatāṃ ca buddhadharmapramuṣitapratiśaraṇacittāśayatāṃ ca saṃsārasrotonuvāhipratiśaraṇacittāśayatāṃ ca mokṣopāyapraṇaṣṭapratiśaraṇacittāśayatāṃ ca | imān daśa cittāśayanupasthāpayati | |

F

sa evaṃ bahūpadravaṃ sattvadhātuṃ samanupaśyan evaṃ vīryamārabhate - mayaivaite sattvāḥ paritrātavyāḥ parimocayitavyāḥ paritoṣayitavyāḥ saṃropayitavyā vinetavyāḥ parinirvāpayitavyā iti |

G

sa evaṃ nirvidanugataśca sarvasaṃskāragatyā upekṣānugataśca sarvasattveṣu anuśaṃsānugataśca sarvajñajñāne tathāgatajñānapratiśaraṇaḥ sarvasattvaparitrāṇāyābhiyuktaḥ evaṃ vyupaparīkṣate - katamena khalu upāyamārgeṇa śakyā ime sattvā evaṃ bahuduḥkhopakleśaprapatitā abhyuddhartum, atyantasukhe ca nirvāṇe pratiṣṭhāpayitum, sarvadharmaniḥsaṃśayatāṃ cānuprāpayitumiti?

H

tasya bodhisattvasyaivaṃ bhavati - nānyatra anāvaraṇavimokṣajñānasthānāt | tacca anāvaraṇajñānavimokṣasthānam nānyatra sarvadharmayathāvadavabodhāt | sa ca sarvadharmayathāvadavabodho nānyatra apracārānutpādacāriṇyāḥ prajñāyāḥ | sa ca prajñāloko nānyatra dhyānakauśalyaviniścayabuddhipratyavekṣaṇāt | tacca dhyānakauśalyaviniścayabuddhipratyavekṣaṇaṃ nānyatra śrutakauśalyāditi | |

I

sa evaṃ pratyavekṣitajñāno bhūyasyā mātrayā saddharmaparyeṣaṇābhiyukto viharati | rātridivaṃ dharmaśravaṇārthiko dharmakāmātṛptāpratiprasrabdho buddhardharmaparyeṣṭihetoḥ | dharmārāmo dharmarato dharmapratiśaraṇo dharmanimno dharmapravaṇo dharmaprāgbhāro dharmaparāyaṇo dharmalayano dharmatrāṇo dharmānudharmacārī |

J

sa evaṃ buddhadharmaparyeṣaṇābhiyukto nāsti tatkiṃcid dravyavittajātaṃ vā dhanadhānyakośakoṣṭhāgārajātaṃ vā hiraṇyasuvarṇamaṇimuktāvajravaiḍūryaśaṅkhaśilāpravālajātarūparajatajātaṃ vā yāvatsarvāṅgapratyaṅgaparityāgo vā yanna parityajati tayā dharmakāmatayā I na ca tasmādduṣkarasaṃjñī bhavati anyatra tasminneva dharmabhāṇakapudgale duṣkarasaṃjñī bhavati yo'syaikadharmapadamapi deśayati I sa dharmahetornāsti tatkiṃcidupātaṃ bāhyaṃ vastu yanna parityajati I nāsti tatkiciṃdādhyātmikaṃ vastu yanna parityajati I nāsti tatkiṃcidguruparicaryopasthānaṃ yannopādatte I nāsti sā kācid mānābhimānotsarganirmāṇopacāratā yāṃ nopādatte I nāsti sā kācitkāyikī pīḍā yāṃ nopādatte I sa citro bhavatyaśrutadharmapada śravaṇena, na tveva trisāhasramahāsāhasralokadhātupratimena ratnarāśipratilambhena I sa citro bhavatyekasubhāṣitagāthāśravaṇena na tveva cakravartirājyapratilambhena I sa citro bhavatyaśrutadharmapadaśravaṇena bodhisattvacaryāpariśodhanena na tveva śakratvabrahmatvapratilambhena bahukalpaśatasahasraparyavasānena I sacedidaṃ kaścidevaṃ brūyāt – evamahaṃ tulyamidaṃ dharmapadaṃ samyaksaṃbuddhopanītaṃ bodhisattvacaryāpariśodhanaṃ saṃśrāvayeyam, sacettvaṃ mahatyāmagnikhadāyāṃ saṃprajvalitāyāmekajvālībhūtāyāmātmānaṃ prapātayeḥ, mahāntaṃ ca duḥkhavedanopakramaṃ svaśarīreṇopādadyā iti I tasyaivaṃ bhavati - utsahe'hamekasyāpi dharmapadasya samyaksaṃbuddhopanītasya bodhisattvacaryāpariśodhanasyārthāya trisāhasramahāsāhasralokadhātāvagniparipūrṇe brahmalokādātmānamutsraṣṭum, kiṃ punaḥ prākṛtāyāṃ agnikhadāyām I api tu khalu punaḥ sarvairnirayāpāyaduḥkhasaṃvāsairapyasmābhirbuddhadharmāḥ paryeṣitavyāḥ, kiṃ punarmanuṣyaduḥkhasaṃvāsairiti I sa evaṃrūpeṇa vīryārambheṇa dharmān paryeṣate I yathāśruteṣu dharmeṣu ca yoniśaḥ pratyavakṣeṇajātīyo bhavati I

K

tāṃśca dharmān śrutvā svacittanidhyaptyā eko rahogata evaṃ mīmāṃsate - dharmānudharmapratipattyā ime buddhadharmā anugantavyā na kevalaṃ vākkarmapariśuddhyeti I so'syāṃ prabhākaryāṃ bodhisattvabhūmau sthito bodhisattvo dharmānudharmapratipattihetorviviktaṃ kāmairviviktaṃ pāpakairakuśaladharmaiḥ savitarkaṃ savicāraṃ vivekajaṃ prītisukhaṃ prathamaṃ dhyānamupasaṃpadya viharati I sa vitarkavicārāṇāṃ vyupaśamādadhyātmasaṃprasādāccetasa ekotībhāvādavitarkamavicāraṃ samādhijaṃ prītisukhaṃ dvitīyaṃ dhyānamupasaṃpadya viharati I sa prīter-virāgādupekṣako viharati smṛtimān saṃprajānan I sukhaṃ ca kāyena pratisaṃvedayati yattadāryā ācakṣante - upekṣakaḥ smṛtimān I sukhavihārī niṣprītikaṃ tṛtīyaṃ dhyānamupasaṃpadya viharati I sa sukhasya ca prahāṇādduḥkhasya ca prahāṇātpūrvam-eva ca saumanasyadaurmanasyayorastaṃgamādaduḥkhāsukham-upekṣāsmṛtipariśuddhaṃ caturthaṃ dhyānamupasaṃpadya viharati I sa sarvaśo rūpasaṃjñānāṃ samatikramāt pratighasaṃjñānām-astaṃgamānnānātvasaṃjñānāmamanasikārādanantakamākāśamityā kāśānantyāyatanamupasaṃpadya viharati I sa sarvaśa ākāśānanty-āyatanasamatikramādanantaṃ vijñānamiti vijñānānantyāyatanam-upasaṃpadya viharati I sa sarvaśo vijñānānantyāyatanasamati-kramānnāsti kiṃcidityākiṃcanyāyatanamupasaṃpadya viharati I sa sarvaśa ākiṃcanyāyatanasamatikramānnaivasaṃjñānāsaṃjñ-āyatanamupasaṃpadya viharati tenānabhiratipadasthānena n-ānyatra dharmānudharmapratipattimupādāya I

L

sa maitrīsahagatena cittena vipulena mahadgatenādvayenāpra-māṇenāvaireṇāsapatnenānāvaraṇenāvyābādhena sarvatrānugatena dharmadhātuparame loke ākāśadhātuparyavasāne sarvāvantaṃ lokaṃ spharitvopasaṃpadya viharati I evaṃ karuṇāsahagatena cittena I muditāsahagatena cittena I upekṣāsahagatena cittena viharati I I

M

so'nekavidhāṃ ṛddhividhiṃ pratyanubhavati I pṛthivīmapi kampayati I eko'pi bhūtvā bahudhā bhavati I bahudhāpi bhūtvaiko bhavati I āvirbhāvaṃ tirobhāvamapi pratyanubhavati I tiraḥ-kuḍyaṃ tiraḥprākāraṃ parvatamapyasajjan gacchati tadyathāpi nāma ākāśe I ākāśe'pi paryaṅkena krāmati tadyathāpi nāma pakṣi-śakuniḥ I pṛthivyāmapyunmajjananimajjanaṃ karoti tadyathāpi nāma udake I udake'pyamañjan gacchati tadyathāpi pṛthivyām I dhūmayati prajvalati, tadyathāpi nāma mahānagniskandhaḥ I sva-kāyādapi mahāvāridhārā utsṛjati tadyathāpi nāma mahāmeghaḥ I yābhirvāridhārābhirayaṃ trisāhasramahāsāhasro lokadhāturādīptaḥ pradīptaḥ saṃprajvalito'gninā ekajvālībhūto nirvāpyate I imāvapi candrasūryāvevaṃmaharddhikau evaṃmahānubhāvau pāṇinā parāmṛśati parimārṣṭi yāvadbrahmalokamapi kāyena vaśaṃ vartayati | |

sa divyena śrotradhātunā [viśuddhenā]tikrāntamānuṣyakena ubhayān śabdān śṛṇoti divyān mānuṣyākān, sūkṣmānaudārikāṃśca | ye dūre'ntike vā antaśo daṃśamaśakakīṭamakṣikāṇāmapi śabdān śṛṇoti | [eṣā divyaśrotrābhijñā] | |

sa parasattvānāṃ parapudgalānāṃ cetasaiva cittaṃ yathābhūtaṃ prajānāti | sarāgaṃ cittaṃ sarāgacittamiti yathābhūtaṃ prajānāti | virāgaṃ cittaṃ virāgacittamiti prajānāti | sadoṣaṃ...vigatadoṣaṃ... samohaṃ...vigatamohaṃ...sakleśaṃ...niḥkleśaṃ...parīttaṃ... vipulaṃ...mahadgataṃ...apramāṇaṃ...saṃkṣiptaṃ...[vistīrṇaṃ]... samāhitaṃ...asamāhitaṃ...vimuktaṃ...avimuktaṃ...sāṅganam... anaṅganam...audārikaṃ cittamaudārikacittamiti yathābhūtaṃ prajānāti | anaudārikaṃ cittamanaudārikaṃ cittamiti yathābhūtaṃ prajānāti | iti parasattvānāṃ parapudgalānāṃ cetasaiva cittaṃ yathābhūtaṃ prajānāti | [ityeṣā paracittajñānāmijñā] | |

so'nekavidhaṃ pūrvanivāsamanusmarati | ekāmapi jātimanusmarati | dve tisraścatasraḥ pañca daśa viṃśatiḥ triṃśataṃ catvāriṃśataṃ pañcāśataṃ jātiśatamanusmarati | anekānyapi jātiśatāni | anekānyapi jātiśatasahasrāṇi | saṃvartakalpamapi vivartakalpamapi | anekānapi saṃvartavivartakalpānapyanusmarati | kalpaśatamapi kalpasahasramapi kalpakoṭīmapi kalpakoṭīśatamapi kalpakoṭīsahasramapi kalpakoṭīśatasahasramapi yāvadanekānyapi kalpakoṭīniyutaśatasahasrāṇyanusmarati - amutrāhamāsaṃ evaṃnāmā | evaṃgotraḥ evaṃjātiḥ evamāhāra evamāyuḥpramāṇaḥ evaṃ cirasthitikaḥ evaṃ sukhaduḥkhapratisaṃvedī | so'haṃ tataścyuto'tropapannaḥ | tataścyuta ihopapannaḥ | iti sākāraṃ soddeśaṃ sanimittamanekavidhaṃ pūrvanivāsamanusmarati | [eṣā pūrvanivāsānusmṛtyabhijñā] | |

sa divyena cakṣuṣā viśuddhenātikrāntamānuṣyakeṇa sattvān paśyati cyavamānānupapadyamānān suvarṇān durvarṇān sugatān durgatān praṇītān hīnān | yathākarmopagān sattvān yathābhūtaṃ prajānāti - ime bhavantaḥ sattvāḥ kāyaduścaritena samanvāgatā vāgduścaritena samanvāgatā [manoduścaritena samanvāgatāḥ] | āryāṇāmapavādakā mithyādṛṣṭayaḥ mithyādṛṣṭikarmasamādānahetostaddhetuṃ tatpratyayaṃ kāyasya bhadātparaṃ maraṇādapāyadurgativinipātanirayeṣūpapadyante I ime punarbhavantaḥ sattvāḥ kāyasucaritena samanvāgatā [vāksucaritena samanvāgatā manaḥsucaritena samanvāgatā] āryāṇāmanapavādakāḥ I samyagdṛṣṭikarmasamādānahetostaddhetuṃ tatpratyayaṃ kāyasya bhedāt paraṃ maraṇātsugatau svarge devalokeṣūpapadyanta iti I [prajānāti I evaṃ] divyena cakṣuṣā viśuddhenātikrāntamanuṣyeṇa sākāraṃ soddeśaṃ sanimittaṃ sattvān paśyati I cyavamānānupapadyamānān...yathābhūtaṃ paśyati I I

sa imāni dhyānāni vimokṣān samādhīn samāpattīśca samāpadyate, vyuttiṣṭhete I na ca teṣāṃ vaśenopapadyate'nyatra yatra bodhyaṅgaparipūriṃ paśyati tatra saṃcintya praṇidhānavaśenopapadyate I tatkasya hetoḥ? tathā hi tasya bodhisattvasyopāyakauśalyābhinirhatā cittasaṃtatiḥ I I

N

tasya asyāṃ prabhākaryāṃ bodhisattvabhūmau sthitasya bodhisattvasya bahavo buddhā ābhāsamāgacchanti I peyālaṃ I pariṇāmayati I tāṃśca tathāgatānarhataḥ samyaksaṃbuddhān paryupāste I teṣāṃ ca dharmadeśanāṃ satkṛtya śṛṇoti udgṛhṇāti dhārayati I śrutvā ca yathābhajamānaṃ pratipattyā samādayati I sa sarvadharmāṇāmasaṃkrāntitāṃ ca avināśitāṃ ca pratītya pratyayatayā vyavalokayati I I

O

tasya bhūyasyā mātrayā sarvāṇi kāmabandhanāni tanūni bhavanti I sarvāṇi rūpabandhanāni sarvāṇi bhavabandhanāni sarvāṇyavidyābandhanāni tanūni bhavanti I dṛṣṭikṛtabandhanāni ca pūrvameva prahīṇāni bhavanti I tasya asyāṃ prabhākaryāṃ bodhisattvabhūmau sthitasya bodhisattvasya...peyālaṃ...anupacayaṃ mithyārāgaḥ prahāṇaṃ gacchati anupacayaṃ mithyādoṣaḥ prahāṇaṃ gacchati, anupacayaṃ mithyāmohaḥ prahāṇaṃ gacchati I tāni cāsya kuśalamūlānyuttapyante pariśuddhyanti karmaṇyāni ca bhavanti I tadyathāpi nāma bhavanto jinaputrāstadeva jātarūpaṃ kuśalasya karmārasya hastagataṃ tulyadharaṇameva pramāṇenāvatiṣṭhate, evameva bhavanto jinaputrā bodhisattvasya asyāṃ prabhākaryāṃ bodhisattvabhūmau sthitasya anekān kalpān yāvadanekāni kalpakoṭiniyutaśatasahasrāṇi....prahāṇaṃ gacchanti I tasya bhūyasyā mātrayā kṣāntisauratyāśayatā ca pariśuddhyati, sākhilyamādhuryāśayatā ca akopyāśayatā ca akṣubhitāśayatā ca alubhitāśayatā ca anunnāmavanāmāśayatā ca sarvakṛtapratikṛtānāṃ niḥkāṅkṣāśayatā ca sattvakṛtapratikṛtānāṃ kāṅkṣāśayatā ca aśāṭhyamāyāvitāśayatā ca agahanāśayatā ca pariśuddhyati I tasya caturbhyaḥ saṃgrahavastubhyo'rthacaryā atiriktatamā bhavati I daśabhyaḥ pāramitābhyaḥ kṣāntipāramitā atiriktatamā bhavati I na ca pariśeṣāsu na samudāgacchati yathābalaṃ yathābhajamānam I iyaṃ bhavanto jinaputrā bodhisattvasya prabhākarī nāma tṛtīyā bodhisattvabhūmiḥ samāsanirdeśataḥ,

P

yasyāṃ pratiṣṭhito bodhisattvo bhūyastvena indro bhavati devarājastridaśādhipatiḥ kṛtī prabhuḥ sattvānāṃ kāmarāgavinivartanopāyopasaṃhārāya kuśalaḥ sattvān kāmapaṅkādabhyuddhartum, yacca kiṃcit...peyālaṃ...yathārūpeṇa vīryārambheṇa ekakṣaṇalavamuhūrtena samādhiśatasahasraṃ ca pratilabhate... I I

prabhākarī nāma tṛtiyā bhūmiḥ I I

[Beginning of third bhūmi's final gathas]

upasaṃhāragāthāḥ |

te śuddhaāśaya guṇākara tīkṣṇacittā
nirviṇṇa rāgavigatā anivartiyāśca |
dṛḍhacitta taptadhṛtiyukti udāravegā
māhātmyatāśayavidū tṛtiyākramanti || 7 ||

atra sthitā vidu prabhākaribhūmideśe
duḥkhaṃ anityamaśuciṃ ca pralopadharmam |
acirasthitāka kṣaṇikaṃ ca nirodhakaṃ ca
vicinanti saṃskṛtagatīkamanāgatīkam || 8 ||

te rogabhūtasahaśokaparadevanaṃ ca
sopāyasaṃ ca priya apriyatānubaddham |
duḥkhadaurmanasyanilayaṃ jvalitāgnikalpaṃ
paśyanti saṃskṛtamananta samujjvalanti || 9 ||

udvigna sarva tribhave anapekṣacittā
jñānābhilāṣa sugatānamananyabuddhiḥ |
avicintiyaṃ atuliyaṃ asamantapāraṃ
saṃpaśyate nirupatāpa jināna jñānam || 10 ||

te buddhajñāna nirupadravamīkṣamāṇā
atrāṇa nātharahitā vrajate caranti |
nityaṃ daridra tribhiragnibhi saṃpradīptā
bhavacārake dukhaśatairvinibaddhacittāḥ || 11 ||

kleśāvṛtāśca avilokana chandahīnāḥ
sugatāna dharmaratanānupranaṣṭa bālāḥ |
saṃsārasrotaanuvāhina mokṣatrastā
me trāyitavya dṛḍha vīrya samārabhante || 12 ||

jñānābhilāṣa anapekṣa jagārthacārī
vyuparīkṣate katama hetu jagasya mokṣe |

nānyatra nāvaraṇajñāna tathāgatānāṃ
jñānaṃ ca prajñaprabhavaṃ sugatānanantam | | 13 | |

prajñā śrutāttu iti cintayi bodhisattvo
jñātvā tamārabhati vīrya śrutārthacārī |
rātriṃdivaṃ śravaṇahetu ananyakarmā
arthārthiko bhavati dharmaparāyaṇaśca | | 14 | |

maṇimuktiratnanilayān priyabāndhavāṃśca
rājyaṃ ananta vividhān pura sthānaśreṣṭhān |
bhāryāsutāṃśca parivāra manonukūlān
anapekṣacittu tyajate vidu dharmahetoḥ | | 15 | |

śira hastapāda nayana svakamātmamāṃsaṃ
jihvā ca daṃṣṭra śrava nāsika śoṇitaṃ ca |
hṛdayaṃ tupādya priya majja parityajanti
nā duṣkaretamatha duṣkara yacchṛṇoti | | 16 | |

yadi kaścidenamupagamya vadeyya evaṃ
yadi agnigarbha prapate jvalitāpi ghoram |
prāpiṣya dharmaratanaṃ sugatopanītaṃ
śrutvā adīnamanasaḥ prapate guṇārthī | | 17 | |

ekasya dharmapada artha sumerumūrdhnā
trisahasra agnirucitaṃ api brahmalokāt |
sūdūrlabhā imi jinasya udārabodhiḥ
ye mānuṣyeṇa sukha labhyati evarūpam | | 18 | |

yāvattareṇa pavararṣiṇa jñānalābha-
stāvattaraṃ dukhamavīcikamutsahyami |
kiṃ vā punarvividhamānuṣaduḥkhaskandhaṃ
hantābhyupemi varadharmipadārthiduḥkham | | 19 | |

dharmaṃ ca śrutva puna yoniṣu cintayāti
dhyānāpramāṇa caturaśca tathā arūpyā |
pañcāpyabhijña pravarā abhinirharanti
nā cāpi teṣu vaśitā upapadya yāti | | 20 | |

atra sthitā guṇadharā bahubuddhakoṭyaḥ
pūjyanti niścitamanā śṛṇuvanti dharmam ।
tanubhūtva mithyapagatāḥ pariśuddhayanti
svarṇe yathā vigatadoṣa pramāṇatulyam ।। 21 ।।

atra sthitā guṇadharāstridaśādhipatyaṃ
kārenti īśvara nivartitu kāmarāgāḥ ।
marusaṃgha nekavividhān kuśalāna mārge
sthāpentyananyamana buddhaguṇābhilāṣe ।। 22 ।।

atra sthitā jinasutā viriyārabhante
labdhvā samādhina sahasraśataṃ anūnam ।
paśyanti buddhavara lakṣaṇacitrigātrāṃ
bhūyo ataḥ praṇidhiśreṣṭha guṇāpramāṇāḥ ।। 23 ।।

ityeṣā tṛtiyā bhūminirdiṣṭā sugatātmajāḥ ।
sarvalokahitaiṣīṇāṃ bodhisattvānanuttamā ।। 24 ।।

[End of third bhūmi's final gathas]

[Beginning of fourth bhūmi's initial gathas]

4 arciṣmatī nāma caturthī bhūmiḥ |

upakramagāthāḥ |

evaṃ śrūṇitva caraṇaṃ vipulaṃ
bhūmyuttamaṃ manuramaṃ pravaram |
saṃharṣitā jinasutāttamanā
abhyokiranti kusumebhi jinam || 1 ||

saṃkampitā lavaṇatoyadharā
iha dharmadeśanamudīrayatām |
marukanyakā abhimanorucirāḥ
saṃgītiyukta varadharmaratāḥ || 2 ||

vaśavarti devapatirāttamanā
maṇiratna divya sugatasya kṣipī |
vācaṃ abhāṣi atha eva jino
utpanna artha guṇapāragato || 3 ||

kiṃ kāraṇaṃ tatha hi dharmavaraṃ
saṃbodhisattvacaraṇaṃ paramam |
bhūmirvidū na iyamadya śrutā
yasyāśravo durlabha kalpaśataiḥ || 4 ||

bhūyaḥ prabhāṣa naradevahitā
caryāvarāṃ jinasutān vidū |
śroṣyanti te marutasaṃghagaṇā
bhūtaṃ viniścayamananyapadam || 5 ||

vimukticandraḥ punarvīro ālapī sugatātmajam |
caturthī saṃkramantānāṃ gocaraṃ bhaṇa uttamam || 6 ||

[End of fourth bhūmi's initial gathas]

4 arciṣmatī nāma caturthī bhūmiḥ |

A

vajragarbha āha - yo'yaṃ bhavanto jinaputrā bodhisattvastṛtīyāyāṃ bodhisattvabhūmau supariśuddhālokaścaturthī bodhisattvabhūmimākramati, sa daśabhirdharmālokapraveśairākramati | katamairdaśabhiḥ? yaduta sattvadhātuvicāraṇālokapraveśena ca lokadhātuvicaraṇālokapraveśena ca dharmadhātuvicāraṇālokapraveśena ākāśadhātuvicāraṇālokapraveśena ca vijñānadhātuvicāraṇā lokapraveśena ca kāmadhātuvicaraṇālokapraveśena ca rūpadhātuvicaraṇālokapraveśena ca ārūpyadhātuvicaraṇālokapraveśena udārāśayādhimuktidhātuvicaraṇālokapraveśena ca māhātmyāśayādhimuktidhātuvicaraṇālokapraveśena | ebhirdaśabhirdharmālokapraveśairākramati | |

B

tatra bhavanto jinaputrā arciṣmatyā bodhisattvabhūmeḥ sahapratilambhena bodhisattvaḥ saṃvṛtto bhavati tathāgatakule tadātmakadharmapratilambhāya daśabhirjñānaparipācakairdharmaiḥ | katamairdaśabhiḥ? yaduta apratyudāvartyāśayatayā ca triratnābhedyaprasādaniṣṭhāgamanatayā ca saṃskārodayavyayavibhāvanatayā ca svabhāvānutpattyāśayatayā ca lokapravṛttinivṛttyāśayatayā ca karmabhavopapattyāśayatayā ca saṃsāranirvāṇāśayatayā ca sattvakṣetrakarmāśayatayā ca pūrvāntāparāntāśayatayā abhāvakṣayāśayatayā ca | ebhirbhavanto jinaputrā daśabhirjñānaparipācakairdharmaiḥ samanvāgato bodhisattvaḥ saṃvṛtto bhavati tathāgatakule tadātmakadharmapratilambhāya |

C

sa khalu punarbhavanto jinaputrā bodhisattvo'syāmarciṣmatyāṃ bodhisattvabhūmau pratiṣṭhito'dhyātmaṃ kāye kāyānudarśī viharati ātāpī saṃprajānan smṛtimān vinīya loke'bhidhyādaurmanasye bahirdhā kāye...adhyātmaṃ bahirdhā kāye | evamevādhyātmaṃ vedanāsu bahirdhā vedanāsu adhyātmaṃ bahirdhā vedanāsu | evamadhyātmaṃ citte bahirdhā citte'dhyātmaṃ citte | adhyātmaṃ dharmeṣu dharmānudarśī...bahirdhā dharmeṣu dharmānudarśī...evamadhyātmaṃ bahirdhā dharmeṣu... | so'nutpannānāṃ pāpakānāmakuśalānāṃ dharmāṇāmanutpādāya cchandaṃ janayati vyāyacchate vīryamārabhate cittaṃ pragṛhṇāti samyakpraṇidadhāti

| utpannānāṃ pāpakānāmakuśalānāṃ dharmāṇāṃ prahāṇāya... | anutpannānāṃ kuśalānāṃ dharmāṇāmutpādāya... | utpannānāṃ kuśalānāṃ dharmāṇāṃ sthitaye'sampramoṣāya vaipulyāya bhūyobhāvāya bhāvanāya paripūraye... | chandasamādhiprahāṇa-saṃskārasamanvāgataṃ ṛddhipādaṃ bhāvayati vivekaniśritaṃ virāganiśritaṃ nirodhaniśritaṃ vyavasargapariṇataṃ vīrya-pariṇataṃ cittapariṇataṃ mīmāṃsāpariṇatam | sa śraddhendriyaṃ bhāvayati vivekaniśritaṃ...vīryendriyaṃ...smṛtīndriyaṃ...-samādhīndriyaṃ...prajñendriyaṃ...sa | śraddhābalaṃ bhāvayati...vīryabalaṃ...smṛtibalaṃ...samādhibalaṃ...prajñābalaṃ... | smṛtisaṃbodhyaṅgaṃ bhāvayati dharmapravicaya...vīrya...prīti-...prasrabdhi...samādhi...upekṣā... | samyakdṛṣṭiṃ bhāvayati-...samyaksaṃkalpaṃ...samyagvācaṃ...samyakkarmāntaṃ...samyagājī vaṃ...samyagvyāyāmaṃ...samyaksmṛtiṃ...samyaksamādhiṃ... ||

D

tacca sarvasattvasāpekṣatayā ca pūrvapraṇidhānābhinirhār-opastabdhatayā ca mahākaruṇāpūrvaṃgamatayā ca mahāmaitry-upetatayā ca sarvajñajñānādhyālambanatayā ca buddhakṣetraviṭha-panālaṃkārābhinirhāratayā ca tathāgatabalavaiśāradyāveṇika-buddhadharmalakṣaṇānuvyañjanasvaraghoṣasaṃpadabhinirhāratay ā ca uttarottaravaiśeṣikadharmaparimārgaṇatayā ca gambhīra-buddhadharmavimokṣaśravaṇānugamanatayā ca mahopāya-kauśalyabalavicāraṇatayā ca |

E

tasya khalu punarbhavanto jinaputrā bodhisattvasya asyām-arciṣmatyāṃ bodhisattvabhūmau sthitasya yānīmāni satkāyadṛṣṭipūrvaṃgamāni ātmasattvajīvapoṣapudgalaskandha-dhātvāyatanābhiniveśasamucchritāni unmiñjitāni nimiñjitāni vicintitāni vitarkitāni kelāyitāni mamāyitāni dhanāyitāni niketa-sthānāni, tāni sarvāṇi vigatāni bhavanti sma |

F

sa yānīmāni karmāṇyakaraṇīyāni samyaksaṃbuddhavivarṇitāni saṃkleśopasaṃhitāni, tāni sarveṇa sarvaṃ prajahāti | yāni cemāni karmāṇi karaṇīyāni samyaksaṃbuddhapraśastāni bodhimārga-saṃbhārānukūlāni, tāni samādāya vartate |

G

sa bhūyasyā mātrayā yathā yathopāyaprajñābhinirhṛtāni mārgasamudāgamāya mārgāṅgāni bhāvayati, tathā tathā snigdhacittaśca bhavati, maducittaśca karmaṇyacittaśca hitasukhāvahacittaśca apakliṣṭacittaśca uttarottaraviśeṣaparimārgaṇacittaśca jñānaviśeṣaṇābhilāṣacittaśca sarvajagatparitrāṇacittaśca gurugauravānukūlacittaśca yathāśrutadharmapratipatticittaśca bhavati ।

H

sa kṛtajñaśca bhavati, kṛtavedī ca sūrataśca sukhasaṃvāsaśca ṛjuśca mṛduśca agahanacārī ca nirmāyanirmāṇaśca suvacāśca pradakṣiṇagrāhī ca bhavati । sa evaṃ kṣamopeta evaṃ damopeta evaṃ śamopeta evaṃ kṣamadamaśamopeta uttarāṇi bhūmipariśodhakāni mārgāṅgāni manasi kurvāṇaḥ samudācaran

I

aprasrabdhavīryaśca bhavati apakliṣṭaḥ । apratyudāvartyavīryaśca vipulavīryaśca anantavīryaśca uttaptavīryaśca asamavīryaśca asaṃhāryavīryaśca sarvasattvaparipācanavīryaśca nayānayavibhaktavīryaśca bhavati ।

J

tasya bhūyasyā mātrayā āśayadhātuśca viśuddhyati, adhyāśayadhātuśca na vipravasati, adhimuktidhātuścottapyate, kuśalamūlavivṛddhiścopajāyate, lokamalakaṣāyatā cāpagacchati, sarv asaṃśayavimatisaṃdehāścāsyocchidyante, niṣkāṅkṣābhimukhatā ca paripūryate, prītiprasabdhī ca samudāgacchati, tathāgatādhiṣṭhānaṃ cābhimukhībhavati, apramāṇacittāśayatā ca samudāgacchāti ।।

K

tasya asyāmarciṣmatyāṃ bodhisattvabhūmau sthitasya bodhisattvasya...peyālaṃ...। bhūyastvena ca teṣāṃ tathāgatānāṃ śāsane pravrajati । tasya bhūyasyā mātrayā āśayādhyāśayādhimuktisamatā viśudhyati । tasya asyāmarciṣmatyāṃ bodhisattvabhūmau sthitasya bodhisattvasya...āśayādhyāśayādhimuktisamatāviśuddhi stiṣṭhati, tāni cāsya kuśalamūlāni sūttaptāni prabhāsvaratarāṇi ca bhavanti । tadyathāpi nāma bhavanto jinaputrāstadeva jātarūpaṃ kuśalena karmāreṇābharaṇīkṛtamasaṃhāryaṃ bhavati tadanyairakṛtābharaṇairjātarūpaiḥ, evameva bhavanto jinaputrā bodhisattvasya asyāmarciṣmatyāṃ bodhisattvabhūmau sthitasya tāni kuśalamūlānyasaṃhāryāṇi bhavanti tadanyeṣāmadharabhūmisthitānāṃ bodhisattvānāṃ kuśalamūlaiḥ ।

tadyathāpi nāma bhavanto jinaputrā maṇiratnaṃ jātaprabhaṃ pariśu ddharaśmimaṇḍalamālokapramuktamasaṃhāryaṃ bhavati tadanyairapi śuddhaprabhai ratnajātaiḥ, anācchedyaprabhaṃ ca bhavati sarvamārutodakapravarṣaiḥ, evameva bhavanto jinaputrā bodhisattvo'syāmarciṣmatyāṃ bodhisattvabhūmau sthitaḥ sannasaṃhāryo bhavati tadanyairadharabhūmisthitairbodhisattvaiḥ, anācchedyajñānaśca bhavati sarvamārakleśasamudācāraiḥ । tasya caturbhyaḥ saṃgrahavastubhyaḥ samānārthatā atiriktatamā bhavati । daśabhyaḥ pāramitābhyo vīryapāramitā atiriktatamā bhavati, na ca pariśeṣāsu na samudāgacchati yathābalaṃ yathābhajamānam । iyaṃ bhavanto jinaputrā bodhisattvasyārciṣmatī nāma caturthī bhūmiḥ samāsanirdeśataḥ, yasyāṃ pratiṣṭhito bodhisattvo bhūyastvena suyāmo bhavati devarājaḥ kṛtī prabhuḥ sattvānāṃ satkāyadṛṣṭisamuddhātāya kuśalaḥ sattvān samyagdarśane pratiṣṭhāpayitum । yacca kiṃcit........।।

arciṣmatī nāma caturthī bhūmiḥ ।।

[Beginning of fourth bhūmi's final gathas]

upasaṃhāragāthāḥ |

parikarmitā tṛtīyabhūmiprabhaṃkarāya
sattvacaryaloka tatha dharma vicāryamāṇaḥ |
ākāśadhātu manadhātu trayaśca dhātu
adhimukti āśaya viśuddhi samākramanti || 7 ||

sahaprāptu arciṣmati bhūmi mahānubhāvaḥ
saṃvṛttu śāstu kulu bhūyu vivartiyatve |
abhedya buddharatane tatha dharmasaṃghe
udayavyayasthiti nirīhaka prekṣamāṇaḥ || 8 ||

lokapravṛtti kriyakarma bhavopapattiṃ
saṃsāranirvṛtivibhāvana kṣetrasattvān |
dharmāñca pūrvamaparānta kṣayānutpādaṃ
saṃvṛttu bhāvayati śāstu kulānuvartī || 9 ||

so eṣu dharmu samupetu hitānukampī
bhāveti kāyamapi vedana cittadharmān |
adhyātmabāhyubhayathā vidu bhāvayāti
smṛtyopasthānabhāvana niketavarjitā || 10 ||

pāpakṣayātkuśaladharmavivardhitā ca
samyakprahāṇa caturo vidu bhāvayanti |
caturṛddhipāda bala indriya bhāvayanti
bodhyaṅgaratna ruciraṃ tatha mārga śreṣṭham || 11 ||

bhāventi tān janayatāṃ samavekṣya buddhim
upastambhayanti praṇidhiṃ kṛtapūrvamaitrāḥ |
sarvajñajñānamabhiprārthana buddhakṣetraṃ
balaśreṣṭhamuttamapathaṃ anucintayantaḥ || 12 ||

vaiśāradaṃ api ca dharma ahārya śāstuḥ
varavuddhaghoṣamabhiprārthayamāna dhīrāḥ |
gambhīramārgaratanaṃ ca vimokṣasthānaṃ

mahatāmupāya samudāgama bhāvayanti || 13 ||

satkāyadṛṣṭivigatāśca dviṣaṣṭidṛṣṭī
attāttamīyavigatāstatha jīvalābham |
skandhāstu dvāra tatha dhātuniketasthānaṃ
sarvaprahāṇa viduṣaṃ catuthāya bhūmyām || 14 ||

so yānimāni sugatena vivarṇitāni
karmāṇi kleśasahajāni anarthakāni |
tāni prahāya vidu āśayato viśuddhā
dharmārabhanti kuśalaṃ jaga–tāyaṇārtham || 15 ||

susnigdhacitta bhavatī vidu apramatto
mṛducittu sārjava hitāsukhaāvahaśca |
aparikliṣṭaśca parimārgati uttamārthaṃ
jñānābhiṣekamabhilāṣi jagārthacārī || 16 ||

gurugauraveṣupagataḥ pratipattikāmo
bhavate kṛtajña sumanāśca akūhakāśca |
nirmāyatāgahana āśayasūrataśca
avivartyavīryu bhavate samudānayantaḥ || 17 ||

tasyātra bhūmi rucirāya pratiṣṭhitasya
adhyāśayaṃ api ca śuddhamupeti dharmam |
adhimukti tapyati vivardhati śukladharmo
malakalmaṣaṃ vimati śaṃśaya sarva yānti || 18 ||

atra sthitā naravararṣabha bodhisattvāḥ
sugatānanekanayutānabhipūjayanti |
śṛṇvanti dharma yatha śāsani pravrajanti
asaṃhārya śakya kṛtakāñcanabhūṣaṇaṃ vā || 19 ||

atra sthitāna vidunā guṇamāśayaṃ ca
jñānaṃ upāya caraṇaṃ ca viśuddhimārgaḥ |
no śakyu māranayutebhi nivartanāya
ratnaprabheva yatha varṣajalairahāryā || 20 ||

atra sthitā naramarudgaṇapūjanārhā
bhontī suyāmapatirīśvara dharmacārī |
sattvāni dṛṣṭigahanādvinivartayanti
saṃbhārayanti kuśalā jinajñānahetoḥ || 21 ||

viryopapeta śatakoṭi mararṣabhāṇāṃ
paśyantyananyamanasaḥ susamāhitatvāt |
tata uttariṃ bahukalpamabhinirharanti
jñānākarā praṇidhiśreṣṭha guṇārthacārī || 22 ||

caturthī itiyaṃ bhūmirviśuddhā śubhacāriṇī |
guṇārthajñānayuktānāṃ nirdiṣṭā sugatātmajāḥ || 23 ||

[End of fourth bhūmi's final gathas]

[Beginning of fifth bhūmi's initial gathas]

5 sudurjayā nāma pañcamī bhūmiḥ ।

upakramagāthāḥ ।

caraṇamatha śruṇitvā bhūmiśreṣṭhāṃ vidūnāṃ
jinasuta parituṣṭā harṣitā dharmahetoḥ ।
gagani kusumavarṣaṃ utsṛjantī udagrāḥ
sādhu sugataputra vyāhṛtaṃ te mahātmā ।। 1 ।।

marupati vaśavartī sārdha devāgaṇena
svagagata sugatasya pūjānārthaṃ udagrā ।
vividharucirameghāḥ snigdhaābhā manojñāḥ
abhikira sugatasya harṣitāḥ prīṇitāśca ।। 2 ।।

gītaruta manojñā vādyatūryābhinādā
devavadhuprayuktāḥ śāstu saṃpūjanārtham ।
jina puna tatharūpaṃ darśayanti sma sthānaṃ
sarvarutasvarebhī eva śabdaḥ prayuktaḥ ।। 3 ।।

sucireṇa āśayu prapūrṇa muneḥ
sucireṇa bodhi śiva prāpta jinaḥ ।
sucireṇa dṛṣṭa naradevahitaḥ
saṃprāpta devapuri śākyamuniḥ ।। 4 ।।

sucireṇa sāgarajalāḥ kṣubhitāḥ
sucireṇa ābha śubha munni jane ।
sucireṇa sattva sukhitāḥ -
sucireṇa śāsu śruta kāruṇikaḥ ।। 5 ।।

sucireṇa saṃgamu mahāmuninā
saṃprāpta sarvagūṇapāramitaḥ ।
mada māna darpa prajahitva tamaṃ
pūjārhu pūjima mahāśramaṇam ।। 6 ।।

(iha pūji kṛtva khagamārgagatā)
iha pūji kṛtva sukha nekavidham ।
iha pūji kṛtva dukhasarvakṣaye
iha pūji kṛtva jina jñānavaram ।। 7 ।।

gaganopamaḥ paramuśuddhu jinu
jagatī aliptu yatha padmu jale ।
abhyudgato udadhi meruriva
harṣitva cittu jina pūjayathā ।। 8 ।।

athābravīdvajragarbhaṃ vimukticandro viśāradaḥ ।
pañcamyā bhūmya ākarān nirdiśasva viśārada ।। 10 ।।

[End of fifth bhūmi's initial gathas]

5 sudurjayā nāma pañcamī bhūmiḥ ।

A

vajragarbha āha - yo'yaṃ bhavanto jinaputrā bodhisattvaścaturthyāṃ bodhisattvabhūmau suparipūrṇamārgaḥ pañcamīṃ bodhisattvabhūmimavatarati, sa daśabhiścittāśayaviśuddhisamatābhiravatarati । katamābhirdaśabhiḥ? yaduta atītabuddhadharmaviśuddhyāśayasamatayā ca anāgatabuddhadharmaviśuddhyāśayasamatayā ca pratyutpannabuddhadharmaviśuddhyāśayasamatayā ca śīlaviśuddhyāśayasamatayā ca cittaviśuddhyāśayasamatayā ca dṛṣṭikāṅkṣāvimativilekhāpanayanaviśuddhyāśayasamatayā ca mārgāmārgajñānaviśuddhyāśayasamatayā ca pratipatprahāṇājñānaviśuddhyāśayasamatayā ca sarvabodhipakṣyadharmottarottaravibhāvanaviśuddhyāśayasamatayā ca sarvasattvaparipācanaviśuddhyāśayasamatayā ca । ābhirdaśabhiścittāśayaviśuddhisamatābhiravatarati ।

B

sa khalu punarbhavanto jinaputrā bodhisattvaḥ pañcamīṃ bodhisattvabhūmimanuprāptaḥ eṣāmeva bodhipakṣyāṇāṃ mārgāṅgānāṃ suparikarmakṛtatvātsupariśodhitādhyāśayatvācca bhūya uttarakālamārgaviśeṣamabhiprārthayamānastathatvānupratipannaśca praṇidhānabalādhānataśca kṛpāmaitrībhyāṃ sarvasattvāparityāgataśca puṇyavijñānasaṃbhāropacayataśca apratiprasrabdhitaśca upāyakauśalyābhinirhārataśca uttarottarabhūmyavabhāsālocanataśca tathāgatādhiṣṭhānasaṃpratyeṣaṇataśca smṛtimatigatibuddhibalādhānataśca apratyudāvartanīyamanasikāro bhūtvā

C

idaṃ duḥkhamāryasatyamiti yathābhūtaṃ prajānāti । ayaṃ duḥkhasamudayaḥ āryasatyamiti yathābhūtaṃ prajānāti । ayaṃ duḥkhanirodhaḥ āryasatyamiti yathābhūtaṃ prajānāti । iyaṃ duḥkhanirodhagāminī pratipadāryasatyamiti yathābhūtaṃ prajānāti । sa saṃvṛtisatyakuśalaśca bhavati । paramārthasatyakuśalaśca bhavati । lakṣaṇasatyakuśalaśca bhavati । vibhāgasatyakuśalaśca bhavati । nistīraṇasatyakuśalaśca bhavati । vastusatyakuśalaśca bhavati । prabhavasatyakuśalaśca bhavati । kṣayānutpādasatyakuśalaśca bhavati । mārgajñānāvatārasatyakuśalaśca bhavati । sarvabodhisattvabhūmikramānusaṃdhiniṣpādanatayā yāvattathāgatajñānasamudayasatyakuśalaśca bhavati | sa parasattvānāṃ yathāśayasaṃtoṣaṇātsaṃvṛtisatyaṃ prajānāti | ekanayasamavasaraṇātparamārthasatyaṃ prajānāti | svasāmanyalakṣaṇānubodhāllakṣaṇasatyaṃ prajānāti | dharmavibhāgavyavasthānānubodhādvibhāgasatyaṃ prajānāti | skandhadhātvāyatanavyavasthānānubodhānnistīraṇasatyaṃ prajānāti | cittaśarīraprapīḍanopanipātitatvādvastusatyam, gatisaṃdhisaṃbandhanatvātprabhavasatyam, sarvajvaraparidāhātyantopaśamātkṣayānutpādasatyam, advayānutpādasatyam, advayābhinirhāranmārgajñānāvatārasatyam, sarvākārābhisaṃbodhitsarvabodhisattvabhūmikramānusaṃdhiniṣpādanatayā yāvattathāgatajñānasamudayasatyaṃ prajānāti adhimuktijñānabalādhānānna khalu punarniravaśeṣajñānāt ||

D

sa evaṃ satyakauśalyajñānābhinirhṛtayā buddhyā sarvasaṃskṛtaṃ riktaṃ tucchaṃ mṛṣā moṣadharma avisaṃvādakaṃ bālālāpanamiti yathābhūtaṃ prajānāti | tasya bhūyasyā mātrayā sattveṣu mahākaruṇā abhimukhībhavati, mahāmaitryālokaśca prādurbhavati ||

E

sa evaṃ jñānabalādhanaprāptaḥ sarvasattvasāpekṣo buddhajñānābhilāṣī pūrvāntāparāntaṃ sarvasaṃskāragatasya pratyavekṣate yathā pūrvāntato'vidyābhavatṛṣṇāprasṛtānāṃ sattvānāṃ saṃsārasroto'nuvāhināṃ skandhālayānucchalitānāṃ duḥkhaskandho vivardhate, nirātmā niḥsattvo nirjīvo niṣpoṣo niṣpudgala ātmātmīyavigataḥ, taṃ yathābhūtaṃ prajānāti | yathā ca anāgatasyaiva asatsaṃmohābhilāṣasya vyavacchedaḥ paryanto niḥsaraṇaṃ nāstyasti ca, tacca yathābhūtaṃ prajānāti ||

F

tasyaivaṃ bhavati - āścaryaṃ yāvadajñānasamūḍhā bateme bālapṛthagjanāḥ, yeṣāmasaṃkhyeyā ātmabhāvā niruddhāḥ, nirudhyante nirotsyante ca | evaṃ ca kṣīyamāṇāḥ kāye na nirvidamutpādayanti | bhūyasyā mātrayā duḥkhayantraṃ vivardhayanti | saṃsārasrotasaśca mahābhayānna nivartante | skandhālayaṃ ca notsṛjanti | dhātūragebhyaśca ga nirvidyante | nandīrāgataścārakaṃ ca nāvabudhyante | ṣaḍāyatanaśūnyagrāmaṃ ca na vyavalokayanti | ahaṃkāramamakārābhiniveśānuśayaṃ ca na prajahanti | mānadṛṣṭiśalyaṃ ca noddharanti | rāgadveṣamohajvalanaṃ ca na praśamayanti | avidyāmohāndhakāraṃ ca na vidhamayanti | tṛṣṇārṇavaṃ ca nocchoṣayanti । daśabalasārthavāhaṃ ca na paryeṣante । mārāśaya-gahanānugataśca saṃsārasāgare vividhākuśalavitarkagrāhākule pariplavante ।

G

apratiśaraṇāstathā saṃvegamāpadyante, bahūni duḥkhāni pratyanubhavanti yaduta jātijarāvyādhimaraṇaśokaparidevaduḥkha-daurmanasyopāyāsān । hanta ahameṣāṃ sattvānāṃ duḥkhārt-ānāmanāthānāmatrāṇānāmaśaraṇānāmalayanānāmaparāyaṇānāman dhānāmavidyāṇḍakośapaṭalaparyavanaddhānāṃ tamobhi-bhūtānāmarthāya eko'dvitīyo bhūtvā tathārūpaṃ puṇyajñānasaṃ-bhāropacayaṃ bibharmi, yathārūpeṇa puṇyajñānasaṃbhār-opacayena saṃbhṛtena ime sarvasattvā atyantaviśuddhim-anuprāpnuyuḥ, yāvaddaśabalabalatāmasaṅgajñānaniṣṭhām-anuprāpnuyuriti ।।

H

sa evaṃ suvilokitajñānābhinirhṛtayā buddhyā yatkiṃcit kuśalamūla-bhārabhate, tatsarvasattvaparitrāṇāyārabhate । sarvasattvahitāya sarvasattvasukhāya sarvasattvānukampāyai sarvasattvānupadravāya sarvasattvaparimocanāya sarvasattvānukarṣāya sarvasattvaprasād-anāya sarvasattvavinayāya sarvasattvaparinirvāṇāyārabhate ।।

I

sa bhūyasyā mātrayā asyāṃ pañcamyāṃ sudurjayāyāṃ bodhisattva-bhūmau sthito bodhisattvaḥ smṛtimāṃśca bhavati, asaṃpramoṣa-dharmatayā matimāṃśca bhavati, suviniścitajñānatayā gatimāṃśca bhavati, sūtrārthagatisaṃdhāyabhāṣitāvabodhatayā hrīmāṃśca bhavati, ātmaparānurakṣaṇatayā dhṛtimāṃśca bhavati, saṃvara-cāritrānutsargatayā buddhimāṃśca bhavati, sthānāsthānakauśalya-suvicāritatayā jñānānugataśca bhavati, aparapraṇeyatayā prajñānu-gataśca bhavati, arthānarthasaṃbhedapadakuśalatayā abhijñānir-hāraprāptaśca bhavati, bhāvanābhinirhārakuśalatayā upāyakuśalaśca bhavati lokānuvartanatayā ।

J

atṛptaśca bhavati puṇyasaṃbhāropacayatayā । apratiprasrabdha-vīryaśca bhavati jñānasaṃbhāraparyeṣaṇatayā । aparikhinnāśayaśca bhavati mahāmaitrīkṛpāsaṃbhārasaṃbhṛtatayā । aśithilaparyeṣaṇ-ābhiyuktaśca bhavati tathāgatabalavaiśāradyāveṇikabuddhadharma-paryeṣaṇatayā । svabhinirhṛtamanasikārānugataśca bhavati buddhakṣetraviṭhapanālaṃkārābhinirhṛtatayā | vicitrakuśalakriyābhiyuktaśca bhavati lakṣaṇānuvyañjanasamudānayanatayā | satatasamitaṃ svabhiyuktaśca bhavati tathāgatakāyavākcittālaṃkāraparyeṣaṇatayā | mahāgauravopasthānaśīlaśca bhavati sarvabodhisattvadharmabhaṇākaśuśrūṣaṇatayā | apratihatacittaśca bhavati bodhicittamahopāyakauśalyasaṃdhyupasaṃhitalokapracāratayā | rātriṃdivamanyacittaparivarjitaśca bhavati sarvasattvaparipācanābhiyogatayā ||

K

sa evamabhiyukto dānenāpi sattvān paripācayati, priyavadyatayāpi, arthakriyayāpi, samānārthatayāpi, rūpakāyasaṃdarśanenāpi, dharmadeśanayāpi, bodhisattvacaryāprabhāvanayāpi, tathāgatamāhātmyaprakāśanatayāpi, saṃsāradoṣasaṃdarśanenāpi, buddhajñānānuśaṃsāparikīrtanenāpi, maharddhivikurvaṇābhinirhāraṇānopacārakriyāprayogairapi sattvān paripācayati | sa evaṃ sattvaparipācanābhiyukto buddhajñānānugatacittasaṃtāno'pratyudāvartanīyakuśalamūlaprayogo vaiśeṣikadharmaparimārgaṇābhiyuktaḥ

L

yānīmāni sattvahitāni loke pracaranti, tadyathā – lipiśāstramudrāsaṃkhyāgaṇanānikṣepādīni nānādhātutantracikitsātantrāṇi śoṣāpasmārabhūtagrahapratiṣedhakāni viṣavetālaprayogapratighātakāni kāvyanāṭakākhyānagāndharvetihāsasaṃpraharṣaṇāni grāmanagarodyānanadīsarastaḍāgapuṣkariṇīpuṣpaphalauṣadhivana ṣaṇḍābhinirhārāṇi suvarṇarūpyamaṇimuktāvaiḍūryaśaṅkhaśilāpravālaratnākaranidarśanāni candrasūryagrahajyotirnakṣatrabhūmicālamṛgaśakunisvapnanimittāni pradeśapraveśāni sarvāṅgapratyaṅgalakṣaṇāni cārānucāraprayoganimittāni saṃvaracāritrasthānadhyānābhijñāpramāṇārūpyasthānāni, yāni cānyānyapi aviheṭhanāvihiṃsāsaṃprayuktāni sarvasattvahitasukhāvahāni, tānyapyabhinirharati kāruṇikatayā anupūrvabuddhadharmapratiṣṭhāpanāya ||

M

tasya asyāṃ sudurjayāyāṃ bodhisattvabhūmau sthitasya bodhisattvasya....peyālaṃ...pariṇāmayati | tāṃśca tathāgatānarhataḥ samyaksaṃbuddhān paryupāsate, teṣāṃ ca sakāśād gauravacitrīkāreṇa satkṛtya dharmadeśanāṃ śṛṇoti udgṛhṇāti dhārayati | śrutvā ca yathābalaṃ yathābhajamānaṃ pratipatyā saṃpādayati |

bhūyastvena ca teṣāṃ tathāgatānāṃ śāsane pravrajati I pravrajitaśca śrutadhārī dharmabhāṇako bhavati I sa bhūyasyā mātrayā śrutācāra-dhāraṇīpratilabdho dharmabhāṇako bhavati anekeṣāṃ ca buddha-koṭiniyutaśatasahasrāṇāmantike anekakalpakoṭiniyutaśatasahasrāṇy-asaṃpramoṣatayā I tasya asyāṃ sudurjayāyāṃ bodhisattvabhūmau sthitasya anekān kalpāṃstāni kuśalamūlānyuttapyante pari-śudhyanti prabhāsvaratarāṇi ca bhavanti, anekāni kalpaśatāni... I tasya tāni kuśalamūlānyuttapyante pariśuddhyanti prabhāsva-ratarāṇi ca bhavanti I tadyathāpi nāma bhavanto jinaputrāstadeva jātarūpaṃ musārgalvasṛṣṭaṃ bhūyasyā mātrayottapyate pari-śudhyati prabhāsvarataraṃ bhavati, evameva bhavanto jinaputrā bodhisattvasya asyāṃ sudurjayāyāṃ bodhisattvabhūmau sthitasya tāni kuśalamūlānyupāyaprajñāvicāritāni bhūyasyā mātrayottapyante pariśuddhyanti, prabhāsvaratarāṇi ca bhavanti, jñānaprayogaguṇ-ābhinirhārādasaṃhāryavicāritatamāni ca bhavanti I tadyathāpi nāma bhavanto jinaputrāścandrasūryagrahajyotirnakṣatrāṇāṃ vimānāloka-prabhavātamaṇḍalībhirasaṃhāryā bhavati mārutāsādhāraṇā ca, evameva bhavanto jinaputrā bodhisattvasya asyāṃ sudurjayāyāṃ bodhisattvabhūmau sthitasya tāni kuśalamūlānyupāyaprajñājñāna-cittavicāraṇānugatānyasaṃhāryāṇi bhavanti, sarvaśrāvakapratyeka-buddhairlaukikāsādhāraṇāni ca bhavanti I tasya daśabhyaḥ pāra-mitābhyo dhyānapāramitā atiriktatamā bhavati, na ca pariśeṣāsu na samudāgacchati yathābalaṃ yathābhajamānam I iyaṃ bhavanto jinaputrā bodhisattvasya sudurjayā nāma pañcamī bodhisattva-bhūmiḥ samāsanirdeśataḥ, yasyāṃ pratiṣṭhito bodhisattvo bhūyastvena saṃtuṣito bhavati, devarājaḥ kṛtī prabhuḥ sattvānāṃ sarvatīrthyāyatanavinivartanāya kuśalaḥ sattvān satyeṣu prati-ṣṭhāpayitum I yatkiṃcit..... I I

sudurjayā nām pañcamī bhūmiḥ I I

[Beginning of fifth bhūmi's final gathas]

upasaṃhāragāthāḥ |

evaṃ viśodhita caturṣu jinacarīṣu
buddhayā triyādhvasamatā anucintayanti |
śīlaṃ ca cittapratipattitu mārgaśuddhiḥ
kāṅkṣāvinīta vidu pañcami ākramanti || 11 ||

smṛti cāpa indriya iṣu anivartitāśca
samyakprahāṇa haya vāhana ṛddhipādāḥ |
pañca balāḥ kavaca sarvapipūabhebyāḥ
śūrāṇivarti vidu pañcami ākramanti || 12 ||

hyapatrāpyavastravidunāṃ śuciśīlagandho
bodhyaṅgamālyavaradhyānavilepanaṃ ca |
prajñāvicāraṇavibhūṣaṇupāyaśreṣṭham
udyānadhāraṇita pañcamimākramanti || 13 ||

caturddhipādacaraṇāḥ smṛtiśuddhigrīvāḥ
kṛpamaitraśreṣṭhanayanā varaprajñadaṃṣṭrā |
nairātmyanāda ripukleśa pradharṣamāṇā
narasiṃha samya vidu pañcamimākramanti || 14 ||

te pañcamīmupagatā varabhūmiśreṣṭhāṃ
pariśuddhamārga śubhamuttari bhāvayanti |
śuddhāśayā vidu jinatvanuprāpaṇārthī
kṛpamaitrakhedavigatā anucintayanti || 15 ||

saṃbhārapuṇyupacayā tatha jñāna śreṣṭhaṃ
naikā upāya abhirocanabhūmya bhāsān |
buddhadhiṣṭhāna smṛtimāṃ matibuddhiprāptā
cattvāri satya nikhilānanucintayanti || 16 ||

paramārthasatyamapi saṃvṛtilakṣaṇaṃ ca
satyavibhāgamatha satyanitīraṇaṃ ca |

tatha vastu sāsrava kṣayaṃ api mārgasatyaṃ
yāvantanāvaraṇasatya samosaranti | | 17 | |

evaṃ ca satya parimārgati sūkṣmabuddhiḥ
na ca tāvadanāvaraṇaprāptu vimokṣaṃ śreṣṭham |
jñānādhimuktivipulāttu guṇākarāṇām
atibhonti sarvajagato arhapratyayānām | | 18 | |

so eva satyaabhinirhṛta tattvabuddhiḥ
jānāti saṃskṛta mṛṣāprakṛtī asāram |
kṛpamaitraābha labhate sugatāna bhūyaḥ
sattvārthikaḥ sugatajñāna gaveṣamāṇaḥ | | 19 | |

pūrvāpare vidu nirīkṣatu saṃskṛtasya
mohāndhakāratamasāvṛta duḥkhalagnā |
abhyuddharoti jagato dukhaskandhavṛddhān
nairātmyajīvarahitāṃstṛṇakāṣṭhatulyān | | 20 | |

kleśādvayena yugapatpunarbhāsi tryadhvaṃ
chedo dukhasya na ca anta samosarantaḥ |
hanto praṇaṣṭa jana te'tidayābhijātā
saṃsārasrota na nivartati niḥsvabhāvam | | 21 | |

skandhālayā uragadhātu kudṛṣṭiśalyāḥ
saṃtapta agnihṛdayāvṛta andhakāre |
tṛṣṇārṇavaprapatitā avalokanatvāt
jinasārthavāhavirahā dukhaarṇavasthāḥ | | 22 | |

evaṃ viditva punarārabhate'pramatto
taccaiva ārabhati sarvajagadvimokṣī |
smṛtimantu bhonti matimān gatimān dhṛtīṃ ca
hrīmāṃśca bhonti tatha buddhina prajñavāṃśca | | 23 | |

avitṛptu puṇyupacaye tatha jñāna śreṣṭhaṃ
no khedavānna śithilo balameṣamāṇaḥ |
kṣetraṃ vidhāya jinalakṣaṇabuddhaghoṣam
avitṛptasarvakriya sattvahitārthayuktaḥ | | 24 | |

paripācanāya jagato vidu śilpasthānān
lipimudrasaṃkhyagaṇadhātucikitsatantrān |
bhūtagrahāviṣamaroganivartanārthaṃ
sthāpenti śastra rucirān kṛpamaitrabuddhī || 25 ||

varakāvyanāṭakamatiṃ vividhaprahaṛṣān
nadyodiyānaphalapuṣpanipadyasthānān |
sthāpenti nekakriya sattvasukhāpanārthaṃ
ratnākarāṃśca upadarśayi naikarūpān || 26 ||

bhūmīcalaṃ ca graha jyotiṣa candrasūryau
sarvāṅgalakṣaṇavicāraṇarājyasthānam |
ārūpyadhyāna tathabhijña athāpramāṇā
abhinirharanti hitasaukhyajagārthakāmāḥ || 27 ||

iha durjayāmupajatā varaprajñacārī
pūjenti buddha nayutā śṛṇuvanti dharmam |
teṣāṃ śubhaṃ punaruttapyati āśayaśca
svarṇaṃ yathā musaragalvayasaṃvimṛṣṭam || 28 ||

ratnāmayā grahavimān vahanti vātā
te yehi tehi tu vahanti asaṃhṛtāśca |
tatha lokadharmi caramāna jagārthacārī
asaṃhārya bhonti yatha padma jale aliptam || 29 ||

atra sthitā tuṣita īśvara te kṛtāvī
nāśenti tīrthyacaraṇān pṛthudṛṣṭisthānān |
yaccācaranti kuśalaṃ jinajñānahetoḥ
sattvāna trāta bhavamo daśabhirbalāḍhyaiḥ || 30 ||

te vīryamuttari samārabhi aramattāḥ
koṭisahasra sugatānabhipūjayanti |
labdhvā samādhi vidu kampayi kṣetrakoṭī
praṇidhīviśeṣu anubhūya guṇākarāṇām || 31 ||

ityeṣā pañcamī bhūmirvicitropāyakoṭibhiḥ |
nirdiṣṭā sattvasārāṇāmuttamā sugatātmajāḥ || 32 ||

[End of fifth bhūmi's final gathas]

[Beginning of sixth bhūmi's initial gathas]

6 abhimukhī nāma ṣaṣṭhī bhūmiḥ |

upakramagāthāḥ |

caraṇavara śruṇitvā bhūmiśreṣṭhaṃ vidūnāṃ
gagani sugataputrā harṣitāḥ puṣpavarṣī |
maṇiratana udārā ābhayuktā viśuddhā
abhikira sugatasya sādhviti vyāharantaḥ || 1 ||

maruta śatasahasrā harṣitā antarīkṣe
diviya rucira citrā ratnacūrṇā udārāḥ |
abhikira sugatebhyo gandhamālyānulepān
chatradhvajāpatākāhāracandrārdhahārān || 2 ||

marupati vaśavartī sarvadevagaṇena
upari khaga paṭhitvā megha ratnāmayāni |
abhikiriṣu prasannaḥ pūjanārthaṃ jinasya
sādhu sugataputrā vyāharī hṛṣṭacittāḥ || 3 ||

amaravadhusahasrāṇyantarīkṣe sthitāni
gīta ruta manojñā vādyasaṃgītiyuktā |
sarvarutasvarebhyo eva śabdā ravante
jina kṛtu sumanojñaiḥ kleśatāpasya hantā || 4 ||

śūnya prakṛtiśāntā sarvadharmānimittāḥ
khagapathasamatulyā nirvikalpā viśuddhāḥ |
gatisthitivinirvṛttā niṣprapañcā aśeṣā
tathatasama tathatvāddharmatā nirvikalpā || 5 ||

yaiḥ punaranubuddhāḥ sarvadharmeva teṣāṃ
bhāvi tatha abhāve iñjanā nāsti kācit |
kṛpa karuṇa jage ca mocanārthaṃ prayuktā-
ste hi sugataputrā aurasā dharmajātāḥ || 6 ||

dānacari carante sarva hitvā nimittaṃ
śīlasudhṛtacittāṃ ādiśāntā praśāntāḥ |
jagati kṛta kṣamante akṣayā dharmajñānī
viriyabalaupetāḥ sarvadharmāviviktāḥ || 7 ||

dhyānanayapraviṣṭā jīrṇakleśā viśuddhāḥ
sarvaviditavastū ādiśūnyādhimuktāḥ |
jñānakriyabalāḍhyā nityayuktā jagārthaṃ
te hi sugataputrāḥ śāntapāpā mahātmāḥ || 8 ||

īdṛśā rutasahasra bhaṇitvā
khe sthitāḥ sumadhurā surakanyāḥ |
tūṣṇibhūta jinamīkṣi prasannā
dharmagauravaratā marukanyāḥ || 9 ||

vimukticandra abravīdvajragarbhaṃ viśāradam |
kīdṛśākāraniṣpattiḥ pañcamāyāmanantaram || 10 ||

[End of sixth bhūmi's initial gathas]

6 abhimukhī nāma ṣaṣṭhī bhūmiḥ ।

A

vajragarmo bodhisattva āha - yo'yaṃ bhavanto jinaputrā bodhisattvaḥ pañcamyāṃ bodhisattvabhūmau suparipūrṇamārgaḥ ṣaṣṭhīṃ bodhisattvabhūmimavatarati । sa daśabhirdharmasamatābhiravatarati । katamābhirdaśabhiḥ? yaduta sarvadharmānimittasamatayā ca sarvadharmālakṣaṇasamatayā ca sarvadharmānutpādasamatayā ca sarvadharmājātatayā ca sarvadharmaviviktasamatayā ca sarvadharmādiviśuddhisamatayā ca sarvadharmaniṣprapañcasamatayā ca sarvadharmānāvyūhānirvyūhasamatayā ca sarvadharmamāyāsvapnapratibhāsapratiśrutkodakacandrapratibimb anirmāṇasamatayā ca sarvadharmabhāvābhāvādvayasamatayā ca । ābhirdaśabhirdharmasamatābhiravatarati ।।

sa evaṃsvabhāvān sarvadharmān pratyavakṣemāṇo'nusṛjan anulomayan avilomayan śraddadhan abhiyan pratiyan avikalpayan anusaran vyavalokayan pratipadyamānaḥ ṣaṣṭhīmabhimukhīṃ bodhisattvabhūmimanuprāpnoti tīkṣṇayā ānulomikyā kṣāntyā । na ca tāvadanutpattikadharmakṣāntimukhamanuprāpnoti ।।

B

sa evaṃsvabhāvān sarvadharmānanugacchan bhūyasyā mātrayā mahākaruṇāpūrvaṃgamatvena mahākaruṇādhipateyatayā mahākaruṇāparipūrṇārthaṃ lokasya saṃbhavaṃ ca vibhavaṃ ca vyavalokayate ।

C

tasya lokasya saṃbhavaṃ ca vibhavaṃ ca vyavalokayata evaṃ bhavati - yāvatyo lokasamudācāropapattayaḥ sarvāḥ, tā ātmābhiniveśato bhavanti । ātmābhiniveśavigamato na bhavanti lokasamudācāropapattaya iti । tasyaivaṃ bhavati - tena khalu punarime bālabuddhya ātmābhiniviṣṭā ajñānatimirāvṛtā bhāvābhāvābhilāṣiṇo-'yoniśomanasikāraprasṛtā vipathaprayātā mithyānucāriṇaḥ puṇyāpuṇyāneñjyānabhisaṃskārānupacinvanti । teṣāṃ taiḥ saṃskārairavaropitaṃ cittabījaṃ sāsravaṃ sopādānamāyatyāṃ jātijarāmaraṇapunarbhavābhinirvṛttisaṃbhavopagataṃ bhavati । karmakṣetrālayamavidyāndhakāraṃ tṛṣṇāsnehamasmimānapariṣyandanataḥ । dṛṣṭikṛtajālapravṛddhyā ca nāmarūpāṅkuraḥ prādurbhavati । prādurbhūto vivardhate I vivṛddhe nāmarūpe pañcānāmindriyāṇāṃ pravṛttirbhavati I pravṛttānāmindriyāṇāmanyonya(saṃ)nipātataḥ sparśaḥ I sparśasya saṃnipātato vedanā prādurbhavati I vedanāyāstata uttare'bhinandanā bhavati I tṛṣṇābhinandanata upādānaṃ vivardhate I upādāne vivṛddhe bhavaḥ saṃbhavati I bhave saṃbhūte skandhapañcakamunmajjati I unmagnaṃ skandhapañcakaṃ gatipañcake'nupūrvaṃ mlāyati I mlānaṃ vigacchati I mlānavigamājjvaraparidāhaḥ I jvaraparidāhanidānāḥ sarvaśokaparidevaduḥkhadaurmanasyopāyāsāḥ samudāgacchanti I teṣāṃ na kaścitsamudānetā I svabhāvānābhogābhyāṃ ca vigacchanti I na caiṣāṃ kaścidvigamayitā I evaṃ bodhisattvo'nulomākāraṃ pratītyasamutpādaṃ pratyavekṣate I I

D

tasyaivaṃ bhavati - satyeṣvanabhijñānaṃ paramārthato'vidyā I avidyāprakṛtasya karmaṇo vipākaḥ saṃskārāḥ I saṃskārasaṃniśritaṃ prathamaṃ cittaṃ vijñānam I vijñānasahajāścatvāra upādānaskandhā nāmarūpam I nāmarūpavivṛddhiḥ ṣaḍāyatanam I indriyaviṣayavijñāgatrayasamavadhānaṃ sāsravaṃ sparśaḥ I sparśasahajā vedanā I vedanādhyavasānaṃ tṛṣṇā I tṛṣṇāvivṛddhirupādānam I upādānaprasṛtaṃ sāsravaṃ karma bhavaḥ I karmaniṣyando jātiḥ skandhonmajjanam I skandhaparipāko jarā I jīrṇasya skandhabhedo maraṇam I mriyamāṇasya vigacchataḥ saṃmūḍhasya sābhiṣvaṅgasya hṛdayasaṃtāpaḥ śokaḥ I śokasamutthitā vākpralāpāḥ paridevaḥ I pañcendriyanipāto duḥkham I manodṛṣṭinipāto daurmanasyam I duḥkhadaurmanasyabahulatvasaṃbhūtā upāyāsāḥ I evamayaṃ kevalo duḥkhaskandho duḥkhavṛkṣo'bhinirvartate kārakavedakavirahita iti I I

tasyaivaṃ bhavati - kārakābhiniveśataḥ kriyāḥ prajñāyante I yatra kārako nāsti, kriyāpi tatra paramārthato nopalabhyate I

E

tasyaivaṃ bhavati - cittamātramidaṃ yadidaṃ traidhātukam I

F

yānyapīmāni dvādaśa bhavāṅgāni tathāgatena prabhedaśo vyākhyātāni, api sarvāṇyeva tāni cittasamāśritāni I tatkasya hetoḥ? yasmin vastuni hi rāgasaṃyuktaṃ cittamutpadyate tadvijñānam I vastusaṃskāre'smimoho'vidyā I avidyācittasahajaṃ nāmarūpam I nāmarūpavivṛddhiḥ ṣaḍāyatanam I ṣaḍāyatanabhāgīyaḥ sparśaḥ I sparśasahajā vedanā I vedayato'vitṛptistṛṣṇā I tṛṣṇārtasya saṃgraho-'parityāga upādānam I eṣāṃ bhavāṅgānāṃ saṃbhavo bhavaḥ I bhavonmajjanaṃ jātiḥ I jātiparipāko jarā I jarāpagamo maraṇamiti I I

G

tatra avidyā dvividhakāryapratyupasthānā bhavati I ālambanataḥ sattvān saṃmohayati, hetuṃ ca dadāti saṃskārābhinirvṛttaye I saṃskārā api dvividhakāryapratyupasthānā bhavanti I anāgatavipākābhinirvṛtti ca kurvanti, hetuṃ ca dadati vijñānābhinirvṛttaye I vijñānamapi dvividhakāryapratyupasthānaṃ bhavati I bhavapratisaṃdhiṃ ca karoti, hetuṃ ca dadāti nāmarūpābhinirvṛttaye I nāmarūpamapi dvividhakāryapratyupasthānaṃ bhavati I anyonyopastambhanaṃ ca karoti, hetuṃ ca dadāti ṣaḍāyatanābhinirvṛttaye I

ṣaḍāyatanamapi dvividhakāryapratyupasthānaṃ bhavati I svaviṣayavibhaktitāṃ cādarśayati, hetuṃ ca dadāti sparśābhinirvṛttaye I sparśo'pi dvividhakāryapratyupasthāno bhavati I ālambanasparśanaṃ ca karoti, hetuṃ ca dadāti vedanābhinirvṛttaye I vedanāpi dvividhakāryapratyupasthānā bhavati I iṣṭāniṣṭobhayavimuktānubhavanaṃ ca karoti, hetuṃ ca dadāti tṛṣṇābhinirvṛttaye I tṛṣṇāpi dvividhakāryapratyupasthānā bhavati I saṃrajanīyavastusaṃrāgaṃ ca karoti, hetuṃ ca dadātyupādānābhinirvṛttaye I upādānamapi dvividhakāryapratyupasthānaṃ bhavati I saṃkleśabandhanaṃ ca karoti, hetuṃ ca dadāti bhavābhinirvṛttaye I

bhavo'pi dvividhakāryapratyupasthāno bhavati I anyabhavagatipratyadhiṣṭhānaṃ ca karoti, hetuṃ ca dadāti jātyabhinirvṛttaye I jātirapi dvividhakāryapratyupasthānā bhavati I skandhonmajjanaṃ ca karoti, hetuṃ ca dadāti jarābhiniṃvṛttaye I jarāpi dvividhakāryapratyupasthānā bhavati I indriyapariṇāmaṃ ca karoti, hetuṃ ca dadāti maraṇasamavadhānābhinirvṛttaye I maraṇamapi dvividhakāryapratyupasthānaṃ bhavati - saṃskāravidhvaṃsanaṃ ca karoti, aparijñānānucchedaṃ ceti I I

H

tatra avidyāpratyayāḥ saṃskārā ityavidyāpratyayatā saṃskārāṇām-anucchedo'nupastambhaśca I saṃskārapratyayaṃ vijñānamiti saṃskārapratyayatā vijñānānāmanucchedo'nupastambhaśca I peyālaṃ...jātipratyayatā jarāmaraṇasyānucchedo'nupastambhaśca I avidyānirodhātsaṃskāranirodha ityavidyāpratyayatābhāvātsaṃskārāṇāṃ vyupaśamo'nupastambhaśca I peyālaṃ...jātipratyayatābhāvājjarāmaraṇasya vyupaśamo'nupastambhaśca I I

I

tatra avidyā tṛṣṇopādānaṃ ca kleśavartmano'vyavacchedaḥ I saṃskārā bhavaśca karmavartmano'vyavacchedaḥ I pariśeṣaṃ duḥkhavartmano'vyavacchedaḥ I pravibhāgataḥ pūrvāntāparāntanirodhavartmano vyavacchedaḥ I evameva trivartma nirātmakamātmātmīyarahitaṃ saṃbhavati ca asaṃbhavayogena, vibhavati ca avibhavayogena svabhāvato naḍakalāpasadṛśam I I

J

api tu khalu punaryaducyate - avidyāpratyayāḥ saṃskārā ityeṣā paurvāntikyapekṣā I vijñānaṃ yāvadvedanetyeṣā pratyutpannāpekṣā I tṛṣṇa yāvadbhava ityeṣā aparāntikyapekṣā I ata urdhvamasya pravṛttiriti I avidyānirodhātsaṃskāranirodha ityapekṣāvyavaccheda eṣaḥ I I

K

api tu khalu punastriduḥkhatā dvādaśa bhavāṅgānyupādāya I tatra avidyā saṃskārā yāvatṣaḍāyatanamityeṣā saṃskāraduḥkhatā I sparśo vedanā caiṣā duḥkhaduḥkhatā I pariśeṣāṇi bhavāṅgānyeṣā pariṇāmaduḥkhatā I avidyānirodhātsaṃskāranirodha iti triduḥkhatāvyavaccheda eṣaḥ I I

L

avidyāpratyayāḥ saṃskārā iti hetupratyayaprabhavatvaṃ saṃskārāṇām I evaṃ pariśeṣāṇām I avidyānirodhātsaṃskāranirodha ityabhāvaḥ saṃskārāṇām I evaṃ pariśeṣāṇām I I

avidyāpratyāḥ saṃskārā ityutpādavinibandha eṣaḥ I evaṃ pariśeṣāṇām I avidyānirodhātsaṃskāranirodha iti vyayavinibandha eṣaḥ I evaṃ pariśeṣāṇām I I

avidyāpratyayāḥ saṃskārā iti bhāvānulomaparīkṣā I evaṃ pariśeṣāṇām I avidyānirodhātsaṃskāranirodha iti kṣayavyayāvinivandha eṣaḥ I evaṃ pariśeṣāṇām I I

M

sa evaṃ dvādaśākāraṃ pratītyasamutpādaṃ pratyavekṣate'nuloma-pratilomaṃ yaduta bhavāṅgānusaṃdhitaśca ekacittasamava-saraṇataśca svakarmāsaṃbhedataśca avinirbhāgataśca trivartm-ānuvartanataśca pūrvāntapratyutpannāparāntāvekṣaṇataśca tri-duḥkhatāsamudayataśca hetupratyayaprabhavataśca utpāda-vyayavinibandhanataśca abhāvākṣayatāpratyavekṣaṇataśca ||

N

tasyaivaṃ dvādaśākāraṃ pratītyasamutpādaṃ pratyavekṣamāṇasya nirātmato niḥsattvato nirjīvato niṣpudgalataḥ kārakavedakarahitato-'svāmikato hetupratyayādhīnataḥ svabhāvaśūnyato viviktato'sva-bhāvataśca prakṛtyā pratyavekṣamāṇasya śūnyatāvimokṣamukham-ājātaṃ bhavati ||

tasyaivaṃ bhavāṅgānāṃ svabhāvanirodhātyantavimokṣapraty-upasthānato na kiṃciddharmanimittamutpadyate | ato'sya ānimitta-vimokṣamukhamājātaṃ bhavati ||

tasyaivaṃ śūnyatānimittamavatīrṇasya na kaścidabhilāṣa utpadyate anyatra mahākaruṇāpūrvakātsattvaparipācanāt | evamasya apraṇi-hitavimokṣamukhamājātaṃ bhavati ||

ya imāni trīṇi vimokṣamukhāni bhāvayan ātmaparasaṃjñāpagato kārakavedakasaṃjñāpagato bhāvābhāvasaṃjñāpagato

O

bhūyasyā mātrayā mahākaruṇāpuraskṛtaḥ prayujyate'pariniṣ-pannānāṃ bodhyaṅgānāṃ pariniṣpattaye, tasyaivaṃ bhavati – saṃyogātsaṃskṛtaṃ pravartate | visaṃyogānna pravartate | sāmagryā saṃskṛtaṃ pravartate | visāmagryā na pravartate | hanta vayamevaṃ bahudoṣaduṣṭaṃ saṃskṛtaṃ viditvā asya saṃyogasya asyāḥ sāmagryā vyavacchedaṃ kariṣyāmaḥ, na cātyantopaśamaṃ sarvasaṃskārāṇāmavirāgayiṣyāmaḥ sattvaparipācanatāyai ||

evamasya bhavanto jinaputrāḥ saṃskāragataṃ bahudoṣaduṣṭaṃ svabhāvarahitamanutpannāniruddhaṃ prakṛtyā pratyav-ekṣamāṇasya mahākaruṇābhinirhārataśca sattvakāryānutsargataśca saṅgajñānābhimukho nāma prajñāpāramitāvihāro'bhimukhībhavatyavabhāsayogena | sa evaṃ jñānasamanvāgataḥ prajñāpāramitāvihārāvabhāsito bodhyaṅgāhārakāṃśca pratyayānupasaṃharati | na ca saṃskṛtasaṃvāsena saṃvasati | svabhāvopaśamaṃ ca saṃskārāṇāṃ pratyavekṣate | na ca tatrāvatiṣṭhate bodhyaṅgāparityaktatvāt | |

P

tasya asyāmabhimukhyāṃ bodhisattvabhūmau sthitasya bodhisattvasya avatāraśūnyatā ca nāma samādhirājāyate | svabhāvaśūnyatā...paramārthaśūnyatā...paramaśūnyatā...mahāśūnyatā...saṃpr ayogaśūnyatā...abhinirhāraśūnyatā yathāvadavikalpaśūnyatā sāpekṣaśūnyatā vinirbhāgāvinirbhāgaśūnyatā nāma samādhirājāyate | tasyaivaṃpramukhāni daśa śūnyatāsamādhimukhaśatasahasrāṇyāmukhībhavanti | evamānimittasamādhimukhaśataśahasrāṇi apraṇihitasamādhimukhaśatasahasrāṇyāmukhībhavanti |

Q

tasya bhūyasyā mātrayā asyāmabhimukhyāṃ bodhisattvabhūmau sthitasya bodhisattvasyabhedyāśayatā ca paripūryate | niyatāśayatā...kalyāṇāśayatā...gambhīrāśayatā...apratyudāvartyāśayatā...apratipra strabdhāśayatā...vimalāśayatā...anantāśayatā...jñānābhilāṣāśayatā...u pāyaprajñāsaṃprayogāśayatā ca paripūryate | |

R

tasyaite daśa bodhisattvāśayāḥ svanugatā bhavanti tathāgatabodhau | apratyudāvartanīyavīryaśca bhavati sarvaparapravādibhiḥ | samavasṛtaśca bhavati jñānabhūmau | vinivṛttaśca bhavati śrāvakapratyekabuddhabhūmibhyaḥ | ekāntikaśca bhavati buddhajñānābhimukhatāyām | asaṃhāryaśca bhavati sarvamārakleśasamudācāraiḥ | supratiṣṭhitaśca bhavati bodhisattvajñānālokatāyām | suparibhāvitaśca bhavati śūnyatānimittāpraṇihitadharmasamudācāraiḥ | saṃprayuktaśca bhavatyupāyaprajñāvicāraiḥ| vyavakīrṇaśca bhavati bodhipākṣikadharmābhinirhāraiḥ| tasya asyāmabhimukhyāṃ bodhisattvabhūmau sthitasya prajñāpāramitāvihāro'tiriktatara ājāto bhavati, tīkṣṇā cānulomikī tṛtīyā kṣāntireṣāṃ dharmāṇāṃ yathāvadanulomatayā na vilomatayā | |

S

tasya asyāmabhimukhyāṃ bodhisattvabhūmau sthitasya bodhisattvasya yathāvatsamāpattiprajñājñānālokatayā prayujyate, pratipattitaścādhārayati | sa bhūyasyā mātrayā tathāgatadharmakośaprāpto bhavati | tasya asyāmabhimukhyāṃ bodhisattvabhūmau sthitasya anekān kalpāṃstāni kuśalamūlāni bhūyasyā mātrayā uttaptaprabhāsvaratarāṇi bhavanti I anekāni kalpaśatāni.... I tāni kuśalamūlāni bhūyasyā mātrayottaptaprabhāsvaratarāṇi bhavanti I tadyathāpi nāma bhavanto jinaputrāstadeva jātarūpaṃ vaiḍūryaparisṛṣṭaṃ bhūyasyā mātrayottaptaprabhāsvarataraṃ bhavati, evameva bhavanto jinaputrā bodhisattvasya asyāmabhimukhyāṃ bodhisattvabhūmau sthitasya tāni kuśalamūlānyupāyaprajñājñānavicāritāni bhūyasyā mātrayottaptaprabhāsvaratarāṇi bhavanti, bhūyo bhūyaśca praśamāsaṃhāryatāṃ gacchanti I tadyathāpi nāma bhavanto jinaputrāścandrābhā sattvāśrayāṃśca prahlādayati asaṃhāryā ca bhavati catasṛbhirvātamaṇḍalībhiḥ, evameva bhavanto jinaputra bodhisattvasya asyāmabhimukhyāṃ bodhisattvabhūmau sthitasya tāni kuśalamūlānyanekeṣāṃ sattvakoṭinayutaśatasahasrāṇāṃ kleśajvālāḥ praśamayanti, prahlādayanti, asaṃhāryāṇi ca bhavanti caturbhirmārāvacaraiḥ I tasya daśabhyaḥ pāramitābhyaḥ prajñāpāramitā atiriktatamā bhavati, na ca pariśeṣā na samudāgacchati yathābalaṃ yathābhajamānam I iyaṃ bhavanto jinaputrā bodhisattvasya abhimukhī nāma ṣaṣṭhī bodhisattvabhūmiḥ samāsanirdeśataḥ, yasyāṃ pratiṣṭhito bodhisattvo bhūyastvena sunirmito bhavati devarājaṃ kṛtī prabhuḥ sattvānāmabhimānapratiprasrabdhaye kuśalaḥ sattvānyābhimānikadharmebhyo vinivartayitum I asaṃhāryaśca bhavati sarvaśrāvakaparipṛcchāyāṃ kuśalaḥ sattvān pratītyasamutpāde'vatārayitum I yacca kiṃcit.... I I

abhimukhī nāma ṣaṣṭī bhūmiḥ I I

[Beginning of sixth bhūmi's final gathas]

upasaṃhāragāthāḥ |

paripūrṇamārgacaraṇā vidu pañcamāyāṃ
dharmānimittata alakṣaṇatā ajātā |
anutpāda ādipariśuddhyatiniṣprapañcā
bhāvetva jñānamati ṣaṣṭhi samākramanti || 11 ||

dharmā vivikta apratigraha nirvikalpā
māyāsvabhāva dvayabhāvatu viprayuktā |
anulomayanta avilomanta dharmanetrī
jñānānvitāḥ pravara ṣaṣṭhi samākramanti || 12 ||

tīkṣṇānulomasthita jñānabalopapetāḥ
samudāgamaṃ vibhavu prekṣiṣu sarvaloke |
mohāndhakāraprabhavaṃ jagasaṃbhavātmā
tasyaiva mohavigamena pravṛti nāsti || 13 ||

vicinanti pratyayakṛtiṃ paramārthaśūnyāṃ
kriya hetupratyayasamajña kriyāvirodhau |
yāthāvataḥ karakapetakriyāṃ viditvā
vicinanti saṃskṛta ghanābhrasamaṃ nirīham || 14 ||

satyeṣu'jñānu paramārthatu sā avidyā
karmā ca cetanabalena vibhāgaprāptam |
cittaṃ niśritya sahajaṃ puna nāmarūpam
evaṃmukhā bhavati yāva dukhasya skandhaḥ || 15 ||

te cittamātra ti traidhātukamotaranti
api cā bhavāṅga iti dvādaśa ekacitte |
saṃrāgu jātu api cittu prabhāvitastu
evaṃ ca saṃbhavakṣayaṃ puna cittabhāgam || 16 ||

kāryaṃ avidyadvaya kurvati mohabhāve
mohebhi hetu vahate puna cetanāyāḥ |

evaṃ ca yāva jaradhvaṃsanaskandhabhedam
anu sarva duḥkhaprabhavaṃ kṣayataḥ abhāvaḥ || 17 ||

ucchedu no bhavati pratyayatāmavidyā
nocchedyatāpi kara prahāya saṃnirodham |
moho teṣu ca upādānaṃ kleśavartma
karma bhavaṃ ca api cetana śeṣa duḥkhā || 18 ||

mohaṃ tu āyatana saṃskṛtaduḥkha teṣāṃ
sparśaṃ ca vedana sukhādukhatāya duḥkhā |
śeṣānamaṅganapariṇāmaduḥkhavṛddhiḥ
vyuccheda tasya duḥkhatā na hi ātmamasti || 19 ||

adhveṣu pūrvaṃ tamacetanasaṃskṛtasya
vijñāna vedana vivartati pratyutpannam
aparāntu teṣu prabhavo dukhasaṃbhaveyam
āpekṣa cchedu prasaraṃ ca nirīkṣayantaḥ || 20 ||

mohasya pratyayatu saṃbhavate vibandhā
vinibandhanavyayakṣaye sati pratyayānām |
hetośca mūlaprabhavaṃ na tu hetubhedaṃ
vyuparīkṣate ca jina jñāna svabhāvaśūnyam || 21 ||

anuloma mohaprabhavaṃ ca prabhāvataśca
pratilomahetu kṣayato bhava sarvacchedyam |
gambhīrapratyayatamasya sato'sataśca
vyuparīkṣate daśavidhaṃ aniketabuddhiḥ || 22 ||

saṃdhī bhavāṅgatu tathāpi ca karmasthānam
avibhāgatastrividhu vartmani pūrvataśca |
triyahetu duḥkhavibhavā udaya vyayaṃ ca
abhāvato'kṣayata pratyaya ānulomam || 23 ||

evaṃ pratītyasamutpāda samotaranti
māyopamaṃ vitatha vedakarmāpanītam |
svapnopamaṃ ca tathatā pratibhāsa caiva
bālāna mohana marīcisamasvabhāvam || 24 ||

yā eva bhāvana sa śūnyata paṇḍitānāṃ
rati pratyayāna bhavate idamānimittam |
jānitva jātu vitathaṃ praṇidhātu nāsti
anyatra sattvakṛpayā upapadyanti || 25 ||

evaṃ vimokṣamukha bhāvayi te mahātmā
kṛpabuddhi bhūya tatha buddhaguṇābhilāṣī |
saṃyogasaṃskṛtikṛta vyuparīkṣamāṇo
niyatāśayo bhavati naikaguṇopapetaḥ || 26 ||

pūrṇā sahasra daśa śūnyataye samādhī
tatha ānimittavaradaṃ ca vimokṣa tāyī || 27[2] ||

pralhādayanti jagadāśaya candraābhā
vahamānu vāta caturo asaṃhāryaprāptā |
atikramya mārapathamābha jinaurasānāṃ
praśamenti kleśaparitāpa dukhārditānām || 28 (29) ||

iha bhūmideśupagatā marutādhipāste
bhontī sunirmita kṛtāvadhimānaghātī |
yaṃ caiva ārabhiṣu jñānapathopapetā
asaṃhārya śrāvakagatī atikrānta dhīrāḥ || 29 (30) ||

ākāṅkṣamāṇu sugatātmaja vīryaprāptāḥ
koṭīśatasahasrapūrṇa samādhi labdhāḥ |
paśyanti ekakṣaṇi buddha daśaddiśāsu
pratapanti sūrya eva madhyagu grīṣmakāle || 30 (31) ||

gambhīra durdṛśā sūkṣma durjñeyā jinaśrāvakaiḥ |
ṣaṣṭhī bhūmirmahātmānāmākhyātā sugatātmajāḥ || 31 (32) ||

[End of sixth bhūmi's final gathas]

[Beginning of seventh bhūmi's initial gathas]

7 dūraṃgamā nāma saptamī bhūmiḥ |

upakramagāthāḥ |

atha vividharucirameghān marudgaṇo'bhikiriṣu vegaprāptāḥ |
pravyāharanti madhurā girivara śubha prītisaṃpūrṇāḥ || 1 ||

sādhu varatīkṣṇacittā guṇaśatasamupetajñānavaśavartim |
varacaraṇaṃ parituṣṭaṃ jagahitavarapuṇḍarīkāṇām || 2 ||

tada pravaramatulamābhā maheśvarāḥ khegatā naravarasya |
vararuciragandhameghānabhikiri kleśaughamapahartum || 3 ||

pravyāharanti madhuraṃ marudgaṇā harṣakararuciraghoṣāḥ |
paramasulabdhalābhāḥ śrutu yairayu bhūminirdeśaḥ || 4 ||

tūrya madhuraghoṣayukta marukanyāḥ prīṇitamanobhiḥ |
sucarasugatānubhāvādvaracaririyamīdṛśī proktā || 5 ||

sumanī sucaraṇaśreṣṭhaḥ sudānta damakāna lokamahitānām |
atikramya sarvalokaṃ lokacariṃ darśayī sūkṣmām || 6 ||

darśenti kāya vividhān kāyākāyāṃśca dharmatopetāḥ |
śamathaḥ samitivibhakto bhaṇati ghoṣaṃ na cākṣaraṃ ravati || 7 ||

kṣetraśatamākramante pūjenti nāyakān paramapūjiyān |
ātmajanitakṣetrasaṃjñā vidhunitvā jñānavaśavartī || 8 ||

paripācayanti sattvānna cātmaparasaṃjña sarvaśa upenti |
śubha saṃcinanti pravaraṃ na cāpi śubhasaṃcayaniketāḥ || 9 ||

rāgarajadoṣamohaiḥ paśyitva sarvaloka jvalamānān |
varjeti sarvasaṃjñā vīryaṃ varamārabhī kṛpayā || 10 ||

marukanyā devasaṃghāśca pūjentā varasvaram |
tūṣṇīṃbhāvaratāḥ sarve prekṣante puruṣarṣabham || 11 ||

pariṣadviprasanneyamavocat sugatātmajam |
saptamyā bhūmerākārān nirdiśasva guṇākara || 12 ||

[End of seventh bhūmi's initial gathas]

7 duraṃgamā nāma saptamī bhūmiḥ ।

A

vajragarbha āha - yo'yaṃ bhavanto jinaputrā bodhisattvaḥ ṣaṣṭyāṃ bodhisattvabhūmau suparipūrṇabodhisattvamārgaḥ saptamīṃ bodhisattvabhūmimākramati, sa daśabhirupāyaprajñājñānābhinirhṛtairmārgāntarārambhaviśeṣairākramati । katamairdaśabhiḥ? yaduta śūnyatānimittāpraṇihitasamādhisuparibhāvitamānasaśca bhavati, mahāpuṇyajñānasambhāropacayaṃ ca saṃbibharti । nairātmyaniḥsattvanirjīvaniṣpudgalatāṃ ca sarvadharmāṇām-avatarati, caturapramāṇābhinirhāraṃ ca notsṛjati । puṇyadharm-occhrayapāramitābhisaṃskāraṃ cābhisaṃskaroti, na ca kiṃcid-dharmamabhiniviśate । sarvatraidhātukavivekaprāptaśca bhavati, traidhātukaviṭhapanālaṃkārābhinirhāraṃ cābhinirharati । atyanta-śāntopaśāntaśca sarvakleśajvālāpagamādbhavati, sarvasattvarāgad-veṣakleśajvālāpraśamābhinirhāraṃ cābhinirharati । māyāmarīci-svapnapratibhāsapratiśrutkodakacandrapratibimbanirmāṇabhāvābh āvasvabhāvādvayānugataśca bhavati, karmakriyāvibhaktyapramāṇā-śayatāṃ cābhinirharati । ākāśasamakṣetrapathasubhāvitamanāśca bhavati, buddhakṣetraviṭhapanālaṃkārābhinirhāraṃ cābhinirharati । prakṛtidharmakāyatāṃ ca sarvabuddhanāmavatarati, rūpakāya-lakṣaṇānuvyañjanaviṭhapanālaṃkārābhinirhāraṃ cābhinirharati ।

anabhilāpyarutaghoṣāpagataṃ ca prakṛtiśāntaṃ tathāgataghoṣam-adhimucyate, sarvasvarāṅgavibhaktiviśuddhyalaṃkārābhinirhāraṃ cābhinirharati । ekakṣaṇatryadhvānubodhaṃ ca buddhānāṃ bhagavatāmavatarati, nānālakṣaṇākalpasaṃkhyāvibhāvanāṃ cānu-praviśati sattvāśayavibhāvanāya । evirbhavanto jinaputrā daśabhir-upāyaprajñājñānābhinirhṛtibhirmārgāntarārambhaviśeṣairbodhisattv aḥ ṣaṣṭhyā bodhisattvabhūmeḥ saptamīṃ bodhisattvabhūmim-ākrānta ityucyate ।।

B

sa saptamyāṃ bodhisattvabhūmau sthito bodhisattvo'pramāṇ-āsattvadhātumavatarati । apramāṇaṃ ca buddhānāṃ bhagavatāṃ sattvaparipācanavinayakarmāvatarati । apramāṇaṃ lokadhātum-avatarati । apramāṇaṃ ca buddhānāṃ bhagavatāṃ kṣetrapari-śuddhimavatarati । apramāṇaṃ ca dharmanānātvamavatarati ।

apramāṇaṃ ca buddhānāṃ bhagavatāṃ jñānābhisaṃbodhim-avatarati | apramāṇaṃ ca kalpasaṃkhyāpraveśamavatarati | apramāṇaṃ ca buddhānāṃ bhagavatāṃ tryadhvānubodham-avatarati | apramāṇaṃ ca sattvānāmadhimuktinānātvaviśeṣam-avatarati | apramāṇaṃ ca buddhānāṃ bhagavatāṃ rūpakāyan-ānātvadarśanamavatarati | apramāṇaṃ ca sattvānāmāśayendriya-nānātvamavatarati | apramāṇaṃ ca buddhānāṃ bhagavatāṃ ghoṣ-odāhārasattvasaṃtoṣaṇamavatarati | apramāṇaṃ sattvānāṃ citta-caritanānātvamavatarati | apramāṇaṃ ca buddhānāṃ bhagavatāṃ jñānaprasarānugamamavatarati | apramāṇaṃ śrāvakayāna-niryāṇāadhimuktinānātvamavatarati | apramāṇaṃ ca buddhānāṃ bhagavatāṃ mārgadeśanāvatāramavatarati | apramāṇaṃ pratyeka-buddhayānasamudāgamaniṣpattimavatarati | apramāṇaṃ ca buddhānāṃ bhagavatāṃ jñānamukhapraveśanirdeśamavatarati | bodhisattvānāṃ bodhisattvacaryāprayogamavatarati | apramāṇaṃ ca buddhānāṃ bhagavatāṃ mahāyānasamudayāvatāranirdeśanām-avatarati | |

C

tasyaivaṃ bhavati - evamapramāṇaḥ khalu punastathāgatānām-arhatāṃ samyaksaṃbuddhānāṃ viṣayo yasya na sukarā saṃkhyā kartuṃ kalpakoṭiśatasahasrairyāvadetāvadbhirapi kalpakoṭiniyuta-śatasahasraiḥ | sarva...viṣayo'smābhiḥ samupasthāpayitavyo-'nābhogato'kalpāvikalpataśca paripūrayitavya iti | sa evaṃ supratyavekṣitajñānābhijñaḥ satatasamitamabhiyuktopāyaprajñā-paribhāviteṣu mārgāntarārambhaviśeṣeṣu supratiṣṭhito bhavaty-avicālyayogena | |

D

sa ekakṣaṇamapi mārgābhinirhārānna vyuttiṣṭhate | sa gacchanneva jñānābhinirhārayukto bhavati | tiṣṭhannapi niṣaṇṇo'pi śayāno'pi svapnāntaragato'pyapagatanīvaraṇaḥ sarveryāpathe sthito'virahito bhavati ebhirevaṃrūpaiḥ saṃjñāmanasikāraiḥ | tasya sarvacitt-otpāde daśānāṃ bodhisattvapāramitānāṃ samudāgamaparipūriḥ samudāgacchati | tatkasmāddhetoḥ? tathā hi sa bodhisattvaḥ sarv-āṃścittotpādānutpannotpannān mahākaruṇāpūrvakān buddha-dharmasamudāgamāya tathāgatajñānāya pariṇāmayati | tatra yaḥ kuśalamūlasya sattvebhya utsargo buddhajñānaṃ paryeṣamāṇasya, iyamasya dānapāramitā | yaḥ praśamaḥ sarvakleśaparidāhānām, iyamasya śīlapāramitā I yā kṛpāmaitrīpūrvagamā sarvasattveṣu kṣāntiḥ, iyamasya kṣāntipāramitā I ya uttarottarakuśaladharmātṛptatayārambhaḥ parākramaḥ, iyamasya vīryapāramitā I yā vipratisāryavisṛtamārgatā sarvajñajñānābhimukhatā, iyamasya dhyānapāramitā I yā sarvadharmāṇāṃ prakṛtyanutpādābhimukhī kṣāntiḥ, iyamasya prajñāpāramitā I yo'pramāṇājñānābhinirhāraḥ, iyamasyopāyakauśalapāramitā I yā sarvaparapravādimārasaṃghairmārgānācchedyatā, iyamasya balapāramitā I yadyathāvatsarvadharmajñānanitīraṇam, iyamasya jñānapāramitā I evamasya bhavanto jinaputrā bodhisattvasya dūraṃgamāyāṃ bodhisattvabhūmau sthitasya imā daśa pāramitāḥ kṣaṇe kṣaṇe paripūryante I evaṃ catvāri saṃgrahavastūni paripūryante, catvāri ca adhiṣṭhānāni, saptatriṃśad bodhipakṣyāśca dharmāḥ, trīṇi ca vimokṣamukhāni, samāsataḥ sarvabodhyaṅgikā dharmāḥ kṣaṇe kṣaṇe paripūryante I I

E

evamukte vimukticandro bodhisattvo vajragarbhaṃ bodhisattvametadavocat - kiṃ punarbho jinaputrā asyāmeva saptamyāṃ bodhisattvabhūmau sthitasya bodhisattvasya sarvabodhyaṅgikā dharmāḥ kṣaṇe kṣaṇe paripūryante, āhosvitsarvāsu daśasu bodhisattvabhūmiṣu? vajragarbha āha - sarvāsu bho jinaputrā daśasu bodhisattvabhūmiṣu bodhisattvasya sarvabodhyaṅgāni kṣaṇe kṣaṇe paripūryante, tadatirekeṇa punarasyāmeva saptamyāṃ bodhisattvabhūmau I tatkasya hetoḥ? iyaṃ bho jinaputrā bodhisattvabhūmiḥ prāyogikacaryāparipūraṇī ca jñānābhijñānacaryākramaṇī ca I api tu khalu punarbho jinaputrāḥ prathamāyāṃ bodhisattvabhūmau sarvapraṇidhānādhyālambena bodhisattvasya sarvabodhyaṅgāni kṣaṇe kṣaṇe paripūryante I dvitīyāyāṃ cittamalāpanayanena I tṛtīyāyāṃ praṇidhānavivardhanatayā dharmāvabhāsapratilambhena ca I caturthyāṃ mārgāvatāreṇa I pañcamyāṃ lokatrayānuvṛtyā I ṣaṣṭyāṃ gambhīradharmamukhapraveśena I asyāṃ tu saptamyāṃ bodhisattvabhūmau sarvabuddhadharmasamutthāpanatayā kṣaṇe kṣaṇe sarvabodhyāṅgāni paripūryante I

F

tatkasya hetoḥ? yāni bodhisattvena prathamāṃ bodhisattvabhūmimupādāya yāvatsaptamī bodhisattvabhūmirityabhinirhṛtāni jñānābhinirhāraprayogāṅgāni, imānyaṣṭamī bodhisattvabhūmimārabhya yāvadatyantaparyavasānamityanābhogena pariniṣpadyante I tadyathāpi nāma bho jinaputrā dvayorlokadhātvoḥ saṃkliṣṭaviśuddhāśayaśca lokadhātorekāntapariśuddhāśayaśca lokadhātorlokāntarikā duratikramā na śakyā yathātathātikramitumanyatra mahābhijñābalādhānāt, evameva bho jinaputra vyāmiśrapariśuddhā bodhisattvacaryāntarikā duratikramā na śakyā yathātathātikramitumanyatra mahāpraṇidhānopāyaprajñābhijñābalādhānāt। vimukticandra āha - kiṃ punarbho jinaputra saptasu bodhisattvabhūmiṣu kleśacaryāsaṃkliṣṭā bodhisattvacaryā pratyetavyā ? vajragarbha āha - prathamāmeva bho jinaputra bodhisattvabhūmimupādāya sarvābodhisattvacaryāpagatakleśakalmāṣā bodhipariṇāmanādhipatyena pratyetavyā । yathābhāgimārgasamatayā, (na ca) tāvatsaptasu bodhisattvabhūmiṣu samatikrāntā kleśacaryetyavācanīyā । tadyathāpi nāma bho jinaputra rājā cakravartī divyaṃ hastiratnamabhirūḍhaścaturo dvīpānākramati, manuṣyaduḥkhadāridryasaṃkleśadoṣāṃśca prajānāti, na ca tairdoṣairlipyate । na ca tāvatsamatikrānto manuṣyabhāvaṃ bhavati । yadā punarmanuṣyāśrayaṃ hitvā brahmalokopapanno bhavati brāhmyavimānamabhirūḍhaḥ, sahasralokadhātumalpakṛcchreṇa paśyatyanuvicarati, brahmapratibhāsaṃ cādarśayati, na ca manuṣya iti prabhāvyate, evameva bhoḥ prathamāṃ bhūmimupādāya bodhisattvaḥ pāramitāyānābhirūḍhaḥ sarvajagadanuvicaran saṃkleśadoṣān prajānāti, na ca tairdoṣairlipyate samyagmārgābhirūḍhatvāt । na ca tāvatsamatikrāntaḥ sarvajagatsaṃkleśadoṣān vaktavyaḥ । saptasu bhūmiṣu sarvaprāyogikacaryāṃ vihāya saptamyā bhūmeraṣṭamīṃ bodhisattvabhūmimavakrānto bhavati, tadā pariśuddhaṃ bodhisattvayānamabhirūḍhaḥ sarvajagadanuvicaran sarvajagatsaṃkleśadoṣān prajānāti, na ca tairdoṣairlipyate samatikrāntatvād lokatriyābhyaḥ । asyāṃ punarbho jinaputra sapyamyāṃ bodhisattvabhūmau sthito bodhisattvo bhūyastvena rāgādipramukhaṃ sarvakleśagaṇaṃ samatikrānto bhavati । so'syāṃ dūraṃgamāyāṃ bodhisattvabhūmau caran bodhisattvo'saṃkleśāniṣkleśa iti vaktavyaḥ । tatkasmāt? asamudācārātsarvakleśānāṃ na saṃkleśa iti vaktavyaḥ । tathāgatajñānābhilāṣādaparipūrṇābhiprāyatvācca na niṣkleśa iti vaktavyaḥ ।।

G

so'syāṃ saptamyāṃ bodhisattvabhūmau sthito bodhisattvo'dhyāśayapariśuddhena kāyakarmaṇā samanvāgato bhavati । adhyāśayapariśuddhena vākkarmaṇā adhyāśayapariśuddhena manaskarmaṇā samanvāgato bhavati I ye ceme daśākuśalāḥ karmapathāstathāgatavivarṇitāḥ, tān sarveṇa sarvaṃ samatikrānto bhavati I ye ceme daśa kuśalāḥ karmapathāḥ samyaksaṃbuddhānubhāvitāḥ, tān satatasamitamanuvartate I yāni laukikāni śilpasthānakarmasthānāni yānyabhinirhṛtāni pañcamyāṃ bodhisattvabhūmau, tānyasya sarvāṇyanābhogata evaṃ pravartante I sa ācāryaḥ saṃmato bhavati trisāhasra mahāsāhasralokadhātau, sthāpayitvā tathāgatānarhataḥ samyaksambuddhān, aṣṭamīṃ bhūmimupādāya ca bodhisattvān I nāsya kaścitsamo bhavatyāśayena vā prayogeṇa vā I yāni cemāni dhyānāni samādhayaḥ samapattayo'bhijñā vimokṣāśca, tānyasya sarveṇa sarvamāmukhībhavanti bhāvanābhinirhārākāreṇa I na ca tāvadvipākataḥ pariniṣpannāni bhavanti tadyathāpi nāma aṣṭamyāṃ bodhisattvabhūmau sthitasya bodhisattvasya I asyāṃ saptamyāṃ bodhisattvabhūmau sthitasya bodhisattvasya sarvacittotpādeṣu prajñopāyabhāvanābalaṃ paripūryate I bhūyasyā mātrayā sarvabodhyaṅgaparipūriṃ pratilabhate I I

H

so'syāṃ saptamyāṃ bodhisattvabhūmau sthitaḥ san suvicitavicayaṃ ca nāma bodhisattvasamādhi samāpadyate I suvicintitārthaṃ ca nāma... I viśeṣamatiṃ ca nāma... I prabhedārthakośaṃ ca... I sarvārthavicayaṃ ca... I supratiṣṭhitadṛḍhamūlaṃ ca... I jñānābhijñāmukhaṃ ca... I dharmadhātu(pari)karmaṃ ca... I tathāgatānuśaṃsaṃ ca... I vicitrārthakośasaṃsāranirvāṇamukhaṃ ca bodhisattvasamādhiṃ samāpadyate I sa evaṃpramukhāni mahābhijñājñānamukhāni paripūrṇāni daśa samādhiśatasahasrāṇi bhūmipariśodhikāni samāpadyate I I

I

sa eṣāṃ samādhīnāmupāyaprajñāsupariśodhitānāṃ pratilambhānmahākaruṇābalena cātikrānto bhavati śrāvakapratyekabuddhabhūmim, abhimukhaśca bhavati prajñājñānavicāraṇābhūmeḥ I I

J

tasya asyāṃ saptamyāṃ bodhisattvabhūmau sthitasya bodhisattvasya apramāṇaṃ kāyakarma nimittāpagataṃ pravartate I apramāṇaṃ vākkarma...manaskarma nimittāpagataṃ pravartate suviśodhitamanutpattikadharmakṣāntyavabhāsitam I vimukticandra āha - nanu bho jinaputra, prathamāyāmeva bodhisattvabhūmau sthitasya bodhisattvasya apramāṇaṃ kāyavāṅmanaskarma sarvaśrāvakapratyekabuddhacaryāṃ samatikrāntaṃ bhavati? vajragarbha āha - bhavati bho jinaputra | tatpunarbuddhadharmādhyālambanamāhātmyena, na punaḥ svabuddhivicāreṇa | asyāṃ tu punaḥ saptamyāṃ bodhisattvabhūmau svabuddhigocaravicārapratilambhādasaṃhāryaṃ śrāvakapratyekabuddhairbhavati | tadyathāpi nāma bhavanto jinaputrā rājakulaprasūto rājaputro rājalakṣaṇasamanvāgato jātamātra eva sarvāmātyagaṇamabhibhavati rājādhipatyena, na punaḥ svabuddhivicāreṇa | yadā punaḥ sa saṃvṛddho bhavati tadā svabuddhibalādhānataḥ sarvāmātyakriyāsamatikrānto bhavati, evameva bho jinaputrā bodhisattvaḥ sahacittotpādena sarvaśrāvakapratyekabuddhānabhibhavatyadhyāśayamāhātmyena, na punaḥ svabuddhivicāreṇa | asyāṃ tu saptamyāṃ bodhisattvabhūmau sthito bodhisattvaḥ svaviṣayajñānaviśeṣamāhātmyāvasthitatvātsarvaśrāvakapratyekabuddhakriyāmatikrānto bhavati ||

K

sa khalu punarbho bodhisattvo'syāṃ saptamyāṃ bodhisattvabhūmau sthito gambhīrasya vivittasyāpracārasya kāyavāṅmanaskarmaṇo lābhī bhavati | na cottaraṃ viśeṣaparimārgaṇābhiyogamavasṛjati | [yena parimārgaṇābhiyogena nirodhaprāptaśca bhavati, na ca nirodhaṃ sākṣātkaroti ||]

L

vimukticandra āha - katamāṃ bhūmimupādāya bodhisattvo nirodhaṃ samāpadyate? vajragarbha āha - ṣaṣṭhīṃ bho jinaputra bodhisattvabhūmimupādāya bodhisattvo nirodhaṃ samāpadyate | asyāṃ punaḥ saptamyāṃ bodhisattvabhūmau pratiṣṭhito bodhisattvaścittakṣaṇe cittakṣaṇe nirodhaṃ samāpadyate ca vyuttiṣṭhate ca | na ca nirodhaḥ sākṣātkṛta iti vaktavyaḥ | tena so'cintyena kāyavāṅmana skarmaṇā samanvāgata ityucyate | āścaryaṃ bho yatra hi nāma bodhisattvo bhūtakoṭivihāreṇa ca viharati, na ca nirodhaṃ sākṣātkaroti | tadyathāpi nāma bho jinaputra puruṣaḥ kuśalo mahāsāgare vārilakṣaṇābhijñaḥ paṇḍito vyakto medhāvī tatropagatayā mīmāṃsayā samanvāgato mahāsāgare mahāyānapātrābhirūḍho vahanakuśalaśca bhavati, vārikuśalaśca bhavati, na ca mahāsamudre vāridoṣairlipyate, evameva bho jinaputra asyāṃ saptamyāṃ bodhisattvabhūmau pratiṣṭhito bodhisattvaḥ sarvajñajñānamahāsāgarāvatīrṇaḥ pāramitāmahāyānapātrābhirūḍho bhūtakoṭivihāreṇa ca viharati, na ca nirodhaṃ sākṣātkaroti, (na ca sasṃkṛtātyantavyupaśamavitarkadoṣairlipyate) । ।

M

sa evaṃ jñānabalādhānaprāptaḥ samādhijñānabalabhāvanābhinirhṛtayā buddhyā mahatopāyaprajñābalādhānena saṃsāramukhaṃ cādarśayati । nirvāṇasatatāśayaśca bhavati । mahāparivāraparivṛtaśca bhavati । satatasamitaṃ ca cittavivekapratilabdho bhavati । traidhātukopapattiṃ ca praṇidhānavaśenābhinirharati sattvaparipācanārtham । na ca lokadoṣairlipyate । śāntapraśāntopaśāntaśca bhavati । upāyena ca jvalati । jvalaṃśca na dahate । saṃvartate ca buddhajñānena । vivartate ca śrāvakapratyekabuddhabhūmibhyām । buddhajñānaviṣayakośaprāptaśca bhavati । māraviṣayagataśca dṛśyate । caturmārapathasamatikrāntaśca bhavati । māraviṣayagocaraṃ cādarśayati । sarvatīrthyāyatanopagataśca dṛśyate । buddhatīrthyāyatanānutsṛṣṭāśayaśca bhavati । sarvalokakriyānugataśca dṛśyate । lokottaradharmagatisamavasaraṇaśca bhavati । sarvadevanāgayakṣagandharvāsuragaruḍakinnaramahoragamanuṣy āmanuṣyaśakrabrahmalokapālātirekavyū-hālaṃkāraviṭhapanāprāptaśca bhavati । sarvabuddhadharmatimanasikāraṃ ca na vijahāti । ।

N

tasyaivaṃ jñānasamanvāgatasya asyāṃ saptasyāṃ dūraṃgamāyāṃ bodhisattvabhūmau sthitasya bodhisattvasya bahavo buddhā ābhāsamāgacchanti... । tāṃśca tathāgatānarhataḥ samyaksaṃbuddhān paryupāsate । teṣāṃ ca sakāśādgauravacitrīkāreṇa satkṛtya dharmadeśanāṃ śṛṇoti, udgṛhṇāti dhārayati । śrutvā ca yathāvatsamāpattiprajñājñānālokena prayujyate । pratipattitaścādhārayati । śāsanasaṃdhārakaśca bhavati teṣāṃ buddhānāṃ mahātmanām । asaṃhāryaśca sarvaśrāvakapratyekabuddhābhisamayaparipṛcchāsu । tasya bhūyasyā mātrayā sattvānugrahāya gambhīradharmakṣāntirviśuddhyati । tasya...anekān kalpāṃstāni kuśalamūlānyuttapyante, pariśuddhyanti, karmaṇyāni ca bhavanti, paryavadānaṃ cāgacchanti । anekāni kalpaśatāni...anekāni kalpakoṭiniyutaśatasahasrāṇi tāni kuśalamūlānyuttapyante, pariśuddhyanti, karmaṇyāni ca bhavanti, paryavadānaṃ cāgacchanti । tadyathāpi nāma bho jinaputrāḥ tadeva jātarūpaṃ sarvaratnapratyuptaṃ bhūyasyā mātrayottaptataraṃ bhavati, prabhāsvarataraṃ bhavati, asaṃhāryataraṃ ca bhavatyanyābhyo bhūṣaṇavikṛtibhyaḥ, evameva bho jinaputrāḥ...tāni kuśalamūlānyupāyaprajñājñānābhinirhṛtāni bhūyasyā mātrayottaptatarāṇi bhavanti prabhāsvaratarāṇi, paryavadātatarāṇi asaṃhāryatarāṇi ca bhavanti sarvaśrāvakapratyekabuddhaiḥ । tadyathāpi nāma bho jinaputrāḥ sūryābhā asaṃhāryā bhavanti sarvajyotirgaṇacandrābhābhiścaturṣu mahādvīpeṣu, sarvasnehagatāni bhūyastvena pariśoṣayanti, sarvaśasyāni paripācayanti, evameva bho jinaputrā...tāni kuśalamūlānyasaṃhāryāṇi bhavanti sarvaśrāvakapratyekabuddhaiḥ, caturviparyāsagatāni ca sarvakleśasnehagatāni bhūyastvena pariśoṣayanti । kleṣāvilāni ca sarvasaṃtānāni paripācayanti । tasya daśabhyaḥ pāramitābhya upāyakauśalyapāramitā atiriktatamā bhavati, na ca pariśeṣā na samudāgacchati yathābalaṃ yathābhajamānam । iyaṃ bho jinaputrā bodhisattvasya dūraṃgamā nāma saptamī bodhisattvabhūmiḥ samāsanirdeśataḥ, yasyāṃ pratiṣṭhito bodhisattvo bhūyastvena vaśavartī bhavati devarājaḥ kṛtī prabhuḥ sattvānāmabhisamayajñānopasaṃhāreṣvaparyantaḥ sarvaśrāvakapratyekabuddhaparipṛcchāsu kuśalaḥ sattvānniyāmamavakrāmayitum । yacca kicit... । ।

dūraṃgamā nāma saptamī bhūmiḥ । ।

[Beginning of seventh bhūmi's final gathas]

upasaṃhāragāthāḥ ।

gambhīrajñāna paramārthapadānusārī
ṣaḍbhūminiścitamatiḥ susamāhitātmā ।
prajñāmupāya yugapadyabhinirharanto
bhūmyākramanti vidu saptami caryaśreṣṭhām ॥ 13 ॥

śūnyānimittapraṇidhīkṛpamaitrayuktā
buddhānudharma sugatānuga pūjayantaḥ ।
jñānena śubhamahapuṇyabalebhyatṛptā-
stāmākramanti vidu saptami bhūmideśam ॥ 14 ॥

traidhātukena adhivāsa vivekaprāptāḥ
śāntaśca kleśabalaśāntijagābhikāṅkṣī ।
pratibhāsa māya supinādvayadharmacārī
kṛpa darśayanti vidu saptamimākramanti ॥ 15 ॥

śodhenti kṣetra khasamāśaya nirvikalpā
jinalakṣanairupāgato'caladharmatāyām ।
abhilāpyaghoṣavigatā jagatoṣaṇārthaṃ
kṣaṇajñāna cittasya jināna samosaranti ॥ 16 ॥

abhāsaprāpta iti dharma vicārayanti
ākrānta bhūmipravarāṃ jagadarthakārāḥ ।
te atra bhūmyasthita sattvacarī anantān
vicinanti karma sugatān niyutāpramāṇān ॥ 17 ॥

kṣetrāṃśca naikavidhadharmatha kalpasaṃkhyān
adhimuktiāśaya ca cittavicitradhārān ।
triyāṇadeśanamananta samosaranti
asmābhi sattva paripācayitavyametat ॥ 18 ॥

ye te jñānanicitā varamārgaprāptā
īryāpathaiścaturbhi prajñamupāyamuktāḥ ।

sarvasmi cittakṣaṇi bodhiguṇānuprāptāḥ
paripūrayanti daśa pāramitāpradeśān || 19 ||

sarveṣu mārgakuśalasya ya eṣa dānaṃ
śīlaṃ ca kleśapraśamaṃ kṣamamakṣatitvam |
vīryaṃ ca bhūyu anu uttari ārabhante
mārge acalyataya dhyānaguṇānvitānām || 20 ||

anutpādakṣānti virajā varaprajña śreṣṭhā
parṇāmupāya praṇidhī bhuyu kāṅkṣi lakṣmī |
ato'mardayitva balajñānanitīraṇatvād
evaṃ khu bodhiguṇa sarvakṣaṇenupenti || 21 ||

ālambanātu prathamā guṇapāripūri
dvitīyā malāpanaya ūrdhva vibandhacchedam |
caturthāya mārgu samatākriya pañcamāya
anutpāda āhvaya viduḥ puna ṣaṣṭhavṛttiḥ || 22 ||

iha saptamīmupagatāḥ sakalaṃ guṇāni
praṇidhāna naikavividhānabhinirharanti |
kiṃ kāraṇaṃ yaduta jñānakriyābhyupenti
sā aṣṭamīprabhṛti sarvaviśuddhyupenti || 23 ||

duratikramā dūraṃgamā bahusthānakarmā
kṣetrāntaradvipathameva yathottaranti |
vicaranti saptasu alipta nṛpo yathaiva
mārgasthitā na puna sarvatikrānta dhīrāḥ || 24 ||

yada aṣṭamīmupagatāḥ puna jñānabhūmim
atikrānta cittaviṣaye sthita jñānakarme |
brahmā na pekṣati jagannaramānuṣātmā
evaṃ caranti vidu padmamivā aliptāḥ || 25 ||

atra sthitā vividhakleśamatikramanti
teṣāṃ na kleśacari no ca kṣayo'nuprāptiḥ |
mārgasthitā na tada kleśacariṃ caranti
saṃpūrṇa āśaya jinajña kṣayo na tāvat || 26 ||

ye laukikā vividhaśilpakriyāprayogā
ājāti sarvavidunā sthita śāstrajñāne |
dhyānā abhijña bala bhāvayanto'bhyupenti
bhūyaḥ samādhi vividhānabhinirharanti || 27 ||

atikrānta śravakacariṃ tatha pratyayānāṃ
sthita bodhisattvacaraṇe vidu apramāṇām |
pūrve hi āśayatayā iha jñānatāyā
nṛpatīsuto yatha vivṛddhabalopapetaḥ || 28 ||

gāmbhīryatāmupagatā bhuyu ārabhanti
cittaṃ nirodhupagatā na ca sākṣikriyāḥ |
yathā sāgare upagatāḥ sthita yānapātre
pratyakṣa sarva udake na ca yānahāniḥ || 29 ||

bhūyo upāyabalaprajñavarābhyupetā
durjñeyasarvajagajñānakriyāguṇāḍhyāḥ |
pūjenti buddha niyutā bhuyu śuddhibhāvā
yathā tadvibhūṣaṇavicitritu naikaratnaiḥ || 30 ||

atra sthitāna vidunāṃ varaprajña ābhā
śoṣenti tṛṣṇasalilaṃ yatha bhāskārābhāḥ |
te atra bhūmyupagatā vaśavartinaśca
bhonti kṛtī kuśala jñānaphalodeśaiḥ || 31 ||

ākāṅkṣamāṇa dṛḍhavīryabalābhyupetāḥ
koṭīnayūtaśata buddhasahasra pūrṇān |
paśyanti sarvadiśatāsu samāhitatvād
bhūyo'pyataḥ praṇidhiśreṣṭha guṇāprameyāḥ || 32 ||

durjñeyā sarvalokena vaśipratyekacāribhiḥ |
ityeṣā saptamī bhūmirupāyaprajñaśodhanā || 33 ||

[End of seventh bhūmi's final gathas]

[Beginning of eighth bhūmi's initial gathas]

8 acalā nāma aṣṭamī bhūmiḥ |

upakramagāthāḥ |

eva śrutva caraṇaṃ viduna śreṣṭhaṃ
devasaṃgha muditā marupatiśca |
bodhisattva bahavo jagaddhitaiṣi
pūjayanti sugataṃ jinasutāṃśca || 1 ||

puṣpamālya rucirā dhvajāpatākā
gandhacūrṇa rucirā ratanavastrā |
chatra naikarucirān maṇipratyuptān
hārameghapravarānabhisṛjanti || 2 ||

manojñaghoṣamadhuraṃ suravandū
mukta naikaturiyapravaranāṭān |
pūjanārthi jinaputra sugatāṃśca
varṇaśreṣṭha munino udāharanti || 3 ||

sarvi darśi vṛṣabhī dvipādaśreṣṭho
darśi buddhaviṣayaṃ jagaddhitārtham |
śabdamegha rucirān pratāḍamānā-
stūryatāla vividhāstada pramuktāḥ || 4 ||

vālakoṭi sugatāḥ śatasahasrā
gaṅgākoṭi nayutā rajaviśiṣṭāḥ |
kṣemamapratisamāḥ pravaraśreṣṭhaṃ
deśayanti vṛṣabhī virajadharmam || 5 ||

preta tirya narakā manujadevāḥ
yakṣa rakṣa bhujagā asurasaṃghā |
....
nānakarmaviṣaye samanubhonti || 6 ||

sarvakṣetraviṣaye dhutarajānāṃ
cakra śreṣṭhapravaraṃ tadanirvṛttam |
deśayanti madhuraṃ sugataghoṣaṃ
saṃjñacitta jagatastatha vicāran || 7 ||

sattvakāyi sugatā vividhakṣetrā
kṣetri sattvapravarāḥ punavipākāḥ |
devamānuṣagatī tatha vicitrā
jñātva sarva sugato bhaṇati dharmam || 8 ||

sūkṣmasaṃjña bhavati vipulakṣetre
vipulasaṃjña bhavati rajanimitte |
evamādi vividhāṃ sugataṛddhiṃ
sarvaloka bhaṇato na kṣepayeyuḥ || 9 ||

īddaśaṃ vacamāhātmyaṃ vacitvā madhurasvaram |
praśāntā pariṣatprītā prekṣate vadatāṃ varam || 10 ||

praśānta parṣadaṃ jñātvā mokṣacandro'bravītpunaḥ |
aṣṭamyā bhūmiākārāṃ praveśaṃ ca nidarśaya || 11 ||

[End of eighth bhūmi's initial gathas]

8 acalā nāma aṣṭamī bhūmiḥ ।

A

vajragarbho bodhisattva āha - yo'yaṃ bhavanto jinaputrā bodhisattvaḥ saptasu bodhisattvabhūmiṣu sukṛtavicayaḥ prajñopāyābhyāṃ supariśodhitamārgaḥ susaṃbhṛtasaṃbhāraḥ suparibaddhamahāpraṇidhānaḥ adhiṣṭhitatathāgatādhiṣṭhānaḥ svakuśalamūlabalādhānaprāptaḥ tathāgatabalavaiśāradyāveṇikabuddhadharmānugatasaṃjñāmanasikāraḥ supariśodhitādhyāśayasaṃkalpa puṇyajñānabalābhyudgataḥ mahākaruṇākṛpābhyāṃ sarvasattvānutsṛṣṭaprayogaḥ apramāṇajñānapathānugataḥ,

B

sa sarvadharmāṇāmādyanutpannatāṃ ca yathābhūtamavatarati । ajātatāṃ ca alakṣaṇatāṃ ca asaṃbhūtatāṃ ca avināśitāṃ ca aniṣṭhitatāṃ ca apravṛttitāṃ ca anabhinivṛttitāṃ ca abhāvasvabhāvatāṃ ca ādimadhyaparyavasānasamatāṃ ca tathatāvikalpasarvajñajñānapraveśatāṃ ca sarvadharmāṇāṃ yathābhūtamavatarati । sa sarvaśaścittamanovijñānavikalpasaṃjñāpagato'navagṛhītākāśasamo'bhyavakāśaprakṛtito'vatīrṇo'nutpattikadharmakṣāntiprāpta ityucyate ।।

C

tatra bhavanto jinaputrā evaṃ kṣāntisamanvāgato bodhisattvaḥ sahapratilambhādacalāyā bodhisattvabhūmergambhīraṃ bodhisattvavihāramanuprāpto bhavati durājñātamasaṃbhinnaṃ sarvanimittāpagataṃ sarvasaṃjñāgrahavyāvṛttamapramāṇamasaṃhāryaṃ sarvaśrāvakapratyekabuddhaiḥ sarvavivekābhimukhībhūtam । tadyathāpi nāma bhavanto jinaputrā bhikṣurṛddhimāṃścetovaśipāramitāprāpto'nupūrveṇa navamaṃ nirodhaṃ samāpannaḥ sarveñjitamanyanāspanditavikalpāpagato bhavati, evameva bhavanto jinaputrā bodhisattvo'syā aṣṭamyā acalāyā bodhisattvabhūmeḥ sahapratilambhātsarvābhogavigato'nābhogadharmatāprāptaḥ kāyavākcittautsukyāpagataḥ sarveñjitamanyanāspanditavikalpāpagato vipākadharmatāvasthito bhavati । tadyathāpi nāma bho jinaputrāḥ puruṣaḥ suptaḥ svapnāntaragato mahaughaprāptamātmānaṃ saṃjānīte । sa tatra mahadvyāyāmautsukyamārabhetottaraṇāya । sa tenaiva mahatā vyāyāmautsukyena vibudhyeta । samanantaravibuddhaśca vyāyāmautsukyabhayāpagato bhavet ।

evameva bho jinaputrā bodhisattvaścaturmahaughaprāptaṃ sattvakāyaṃ saṃjānāna uttaraṇābhiprāyaḥ sarvajñajñānābhisaṃbodhāya mahadvyāyāmautsukyamārabhate I sa mahāvīryārambhaprāptaḥ samanantaramanuprāpta imāmacalāṃ bodhisattvabhūmiṃ sarvābhogavigato bhavati I tasya sarveṇa sarvaṃ dvayasamudācāro vā nimittasamudācāro vā nābhāsībhavati I tadyathāpi nāma bho jinaputrā brahmalokopapattisthitaḥ kāmāvacarān kleśān na samudācarati, evameva bho jinaputrā bodhisattvo'calāyāṃ bodhisattvabhūmau sthitaḥ sarvacittamanovijñānasamudācārānna samudācarati I sarvabuddhasamudācāramapi...bodhisamudācāramapi...-bodhisattvasamudācāramapi...pratyekabuddhasamudācāramapi...śrā vakasamudācāramapi...nirvāṇasamudācāramapi...arhatsamudācāram api...anāgāmisamudācāramapi...nirvāṇasamudācāramapi...arhatsamu dācāramapi...anāgāmisamudācāramapi...sakṛdāgāmisamudācāramap i...-srotaāpannasamudācāramapi na samudācarati I kaḥ punarvādo laukikān samudācārān samudācariṣyatīti I I

D

tasya khalu bho jinaputra bodhisattvasya evamimāmacalāṃ bodhisattvabhūmimanugatasya pūrvapraṇidhānabalādhānasthitasya buddhā bhagavantastasmin dharmamukhasrotasi tathāgatajñānopasaṃhāraṃ kurvanti I evaṃ cainaṃ bruvanti - sādhu sādhu kulaputra I eṣā paramārthakṣāntirbuddhadharmānugamāya I api tu khalu punaḥ kulaputra yā asmākaṃ daśabalacaturvaiśāradyabuddhadharmasamṛddhiḥ, sā tava nāsti I tasyā buddhadharmasamṛddheḥ paryeṣaṇāya abhiyogaṃ kuru, vīryamārabhasva I etadeva kṣāntimukhaṃ monmokṣīḥ I

E

api tu khalu punaḥ kulaputra kiṃcāpi tvayaivaṃ śāntavimokṣavihāro'nuprāptaḥ, imān punaraśāntānapraśāntān bālapṛthagjanān nānākleśasamudācāraprāptān vividhavitarkopahatamānasān samanvāhara, apekṣasva I

F

api tu khalu punaḥ kulaputra pūrvapraṇidhānamanusmara sattvārthasaṃprāpaṇaṃ jñānamukhācintyatāṃ ca I

G

api tu khalu punaḥ kulaputra eṣā sarvadharmāṇāṃ dharmatā I utpādādvā tathāgatānāmanutpādādvā sthitaivaiṣā dharmatā dharmadhātusthitiḥ yadidaṃ sarvadharmaśūnyatā sarvadharmānupalabdhiḥ । naitayā tathāgatā eva kevalaṃ prabhāvyante, sarvaśrāvakapratyekabuddhā api hyetāmavikalpadharmatāmanuprāpnuvanti ।

H

api tu khalu punaḥ kulaputra prekṣasva tāvat tvamasmākaṃ kāyāpramāṇatāṃ ca jñānāpramāṇatāṃ ca buddhakṣetrāpramāṇatāṃ ca jñānābhinirhārāpramāṇatāṃ ca prabhāmaṇḍalāpramāṇatāṃ ca svarāṅgaviśuddhyapramāṇatāṃ ca । tathaiva tvamapyabhinirhāramutpādaya ।

I

api tu khalu punaḥ kulaputra ekastveṣa āloko yo'yaṃ sarvadharmanirvikalpālokaḥ । īdṛśāstu kulaputra dharmālokāstathāgatānāmaparyantagatā aparyantakṛtā aparyantabaddhāḥ, yeṣāṃ saṃkhyā nāsti, gaṇanā pramāṇamupaniṣadaupamyaṃ nāsti, teṣāmadhigamāya abhinirhāramutpādaya ।

J

api tu khalu punaḥ kulaputra prekṣasva tāvaddaśasu dikṣu apramāṇakṣetratāṃ ca apramāṇasattvatāṃ ca apramāṇadharmavibhaktitāṃ ca । tatsarvamanugaṇaya । yathāvattayā abhinirhāramutpādaya । iti hi bho jinaputra te buddhā bhagavanta evaṃbhūmyanugatasya bodhisattvasya evaṃ pramukhānyaprameyāṇyasaṃkhyeyāni jñānābhinirhāramukhānyupasaṃharanti, yairjñānābhinirhāramukhairbodhisattvo'pramāṇajñānavibhaktito'bhinirhārakarmābhiniṣpādayati ।।

K

ārocayāmi te bho jinaputra, prativedayāmi । te cedbuddhā bhagavantastaṃ bodhisattvamevaṃ sarvajñajñānābhinirhāramukheṣu nāvatārayeyuḥ, tadevāsya parinirvāṇaṃ bhavetsarvasattvakāryapratiprasrabdhiśca । tena khalu punarbuddhā bhagavantastasya bodhisattvasya tāvadapramāṇaṃ jñānābhinirhārakarmopasaṃharanti, yasyaikakṣaṇābhinirhṛtasya jñānābhinirhārakarmaṇaḥ sa pūrvakaḥ prathamacittotpādamupādāya yāvatsaptamīṃ bhūmipratiṣṭhāmupāgata ārambhaḥ śatatamīmapi kalāṃ nopeti, sahasratamīmapi, śatasahasratamīmapi...peyālaṃ... koṭīniyutaśatasahasratamīmapi kalāṃ nopeti, saṃkhyāmapi, gaṇanāmapi, upamāmapi, upanisāmapi, yāvadaupamyamapi na kṣamate | tatkasya hetoḥ? tathā hi bho jinaputra pūrvamekakāyābhinirhāratayā caryābhinirhāro'bhūt | imāṃ punarbhūmiṃ samārūḍhasya bodhisattvasya apramāṇakāyavibhaktito bodhisattvacaryābalaṃ samudāgacchati | apramāṇaghoṣābhinirhārataḥ apramāṇajñānābhinirhārataḥ apramāṇopapattyabhinirhārataḥ apramāṇakṣetrapariśodhanataḥ apramāṇasattvaparipācanataḥ apramāṇabuddhapūjopasthānataḥ apramāṇadharmakāyānubodhataḥ apramāṇābhijñābalādhānābhinirhārataḥ apramāṇaparṣanmaṇḍalavibhaktyabhinirhārataśca apramāṇānugatena kāyavāṅmanaskarmābhinirhāreṇa sarvabodhisattvacaryābalaṃ samudāgacchatyavicālyayogena | tadyathāpi nāma bho jinaputra mahāsamudragāmī poto'prāpto mahāsamudraṃ sābhogavāhano bhavati | sa eva samanantaramanuprāpto mahāsamudramanābhogavāhano vātamaṇḍalīpraṇīto yadekadivasena mahāsamudre kramate, tatsarvasābhogavāhanatayā na śakyaṃ varṣaśatenāpi tāvadaprameyamanuprāptum | evameva bho jinaputra bodhisattvaḥ susaṃbhṛtamahākuśalamūlasaṃbhāro mahāyānasamudāgamābhirūḍho mahābodhisattvacaryāsāgaramanuprāpto yadekamuhūrtena jñānānābhogatayā sarvajñajñānenākramati, tanna śakyaṃ pūrvakeṇa sābhogakarmaṇā kalpaśatasahasreṇāpi tāvadaprameyamanuprāptum ||

L

tatra bho jinaputra bodhisattvo'ṣṭamīṃ bodhisattvabhūmimanuprāpto mahatyā upāyakauśalyajñānābhinirhārānābhogaprasṛtayā bodhisattvabuddhyā sarvajñajñānaṃ vicārayan lokadhātusaṃbhavaṃ ca vicārayati, lokadhātuvibhavaṃ ca vicārayati | sa yathā ca lokaḥ saṃvartate, taṃ ca prajānāti | yathā ca loko vivartate,... | yena ca karmopacayena lokaḥ saṃvartate,... | yena ca karmakṣayeṇa loko vivartate,... | yāvatkālaṃ ca lokaḥ saṃvartate, ... | yāvatkālaṃ ca loko vivartate, ... | yāvatkālaṃ ca lokaṃ saṃvṛttastiṣṭhati,... | yāvatkālaṃ ca loko vivṛttastiṣṭhati, taṃ ca prajānāti sarvatra cānavaśeṣataḥ | sa pṛthivīdhātuparīttatāṃ ca prajānāti mahadgatatāṃ ca...apramāṇatāṃ ca...vibhaktitāṃ ca prajānāti | abdhātu... | tejodhātu... | vāyudhātu... | sa paramāṇurajaḥsūkṣmatāṃ ca prajānāti, mahadgatatāṃ ca apramāṇatāṃ ca vibhaktitāṃ ca prajānāti |

apramāṇaparamāṇurajovibhaktikauśalyaṃ ca prajānāti | asyāṃ ca lokadhātau yāvanti pṛthivīdhātoḥ paramāṇurajāṃsi tāni prajānāti I yāvanti abdhātoḥ... I tejodhātoḥ... I vāyudhātoḥ... I yāvantyo ratnavibhaktayo yāvanti ca ratnaparamāṇurajāṃsi tāni prajānāti I sattvakāya... I kṣetrakāya... I sa sattvānāṃ kāyaudārikatāṃ ca kāyasūkṣmatāṃ ca kāyavibhaktitāṃ ca prajānāti I yāvanti paramāṇurajāṃsi saṃbhūtāni nairayikakāyāśrayatastāni prajānāti I tiryagyonikāyāśrayataḥ... I ...yamalokakāyāśrayataḥ... I ...asuralokakāyāśrayataḥ.... I devalokakāyāśrayataḥ .... I manuṣyalokakāyāśrayataḥ.... I sa evaṃ paramāṇurajaḥprabhedajñānāvatīrṇaḥ kāmadhātusaṃvartaṃ ca prajānāti I rūpadhātuvivartaṃ... I ārūpyadhātuvivartaṃ ca prajānāti I rūpadhātuparīttatāṃ.... ārūpyadhātuparīttatāṃ... I āmadhātuparīttatāṃ ca mahadgatatāṃ ca apramāṇatāṃ ca vibhaktitāṃ ca prajānāti I rūpadhātuparīttatāṃ... ārūpyadhātuparīttataṃ... I kāmadhātuparīttatāṃ ca mahadgatatāṃ ca apramāṇatāṃ ca vibhaktitāṃ ca prajānāti I rūpadhātvārūpyadhātuparīttatāṃ... I traidhātukavicārajñānānugame svabhinirhṛtajñānālokaḥ sattvakāyaprabhedajñānakuśalaḥ kṣetrakāyavibhāgajñānakuśalaśca sattvopapattyāyatanābhinirhāre buddhiṃ cārayati I sa yādṛśī sattvānāmupapattiśca kāyasamudāgamaśca, tādṛśameva svakāyamadhitiṣṭhati sattvaparipācanāya I sa ekāmapi trisāhasramahāsāhasrāṃ lokadhātuṃ spharitvā sattvānāṃ svakāyaṃ vibhaktyadhimuktiṣu tathatvāyopapattaye'bhinirharati pratibhāsajñānānugamanatayā (yathā sattvāḥ paripākaṃ gacchantyanuttarasamyaksaṃbodhivimuktaye) I evaṃ dve vā tisro vā catasro vā pañca vā daśa vā viṃśatirvā triṃśadvā catvāriṃśadvā pañcāśadvā śataṃ vā yāvadanabhilāpyā api trisāhasramahāsāhasrā lokadhātūḥ spharitvā sattvānāṃ svakāyaṃ...peyālaṃ...pratibhāsajñānānugamanatayā I sa evaṃjñānasamanvāgato'syāṃ bhūmau supratiṣṭhita ekabuddhakṣetrācca na calati, anabhilāpyeṣu buddhakṣetreṣu tathāgataparṣanmaṇḍaleṣu ca pratibhāsaprāpto bhavati I I

M

yādṛśī sattvānāṃ kāyavibhaktiśca varṇaliṅgasaṃsthānārohapariṇāhādhimuktyadhyāśayaśca teṣu buddhakṣetreṣu teṣu ca parṣanmaṇḍaleṣu tatra tatra tathā tathā svakāyamādarśayati I sa śramaṇaparṣanmaṇḍaleṣu śramaṇavarṇarūpamādarśayati I brāhmaṇaparṣanmaṇḍaleṣu brāhmaṇavarṇarūpamādarśayati I kṣatriya... I vaiśya... I śūdra... I gṛhapati... I cāturmahārājika... I trāyastriṃśa... I evaṃ yāma... I tuṣita... I nirmāṇarati... I paranirmitavaśavarti... I māra... I brahma... I yāvadakaniṣṭha... I śrāvakavaineyikānāṃ sattvānāṃ śrāvakakāyavarṇarūpamādarśayati I pratyekabuddhavaineyikānāṃ sattvānāṃ pratyekabuddhakāyavarṇarūpamādarśayati I bodhisattva... I tathāgata... I iti hi bho jinaputra yāvanto-'nabhilāpyeṣu buddhakṣetreṣu sattvānāmupapattyāyatanādhimuktiprasarāsteṣu tathatvāya svakāyavibhaktimādarśayati I I

N

sa sarvakāyavikalpāpagataḥ kāyasamatāprāptaḥ (taccāsya kāyasaṃdarśanamakṣūṇamavandhyaṃ ca sattvaparipākavinayāya) sa sattvakāyaṃ ca prajānāti I kṣetrakāyaṃ ca... I karmavipākakāyaṃ ca... I śrāvakakāyaṃ ca... I pratyekabuddhakāyaṃ ca ... I bodhisattvakāyaṃ ca... I tathāgatakāyaṃ ca... I jñānakāyaṃ ca... I dharmakāyaṃ ca... I ākāśakāyaṃ ca prajānāti I sa sattvānāṃ cittāśayābhinirhāramājñāya yathākālaparipākavinayānatikramādākāṅkṣan sattvakāyaṃ svakāyamadhitiṣṭhati I evaṃ kṣetrakāyaṃ karmavipākakāyaṃ...ātmakāyamadhitiṣṭhati I sa sattvānāṃ cittāśayābhinirhāramājñāya yaṃ yameva kāyaṃ yasmin yasmin kāye ākāṅkṣati, taṃ tameva kāyaṃ tasmin tasmin kāye (svakāyaṃ) adhitiṣṭhati I sa sattvakāyānāṃ karmakāyatāṃ ca prajānāti I vipākakāyatāṃ ca... I kleśakāyatāṃ ca... I rūpakāyatāṃ ca... I ārūpyakāyatāṃ ca prajānāti I kṣetrakāyānāṃ parīttatāṃ ca prajānāti, mahadgatatāṃ ca apramāṇatāṃ ca saṃkliṣṭatāṃ ca viśuddhatāṃ ca vyatyastatāṃ ca adhomūrdhatāṃ ca samatalatāṃ ca samavasaraṇatāṃ ca digjālavibhāgatāṃ ca prajānāti I karmavipākakāyānāṃ vibhaktisaṃketaṃ prajānāti I evaṃ śrāvakākāyānāṃ pratyekabuddhakāyānāṃ bodhisattvakāyānāṃ vibhaktisaṃketaṃ prajānāti I tathāgatakāyānāmabhisaṃbodhikāyatāṃ ca prajānāti I praṇidhānakāyatāṃ ca... I nirmāṇakāyatāṃ ca I adhiṣṭhānakāyatāṃ ca I rūpalakṣaṇānuvyañjanavicitrālaṃkārakāyatāṃ ca I prabhākāyatāṃ ca I manomayakāyatāṃ ca I puṇyakāyatāṃ ca I jñānakāyatāṃ ca I dharmakāyatāṃ ca prajānāti I jñānakāyānāṃ suvicāritatāṃ ca prajānāti I yathāvannistīraṇatāṃ ca phalaprayogasaṃgṛhītatāṃ ca laukikalokottaravibhāgatāṃ ca triyāṇavyavasthānatāṃ ca sādhāraṇāsādhāraṇatāṃ ca nairyāṇikānairyāṇikatāṃ ca śaikṣāśaikṣatāṃ ca prajānāti I dharmakāyānāṃ samatāṃ ca prajānāti I avikopanatāṃ ca avasthānasaṃketasaṃvṛttivyavasthānatāṃ ca sattvāsattvadharmavyavasthānatāṃ ca buddhadharmāryasaṃghavyavasthānatāṃ ca prajānāti | ākāśakāyānāmapramāṇatāṃ ca sarvatrānugatatāṃ ca aśarīratāṃ ca avitathānantatāṃ ca rūpakāyābhivyaktitāṃ ca prajānāti ||

O

sa evaṃ kāyajñānābhinirhāraprāpto vaśavartī bhavati sarvasattveṣu | āyurvaśitāṃ ca pratilabhate'nabhilāpyānabhilāpyakalpāyuḥ-pramāṇādhiṣṭhānatayā | cetovaśitāṃ ca pratilabhate'pramāṇ-āsaṃkhyeyasamādhinidhyaptijñānapraveśatayā | pariṣkāravaśitāṃ ca sarvalokadhātvanekavyūhālaṃkārapratimaṇḍitādhiṣṭhāna-saṃdarśanatayā | karmavaśitāṃ ca yathākālaṃ karmavipākādhi-ṣṭhānasaṃdarśanatayā | upapattivaśitāṃ ca sarvalokadhātūpapatti-saṃdarśanatayā adhimuktisaṃdarśanatayā sarvalokadhātubuddha-pratipūrṇasaṃdarśanatayā praṇidhānasaṃdarśanatayā yatheṣṭa-buddhakṣetrakālābhisaṃbodhisaṃdarśanatayā ṛddhisaṃ-darśanatayā sarvabuddhakṣetraṛddhivikurvaṇasaṃdarśanatayā dharmasaṃdarśanatayā anantamadhyadharmamukhāloka-saṃdarśanatayā jñānasaṃdarśanatayā tathāgatabalavaiśārady-āveṇikabuddhadharmalakṣaṇānuvyañjanābhisaṃbodhisaṃdarśanat ayā ||

P

sa āsāṃ daśānāṃ bodhisattvavaśitānāṃ sahapratilambhena acintya-jñānī ca bhavati atulyajñānī ca aprameyajñānī ca vipulajñānī ca asaṃ-hāryajñānī ca bhavati | tasyaivaṃbhūmyanugatasya evaṃ jñānasam-anvāgatasya atyantāgavadyaḥ kāyakarmasamudācāraḥ pravartate, atyantānavadyaśca vāk... | atyantānavadyaśca manaḥsamudācāraḥ pravartate | jñānapūrvaṃgamo jñānānuparivartī prajñāpāramit-ādhipateyo mahākaruṇāpūrvaka upāyakauśalyasuvibhaktaḥ praṇi-dhānasvabhinirhṛtastathāgatādhiṣṭhānasvadhiṣṭhito'pratiprasrabdha sattvārthaprayogo'paryantalokadhātuvibhaktigataḥ | samāsato bho jinaputra bodhisattvasya imāmacalāṃ bodhisattvabhūmimanu-prāptasya sarvabuddhadharmasamudānayanāya kāyavāṅmanas-karmasamudācāraḥ pravartate | sa evamimāmacalāṃ bodhisattva-bhūmimanuprāptaḥ supratiṣṭhitāśayabalaśca bhavati sarvakleśasam-udācārāpagatatvāt | supratiṣṭhitādhyāśayabalaśca bhavati mārgāvi-pravāsitatvāt | mahākaruṇābalasupratiṣṭhitaśca bhavati sattvārthān-utsargatvāt | mahāmaitrībala...sarvajagatparitrāṇatvāt | dhāraṇībala-

...asaṃpramoṣadharmatvāt I pratibhānabala...sarvabuddhadharma-pravicayavibhāgakuśalatvāt I abhijñābala...aparyantalokadhātu-caryāvibhāgakuśalatvāt I praṇidhānabala...sarvabodhisattvakriyān-utsargatvāt I pāramitābala...sarvabuddhadharmasamudānayanatvāt I tathāgatādhiṣṭhānabala...sarvākārasarvajñānābhimukhatvāt I sa evaṃbalādhānaprāptaḥ sarvakriyāśca saṃdarśayati, sarvakriyāsu ca anavadyo bhavatyanupaliptaśca I I

Q

iyaṃ bho jinaputra bodhisattvasya aṣṭamī jñānabhūmiracalety-ucyate'saṃhāryatvāt I avivartyabhūmirityucyate jñānāvivartyatvāt I durāsadabhūmirityucyate sarvajagad-durjñānatvāt I kumārabhūmir-ityucyate anavadyatvāt I janmabhūmirityucyate yathābhiprāyavaśa-vartitvāt I pariniṣpannabhūmirityucyate apunaḥkāryatvāt I pari-niṣṭhitabhūmirityucyate I sukṛtajñānavicayatvāt I nirmāṇabhūmir-ityucyate svabhinirhṛtapraṇidhānatvāt I adhiṣṭhānabhūmirityucyate I parāvikopanatvāt I anābhogabhūmirityucyate pūrvāntābhinir-hṛtatvāt I I

R

evaṃ jñānasvabhinirhṛtaḥ khalu punarbho jinaputra bodhisattvo buddhagotrānugato buddhaguṇaprabhāvabhāsitastathāgat-eryāpathacaryācāritrānugato buddhaviṣayābhimukhaḥ satata-samitaṃ svadhiṣṭhitatathāgatādhiṣṭhānaśca bhavati śakrabrahma-lokapālapratyudgataśca vajrapāṇisatatānubaddhaśca samādhibalān-utsṛṣṭaśca ca apramāṇakāyavibhaktyabhinirhṛtaśca sarvakāyacaryā-balopagataśca mahābhijñāvipākapariniṣpannaśca anantasamādhi-vaśavartī ca apramāṇavyākaraṇapratyeṣakaśca yathāparipavakka-jagadabhisaṃbodhinidarśakaśca bhavati I sa evaṃ jñānabhūmy-anugato mahāyānamaṇḍalānupraviṣṭaḥ suvicāritamahājñānābhijñaḥ satatasamitaṃ pramuktaprajñālokaraśmirasaṅgadharmadhātupath-āvatīrṇo lokadhātupathavibhaktikovidaḥ sarvākāraguṇasaṃ-darśakaḥ svacittotpādavaśavartī pūrvāntāparāntasuvicitajñānaḥ sarvamārapathāvartanavivartanajñānānugataḥ sarvatathāgata-viṣayagocarānupraviṣṭo'paryantalokadhātuprasareṣu bodhisattva-caryāṃ caratyapratyudāvartyayogena I tata ucyate bodhisattvo-'calāṃ bodhisattvabhūmimanuprāpta iti I I

S

tatra bho jinaputra acalāṃ bodhisattvabhūmimanuprāpto bodhisattvaḥ satatasamitamaparyantatathāgatadarśanāvirahito bhavati samādhibalasvabhinirhṛtatvāt I audārikaṃ buddhadarśanapūjopasthānaṃ notsṛjati I sa ekaikasmin kalpe ekaikasmin lokadhātuprasare anekān buddhān, anekāni buddhaśatāni...peyālaṃ...anekāni buddhakoṭīnayutaśatasahasrāṇi satkaroti gurukaroti mānayati pūjayati sarvākārapūjābhinirhāraṃ copasaṃharati I tāṃśca tathāgatān paryupāste, lokadhātuvibhaktipūrvakaṃ ca dharmālokopasaṃhāraṃ pratīcchati I sa bhūyasyā mātrayā tathāgatadharmakośaprāpto'saṃhāryo bhavati lokadhātuparipṛcchānirdeśeṣu I tāni cāsya kuśalamūlānyanekān kalpānuttapyante... I tadyathāpi nāma bho jinaputra tadeva jātarūpaṃ supariniṣṭhitaṃ kuśalena karmāreṇa suparikarmakṛtaṃ jambūdvīpasvāminaḥ kaṇṭhe śirasi vā ābaddhamasaṃhāryaṃ bhavati sarvajambūdvīpakānāṃ sattvānāmābharaṇavikṛtaiḥ, evameva bho jinaputra asyāmacalāyāṃ bodhisattvabhūmau sthitasya bodhisattvasya tāni kuśalamūlānyasaṃhāryāṇi bhavanti sarvaśrāvakapratyekabuddhairyāvatsaptamībhūmisthitaiśca bodhisattvaiḥ I imāṃ ca bhūmimanugatasya bodhisattvasya mahatī prajñājñānaprabhā sattvānāṃ kleśatamāṃsi praśamayati suvibhaktajñānamukhābhinirhāratayā I tadyathāpi nāma bho jinaputra sāhasriko mahābrahmā sāhasra lokadhātuṃ maitryā spharitvā prabhayāvabhāsayati, evameva bho jinaputra bodhisattvo'syāmacalāyāṃ bodhisattvabhūmau sthito yāvaddaśabuddhakṣetraśatasahasraparamāṇurajaḥsamān lokadhātūn mahatā maitryavabhāsena spharitvā sattvānāṃ kleśaparidāhānanupūrveṇa praśamayati, āśrayāṃśca prahlādayati I tasya daśabhyaḥ pāramitābhyaḥ praṇidhānapāramitā atiriktatamā bhavati, na ca pariśeṣāsu na samudāgacchati yathābalaṃ yathābhajamānam I iyaṃ bhavanto jinaputrā bodhisattvasya acalā nāma aṣṭamī bodhisattvabhūmiḥ samāsanirdeśataḥ I vistaraśaḥ punaraparyantakalpanirdeśaniṣṭhāto'nugantavyā I yasyāṃ pratiṣṭhito bodhisattvo bhūyastvena mahābrahmā bhavati sāhasrādhipatiḥ I abhibhūranabhibhūto'nvarthadarśī vaśiprāptaḥ kṛtī prabhuḥ sattvānāṃ sarvaśrāvakapratyekabuddhabodhisattvapāramitopadeśopasaṃhāreṣu asaṃhāryo lokadhātuvibhaktiparipṛcchānirdeśeṣu I yacca kiṃcit... I I

acalā nāma aṣṭamī bhūmiḥ I I

[Beginning of eighth bhūmi's final gathas]

upasaṃhāragāthāḥ |

te bhūmya saptasu viśodhita prajñupāyā
mārgā susaṃbhṛta mahāpraṇidhānabaddhāḥ |
supratiṣṭhitā naravarāḥ kuśalopapetā
jñānābhilāṣi vidu aṣṭamimākramanti || 12 ||

te puṇyajñānupagatāḥ kṛpamaitrayuktā
jñānāpramāṇapathagāḥ khagabuddhikalpāḥ |
śrutadharma niścitabalopagatā maharṣī
kṣāntiṃ labhanti anutpādapraśāntisūkṣmām || 13 ||

ādāvajāta anutpāda alakṣaṇaṃ ca
asaṃbhūtatamavinaṣṭata cāpravṛttam |
bhāvasvabhāvavigatā tathatāvikalpā
mama cittacāravigatāḥ khagatulyakalpāḥ || 14 ||

te eva kṣāntisamanvāgata niṣprapañcā
gambhīracālya vidu śāntavicāraprāptāḥ |
durjñeya sarvajagatārahapratyayaiśca
cittaṃ nimittagrahasaṃjñavibhāvitatvāt || 15 ||

evaṃ sthitānamanucintavikalpa nāsti
bhikṣurnirodhyupagato'paprakalpaprāptaḥ |
svapnoghaprāpta pratibuddha tathāvikalpā
brahmāpure ratisaṅgarahito tathaiva || 16 ||

pūrvādhiṣṭhāna sugatā puna codayanti
eṣā sa kṣānti paramā sugatābhiṣeke |
asmāku jñāna vipulaṃ varabuddhadharmā
te tubhya nāsti ta hi vīryu samārabhāyam || 17 ||

kiṃcāpi śānta tava sarvakileśajvālā
jvalitaṃ niśamya puna kleśagatibhya lokam |

praṇidhāna pūrva smara sattvahitaṃ vicārya
jñānārthi prārthita kriyā jagamokṣahetoḥ || 18 ||

sada eṣa dharmata sthitā tathatāvikalpā
sarveṣu buddhajinaśrāvakapratyayānam |
na hi etinā daśabalāna prabhāvu loke
nānyatra jñānavipulaṃ tribhi adhvasaṅgam || 19 ||

evaṃ tamapratisamā naradevapūjyā
upasaṃharanti bahujñānamukhā vicārān |
jinadharmaniṣpattipraveśamanantapāraṃ
yasyā kalā na bhavate puna bodhicaryā || 20 ||

etāni prāpta vṛṣabhī varajñānabhūmim
ekakṣaṇena spharate diśatāḥ samantān |
jñānapraveśupagatā varabhijñaprāptā
yatha sāgare vahanu mārutayānaprāptaḥ || 21 ||

sābhogacittavigatāḥ sthitajñānakarma
vicinanti kṣetraprabhavaṃ vibhavasthitiṃ ca |
dhātuścatvāri vinibhāgagatāna tāṃśca
sūkṣmaṃ mahadgata vibhakti samosaranti || 22 ||

trisahasri sarvaparamāṇurajo taranti
catvāri dhātu jagakāyi vibhaktitaśca |
ratnā vibhaktiparamāṇu suvargatīṣu
bhinditva jñānaviṣayena gaṇentyaśeṣam || 23 ||

jñāne vibhāvitamanā vidu sarvakāyān
sve kāyi tatra upanenti jagārthahetoḥ |
trisahasra sarva ca spharitva vicitrarūpān
darśenti kāya vividhān tathanantaloke || 24 ||

sūryaṃ śaśiṃ ca vahni māruta antarīkṣe
svakamaṇḍalusya udake pratibhāsaprāptā |
jñānottame sthita tathācaladharmatāyāṃ
jaga śuddhaaśaya vidū pratibhāsaprāptā || 25 ||

yathaāśayaṃ jagata kāyavibhaktitāṃ ca
darśenti sarvapariṣe bhuvi sarvaloke |
vaśipratyayāśraya jinātmajaśrāvakānāṃ
darśenti te sugatakāya vibhūṣitāṅgān || 26 ||

sattvāṃśca kṣetra tatha karmavipāka kāyān
āryāśrayān vividhadharmajñānakāyān |
ākāśakāya vṛṣabhī samatāmupetaṃ
darśenti ṛddhi vividhān jagatoṣaṇārtham || 27 ||

vaśitā daśo vimalajñānavicāraprāptā
anuprāpta jñānakṛta maitrakṛpānukūlāḥ |
yāvacca sarvajinadharmamupādakarmā
trisaṃvaraiḥ susthitameka acalyakalpāḥ || 28 ||

ye cā balā jinasutāna daśa akṣobhyā
tehī upeta avibandhiya sarvamāraiḥ |
buddhairadhiṣṭhita namaskṛta śakrabrahmai-
statha vajrapāṇibalakaiḥ satatānubaddhāḥ || 29 ||

ima bhūmideśupagatā na guṇānamanto
no śakyate kṣayitu kalpasahasrakoṭyaiḥ |
te bhūya buddha niyutān samupāsayante
bhonto utapta yatha bhūṣaṇu rājamūrdhni || 30 ||

ima bhūmideśupagatā vidu bodhisattvā
mahabrahma bhonti sahasrādhipatī guṇāḍhyāḥ |
trayayānadeśana akṣobhyasaṃhāraprāptā
maitrāyanaḥ śubhaprabhā jagakleśaghātī || 31 ||

ekakṣaṇena daśakṣetraśataḥsahasrā
yāvā rajodhātu tattaka samādhyupenti |
paśyanti tattaka daśadiśi sattvasārān
bhūyo ataḥ praṇidhiśreṣṭha vyūha nekāḥ || 32 ||

saṃkṣepa eṣa nirdiṣṭo aṣṭamāyā jinātmajāḥ |

vistaraḥ kalpakoṭībhirna śakyaḥ sarva bhāṣitum || 33 ||

[End of eighth bhūmi's final gathas]

[Beginning of ninth bhūmi's initial gathas]

9 sādhumatī nāma navamī bhūmiḥ ।

upakramagāthāḥ ।

imāṃ bhūmiṃ prabhāṣatā kampitāḥ kṣetrakoṭayaḥ ।
adhiṣṭhānā narendrasya aprameyā acintiyā ।। 1 ।।

ābhāsa rucirā muktāḥ kāyataḥ sarvadarśino ।
tayāvabhāsitāḥ kṣetrāḥ sattvāśca sukhitāstayā ।। 2 ।।

bodhisattvasahasrāṇi antarikṣe sthitāni ca ।
divyātikrāntapūjāya pūjyante vadatāṃ varam ।। 3 ।।

maheśvarā devaputrā vaśavartī praharṣitāḥ ।
nānāprakārapūjābhiḥ pūjenti guṇasāgaram ।। 4 ।।

tato'psaraḥsahasrāṇi harṣitāḥ prīṇitendriyāḥ ।
divyā suyattā saṃgītāḥ śāstu pūjāmajagrayam ।। 5 ।।

tebhyaśca tūryanādebhya anubhāvānmaharṣiṇaḥ ।
īdṛśā rutasahasrā ravantī madhurasvarāḥ ।। 6 ।।

imi sarve jinasutā khilamalavigatā
upagata bhuvi varasuruciracaraṇāḥ ।
jagahita vicarati daśadiśa vṛṣabhī
darśayi jinacari khagasamamanasā ।। 7 ।।

narapuri marupuri bhujagapativiṣaye
viyuha daśadiśi puṇyabalamudīritāḥ ।
tata tu bhuyu jinasuta darśayi atulī
jinasutaprabhava jinanupathaniratā ।। 8 ।।

ekakṣetri acalita sarvakṣetravirajā
anugata jagahita śaśiriva pratibhā ।

sarvaghoṣahānacitta praśamitamanasā
viyahari kṛtaśataśrutipathagiribhiḥ | | 9 | |

yatra sattva hīnacitta dīna mānaniratā-
statra vidu śrāvakācarī deśeti vṛṣabhī |
yatra sattva tīkṣṇacitta pratyayānaniratā-
statra jñāna pratyayāna darśayanti virajā | | 10 | |

ye tu sattvahitamaitramanasā (abhiratās)
tatra tyaṃ(tvaṃ) jinaputrāna darśayanti caraṇam |
ye tu sattva agra śreṣṭha matimānaniratā-
statra amī buddhakāya darśayanti atulam | | 11 | |

māyā yathā māyakāro darśeti jagahite
yāya koṭi naikavidyā sarvabhāvavigatā |
eva vidū buddhasutā jñānamāyaniratā
darśayanti sarvacarī sarvabhāvavigatā | | 12 | |

etādṛśā rutasahasrān bhaṇitva madhurāṃ-
stadā marukanyakā jinaṃ dṛṣṭvā tūṣṇīṃbhūtāḥ |
parṣadviprasanneyamavocatsugatātmajam
aṣṭamāyā bhaṇa ūrdhvaṃ cariṃ saddharmarājinām | | 13 | |

[End of ninth bhūmi's initial gathas]

9 sādhumatī nāma navamī bhūmiḥ ।

A

vajragarbho bodhisattva āha - yo'yaṃ bhavanto jinaputrā bodhisattva evamapramāṇajñeyavicāritayā buddhyā bhūyaścottarān śāntān vimokṣānadhyavasyan adhyālambamānaḥ bhūyaścottaraṃ tathāgatajñānaṃ susamāptaṃ vicārayan tathāgataguhyānupraveśaṃ cāvataran acintyajñānamāhātmyaṃ ca pravicinvan dhāraṇīsamādhipravicayaṃ ca pariśodhayan abhijñāvaipulyaṃ cābhinirharan lokadhātuvibhaktiṃ cānugacchan tathāgatabalavaiśādyāveṇikabuddhadharmāsaṃhāryatāṃ ca parikarmayan tathāgatadharmacakrapravartanavṛṣabhatāṃ cānukramamāṇaḥ mahākaruṇādhiṣṭhānapratilambhaṃ cānutsṛjan navamīṃ bodhisattvabhūmimākramati ।

B

so'syāṃ sādhumatyāṃ bodhisattvabhūmau sthitaḥ kuśalākuśalāvyākṛtadharmābhisaṃskāraṃ ca yathābhūtaṃ prajānāti । sāsravānāsravadharmābhisaṃskāraṃ ca... । laukikalokottaradharmābhisaṃskāraṃ ca... । cintyācintyadharmābhisaṃskāraṃ ca... । niyatāniyatadharmābhisaṃskāraṃ ca... । śrāvakapratyekabuddhadharmābhisaṃskāraṃ ca... । bodhisattvacaryādharmābhisaṃskāraṃ ca... । tathāgatabhūmidharmābhisaṃskāraṃ ca... । saṃskṛtadharmābhisaṃskāraṃ ca.. । asaṃskṛtadharmābhisaṃskāraṃ ca yathābhūtaṃ prajānāti । ।

C

sa evaṃjñānānugatayā buddhyā sattvacittagahanopacāraṃ ca yathābhūtaṃ prajānāti । kleśagahanopacāraṃ ca... । karmagahanopacāraṃ ca... । indriyagahanopacāraṃ ca ... । adhimuktigahanopacāraṃ ca... । dhātugahanopacāraṃ ca... । āśayānuśayagahanopacāraṃ ca... । upapattigahanopacāraṃ ca... । vāsanānusaṃdhigahanopacāraṃ ca... । trirāśivyavasthānagahanopacāraṃ ca yathābhūtaṃ prajānāti ।

D

sa sattvānāṃ cittavaimātratāṃ ca yathābhūtaṃ prajānāti । cittavicitratāṃ ca cittakṣaṇalaghuparivartabhaṅgabhaṅgatāṃ ca cittaśarīratāṃ ca cittānantyasarvataḥprabhūtatāṃ ca cittaprabhāsvaratāṃ ca cittasaṃkleśaniḥkleśatāṃ ca cittabandhavimokṣatāṃ ca cittamāyāviṭhapanatāṃ ca cittayathāgatipratyupasthānatāṃ ca yāvadanekāni cittanānātvasahasrāṇi yathābhūtaṃ prajānāti I

E

sa kleśānāṃ dūrānugatatāṃ ca yathābhūtaṃ prajānāti I prayogānantatāṃ ca... I sahajāvinirbhāgatāṃ ca... I anuśayaparyutthānaikārthatāṃ ca... I cittasaṃprayogāsaṃprayogatāṃ ca... I upapattisaṃdhiyathāgatipratyupasthānatāṃ ca... I traidhātukavibhaktitāṃ ca... I tṛṣṇāvidyādṛṣṭiśalyamānamahāsāvadyatāṃ ca... I trividhakarmaṇi dānānupacchedatāṃ ca... I samāsato yāvaccaturaśītikleśacaritanānātvasahasrānupraveśatāṃ ca yathābhūtaṃ prajānāti I

F

sa karmaṇāṃ kuśalākuśalāvyākṛtatāṃ ca... I vijñaptyavijñaptitāṃ ca... I cittasahajāvinirbhāgatāṃ ca... I svarasakṣaṇakṣīṇabhaṅgopacayāvipraṇāśaphalānusaṃdhitāṃ ca... I vipākavipākatāṃ ca... kṛṣṇaśuklākṛṣṇaśuklānekadeśakarmasamādānavaimātratāṃ ca... I karmakṣetrāpramāṇatāṃ ca... I āryalaukikapravibhaktitāṃ ca... I lokottaradharmavyavasthānatāṃ ca... I (sopādānānupādānatāṃ ca... I saṃskṛtāsaṃskṛtatāṃ ca I) dṛṣṭadharmopapadyāparaparyāyavedanīyatāṃ ca... I yānāyānaniyatāniyatatāṃ ca... I samāsato yāvaccaturaśītikarmanānātvasahasrapravibhaktivicayakauśalyaṃ ca yathābhūtaṃ prajānāti I

G

sa indriyāṇāṃ mṛdumadhyādhimātratāṃ ca... I pūrvāntāparāntasaṃbhedāsaṃbhedatāṃ ca... I udāramadhyanikṛṣṭatāṃ ca... I kleśasahajāvinirbhāgatāṃ ca... I yānāyānaniyatāniyatatāṃ ca... I yathāparipavkāparipakvavaineyikatāṃ ca... I indriyajālānuparivartanalaghubhaṅganimittagrahaṇatāṃ ca... I indriyādhipatyānavamardanīyatāṃ ca... I vivartyāvivartyendriyapravibhāgatāṃ ca... I dūrānugatasahajāvinirbhāganānātvavimātratāṃ ca, samāsato yāvadanekānīndriyanānātvasahasrāṇi prajānāti I so'dhimuktīnāṃ mṛdumadhyādhimātratāṃ ca...yāvadanekānyadhimuktinānātvasahasrāṇi prajānāti I sa dhātūnāṃ.... I sa āśayānāṃ.... I

H

so'nuśayānāmāśayasahajacittasahajatāṃ ca.... I cittasaṃprayogatāṃ ca... I viprayogavibhāgadūrānugatatāṃ ca... I anādikālānuddhaṭitatāṃ ca... I sarvadhyānavimokṣasamādhisamāpattyabhijñāprasahyatāṃ ca I traidhātukasaṃdhisunibaddhatāṃ ca I anādikālacittanibandhasamudācāratāṃ ca I āyatanadvārasamudayavijñaptitāṃ ca I pratipakṣālābhādravyabhūtatāṃ ca I bhūmyāyatanasamavadhānāsamavadhānatāṃ ca I ananyāryamārgasamuddhaṭanatāṃ ca prajānāti I

I

sa upapattinānātvatāṃ ca I yathākarmopapattitāṃ ca I nirayatiryagyonipretāsuramanuṣyadevavyavasthānatāṃ ca I rūpārūpyopapattitāṃ ca I saṃjñāsaṃjñopapattitāṃ ca I karmakṣetratṛṣṇāsnehāvidyāndhakāravijñānabījapunarbhavaprarohaṇatāṃ ca I nāmarūpasahajāvinirbhāgatāṃ ca I bhavasaṃmohatṛṣṇābhilāṣasaṃdhitāṃ ca I bhoktukāmabhavitukāmasattvaratyanavarāgratāṃ ca I traidhātukāvagrahaṇasaṃjñāniṣkarṣaṇatāṃ ca prajānāti I

J

sa vāsanānāmupacārānupacāratāṃ ca... I yathāgatisaṃbandhavāsanāvāsitatāṃ ca I yathāsattvacaryācaraṇavāsitatāṃ ca I yathākarmakleśābhyāsavāsitatāṃ ca I kuśalākuśalāvyākṛtadharmābhyāsavāsitatāṃ ca I punarbhavagamanādhivāsitatāṃ ca... I anupūrvādhivāsitatāṃ ca I dūrānugatānupacchedakleśopakarṣaṇavikārānuddharaṇavāsitatāṃ ca I dravyabhūtādravyabhūtavāsitatāṃ ca I śrāvakapratyekabuddhabodhisattvatathāgatadarśanaśravaṇasaṃvās avāsitatāṃ ca prajānāti I

K

sa sattvarāśīnāṃ samyaktvaniyatatāṃ ca prajānāti mithyātvaniyatatāṃ ca I ubhayatvāniyatatāṃ ca... I samyagdṛṣṭisamyagniyatatāṃ ca mithyādṛṣṭimithyā...niyatatāṃ ca I tadubhayavigamādaniyatatāṃ ca pañcānantaryānyatamamithyādṛṣṭiniyatatāṃ ca... I pañcendriyasamyagniyatatāṃ ca... I aṣṭamithyātvamithyāniyatatāṃ ca... I samyaktvasamyagniyatatāṃ ca... I apunaḥkāritatāṃ ca... I mātsaryerṣyāghṛṇopacārāvinivṛttyā mithyāniyatatāṃ ca... I āryānuttaramārgabhāvanopasaṃhārasamyaktvaniyatatāṃ ca... I tadubhayavigamādaniyatarāśyupadeśatāṃ ca prajānāti I iti hi bho jinaputra evaṃjñānānugato bodhisattvaḥ sādhumatyāṃ bodhisattvabhūmau pratiṣṭhita ityucyate I I

L

so'syāṃ sādhumatyāṃ bodhisattvabhūmau sthita evaṃ caryāvimātratāṃ sattvānāmajñāya tathaiva mokṣopasaṃhāramupasaṃharati I sa sattvaparipākaṃ prajānāti I sattvavinayaṃ ca... I śrāvakayānadeśanāṃ ca I pratyekabuddhayānadeśanāṃ ca I bodhisattvayānadeśanāṃ ca । tathāgatabhūmideśanāṃ ca prajānāti । sa evaṃ jñātvā tathatvāya sattvebhyo dharmaṃ deśayati ।

yathāśayavibhaktito yathānuśayavibhaktito yathendriyavibhaktito yathādhimuktivibhaktito yathāgocaravibhāgajñānopasaṃhārataḥ sarvagocarajñānānugamanato yathādhātugahanopacārānugamanato yathāgatyupapattikleśakarmavāsanānuvartanato yathārāśivyavasthānānugamanato yathāyānādhimokṣavimuktiprāptito'nantavarṇarūpakāyasaṃdarśanataḥ sarvalokadhātumanojñasvaravijñāpanataḥ sarvarutaravitaparijñānataḥ sarvapratisaṃvidviniścayakauśalyataśca dharmaṃ deśayati ।।

M

so'syāṃ sādhumatyāṃ bodhisattvabhūmau sthitaḥ san bodhisattvo dharmabhāṇakatvaṃ kārayati, tathāgatadharmakośaṃ ca rakṣati ।

N

sa dharmābhāṇakagatimupagato'pramāṇajñānānugatena kauśalyena catuḥpratisaṃvidabhinirhṛtayā bodhisattvavācā dharmaṃ deśayati । tasya satatasamitamasaṃbhinnāścatasro bodhisattvapratisaṃvido-'nupravartante । katamāścatasraḥ? yaduta dharmapratisaṃvit arthapratisaṃvit niruktipratisaṃvit pratibhānapratisaṃvit ।।

O

sa dharmapratisaṃvidā svalakṣaṇaṃ dharmāṇāṃ prajānāti । arthapratisaṃvidā vibhaktiṃ dharmāṇāṃ prajānāti । niruktipratisaṃvidā asaṃbhedadeśanāṃ dharmāṇāṃ prajānāti । pratibhānapratisaṃvidā anuprabandhānupacchedatāṃ dharmāṇāṃ prajānāti ।।

P

punaraparaṃ dharmapratisaṃvidā abhāvaśarīraṃ dharmāṇāṃ prajānāti । arthapratisaṃvidā udayāstagamanaṃ dharmāṇāṃ prajānāti । niruktipratisaṃvidā sarvadharmaprajñaptyacchedanadharmaṃ deśayati । pratibhānapratisaṃvidā yathāprajñaptyavikopanatāparyantatayā dharmaṃ deśayati ।।

Q

punaraparaṃ dharmapratisaṃvidā pratyutpannavibhaktiṃ dharmāṇāṃ prajānāti । arthapratisaṃvidā atītānāgatavibhaktiṃ dharmāṇāṃ prajānāti । niruktipratisaṃvidā atītānāgapratyutpannāsaṃbhedato dharmaṃ deśayati । pratibhānapratisaṃvidā ekaikamadhvānamārabhya aparyantadharmālokatayā dharmaṃ deśayati

| |

R

punaraparaṃ dharmapratisaṃvidā dharmaprabhedaṃ prajānāti | arthapratisaṃvidā arthaprabhedaṃ prajānāti | niruktipratisaṃvidā yathārutadeśanatayā dharmaṃ deśayati | pratibhānapratisaṃvidā yathānuśayajñānaṃ deśayati | |

S

punaraparaṃ dharmapratisaṃvidā dharmajñānavibhaktyasaṃbhedakauśalyaṃ prajānāti | arthapratisaṃvidā anvayajñānatathātvavyavasthānaṃ prajānāti | niruktipratisaṃvidā saṃvṛtijñānasaṃdarśanāsaṃbhedatayā nirdiśati | pratibhānapratisaṃvidā paramārthajñānakauśalyena dharmaṃ deśayati | |

T

punaraparaṃ dharmapratisaṃvidā ekanayāvikopaṃ dharmāṇāṃ prajānāti | arthapratisaṃvidā skandhadhātvāyatanasatyapratītyasamutpādakauśalyānugamamavatarati | niruktipratisaṃvidā sarvajagadabhigamanīyasumadhuragirinirghoṣākṣarairnirdiśati | pratibhānapratisaṃvidā bhūyo bhūyo'paryantadharmāvabhāsatayā nirdiśati | |

U

punaraparaṃ dharmapratisaṃvidā ekayānasamavasaraṇanānātvaṃ prajānāti | arthapratisaṃvidā pravibhaktayānavimātratāṃ prajānāti | niruktipratisaṃvidā sarvayānānyabhedena nirdiśati | pratibhānapratisaṃvidā ekaikaṃ yānamaparyantadharmābhāsena deśayati | |

V

punaraparaṃ dharmapratisaṃvidā sarvabodhisattvacarijñānacaridharmacarijñānānugamamavatarati | arthapratisaṃvidā daśabhūmivyavasthānanirdeśapravibhaktimavatarati | niruktipratisaṃvidā yathābhūmimārgopasaṃhārasaṃbhedena nirdiśati | pratibhānapratisaṃvidā ekaikāṃ bhūmimaparyantākāreṇa nirdiśati | |

W

punaraparaṃ dharmapratisaṃvidā sarvatathāgataikalakṣaṇānubodhamavatarati | arthapratisaṃvidā nānākālavastulakṣaṇavibhaṅgānugamaṃ prajānāti | niruktipratisaṃvidā yathābhisaṃbodhiṃ vibhaktinirdeśena nirdiśati | pratibhānapratisaṃvidā ekaikaṃ dharmapadamaparyantakalpāvyavacchedena nirdiśati | |

X

punaraparaṃ dharmapratisaṃvidā sarvatathāgatavāgbalavaiś-arādyabuddhadharmamahākaruṇāpratisaṃvitprayogadharmacakrān upravartamānasarvajñajñānānugamaṃ prajānāti I arthapratisaṃvidā caturaśītisattvacaritasahasrāṇāṃ yathāśayaṃ yathendriyaṃ yathā-dhimuktivibhaktitastathāgataghoṣaṃ prajānati I niruktipratisaṃvidā sarvasattvacaryāsaṃbhedatastathāgataghoṣānuraveṇa nirdiśati I pratibhānapratisaṃvidā tathāgatajñānaprabhācaryāmaṇḍal-ādhimukttyā dharmaṃ deśayati I I

Y

sa evaṃ pratisaṃvidā jñānābhinirhārakuśalo bho jinaputra bodhisattvo navamīṃ bodhisattvabhūmimanuprāptastathā-gatadharmakośaprāpto mahādharmabhāṇakatvaṃ ca kurvāṇaḥ arthavatīdhāraṇīpratilabdhaśca bhavati I dharmavatī... I jñānābhi-nirhāravatī... I avabhāsavatī... I vasumatīdhāraṇī... I sumatidhāraṇī... I tejodhāraṇī... I asaṅgamukhadhāraṇī... I ananta... I vicitrārthakośa... I sa evamādīnāṃ dhāraṇīpadānāṃ paripūrṇāni daśadhāraṇīmukh-āsaṃkhyeyaśatasahasrāṇi pratilabhate I tathā asaṃkhyeyaśata-sahasrānugatenaiva svarāṅgakauśalyena tāvadapramāṇānugatenaiva pratibhānavibhaktimukhena dharmaṃ deśayati I sa evam-apramāṇairdhāraṇīmukhāsaṃkhyeyaśatasahasrairdaśasu dikṣu aprameyāṇāṃ buddhānāṃ bhagavatāṃ sakāśāddharmaṃ śṛṇoti I śrutvā ca na vismārayati I yathāśrutaṃ ca apramāṇavibhaktita evaṃ nirdiśati I I

Z

sa ekasya tathāgatasya sakāśāddaśabhirdhāraṇīmukhāsaṃkhyeya-śatasahasrairdharmān paryavāpnoti I yathā caikasya, evamapary-antānāṃ tathāgatānām I sa praṇidhānamātreṇa bahutaraṃ samyak-saṃbuddhasakāśāddharmamukhālokaṃ saṃpratīcchati, na tveva mahābāhuśrutyaprāptaḥ śrāvakaḥ śrutodgrahaṇadhāraṇīprati-labdhaḥ kalpaśatasahasrodgrahaṇādhiṣṭhānena I sa evaṃ dhāraṇī-prāptaśca bhavati pratibhānaprāptaśca dharmasāṃkathyaṃ saṃ-niṣaṇṇaḥ sarvāvatīṃ trisāhasramahāsāhasralokadhātuṃ spharitvā yathāśayavibhaktitaḥ sattvebhyo dharmaṃ deśayati dharmāsane niṣaṇṇaḥ I dharmāsanaṃ cāsya tathāgatānabhiṣekabhūmiprāptān bodhisattvān sthāpayitvā sarvato viśiṣṭamapramāṇāvabhāsaprāptaṃ bhavati I sa dharmāsane niṣaṇṇa ākāṅkṣan ekaghoṣodāhāreṇa sarvaparṣadaṃ nānāghoṣarutavimātratayā saṃjñāpayati | ākāṅkṣan nānāghoṣanānāsvarāṅgavibhaktibhirājñāpayati | ākāṅkṣan raśmimukhopasaṃhārairdharmamukhāni niścārayati | ākāṅkṣan sarvaromakūpebhyo ghoṣānniścārayati | ākāṅkṣan yāvattrisāhasramahāsāhasrāyāṃ lokadhātau rūpāvabhāsāstebhyaḥ sarvarūpāvabhāsebhyo dharmarutāni niścārayati | ākāṅkṣan ekasvararutena sarvadharmadhātuṃ vijñāpayati | ākāṅkṣan sarvarutanirghoṣeṣu dharmarutamadhitiṣṭhati | ākāṅkṣan sarvalokadhātuparyāpannebhyo gītāvādyatūryaśabdebhyo dharmarutaṃ niścārayati | ākāṅkṣan ekākṣararutātsarvadharmapadaprabhedarutaṃ niścārayati | ākāṅkṣan anabhilāpyānabhilāpyalokadhātvaparyantataḥ pṛthivyaptejovāyuskandhebhyaḥ sūkṣmaparamāṇurajaḥprabhedata ekaikaparamāṇurajonabhilāpyāni dharmamukhāni niścārayati | sacettaṃ trisāhasramahāsāhasralokadhātuparyāpannaḥ sarvasattvā upasaṃkramya ekakṣaṇalavamuhūrtena praśnān paripṛccheyuḥ, ekaikaśca teṣāmapramāṇarutavimātratayā paripṛcchet, yaṃ caikaḥ sattvaḥ paripṛcchenna taṃ dvitīyaḥ, taṃ bodhisattvaḥ sarvasattvarutapadavyañjanamudgṛhṇiyāt | udgṛhya caikarutābhivyāhāreṇa teṣāṃ sarvasattvānāṃ cittāśayān paritoṣayet (yāvadanabhilāpyalokadhāturpayāpannā vā sattvā upasaṃkramya ekakṣaṇalavamuhūrtena praśnān paripṛccheyuḥ, ekaikaśca teṣāmapramāṇarutavimātratayā paripṛcchet, yaṃ caikaḥ paripṛcchenna taṃ dvitīyaḥ, taṃ bodhisattva ekakṣaṇalavamuhūrtenaiva sarvamudgṛhya ekodāhāreṇaiva sarvānājñāpayet | yāvadanabhilāpyānapi lokadhātūn spharitvā yathāśayendriyādhimuktitaḥ sattvebhyo dharmaṃ deśayati | dharmasāṃkathyaṃ niṣaṇṇaśca tathāgatādhiṣṭhānasaṃpratyeṣakaḥ sakalena buddhakāryeṇa sarvasattvānāṃ pratyupasthito bhavati | sa bhūyasyā mātrayā evaṃ jñānāvabhāsapragrahaṇamārabhate | sacedekasmin vālāgraprasare yāvantyanabhilāpyeṣu lokadhātuṣu paramāṇurajāṃsi tāvantastathāgatāstāvadapramāṇaprāpteṣveva parṣanmaṇḍaleṣu dharmaṃ deśayeyuḥ | ekaikaśca tathāgatastāvadapramāṇaprāptebhyaḥ sarvasattvebhyo nānātvato dharmaṃ deśayet, ekaikasmiṃśca sattvāśayasaṃtāne tāvadapramāṇameva dharmopasaṃhāramupasaṃharet | yathā caikastathāgataḥ parṣanmaṇḍale tathā te sarve tathāgatāḥ | yathā caikasmin vālāgraprasare tathā sarvasmin dharmadhātau | tatrāsmābhistādṛśaṃ smṛtivaipulyamabhinirhartavyaṃ yathaikakṣaṇena sarvatathāgatānāṃ sakāśāddharmāvabhāsaṃ pratyeṣemahi ekarutāvyatirekāt | yāvanti ca tāni yathāparikīrtitāni parṣanmaṇḍalāni nānānikāyadharmapravaṇaika-paripūrṇāni, tatrāsmābhistādṛśaṃ prajñāvabhāsaviniścayaprati-bhānaṃ pariśodhyaṃ yadekakṣaṇena sarvasattvān paritoṣayet, kiṃ punariyatsu lokadhātuṣu sattvāni | |

sa imāṃ sādhumatīṃ bodhisattvabhūmimanuprāpto bodhisattvo bhūyasyā mātrayā rātriṃdivamananyamanasikāraprayukto bhūtvā buddhagocarānupraviṣṭastathāgatasamavadhānaprāpto gambhīra-bodhisattvavimokṣānuprāpto bhavati | sa evaṃjñānānugato bodhi-sattvaḥ samāhitastathāgatadarśanaṃ na vijahāti | ekaikāsmiṃśca kalpe'nekān buddhān, anekāni buddhaśatāni...anekāni buddhakoṭi-nayutaśatasahasrāṇi... | dṛṣṭvā ca satkaroti gurukaroti mānayati pūjayati | audārikena buddhadarśanena pūjopasthānaṃ notsṛjati | tāṃśca tathāgatān praśnān paripṛcchati | sa dharmadharaṇīnirdeś-ābhinirjāto bhavati | tasya bhūyasyā mātrayā tāni kuśalamūlāny-uttaptatamānyasaṃhāryāṇi bhavanti | tadyathāpi nāma bho jina-putrāstadeva jātarūpamābharaṇīkṛtaṃ supariniṣṭhitaṃ kuśalena karmāreṇa rājñaścakravartina uttamāṅge kaṇṭhe vā ābaddham-asaṃhārya bhavati sarvakoṭṭarājānāṃ cāturdvipakānāṃ ca sattvānāmābharaṇavikṛtaiḥ, evameva bho jinaputrā bodhisattvasya asyāṃ sādhumatyāṃ bodhisattvabhūmau sthitasya tāni kuśala-mūlāni mahājñānāloka suvibhaktānyuttapyante, asaṃhāryāṇi bhavanti sarvaśrāvakapratyekabuddhairadharabhūmisthitaiśca bodhisattvaiḥ | tasya sā kuśalamūlābhā sattvānāṃ kleśacitta-gahanānyavabhāsya tata eva vyāvartate | tadyathāpi nāma bho jina-putrā dvisāhasriko mahābrahmā sarvasmin dvisāhasrike lokadhātau gahananimnopacārānavabhāsayati, evameva bho jinaputrā bodhi-sattvasya asyāṃ sādhumatyāṃ bodhisattvabhūmau sthitasya sā kuśalamūlābhā sattvānāṃ kleśacittagahanānyavabhāsya tata eva vyāvartate | tasya daśabhyaḥ pāramitābhyo balapāramitā atirikta-tamā bhavati, na ca pariśeṣāsu na samudācarati yathābalaṃ yathā-bhajamānam | iyaṃ bhavanto jinaputrā bodhisattvasya sādhumatī nāma navamī bodhisattvabhūmiḥ...mahābrahmā bhavati mahābala-sthāmaprāpto dvisāhasrādhipatirabhibhūḥ...pāramitopadeśeṣv-asaṃhāryaḥ sattvāśayaparipṛcchānirdeśaiḥ | yacca kiṃcit... | |

sādhumatī nāma navamī bhūmiḥ | |

[Beginning of ninth bhūmi's final gathas]

upasaṃhāragāthāḥ ।

te apramāṇabalabuddhi vicārayantaḥ
susūkṣmajñānaparamā jagatā durjñeyā ।
tatha guhyasthāna sugatāna samosaranto
bhūmiṃ kramanti navamīṃ jagato'rthakarīm ।। 14 ।।

te dhāraṇīmukhi samādhisamāhitāgrā
vipulā abhijñā api kṣetrapraveśanantam ।
balajñānaniścayamapi jinu dhairyasthānaṃ
praṇidhīkṛpāśayavidū navamotaranti ।। 15 ।।

te atra bhūmyanugatā jinakośadhārī
kuśalāśca dharmakuśalāśca avyākṛtāśca ।
ye sāsravā api ca laukika ye ca āryā-
ścintyā acintiya vidū anubuddhyayanti ।। 16 ।।

niyatāṃśca dharmaniyatāṃ pravicārayanti
trayayānasaṃpadakriyā paritārayanti ।
bhūmidharma yathāadhimukti pracāratasca
abhisaṃskaronti yatha lokya tathotaranti ।। 17 ।।

te evajñānanugatā varasūkṣmabuddhī
sattvāna cittagahanaṃ parimārgayanti ।
(cittaṃ vicitrakṣaṇavartanivartatāṃ ca)
cittaṃ anantaprabhavaṃ sada otaranti ।। 18 ।।

kleśānanādina prayogasahāyatāśca
ye paryutthānanuśayā gatisaṃdhitaśca ।
tatha karmapraveśa vicitravibhaktitaśca
hetū niruddhaphalanāśa samotaranti ।। 19 ।।

indriya yā mṛdukamadhya udāratasca
saṃbhedapūrvamaparānta samotaranti ।

adhimukti naika vividhā śubha āśubhataśca
catvāri āśīti sahasra samotaranti | | 20 | |

dhātūpraveśa jaga bhāvitakleśadṛṣṭī
gahanaṃ gatā anavarāgra acchedataśca |
ye āśayā anuśayā sahajapracārī
cittāsamosṛta nibaddha accheda tanti | | 21 | |

cittaṃ yathā anuśayā na ca dravyabhūto
na ca deśasthā na ca vipravasanti āśayā |
durheya dhyānaviṣayānabhivartiyāśca
chedaśca mārga vinayena na cānyamasti | | 22 | |

upapatti ṣaḍgati vibhaktipraveśataśca
snehaṃ ca tṛṣṇamavidyāndhaka karmakṣetrā |
vijñānabījasahajāṅkuranāmarūpaṃ
traidhātuke anavarāgra samotaranti | | 23 | |

te vāsanāgati kileśa ca karma cittā
suvihāratāya na punargatisanta kāmā |
rāśitribhirniyatasattva samotaranti
dṛṣṭīnimagnamapi jñāna samotaranti | | 24 | |

evaṃ visaraṇagatāḥ sthita atra bhūmyāṃ
sarvasattva āśaya yathendriya yādhimuktiḥ |
teṣāmarthe dharmavibhakti prakāśayanti
pratisaṃvidarthakuśalāḥ pratibhā nirukti | | 25 | |

te dharmabhāṇaka gatī anuprāpta (sthānaṃ)
siṃhariṣabhanibhā girirājakalpāḥ |
abhipravarṣanti madhuramamṛtasya varṣaṃ
bhujagendrasāgara yathā anupūrayanti | | 26 | |

hitārthajñānakuśalāstatha dharmatāyāṃ
sarvaṃ niruktyanugatāḥ pratibhānaprāptāḥ |
te dhāraṇī daśa asaṃkhyasahasra labdhā
dhāranti dharma yatha (sāgara varṣadhārī) | | 27 | |

evaṃ ca dhāraṇiviśuddhisamādhiprāptā
ekakṣaṇena daśabuddhasahasra dṛṣṭāḥ |
śravaṇena dharmaratanaṃ ca nideśayanti
(ekaikamaṇḍalaviśuddhisvarāṅgagatāḥ) || 28 ||

vyohārate trisahasramahalokadhātuṃ
pariśeṣa sattva vividhāstrayaratanebhyaḥ |
toṣenti sarva yathaindriyaāśayāśca
catudvīpasāgara varṣā sama modayanti || 29 ||

(bhūyottariṃ guṇinu vīrya samārabhante)
cittaanti vālaprasara asmi sucetanantāḥ |
deśeyu dharma sugatāḥ puna nānasattvaṃ
śrutvā dharema yatha sarvada (bījadhārī) || 30 ||

(yāvatakā) jagadiha praviśanti sattvāḥ
(te sarva ekapariṣanmaṇḍale niṣaṇṇāśca) |
eṣāṃ ca ekakṣaṇi sarvi samotaritvā
ekāṃ rutena imi tarpayitavya sarve || 31 ||

(atra sthitā naramaruttama dharmarājā)
bhontī dharmairjinasutāḥ paricālayanti |
rātriṃdivaṃ sada jinaiḥ śamathānuprāptā
gambhīra śānta sthita jñānavimokṣadhīrā || 32 ||

(te'nekabuddhaniyutān paryupāsayante)
bhontī uttapta paṇu (pāṇḍu) cakravartaḥprabhāvā |
tasya kleśagahanāni prabhā samājya
brahmaṇo va dvisahasrikalokadhātuḥ || 33 ||

(atra sthitā guṇadharā) mahabrahmaloke
bhontī (triyānadeśanaṃ viditānubhāvā |)
yaṃ caivamārabhati sarvajagaddhitāya
sarvajñajñānupagatā guṇajñānaprāptā || 34 ||

(kṣetrāpramāṇaparyāpanna) ekā rajāgre

kṣaṇi eki (tattakasamādhi u)penti dhīrāḥ |
(dṛṣṭvā sarve diśi jināṃśca vacaḥ śṛṇonti)
tato vikurvi praṇidhānanvitāpramāṇāḥ || 35 ||

ityeṣā navamī bhūmirmahājñānavicāriṇā |
gambhīrā durdṛśā sūkṣmā nirdiṣṭā sugatātmajāḥ || 36 ||

[End of ninth bhūmi's final gathas]

[Beginning of tenth bhūmi's initial gathas]
10 dharmameghā nāma daśamī bhūmiḥ |

upakramagāthāḥ |

eva śrutva caraṇamanuttamaṃ
śuddhavāsanayutāḥ praharṣitāḥ |
antarīkṣasthita prīṇitendriyāḥ
pūjayanti sugataṃ tathāgatam || 1 ||

bodhisattvanayutā acintiyā
antarīkṣagatiprāptiharṣitāḥ |
gandhamegha atulān manomayān
dhūpayanti sattvakleśaghātinaḥ || 2 ||

devarāja vaśavarti prīṇito
antarīkṣa trisahasrakoṭibhiḥ |
vastrakaiḥ samakarī sagauravā
bhrāmayanti rucirān varān śatam || 3 ||

apsarā bahava prīṇitendriyāḥ
pūjayanti sugataṃ sagauravāḥ |
tūryakoṭinayutāḥ pravāditā
evarūpa ravuyukta rāvataḥ || 4 ||

ekakṣetra sugato niṣaṇṇakaḥ
sarvakṣetri pratibhāsa darśayī |
kāyakoṭi vividhā manoramā
dharmadhātuvipulān spharitvana || 5 ||

ekaromu sugatasya raśmayo
niścaranti jagakleśa śāmyati |
śakyu (kṣetra-raja-dhātu'pi) kṣayī
tasya raśmigaṇanā tvajānitum || 6 ||

keci buddhavaralakṣaṇaṃ viduḥ

paśyayanti varacakravartinaḥ |
anyakṣetravaracarya uttamāṃ
śodhayanti dvipadendra dṛśyate || 7 ||

(tuṣitāyatanaprāpta nāyako)
cyavamānu caṃkramāṇa dṛśyate |
garbhaprāpta bahukṣetrakoṭiṣu
jāyamāna kvaci kṣetra dṛśyate || 8 ||

niṣkramanta jagahetu nāyako
budhyamāna puna bodhimuttamām |
(dharmacakravartanirvṛtāgato)
dṛśyamāna buddhakṣetrakoṭiṣu || 9 ||

māyakāra yatha vidyaśikṣito
jīvikārtha bahukāya darśayī |
tadva śāstu varaprajñaśikṣito
sarvakāyabhinihartu (sattvana) || 10 ||

śūnya śānta gatadharmalakṣaṇā
antarīkṣasamaprāptadharmatām |
buddhaśāstu paramārthatattvataṃ
darśayī pravarabuddhagocaram || 11 ||

yatha svabhāvu sugatānagocarā
sarvasattva tatha prāpta dharmatām |
lakṣalakṣa samalakṣa tādṛśā
sarvadharma paramārthalakṣaṇāḥ || 12 ||

ye tu jñāna sugatāna arthiṃke
kalpakalpaparikalpavarjitam |
bhāvabhāvasamabhāvabuddhayaḥ
kṣipra bheṣyati nareśa uttamāḥ || 13 ||

īdṛśān rutasahasrān bhaṇitva madhurasvarāḥ |
marukanyā jinaṃ lokya tūṣṇībhūtāḥ śame ratāḥ || 14 ||

prasannaṃ parṣadaṃ jñātvā mokṣacandro viśāradaḥ |
vajragarbhaṃ tridhāpṛcchajjinaputraṃ viśāradam || 15 ||

daśamī saṃkramantānāṃ kīdṛśaṃ guṇagocaram |
nimittaprātihāryāṃśca sarvamākhyā(hi) parikrama || 16 ||

atha khalu vajragarbho bodhisattvo daśadiśaṃ vyavalokya sarvāvatīṃ parṣadaṃ vyavalokya dharmadhātuṃ ca vyavalokayan sarvajñatācittotpādaṃ ca saṃvarṇayan bodhisattvaviṣayamādarśayan caryābalaṃ pariśodhayan sarvākārajñatāsaṃgrahamanuvyāha ran sarvalokamalamapakarṣayan sarvajñajñānamupasaṃharan acintyajñānaniryūhamādarśayan bodhisattvaguṇān prabhāvayan evameva bhūmyarthaṃ prarūpayamāṇo buddhānubhāvena tasyāṃ velāyāmimā gāthā abhāṣata -

[End of tenth bhūmi's initial gathas]

10 dharmameghā nāma daśamī bhūmiḥ |

A

vajragarbho bodhisattva āha - yo'yaṃ bhavanto jinaputrā bodhisattva evamapramāṇajñeyavicāritayā buddhyā yāvannavamī bodhisattvabhūmiriti suvicitavicayaḥ suparipūrṇaśukladharmaḥ paryantasaṃbhāropacayopacitaḥ suparigṛhītamahāpuṇyajñānasaṃbhāraḥ mahākaruṇāvaipulyādhigataḥ lokadhātuvibhaktivaimātryakovidaḥ sattvadhātupraviṣṭagahanopacāraḥ tathāgatagocarapraveśānugatasaṃjñāmanasikāraḥ balavaiśāradyabuddhadharmādhyālambanānugataḥ sarvākārasarvajñajñānābhiṣekabhūmiprāpta ityucyate ||

B

tasya khalu punarbhavanto jinaputrā evaṃjñānānugatasya bodhisattvasya abhiṣekabhūmisamāpannasya vimalo nāma samādhirāmukhībhavati | dharmadhātuvibhaktipraveśaśca nāma | bodhimaṇḍālaṃkāravyūhaśca nāma | sarvākāraraśmikusumaśca nāma | sāgaragarbhaśca nāma | sāgarasamṛddhiśca nāma | ākāśadhātuvipulaśca nāma | sarvadharmasvabhāvavicayaśca nāma | sarvasattvacittacaritānugataśca nāma | pratyutpannasarvabuddhasaṃmukhāvasthitaśca nāma bodhisattvasamādhirāmukhībhavati | tasaivaṃpramukhāni daśa samādhyasaṃkhyeyaśatasahasrāṇyāmukhībhavanti | sa tān sarvān samādhīn samāpadyate ca vyuttiṣṭhate ca, samādhikauśalyānugataśca yāvatsamādhikāryaṃ tatsarvaṃ pratyanubhavati | tasya yāvaddaśasamādhyasaṃkhyeyaśatasahasrāṇāṃ paryante sarvajñajñānaviśeṣābhiṣekavānnāma bodhisattvasamādhirāmukhībhavati ||

C

yasmin samanantarābhimukhībhūte daśatrisāhasraśatasahasrāparyantapramāṇaṃ mahāratnarājapadmaṃ prādurbhavati sarvākārararatnapratyarpitaṃ sarvalokaviṣayasamatikrāntaṃ lokottarakuśalamūlasaṃbhūtaṃ māyāsvabhāvagocarapariniṣpannaṃ dharmadhātusuvyavasthitāvabhāsaṃ divyaviṣayasamatikrāntaṃ mahāvaiḍūryamaṇiratnadaṇḍamatulyacandanarājakarṇikaṃ mahāśmagarbhakesaraṃ jāmbūnadasuvarṇāvabhāsapatramaparimitaraśmisaṃkusumitaśarīraṃ sarvapravararatnapratyuptagarbhamaparyantamahāratnajālasaṃchannaṃ paripūrṇadaśatrisāhasraśatasahasraparamāṇurajaḥsamamahāratnapadmaparivāram | tadanugatastadanurūpaśca tasya bodhisattvasya kāyaḥ saṃtiṣṭhate I sa tasya sarvajñajñānaviśeṣābhiṣekavataḥ samādheḥ sahapratilambhāttasminmahāratnarājapadme niṣaṇṇaḥ saṃdṛśyate I samanantaraniṣaṇṇaśca sa bodhisattvastasmin mahāratnarājapadme, atha yāvanti tasya mahāratnarājapadmasya mahāpadmāni parivāraḥ prādurbhūtaḥ, tāvanto bodhisattvā daśadiglokadhātusaṃnipatitāstaṃ bodhisattvamanuparivārya teṣu mahāratnapadmeṣu niṣīdanti I ekaikaśca teṣāṃ daśa samādhiśatasahasrāṇi samāpadyate tameva bodhisattvaṃ nirīkṣamāṇaḥ I I

D

samanantarasamāpanne ca tasmin bodhisattve teṣu ca bodhisattveṣu niravaśeṣam, atha sarvalokadhātusaṃprakampanaṃ bhavati I sarvāpāyapratiprasrambhaṇaṃ ca, sarvadharmadhātvavabhāsakaraṇaṃ ca, sarvalokadhātupariśodhanaṃ ca, sarvabuddhakṣetranāmadheyarutānanuravaṇaṃ ca, sarvasabhāgacaritabodhisattvasaṃnipātanaṃ ca sarvalokadhātudevamanuṣyatūryasaṃgītisaṃpravādanaṃ ca sarvasattvasukhasaṃjananaṃ ca sarvasamyaksaṃbuddhācintyapūjopasthānapravartanaṃ ca sarvatathāgataparṣanmaṇḍalavijñāpanaṃ ca bhavati I tatkasya hetoḥ? tathā hi bho jinaputrāstasya bodhisattvasya samanantaraniṣaṇṇasya tasmin mahāratnarājapadme adhastāccaraṇatalābhyāṃ daśaraśmyasaṃkhyeyaśatasahasrāṇi niścaranti I niścarya daśadiśamavīciparyantān mahānirayānavabhāsayanti I nairayikānāṃ sattvānāṃ sarvaduḥkhāni pratiprasrambhayati I jānumaṇḍalābhyāṃ daśa...daśadiśaṃ sarvatiryagyonibhavanānyavabhāsayanti, sarvatiryagyoniduḥkhāni ca praśamayanti I nābhimaṇḍalād daśa...sarvayamalokabhavanāni avabhāsayanti, sarvayamalaukikānāṃ sattvānāṃ duḥkhāni ca praśamayanti I vāmadakṣiṇābhyāṃ pārśvābhyāṃ...manuṣyāśrayān...manuṣya... I ubhābhyāṃ pāṇibhyāṃ devāsurabhavanāni...devāsura... I aṃsābhyāṃ...śrāvakayānīyāśrayānavabhāsayanti, dharmālokamukhaṃ copasaṃharanti I pṛṣṭhato grīvāyāśca...pratyekabuddhāśrayānavabhāsayanti, śāntisamādhimukhanayaṃ copasaṃharanti I mukhadvārād...prathamacittopādamupādāya yāvannavamīṃ bhūmimanuprāptān bodhisattvānavabhāsayanti, prajñopāyakauśalyanayaṃ copasaṃharanti I ūrṇākośāddaśaraśmyasaṃkhyeyaśatasahasrāṇi niścaranti, niścarya daśasu dikṣu sarvamārabhavanānyavabhāsya dhyāmīkṛtya abhiṣekabhūmiprāptān bodhisattvān avabhāsya tatkāyeṣvevāstaṃ gacchanti I uparyuttamāṅgāt paripūrṇadaśatrisāhasrāsaṃkhyeyaśatasahasraparamāṇurajaḥsamā raśmayo niścaranti, niścarya daśasu dikṣu dharmadhātupramāṇānyākāśadhātuparyavasānāni sarvatathāgataparṣanmaṇḍalānyavabhāsya daśākāraṃ lokaṃ pradakṣiṇīkṛtya uparikhagapathe sthitvā mahāraśmijālamaṇḍalāni kṛtvā uttaptaprabhāsaṃ nāma mahattathāgatapūjopasthānaṃ sarvatathāgatānāmanupravartayanti I tasya pūjopasthānasya prathamacittotpādamupādāya yāvannavamībhūmyanupravartitam tathāgatapūjopasthānaṃ... I tataḥ khalvapi mahāraśmijālamaṇḍalādyāvatī daśasu dikṣu niravaśeṣasarvadharmadhātvantargatā puṣpaprajñaptirvā gandhadhūpamālyavilepanacūrṇacīvaracchatradhvajapatākāvastrābharaṇamaṇiratnaprajñaptirvā, tato'tiriktatarāḥ sarvalokaviṣayasamatikrāntā lokottarakuśalamūlasaṃbhārādhipatyābhinirvṛttāḥ sarvākāraguṇasaṃpannā acintyanirvāṇādhiṣṭhānādhiṣṭhitā nānāvyūhamahāratnavarṣā iva ekaikatathāgataparṣanmaṇḍale mahāmeghā ivābhipravarṣanti sma I tāṃ ca ye sattvāḥ pūjāṃ saṃjānante, te sarve niyatā bhavantyanuttarāyāṃ samyaksaṃbodhau I evaṃrūpaṃ pūjopasthānaṃ pravartya tā raśmayaḥ punareva sarvāvanti tathāgataparṣanmaṇḍalānyavabhāsya daśākāraṃ lokaṃ pradakṣiṇīkṛtya teṣāṃ tathāgatānāmarhatāṃ samyaksaṃbuddhānāmadhastātkramataleṣu astaṃ gacchanti I tatasteṣāṃ tathāgatānāṃ teṣāṃ ca bodhisattvānāṃ viditaṃ bhavati - amuṣmin lokadhātuprasare evaṃcaryānugato bodhisattvo'bhiṣekakālaprāpta iti I tatra bho jinaputrā daśabhyo digbhyo'paryantebhyo lokadhātuprasarebhyo'prameyāsaṃkhyeyāparyantā bodhisattvā yāvannavamībodhisattvabhūmipratiṣṭhitā āgatya taṃ bodhisattvamanuparivārya mahatīṃ pūjāṃ kṛtvā tameva bodhisattvaṃ nirīkṣamāṇā daśa samādhiśatasahasrāṇi samāpadyante I abhiṣekabhūmiprāptānāṃ ca bodhisattvānāṃ kāyebhyaḥ śrīvatsālaṃkārādvajrasvastikāt sarvamāraśatruvijayo nāmaikaikā mahāraśmirdaśaraśmyasaṃkhyeyaśatasahasraparivārā niścarati, niścarya daśadiśo'vabhāsya aparyantāni prātihāryāṇi saṃdarśya tasya bodhisattvasya śrīvatsālaṃkāre vajrasvastika evāstaṃ gacchati I samanantarādastamitāyāśca tasyā raśmyāḥ śatasahasraguṇottarā tasya bodhisattvasya balasthāmābhivṛddhiḥ prajñāyate I I

E

atha khalu bho jinaputrāḥ sarvajñatābhijñāvatyo nāma raśmayasteṣāṃ tathāgatānāmarhatāṃ samyaksaṃbuddhānāmūrṇākośebhyo niścarantyasaṃkhyeyaoparivārāḥ I tāḥ sarvāsu daśasu dikṣu aśeṣataḥ sarvalokadhātūnavabhāsya daśākāraṃ lokaṃ pradakṣiṇīkṛtya mahānti tathāgatavikurvitāni saṃdarśya bahūni bodhisattvakoṭiniyutaśatasahasrāṇi saṃcodya sarvabuddhakṣetraprasarān ṣaḍvikāraṃ saṃprakampya sarvāpāyacyutigatyupapattīḥ praśamya sarvamārabhavanāni dhyāmīkṛtya sarvatathāgatābhisaṃbodhivibuddhabuddhāsanānyupasaṃdarśya sarvabuddhaparṣanmaṇḍalavyūhaprabhāvaṃ nidarśya dharmadhātuparamānākāśadhātuparyavasānān sarvalokadhātūnavabhāsya punarevāgatya taṃ sarvāvantaṃ bodhisattvaparṣatsaṃnipātamuparyuparipradakṣiṇīkṛtya mahāvyuhānnidarśya tā raśmayastasya bodhisattvasyottamāṅge'staṃ gacchanti I tatparivāraraśmayaśca tathā saṃnipatitānāṃ teṣāṃ bodhisattvānāṃ śirassvantardhīyante sma I samanantarasaṃnipatitābhiśca tābhī raśmibhiste bodhisattvā apratilabdhapūrvāṇi daśa samādhiśatasahasrāṇi pratilabhante I tāśca raśmayastulyakālaṃ tasya bodhisattvasyottamāṅge nipatitā bhavanti I sa ca bodhisattvo'bhiṣikta ityucyate samyaksaṃbuddhaviṣaye I daśabalaparipūryā tu samyaksaṃbuddha iti saṃkhyāṃ gacchati I tadyathāpi nāma bho jinaputrā yo rājñaścakravartinaḥ putro jyeṣṭhaḥ kumāro›gryamahiṣīprasūtaścakravartirājalakṣaṇasamanvāgato bhavati, taṃ rājā cakravartī divye hastisauvarṇe bhadrapīṭhe niṣādya, caturbhyo mahāsamudrebhyo vāryānīya, upariratnavimānena dhāryamāṇena mahatā puṣpadhūpagandhadīpamālyavilepanacūrṇacīvaracchatradhvajapatākātūryatālāvacarasaṃgitivyūhena sauvarṇaṃ bhṛṅgāraṃ gṛhītvā tena vāriṇā taṃ kumāraṃ mūrdhanyabhiṣiñcati I samanantarābhiṣiktaśca rājā kṣatriyo mūrdhabhiṣikta iti saṃkhyāṃ gacchati I daśakuśalakarmapathaparipūryā tu cakravartīti saṃjñāṃ pratilabhate I evameva bho jinaputrāḥ samanantarābhiṣikto bodhisattvastairbuddhairbhagavadbhirmahājñānābhiṣekābhiṣikta ityucyate I samyaksaṃbuddhābhiṣekeṇa daśabalaparipūryā tu samyaksaṃbuddha iti saṃkhyāṃ gacchati I ayaṃ bho jinaputrā bodhisattvasya mahājñānābhiṣeko yasyārthe bodhisattvo'nekāni duṣkaraśatasahasrāṇyārabhate I sa evamabhiṣikto›prameyaguṇajñānavivardhito dharmameghāyāṃ bodhisattvabhūmau pratiṣṭhita ityucyate I I

F

so'syāṃ dharmameghāyāṃ bodhisattvabhūmau pratiṣṭhito bodhisattvo dharmadhātusamudāgamaṃ ca yathābhūtaṃ prajānāti | kāmadhātusamudāgamaṃ ca yathābhūtaṃ prajānāti | rūpadhātusamudāgamaṃ ca yathābhūtaṃ prajānāti | ārūpyadhātusamudāgamaṃ ca yathābhūtaṃ prajānāti | lokadhātusamudāgamaṃ ca yathābhūtaṃ prajānāti | sarvasattvadhātusamudāgamaṃ ca yathābhūtaṃ prajānāti | vijñānadhātusamudāgamaṃ ca yathābhūtaṃ prajānāti | saṃskṛtāsaṃskṛtadhātusamudāgamaṃ ca yathābhūtaṃ prajānāti | ākāśadhātusamudāgamaṃ ca yathābhūtaṃ prajānāti | bhūtābhūtadeśanāṃ ca yathābhūtaṃ prajānāti | nirvāṇaṃ ca yathābhūtaṃ prajānāti | dṛṣṭikleśasamudāgamaṃ ca yathābhūtaṃ prajānāti | lokadhātupravṛttinivṛttisamudāgamaṃ ca yathābhūtaṃ prajānāti | śrāvakacaryāsamudāgamaṃ ca yathābhūtaṃ prajānāti | pratyekabuddhacaryāsamudāgamaṃ ca yathābhūtaṃ prajānāti | bodhisattvacaryāsamudāgamaṃ ca yathābhūtaṃ prajānāti |

tathāgatabalavaiśāradyāveṇikabuddhadharmarūpakāyadharmakāya samudāgamaṃ ca yathābhūtaṃ prajānāti | sarvākārasarvajñajñānasamudāgamaṃ ca yathābhūtaṃ prajānāti | abhisaṃbodhidharma-cakrapravṛttisaṃdarśanasamudāgamaṃ ca yathābhūtaṃ prajānāti | samāsataḥ sarvadharmapraveśavibhaktiniṣṭīrṇasamudāgamaṃ ca yathābhūtaṃ prajānāti | sa evaṃjñānānugatayā buddhyā uttari sattvakāyanirmāṇaṃ ca yathābhūtaṃ prajānāti | kleśakāyanirmāṇaṃ ca yathābhūtaṃ prajānāti | dṛṣṭikṛtanirmāṇaṃ ca... lokadhātunirmāṇaṃ ca...dharmadhātunirmāṇaṃ ca...śrāvakanirmāṇaṃ ca...pratyekabuddhanirmāṇaṃ ca...bodhisattvanirmāṇaṃ ca...tathāgatanirmāṇaṃ ca...sarvanirmāṇakalpākalpatāṃ ca yathābhūtaṃ prajānāti | sarvabuddhādhiṣṭhānaṃ ca...dharmādhiṣṭhānaṃ ca...saṃghādhiṣṭhānaṃ ca...karmādhiṣṭhānaṃ ca kleśādhiṣṭhānaṃ ca...kālādhiṣṭhānaṃ ca...praṇidhānādhiṣṭhānaṃ ca...pūjādhiṣṭhānaṃ ca...caryādhiṣṭhānaṃ ca...kalpādhiṣṭhānaṃ ca...jñānādhiṣṭhānaṃ ca prajānāti | sa yānīmāni tathāgatānāmarhatāṃ samyaksaṃbuddhānāṃ sūkṣmapraveśajñānāni yaduta caryāsūkṣmapraveśajñānaṃ vā, cyutyupapattisukṣmapraveśajñānaṃ vā, janmasūkṣmapraveśajñānaṃ vā, abhiniṣkramaṇasūkṣmapraveśajñānaṃ vā, abhisaṃbodhisūkṣmapraveśajñānaṃ vā, vikurvaṇasukṣmapraveśa-

jñānaṃ vā, dharmacakrapravartanasūkṣmapraveśajñānaṃ vā, dharmadeśanāsukṣmapraveśajñāna vā, dharmavistarasūkṣmapraveśajñānaṃ vā, āyuḥpramāṇādhiṣṭhānajñānaṃ vā, varṇarūpakāyasaṃdarśanajñānaṃ vā, sarvasattvavinayātikramaṇajñānaṃ vā, sarvalokadhātuspharaṇajñānaṃ vā, sarvasattvacittacaritavyavalokanajñānaṃ vā, ekakṣaṇe tryadhvavyavalokanajñānaṃ vā, pūrvāntāparāntaniravaśeṣajñānaṃ vā, sarvasattvacittacaritanānātvasamantajñānaṃ vā, tathāgatabalavaiśāradyabuddhadharmācint ya-
jñānaṃ vā, tathāgataparinirvāṇajñānaṃ vā, śāsanādhiṣṭhānasaddharmasthitijñānaṃ vā, evaṃpramukhānyaprameyāsaṃkhyeyāni tathāgatānāṃ sukṣmapraveśajñānāni, tāni sarvāṇi yathābhūtaṃ prajānāti | sa yānīmāni tathāgatānāmarhatāṃ samyaksaṃbuddhānāṃ guhyasthānāni yaduta kāyaguhyaṃ vā vāgguhyaṃ vā cittaguhyaṃ vā kālākālavicāraṇāguhyaṃ vā bodhisattvavyākaraṇaguhyaṃ vā sattvasaṃgrahanigrahaguhyaṃ vā vineyotsādanāvasānaguhyaṃ vā yathākālāvavādānuśāsanādhyupekṣaṇaṃ vā yānanānātvavyavasthāpanaguhyaṃ vā sattvacaryendriyavibhaktiguhyaṃ vā sattvakarmakriyāvatāraguhyaṃ vā bodhisattvacaryendriyavibhaktiguhyaṃ vā caryābhisaṃbodhisvabhāvaprabhāvānubodhiguhyaṃ vā svabhāvābhisaṃbodhyadhiṣṭhānaguhyaṃ vā avatārottāraṇaguhyaṃ vā ākarṣaṇasaṃpreṣaṇaguhyaṃ vā sthānacaṃkramaṇaniṣadyāśayyāsanasaṃdarśanaguhyaṃ vā āhāraparibhogakāyopakaraṇapratisevanaguhyaṃ vā bhāṣitatūṣṇīṃbhāvadhyānavimokṣasamādhisamāpattisaṃdarśanaguhyaṃ vā, evaṃpramukhānyaprameyāsaṃkhyeyāni tathāgatānāṃ guhyasthānāni, tāni sarvāṇi yathābhūtaṃ prajānāti | sa yānīmāni tathāgatānāṃ kalpapraveśasamavasaraṇajñānāni yaduta ekakalpāsaṃkhyeyakalpasamavasaraṇatā | asaṃkhyeyakalpaikakalpasamavasaraṇatā | saṃkhyeyakalpāsaṃkhyeyakalpasamavasaraṇatā | asaṃkhyeyakalpasaṃkhyeyakalpasamavasaraṇatā | cittakṣaṇakalpasamavasaraṇatā | kalpacittakṣaṇasamavasaraṇatā | kalpākalpasamavasaraṇatā | akalpakalpasamavasaraṇatā | sabuddhakakalpābuddhakakalpasamavasaraṇatā | abuddhakakalpasabuddhakakalpasamavasaraṇatā | atītānāgatakalpapratyutpannakalpasamavasaraṇatā | pratyutpannakalpātītānāgatakalpasamavasaraṇatā | atītakalpānāgatakalpasamavasaraṇatā | anāgatakalpātītakalpasamavasaraṇatā | dīrgha-

kalpahrasvakalpasamavasaraṇatā | hrasvakalpadīrghakalpasamavasaraṇatā | sarvakalpeṣu saṃjñākṛtasamavasaraṇatā | sarvasaṃjñākṛteṣu kalpasamavasaraṇatā | evaṃ pramukhānyaprameyāṇyasaṃkhyeyāni kalpapraveśasamavasaraṇāni, tāni sarvāni yathābhūtaṃ prajānāti | sa yānīmāni tathāgatānāmarhatāṃ samyaksaṃbuddhānāmavatārajñānāni yaduta vālapathāvatārajñānaṃ vā paramāṇurajovatārajñānaṃ vā buddhakṣetrakāyābhisaṃbodhyavatārajñānaṃ vā sattvakāyacittābhisaṃbodhyavatārajñānaṃ vā sarvatrānugatābhisaṃbodhyavatārajñānaṃ vā vyatyastacarisaṃdarśanāvatārajñānaṃ vā anulomacarisaṃdarśanāvatārajñānaṃ vā pratilomacarisaṃdarśanāvatārajñānaṃ cintyācintyalokavijñeyavijñeyaṃ carisaṃdarśanāvatārajñānaṃ vā śrāvakavijñeyapratyekabuddhavijñeyabodhisattvavijñeyatathāgatavijñeyacarisaṃdarśanāvat ārajñānaṃ vā, tāni sarvāṇi yathābhūtaṃ prajānāti | iti hi bho jinaputrā aprameyaṃ buddhānāṃ bhagavatāṃ jñānavaipulyamapramāṇamevāsyāṃ bhūmau sthitasya bodhisattvasyāvatārajñānam ||

G

sa khalu punarbho jinaputrā bodhisattva evamimāṃ bodhisattvabhūmimanugato'cintyaṃ ca nāma bodhisattvavimokṣaṃ pratilabhate | anāvaraṇaṃ ca nāma viśuddhivicayaṃ ca nāma samantamukhāvabhāsaṃ ca nāma tathāgatakośaṃ ca nāma apratihatacakrānugataṃ ca nāma tryadhvānugataṃ ca nāma dharmadhātugarbhaṃ ca nāma vimuktimaṇḍalaprabhāsaṃ ca nāma aśeṣaviṣayagamaṃ ca nāma bodhisattvavimokṣaṃ pratilabhate | iti hi bho jinaputrā imān daśa bodhisattvavimokṣān pramukhān kṛtvā aprameyāsaṃkhyeyāni bodhisattvavimokṣamukhaśatasahasrāṇi bodhisattvo'syāṃ daśamyāṃ bodhisattvabhūmau pratiṣṭhitaḥ pratilabhate | evaṃ yāvatsamādhiśatasahasrāṇi dhāraṇīśatasahasrāṇi abhijñābhinirhāraśatasahasrāṇi pratilabhate | jñānālokaśatasahasrāṇi vikurvaṇaśatasahasrāṇi prasaṃvinnirhāraśatasahasrāṇi upāyaprajñāvikrīḍitaśatasahasrāṇi gambhīradharmanayapraveśaśatasahasrāṇi mahākaruṇāvegaśatasahasrāṇi bodhisattvavaśitāpraveśaśatasahasrāṇi pratilabhate ||

H

sa evaṃjñānānugatayā buddhyā apramāṇānugatena smṛtikauśalyena samanvāgato bhavati | sa daśabhyo digbhyo'prameyāṇāṃ buddhānāṃ bhagavatāṃ sakāśādekakṣaṇalavamuhūrtenā apramāṇān mahādharmāvabhāsān mahādharmālokān mahādharmameghān sahate saṃpratīcchati svīkaroti saṃghārayati I tadyathāpi nāma bho jinaputrāḥ sāgaranāgarājameghavisṛṣṭo mahānapskandho na sukaro'nyena pṛthivīpradeśena soḍhuṃ vā saṃpratyeṣituṃ vā svīkartuṃ vā saṃdhārayituṃ vā anyatra mahāsamudrāt, evameva bho jinaputrā ye te tathāgatānāṃ bhagavatāṃ guhyānupraveśā yaduta mahādharmāvabhāsā mahādharmālokā mahādharmāmeghāḥ, te na sukarāḥ sarvasattvaiḥ sarvaśrāvakapratyekabuddhaiḥ prathamāṃ bhūmimupādāya yāvannavamībhūmipratiṣṭhitairapi bodhisattvaiḥ, tān bodhisattvo'syāṃ dharmameghāyāṃ bodhisattvabhūmau sthitaḥ sarvān sahate saṃpratīcchati svīkaroti saṃdhārayati I tadyathāpi nāma bho jinaputrā mahāsamudra ekasyāpi mahābhujagendrasya mahāmeghān sahate...dvayorapi trayāṇāmapi yāvadaparimānāṇāmapi bhujagendrāṇāmekakṣaṇalavamuhūrtenāprameyān mahāmeghān sahate... I tatkasya hetoḥ? apramāṇavipulavistīrṇatvānmahāsamudrasya I evameva bho jinaputrā asyāṃ dharmameghāyām bodhisattvabhūmau pratiṣṭhito bodhisattva ekasyāpi tathāgatasya sakāśādekakṣaṇa...dvayorapi trayānāmapi yāvadaparimānāṇāmapi tathāgatānāṃ sakāśādekakṣaṇa... I tata ucyata iyaṃ bhūmirdharmamegheti I I

vimukticandro bodhisattva āha - śakyaṃ punarbho jinaputra saṃkhyāṃ kartuṃ kiyatāṃ tathāgatānāmantikebhyo bodhisattvaikakṣaṇa...? vajragarbho bodhisattva āha - na sukarā bho jinaputra saṃkhyā kartu gaṇanānirdeśena - iyatāṃ tathāgatānāmantikebhyo bodhisattvaikakṣaṇa... I api tu khalvaupamyaṃ kariṣyāmi I tadyathāpi nāma bho jinaputra daśasu dikṣu daśabuddhakṣetrānabhilāpyakoṭiniyutaśatasahasraparamāṇurajaḥsamāsu lokadhātuṣu yāvat sattvadhātuniravaśeṣayogena saṃvidyate I tata ekaḥ sattvaḥ śrutagrahaṇadhāraṇīpratilabdho bhavettathāgatānāmupasthāuyako mahāśrāvako›gryaḥ śrutadharāṇām I tadyathāpi nāma bhagavato vajrapadmottarasya tathāgatasyārhataḥ samyaksaṃbuddhasya mahāvijayo nāma bhikṣurevaṃrūpeṇa śrutakauśalyabalādhānena sa ekaḥ sattvaḥ samanvāgato bhavet I yathā ca sa ekaḥ sattvastathā niravaśeṣāsu sarvāsu lokadhātuṣu te sarve sattvāḥ samanvāgatā bhaveyuḥ I yaccaikenodgṛhītaṃ syānna dvitīyena I tatkiṃ manyase bho jinaputra bahutaraṃ teṣāmaprameyāpramāṇaṃ vā śrutakauśalyaṃ bhavet? vimukticandro bodhisattva āha - bahu bho jinaputra apramāṇaṃ tatteṣāṃ sarvasattvānāṃ śrutakauśalyaṃ bhavet I vajragarbho bodhisattva āha - ārocayāmi te bho jinaputra, prativedayāmi I yaṃ dharmameghāyāṃ bodhisattvabhūmau pratiṣṭhito bodhisattva ekakṣaṇalavamuhūrtenaikasyaiva tāvattathāgatasya sakāśāddharmadhātutryadhvakośaṃ nāma mahādharmāvabhāsālokameghaṃ sahate... I yasya mahādharmāvabhāsālokamegha-saṃdhāraṇakauśalyasya tat pūrvakaṃ śrutakauśalyaṃ...kṣamate I yathā caikasya tathāgatasya sakāśāttathā daśasu dikṣu yāvanti tāsu pūrvikāsu lokadhātuṣu paramāṇurajāṃsi saṃvidyante, tāvatāṃ samyaksaṃbuddhānāṃ tato›pi bhūya uttari aprameyāṇāṃ tathāgatānāṃ sakāśādekakṣaṇalavamuhūrtena dharmadhātutryadhvakośaṃ nāma mahādharmāvabhāsālokameghaṃ sahate... I tata ucyata iyaṃ bhūmirdharmamegheti I I

punaraparaṃ bho jinaputra dharmameghāyāṃ bodhisattvabhūmau pratiṣṭhito bodhisattvaḥ svapraṇidhānabalādhānato mahākṛpākaruṇāmeghaṃ samutthāpya mahādharmāvabhāsagarjanamabhijñāvidyāvaiśāradyavidyudvidyotitaṃ mahāraśmimārutasamīritaṃ mahāpuṇyajñānaghanābhrajālasaṃdarśanaṃ vividhakāyaghanāvarta-saṃdarśanaṃ mahādharmanirnādanaṃ namuciparṣadvidrāvaṇam-ekakṣaṇalavamuhūrtena daśasu dikṣu yāvanti tāsu lokadhātuṣu tāni paramāṇurajāṃsi saṃvidyante tāvanti lokadhātukoṭinayutaśata-sahasrāṇi spharitvā tebhyo'pi bhūyo'prameyāṇi lokadhātukoṭinayutaśatasahasrāṇi spharitvā mahāmṛtakuśaladhārābhipravarṣaṇena yathāśayataḥ sattvānāmajñānasamutthitāḥ sarvakleśarajojvālāḥ praśamayati I tata ucyata iyaṃ bhūmirdharmamegheti I I

punaraparaṃ bho jinaputra dharmameghāyāṃ bodhisattva ekasyāmapi lokadhātau tuṣitavarabhavanavāsamupādāya cyavanācaṃkramaṇagarbhasthitijanmābhiniṣkramaṇābhisaṃbodhyadhyeṣaṇamahādharmacakrapravartana-mahāparinirvāṇabhūmiriti sarvatathāgatakāryamadhitiṣṭhati yathāśayeṣu sattveṣu yathāvaineyikeṣu, evaṃ dvayorapi yāvadyāvanti tāsu lokadhātuṣu paramāṇurajāṃsi saṃvidyante, tato'pi bhūyo'prameyeṣu lokadhātukoṭiniyutaśata-sahasreṣu tāni paramāṇu... vaineyikeṣu I I

I

sa evaṃjñānavaśitāprāptaḥ suviniścitamahājñānābhijña ākāṅkṣan saṃkliṣṭāyā lokadhātoḥ pariśuddhatāmadhitiṣṭhati I pariśuddhāyā lokadhātoḥ saṃkliṣṭatāmadhitiṣṭhati I saṃkṣiptāyā lokadhātorvistīrṇatāmadhitiṣṭhati I vistīrṇāyāḥ saṃkṣiptatāmadhitiṣṭhati I evaṃ vipulamahadgatāpramāṇasūkṣmaudārikavyatyastāvamūrdhamatalādīnāṃ sarvalokadhātūnāṃ vṛṣabhatayānantam-abhinirhāramadhitiṣṭhati I ākāṅkṣan ekasmin paramāṇurajasyekām-api lokadhātuṃ sarvāvatīṃ sacakravālaparikhāmadhitiṣṭhati I tacca paramāṇurajo na vardhayati tāṃ ca kriyāmādarśayati I dve'pi tisro-'pi catasro'pi pañcāpi yāvadanabhilāpyāpi lokadhāturekasmin paramāṇurajasi sarvāḥ sacakravālaparikhā adhitiṣṭhati I ākāṅkṣan ekasyāṃ lokadhātau dvilokadhātuvyūhamādarśayati I ākāṅkṣan yāvadanabhilāpyalokadhātuvyūhamādarśayati I ākāṅkṣan ekalokadhātuvyūhaṃ dvayorlokadhātvorādarśayati I yāvadanabhilāpyāsu lokadhātuṣvādarśayati I ākāṅkṣan yāvadanabhilāpyāsu lokadhātuṣu yaḥ sattvadhātustamekasyāṃ lokadhātau saṃdadhāti, na ca sattvān viheṭhayati I ākāṅkṣan ekasyāṃ lokadhātau yāvān sattvadhātustamanabhilāpyāsu lokadhātuṣu saṃdadhāti... I ākāṅkṣan anabhilāpyalokadhātugatān sattvānekavālapathe saṃdadhāti... I ākāṅkṣan ekavālapathe ekaṃ sarvabuddhaviṣayavyūhamādarśayati I ākāṅkṣan yāvadanabhilāpyān sarvākārabuddhaviṣayavyūhānādarśayati I ākāṅkṣan yāvantyanabhilāpyāsu lokadhātuṣu paramāṇurajāṃsi tāvata ātmabhāvānekakṣaṇalavamuhūrtena nirmimīte I ekaikasmiṃśca ātmabhāve tāvata eva pāṇīn saṃdarśayati I taiśca pāṇibhirdaśasu dikṣu buddhapūjāyāṃ prayujyate I ekaikena ca pāṇinā gaṅgānadīvālikāsamān puṣpapuṭāṃsteṣāṃ buddhānāṃ bhagavatāṃ kṣipati I yathā puṣpāṇāmevaṃ gandhānāṃ mālyānāṃ vilepanānāṃ cūrṇānāṃ cīvarāṇāṃ chatrāṇāṃ dhvajānāṃ patākānāmevaṃ sarvavyūhānām I ekaikasmiṃśca kāye tāvantyeva śirāṃsi adhitiṣṭhati I ekaikasmiṃśca śirasi tāvatīreva jihvā adhitiṣṭhati I tābhisteṣāṃ buddhānāṃ bhagavatāṃ varṇaṃ bhāṣate I cittotpāde ca daśadikpharaṇaṃ gacchāti I cittakṣaṇe cāpramāṇā abhisaṃbodhīryāvanmahāparinirvāṇāvyūhānadhitiṣṭhati I apramāṇakāyatāṃ ca trayadhvatāyāmadhitiṣṭhati I svakāye cāpramāṇānāṃ buddhānāṃ bhagavatāmaprameyān buddhakṣetraguṇavyūhān-adhitiṣṭhati I sarvalokadhātusaṃvartavivartavyūhāṃśca svakāye-

'dhitiṣṭhati I sarvā vātamaṇḍalīścaikaromakūpādutsṛjati I na ca sattvān viheṭhayati I ākāṅkṣaṃścaikāmapskandhaparyantaṃ lokadhātumadhitiṣṭhati I tasyāṃ ca mahāpadmamadhitiṣṭhati I tasya ca mahāpadmasya prabhāvabhāsavyūhena anantā lokadhātūḥ spharati I tatra ca mahābodhivṛkṣamādarśayati I yāvatsarvākāravaropetaṃ sarvajñānatvaṃ saṃdarśayati I svakāye daśadiṅmaṇividyuccandrasūryaprabhā yāvatsarvāvabhāsaprabhā adhitiṣṭhati I ekamukhavātena caikaikasyā diśaḥ pratidiśamanantā lokadhātūḥ kampayati, na ca sattvānuttrāsayati I daśadiśaṃ ca vātasaṃvartanīṃ tejaḥsaṃvartanīmapsaṃvartanīmadhitiṣṭhati I sarvasattvāṃśca ākāṅkṣan yathābhiprāyaṃ rūpāśrayālaṃkṛtānadhitiṣṭhati I svakāye ca tathāgatakāyamadhitiṣṭhati I tathāgatakāye ca svakāyamadhitiṣṭhati I tathāgatakāye svabuddhakṣetramadhitiṣṭhati I svabuddhakṣetre ca tathāgatakāyamadhitiṣṭhati I iti hi bho jinaputra dharmameghāyāṃ bodhisattvabhūmau pratiṣṭhito bodhisattva imāni cānyāni cāprameyāsaṃkhyeyāni ṛddhivikurvaṇakoṭinayutaśatasahasrāṇyādarśayati I I

J

atha khalu tasyāḥ parṣadaḥ keṣāṃcidbodhisattvānāṃ keṣāṃciddevanāgayakṣagandharvāsuragaruḍakinnaramahoragaśakrabrahmalokapālamaheśvaraśuddhāvāsānāmetadabhavat - yadi tāvadbodhisattvasyaivamapramāṇa ṛddhyabhisaṃskāragocaraḥ, tathāgatānāṃ punaḥ kiṃrūpo bhaviṣyatīti ? atha khalu vimukticandro bodhisattvastasyāḥ parṣadaścittāśayavicāramājñāya vajragarbhaṃ bodhisattvametadavocat - saṃśayitā bateyaṃ bho jinaputra parṣat I sādhu, asyāḥ saṃśayacchityarthaṃ kiṃcinmātraṃ bodhisattvavyūhaprātihāryaṃ saṃdarśaya I atha khalu vajragarbho bodhisattvastasyāṃ velāyāṃ sarvabuddhakṣetrakāyasvabhāvasaṃdarśanaṃ nāma bodhisattvasamādhiṃ samāpadyate I samanantarasamāpanne vajragarbhe bodhisattve sarvabuddhakṣetrakāyasvabhāvasaṃdarśanaṃ bodhisattvasamādhim, atha tāvadeva sā sarvāvatī bodhisattvaparṣat sā ca devanāgayakṣaśuddhāvāsaparṣad vajra-garbhasya bodhisattvasya kāyāntarībhūtamātmānaṃ saṃjānīte sma, tatra ca buddhakṣetramabhinirvṛtaṃ saṃjānīte sma I tasmiṃśca buddhakṣetre ye ākāravyūhāste na sukarāḥ paripūrṇayāpi kalpakoṭyā prabhāvayitum I tatra ca bodhivṛkṣaṃ daśatrisāhasraśatasahasraviṣkambhaskandhaṃ paripūrṇatrisāhasrakoṭivipulāpramāṇaviṭapodviddhaśikharaṃ tadanurūpaṃ ca tasmin bodhimaṇḍe siṃhāsanavaipulyaṃ tatra sarvābhijñāmatirājaṃ nāma tathāgataṃ bodhimaṇḍavaragataṃ samapaśyat । iti hi yāvantastatra vyūhāḥ saṃdṛśyante te na sukarāḥ paripūrṇayāpi kalpakoṭyā prabhāvayitum । sa idaṃ mahāprātihāryaṃ saṃdarśya tāṃ sarvāvatīṃ bodhisattva-parṣadaṃ tāṃ ca devanāga... śuddhāvāsaparṣadaṃ punareva yathā-sthāne sthāpayāmāsa । atha khalu sā sarvāvatī parṣadāścaryaprāptā tūṣṇīṃbhūtā tameva vajragarbhaṃ bodhisattvaṃ nidhyāyantī sthit-ābhūt । atha khalu vimukticandro bodhisattvo vajragarbhaṃ bodhi-sattvametadavocat - āścaryamidaṃ bho jinaputra, adbhutaṃ yāvad-acintyopamasya samādhernimeṣavyūhaprabhāvaḥ । tatko nāmāyaṃ bho jinaputra samādhiḥ? vajragarbho bodhisattva āha – sarva-buddhakṣetrakāyasvabhāvasaṃdarśano nāmāyaṃ bho jinaputra samādhiḥ । vimukticandro bodhisattva āha - kaḥ punarbho jinaputra asya samādhergocaraviṣayavyūhaḥ ? vajragarbho bodhisattva āha – ākāṅkṣan bho jinaputra bodhisattvo'sya samādheḥ suparibhāvita-tvādgaṅgānadīvālikāsamalokadhātuparamāṇurajaḥsamāni daśa buddhakṣetrāṇi svakāye ādarśayet, ato vā bhūya uttari । īdṛśānāṃ bho jinaputra bodhisattvasamādhīnāṃ dharmameghāyāṃ bodhi-sattvabhūmau sthito bodhisattvo bahūni śatasahasrāṇi pratilabhate । tena tasya bodhisattvasya yāvad yauvarājyaprāptairapi bodhi-sattvaiḥ sādhumatībodhisattvabhūmau pratiṣṭhitairna sukaraḥ kāyaḥ kāyakarma vā jñātum । na sukarā vāgvākkarma vā jñātum । na sukaraṃ mano manaskarma vā jñātum । na sukararddhirjñātum । na sukaraṃ tryadhvavilokitaṃ jñātum । na sukaraḥ samādhigocarānu-praveśo jñātum । na sukaro jñānaviṣayo jñātum । na sukaraṃ vimokṣavikrīḍitaṃ jñātum । na sukaraṃ nirmāṇakarma vā adhi-ṣṭhānakarma vā prabhākarma vā prabhākarma vā jñātum । na sukaraṃ yāvatsamāsataḥ kramotkṣepanikṣepakarmāpi jñātum । yāvat yauvarājya... । evamapramāṇā bho jinaputra iyaṃ dharma-meghā bodhisattvabhūmiḥ samāsanirdeśataḥ । vistaraśaḥ punar-asaṃkhyeyakalpaśatasahasranirdeśāparyantākārato draṣṭavyā ।।

vimukticandro bodhisattva āha - kidṛśo bho jinaputra tathāgata-gocaraviṣayapraveśo yatredaṃ bodhisattvānāṃ caryāviṣayādhi-ṣṭhānamevamaopramāṇam? vajragarbho bodhisattva āha – tadyath-āpi nāma syādbho jinaputra kaścideva puruṣaścaturdvīpikāyā loka-dhātordvau trīn vā kolāsthimātrān pāṣāṇān gṛhitvaivaṃ vadet –

kiyatī nu khalu sā pṛthivīdhāturaparyantāsu lokadhātuṣu itaḥ pāṣāṇebhyo mahadgatatayā vā pramāṇatveneti? īdṛśamidaṃ mama tvadvacanaṃ pratibhāti ǀ yastvamapramāṇajñāninām tathāgatānāmarhatāṃ samyaksaṃbuddhānāṃ dharmatāṃ bodhisattvadharmatayā tulayasi ǀ api tu khalu punarbho jinaputra yathā cāturdvīpikāyā lokadhātoḥ parīttā pṛthivīdhāturyā udgṛhītāpramāṇāvaśiṣṭā, evameva bho jinaputra asyā eva tāvaddharmameghāyā bodhisattvabhūmerapremeyān kalpānnirdiśyamānāyāḥ pradeśamātraṃ nirdiṣṭaṃ syāt, kaḥ punarvādastathāgatabhūmeḥ ǀ ārocayāmi te bho jinaputra, prativedayāmi ǀ ayaṃ me tathāgataḥ purataḥ sthitaḥ sākṣībhūtaḥ ǀ sacedbho jinaputra daśasu dikṣu ekaikasyāṃ diśi aparyantalokadhātuparamāṇurajaḥsamāni buddhakṣetrāṇyevaṃbhūmiprāptairbodhisattvaiḥ pūrṇāni bhaveyuryathekṣuvanaṃ vā naḍavanaṃ vā veṇuvanaṃ vā tilavanaṃ vā śālivanaṃ va, teṣāmaparyantakalpābhinirhṛto bodhisattvacaryābhinirhāratathāgatasyaikakṣaṇajñānaprasṛtasya tathāgataviṣayasya... ǀ iti hi bho jinaputra evaṃjñānānugato bodhisattvastathāgatādvayakāyavākcitto bodhisattvasamādhibalaṃ ca notsṛjati buddhadarśanapūjopasthānaṃ ca karoti ǀ sa ekaikasmin kalpe'paryantāṃstathāgatān sarvākārābhinirhārapūjābhiḥ pūjayati ǀ audārikānugatayā pūjayā teṣāṃ ca buddhānāṃ bhagavatāmadhiṣṭhānāvabhāsaṃ saṃpratīcchati ǀ sa bhūyasyā mātrayā asaṃhāryo bhavati dharmadhātuvibhaktiparipṛcchānirdeśaiḥ ǀ anekān kalpānanekāni kalpaśatāni...anekāni kalpakoṭinayutaśatasahasrāṇi ǀ tadyathāpi nāma bho jinaputra divyakarmārakṛtaṃ mahābharaṇopacāraṃ mahāmaṇiratnapratyuptaṃ vaśavartino devarājasyottamāṅge kaṇṭhe vā āvaddhamasaṃhāryaṃ bhavati tadanyairdivyamānuṣyakairābharaṇavibhūṣaṇopacāraiḥ, evameva bho jinaputra bodhisattvasyemāṃ daśamīṃ dharmameghāṃ bhodhisattvabhūmimanuprāptasya te bodhisattvajñanopacārā asaṃhāryā bhavanti sarvasattvaiḥ sarvaśrāvakapratyekabuddhaiḥ prathamāṃ bodhisattvabhūmimupādāya yāvannavamīṃ bodhisattvabhūmimanuprāptairbodhisattvaiḥ ǀ asyāṃ ca bodhisattvabhūmau sthitasya bodhisattvasya jñānavabhāsaḥ sattvānāṃ yāvatsarvajñajñānāvatārāya saṃvartate›saṃhāryastadanyairjñānāvabhāsaiḥ ǀ tadyathāpi nāma bho jinaputra maheśvarasya devarājasyābhā atikrāntā bhavati sarvopapattyāyatanāni, sattvānāṃ ca kāyāśrayān prahlādayati, evameva bho jinaputra bodhisattvasya asyāṃ daśabhyāṃ dharmameghāyāṃ bodhisattvabhūmau sthitasya jñānābhā asaṃhāryā bhavati sarvaśrāvakapratyekabuddhaiḥ prathamāṃ bodhisattvabhūmimupādāya yāvannavamībodhisattvabhūmipratiṣṭhitairbodhisattvairyāvatsarvajñajñānadharmatāyāṃ ca sattvān pratiṣṭhāpayati । sa khalu punarbho jinaputra bodhisattva evaṃjñānānugato buddhairbhagavadbhistryadhvajñānaṃ ca saṃśrāvyate । dharmadhātuprabhedajñānaṃ ca sarvalokadhātuspharaṇaṃ ca sarvalokadhātvavabhāsādhiṣṭhānaṃ ca sarvasattvakṣetradharmaparijñānaṃ ca sarvasattvacittacaritānupraveśajñānaṃ ca sarvasattvayathākālaparipākajñānaṃ ca vinayānatikramaṇaṃ ca sarvadharmapravicayavibhaktijñānakauśalyaṃ ca samāsato yāvatsarvajñajñānāpramāṇatāṃ ca saṃśrāvyate । tasya daśabhyaḥ pāramitābhyo jñānapāramitā atiriktatamā bhavati, na ca pariśeṣāsu na samudāgacchati yathābalaṃ yathābhajamānam । iyaṃ bho jinaputra bodhisattvasya dharmameghā nāma daśamī bodhisattvabhūmiḥ samāsanirdeśataḥ । vistaraśaḥ punarasaṃkhyeyāparyantakalpanirdeśaniṣṭhāto'nugantavyā । yasyāṃ pratiṣṭhito bodhisattvo bhūyastvena maheśvaro bhavati devarājaḥ kṛtī prabhuḥ sattvānāṃ sarvaśrāvakapratyekabuddhabodhisattvapāramitopadeśeṣvasaṃhār yo dharmadhātuvibhaktiparipṛcchānirdeśaiḥ । yacca kiṃcit... ।।

dharmameghā nāma bodhisattvabhūmirdaśamī ।।

[Beginning of tenth bhūmi's final gathas]

upasaṃhāragāthāḥ ।

śamadamaniratānāṃ śāntadāntāśayānāṃ
khagapathasadṛśānāmantarīkṣasamānām ।
khilamanavidhutānāṃ mārgajñāne sthitānāṃ
śṛṇuta cariviśeṣān bodhisattvāna śreṣṭhān ।। 17 ।।

kuśalaśatasahasraṃ saṃciyā kalpakoṭyā
buddhaśatasahasrān pūjayitvā maharṣīn ।
pratyayajinavaśīṃścāpūjayitvā anantān
sarvajagatahitāyā jāyate bodhicittam ।। 18 ।।

vratatapatapitānāṃ kṣāntipāraṃgatānāṃ
hiriśiricaritānāṃ puṇyajñānodgatānām ।
vipulagatimatīnāṃ buddhajñānāśayānāṃ
daśabalasamatulyaṃ jāyate bodhicittam ।। 19 ।।

yāva jina triyadhvā pūjanārthāya pūjaṃ
khagapathapariṇāmaṃ śodhanaṃ sarvakṣetram ।
samyaganugatārthe yāvatā sarvadharmān
mokṣa jagata arthe jāyate bodhicittam ।। 20 ।।

pramuditasamutīnāṃ dānadharmāratānāṃ
sakalajagahitārthe nityamevodyatānām ।
jinaguṇaniratānāṃ sattvarakṣāvratānāṃ
tribhuvanahitakārye jāyate bodhicittam ।। 21 ।।

akuśalaviratānāṃ śuddhaśīlāvratānāṃ
vrataniyamaratānāṃ śāntasaumyendriyāṇām ।
jinaśaraṇagatānāṃ bodhicaryāśayānāṃ
tribhuvanahitasādhyaṃ jāyate bodhicittam ।। 22 ।।

anugatakuśalānāṃ kṣāntisauratyabhājāṃ
viditaguṇarasānāṃ tyaktamānotsavānām ।

nihitaśubhamatīnāṃ dāntusaumyāśayānāṃ
sakalahitavidhāne jāyate bodhicittam | | 23 | |

pracalitaśubhakāryā dhīravīryotsahā ye
nikhilajanahitārthe prodyayāmāna siṃhāḥ |
avirataguṇasādhyā nirjitakleśasaṃghā
jhaṭiti manasi teṣāṃ jāyate bodhicittam | | 24 | |

susamavahitacittā dhvastamohāndhakārā
vigalitamadamānā tyaktasaṃkliṣṭamārgāḥ |
śamasukhaniratā ye tyaktasaṃsārasaṅgā
jhaṭiti manasi teṣāṃ jāyate bodhicittam | | 25 | |

vimalakhasamacittā jñānavijñānavijñā
nihatanamucimārā vāntakleśābhimānāḥ |
jinapadaśaraṇasthā labdhatattvārthakā ye
sapadi manasi teṣāṃ jāyate bodhicittam | | 26 | |

tribhuvanaśivasādhyopāyavijñānadhīrāḥ
kalibalaparihāropāyavidyarddhimantaḥ |
sugataguṇasamīhā ye ca puṇyānurāgāḥ
sapadi manasi teṣāṃ jāyate bodhicittam | | 27 | |

tribhuvanahitakāmā bodhisaṃbhārapūrye
praṇihitamanasā ye duṣkare'pi caranti |
aviratаśubhakarmaprodyatā bodhisattvāḥ
sapadi manasi teṣāṃ jāyate bodhicittam | | 28 | |

daśabalaguṇakāmā bodhicaryānuraktā
vijitakalibalaughāstyaktamānānuṣaṅgāḥ |
anugataśubhamārgā labdhadharmārthakāmā
jhaṭiti manasi teṣāṃ jāyate bodhicittam | | 29 | |

iti gaṇitaguṇāṃśā bodhicaryāścarantu
jinapadapraṇidhānāḥ satsamṛddhiṃ labhantu |
triguṇapariviśuddhā bodhicittaṃ labhantu
triśaraṇapariśuddhā bodhisattvā bhavantu | | 30 | |

daśa pāramitāḥ pūrya daśabhūmīśvaro bhavet I
bhūyo'pi kathyate hyetacchruṇutaivaṃ samāsataḥ I I 31 I I

bodhicittaṃ yadāsādya saṃpradānaṃ karoti yaḥ I
tadā pramuditāṃ prāpto jambūdvīpeśvaro bhavet I I 32 I I

tatrasthaḥ pālayan sattvān yathecchāpratipādanaiḥ I
svayaṃ dāne pratiṣṭhitvā parāṃścāpi niyojayet I I 33 I I

sarvān bodhau pratiṣṭhāpya saṃpūrṇā dānapāragaḥ I
etaddharmānubhāvena saṃvaraṃ samupācaret I I 34 I I

samyakśīlaṃ samādhāya saṃvarakuśalī bhavet I
tataḥ sa vimalāṃ prāptaścāturdvīpeśvaro bhavet I I 35 I I

tatrasthaḥ pālayan sattvān akuśalanivāraṇaiḥ I
svayaṃ śīle pratiṣṭhitvā parāṃścāpi niyojayet I I 36 I I

sarvān bodhau pratiṣṭhāpya saṃpūrṇaśīlapāragaḥ I
etaddharmavipākena kṣāntivratamupāśrayet I I 37 I I

samyakkṣāntivrataṃ dhṛtvā kṣāntibhṛtkuśalī bhavet I
tataḥ prabhākarīprāptastrayastriṃśādhipo bhavet I I 38 I I

tatrasthaḥ pālayan sattvān kleśamārganivāraṇaiḥ I
svayaṃ kṣāntivrate sthitvā parāṃścāpi niyojayet I I 39 I I

sattvān bodhau pratiṣṭhāpya kṣāntipāraṃgato bhavet I
etatpuṇyavipākaiḥ sa vīryavratamupāśrayet I I 40 I I

samyagvīryaṃ samādhāya vīryabhṛt kuśalī bhavet I
tataścārciṣmatīprāptaḥ suyāmādhipatirbhavet I I 41 I I

tatrasthaḥ pālayan sattvān kudṛṣṭisaṃnivāraṇaiḥ I
samyagdṛṣṭau pratiṣṭhāpya bodhayitvā prayatnataḥ I I 42 I I

svayaṃ vīryavrate sthitvā parāṃścāpi niyojayet |
sarvān bodhau pratiṣṭhāpya vīryapāraṃgato bhavet || 43 ||

etatpuṇyavipākaiśca dhyānavrataṃ samāśrayet |
sarvakleśān vinirjitya samādhisuṣṭhito bhavet || 44 ||

samyag dhyānaṃ samādhāya samādhikuśalī bhavet |
tataḥ sudurjayāprāptaḥ saṃtuṣitādhipo bhavet || 45 ||

tatrasthaḥ pālayan sattvān tīrthyamārganivāraṇaiḥ |
satyadharmaṃ pratiṣṭhāpya bodhayitvā prayatnataḥ || 46 ||

svayaṃ dhyānavrate sthitvā parāṃścāpi niyojayet |
sarvān bodhau pratiṣṭhāpya dhyānapāraṃgato bhavet || 47 ||

etatpuṇyavipākaiśca prajñāvratamupāśrayet |
sarvamārān vinirjitya prajñābhijñasamṛddhimān || 48 ||

samyakprajñāṃ samādhāya svabhijñākuśalī bhavet |
tataścābhimukhīprāptaḥ sunirmitādhipo bhavet || 49 ||

tatrasthaḥ pālayan sattvān abhimānanivāraṇaiḥ |
śūnyatāsu pratiṣṭhāpya bodhayitvā prayatnataḥ || 50 ||

svayaṃ prajñāvrate sthitvā parāṃścāpi niyojayet |
sarvān bodhau pratiṣṭhāpya prajñāpāraṃgato bhavet || 51 ||

etatpuṇyavipākaiśca sa supāyavrataṃ caret |
sarvaduṣṭān vinirjitya saddharmakuśalī bhavet || 52 ||

sa supāyavidhānena sattvān bodhau niyojayet |
tato dūraṃgamāprāpto vaśavartīśvaro bhavet || 53 ||

tatrasthaḥ pālayan sattvānabhisamayabodhanaiḥ |
bodhisattvaniyāmeṣu pratiṣṭhāpya prabodhayan || 54 ||

tatropāye svayaṃ sthitvā parāṃścāpi niyojayet |

sarvān bodhau pratiṣṭhāpya hyupāyapārago bhavet | | 55 | |

etatpuṇyānubhāvaiśca supraṇidhimupāśrayet |
mithyādṛṣṭiṃ vinirjitya samyagdṛṣṭikṛtī budhaḥ | | 56 | |

supraṇihitacittena samyagbodhau pratiṣṭhitaḥ |
tataścāpyacalāprāpto brahmā sāhasrikādhipaḥ | | 57 | |

tatrasthaḥ pālayan sattvān triyānasaṃpraveśanaiḥ |
lokadhātuparijñāne pratiṣṭhāpya prabodhayan | | 58 | |

supraṇidhau svayaṃ sthitvā parāṃścāpi niyojayet |
sarvān bodhau pratiṣṭhāpya praṇidhipārago bhavet | | 59 | |

etatpuṇyānusāraiśca balavratamupāśrayet |
sarvaduṣṭān vinirjitya saṃbodhau kṛtaniścayaḥ | | 60 | |

samyagbalasamutsāhaiḥ sarvatīrthyān vinirjayet |
tataḥ sādhumatīprāpto mahābrahmā bhavet kṛtī | | 61 | |

tatrasthaḥ pālayan sattvān buddhayānopadarśanaiḥ |
sattvāśayaparijñāne pratiṣṭhāpya prabodhayan | | 62 | |

svayaṃ bale pratiṣṭhitvā paraṃścāpi niyojayet |
sarvān bodhau pratiṣṭhāpya balapāraṃgato bhavet | | 63 | |

etatpuṇyavipākaiśca jñānavratamupāśrayet |
caturmārān vinirjitya bodhisattvo guṇākaraḥ | | 64 | |

samyag jñānaṃ samāsādya saddharmakuśalī bhavet |
dharmameghāṃ tataḥ prāpto maheśvaro bhavet kṛtī | | 65 | |

tatrasthaḥ pālayan sattvān sarvākārānubodhanaiḥ |
sarvākāravare jñāne pratiṣṭhāpya prabodhayan | | 66 | |

svayaṃ jñāne pratiṣṭhitvā parāṃścāpi niyojayet |
sarvān bodhau pratiṣṭhāpya jñānapāraṃgato bhavet | | 67 | |

etatpuṇyānubhāvaiśca daśabhūmīśvaro jinaḥ ।
sarvākāraguṇādhāraḥ sarvajño dharmarāḍ bhavet ।। 68 ।।

iti matvā bhavadbhiśca saṃbodhipadalabdhaye ।
daśapāramitāpūryai caritavyaṃ samāhitaiḥ ।। 69 ।।

tathā bodhiṃ śivāṃ prāpya caturmārān vijitya ca ।
sarvān bodhau pratiṣṭhāpya nirvṛtiṃ samavāpsyatha ।। 70 ।।

etatcchrutvā parijñāya caradhvaṃ bodhisādhane ।
nirvighnaṃ bodhimāsādya labhadhvaṃ saugatāṃ gatim ।। 71 ।।

[End of tenth bhūmi's final gathas]

[Beginning of parīndanāparivartaḥ's gathas]

11 parīndanāparivartaḥ |

upakramaḥ |

etāstāḥ khalu punarbho jinaputrā daśa bodhisattvabhūmayaḥ samāsato nirdiṣṭāḥ sarvākāravaropetasarvajñajñānānugatā draṣṭavyāḥ | tasyāṃ velāyāmayaṃ trisāhasramahāsāhasro lokadhātuḥ ṣaḍvikāraṃ prākampat | vividhāni ca puṣpāṇi viyato nyapatan | divyamānuṣyakāni ca tūryāṇi saṃpravāditānyabhūvan | anumodanāśabdena ca yāvadakaniṣṭhabhuvanaṃ vijñaptamabhūt ||

atha tasmin samaye bhagavāṃstān vimukticandrapramukhān sarvān bodhisattvānāmantrya evamādiśat - imāmahaṃ mārṣā asaṃkhyeyakalpakoṭīnayutaśatasahasrasamudānītāmanuttarāṃ samyaksaṃbodhiṃ yuṣmākaṃ haste parindāmi anuparindāmi paramayā parindanayā | tadyūyaṃ sarve svayaṃ caivamimaṃ dharmaparyāyaṃ dhārayata, parebhyaśca vistareṇa saṃprakāśayata | saṃkṣepānmārṣā yadi tathāgataḥ kalpasthitikenāyuḥpramāṇena rātriṃdivamadhitiṣṭhamāno'sya dharmaparyāyasya varṇaṃ bhāṣate, naivāsya dharmaparyāyasya varṇaparyanto bhavet, na ca tathāgatapratibhānakṣayo bhavet | yathā tathāgataśīlasamādhiprajñāvimuktijñānadarśanamapramāṇamaparyantam, evameva mārṣā ya imaṃ dharmaparyāyamudgrahīṣyati dhārayiṣyati vācayiṣyati likhiṣyati likhāpayiṣyati paryavāpsyati pravartayiṣyati, parṣanmadhye ca vistareṇa saṃprakāśayiṣyati - anena cittena kathamamī sattvā evamudāradharmasya lābhinaḥ syuriti śraddhayā satkṛtya śrāvayiṣyanti śroṣyanti ca yoniśo manasi bhāvayiṣyanti ca | pustakalikhitaṃ kṛtvā gṛhe dhārayiṣyati satkariṣyati gurukariṣyati mānayiṣyati pūjayiṣyati | amātsaryacittatayā asya dharmaparyāyasya varṇaṃ bhāṣitvā likhanāya vācanāya svādhyayanāya pūjanāya darśanāya dāsyati, teṣāmapi nāsti puṇyaparyantaḥ ||

atha khalu bhagavānasyaiva dharmaparyāyasya bhūyasyā mātrayā anuparindanārthaṃ tasyāṃ velāyāmimā gāthā abhāṣata –

sattvā dṛṣṭā ye mayā buddhadṛṣṭyā
te'rhantaḥ syuḥ śāriputreṇa tulyāḥ ।
tāṃ cetkaścitpūjayetkalpakoṭyā
tulyān gaṅgāvālukābhiryathaiva ।। 1 ।।

pratyekabuddhāya tu yaśca pūjāṃ
kuryādahorātramapi prahṛṣṭaḥ ।
mālyaprakāraiśca tathāmbaraiśca
tasmādayaṃ puṇyakṛto viśiṣṭaḥ ।। 2 ।।

sarve'pi pratyekajinā yadi syu-
stān pūjayet kaścidihāpramattaḥ ।
puṣpaiśca gandhaiśca vilepanaiśca
kalpānanekān śayanānnapānaiḥ ।। 3 ।।

ekasya yaścaiva tathāgatasya
kuryāt praṇāmamapi caikavāram ।
prasannacitto'tha vadennamo'rhan
tasmādidaṃ śreṣṭhataraṃ ca puṇyam ।। 4 ।।

buddhā bhaveyuryadi sarvasattvā-
stān pūjayet yaśca yathaiva pūrvam ।
divyaiśca puṣpairatha mānuṣaiśca
kalpānanekān bahubhiḥ prakāraiḥ ।। 5 ।।

yaścaiva saddharmavilopakāle
tyaktvā svakāyaṃ ca tathātmajīvam ।
dadyādahorātramidaṃ hi sūtraṃ
viśiṣyate puṇyamidaṃ hi tasmāt ।। 6 ।।

yasyepsitaṃ pūjayituṃ jinendrān
pratyekabuddhānapi śrāvakāṃśca ।
dṛḍhaṃ samutpādya sa bodhicittam
idaṃ sadā sūtravaraṃ dadātu ।। 7 ।।

rājā hyayaṃ sarvasubhāṣitānāṃ

so'bhudgataḥ sarvatathāgatānāma |
gṛhe sthitastasya tathāgataḥ sa
tiṣṭhedidaṃ yatra hi sūtraratnam || 8 ||

prabhāṃ sa prāpnoti śubhāmanantām
ekaṃ padaṃ vādi śatīhayaśca |
na vyañjanād grasyati nāpi cārthād
dadāti yaḥ sūtramidaṃ parebhyaḥ || 9 ||

anuttarāsau naranāyakānāṃ
sattvo na kaścit sadṛśo'sya vidyate |
bhavetsamudreṇa samaśca so'kṣayaḥ
śrutvā hi yo dharmamimaṃ prapadyate || 10 ||

[End of parīndanāparivartaḥ's gathas]

11 parīndanāparivartaḥ ।

A

imāstāḥ khalu punarbho jinaputrā daśa bodhisattvabhūmayaḥ samāsanirdeśato nirdiṣṭāḥ । vistaraśaḥ punaraparyantakalpa-nirdeśaniṣṭhāto'nugatavyāḥ । yā atītānāgatapratyutpannairbuddhair-bhagavadbhirbhāṣitāśca bhāṣiṣyante ca bhāṣyante ca, tāḥ khalu punarbho jinaputra, etā daśa bodhisattvabhūmayaḥ sarvākārasarva-jñajñānānugatā draṣṭavyā anupūrvābhimukhatvāt । tadyathāpi nāma bho jinaputra anavataptahradaprabhavaṃ pravahadvāri caturbhir-mahānadīsrotomukhairjambūdvīpaṃ saṃtarpya akṣayaṃ bhūyo vivṛddhamaprameyāṇāṃ sattvānāmupakārībhūtaṃ yāvanmahā-samudramarpayati, tacca vāri ādita eva mahāsāgarābhimukham, evameva bho jinaputra bodhicittamahāhradaprabhavaṃ pravahat kuśalamūlavāri mahāpraṇidhānanadīsrotomukhaiścaturbhiḥ saṃ-grahavastubhiḥ sarvasattvadhātu saṃtarpya akṣayaṃ bhūya uttari vivṛddham aprameyāṇāṃ sattvānāmupakārībhūtaṃ yāvatsarvākāra-sarvajñajñānamahāsamudramarpayati । tacca kuśalamūlavāri ādita eva sarvajñatāmahāsāgarābhimukham ।।

B

tāḥ khalu bho jinaputra etā daśa bhūmayo buddhajñānaṃ pratītya prajñāyante । tadyathāpi nāma bho jinaputra mahāpṛthivīṃ pratītya daśa mahāratnaparvatarājāḥ prajñāyante । tadyathā himavān parvatarājo gandhamādano vaidalya ṛṣigiriryugaṃdharo'śvakarṇa-girirnimiṃdharaścakravālaḥ ketumān sumeruśca mahāparvatarājaḥ । tara bho jinaputra tadyathāpi nāma himavān parvatarāja ākaraḥ sarvabhaiṣajyajātīnāmaparyantaḥ sarvabhaiṣajyajātigrahaṇatayā, evameva bho jinaputra pramuditāyāṃ bodhisattvabhūmau sthito bodhisattva ākaro bhavati sarvalaukikakāvyaśāstramantravidy-āsthānānāmaparyantaḥ sarvalaukikakāvyaśāstramantravidyopāyena । tadyathāpi nāma bho jinaputra gandhamādano mahāparvatarāja ākaraḥ sarvagandhajātīnāmaparyantaḥ sarvagandhajātigrahaṇena, evameva bho jinaputra vimalāyāṃ bodhisattvabhūmau sthito bodhi-sattva ākaro bhavati sarvabodhisattvaśīlasaṃvaracāritragandhānām-aparyantaḥ sarvabodhisattvaśīlasaṃvaracāritragandhasaṃgrahaṇena । tadyathāpi nāma bho jinaputra vaidalyo mahāparvatarājaḥ śuddho ratnamaya ākaraḥ sarvaratnajātīnāmaparyantaḥ sarvalaukikaratnajātigrahaṇena, evameva bho jinaputra prabhākaryāṃ buddhabhūmau sarvalaukikadhyānābhijñāvimokṣasamādhisamāpattīnām, aparyantaḥ sarvalaukikadhyānābhijñāvimokṣasamādhisamāpattīnām, aparyantaḥ sarvalaukikadhyānābhijñāvimokṣasamādhisamāpattiparipṛcchānirdeśaiḥ | tadyathāpi nāma bho jinaputra ṛṣigirirmahāparvatarājaḥ pañcābhijñānāmṛṣīṇāmaparyantaḥ pañcābhijñarṣigaṇanayā, evameva bho jinaputra arciṣmatyāṃ buddhabhūmau sarvamārgāmārgāntarāvatāranirdeśaviśeṣajñānānāmaparyantaḥ sarvamārgāmārgāntaraviśeṣajñānaparipṛcchānirdeśaiḥ | tadyathāpi nāma bho jinaputra yugaṃdharo mahāparvatarājaḥ sarvayakṣamaharddhikānāmaparyantaḥ sarvayakṣamaharddhikagaṇanayā, evameva bho jinaputra sudurjayāyāṃ buddhabhūmau sarvābhijñarddhivikurvaṇaprātihāryāṇāmaparyantaḥ sarvābhijñarddhivikurvaṇaprātihāryaparipṛcchānirdeśaiḥ | tadyathāpi nāma bho aśvakarṇagirirmahāparvatarājaḥ sarvaphalajātīnāmaparyantaḥ sarvaphalajātigrahaṇena, evameva bho jinaputra abhimukhyāṃ buddhabhūmau pratītyasamutpādāvatāranirdeśānāmaparyantaḥ śrāvakaphalābhisamayaparipṛcchānirdeśaiḥ | tadyathāpi nāma bho jinaputra nimiṃdharo nāma mahāparvatarājaḥ sarvanāgamaharddhikānāmaparyantaḥ sarvanāgamaharddhigaṇanayā, evameva bho jinaputra dūraṃgamāyāṃ buddhabhūmau upāyaprajñānirdeśānāmaparyantaḥ pratyekabuddhaphalābhisamayaparipṛcchāanirdeśaiḥ | tadyathāpi nāma bho jinaputra cakravālo nāma mahāparvatarājaḥ vaśībhūtānāmaparyanto vaśībhūtagaṇanayā, evameva bho jinaputra acalāyāṃ buddhabhūmau sarvabodhisattvavaśitābhinirhārāṇāmaparyanto lokadhātuvibhaktiparipṛcchānirdeśaiḥ | tadyathāpi bho jinaputra ketumān nāma mahāparvatarājaḥ asuramaharddhikānāmaparyanto'suramaharddhikagaṇanayā, evameva bho jinaputra sādhumatyāṃ buddhabhūmau sarvasattvapravṛttinivṛttijñānopacārāṇāmaparyantaḥ sarvajagatsaṃbhavavibhavaparipṛcchānirdeśaiḥ | tadyathāpi bho jinaputra sumerurmahāparvatarājaḥ sarvadevamaharddhikānāmaparyantaḥ sarvadevamaharddhikagaṇanayā, evameva bho jinaputra dharmameghāyāṃ buddhabhūmau tathāgatabalavaiśaradyāveṇikabuddhadharmāṇāmaparyanto buddhakāyasaṃdarśanaparipṛcchānirdeśaiḥ | yathā khalu punarime bho jinaputra daśa mahāratnaparvatā mahāsamudrasaṃbhūtā mahāsamudraprabhāvitāḥ, evameva bho jinaputra imā api daśa bhūmayaṃ sarvajñatāsaṃbhūtāḥ sarvajñatāprabhāvitāḥ | |

C

tadyathāpi bho jinaputra mahāsamudro daśabhirākāraiḥ saṃkhyāṃ gacchatyasaṃhāryatayā | katamairdaśabhiḥ? yaduta anupūrvanimnataśca mṛtakuṇapāsaṃvāsataśca anyavārisaṃkhyātyajanataśca ekarasataśca bahuratnataśca gambhīraduravagāhataśca vipulāpramāṇataśca mahābhūtāvāsataśca sthitavelānatikramaṇataśca sarvameghavārisaṃpratyeṣaṇātṛptitaśca, evameva bho jinaputra bodhisattvacaryā daśabhirākāraiḥ saṃkhyāṃ gacchatyasaṃhāryatayā | katamairdaśabhiḥ ? yaduta pramuditāyāṃ bodhisattvabhūmau anupūrvamahāpraṇidhānābhinirhāranimnataḥ | vimalāyāṃ bodhisattvabhūmau dauḥśīlyamṛtakuṇapāsaṃvāsataḥ | prabhākaryāṃ bodhisattvabhūmau laukikaprajñaptisaṃkhyātyāgataḥ | arciṣmatyāṃ bodhisattvabhūmau buddhabhedyaprasādaikarasataḥ | sudurjayāyāṃ bodhisattvabhūmau apramāṇopāyābhijñālokakriyābhinirhārabahuratnataḥ | abhimukhyāṃ bodhisattvabhūmau pratītyasamutpādapratyavekṣaṇaduravagāhagāmbhīryataḥ | dūraṃgamāyāṃ bodhisattvabhūmau buddhipravicayakauśalyavipulāpramāṇataḥ | acalāyāṃ bodhisattvabhūmau mahāvyūhābhinirhārasaṃdarśanamahābhūtāvāsataḥ | sādhumatyāṃ bodhisattvabhūmau gambhīravimokṣajagaccaritayathāvatprativedhasthitavelānatikramaṇ ataḥ | dharmameghāyāṃ bodhisattvabhūmau sarvatathāgatadharmāvabhāsamahāmeghavārisaṃpratyeṣaṇātṛptitaḥ | |

D

tadyathāpi bho jinaputra mahāmaṇiratnaṃ yadā daśa ratnagotrāṇyatikramya abhyutkṣiptaṃ ca bhavati kuśalakarmārasuparitāpitaṃ ca suparipiṇḍitaṃ ca supariśodhitaṃ ca suparyavadāpitaṃ ca sunirviddhaṃ ca ratnasūtrasvāviddhaṃ ca uccavaiḍūryamaṇiratnadaṇḍadhvajāgrāvaropitaṃ ca sarvāvabhāsapramuktaṃ ca rājānujñātaṃ ca bhavati, tadā sarvasattvānāṃ sarvaratnasaṃgrahāya pratyupasthitaṃ bhavati, evameva bho jinaputra yadā bodhisattvānāṃ sarvajñatāratnacittotpādo daśāryaratnagotrāṇyatikramyotpanno bhavati dhūtaguṇasaṃlekhaśīlavratatapaḥsuparitāpitaśca dhyānasamādhisamāpattisuparipiṇḍitaśca mārgāṅgākārasupariśodhitaśca upāyābhijñāsuparyavadāpitaśca pratītyasamutpādasunirviddhaśca upāyaprajñāvicitraratnasūtrasvāviddhaśca vaśitāmahāvaiḍūryamaṇiratnadaṇḍadhvajāgrāvaropitaśca sattvacaritapratyavekṣaṇaśrutajñānāvabhāsasaṃprayuktaśca tathāgatadharmarājasamyaksaṃbuddhajñānābhiṣekānugataśca bhavati, tadā sarvasattvānāṃ sarvabuddhakāryaratnasaṃgrahāya pratyupasthito bhavati, tadā ca sarvajña ityākhyāyate ||

E

ayaṃ khalu punarbho jinaputra bodhisattvacaryāsamudānayanaḥ sarvākārasarvajñajñānaguṇasaṃcayo dharmamukhaparivarto nānavaropitakuśālamūlānāṃ sattvānāṃ śravaṇāvabhāsamāgamiṣyati || vimukticandro bodhisattva āha - yeṣāṃ punarbho jinaputra ayaṃ sarvākārasarvajñajñānaguṇasaṃcayo dharmamukhaparivartaḥ śravaṇāvabhāsamāgamiṣyati, te kiyatā puṇyopacayena samanvāgatā bhaviṣyanti? vajragarbho bodhisattva āha – yāvān bho jinaputra sarvajñajñānasya prabhāvastāvān sarvajñatācittotpādasaṃgrahālambanātpuṇyopacayaḥ syāt | yāvān sarvajñatācittotpādasaṃgrahālambanataḥ puṇyopacayastāvānevāsya dharmamukhaparivartasyābhimukhaḥ puṇyopacayo'nugantavyaḥ | tatkasya hetoḥ? na hi bho jinaputra śakyaṃ anyatra bodhisattvena ayaṃ sarvākārasarvajñajñānaguṇasaṃcayo dharmamukhaparivartaḥ śrotuṃ vā adhimoktuṃ vā pratyetuṃ vā udgrahītuṃ vā dhārayituṃ vā saṃdhārayituṃ vā | kaḥ punarvādo bhāvanākāraprayogodyoganiṣpādaneṣu? tasmāttarhi bho jinaputra sarvajñajñānamukhānugatāste saṃdhārayitavyāḥ, ye imaṃ sarvajñajñānaguṇasaṃcayadharmamukhaparivartaṃ śropyati, śrutvā cādhimokṣyante, adhimucya cādhārayiṣyanti, bhāvanākāreṇa prayokṣyante || atha khalu tasyāṃ velāyāṃ buddhānubhāvena dharmatāpratilambhena ca daśadiglokadaśabuddhakṣetrakoṭiparamāṇurajaḥsamā lokadhātavaḥ ṣaḍvikāramaṣṭādaśamahānimittamakampanta prākampanta saṃprākampanta | acalan prācalan saṃprācalan | avedhanta prāvedhanta saṃprāvedhanta | araṇan prāraṇan saṃprāraṇan | akṣumyan prākṣubhyan saṃprākṣumyan | agarjan prāgarjan saṃprāgarjan | divyāśca puṣpagandhamālyameghā abhiprāvarṣan | divyāśca vastrameghā divyāścūrṇameghā divyā ratnameghā divyā ābharaṇameghā divyā chatrameghā divyā dhvajameghā divyā patākāmeghā abhiprāvarṣan | divyaṃ ca sūryacakrātmabhāvamaṇḍalamaṇirājasumerumeghavarṣamabhiprāvarṣan | divyaṃ ca sarvarutaravitavādyamaṇirājasumerumeghavarṣamabhiprāvarṣan | divyaṃ ca jāmbūnadakanakavarṇaprabhāmaṇḍalamaṇirājasumerumeghavarṣamabhiprāvarṣan I divyāśca tūryatālāvacarasaṃgītimeghā nadanti sma I divyasamatikrāntāḥ sarvajñatābhūmyabhiṣṭavasaṃgītimeghā nadanti sma I yathā cāsyāṃ lokadhātau cāturdvīpikāyāṃ paranirmitavaśavartino devarājasya vimāne maṇiratnagarbhaprāsāde, tathā sarvalokadhātuṣu daśa diśaḥ spharitvā iyameva dharmadeśanā sarvatraiva pravartate sma I ...daśabhyo digbhyo daśabuddhakṣetrakoṭiparamāṇurajaḥsamānāṃ lokadhātūnāṃ pareṇa daśabuddhakṣetrakoṭiparamāṇurajaḥsamā bodhisattvā āgacchanti daśadiśaṃ spharantaḥ I te ca āgatyaivamāhuḥ - sādhu sādhu bho jinaputra, yastvamimāṃ bodhisattvabhūmidharmatāṃ sūcayati I vayamapi bho jinaputra sarve vajragarbhasamanāmakā eva vajraśrīnāmikābhyo nānālokadhātubhya ihāgatā vajradhvajanāmakānāṃ tathāgatānāmantikebhyaḥ I sarvāsu ca tāsu lokadhātuṣu iyameva dharmadeśanā pravartate buddhānubhāvena evaṃrūpāsveva parṣatsu I ebhireva padairebhireva vyañjanairebhireva niruktairetamevārthamabhilaṣadbhiranūnamanadhikamanatiriktam, te vayaṃ bho jinaputra sākṣībhūtā buddhānubhāvenemāṃ parṣadaṃ saṃprāptāḥ I yathā ca bho jinaputra vayamimāṃ lokadhātuṃ saṃprāptāstathā ca daśasu dikṣu sarvalokadhātuṣvekaikasyāṃ lokadhātau cāturdvīpikāyāṃ paranirmitavaśavartibhavane vaśavartino devarājasya vimāne maṇiratnagarbhaprāsāde saṃprāptā iti I I idamavocadvajragarbho bodhisattvo mahāsattvo'bhyanujñātastathāgatena I āttamanāḥ sā ca sarvāvatī bodhisattvaparṣat sā ca devanāga...śuddhāvāsaparṣad bhagavāṃśca paranirmitavaśavartiṣu deveṣu viharannacirābhisaṃbuddho dvitīye saptāhe vaśavartino devarājasya vimāne maṇiratnagarbhe vajragarbhasya bodhisattvasya bhāṣitamabhyanandanniti I I iti parīndanāparivarto nāmaikādaśaḥ I I iti śrībodhisattvacaryāprasthāno daśabhūmīśvaro nāma mahāyānasūtraratnarājaḥ samāptaḥ I I

Endnotes

1. Use of this Sanskrit text here is by the kind permission of Dr. Miroj Shakya, Project Coordinator, Digital Sanskrit Buddhist Canon Project and Rare Buddhist Sanskrit Manuscript Preservation Project, University of the West, Rosemead, CA. Sandhi-compliant line breaks were added in-house by Kalavinka Press.
2. Although not noted in the DSBC text's numbering, apparently the last half of verse 27 and all of verse 28 have been lost from the Sanskrit. I have appended the original numbering of each remaining verse in parentheses.

About the Translator

Bhikshu Dharmamitra (ordination name "Heng Shou" – 釋恆授) is a Chinese-tradition translator-monk and one of the earliest American disciples (since 1968) of the late Guiyang Ch'an patriarch, Dharma teacher, and pioneer of Buddhism in the West, the Venerable Master Hsuan Hua (宣化上人). He has a total of 34 years in robes during two periods as a monastic (1969–1975 & 1991 to the present).

Dharmamitra's principal educational foundations as a translator of Sino-Buddhist Classical Chinese lie in four years of intensive monastic training and Chinese-language study of classic Mahāyāna texts in a small-group setting under Master Hsuan Hua (1968–1972), undergraduate Chinese language study at Portland State University, a year of intensive one-on-one Classical Chinese study at the Fu Jen University Language Center near Taipei, two years of course work at the University of Washington's Department of Asian Languages and Literature (1988–90), and an additional three years of auditing graduate courses and seminars in Classical Chinese readings, again at UW's Department of Asian Languages and Literature.

Since taking robes again under Master Hua in 1991, Dharmamitra has devoted his energies primarily to study and translation of classic Mahāyāna texts with a special interest in works by Ārya Nāgārjuna and related authors. To date, he has translated more than fifteen important texts comprising approximately 150 fascicles, including most recently the 80-fascicle *Avataṃsaka Sūtra* (the "Flower Adornment Sutra"), Nāgārjuna's 17-fascicle *Daśabhūmika Vibhāṣa* ("Treatise on the Ten Grounds"), and the *Daśabhūmika Sūtra* (the "Ten Grounds Sutra"), all of which are current or upcoming Kalavinka Press publications.

Kalavinka Buddhist Classics

(www.kalavinkapress.org)

Fall, 2019 Title List

Meditation Instruction Texts

The Essentials of Buddhist Meditation

A marvelously complete classic *śamathā-vipaśyanā* (calming-and-insight) meditation manual. By Tiantai Śramaṇa Zhiyi (538–597).

Six Gates to the Sublime

The early Indian Buddhist meditation method involving six practices used in calming-and-insight meditation. By Śramaṇa Zhiyi

Bodhisattva Path Texts

On Generating the Resolve to Become a Buddha

On the Resolve to Become a Buddha by Ārya Nāgārjuna
Exhortation to Resolve on Buddhahood by Patriarch Sheng'an Shixian
Exhortation to Resolve on Buddhahood by the Tang Literatus, Peixiu

Letter from a Friend - The Three Earliest Editions

The earliest extant editions of Ārya Nāgārjuna's *Suhṛlekkha*:
Translated by Tripiṭaka Master Guṇavarman (*ca* 425 CE)
Translated by Tripiṭaka Master Saṇghavarman (*ca* 450 CE)
Translated by Tripiṭaka Master Yijing (*ca* 675 CE).

Marvelous Stories from the Perfection of Wisdom

130 Stories from Ārya Nāgārjuna's *Mahāprājñāpāramitā Upadeśa.*

Nāgārjuna's Guide to the Bodhisattva Path

The *Bodhisaṃbhāra Treatise* with abridged Vaśitva commentary.

The Bodhisaṃbhāra Treatise Commentary

The complete exegesis by the Indian Bhikshu Vaśitva (*ca* 300–500).

Nāgārjuna on Mindfulness of the Buddha

Ch. 9 and Chs. 20–25 of Nāgārjuna's *Daśabhūmika Vibhāṣā*
Ch. 1, Subchapter 36a of Nāgārjuna's *Mahāprājñāpāramitā Upadeśa.*

Nāgārjuna on the Six Perfections

Chapters 17–30 of Ārya Nāgārjuna's *Mahāprājñāpāramitā Upadeśa.*

A Strand of Dharma Jewels (Ārya Nāgārjuna's *Ratnāvalī*)

The earliest extant edition, translated by Paramārtha: *ca* 550 CE

The Ten Bodhisattva Grounds

Śikṣānanda's translation of The Flower Adornment Sutra, Ch. 26

The Ten Grounds Treatise
Nāgārjuna's 35-chapter *Daśabhūmika Vibhāṣā*

The Ten Grounds Sutra
Kumārajīva's translation of the *Daśabhūmika Sūtra*

Vasubandhu's Treatise on the Bodhisattva Vow
By Vasubandhu Bodhisattva (*ca* 300 CE)

CPSIA information can be obtained
at www.ICGtesting.com
Printed in the USA
LVHW091352011119
635851LV00035B/25/P

9 781935 413110